100
DAYS TO
VICTORY

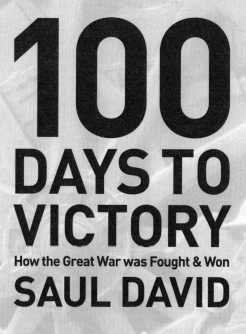

100
DAYS TO
VICTORY

How the Great War was Fought & Won

SAUL DAVID

HODDER &
STOUGHTON

For my darling Natasha.

CONTENTS

INTRODUCTION

My earliest memory of my grandparents' large but ramshackle country house in the Welsh Borders is of the broad staircase up to the first-floor landing where two imposing pictures always caught my attention. Both were of serious young men in uniform, wearing smart military caps, Sam Browne cross-belts and moustaches. Later I discovered they were my grandmother's two elder brothers, and that both had fought in the First World War.

Another prominent image in my grandparents' house was of an elderly man sitting with a Springer spaniel at his feet. He was not in uniform, and was clearly too old to fight, yet I surmised from his faraway, slightly doleful expression that he had seen things he would prefer to forget. The photograph was of my paternal great-grandfather who survived four years of service on the Western Front.

The fortunes of my ancestors during the First World War were fairly typical: some paid the ultimate price; others had the good luck to return from the fighting, sound in body if not always in mind. But all played their part, as did the millions of Britons mobilized on the Home Front, in gaining for the Allies the consolation of eventual Victory.

My family, like so many others, was both bystander and participant in the Great War, a war supposedly to end all wars. It now seems scarcely credible that more than five million British men were sent to fight (and 702,000 of them to die) in battlefields as far afield as Flanders, Greece, Mesopotamia, Palestine, Egypt, German East Africa (Tanzania), Italy, Turkey, Bulgaria and China. Even in Britain the effects of this first industrialized or total war were far-reaching. Civilian communities were bombed from the air and bombarded from sea. With so many men in uniform, women took on traditional male jobs as firemen, coalmen, bus conductors, munitions workers and so on. They joined the Women's Land Army to help with agricultural production, and were recruited as

1

nurses into the Voluntary Aid Detachments (VADs) or First Aid Nursing Yeomanry (FANY), and as drivers, cooks and telephonists in the Women's Army Auxiliary Corps (WAAC), the Women's Royal Naval Service (WRNS) and the Women's Royal Air Force (WRAF). This huge female contribution to the war effort was to have profound social, economic and political consequences in Britain, not least the introduction of female suffrage in February 1918.

The government realized what as at stake in 1914 by appealing for enormous numbers of volunteer soldiers and, when that proved insufficient, introducing conscription for the first time in our history (a move that was opposed on religious and moral grounds by 16,000 conscientious objectors). It passed the Defence of the Realm Act (DORA), which gave it wide-ranging powers to censor and suppress sensitive information, try suspected spies by court martial and commandeer economic resources for the war effort. It worked with trade unions to prevent strikes and set up vast state-run munitions factories to feed the seemingly insatiable demand for shells and bullets. It introduced rationing and Daylight Summer Time (to give more working hours). And it made a vital, if heavy-handed, contribution to the propaganda war by censoring soldiers' letters, closing down radical newspapers (including the socialist *Tribune*), spreading misinformation about enemy atrocities, and using posters and information films (notably *The Somme*) to boost morale and bolster public support for the war.

Today the overriding popular perception of the fighting – particularly on the Western Front where more than two million British soldiers were killed or wounded – is still one of futility and waste, a case of 'Lions led by Donkeys'. In fact, as this book will show, the truth is much more nuanced: many mistakes were made by senior commanders but, far from all being 'Donkeys', some like Haig, Allenby, Plumer and Byng made a positive contribution in very difficult circumstances; battles like the Somme and Passchendaele may have exacted a terrible cost in lives lost, but they also played a vital role in wearing the Germans down in a long war of attrition; and the trench warfare on the Western Front was not simply a case of two sides banging their heads unimaginatively against a brick wall, but rather an extraordinarily fertile period of military innovation in terms of weapons, tactics, training, logistics and the treatment of casualties – innovations that in 1918 would help the Allies to pierce the German lines and win the war.

Moreover the vast majority of ordinary soldiers never stopped believing in the justice of the cause they were fighting for. The trenches were for many a brutal and inhuman experience. But even combat soldiers – a small proportion of the total number in uniform – spent only a third of their time in the front line, with the remainder spent training, resting and in reserve; and some were even invigorated by the comradeship and excitement of ever-present danger.

Captain Markham David, the author's
great-grandfather.

All of these themes are covered by my choice of the hundred key dates and events – some directly involving my family – that best illustrate the lasting and irrevocable impact the war had on civilians and soldiers across the globe. While all the entries concentrate on a single day, they necessarily include information from a broader time span to give the narrative its context. In this way, and by combining a variety of first-hand sources with the most recent scholarship, I have tried to produce a one-volume history of this highly complex and much misunderstood conflict that is modern, vivid and accessible.

*   *   *

No aspect of the war is more contested by historians than its origins. In the space of exactly a month – from the assassination of the Archduke Franz Ferdinand and his wife in Sarajevo on 28 June 1914 to the Austro-Hungarian declaration of war on Serbia on 28 July (a step that, thanks to Europe's alliance system, was almost bound to drag in the other great powers) – Europe went from peaceful prosperity to the brink of a war that would bring down four empires and cost more than fifteen million lives. It would also, thanks to the harshness of its peace settlement (signed at Versailles in 1919), sow the seeds for a second and even more destructive global conflict, which in turn gave rise to the Cold War.

The causes of the war in 1914 are therefore immensely significant. Was it inevitable after the Sarajevo assassinations, or did Europe's monarchs and politicians have an element of choice in their decisions? Convinced of the former scenario was a near-destitute twenty-five-year-old Austrian artist who for the previous year had been eking out a meagre living as a watercolourist in the Bavarian capital of Munich. A fervent German nationalist, he later described the political atmosphere in Europe, prior to the assassinations, as 'oppressive and foreboding; so much so that the sense of an impending catastrophe became transformed into a feeling of impatient expectance'. He added:

> When the news came to Munich that the Archduke Franz Ferdinand had been murdered, I had been at home all day and did not get the particulars of how it happened. At first I feared that the shots may have been fired by some German-Austrian students who had been aroused to a state of furious indignation by the persistent pro-Slav activities of the Heir to the Hapsburg Throne and therefore wished to liberate the German population from this internal enemy ... But soon afterwards I heard the names of the presumed assassins and also that they were known to be Serbs. I felt somewhat dumbfounded in the face of the inexorable vengeance which Destiny had wrought. The greatest friend of the Slavs had fallen victim to the bullets of Slav patriots.[1]

The young artist's relief at learning the identity of the assassins was matched by a conviction that war was now both 'absolutely inevitable' and welcome. It would not be, in his view, merely a war of retribution against the independent state of Serbia – which was perceived (with some justification) to be behind the killings – but 'rather a case of

Germany fighting for her own existence'.[2] The artist's name was Adolf Hitler.

Contrary to Hitler's assertion, however, the outbreak of a European war was not bound to follow the Sarajevo assassinations. Internal politics, the weight of public opinion, a complex system of alliances and a sense in some European capitals that it was better to fight sooner rather than later encouraged European monarchs and politicians to take their countries to the edge of the abyss. What prevented them from drawing back, and ultimately tipped them over, was the urgency of mobilization timetables.

Austria-Hungary's tardy reaction to the assassinations was to present Serbia, which it accused of complicity in the plot, with a harsh ultimatum on 23 July. Its demands included the denunciation of all separatist activities, the banning of publications and organizations hostile to Austria-Hungary and co-operation with Habsburg officials in suppressing subversion and conducting a judicial inquiry.[3] 'A state accepting such terms,' declared Sir Edward Grey, the British Foreign Secretary, 'would cease to count among independent states.'[4]

Yet Serbia's measured reply, delivered shortly before the expiry of the forty-eight-hour deadline, was to agree to almost all the demands. The only caveat was that the joint Austro-Serbian judicial inquiry would have to be subject to Serbia's constitution and international law. This was enough for the Austrians to reject the ultimatum, break off relations and, on 28 July, mobilize their troops in the Balkans and declare war on Serbia.[5] Emperor Franz Joseph signed the declaration with an ostrich-feather quill at the desk of his study in the imperial villa at Bad Ischl. It read:

> To my peoples! It was my fervent wish to consecrate the years which, by the Grace of God, still remain to me, to the works of peace and to protect my peoples from the heavy sacrifices and burdens of war. Providence, in its wisdom, has decreed otherwise. The intrigues of a malevolent opponent compel me, in the defence of the honour of my Monarchy, for the protection of its dignity and its position as a power, for the security of its possessions, to grasp the sword after long years of peace.[6]

Why did the Vienna government take such a hard line? Firstly because its suspicions of Serbian complicity were, at least in part, justified. Sarajevo was the capital of Bosnia-Herzogovina, part of the Austro-Hungarian

Empire. More than two-fifths of Bosnia's population was ethnic Serb, many of whom yearned for independence from Austria and union with a Greater Serbia. Nor were the secret organizations dedicated to achieving that end – like the 'Young Bosnia' group to which the Sarajevo assassins belonged – to be found solely on Austrian territory. In Serbia itself, many army officers and government officials belonged to the Black Hand, a group determined to unite all Serbs by violence. The Austrians – swallowing the red herring told them by the assassins during interrogation – blamed a Serb propaganda body known as the Narodna Odbrana ('People's Defence') for orchestrating the assassinations. In fact it was the Black Hand, led by Colonel Dragutin Dimitrijević (or 'Apis'), the Serbian military intelligence chief, that provided Gavrilo Princip and the other assassins with weapons, trained them in their use and helped to smuggle them back into Bosnia. While there is no evidence that the Serb government of Nikola Pašić was part of the plot – he, after all, was a political opponent of Dimitrijević – the Austrians were right to accuse some Serb officials of working to destabilize their Slavic provinces. The irony is that Dimitrijević and other Serb hardliners sanctioned Franz Ferdinand's killing because they regarded him as a hawk dedicated to Serbia's destruction. In fact, as Hitler also recognized, he was 'the foremost advocate of restraint'.[7]

Pašić's moderate response to Austria's ultimatum was based on a sober assessment of Serbia's military capacity. The recent successful Balkan Wars of 1912 and 1913* may have doubled Serbia's territory and increased its population from 2.9 to 4.4 million, but they also emptied its treasury and military arsenal. Rifles were in particularly scarce supply. Needing time to rearm, Pašić was determined to avoid a war.[8]

Many in the Austro-Hungarian government and military, on the other hand, felt the time was opportune. They were convinced that unless Serbia's intrigues were stopped by force, their polyglot Empire – made up of no fewer than eleven ethnic groups† – was in danger of disintegration. They

---

* In 1912–13, Serbia, Bulgaria, Greece and Montenegro had beaten Turkey in the First Balkan War; in the Second, in 1913, Bulgaria attacked its former allies (and Romania) and was itself defeated.
† Including Germans (12 million), Hungarians (10), Czechs (6.6), Poles (5), Ruthenians (4), Croats (3.2), Romanians (2.9), Slovaks (2) and Serbs (2) (Stevenson, *1914–1918*, p. 13).

feared a Pan-Slav movement, spearheaded by Serbia (and backed by its great-power ally Russia), and were determined, in the words of Foreign Minister Leopold von Berchtold, to 'tear away with a strong hand the net in which its enemy seeks to entangle it'.[9]

Yet before Austria-Hungary could risk a war with Serbia, it needed Germany's backing. Their defensive alliance dated back to 1879, and was directed primarily against Russia. The Russians, in turn, had concluded a similar treaty with France in 1894 to counteract the threat from Germany. One by one the other European powers had joined or become loosely associated with one alliance bloc or the other: Italy with the Central Powers – that is, Germany and Austria-Hungary – in 1882; and Britain with France and Russia in 1904 and 1907 respectively (a bloc known as the Triple Entente).

Only too aware of these alliances, the German government knew it had to tread carefully in the days following the assassinations if it wanted to avoid a continental (which of course, given the extent of the European powers' imperial possessions, meant a global) conflict. Instead, at least at first, it encouraged Austria to take firm action. On 5 July, responding to Emperor Franz Joseph's assertion that Serbia needed to be eliminated 'as a political factor',[10] the German Kaiser Wilhelm II assured the Austrian envoy Count von Hoyos that his country had Germany's backing to 'march into Serbia', even if war with Russia resulted. A day later, the German Chancellor Theobald von Bethmann Hollweg repeated this secret assurance, known to historians as the 'blank cheque'.[11]

In many ways, Germany had the most to lose from a general war. 'In the previous round of wars,' noted a leading historian of the period, 'it had humbled Austria and France and expanded its territory: its economy was one of the fastest growing in Europe. Otto von Bismarck, the first Chancellor of united Germany, recognized that it stood to gain nothing from a new war, unless it be to forestall French recovery after 1870; but the French rebuilt their defences and the moment for pre-emption passed.'[12]

The key moment was Bismarck's forced retirement in 1890. Thereafter (and particularly during the years 1897–1908) the Kaiser became the dominant force in German politics, exerting 'considerable influence over diplomacy and in military and naval matters'.[13] It was his vainglory that authorized the disastrous *Weltpolitik* ('world policy') in the late 1890s, ushering in a naval arms race against Britain, the dominant maritime and imperial power, which Germany could not win. The policy, moreover, had serious financial, political and diplomatic consequences for Germany's ruling elite: it pushed the imperial budget into deficit, triggering political infighting over the inevitable tax increases, and ensuring that the left-wing Social Democratic Party (SPD) was by 1912 the largest in the Reichstag; and it drove a resentful Britain into the arms of its former enemies France and Russia, thus completing the 'encirclement' of the Central Powers.

With Austria its only 'dependable' great-power ally, and fearful that a huge increase in Russian military expenditure (announced in 1910) would jeopardize its secret war strategy of avoiding a war on two fronts by first defeating the French Army before turning to deal with the less sophisticated Russians,* Germany's political and military leaders became convinced that the sooner a European war began the better. Helmuth von Moltke the Younger, Chief of the German General Staff, said as much during the infamous 'War Council' of December 1912, to which no civilians were invited. His naval counterpart Alfred von Tirpitz was more circumspect, saying the navy needed another twelve to eighteen months to prepare. That time had now elapsed and even Bethmann saw the need to back Austria in its showdown with Serbia.[14] The ideal outcome for him and Gottlieb von Jagow, the German Foreign Secretary, was a localized Balkan war that neutered Serbia, bolstered Austria and split the Triple Entente. But they also knew that if Russia intervened a continental war was inevitable.

The question on everyone's lips following Austria's declaration of war on Serbia on 28 July was how would St Petersburg react? There was no alliance treaty that impelled Russia to come to Serbia's assistance; nor did it have much of an economic stake in the Balkan country. On the other hand, Russia did have a vital strategic interest in the region, notably the passage of its trade through the Straits of Constantinople (which its military leaders had been planning to seize from the Ottomans since the

---

* A strategy known to historians as the Schlieffen plan, after its creator Alfred von Schlieffen, Chief of the German General Staff from 1890 to 1905 – though in reality it was heavily, and some would say disastrously, modified by Schlieffen's successor, Helmuth von Moltke the Younger.

1890s), and it needed a strong and independent Serbia to counterbalance Austro-Hungarian forces in the event of war. Yet perhaps the most telling issue for Tsar Nicholas II and his ministers, in the immediate aftermath of Austria's declaration, was the strength of Russian public opinion. Responding to Kaiser Wilhelm II's belated attempt to mediate, the Tsar replied on 29 July: 'An ignoble war has been declared on a weak country. The indignation in Russia, fully shared by me, is enormous. I foresee that very soon I shall be overwhelmed by the pressure brought upon me and be forced to take extreme measures which will lead to war.'[15]

The Tsar was referring, of course, to troop mobilization: the calling up of reservists – a measure that, typically, would increase the size of a European standing army by three to four times – and providing them with horse and motor transport.* Already, on 24 and 25 July, he and his council of ministers had ordered four military districts – Kiev, Odessa, Moscow and Kazan – to take preliminary steps such as cancelling leave and clearing the frontier railway lines. A day later the Russian army recalled its reservists; and towards midnight on 29 July, in response to Austria-Hungary's mobilization against Serbia, the four districts already alerted were told to mobilize.[16] This partial mobilization was seen by Russian ministers, according to historian Hew Strachan, as a 'buttress' to diplomacy, rather than an 'inevitable progression to war itself'.[17] A similar tactic had been used during a previous Balkan crisis in November 1912 and did not lead to war. It was deemed necessary because the Russian Army was notoriously slow to mobilize, with a minimum delay of fifteen days from the mobilization order to the point at which the army could actually start fighting (and almost a month needed to complete full mobilization). During this time, reckoned Russian ministers, there would be plenty of opportunity for further negotiation.[18]

Yet even partial mobilization – while questionable from a military point of view because it did not involve the key area of Warsaw that bordered both Germany and Austria-Hungary – produced a momentum of its own. It gave Serbia an assurance that it would not fight alone; and, more importantly, it put pressure on Germany to mobilize. Germany's plan to defeat first France before turning on Russia depended upon 'that

---

* Mobilization preceded 'concentration', the movement of troops to the frontier (normally by rail), which was followed in turn by deployment for combat.

very delay in Russian mobilization which the decisions of 24 and 25 July were calculated to eliminate'. If they allowed the Russians to get too much of a head start, 'they would risk defeat in the east before they had won in the west'.[19]

It was for this reason that Count Pourtalès, the German ambassador to St Petersburg, warned the Russian Foreign Minister Sergei Sazonov on 29 July that if Russia continued its military preparations, Germany would be forced to do likewise. Viewing the threat as an ultimatum, the Foreign Minister replied: 'Now I am in no doubt as to the true cause of Austrian intransigence.'[20] This was the moment, according to the historian Christopher Clark, that Sazonov became convinced of the need for full mobilization against both Austria-Hungary and Germany. If Austria's aggression towards Serbia 'was in fact German policy', he reasoned, partial mobilization was pointless. The Foreign Minister was also influenced by the claim by the Russian high command (or Stavka) that it was technically impossible to combine 'partial mobilization (for which no proper plan existed) with the option of a general mobilization thereafter'; and he was emboldened by the assurance given on 28 July by the French ambassador, Maurice Paléogue, that the Russians could count 'in case of necessity' on 'the complete readiness of France to fulfil her obligations as an ally'.[21]

By the evening of the 29th, Sazonov had convinced the Tsar of the need for general mobilization and the necessary telegrams were minutes from being despatched when, incredibly, Nicholas II changed his mind. He had been swayed by the timely arrival of a telegram from Kaiser Wilhelm II, his third cousin, which suggested that 'a direct understanding between your Government and Vienna is possible and desirable', and that Germany was 'continuing its exertions to promote it'.[22] This brought the Tsar to his senses. 'I will not be responsible for a monstrous slaughter,' he exclaimed, before ordering the mobilization to be scaled down from general to partial.[23]

The following day, in an attempt to explain his mobilization of troops against Austria-Hungary, Nicholas II wrote to the Kaiser: 'The military measures which have now come into force were decided five days ago for reasons of defence on account of Austria's preparations. I hope from all my heart that these measures won't in any way interfere with your part as a mediator.'[24]

The Kaiser's response, also sent on the 30th, was to repeat the threat his ambassador had made the day before:

> Count Portales [sic] was instructed to draw the attention of your Government to the danger and grave consequences involved by a mobilization . . . Austria has only mobilized against Serbia and only a part of her army. If, as is now the case, according to the communication by you and your Government, Russia mobilizes against Austria, my role as mediator, which you kindly entrusted me with, and which I accepted at your express prayer, will be endangered if not ruined. The whole weight of the decision lies solely on your shoulders now, who have to bear the responsibility for Peace or War.[25]

It was this telegram that persuaded the Tsar that Sazonov was right. 'They [the Germans] don't want to acknowledge that Austria mobilized before we did,' he told his Foreign Minister at an afternoon meeting in the Peterhof Palace. 'Now they demand that our mobilization be stopped, without mentioning that of the Austrians . . . At present if I accepted Germany's demands, we would be disarmed against Austria.'[26]

This was a miscalculation. At this stage, Austria had confined its military preparations to defeating Serbia. But the Tsar was not alone in assuming that the Austrians were mobilizing against Russia by stealth: most of his ministers and generals thought likewise. Having listened to Sazonov's arguments, the Tsar concluded: 'You are right, there is nothing else left than to prepare ourselves for an attack. Transmit to the chief of the general staff my orders of [general] mobilization.'[27] The relevant telegrams were despatched from St Petersburg at 6 p.m. on 30 July.

The German government's reaction on 31 July was predictable: having ordered an intensification of its own military preparations, it sent the Russian government an ultimatum to cancel its mobilization within twelve hours or face the consequences. Russia refused and on 1 August, the same day it and Austria-Hungary began their own general mobilizations, Germany declared war. 'If Germany threw down the gauntlet,' wrote the historian David Stevenson, 'Russia picked it up.'[28]

What, though, of Russia's ally France? Was there a possibility of it staying neutral in a Russo-German war, as the Germans demanded on 31 July? Not if it wanted to remain a great power, its leaders reasoned, convinced as they were that the preservation of the Triple Entente 'was a more important objective in French foreign policy than the avoidance of war' (not least because they feared that the loss of Russia as any ally would have made France extremely vulnerable to German aggression).[29] They had made no attempt to restrain their ally Russia in the crucial days after the delivery of Austria's ultimatum to Serbia, and were not about to abandon it now. They duly rejected Germany's ultimatum and began their own mobilization, though the army was ordered to keep ten kilometres back from the Franco-Belgian border (the anticipated direction of a German attack) so as not to threaten Belgian neutrality. With the die cast, and using the pretext that French troops had violated its territory, Germany declared war on France on 3 August. The date of no return, however, and the day a European (if not yet a world) war became inevitable, was when the Tsar authorized full Russian mobilization on 30 July 1914.

Who, then, was chiefly responsible? Since the publication of Fritz Fischer's groundbreaking *Germany's Aims in the First World War* in 1961, historians have tended to blame the Kaiser and his chief military advisers.[30] More recently the spotlight has shifted towards the Austro-Hungarians, the Russians and, to a lesser extent, the Serbians.[31] A recent book on what is known as the July Crisis, by Christopher Clark, has claimed that the governments of all the main powers preferred war to diplomatic defeat that month, and it is hard to point the finger at any single participant. 'There is no smoking gun in this story,' wrote Clark, 'or, rather, there is one in the hands of every major character. Viewed in this light, the outbreak of war was a tragedy, not a crime.' He added: 'The protagonists of 1914 were sleepwalkers, watchful but unseeing, haunted by dreams, yet blind to the reality of the horror they were about to bring into the world.'[32]

This is going too far. None of the major powers worked as hard as they could have done to prevent war; but the decision taken by Austria-Hungary, crucially backed by Germany, to emasculate Serbia by either diplomatic or military means in the wake of the Sarajevo assassinations was the moment at which a general conflict became very likely if not inevitable. It was taken in the firm belief that if the Entente powers chose to fight they would be defeated; and if they did not the Entente would collapse. Either way, the Central Powers could not lose – or so they thought.

The reaction to the war across Europe was mixed. A young Heinrich

Himmler, living in Landshut in Lower Bavaria, complained in his diary about the number of locals openly weeping.[33] Yet in many large cities – from St Petersburg to Berlin, Paris to Vienna – the news of the war was greeted by cheering crowds of all social classes. In a photograph of one, taken in Munich on 2 August, can be seen the distinctive face of the young Adolf Hitler. 'I was carried away by the enthusiasm of the moment,' he wrote in *Mein Kampf*, 'and . . . sank down upon my knees and thanked Heaven out of the fullness of my heart for the favour of having been permitted to live in such a time.'[34] Three days later, though of Austrian nationality, he volunteered for service in the Bavarian Army. When word of his acceptance came through on the 16th, he was ecstatic. 'No words of mine', he wrote, 'could now describe the satisfaction I felt on reading that I was instructed to report to a Bavarian [infantry] regiment. Within a few days I was wearing that uniform which I was not to put off for nearly six years.'[35]

PROLOGUE

'Sophie, Sophie, don't die, stay alive for our children!'

At 9.20 a.m. on 28 June 1914, shortly before leaving the Hotel Bosna in Ilidze for the train that would take him and his wife to Sarajevo, Archduke Franz Ferdinand, heir apparent to the Austro-Hungarian throne, dictated a telegram to his eldest daughter Sophie (named after her mother):

> Mama and I are very well. Weather warm and fine. We gave a large dinner party yesterday and this morning there is the big reception in Sarajevo. Another large dinner party after that and then we are leaving on the *Viribus Unitis*. Dearest love to you all. Papa.[1]

At 9.50 a.m., exactly on schedule, the royal couple arrived at Sarajevo railway station and were welcomed by General Oskar Potiorek, military governor of Bosnia-Herzogovina, and a guard of honour. The fifty-year-old archduke was wearing the elaborate uniform of a general of hussars: black shiny boots with spurs, black trousers with a red stripe down the outer seam, a blue serge tunic with three stars on its raised collar, white gloves and a black peaked helmet topped with light-green peacock feathers. His wife Sophie was in a full-length white dress, gathered at the waist by a red sash, and a fur of ermine tails, her face partly obscured by a wide-brimmed hat and veil.[2]

At 10 a.m., having inspected the guard of honour, the couple joined General Potiorek in an open-top Gräf and Stift sports coupé for the short drive down the Appel Quay, a broad boulevard that runs through the centre of Sarajevo, to the town hall where a welcome reception was planned. Their car – with the archduke and his wife in the back seat, and facing Potiorek who was on a pull-down bench – was the third of seven; the remainder contained aides, gendarmes and sundry local officials.

The sun was shining, after two days of cold drizzle, and the bulk of the watching crowd was gathered to the left of the procession, sheltering in the shade of the houses and trees on the city side of the quay. Only a handful of people were standing on an unshaded narrow pavement to the right of the quay where a low embankment separated the road from the River Miljacka, fifteen to twenty feet below. Despite the warnings of the local police chief, who feared an assassination attempt, there had been no repeat of the elaborate security precautions for the Emperor's visit four years earlier when a cordon of soldiers had lined the streets. Instead, 120 policemen and a handful of gendarmes were dotted along the route, facing the crowd in case of trouble.

With the cars spaced fifty yards apart, the procession moved past cheering Sarajevans and houses and shops flying the Habsburg black and yellow and Bosnian red and yellow banners. The archducal car was about halfway down the quay when the driver heard a bang and noticed a dark object flying towards him from the right. Suspecting a bomb had been detonated, he accelerated, causing the missile to hit the folded roof of the car, bounce off and fall to the ground. Seconds later it exploded in front of the next car's left rear wheel, injuring two of its occupants and seven spectators, and leaving a small crater in the road.

Even before the bulk of the motorcade had come to a halt – the first two cars, unaware of the drama, continued on to the town hall – the would-be assassin, a nineteen-year-old Bosnian Serb ultra-nationalist called Nedeljko Čabrinović, had taken a double-dose of cyanide and jumped into the neighbouring Miljacka River. But the poison failed to kill him, the water was shallow, and he was quickly arrested. Did he have any accomplices? he was asked in a nearby police station. He refused to answer.

Meanwhile the archduke, the target of the attack, had bravely decided not to cancel the rest of the day's engagements, including a reception in the town hall, the opening of a new museum on Franz Josef Street, and lunch in the governor's palace, the Konak. 'I thought something like this might happen,' he told Potiorek. 'The fellow must be insane, let us proceed with our programme.'[3]

Franz Ferdinand can only be admired for his sangfroid. But was it

16

wise for him to have travelled to Bosnia-Herzogovina in the first place? He had been warned as early as 1911 – just three years after they became Austrian possessions – that the twin Balkan provinces were 'politically unconsolidated, culturally and economically underdeveloped, rent by political dissension and wide open to foreign subversive influences'.[4] Moreover the date chosen for the royal couple's visit to Sarajevo, 28 June, was not an auspicious one. It was St Vitus' Day, the anniversary of the Battle of Kosovo Field in 1389 when a Serb-led army had been defeated by the Ottoman Turks (marking the end of the Serb Empire in the Balkans and the start of five centuries of Muslim domination), and a date heavy with symbolism for the many Bosnian Serbs who yearned for inclusion in a Greater Serbia. They remembered not only the defeat, but also the aftermath when a single Serb penetrated the enemy camp and assassinated the Turkish Sultan.

Yet the archduke was determined to fulfil his role as inspector-general of the Austro-Hungarian Army by attending the annual manoeuvres in Bosnia, and felt that his liberal reforming politics and pro-Slav leanings – he supported, for example, the creation of a south Slav kingdom under Austrian suzerainty – made him an unlikely target for Serb terrorists. The trip had another attraction for Franz Ferdinand in that its military nature would allow his Czech-born wife Sophie, styled the Duchess of Hohenburg but not accorded royal status by the now octogenarian Emperor Franz Joseph (nor were their children allowed to succeed him to the Austrian throne), to accompany him as an equal.

The first two days of the visit passed without incident as the archduke watched the army go through its paces in the hills west of Ilidze, while his wife made two visits to Sarajevo. During the evening of the 27th, following a sumptuous dinner in the Hotel Bosna, some of the archduke's staff advised him to cancel his own trip to Sarajevo the following day. They were worried about hostile crowds at a time of heightened national emotion for the Serbs, they told him, and felt a third visit to the Bosnian capital would be tempting fate. The archduke seemed convinced by the argument until a local official, Colonel Merizzi, pointed out that an early departure would offend the Bosnian Croat loyalists and be seen as a sign of weakness. This persuaded the archduke to stick to the original schedule.

Now, in the wake of the bomb attack, he must have regretted that decision. Yet so determined was he to appear unruffled that, after a somewhat muted reception at the town hall, he rejected Potiorek's advice to cut short the visit by proceeding straight to the Konak, or even back to his hotel at Ilidze. Instead Franz Ferdinand – described by one historian as 'an unattractive man, authoritarian, choleric, and xenophobic'[5] – insisted on visiting the most seriously wounded officer in the hospital. Only his wife would be taken to the safety of the Konak. But when told of this she demurred: 'I will go with you to the hospital.'[6]

To avoid driving through the narrow streets of the city centre, the archduke's staff decided to take the long way round to the hospital by retracing their steps down the Appel Quay. Only this time Count von Harrach, the archduke's bodyguard, would move from his place next to the driver to the left running board from where he could shield the heir to the throne. He could do nothing, however, if an attack came from the right side.

It was 10.45 a.m. as the procession – now just six cars with the Archduke's second in line – left the town hall and proceeded down the Appel Quay. But as it drew level with the Latin Bridge to its left, the lead vehicle turned right into Franz Josef Street, as originally planned, instead of continuing straight ahead. Confused, the archduke's driver began to follow until Potiorek shouted at him to stop. 'This is the wrong way! We are supposed to take the Appel Quay!'

The driver braked and put the car into neutral (it had no reverse gear) so that it could be pushed back on to the main thoroughfare. As fate would have it, the car had come to a temporary halt opposite Schiller's general store, in front of which stood one of Čabrinović's accomplices, the nineteen-year-old Gavrilo Princip. Described by an eyewitness as short and hollow-eyed, Princip was barely six feet from the unprotected right side of the royal car when he drew a Browning semi-automatic pistol from his pocket and fired twice. He later insisted that the presence of the duchess had caused him to hesitate. 'Where I aimed I do not know. But I know that I aimed at the Heir Apparent,' he told investigators. 'Whether I hit the victim or not, I cannot tell, because instantly people turned around to hit me.' He claimed he had then raised the gun to his head, intending to commit suicide, but it was knocked away by a spectator who, with others, tried to lynch him. Eventually rescued by gendarmes, he was beaten 'again, in order not to be unavenged'.[7]

Princip's shots, however, had found their mark. The first had passed through the car door and into the duchess's abdomen, severing the stomach artery; the second had hit the archduke in the neck, tearing the jugular vein and lodging in his spine. As the car swept over the Latin Bridge towards the Konak, Sophie collapsed on to the archduke's lap. Fearful that he himself was mortally wounded, Franz Ferdinand implored his wife: 'Sophie, Sophie, don't die, stay alive for our children!' But she was silent and, after assuring Harrach who was still on the running board that he was not in pain, the archduke also lost consciousness.[8]

Sophie had stopped breathing by the time they reached the Konak. Her husband survived her by a matter of minutes, his blood staining the clothes of his valet as the latter cut open his uniform to ease his breathing. They were both pronounced dead at a few minutes past eleven.[9] As the bells of Sarajevo tolled in honour of the slain, and the news of the assassinations spread by telegraph across Europe, few could have anticipated that within five weeks of this act of terrorism the world would be at war.

PART ONE
1914

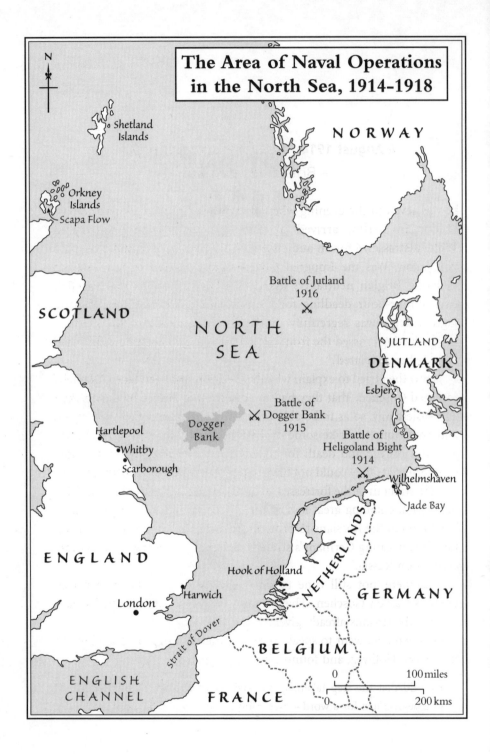

The Area of Naval Operations in the North Sea, 1914–1918

N

NORWAY

Shetland
Islands

Orkney
Islands
Scapa Flow

Battle of Jutland
1916
✕

SCOTLAND

NORTH
SEA

JUTLAND

DENMARK

Esbjerg

Battle of
✕ Dogger Bank
1915

Dogger
Bank

Hartlepool
Whitby
Scarborough

Battle of
Heligoland Bight
1914
✕

Wilhelmshaven

Jade Bay

NETHERLANDS

Hook of Holland

ENGLAND

London   Harwich

GERMANY

Strait of Dover

BELGIUM

ENGLISH
CHANNEL

FRANCE

0   100 miles

0   200 kms

4 August 1914: *'Just for a scrap of paper'*
– Britain declares war

I t was seven in the evening when Sir Edward Goschen, British ambassador in Berlin, arrived at the German Foreign Ministry at
Wilhelmstrasse 76 for an audience with the Secretary of State, Gottlieb
von Jagow. Was the Imperial Government prepared to refrain from
violating Belgian neutrality? asked Goschen, conscious that Britain's
twenty-four-hour deadline for Germany to do so had now elapsed.
Jagow's reply was regretfully no, 'as in consequence of the German
troops having crossed the frontier that morning, Belgian neutrality had
already been violated'.[1]

Jagow then tried to explain why this decision had been taken. 'Namely,'
reported Goschen, 'that they had to advance into France by the quickest
and easiest way, so as to be able to get well ahead with their operations
and endeavour to strike some decisive blow as early as possible. It was
a matter of life and death for them, as if they had gone by the more
southern route they could not have hoped, in view of the paucity of roads
and the strength of the fortresses, to have got through without formidable
opposition entailing great loss of time.' This in turn, said Jagow, would
have allowed the Russians to bring more troops up to the German frontier, thus negating Germany's strategy of rapidly defeating France before
turning on Russia.[2]

Was there 'not still time to draw back and avoid possible consequences'? asked Goschen. That was no longer possible, replied Jagow,
and for the reasons already given.[3]

Goschen next went to speak to the German Chancellor, Theodor von
Bethmann Hollweg, and found him 'very agitated':

> He said that the step taken by his Majesty's Government was terrible
> to a degree; just for a word – 'neutrality', a word which in war time had

so often been disregarded – just for a scrap of paper* Great Britain was going to make war on a kindred nation who desired nothing better than to be friends with her . . . What we had done was unthinkable; it was like striking a man from behind while he was fighting for his life against two assailants . . . I protested strongly against that statement, and said . . . it was, so to speak, a matter of 'life and death' for the honour of Great Britain that she should keep her solemn engagement to do her utmost to defend Belgium's neutrality if attacked.[4]

But was Belgian neutrality the real reason that Britain went to war, as Goschen told Bethmann? Or did it provide a convenient cloak for other less noble considerations? And, more significantly, did Britain's ineffectual diplomacy actually muddy the waters for the other powers and make a peaceful solution to the July Crisis even less likely?

Sir Edward Grey, the British Foreign Secretary, has traditionally been portrayed as a peacemaker. On 29 July, for example, he had told the German ambassador Prince Lichnowsky that 'mediation was an urgent necessity if those concerned did not wish to have things become a European catastrophe'.[5] Yet the message was mixed: on the one hand he warned Lichnowsky that Britain might be forced to take precipitate action if Germany and France were drawn into the war; while on the other he said Britain had no legal obligations to its Entente partners.[6]

Thus encouraged by Grey's non-committal stance, Bethmann made a clumsy attempt to ensure Britain's neutrality by offering to guarantee in return both France and Belgium's territorial integrity in Europe – but not the former's colonies nor the latter's neutrality. This Herbert Asquith's Liberal government would not countenance. 'Such a proposal is unacceptable,' Grey informed the German ambassador on 1 August, 'for France, without further territory in Europe being taken from her, could be so crushed as to lose her position as a Great Power, and become subordinate to Germany policy. Altogether apart from that, it would be a disgrace for us to make this bargain with Germany at the expense of France, a disgrace from which the good name of this country would never recover.' Nor was, Grey added, the government prepared to

---

* Bethmann was referring to the Treaty of 1839 – signed by plenipotentiaries from Britain, Belgium, France, Prussia and Russia – that had guaranteed Belgian neutrality.

'bargain' away Belgium's neutrality. Clutching at straws, the ambassador asked for a 'definite declaration that Great Britain would remain neutral' if Germany did not invade Belgium. Grey, rightly, refused to give it.[7]

What Grey had been prepared to offer at an earlier meeting that day, and without any authorization from his fellow Cabinet members, was not just for Britain to stay neutral if Germany refrained from attacking France, but to vouch for French neutrality as well. Would Germany, he asked Lichnowsky, 'in the event of France remaining neutral in a war between Russia and Germany', agree not to attack the French? Surprised and delighted by this extraordinary proposal, Lichnowsky said yes, he 'could take the responsibility for such a guarantee'.[8]

When word of the offer reached Berlin, the Kaiser called for champagne and ordered Moltke, his army chief of staff, to halt mobilization against France (a move that Moltke, knowing the importance of railway time-tables, tried desperately to resist). But Lichnowsky soon put a dampener on these celebrations, and triggered a reversal of the order to stop mobi-lization, when he reported that evening that Grey's offer had been with-drawn. 'There is,' he wrote, 'no British proposal at all.'[9]

In truth, the French would never have agreed to stand aside while Germany and Austria attacked its ally Russia, a position made very clear to Grey that day by the British ambassador in Paris, Sir Francis Bertie. 'If France undertook to remain so,' cabled Bertie, 'the Germans would first attack the Russians and, if they defeated them, then turn round on the French.'[10]

By now Grey had come to his senses and, from this point on, Germany's leaders must have known that Britain would not stand aloof from a European war. Any final doubts were dispelled by Grey's confession to the House of Commons on 3 August that, a day earlier, he had assured the French ambassador 'that if the German fleet comes into the Channel or through the North Sea to undertake hostile operations against the French coasts or shipping, the British fleet will give all the protection in its power'.[11] In the same speech he informed the House that the Belgian government had just been given an ultimatum by Germany to 'facilitate the passage of German troops' through its territory or face the conse-quences. For Grey, and for the government, the only course available was to resist German aggression. The alternative – to 'stand aside' and ignore 'the Belgian treaty obligations, the possible [naval] position in the

Mediterranean, with damage to British interests, and what may happen to France from our failure to support France' – would, in Grey's opinion, 'sacrifice our respect and good name and reputation before the world, and should not escape the most serious and grave economic consequences'.[12]

In the event it was Britain that declared war on Germany, at 11 p.m. on 4 August, and not the other way around. The ostensible reason was Germany's invasion of Belgium earlier that day, an act made necessary by the requirements of the Schlieffen plan. In fact, Belgian neutrality was a pretext – and a particularly useful one for a Cabinet that, until 2 August, had been divided over the need to get involved.* 'The vital point', wrote David Stevenson, 'was not the invasion, but that Germany was the invader, and the British government and much of the public saw German domination of Western Europe as dangerous.'[13] The Cabinet feared the Germans dominating the continent and winning control of the Channel ports; it also feared for the security of Britain's Empire and trade if, having failed to support France and Russia, 'its links with them would have been forfeit, and the reopening and deepening of those old and more traditional rivalries would have driven Britain into the only alternative, an Anglo-German alliance'.[14] And yet the issue of Belgian neutrality is what united the Cabinet,† Parliament and the country behind intervention: it became, in Hew Strachan's words, 'the bridge which allowed *Realpolitik* and liberalism to join forces'.

6 August 1914: *'Have they all gone to the war?'*
– The Cabinet agrees to send the BEF to France

Two days after Britain's declaration of war my great-uncle Hugh Neely, a personable twenty-six-year-old Roman Catholic dentist and county footballer, closed his thriving practice in Southampton and travelled up

---

* Before 2 August, when Germany sent its ultimatum to Belgium, only a minority of the Cabinet – albeit its senior figures, including Asquith, Grey, Lloyd George and Winston Churchill – were determined to fight if France was attacked.
† In fact two radical ministers resigned, but the rest were now solidly pro-war.

to London to rejoin his former unit of Territorials, the 1/28th County of London Regiment, better known as the Artists' Rifles.

The son of the founder of William Neely & Co., a successful London stationery business, Hugh had enjoyed a privileged upbringing with his three brothers and single sister in a large house in Bromley, Kent. The second son, he followed in the footsteps of his elder brother Clive by winning an exhibition to Lancing College where he gained the rank of sergeant in the Officer Training Corps (OTC). On leaving Lancing, he joined Clive in the professions, training first as an architect and then switching in 1908 to Guy's Hospital to learn dentistry; Clive would qualify as a certified accountant a year later. But Hugh was the star of the family: he could play the piano, sing and was a superb amateur footballer. During his four years as a dental student at Guy's he won his colours for the United Hospitals' team and represented Surrey on five occasions.[1] A 1912 report in the *Daily Express* described him as 'General Utility Neely', a man who could 'play in any position', a 'long hard kicker' and a 'keen tackler'.[2]

Hugh's next brother Guy, a twenty-four-year-old trainee doctor, also volunteered for service in August 1914, gaining a commission in the

Second Lieutenants Clive and Hugh Neely, the author's great-uncles.

Royal Army Medical Corps; and Clive would certainly have joined up if he had had the opportunity. He had been working for a firm of accountants in Kuala Lumpur since 1910. When war broke out, Clive at once applied for leave; but it was refused, much to his chagrin. 'I wish I was there to make a third,' he wrote to his mother. 'You would be in a hot bed of militarism then me old mum!' Instead he had to make do with serving as a private in the local Malay militia, doing his best to keep his 'gun (sorry rifle) clean', and scolding his young Javanese servant 'if it hasn't been attended to!'[3]

That left just one Neely brother not in uniform: thirteen-year-old Jack who was at boarding school in Lancashire. His pretty flame-haired sister Phyllis* (or 'Phyl' as the family called her), three years his senior, had recently been expelled from her convent school in Haywards Heath and was living at home that August. A high-spirited teenager who enjoyed tennis and parties, she was particularly close to her sporty brother Hugh and understandably worried when he volunteered for the infantry. Only a few months earlier she had sent Hugh a jaunty picture postcard of her and her friends in the garden of their school, asking him to pray for her as she embarked upon her leaving exams, and sending 'much love to you both'. She does not name the other recipient of her love but, as will become clear, it was probably Hugh's sweetheart (and soon to be fiancée) Dorothy.

As for Phyl's exams, she obviously did well because a few months later, with the war barely four weeks old, she received a letter of congratulation for winning so many prizes from a Dutch former schoolfriend. 'I am sure you are first of the juniors, are not you?' asked the friend, before turning to more sobering matters: 'Oh, Phyl, I suddenly think of your brothers. Have they all gone to the war? I do hope they haven't. It would be dreadful for you and your dear mother. I am so glad that Holland is still in peace, but for how long?'[4]

Despite its declaration of war, Asquith's government did not make a final decision to despatch a British army to France until 6 August. Why the delay? After all, as the diary of Lieutenant-General Sir Douglas Haig makes clear, 'Precautionary Measures' for mobilization – such as the

* Born in 1898, Phyllis was my paternal grandmother.

writing up of the relevant telegrams – had been ordered by the War Office as early as 29 July. So six days later, when full mobilization was ordered – the single-word telegram reaching Haig's Aldershot headquarters at 5.05 p.m. on 4 August – it was simply a matter of dating and despatching the telegrams. 'These orders were put in force and methodically acted upon without friction and without flurry,' Haig noted in his diary. 'Everything had been so well thought out and foreseen that I, as "C-in-C [Commander-in-Chief] Aldershot", was never called upon for a decision. I had thus all my time free to make arrangements for my own departure for the front.'[5]

The question was: which front? Because, unbeknown to Haig – a fifty-three-year-old veteran of the Sudan and Boer Wars, and the scion of the Scottish whisky family – the British Cabinet's acceptance of belligerence on 4 August had been on the assumption that it would not be necessary to send an expeditionary force to France. Instead ministers envisaged a war fought in the traditional fashion – naval, colonial and financial – with perhaps only a small professional force sent to the continent.[6]

Most of the politicians, in turn, were unaware that Franco-British staff talks had been ongoing since 1912, and that the War Office's Directorate of Operations, headed by Major-General Henry Wilson, had with the French drawn up a plan for sending a British Expeditionary Force (BEF) to the continent in the event of war with Germany. Wilson was convinced that the BEF could tip the balance, and that it needed to be sent as quickly as possible. But nothing had been agreed with the politicians – though Grey and one or two others were aware of the plan – and it was to discuss the options that a War Council was held at 10 Downing Street at 4 p.m. on 5 August.

Among those present were Asquith (in the chair), Grey and most of the Cabinet, notably the newly appointed War Secretary, Field Marshal Earl Kitchener of Khartoum. The soldiers included the Chief of the Imperial General Staff (CIGS), Sir Charles Douglas; the commander-designate of the BEF, Field Marshal Sir John French; his chief of staff, Sir Archibald Murray; the two BEF corps commanders, Haig and Jimmy Grierson; and Henry Wilson.

After a brief assessment of the political situation by Asquith, French presented the prearranged plan that had been 'worked out between the British and French General Staffs'. Haig recorded:

Briefly stated, it was hoped that the Expeditionary Force would mobilize simultaneously with the French, and would be concentrated behind the French left at Mauberge by the fifteenth day of mobilization. The intention was then to move eastwards towards the Meuse, and act on the left of the French against the German right flank. We were now, however, late in mobilizing, and so this plan was no longer possible.[7]

French's solution was for the BEF to concentrate at Amiens, fifty miles south-west of Mauberge, where it would be in less danger. In any event, said French, it was vital that the BEF was sent to France intact, and as rapidly as possible.[8] He then contradicted himself, and infuriated Wilson and Haig, by suggesting an alternative to the prearranged plan: that of operating from Antwerp, in collusion with 'the Belgian and possibly Dutch Armies'.[9]

The absurdity of French's Antwerp option was quickly revealed. Winston Churchill, First Lord of the Admiralty,* said that the Royal Navy could not protect the many troop transports needed to send the whole of the BEF across the longer North Sea passage to the Scheldt; Douglas pointed out that all the planning had been for embarkations across the Channel, that the French had 'arranged for rolling stock and prepared railway timetables for the movement of our units', and that any change of destination at the last moment 'would have serious consequences'; and Haig spoke of the risk of 'defeat in detail' if the BEF was 'separated from the French'.[10]

Haig went further, arguing that the war was 'bound' to be a long one and that it was necessary for Britain to organize its resources 'for a *war of several years*'. First and foremost it needed to create a mass army of at least a million men, and to this end it might be prudent to hold back a 'considerable portion of officers and NCOs' from the BEF to form an experienced nucleus. Yet he supported the sending of a BEF to join French forces, the sooner the better.[11]

Most of the Council of War was now convinced that it was best to stick to the original plan, though a definite decision to send the BEF was not taken by the Cabinet until the morning of 6 August. It remained only for a second Council of War, held that afternoon, to discuss the

---

* In effect, the Secretary of State for the Navy.

size of the BEF.[12] French foresaw a short war and wanted at least five infantry divisions; but Kitchener, agreeing with Haig's sentiments if not his conclusions, said the war would last several years and urged caution. French was overruled and it was agreed to send four infantry divisions and one cavalry division, giving a total BEF (with supporting troops) of 100,000 men. 'The suspicion', wrote Richard Holmes, 'that Kitchener was trying to starve him of troops was implanted in [French's] receptive brain then, long before the first shot was fired.'[13]

8 August 1914: *'Your Country Needs You!'*
– Kitchener appeals for volunteers

On Lord Kitchener's first day in the War Office, he declared: 'There is no army!' By that he meant a force capable of fighting a major conflict on the continent and, given that that was the course to which the BEF was now committed, he was right to be worried. The regular British Army at the time, not including reservists, numbered only 247,000 officers and men, a third of whom were in India. Even when Kitchener took into account the part-time Special Reserve and Territorial Force (formerly the Militia and Volunteers respectively), the total was only 733,000, a fraction of the size of the conscript armies that France, Germany, Austria-Hungary and Russia were mobilizing for war.

Kitchener, like Haig, was also convinced that the war would be long and that, as he told *The Times* military correspondent Colonel Charles à Court Repington, Germany would 'fight to the last breath and the last horse'. France could shoulder the burden only for so long, he added, and it was up to its allies Russia and Britain to assist it in defeating the Central Powers.[1] To this end Kitchener was determined to raise up to seventy new infantry divisions by the third year of the war.* His preference was

---

* In the event, between 1914 and 1918, the British Empire raised 104 infantry divisions: twelve Regular, one Royal Naval, thirty-two Territorial Force (including eight home defence divisions), thirty New Army, eighteen Indian and eleven imperial (Philpott, *Bloody Victory*, p. 44).

to introduce conscription for the first time in Britain's history; but his Cabinet colleagues argued, persuasively, that such an option would create social unrest and threaten national unity. So instead, on 8 August, he made his famous appeal for the first 100,000 volunteers.

The plan was to create a series of New Armies, complete in all their branches, with each one replicating the six infantry divisions of the original BEF (though, initially, only four were sent to France). This was to be done through the normal regular recruiting channels, rather than through the Territorial Force, and the scheme for the first New Army, or New Expeditionary Force as it was originally called, was announced on 12 August. Six of the eight regional commands – the exceptions were Aldershot and the London District – would each provide an infantry division by recruiting at least one service battalion for every line regiment in their area.

At first the response to Kitchener's iconic 'Your Country Needs You' recruiting poster was sluggish. But it soon picked up with the daily total rising from 7,000 on 11 August to almost 10,000 a week later, and peaking at 33,000 on 3 September, the highest number of recruits achieved on a single day during the whole war. In the first eight weeks, more than 750,000 men between the ages of nineteen and forty had volunteered to serve for three years or the duration of the war.[2]

Departure of the Liverpool Scottish for the front in 1914.

The volunteers came from every walk of life – from City workers to manual labourers – and their motivations, according to one historian, 'were many and varied'. He added: 'A simple patriotism and a genuine desire to stand up against the foe for "King and Country" was undoubtedly present for many. For others it was a simple zest for adventure: a change from the tedium of the office, the hard graft of the shop floor, the loneliness of the farmyard, the filth and ever-present dangers of the pit.'[3]

Others joined up because their friends had done so, with whole units known as 'Pals' battalions raised in a single locality and often from men of the same occupation. London's regiment, the Royal Fusiliers, recruited 'Stockbrokers', 'Public Schools' and 'Jewish' battalions. Further north the newly formed 10th Lincolns and 11th East Lancs were known, respectively, as the 'Grimsby Chums' and the 'Accrington Pals'. The latter battalion, 1,100 strong, was embodied within ten days of the *Accrington Observer and Times* announcing on 8 August a 'Great Rally to the Flag'.[4] There were, in addition, units known as the 'Post Office Rifles', the 'Hull Commercials' and even two 'Sportsmen's' battalions.

Private Arthur Dalby, who joined the 'Leeds Pals' (otherwise known as the 15th Battalion, West Yorkshire Regiment), recalled:

> I saw this lot in the paper and it said it was all Leeds people, and I joined up. I didn't even know that infantry walked, to be quite truthful with you, I didn't know anything about soldiers. I ought to have joined the cavalry lot, being brought up with horses, but it appealed to me and I went and I've never regretted a moment of it really, because I never met a finer lot of fellows in my life.[5]

A young man who at first had rather less success when he tried to answer Kitchener's call was the nineteen-year-old Roland Leighton, a brilliant scholar and poet who had carried off almost all the academic prizes in his last year at Uppingham School, and who was due to take up a place at Oxford to read Classics. Brought up in East Anglia, the son of two successful authors, Leighton applied for a commission in the Norfolk Regiment but was rejected 'on account of imperfect eyesight'. He next tried the Royal Artillery and even the distinctly unglamorous Army Service Corps, and was still refused. So he went back to the infantry and, finally, was told he might be accepted in the Norfolks after all. He explained the reasons behind his determination to join up in a letter to twenty-year-old Vera Brittain, the pretty bluestocking sister of his best friend, who had won an exhibition to study English at Somerville College, Oxford:

> I don't think in the circumstances I could easily bring myself to endure a secluded life of scholastic vegetation. It would seem a somewhat cowardly shirking of my obvious duty . . . I feel that I am meant to take an active part in this War. It is to me a very fascinating thing – something, if often horrible, yet very ennobling and very beautiful, something whose elemental reality raises it above the reach of all cold theorising. You will call me a militarist. You may be right.[6]

Though in love with Leighton, Brittain was nettled by his jibe about 'scholastic vegetation'. 'It seemed', she wrote later, 'so definitely to put me outside everything that now counted in life, as well as outside his own interests, and his own career. I felt it altogether contrary to his professed feminism – but then so was the War.' She replied to Leighton:

> Women get all the dreariness of war, and none of its exhilaration. This, which you say is the only thing that counts at present, is the one field in which women have made no progress – perhaps never will . . . I sometimes feel that work at Oxford, which will only bear fruit in the future and lacks the stimulus of direct connection with the War, will require a restraint I am scarcely capable of. It is strange how what we both so worked for should now seem so little.[7]

Brittain's brother Edward had also decided to join the army rather than take up his place at Oxford, as had Victor Richardson, the third of the tight-knit and talented group of friends from Uppingham School that Roland's mother had dubbed 'The Three Musketeers'. Yet, like Roland, both failed their initial medicals, and when Vera Brittain duly went up to Somerville in October 1914 she thought the possibility of the war affecting her 'personally' had 'become quite remote'.[8]

Even those volunteers who had been accepted in August were not thrown straight into battle. First they had to be trained by professionals and given the right equipment – and both were in short supply, as the diary of Neil Weir, a young Oxford undergraduate who joined the 10th (Service) Battalion, the Argyll & Sutherland Highlanders, makes clear:

Most of our senior officers were regular soldiers who had been held back when their Battalions had been sent to the front to train our hastily raised mobs. What a prospect for them who had been used to smartness, cleanliness and obedience. The Officers and men now working under them had to be taught all these things and with the extra disadvantages of no uniform, no rifles, no training grounds, no band and no recreations.[9]

Despite these difficulties, the volunteers were united in their willingness to risk their lives for a cause they saw as patriotic, selfless and just. This almost mystical fervour was best expressed in the poetry of Rupert Brooke, aged twenty-seven, the Rugby- and Cambridge-educated former socialist who had accepted a commission in Winston Churchill's newly created Royal Naval Division. In mid-October, after experiencing combat for the first time at Antwerp, Brooke wrote the sonnet that would make him famous, and that so perfectly captured the country's mood of stern resolution:*

> Now, God be thanked Who has matched us with His hour,
>   And caught our youth, and wakened us from sleeping,
> With hand made sure, clear eye, and sharpened power,
>   To turn, as swimmers into cleanness leaping,
> Glad from a world grown old and cold and weary,
>   Leave the sick hearts that honour could not move,
> And half-men, and their dirty songs and dreary,
>   And all the little emptiness of love![10]

23 August 1914: *'Every shot was meant'*
– The Battle of Mons

At 6 a.m., having reached the banks of the Mons–Condé Canal in Belgium the night before, the sentries of the forward battalions of the BEF's II Corps were peering across the water into the morning mist

---

* Among the other European intellectuals who welcomed war as spiritually cleansing were the Austrian poet Rainer Maria Rilke, and the German novelists Hermann Hesse and Thomas Mann, the latter describing war as a 'purification, liberation' from the 'toxic comfort of peace'.

when they caught the first sight of movement. It was a German cavalry patrol, moving cautiously down the Nimy Road towards the canal. An officer cried out, 'At five hundred yards – five rounds rapid – Fire!'

The well-trained infantrymen of the 4th Royal Fusiliers, capable like all British professionals of firing fifteen rounds a minutes with their excellent Short Magazine Lee Enfield (SMLE) .303 rifles, did as they were instructed and it was not long before the German cavalry were retiring in disorder. A couple of hours later, after a preliminary bombardment, the German infantry attacked in a dense grey mass, pressing hard against the 4th Royal Fusiliers and the 4th Middlesex Regiment at the apex of the salient the BEF was holding round the mining town of Mons. A corporal of the 4th Royal Fusiliers recalled:

> Bloody Hell! You couldn't see the earth for them, there were that many. Time after time they gave the order '*Rapid Fire*'. Well, you didn't wait for the order, really! You'd see a lot of them coming in a mass on the other side of the canal and you just let them have it. They kept retreating, and then coming forward, and then retreating again. Of course we were losing men and a *lot* of the officers, especially when the Germans started this shrapnel shelling and, of course, *they* had machine-guns – masses of them! . . . I don't know how many times we saw them off.[1]

But the Germans kept coming in waves, and by mid-afternoon an order had reached the forward battalions to fall back to a position behind Mons, near the mining villages of Framières and Paturages. Private Sidney Godley of the 4th Royal Fusiliers ignored the order. For two hours, manning one of his battalion's two Maxim machine-guns, he had single-handedly kept the Germans from crossing the bridge over the canal at Nimy. Now, though twice wounded, he covered the retreat of his comrades and only ceased firing as the Germans stormed the bridge. His last act 'was to destroy the gun and throw the pieces into the canal'.[*2]

Sir John French's men fought splendidly at Mons, inflicting more than 5,000 casualties to 1,850 of their own.[3] So rapid was the firing from the British rifles that the Germans mistook them for machine-guns. This was

---

* Godley remained a prisoner of war until November 1918. The officer in charge of the machine-gun section, Lieutenant Maurice Dease, died of his wounds. Both were awarded Victoria Crosses, the first of the conflict.

the result of huge improvements in training since the Anglo-Boer War (1899–1902). As well as spending more time on the rifle range – achieving rates of fire that were far superior to the great conscript armies of Europe – British soldiers laboriously practised the principles of fire and move-ment in attack, and of regulated fire from defensive positions. They also had the advantage of a rifle with a ten-shot magazine, compared to the five-shot German Mauser, and one whose crooked bolt enabled them to keep their eye on the target as they reloaded, whereas the straight bolt on the Mauser caused the firer to avert his gaze, so slowing his rate of fire. The benefits to the British were reaped at Mons. 'We killed a tremen-dous number of them,' wrote a Private P. Case of the 1st King's (Liverpool) Regiment, holding the canal to the west of Mons, 'and owing to their massed formation they were practically standing up dead before us.'[4]

The BEF fought off a German attacking force of at least three times its size at Mons on 23 August. That it had been placed in such jeopardy in the first place, however, was entirely the fault of its commander Sir John French. Following a cordial meeting on the 16th with General Joseph Joffre, the French Commander-in-Chief, Sir John had agreed not only to forget his initial misgivings and concentrate his troops at Mauberge (as per the original intention), but also to conform to Joffre's general plan to attack the German forces advancing through Belgium. The intention was for the BEF to protect the open left flank of the French Fifth Army. What French and Joffre were not expecting, however, was that the German right wing in Belgium would be composed of no fewer than sixteen corps, six Landwehr (or militia) brigades and five cavalry divisions 'poised to fall, like the headsman's axe, on the BEF and the 5th Army' on the 23rd.[5]

That evening, with his bloodied but undefeated troops occupying their new defensive position to the south of Mons, French was determined to hold his ground. But he changed his mind when, at midnight, he received word that the French Fifth Army had fallen back without telling him, thus exposing his right flank while his left was barely covered by a weak French cavalry force. Orders were at once despatched for the BEF to make a general retreat of eight miles. This difficult night manoeuvre caused confusion but no loss of life; far more serious was the damage done to Anglo-French relations. The incident convinced the British field marshal, wrote his biog-rapher, 'that the French were basically untrustworthy as Allies, and sowed the seeds of distrust which, from time to time, bore bitter fruit'.[6]

A company of the 4th Royal Fusiliers resting in the Grand Place, Mons,
on 22 August 1914.

The Battle of Mons was one of the few setbacks experienced by the
German Army in its attempt to win a quick and decisive victory over
France in August 1914. In line with the Schlieffen–Moltke plan, it had
committed the vast bulk of its forces – a total of seventy-eight infantry
divisions and ten cavalry divisions, grouped in seven armies – to the
western theatre; and of those, no fewer than fifty-two divisions were
earmarked to advance through Belgium and Luxembourg while the
balance held their ground to the south.[7]

At first the Germans troops made good progress as the main Belgian
field army, unsupported by the French and British, withdrew into the
fortified national redoubt at Antwerp. Liège (after a brave but ultimately
futile eleven-day resistance), Namur and Brussels had all fallen by 20
August, enabling the Germans to concentrate their forces for the advance
into France. Richard Harding Davis, the celebrated American novelist
and war correspondent, described the German Army's entry into Brussels
as 'not men marching, but a force of nature like a tidal wave, an avalanche
or a river flooding its banks'. He added:

> For seven hours the army passed in such solid column that not once
> might a taxicab or trolley car pass through the city. Like a river of steel
> it flowed, gray and ghostlike. Then, as dusk came and thousands of

horses' hoofs and thousands of iron boots continued to tramp forward, they struck tiny sparks from the stones, but the horses and men who beat out the sparks were invisible.[8]

The seemingly inexorable German advance had been assisted by the preoccupation of the GQG (Grand Quartier Général, or French high command) with its own offensives further south: the first was into the lost provinces of Alsace-Lorraine where on 20 August, after initial gains, it was stopped in its tracks at the Battle of Morhange-Sarrebourg and eventually driven back across the border with the loss of 20,000 prisoners and 150 guns; an even more serious defeat was inflicted on French troops advancing against the German centre in the Ardennes on 22 August, the day Lanzerac's Fifth Army was bested further north at Charleroi. A day later the BEF felt the full force of the German right wing at Mons before it, too, began the long retreat to the Marne river.

29 August 1914: *'The booty is immense'*
– The Germans triumph at Tannenberg

As night fell General Alexander Samsonov, commander of the Russian Second Army, and five members of his personal staff were making their way on horseback through the thick forests of East Prussia towards the Russian frontier when they were fired on by German machine-guns. 'Amidst a hail of bullets,' wrote a Russian officer, 'the party dismounted and continued their way on foot, into another belt of forest.' He added:

> Utter darkness surrounded them. The sounds of fighting died away, and all that could be heard was the trampling of the undergrowth and an occasional voice as members of the little party called out to each other in order to keep together. From time to time a halt was called and all drew closer to make sure that nobody was missing. General Samsonov, who suffered from heart trouble, and found his breathing more and more difficult, lagged behind. There came a time when everybody had been called and all had answered but Samsonov. General Postovski, the

Chief of his Staff, immediately called a halt and in the thick darkness led a search for the missing general. It was fruitless.[1]

Samsonov's corpse was discovered by the enemy two days later. He had shot himself, preferring death to the disgrace of capture and the shame of having lost the first great battle of the war against an enemy that was supposed to be outnumbered and acting on the defensive. How had it happened?

At the start of the war the Germans had assigned only a single army, the Eighth under General Max von Prittwitz, to defend East Prussia against the Prussians. It comprised thirteen infantry divisions and one cavalry division, all of them second rate, with 774 guns – about a tenth of the German Army's total strength.[2] The Russians had mobilized, on the other hand, a total of ninety-eight infantry divisions and thirty-seven cavalry divisions on their western frontier, but the bulk of those forces were directed against Austria-Hungary.[3] This was a mistake. 'Strategically,' wrote David Stevenson, 'the Russians would have been prudent to stay on the defensive against Austria-Hungary and focus on Germany, in order to threaten Berlin and co-ordinate pressure with the French. But politically they felt compelled to assist Serbia.'[4]

So while the Russians' major offensive in August 1914 was directed against Austria-Hungary, a secondary attack was ordered into East Prussia by the Russian First and Second Armies under, respectively, Generals Paul von Rennenkampf and Alexander Samsonov. It did not help that these two men loathed each other (having once come to blows), nor that East Prussia's difficult terrain – chiefly the presence of a fifty-mile-wide chain of lakes in the centre of the province – dictated two separate lines of advance which would give the Germans the opportunity to defeat them one after the other.

Not that the forty-four-year-old Samsonov was concerned. Alone his army of fourteen and a half infantry divisions, four cavalry divisions and 1,160 guns was bigger than Prittwitz's. Rennenkampf had a smaller force – six and a half infantry divisions, five and a half cavalry divisions and 492 guns – but it was assumed he could hold his own until Samsonov came to his assistance. Neither was particularly worried by his army's poor logistics and communications – notably a reliance on wireless messages that were often sent *en clair* – and each began the campaign with his confidence high.[5]

At first that optimism seemed justified. On 20 August, at the encounter battle of Gumbinnen near the East Prussian frontier, Rennenkampf's advance guard repulsed an attack by two of Prittwitz's corps, inflicting 8,000 casualties on a force of just 30,000. Shaken by this setback (caused primarily by the impatience of his I Corps commander, General Hermann von François), and mindful of signal and aerial reconnaissance that Samsonov's advance further south was threatening his lines of communication, Prittwitz ordered a withdrawal to the Vistula. But it was too late. Samsonov was nearing the rearmost corps of the Eighth Army and was bound to win the race to the Vistula. If Prittwitz was to secure his line of retreat he would first have to overcome the Russian Second Army.[6]

The original plan – suggested by Prittwitz's chief of staff, Max Hoffmann – was to switch part of his army by rail to face Samsonov's left wing; the rest of the army would then disengage from Rennenkampf and march into a position to attack Samsonov's right. But it was a highly risky manoeuvre: if Rennenkampf got wind of what was happening he would be able to attack the withdrawing Germans in the flank and rear. They would be caught between the two Russian armies. Everything depended upon secrecy and Russian inertia.

At first all went well and by 23 August the whole of the German Eighth Army, bar its cavalry division, had broken contact with Rennenkampf who did not appear to notice. Yet by now Helmuth von Moltke and the OHL (Oberste Heeresleitung, or Supreme Army Command) had grown tired of Prittwitz's gloomy reports and replaced him with Paul von Hindenburg, a veteran of the Austro-Prussian war, and General Erich Ludendorff, the hero of Liège, as chief of staff. The pair reached East Prussia on 24 August and immediately authorized Hoffmann's plan: 'they were not its originators', wrote Hew Strachan, but rather 'its executors and each made a vital personal contribution'. On 24 August, when it was clear that Rennenkampf was not in pursuit, Ludendorff ordered the two marching corps to close with Samsonov's right. The imperturbable Hindenburg, meanwhile, calmed his brilliant but nervy subordinate's fears that Rennenkampf could still intervene and rob them of victory.[7]

Fortunately communications between the two Russian armies were virtually non-existent, and Samsonov's, having marched non-stop for more than a week, was disorganized and close to collapse. On 24 August his lead corps came into contact with the Eighth Army's XX Corps and a fierce battle developed. A day later, under pressure from a second Russian corps, XX Corps withdrew closer to its supports. Samsonov assumed this was part of a general retreat and, in an attempt to outflank it, detached another corps and sent it further to the west. He realized his mistake too late.

On 26 August the two marching German corps struck Samsonov's right corps in the flank and forced it to retreat in disorder. The following day, the German I Corps, transported by rail, infiltrated the gap between the right of Samsonov's army and its centre. 'Moreover,' wrote Hindenburg, 'we learned that it was only in the imagination of an airman that Rennenkampf was marching in our rear. The cold truth was that he was slowly pressing on to Königsberg. Did he, or would he, not see that Samsonov's right flank was increasingly threatened with utter ruin and that the danger to his left wing also was increasing from hour to hour?'[8]

By 28 August both Russian flanking corps had been defeated and the two corps that made up the centre of Samsonov's army were in danger of being enveloped. The net closed on the 29th as, according to a Russian officer, the remaining two corps 'fell back into the shades of Tannenberg Wood, absolutely helpless and unable to use their artillery'. He added: 'The result of this disaster was that the Germans captured, almost in full strength, two army corps with all their officers, and recovered possession of their own troops who had been captured earlier during the battle.'[9]

It was during the night of 29/30 August that Samsonov and thousands of other Russians tried to escape the encirclement. More desperate break-outs were attempted the following day, but few of them succeeded. By the 31st, the Germans could claim the capture of 92,000 prisoners and nearly 400 guns. A further 50,000 Russians had been killed. Hindenburg boasted to the Kaiser: 'The guns are still in the forests and are now being brought in. The booty is immense.'[10]

At a thanksgiving service in the church at Allenstein, the German commander noticed young soldiers and elderly reservists sink to their knees, overcome with emotion. It was, he thought, 'a worthy curtain to their heroic achievements'.[11]

Hindenburg was right. His troops had won an astonishing victory, arguably the most decisive of the conflict, and all the more noteworthy given the low priority that Germany had given to its Eastern Front. But the Central Powers were not having it all their own way. Only days later,

General Hermann von François, commanding the German I Corps, inspects
a destroyed Russian column at Tannenberg in late August 1914.

having defeated the Austrians at the Battle of Gnila Lipa, the Russian
Eighth Army took the vital fortress of Lemburg in Austrian Galicia. In
Serbia, too, the Austrians' overconfidence had proved costly as their
invading Fifth Army was surprised by a night attack at Çer Mountain, a
battle that raged for three days before the Austrians withdrew. By 24
August they had evacuated Serbian territory.

Yet Hindenburg's victory at Tannenberg – confirmed by the encirclement
of Samsonov's army on 29 August – had given the German armies in the
west a vital breathing space in which to complete the conquest of France.

30 August 1914: *'I have seen the broken bits of many regiments'*
– The Amiens Despatch

Vera Brittain was having supper at her family home in the spa town
of Buxton, Derbyshire, when her father and brother Edward – who

was still waiting for his commission – began discussing 'a very dismal article in the Sunday Times, speaking of the tremendous losses in the British Army & the apparent invincibleness of the Germans all round'. The 'situation', noted Brittain in her diary, 'seems very grave indeed'.[1]

The article had been filed in Amiens the day before by Arthur Moore of *The Times*. Headlined 'BROKEN BRITISH REGIMENTS. BATTLING AGAINST THE ODDS. MORE MEN NEEDED', it read in part:

> Since Monday last the German advance has been one of almost incredible rapidity. As I have already written you, the British Force fought a terrible fight – which may be called the action of Mons, though it covered a big front – on Sunday . . .
>
> Regiments were grievously injured, and the broken army fought its way backwards by the sheer unconquerable mass of numbers of an enemy prepared to throw away three or four men for the life of every British soldier . . . To sum up, the first great German effort has succeeded. We have to face the fact that the British Expeditionary Force, which bore the great weight of the blow, has suffered terrible losses and requires immediate and immense reinforcement. The [BEF] has won indeed imperishable glory, but it needs men, men, and yet more men.[2]

Moore was one of a number of unofficial war correspondents who were reporting from behind the front lines in France. When war broke out, the War Office had created a register for approved correspondents who were to accompany the BEF. But Lord Kitchener, remembering his own run-in with journalists during the Boer War, chose to ban them from the military zone; moreover, he ruled, any despatches from France were to be censored by a new Press Bureau, set up under F. E. Smith (later Lord Birkenhead). The Bureau's bland communiqués – with their minimal facts and complete lack of human interest – did little to assuage the public's insatiable appetite for news of the fighting. Which is why enterprising men like Moore, Philip Gibbs of the *Daily Chronicle* and William Beach Thomas of the *Daily Mail* were prepared to risk arrest to find out the truth.[3]

Assuming that Moore's Amiens Despatch would be rejected by F. E. Smith, the senior staff at *The Times* had chosen to tone it down and delete certain passages before sending it to the Press Bureau on 29 August. Yet it came back with the deleted paragraphs reinstated and its conclusion rewritten to emphasize the need for reinforcements. Smith's remit to withhold and censor bad news from the front had been overridden by the War Office's wish to boost recruitment. Yet by allowing the Amiens Despatch to be published in its unexpurgated form, Smith revealed the contrast between the official version of events and that which, belatedly, had found its way into the daily newspapers.[4]

The subsequent storm in Parliament – with Asquith acknowledging the public's right to hear 'prompt and authentic information' from the front – resulted in Smith's resignation and the appointment of Colonel Ernest Swinton, a talented staff officer (and later the 'father' of armoured warfare), as the army's first official journalist. Attached to French's GHQ, his task was to write 'Eyewitness' accounts of military operations that would be censored first in France and then by Kitchener himself before being released to the press. 'This was the start', wrote one historian of war reporting, 'of a period of conspiracy, of deliberate lies and the suppression of truth; the foundations of a propaganda process with which we are still familiar today.'[5]

Swinton knew exactly what he was doing. 'The principle which guided me in my work', he wrote later, 'was above all to prevent helping the enemy. This appeared to me even more important than the purveyance of news to our own people.'[6]

Only in May 1915, after complaints from the United States, did the government allow selected civilian journalists to report from the front. They had to agree to submit their copy to an army censor and, in a clever move by the War Office, to accept temporary commissions and wear uniforms. Official war reporting, as a result, was far from objective.

5 September 1914: *'All that men can do our fellows will do'*
– Sir John French commits the BEF to the offensive

At 2 p.m., General Joffre arrived at the BEF's headquarters in the Château de Vaux-le-Pénil, south of the River Marne, and was ushered into a small room to meet Sir John French and his senior staff. Joffre put his cap on the table, faced the British commander and thanked him for taking a decision that would settle the fate of Europe. He then proceeded to outline his plan of attack – known as Instruction Générale No. 6 – for the following day. The Sixth Army would cross the Ourcq in the direction of Château-Thierry; the BEF was to advance east towards Montmirail; the Fifth Army was to turn north, though not until it had linked up with the BEF; and the Ninth Army was to protect the Fifth's flank.[1] Joffre was ready to throw his last company into the battle to save France, he told Sir John, but he needed the full support of the BEF. Clasping Sir John's hands powerfully in his, he concluded: 'Monsieur le Maréchal, c'est la France qui vous supplie.'[2]

Overcome with emotion, Sir John seemed lost for words as tears stained his flushed cheeks. At last, turning to a liaison officer, he exclaimed: 'Damn it, I can't explain. Tell him that all that men can do our fellows will do.'

When Sir John's chief of staff then intervened to say that the BEF could not start its advance as early as the French commander wished, Joffre was unperturbed. 'It cannot be helped,' he said, shrugging his shoulders. 'Let them start as soon as they can. I have the Marshal's word, that is enough for me.'[3]

For the previous two weeks – ever since the Battle of Mons – the Allied armies in Belgium and north-eastern France had been in retreat. So little did Sir John French trust the French after the events of the 23rd, and so serious did he regard his losses at Mons and a second major action at Le Cateau on 26 August (where British casualties were 8,000), that at one point he refused to take part in an Allied counter-attack; worse still, on the 30th he informed General Joffre that the battered BEF needed to retire behind the Seine to refit, and would not return to the battle 'for at least 10 days'. Only Lord Kitchener's personal intervention on 1 September had kept the BEF in the front line, much to Sir John French's fury and Joffre's relief.[4]

Meanwhile, on 31 August, Joffre had learned from intercepted signals and aerial reconnaissance that General von Kluck's First Army, on the German right, was now marching to the east and not the west of Paris. Thus developed in Joffre's mind the possibility of taking Kluck's army in the flank.* He knew the German troops were exhausted after five weeks

---

* General Gallieni, commander of the Paris garrison, came to a similar conclusion after ordering aerial observation of Kluck's army on 3 August.

of constant marching and fighting, and were at the end of their supply lines. His soldiers, on the other hand, were drawing closer to their supply depots, and he had been able to use France's excellent transverse railways to move troops from the right of his line to form a new Sixth Army of nine infantry and two cavalry divisions, under General Michel-Joseph Maunoury, on the outskirts of Paris.[5]

The only fly in the ointment was Sir John French. Would he, or would he not, let the BEF take part in the coming offensive? Joffre received his answer at their historic meeting on the 5th.

French reinforcements arrive in taxicabs from Paris to prevent a German breakthrough on the Marne on 7 September 1914.

Though there was some fighting that evening near the River Ourcq, the main Allied offensive did not begin until the following day. It was the start of a four-day swirling battle that became known as 'the Miracle of the Marne'. At first an Allied victory seemed unlikely as a series of assaults against the centre and flanks of the German position were repulsed. On 7 August it was Kluck's turn to attack Maunoury's Sixth Army with two corps that had been force-marched from his left wing. But for desperate measures by General Gallieni, the commander of the Paris garrison, who used taxicabs to send more than 2,000 reinforcements to Maunoury's assistance, the Germans might have broken through on the 7th. Elsewhere the situation was more favourable for the Allies as the transfer of two corps from Kluck's left wing had opened up a dangerous gap between the German First and Second Armies (the latter commanded by General von Bülow) into which the BEF marched.[6]

Even so the Germans might still have stabilized the situation had not their Chief of the General Staff, Moltke, lost his nerve. Stationed in Luxembourg, and out of contact with his army commanders, Moltke sent a staff officer, Colonel Hentsch, to assess the situation. Hentsch had the authority to order a withdrawal if he felt the forward armies were losing contact with each other, and that was the conclusion he came to when he reached Bülow's headquarters and learned of the British advance. He agreed with Bülow that the Second Army would retreat if the BEF crossed the Marne; it did so on 9 September, triggering not only the Second Army's withdrawal but also that of the First. Two days later, Moltke ordered the Third, Fourth and Fifth armies to retreat as well.[7] (The failure of the Schlieffen–Moltke plan caused its co-author to suffer a nervous breakdown. He was replaced on 14 September by the War Minister, Erich von Falkenhayn, who acted in both capacities until the following January when he relinquished the political post to his deputy.)

The Germans fell back to the 400-feet-high Chemin des Dames* ridge beyond the River Aisne, a defensive position that Moltke had earlier identified as naturally strong. To make it more so, the German infantry and field engineers were ordered to dig trenches and protect them with parapets (a skill they had regularly practised while on peacetime manoeuvres). On 14 September, Joffre ordered a general attack on the ridge; but only in the British sector did it almost succeed. 'The 1st Division on the right gained ground,' noted General Haig in his diary,

> but could not maintain itself in the face of the opposition encountered. Only in the centre the 5 Brigade, moving along the eastern slopes of the Beaulne ridges, was able to get forward and continue its advance until it reached the ridge about Tilleul de Courtacon. In the dark General Haking† failed to get in touch with the 1st Division, but his

---

* 'Ladies' Way', named after the route regularly taken by Louis XV's daughters.
† Brigadier-General Richard Haking, commander of 5 Brigade.

patrols found German outposts on both flanks. He consequently drew back his troops under cover of darkness to the neighbourhood of Verneuil.[8]

'I think it is very likely', wrote Sir John French on the 14th, 'that the enemy is making a determined stand on the Aisne.'[9] That evening he ordered his men to dig in.

The BEF did not remain long on the Aisne. In October it was sent north into Flanders as part of a series of operations known as the 'Race to the Sea', with both the Allies and the Germans trying (and failing) to outflank each other before the trench lines connected up from Switzerland to the Channel coast. Thereafter the BEF held various sectors (originally in Flanders and Artois, but later extending as far south as the Somme) of the Allied front line that ran for 475 miles, in the shape of a reversed S, from Nieuport in Belgium to the Swiss border. It was a trench line that, despite countless offensives and the loss of millions of soldiers, would barely alter for much of the next three and half years.

That was all in the future. In early September 1914, the fate of France hung in the balance. The German strategy of risking all on a rapid victory in the west, before turning to deal with the Russians, seemed close to paying off. It all hinged on Joffre's counter-attack, planned for 6 September, and that in turn depended on Sir John French's response to his emotional appeal for British assistance on the 5th. Fortunately for the Allies, that appeal succeeded and within days the 'Miracle of the Marne' had turned the tide.

President Raymond Poincaré of France justly acknowledged the part that both French and British troops had played in this victory in a letter of congratulation to the French Minister of War on 11 September. 'Far from being fatigued by long weeks of marching and unceasing battle,' he wrote, 'our troops have shown more endurance and keenness than ever. With the vigorous assistance of our English allies they have forced back the enemy to the east of Paris, and the brilliant successes they have gained and the magnificent qualities they have shown are sure guarantees of decisive victories.'[10]

8 September 1914: *'All I have . . . I leave to Miss Mary MacNulty'*
– Shot at dawn

At 6.22 a.m., a young British private was dozing in his cell in the Château Combreaux at Tournan-en-Brie, twenty-five miles south-east of Paris, when the door was unlocked and two men entered: Captain J. Monteath, the 5th Division's Assistant Provost Marshal; and an unidentified army padre. Reading from a sheet of paper, Monteath announced: 'Private Thomas Highgate, regimental number 10061, of the 1st Battalion, The Royal West Kent Regiment, you have been found guilty of desertion by a Field General Court Martial and sentenced to suffer death by being shot.'[1]

As a stunned Highgate tried to take in the awful news, Monteath explained that the sentence would be carried out by firing squad in exactly forty-five minutes, and that the prisoner was advised to use that time to make peace with his Maker. He then left the room.

Highgate was just nineteen years old. Born in Shoreham in Kent, the only son of a farm labourer, he had followed the same occupation before joining his local regiment at the age of seventeen years and nine months in February 1913. When war broke out, Highgate's battalion was quartered in Richmond Barracks, Dublin. It arrived in France on 15 August as part of the BEF's 5th Division that, along with the 3rd, made up II Corps under Lieutenant-General Sir James Grierson. Tragically Grierson died of a heart attack two days later, on a train heading for the BEF's concentration area, and was replaced by Lieutenant-General Sir Horace Smith-Dorrien.

Highgate had been in France for less than three weeks when he went missing from his battalion in the early hours of 6 September. The nightmare retreat from Mons had finally come to an end the day before, near the banks of the Marne, and the 1st Royal West Kents had spent the night in a stubble field a mile south of Tournan-en-Brie. Next morning, in accordance with Sir John French's promise to Joffre that the BEF would support his general offensive, the 1st Royal West Kents began its march north. As it did so, Highgate went missing.

He was found an hour or two later, wearing civilian clothes, by Thomas

Fermor, an English gamekeeper to Baron Edward de Rothschild (whose estate bordered Tournan), and handed over to the French gendarmerie. They, in turn, informed the British military. Within hours he had been tried and sentenced to death for desertion. But various questions remain: were there extenuating reasons for Highgate's absence from his battalion? And did he receive a fair trial?

The answer to the first question is almost certainly yes. Highgate was a young and inexperienced soldier and the Battle of Mons, where his battalion suffered more than a hundred casualties holding a section of canal near the railway bridge, was a shocking introduction to war. At first the men of the Royal West Kents held their own, using disciplined rifle fire to tear to pieces the attacking troops of the 12th Brandenburg Grenadiers. 'Wherever I looked,' wrote the novelist Walter Bloem, a captain in the 12th, 'right or left, were dead and wounded, quivering in convulsions, groaning terribly, blood oozing from fresh wounds.' He added: 'They apparently knew something about war, these cursed English, a fact soon confirmed on all sides.'[2]

But retaliation came in the form of a heavy artillery bombardment by 5.9-inch German shells that shattered the shallow trenches of the Royal West Kents and forced them to withdraw, taking their wounded with them. Three days later, Highgate and his battalion were again in action at Le Cateau, an even more desperate struggle. Thereafter, they were part of the 'fighting retreat' to the Marne – covering more than 250 miles in under two weeks – an exhausting and dispiriting experience that, coming so soon after his brutal initiation to war at Mons and Le Cateau, must have broken Highgate's spirit.

A corporal in the 1st Royal Berkshires wrote of the withdrawal:

September 3rd: The first four or five hours we did without a single halt or rest, as we had to cross a bridge over the Aisne before the Royal Engineers blew it up. It was the most terrible march I have ever done. Men were falling down like ninepins. They would fall flat on their faces on the road, while the rest of us staggered round them, as we couldn't lift our feet high enough to step over them, and, as for picking them up, that was impossible, as to bend meant to fall.[3]

Many British soldiers lost contact with their units during the retreat to the Marne. In one infamous instance, at Saint-Quentin on 27 August, two commanding officers* tried to surrender their disgruntled battalions en masse to the Germans, but a cavalry major intervened and led the men to safety.[4]

George Roupell, a lieutenant in the East Surrey Regiment who would win a Victoria Cross in 1915, recorded in his diary that instances of indiscipline were inevitable after the rigours of the retreat:

> Since our fight at Mons on August 23rd we had not a single day's rest. When we were not fighting, we were marching as hard as we could. Men were physically weak from the long marches and mentally weak from the continual strain of never being out of reach of the enemy's guns . . . It is scarcely surprising that under these conditions traces of panic and loss of self-control occurred.[5]

The military authorities, on the other hand, were fearful that this panic and indiscipline might spread. By 5 September, the BEF had lost nearly 20,000 men: killed, wounded, missing in action or just plain disappeared. Of these, almost 3,000 were listed as stragglers, including 291 from a single battalion, the 1st Royal Warwicks, and 246 from the 2nd Argyll & Sutherland Highlanders. Highgate's battalion, on the other hand, had reported only ten absent.[6]

On 4 September, to try and stop the rot, Sir John French had stated in Army Orders that he 'viewed with grave displeasure the straggling which still continues . . . and has reason to think that in certain cases sufficient effort is not being made to rejoin units'. All ranks, he continued, will face 'severe punishment if there is reason to suppose that every effort has not been made to rejoin'.[7]

The first inkling that the British military had of Highgate's defection was a signal received in II Corps headquarters at 8.50 a.m. on the 6 September. It read: 'Civilian reports an English deserter in plain clothes at the farm of M Poirier, rue de Martry, Tournan, and can you deal?'[8]

---

* The officers involved were Lieutenant-Colonels Ellington and Mainwaring of the 1st Royal Warwickshires and 2nd Dublin Fusiliers respectively. On 9 September they were court-martialled, found guilty of 'shamefully delivering up a garrison to the enemy' and cashiered. Mainwaring later joined the French Foreign Legion, using a pseudonym, and won the Croix de Guerre and promotion to sergeant for his bravery on the Western Front. In the early 1930s, he was restored to his former rank by George V.

Within a very short time, General Smith-Dorrien had convened an immediate field general court martial (requiring a panel of just three officers, rather than the usual five) and signed an army form (No. 49) that stated that 'military exigencies' such as, in this case, the 'proximity of the enemy' made it 'inexpedient' to observe the provisions of various rules, notably giving the defendant the 'proper opportunity of preparing his defence, and a copy of the summary of evidence against him'.[9] Conscious that II Corps was heading back into battle, Smith-Dorrien was determined to bring Highgate to justice as quickly as possible.

Highgate's crime, in the eyes of his superiors, was not simply that he had fallen out of the line of march – something he admitted at his trial – but that he had no intention of rejoining his battalion. The absolute proof of this, they felt, was that he was found wearing civilian clothes. From this point on his fate was as good as sealed.

With almost indecent haste, Highgate was passed mentally and physically fit for trial by a Captain Moss of the Royal Army Medical Corps and then brought before the court martial in the Château Cambreaux, a mile south of Tournan, during the afternoon of the 6th. The court was comprised of a president, Colonel A. B. Dunsterville (commanding II Corps' attached troops), and a captain and lieutenant of the 1st Cameron Highlanders. The prosecutor was the Assistant Provost Marshal of II Corps. Highgate, with no officer to defend him, pleaded not guilty to the charge of 'deserting His Majesty's Service' when on active service.

The first witness was Thomas Fermor who said that at 8.15 a.m. that day he had been searching for a bicycle and 'from information received' had gone towards the 'Madeleine' where he found the accused there 'dressed in civilian clothes'. When he asked him what he was doing, Highgate had replied: 'I have lost my Army, and I mean to get out of it,' or, as Fermor put it, 'words to that effect'. Fermor added: 'I searched him and found on him the [pay] book which I produce . . . We found his clothes [uniform] in a woodshed, the rifle & cartridges were missing. I took him to the Mairie and gave him up to the French police.'[10]

Aware that he had to challenge Fermor's incriminating evidence, Highgate asked him in cross-examination: 'Did I say I wanted to get out of it, or that I wanted to find my way out of it?'

Fermor replied: 'You said "I have had enough of it. I want to get out of it, and this is how I am doing it."'

The second prosecution witness, a staff officer called Captain Milward, testified that when he went to collect the accused from the Mairie he was 'dressed in plain clothes, just as he is now'. When he asked him why he had run away, the accused replied 'that he left his bivouac that morning and remembered nothing more'.

Declining to cross-examine Milward, and with no witnesses of his own, Highgate gave a statement to the court under oath. He had left his regiment during a stop on the march north to 'ease' himself, and by the time he had finished the regiment had gone on. He explained:

> I went out but could not find them, got strolling about, went down into a farm, lay down in an empty house, and have a slight remembrance of putting some civilian clothes on, but do not remember exactly what happened until the man came down to arrest me. I was coming back then to see if I could find my clothes, and my Regiment, but I was taken to the police station before I could get back. When I was asked by the man who arrested me who I was, I answered him at once and told him who I was.

In cross-examination, the prosecutor asked: 'Why did you say to Mr Fermor you "wanted to get out of it and that was how you were doing it", or words to that effect?'

Highgate replied: 'I told him that I was trying to get out of it, meaning that I had lost my way and wanted to get out of the place in which I was, and wanted to rejoin my Regiment. I cannot say why I was in civilian clothes.'[11]

This was the nub and, without a credible reason for abandoning his uniform, Highgate had little chance of an acquittal. The court duly found him guilty as charged and sentenced him 'to suffer death by being shot' with no recommendation to mercy. The sentence was confirmed by Smith-Dorrien on the 6th, and by Sir John French a day later, with the former insisting that the execution be carried out 'as publicly as convenient'.[12]

Shortly after 7 a.m. on 8 September, Highgate was blindfolded, tied to a post and shot by firing squad in the grounds of the Château Cambreaux. Forced to watch this grim spectacle, in accordance with Smith-Dorrien's orders, were 400 men of the Dorset and Cheshire Regiments, fellow members of the 5th Division. Highgate was then cut down and buried in an unmarked grave. On page 14 of his pay book, he had scrawled his makeshift will: 'If I get killed all I have to come from the Government for my services to Miss Mary MacNulty, No. 3 Leinster St, Phibsborough, Dublin.'[13] The sweetheart he had met while stationed in Ireland would never know the truth.

By modern standards, Highgate was the victim of rough justice: he had no time to prepare a defence and no defending officer; there were, moreover, mitigating circumstances to his crime in terms of his age, inexperience and the trauma of his fight at and retreat from Mons. On the other hand the evidence – notably his shedding of his uniform and his comment that he had 'had enough' and wanted 'to get out of it' – did support the charge of desertion.

At the time of Highgate's execution the Battle of the Marne was still in the balance and the BEF, his battalion included, was fighting for its life. Under the circumstances, French and Smith-Dorrien were keen to make an example of Highgate to encourage the others. That is why his execution was witnessed by two companies of soldiers, and announced in Army Routine Orders on 10 September. Four days later, French warned: 'Failure to maintain the highest standard of discipline will result in the infliction of the most severe punishment.'[14]

Highgate was the first of 309 British and Empire soldiers to be executed for military offences committed while on active service during the conflict (a further thirty-seven were shot for murder). Like Highgate, the vast majority were found guilty of desertion (266), with cowardice (18), quitting a post (7), striking a superior officer (6) and disobedience of a lawful order (5) the next most prevalent categories. The figures sound shocking but they need to be put into context. More than 5,250,000 men served in the British Army in the First World War, of whom 702,000 were killed and 1.66 million wounded. During the period 4 August 1914 to October 1918, there were 238,000 courts martial, yet only 3,080 resulted in death sentences. Of those, only 346 (11 per cent, including for murder) were carried out. In the case of desertion, only a tiny fraction (3.6 per cent) of the soldiers tried for that crime were actually executed. 'These statistics show with lucid clarity', wrote the co-authors of a recent book on the subject, 'just how sparingly the final sanction of military law was employed by a massive army fighting for its life.'[15]

Nevertheless in 2006, after a long campaign by relatives and citizens' groups, Des Browne, then Secretary of State for Defence, acknowledged that the evidence no longer existed to assess each of the cases individually, and that the best way to acknowledge that an injustice had been done in some instances was to grant a posthumous pardon to all 309 men executed for military offences. In Highgate's file, like all the others, was placed a note from Browne confirming that the pardon stood 'as recognition that he was one of the victims of the First World War and that execution was not a fate he deserved'.[16]

22 September 1914: *'We were woken by a terrific crash'* – First blood to the U-boats

At 6.10 a.m., the German submarine *U-9* was eighteen miles north-west of the Hook of Holland, partly submerged but with five feet of its periscope visible, when it caught sight of three Royal Navy cruisers. 'I submerged completely,' wrote the U-boat's skipper, Kapitänleutnant Otto Weddigen, 'and laid my course so as to bring up in the centre of the trio, which held a sort of triangular formation. I could see their gray-black sides riding high over the water.'[1]

Built in Danzig in 1908, Weddigen's petrol-driven *U-9* was one of the oldest of the twenty operational submarines in the German High Seas Fleet at the start of the war. One hundred and ninety feet long, with a crew of thirty-five and a submerged top speed of just 8 knots, it was much smaller and less heavily armed than the more famous U-boats of the Second World War. It had, moreover, suffered engine failure on a recent mission to attack the British Grand Fleet at Scapa Flow.[2] Yet on 22 September it was, wrote Weddigen, 'behaving beautifully'. He added:

> When I first sighted them they were near enough for torpedo work, but I wanted to make my aim sure, so I went down and in on them. I had taken the position of the three ships before submerging, and I succeeded in getting another flash through my periscope before I began action. I soon reached what I regarded as a good shooting point.
>
> Then I loosed one of my [six] torpedoes at the middle ship. I was then about twelve feet under water, and got the shot off in good shape,

my men handling the boat as if she had been a skiff. I climbed to the surface to get a sight through the tube of the effect, and discovered that the shot had gone straight and true, striking the ship, which I later learned was the 'Aboukir'.[3]

HMS *Aboukir* was one of three old Cressy-class armoured cruisers that had been given the dangerous, and some felt suicidal, task of patrolling the area of the North Sea known as the Broad Fourteens. Its crew, like that of its sister ships *Cressy* and *Hogue*, was chiefly composed of middle-aged reservists, but included a sprinkling of young cadets from Dartmouth like fifteen-year-old 'Kit' Wykeham-Musgrave who was asleep when the torpedo struck. He recalled:

We were woken by a terrific crash and the whole ship shook and all the crockery in the pantry fell. Of course we thought it was a mine, and rushed up on deck. We had all the scuttles and watertight doors closed at once, and everything that would float brought up and thrown over-board . . . She then started to list heavily.[4]

Unaware that *Aboukir* had been torpedoed, and that danger still lurked, *Cressy* and *Hogue* steamed at once to their sister ship's assistance. On board *Hogue*, which stopped a quarter of a mile off the stricken ship's starboard beam, was another fifteen-year-old cadet, Hereward Hook:

In about ten minutes [he wrote] *Aboukir* had taken a heavy list to port, and in about fifteen her condition was hopeless. It was my first sight of men struggling for their lives. The bilge keel and part of the ship's bottom were exposed to view, with hundreds of men's heads bobbing about in the water, while a continuous stream of very scantily clad men appeared from the upper deck and started tobogganing down the ship's side, stopping suddenly when they came to the bilge keel, climbing over it, and continuing their slide until they reached the water with a splash.[5]

Escaping by this route, Wykeham-Musgrave swam to *Hogue* and was 'just going on board' when she was hit amidships by two torpedoes.[6] 'The whole ship seemed to jump at least six inches out of the water,' recalled Hook, 'and an enormous column of water was sent up, some of which descended with considerable force on my back and shoulders. The second torpedo must have gone through the hole made in the ship's side by the first, thereby nearly cutting the ship in halves, as No. 3 funnel suddenly collapsed like a house of cards.'[7]

The ship sank in 'six or seven minutes', wrote Hook, but there was no panic among the veteran crew. He was rescued by a launch; Wykeham-Musgrave managed to swim to *Cressy* and was hauled on board by a rope and given a mug of cocoa.[8] Aware by now that a U-boat was responsible, *Cressy*'s captain bravely chose to stand and fight, firing her torpedo defence batteries and steaming in a zig-zag course. 'This made it necessary for me to get nearer to the "Cressy",' noted Weddigen.

> I had come to the surface for a view and saw how wildly the fire was being sent from the ship. Small wonder that was when they did not know where to shoot, although one shot went unpleasantly near us.
>
> When I got within suitable range I sent away my third attack . . . My crew were aiming like sharpshooters and both torpedoes went to the bull's-eye . . . The enemy was made useless and at once began sinking by her head. Then she careened far over, but all the while her men stayed at the guns looking for their invisible foe. They were brave and true to their country's sea traditions. Then she eventually suffered a boiler explosion and completely turned turtle.[9]

Incredibly, young Wykeham-Musgrave survived this third sinking and was later rescued by a Dutch trawler. He and Hook, who was picked up by a fishing-boat, were among the 300 or so survivors from the three cruisers; a further 1,459 officers and crew were killed. The disaster would have been prevented if the Admiralty had heeded Commodore Roger Keyes' warning that the patrol was unnecessary and highly dangerous. But Keyes was overruled by the Chief of the Admiralty War Staff, Vice-Admiral Sir Frederick Sturdee, who felt that the Scheldt estuary had to be kept open to traffic, and cited the seventeenth-century Anglo-Dutch Wars as the precedent for maintaining a patrol of the Broad Fourteens.[10]

After sinking the three cruisers, *U-9* was chased by Royal Navy destroyers but made good its escape. On 24 September Kapitänleutnant Weddigen was decorated with two Iron Crosses, First and Second Class, by the Kaiser himself. In late October, for sinking the cruiser HMS *Hawke*, Weddigen was given Imperial Germany's highest award for gallantry, the

Pour le Mérite (or 'Blue Max'). His luck ran out on 18 March 1915, however, when his new command, *U-29*, was sunk in the Pentland Firth with all hands.

6 October 1914: *'Spy mania everywhere'*
– The Fall of Antwerp

It was early morning when Benbow Battalion of the 1st Royal Naval Brigade finally reached Antwerp after a long voyage from Deal in Kent. 'We were marched through the town,' recalled Able Seaman Jeremy Bentham, 'and out into the country, told to dig a light trench and stand by for a Uhlan [German irregular cavalry] charge. We said, "What's that? Never heard of it." For none of us had ever fired a gun and hardly knew one end of a rifle from the other.'[1]

Bentham and his colleagues had been sent to Antwerp because of its vital strategic importance. 'Antwerp', wrote Winston Churchill, First Lord of the Admiralty, 'was not only the sole stronghold of the Belgian nation; it was also the true left flank of the Allied front in the west. It guarded the whole line of the Channel ports. It threatened the flank and even the rear of the German Armies in France . . . No German advance to the sea coast, upon Ostend, upon Dunkirk, upon Calais and Boulogne seemed possible while Antwerp was unconquered.'[2]

As long as the bulk of the Belgian Army remained behind Antwerp's defences, Churchill and his Cabinet colleagues assumed the fortress was secure. But on 2 October, four days after heavy German howitzers had begun to reduce Antwerp's defences, the Belgian government informed London that it was about to withdraw its army to Ostend, thus surrendering the fortress to the Germans. Determined to prevent this, Asquith's government persuaded the Belgians to delay their departure so that British troops could take their place.[3]

The first reinforcements sent were 2,000 Royal Marines of the Naval Division who reached Antwerp during the night of the 3rd. They were followed, during the night of the 5th, by Bentham and his colleagues in the 1st and 2nd Royal Naval Brigades, both composed of reserves with little infantry training. The plan was for them to defend Antwerp until the last remaining regular division, the 7th, could join them. The 7th had been due to join the newly expanded BEF – now consisting of three infantry and one cavalry corps, each of two divisions – as it relocated to the area around Ypres, and Sir John French was predictably furious when these extra troops were earmarked for Antwerp, telling Churchill that he opposed the concept of 'putting mobile troops *inside* a fortress'.[4] This was, of course, a volte-face from French's earlier enthusiasm for the Antwerp option; but *then* it had involved the whole BEF, whereas *now* it would involve a dissipation of his total force.

The First Lord of the Admiralty disagreed, and went himself to Antwerp on 3 October to convince the Belgian King and government to hold on. 'He dominated the whole place; the King, ministers, soldiers, sailors,' recalled Colonel J. E. B. Seely, the ex-War Minister who had arrived in Antwerp as Sir John French's representative. 'So great was his influence that I am convinced that with 20,000 British troops he could have held Antwerp against any onslaught.'[5]

Bizarrely dressed in the faux military uniform of Trinity House* – a blue jacket with a double row of brass buttons, and a military-style peaked cap with gold braid – Churchill admitted later that his intention all along had been to command troops in battle.[6] To that end he cabled Asquith on 5 October, offering to resign from the Cabinet and remain in Antwerp in a military capacity. 'I feel it my duty to offer my services,' he wrote, 'because I am sure this arrangement will afford the best prospects of a victorious result to an enterprise in which I am deeply involved.'[7]

His offer was rejected, not least because the War Office knew that German infantry had breached the outer ring of Antwerp's defences, and instead Churchill was told to arrange an orderly evacuation of the city. It began during the evening of the 6th. The retreat was like a scene from Dante's hell, lit by 'hills and spires of flame', wrote Rupert Brooke who was serving with Oc Asquith (son of the Prime Minister) as a sub-lieutenant in Anson Battalion of the Royal Naval Division. Brooke added:

* The City of London corporation with responsibility for pilotage and lighthouses, of which Churchill had been appointed an Elder Brother in 1913.

Thousands of refugees, their goods on barrows and hand-carts and perambulators and wagons, moving with uniform slowness out into the night, two unending lines of them, the old men mostly weeping, the women with hard drawn faces, the children praying or crying or sleeping. That's what Belgium is now: the country where three civilians have been killed to every one soldier . . . It's queer to think that one has been a witness to one of the greatest crimes of history. Has ever a nation been treated like that? And how can such a stain be wiped out?[8]

Brooke and his battalion made it safely over the Scheldt to the railhead at Saint-Gilles where they escaped on a train to Ostend via Bruges. But not everyone got away. Sarah Macnaughton, a British nurse helping with a private ambulance unit, remembered shells exploding in the hospital grounds as staff searched frantically for transport to move their seventy wounded patients. 'At last we got a motor ambulance,' she wrote, 'and packed in twenty men. We told them to go as far as the bridge [over the Scheldt] and send it back for us. It never came. Nothing seemed to come.'[9]

Likewise, Able Seaman Bentham's platoon never received an order to quit the trenches, and several hours had passed before they realized that everyone else had gone. 'It was a ghastly march,' he recalled, 'because everyone was very hungry and very tired and we didn't dare go to sleep when we stopped for a rest in case we might be left behind and find ourselves taken by the Germans.' He added:

> The atmosphere in Antwerp was absolutely chaotic, crowds of refugees taking up most of the road and spy mania everywhere. We guessed that because we even saw a few corpses hanging from lamp posts. Eventually we got to the Scheldt, but we'd missed the bridge and we'd no idea how to get across. After a long search someone found a boat and somehow or other we all crammed into it. It was a wonder we got to the other side!

Once across the river they were supposed to board trains to take them south to Ostend. But the trains had left and the only option now was to walk, a march that took them to the Dutch frontier where they were told they would be given twenty-four hours 'to get out of the country'. But it was 'all poppycock, of course', noted Bentham, and once he and his comrades had surrendered their weapons they and most of the 1st Naval Brigade – a total of thirty-seven officers and 1,442 men – were arrested and interned in Groningen in northern Holland.[10] A further five officers and 931 men, mostly Marines, were captured by the Germans en route south.[11] Antwerp fell to the Germans on 10 October.

Wrecked transport and equipment left in the streets of Antwerp by retreating Belgian soldiers in October 1914.

Could Churchill's plan have succeeded? Colonel Seely thought so, noting 'we could probably have held the place for many weeks, and if so, it would have altered the whole course of the war'. But he was also convinced that the expedition, however brief, was worthwhile. 'From all I learned and from all I saw,' he wrote, 'I think it very possible that had Winston not brought his naval men to Antwerp the Belgian Field Army [30,000–40,000 men] would not have escaped. Had Winston been vigorously supported, even this late in the day, the Germans would have been forced to detach such large forces that their advance on Ypres would have been stayed, and might have been prevented altogether.'[12]

Churchill himself thought the effects of his expedition even further reaching. 'Had the German Siege Army been released on the 5th,' he wrote, 'and, followed by their great reinforcements already available, advanced at once, nothing could have saved Dunkirk, and perhaps Calais and Boulogne. The loss of Dunkirk was certain and that of both Calais and Boulogne probable. Ten days were wanted, and ten days were won.'[13]

25 October 1914: *'He was dragged off the field'*
– The Indian Corps to the rescue

After dark, a young Afridi Pashtun by the name of Usman Khan played a key role in driving off a German attack on the Messines–Wytschaete feature south of Ypres in Flanders. 'Usman Khan', wrote the official historian,

> was wounded twice during the night and was ordered back to the regimental Aid Post . . . He refused to go . . . in his opinion, his wounds were slight and he could fire his rifle perfectly well as long as he remained in the lying position. He was once again wounded; rather more seriously now, for a bullet removed a sizeable portion of both his thighs, causing serious bleeding. This time he was not given the choice and was dragged off the field, protesting feebly that he could still fire his rifle. He was subsequently awarded the Indian Distinguished Service Medal.[1]

Khan's battalion, the 57th (Wilde's) Rifles, was seeing action for the first time since it had arrived in Marseilles as part of the 3rd (Lahore) Division of the Indian Corps in late September. It and other battalions of the Ferozepore Brigade were thrown piecemeal into the line south of Ypres to help stem a massive German offensive that had begun on 19 October from La Bassée Canal in the south to the estuary of the Yser in the north, with twenty-four divisions against nineteen Allied (though the latter total included six weakened Belgian divisions). The heaviest fighting was between fourteen German divisions and seven British, with three

British cavalry divisions fighting as infantry, and a hotch-potch of French sailors, Territorials and cavalry defending the gap between the British and the Belgians on the sea.

The battle that came to be known as First Ypres was fought in field ditches and rudimentary trenches barely three feet deep, both frequently waterlogged and unprotected by barbed wire. In the absence of solid defences, 'it was the curtain of rifle bullets, crashing out in a density the Germans often mistook for machine-gun fire, that broke up attacks and drove the survivors of an assault to ground or sent them crawling back to cover on their start lines'.[2]

The Indian soldiers played their part in this doughty defence, though Major-General James Willocks, commanding the Indian Corps, regretted the break-up of his divisions as emergency stopgaps. 'Where is my Lahore Division?' he wrote in his diary on 29 October.[3]

Two days later the 129th (Duke of Connaught's Own) Baluchis, also of the Ferozepore Brigade but attached to the British Cavalry Corps, gained everlasting renown when one of its sepoys, twenty-six-year-old Khudadad Khan from Jhelum in the Punjab, became the first Indian soldier to win a Victoria Cross. His citation read:

> On 31st October, 1914, at Hollebeke, Belgium, the British Officer in charge of the detachment having been wounded, and the other gun put out of action by a shell, Sepoy Khudadad, though himself wounded, remained working his gun until all the other five men of the gun detachment had been killed.[4]

When overrun by the Germans, Khan 'feigned death and was able to crawl away and rejoin his unit'.[5] Thanks to his bravery, and that of his fellow Baluchis, the Germans were held up long enough for Indian and British reinforcements to arrive and prevent a final breakthrough.*

General Willocks was astonished at how well Usman and Khudadad Khan's battalions performed given the difficulties they were operating under. 'Here were two Indian battalions,' he wrote, 'suddenly dumped down in a maelstrom, depending for guidance entirely on their few British officers, split up into half companies, attached to various British corps

---

* Khan later recovered from his wounds in an English hospital and was awarded the VC by King George V at Buckingham Palace on 26 January 1915.

in turn, cavalry, infantry, guns; hurried from one trench to another, from one front to another, hardly realising the meaning or object of it all.' And yet, despite losing most of their officers, they fought on 'in those few but stormy days of Ypres'.[6]

The 129th Baluchis in makeshift trenches on the edge of Wytschaete, Flanders, in late October 1914. On the 31st, near Hollebeke, Sepoy Khudadad Khan of the 129th became the first Indian soldier to win the Victoria Cross.

Usman and Khudadad Khan were just two of more than 138,000 Indian soldiers – drawn from the many races that the British had designated as 'martial', including Punjabis, Baluchis, Sikhs, Jats, Dogras, Gurkhas, Pathans and Garhwalis – who served on the Western Front during the first year of the war. By 1 December their casualties numbered 133 British and 95 Indian officers and 4,735 other ranks. Some, particularly the Pathans, seemed to enjoy the fighting; many were genuinely proud to be serving the Empire in its time of need. But as their casualties mounted, and the weather deteriorated, morale began to fall. There was an especially high incidence of self-inflicted wounds, mostly in the left hand, and some sepoys plotted sedition. When the Indian Corps was finally withdrawn from France in October 1915, it was sent to Mesopotamia and not home for 'fear of unrest'.[7]

A total of almost 1.5 million Indians fought for Britain in various theatres during the First World War. Nor were they the only imperial contribution. No sooner had war been declared than the Dominions and colonies offered their unequivocal support. 'When Great Britain is at war,' declared Sir Wilfrid Laurier, the former Prime Minister of Canada, 'we are at war.' His countrymen agreed, with no fewer than 630,000 volunteering for foreign service (though only 30,000 were French Canadians). Australia and New Zealand raised sizeable contingents (the Anzacs), as did South Africa (though the latter also experienced the only rebellion *against* participation by disaffected Boers who were defeated in a brief but bloody civil war). Even Catholic Ireland contributed 135,000 volunteers to Kitchener's New Army. 'Recruits', wrote one imperial historian, 'flooded in from all parts of the empire and beyond: Maoris and Fijians, West Indians and Falkland Islanders, Moosejaw frontiersmen and Khyber Pathans, Chinese coolies and African askaris, Dutch farmers from the Cape and Scottish shepherds from Patagonia . . . Flung into the scales of war, the imperial sword may have tipped the balance.'[8]

31 October 1914: *'The Worcesters saved the Empire'*
– First Battle of Ypres

At 1.45 p.m., Sir John French was forced to leave his car amid the chaos of a beaten army. 'It was a regular debacle,' he noted. 'The heavy guns were trotting. When a heavy field gun trots you may be sure things are pretty bad.'[1]

Continuing on foot up the Menin Road, French reached General Haig's I Corps headquarters in the White Château at the foot of Hooge Ridge at 2 p.m. He found his corps commander 'very white but quite calm'. Haig explained: 'They have broken us right in and are pouring through the gap.'[2]

To make matters worse, said Haig, a German shell had just decapitated the staffs of his 1st and 2nd Divisions, killing General Lomax and wounding General Monro. With only rear-echelon troops standing between the Germans and the ancient Belgian cloth town of Ypres, and beyond that the unprotected supply ports of Boulogne and Nieuport, the fate of the BEF was hanging in the balance. French slumped into a chair, pale with shock. It was, he claimed later, the worst half-hour of his life.[3]

He discussed with Haig the possibility of retreat. But this was not Mons. With Ypres and the River Yser at their backs, few major roads and bridges, and the troops exhausted, they realized there was no chance of an orderly withdrawal. Their only hope was to request French reinforcements and pray they arrived in time. Sir John left for General Foch's headquarters, but as he hurried back down the Menin Road to find his car he was deeply despondent and in no doubt that 'the last barrier between the Germans and the Channel seaboard was broken down'.[4]

French was approaching his car when he heard footsteps and his name called. He turned to see a breathless Lieutenant Straker, Haig's aide-de-camp (ADC), dodging between ambulances, wagons and walking wounded. Straker had momentous news: a single battalion, the 2nd Worcesters, had retaken Gheluvelt and plugged the gap. French was in no doubt about the significance of the moment. 'The Worcesters', he claimed later, 'saved the Empire.'[5]

A private in the 2nd Worcesters recalled:

> They fled in a solid grey mass and we watched the boys winkling them out. Remorseless. It was slaughter. At one point in the sunken road [near Gheluvelt Château] we were firing the machine-gun, using dead bodies for cover . . . Our lines weren't established and it was dangerous to hang around because the Germans were sweeping this sunken road with enfilade fire from Gheluvelt village. We linked up with the Welsh [South Wales Borderers] and had to send forward fighting patrols to clear them out of it – and we did it (apart from a few fanatics in a few pockets who held on and kept firing). We plugged the gap to Calais.[6]

This extraordinary counter-attack by the 2nd Worcesters was the pivotal moment in the First Battle of Ypres. By 2 November, the main German offensive had been repulsed – albeit narrowly – with heavy casualties, particularly to the German volunteer corps (including 25,000 university students killed on 22 October in an engagement at Langemarck known as the *Kindermord*, or 'massacre of the innocents'). After the failure of another large-scale offensive on 11 November, the German attacks became more sporadic and were finally ended on the 22nd when the Kaiser accepted his generals' advice to switch the focus of military operations to the Eastern Front. They had lost 130,000 men; the Allies a similar number, though the comparatively high British share (58,000 to 50,000 French and 20,000 Belgians) meant the original BEF had virtually ceased to exist.[7]

Among the inexperienced German soldiers blooded at First Ypres was Adolf Hitler. Assigned to the newly formed Bavarian Reserve Infantry Regiment 16 (known, after its colonel, as the List Regiment), he had finally left for the front in late October. His baptism of fire was on the 29th, at Gheluvelt near the Menin Road, where in four days of fighting his regiment lost its colonel and nearly 2,250 (or 75 per cent) of its 3,000 men.[8] On 3 November, chiefly because of these heavy losses, Hitler was made a Gefreiter (the equivalent of private first class in the US Army, there being no similar position for British troops), a rank that conferred no powers of command over other soldiers. Already his initial enthusiasm for war had been replaced by a grim realization that 'life is a constant horrible struggle'. A couple of weeks later, by which time he was a runner attached to the regimental staff, he helped to save his new colonel's life, an act of gallantry for which he was awarded the Iron Cross, Second Class on 2 December. He described it as 'the happiest day of my life'.[9]

4 November 1914: *'The action of a lunatic'*
– Lettow-Vorbeck repulses the British at Tanga

At 2.30 p.m., as it struggled through thick bush towards the outskirts of the German East African port of Tanga,* Major-General Arthur Aitken's 8,000-strong Indian Expeditionary Force B came under sustained rifle and machine-gun fire from fewer than 1,000 defenders, most of them African askaris. Assuming the town was unprotected, Aitken had ordered his seven battalions to advance in one long line, a formation which

* The first move in Britain's attempt to bring the whole of German East Africa under its authority.

'staggered' one of his intelligence officers and reminded him 'of days long past'. Nor had the commander bothered to land field guns, leaving his men without artillery support.[1]

His best troops on the right – the 2nd Loyal North Lancs (the only British unit in the force), one and a half battalions of Kashmir Rifles and the 13th Rajputs – drove back the German outposts, captured a machine-gun and entered the town. Some Rajputs even managed to occupy the Kaiserhof Hotel and lower the two German flags on its roof. But in the centre and on the left of Aitken's line the seasick and inexperienced Indian battalions disintegrated. The Palamcottahs from western India (an area not considered 'martial' by the British) were the first to break, hastened in their flight by a swarm of angry bees. This, in turn, isolated the 101st Grenadiers on the British left and forced them to wheel to the right to maintain contact with the Loyal North Lancs. If they had kept on their original compass bearing they might have outflanked the German defenders at the railway station. Instead, they came under heavy machine-gun fire from well-dug-in positions near railway workshops, and exposed their own left flank to a 'right hook' counter-attack that was launched by the skilful German commander Colonel Paul von Lettow-Vorbeck. Within minutes all of the 101st's British officers, five Indian officers and a third of the rank and file were dead. The survivors were soon scattered in the bush.[2]

By 5.30 p.m., exhausted by vicious street fighting, most of the rest of Aitken's force were in retreat, leaving the Rajputs and the Kashmiris clinging to defensive positions on the seafront. What saved them from annihilation was a mistaken bugle call by an askari trumpeter for the whole German force to move back to its assembly point. 'In some inexplicable way,' wrote Lettow-Vorbeck, 'the troops imagined a Headquarters order had been issued that they were to return to their old camp west of Tanga.' It deprived him, at a vital moment, of enough troops to pursue the beaten enemy.[3]

That evening, with Tanga empty of German troops, Aitken gave orders for the re-embarkation of his entire force. They left in such haste that all heavy stores were abandoned, gifting to Lettow-Vorbeck eight machine-guns, 455 rifles, half a million rounds of ammunition, telephone equipment, coats, blankets and even uniforms. The British casualties were 817 men killed, wounded and missing; the Germans just 125. 'So ended', wrote one British officer, 'one of the most ignominious defeats ever inflicted on a British Army.'[4]

Another participant was quick to apportion blame. 'To land a large force without reconnaissance,' he wrote on 11 November, 'to see whether any of the enemy were about appears the action of a lunatic.'[5] Aitken was duly sacked and overall responsibility for the East African theatre was switched from India to the War Office.

Lettow-Vorbeck, on the other hand, won instant fame in Germany. Nor was Tanga an isolated success. During the next four years, with a force that never exceeded 14,000 (3,000 Germans and 11,000 Africans), Lettow-Vorbeck held at bay more than 300,000 British, Belgian and Portuguese troops. He never lost a battle, though in late 1917 weight of numbers forced him to leave German East Africa (modern Tanzania) for Portuguese Mozambique, and only after the Armistice had been signed in Europe in November 1918 did he agree to surrender his tiny but undefeated army of 155 Germans and 1,100 askaris to the British at Abercorn in Northern Rhodesia (Zambia today). The only German commander to occupy British territory during the conflict, he and his men were given a heroes' welcome when they returned to Germany in 1919.[6]

6 November 1914: *'May my life be honoured'*
– The shooting of a spy

Shortly before Carl Hans Lody was due to be shot in the Tower of London, the first execution there for a century and a half,* he asked the presiding Assistant Provost Marshal: 'I suppose you will not shake hands with a spy?'

The officer replied: 'No, but I will shake hands with a brave man.'[1]

Lody was a German naval reserve officer who had left the regular service in his twenties to become a tour guide overseas. He had, as a result, travelled widely and spoke fluent English with an American accent. In July 1914, with war imminent, he volunteered his services to German

---

* The previous execution had been the beheading of the Jacobite Lord Lovat in 1747.

naval intelligence (Nachrichten-Abteilung or 'N'). A month later, using a genuine American passport in the name of Charles A. Inglis, he was sent to Britain via Norway to gather intelligence on the Royal Navy, particularly its losses in the anticipated showdown with the German High Seas Fleet.[2]

With no experience and little training, Lody proved to be a hopelessly inept spy. He hired a bicycle to get to naval installations, taking notes and asking questions.[3] On 4 September, a week after arriving in Edinburgh, he sent an uncoded letter to a German recipient at an address in Stockholm that was known to be used by 'N', giving incorrect information about the alleged landing of large numbers of Russian troops in Aberdeen two days earlier.[4] The letter was intercepted by MO5 (the forerunner of MI5) – whose counter-espionage agents were routinely targeting mail sent to neutral countries – as were subsequent messages sent from London and Liverpool. He was arrested on 2 October in Killarney, en route to Queenstown, the main British naval base in Ireland, and brought back to London for trial.[5]

Reginald Drake, MO5's head of counter-espionage, wanted the court martial to take place *in camera* so that either Lody could be turned and used as a double-agent or disinformation sent in his name. (A similar type of 'Double-Cross System' would be used to great effect in the Second World War.) But Drake was overruled by a government keen to trumpet its success in dealing with German espionage, and a public court martial took place at the Middlesex Guildhall in late October. It duly found Lody guilty of spying and condemned him to death on 2 November.[6]

There were some at MO5 who questioned whether it was 'sound policy to execute spies and to begin with a patriotic spy like Lody'. They included MO5's chief Sir Vernon Kell who, according to his wife, regarded Lody as a 'really fine man' and 'felt it deeply that so brave a man should have to pay the death penalty'. Lody had accepted his fate with calmness and grace, writing to thank the officer in charge of Wellington Barracks for the 'kind and considered treatment' he had received during his incarceration there.[7]

At 7 a.m. on 6 November, three days after the confirmation of his sentence by King George V, Lody was led into the Tower's indoor firing-range, blindfolded and placed on a chair. He was then shot by an eight-man squad, the officer in command delivering the coup de grâce with a revolver.[8] 'May my life be honoured', he had written in his last letter to relations in Stuttgart, 'as a humble offering on the altar of the Fatherland'.[9] It was, but not until the Second World War when a German destroyer was named after him.

Carl Hans Lody of German naval intelligence who was executed in the Tower of London for spying on 6 November 1914.

Lody's military trial and execution had been authorized by a piece of emergency legislation that, in the name of national security, was destined to curtail many of the civil liberties that Britons took for granted. Dubbed the Defence of the Realm Act (DORA), it had been passed by the House of Commons without debate on 8 August. In its initial form – it was amended and extended no fewer than six times during the war – it sought to give the authorities the power to try by court martial anyone 'communicating with the enemy' or 'obtaining information' for the purpose of jeopardizing military operations or assisting the enemy; and also those who threatened the 'safety of any means of communication, or of railways, docks or harbours'.[10]

These powers of martial law were extended on 27 November 1914 when the Defence of the Realm Consolidation Act replaced the existing legislation. This new act gave the government wide-ranging powers to suppress published criticism, to imprison without trial and to commandeer economic resources for the war effort. Among the seemingly harmless acts that became criminal offences were flying kites, lighting bonfires, buying binoculars, discussing naval and military matters and buying alcohol on public transport. Pub opening hours* were limited from noon to 3 p.m. and from 6.30 p.m. to 9.30 p.m. (the afternoon closure was kept until 1988), and drinks were watered down.[11]

But the most invidious section allowed for the censorship of oral or written information 'likely to cause disaffection or alarm'. As this could apply to just about any form of anti-government criticism, it was open to the type of political misuse that resulted in the police raiding the offices of Keir Hardie's Independent Labour Party in 1915 and charging the organization with publishing seditious material. The fact that the government lost the case was never made public because the trial, unlike Lody's, was held in secret.[12]

9 November 1914: *'The result . . . was never in doubt'*
– The sinking of the *Emden*

At 6.30 a.m., the Australian cruiser HMAS *Sydney* was on troopship escort duty in the South Seas when it received an urgent wireless message that a 'foreign warship' was 'off the entrance' to Port Refuge on the nearby Cocos Islands. Its captain, John Glossop, at once gave the order to head there at maximum speed, sighting both land and the smoke of a ship at 9.15 a.m.[1]

It was the notorious German light cruiser HIGMS *Emden*. Since sailing from the treaty port of Tsingtao in northern China in early August, the *Emden* had left a trail of Allied destruction in its wake. Despite being chased by British, Russian, French and Japanese† warships as it criss-crossed the

---

* Before the war, pubs could open from 5 a.m. to 12.30 a.m.
† Japan had entered the war on the side of the Allies on 25 August 1914.

Pacific and Indian Oceans, the *Emden* had sunk no fewer than sixteen British merchant ships, burned the oil storage tanks at Madras and, on 28 October, torpedoed the Russian light cruiser *Zhemtchug* and the French destroyer *Mousquet* in a raid on the Malay port of Penang. This last daring act was mentioned by my great-uncle Clive Neely – still living down the coast at Kuala Lumpur while he waited for leave from work to return to England – in a letter to his mother. 'The German cruiser "Emden" gaily sailed into Penang one night,' he wrote, 'anchored & at daybreak moved off' and 'sank a Russian cruiser at anchor'. Later, having bombarded Penang's oil tanks, she met and sank 'a French boat' after '20 minutes firing'. But, added Neely, it was the German captain's chivalry that most impressed the skipper of a merchant ship who was allowed to escape when the French warship appeared. 'Well goodbye for now skipper,' Captain Karl von Müller is reported to have said. 'See you later!'[2]

On 9 November, Müller's luck ran out. His ship had been using a fake funnel to hide its identity; but the wireless station at Port Refuge saw through the disguise and sent a message for help before German sailors could destroy its equipment. Lieutenant Hellmuth von Mücke and the boarding party were rowing back to the *Emden* when HMAS *Sydney* appeared. Mücke recalled:

> In a few minutes the 'Emden' hoisted her battleflags and opened fire on an opponent that could not be seen from the boats. Its presence however was denoted by the high splashes. It proved to be the English-Australian cruiser 'Sydney', one and a half times larger, five years younger, equipped with side-armour, and carrying a battery with the same number of guns per broadside as the 'Emden', but each gun one and a half times larger. Having the superior speed, the result of this engagement was never in doubt.[3]

Firing 'very accurate and rapid' salvoes, the *Emden* drew first blood.[4] But soon *Sydney*'s heavier firepower told, her shells easily penetrating her opponent's 'unarmoured sides, causing extraordinary damage'. Having moved out of the range of the *Emden*'s smaller guns, the Australian ship could fire at will. 'A shell knocked the forward smokepipe down,' recorded Mücke. 'This huge, bulky mass lay athwart the forecastle. Almost at the same time another shell carried the foremast by the board. When

I saw this I knew that at least one of my comrades lived no more – the control officer in the foretop.'[5]

The charred hulk of the German light cruiser *Emden* off the Cocos Islands on 9 November 1914. It later sank.

After grounding on the beach of North Keeling Island at 11.35 a.m., the burning *Emden* was given a brief respite while the *Sydney* broke off the attack to pursue 'a merchant ship which had come up during the action'. When she returned at 4.30 p.m. the *Emden* was still flying her colours. But a final five-minute salvo persuaded Müller to strike them, and he and most of the surviving crew were rescued from the shattered ship a day later.[6] By then, however, Mücke and the boarding party had escaped from the Cocos in a requisitioned seventy-ton schooner. Sailing first to the neutral Dutch East Indies, they joined a German steamer to Yemen and, having fought off Bedouin tribesmen, finally reached Constantinople via the Hejaz railway in June 1915.[7]

11 November 1914: *'Not a very pleasant bivouac'*
– A sapper goes to war

At 2.30 p.m, after a particularly rough overnight crossing from Southampton, the Nos 2 and 3 (Railway) Companies of the Royal Monmouthshire Royal Engineers, the oldest militia regiment in the British Army, arrived at the French port of Le Havre in the SS *Manchester Importer*. Having paraded on the quayside, the companies – each comprising six officers and 280 or so men – were ordered to bivouac for the night in a large hangar or shed. 'Not a very pleasant bivouac,' wrote my great-grandfather Captain Markham David, the officer commanding No. 2 Company. 'Very smelly, draughty and cold. No time to disembark the kits so no mackintosh sheets or blankets for the men.'[1]

Three parts Armenian and one English, David had been born in Dacca, East Bengal (now Bangladesh), in 1877. His mother Elizabeth died of cholera a year later at the age of twenty-nine, prompting his heartbroken father Marcar David (shortened from the original Davidian)* to sell his successful jute business and move his six surviving children to England where they lived in a large house in Prince's Square, Paddington.

Keen for his three sons to become English gentlemen, Marcar sent them to the leading public schools: the elder pair to Harrow; and Markham, the youngest, to Cheltenham, and later to Clare College, Cambridge. In 1899, shortly after graduating, Markham married Celestine ('Nona') Wharton, the younger sister of a fellow student (and a direct descendant of Oliver Cromwell's sister and the regicide Valentine Wharton). Within four years they had produced three children – Charles, Hugh and Aubrey – and moved to a country house in Monmouthshire on the Welsh marches. Left a private income of £800 a year by his father (who had died in 1893), Markham could afford to employ four household servants and a gardener. He enjoyed the leisurely life of a country gentleman – shooting, fishing and playing golf – and his only

---

* Marcar's father was David Khan Davidian (1795–1851), court physician to Fat'h Ali Shah of Persia, and descended from Armenians who had been forced to move from their homeland in eastern Anatolia (modern Turkey) to New Julfa near Isfahan in Persia by Shah Abbas the Great in the early seventeenth century. Davidian's portrait still hangs on the wall of the Armenian cathedral in New Julfa.

commitments were the odd weekend of drilling and a two-week camp in the summer with the local militia regiment, the Royal Monmouthshire Royal Engineers (RMRE), which he had joined as a young second lieutenant in 1903. This, more than anything, had signalled his acceptance in county society – an extraordinary achievement for a man whose sallow skin and thick black eyebrows betrayed his 'eastern' origins.

Though he and his family moved away from Monmouthshire in 1907, to live near his wife's parents who ran the prep school for Wellington College in Berkshire, Markham remained a member of the RMRE and was called up as a Special Reserve officer in August 1914. Now, having endured ten weeks' training at Longmoor Camp in Hampshire, he was keen to enter the fray. 'We paraded early in the Hangar and I took the company for a run,' he noted on 14 November. 'Men are all looking well and are keen to move on. Weather becomes very bad indeed, great storm of wind and rain and we are lucky to have a roof over us.'[2]

That night he received orders to move his men the following day by train to Saint-Omer, the site of Sir John French's General Headquarters. They arrived on the 16th, having linked trains with some 'very fine looking' Gurkhas and Sikhs of the Indian Corps en route, and were marched to their billets in villages and farms to the east of the town, the officers in farmhouses and the men in corn barns where there was a 'plentiful supply of clean straw'. To help prevent a breakthrough of the type that had almost occurred at Ypres on 31 October, they were given the unglamorous but vital task of constructing a reserve system of trenches southwards from Dunkirk. 'Concealment and drainage are the all important factors,' wrote Captain David on 17 November, 'and a field of fire of 200 yards is all that is required in selecting positions, provided the other requirements can be secured. Concealed flank trenches are being used wherever possible and these can also be used as communicating trenches.'[3]

His main concern was not enemy fire but the weather – snow began to fall on the 18th – and the fact that some of his men's boots were beginning to come apart. 'These are the worst quality I have ever seen,' he noted, 'and in one case I tore the leather easily in my hands. It was very little stronger than brown paper.'[4] These difficulties notwithstanding, Captain David and his men set to work digging trenches that, at this early stage of the war, were just twenty inches wide, three feet deep and with a nine-inch-high earth parapet above the forward lip. Already, however, they were being built in the familiar zig-zag pattern – with twelve-feet stretches of trench followed by six feet traverses – to protect the defenders against flanking fire and artillery bursts. Though later trenches would be deeper, wider and with higher parapets and paradoses (the smaller lip to the rear), this basic design would not change for the rest of the war.

No. 2 Company made good early progress on its first stretch of trenches and concealed machine-gun posts in late November. But as the weather deteriorated, their work slowed to a crawl. 'Pouring with rain and blowing a gale,' wrote Captain David on 7 December. 'We find trenches still half full of water. The sides have fallen in in places. So a large party is detailed to cut brushwood for revetting, the remainder on drainage.' Worse was to come on the 12th when, with one large barn they were using as a billet in danger of collapsing, the company was ordered to move to another village. David noted: 'I went in advance on a motor cycle and on arrival . . . found the whole village occupied by French troops and the billets arranged for us had been commandeered.' The company eventually found space in a separate village, the 'men in the buildings just evacuated by the French [140th Regiment] and the officers in the chateau'.[5]

Back in England, meanwhile, my great-uncle Hugh Neely was still waiting to be sent to France. After rejoining the Artists' Rifles, he switched to the Suffolk Regiment and was given a temporary commission in its 3rd (Reserve) Battalion on 6 October. Ever since he had been training with the battalion at Felixstowe and Hythe (where he was sent on a heavy-machine-gun course). He wrote to his sister Phyl in December:

> Leave will be more difficult than ever for me after now, as they have just started a new company & self & two others (only) have been posted to it. The new company will be absolutely all raw recruits & I think it is rather a compliment they've paid me. The man who is the acting captain is the best subaltern in the corps, the 2nd is also thought a lot of by the Colonel & I am the 3rd, & I don't think they would put anyone, who they thought no use, there. It will mean a devil of a lot more work but much better experience than being one of 12 as I am at present.[6]

His chief concern was his sweetheart Dorothy Averill who, having joined the Voluntary Aid Detachment as a nurse, was looking for suitable employment in the Southampton area. 'She had,' he informed Phyl, 'rather a trying experience taking some poor wounded soldiers up to Scotland. She says their sufferings were awful & she never left them all day Friday, Friday night, Saturday & Saturday night. Pretty good. Do you write to her ever, kid? You might be a pal & do so sometimes. Don't know when I shall see her again. Southampton is ever so far away.'[7]

8 December 1914: *'Revenge is sweet'*
– The Battle of the Falklands

Vice-Admiral Sir Frederick Sturdee's South Atlantic Squadron was taking on coal at Ports Stanley and William in the Falklands when, at 8 a.m., a 'four-funnelled man-of-war' was sighted on the horizon. 'We did not think anything of this,' wrote a young midshipman on Sturdee's flagship, the battlecruiser *Invincible*, 'but ate a fair breakfast, and started coaling again. At 9 a.m. two ships came close to Port William where we were coaling. The [battleship] *Canopus* – the ship stationed at Port Stanley – fired on them. The ships made off at once.'[1]

The two ships that HMS *Canopus* had fired on, at a range of 11,000 yards, were the armoured cruiser *Gneisenau* and the light cruiser *Nürnberg*, part of the same German East Asiatic Squadron under Admiral Count von Spee that the *Emden* had belonged to at the start of the war. Since parting from the *Emden*, Spee's squadron had steamed across the Pacific and, on 1 November, scored a notable victory at the Battle of Coronel off Chile when it sank Rear Admiral Sir Christopher Cradock's flagship HMS *Monmouth* and another armoured cruiser *Good Hope* (with the loss of all 1,600 hands). It was to avenge this defeat and restore British naval superiority in the South Atlantic that the Admiralty despatched Sturdee with two modern battlecruisers – *Invincible* and *Inflexible* – to hunt down Spee. Now, by luck, they had found him.

Totally unaware of the presence of Sturdee's powerful squadron, Spee had sent *Gneisenau* and *Nürnberg* to reconnoitre Port Stanley, prior to landing and destroying the wireless station and any stocks of coal. They soon spotted the telltale tripod masts of the British battlecruisers and turned to flee. Spee knew, however, that his light cruisers could not outrun the much faster British ships and so gave orders for them to escape to the west while he took on the battlecruisers with his armoured cruisers *Scharnhorst* and *Gneisenau*.

Sturdee countered by sending the *Kent*, *Glasgow* and *Cornwall* in pursuit of the three fleeing German light cruisers while his remaining ships prepared for battle. He knew that if he kept beyond the maximum range of Spee's 8.2-inch guns (13,500 yards), and inside that of his own 12-inch guns (16,400 yards), he could not lose. Spee, on the other hand, was determined to close to around 12,000 yards where his additional 5.9 inch guns would outrange Sturdee's 4-inch secondary armament.

Spee won this initial duel by closing the range and landing several shells on the battlecruisers. 'Their firing was beautiful to watch,' wrote Lieutenant Frederick Giffard on the *Inflexible*. 'Perfect ripple salvo all along their sides. A brown coloured puff with a centre of flames masking each gun as it fired . . . They straddled us time after time. One could hear the shell coming with a curious shrill whine which gradually got deeper and then pop, pop as they burst.'[2]

A paymaster on the *Invincible* remembered occasional hits as the ship 'seemed to stagger and tremble'. He added:

> Suddenly, without warning, the atmosphere became thick with smoke . . . We quickly raised the hatch above to the mess decks, got out and were stumbling about in a thick fog of dust, steam and smoke. The hoses were running full on, and the mess was indescribable. The mess stools and tables and all the gear were lying in pools of water . . . The fire was located in the sick bay but it was some time before it was got under control.[3]

Meanwhile the British counter-fire 'looked very wild', wrote an officer on the light cruiser *Cornwall*, and the Germans 'did not seem to be hit'.[4] But gradually, as the fight wore on, the heavier weight of British shell began to tell. By 3.30 p.m. the *Scharnhorst* changed course. 'Just previously,' noted Sturdee, 'her fire had slackened perceptibly, and one shell had shot away her third funnel; some guns were not firing, and it would appear that the turn was dictated by a desire to bring her starboard guns into action. The effect of the fire on the "Scharnhorst" became more and more apparent in consequence of smoke from fires, and also escaping steam; at times a shell would cause a large hole to appear in her side, through which could be seen a dull red glow of flame.'[5]

Admiral Graf von Spee's cruiser squadron steaming in rough seas in the South Atlantic in November 1914, with Spee's flagship *Scharnhorst* in the foreground.

Aware that the ship was doomed, Sturdee signalled the *Scharnhorst* to strike its colours. But Spee refused and, at 4.47 p.m., his flagship sank with all hands. Both battlecruisers then turned their attention to the *Gneisenau* which took at least fifty hits by 12-inch shells before her captain ordered her to be scuttled at 6 p.m. At least 200 men made it safely into the water but, according to Lieutenant Giffard, many 'must have drowned from sheer cold'.[6] Of the handful rescued by *Inflexible*, 'most could not sleep that first night – the scenes on their ship were so terrible'. Giffard added: 'It was impossible for them to get from one end of the ship to the other, there was no upper or main deck left at all, and the lower (armoured) deck was full of holes and very hot. Over 2000 of them have been killed or drowned with all their cherished possessions, and their good ships . . . They said our 12-inch shell made their whole ship shake and they could feel the decks rippling like a caterpillar.'[7]

Of the other German ships involved, the *Nürnberg* and *Leipzig* were also sunk and only the *Dresden* escaped. 'Still black with coal dust but happy,' noted an *Invincible* torpedoman in his diary. 'Revenge is sweet.'[8] His ship had suffered twenty-two hits; *Inflexible* only two.

The battle was, wrote Hew Strachan, 'the most decisive naval engagement' of the war. It had, moreover, vindicated Admiral Jackie Fisher's advocacy of the battlecruiser: 'the combination of speed and long-range gunnery had proved decisive'. And yet it had taken 'five hours' shooting and 1,174 12-inch shells – or one hit per gun every seventy-five minutes – to sink two German armoured cruisers'. Such inaccurate shooting would prove more costly for the Royal Navy in the sea battles to come.[9]

Even so, the destruction of Spee's East Asiatic Squadron had wiped out the shame of Coronel and ended the threat from the German raiders. Sturdee was rewarded with a baronetcy, the first for a successful action at sea since 1814.

16 December 1914: ' "Run!" came the order – and we ran'
– German battlecruisers shell Scarborough

The school day at St Margaret's in Scarborough, East Yorkshire, was just beginning when explosions were heard near by. A sixteen-year-old pupil, the future novelist and reformer Winifred Holtby, knew at once the culprit: the warships of the German Imperial Navy. 'Just as we got through the gate,' she wrote to a friend,

> another shell burst quite near, and 'Run!' came the order – and we ran. Ran, under the early morning sky, on the muddy, uneven road, with the deafening noise in our ears, the echo ringing even when the actual firing stopped for a moment – it never stopped for more; ran, though our hastily clad feet slipped on the muddy road. Over the town hung a mantle of heavy smoke, yellow, unreal, which make the place look like a dream city, far, far away. Only the road was real – it was not fear, but something inexplicable that hurt, and yet in some strange way was not wholly unpleasant.[1]

Moments later, Holtby 'heard the roar of a gun, and the next instant there was a crash, and a thick cloud of black smoke enveloped one of the houses in Seamer Road; a tiny spurt of red flame shot out'. Panicked townspeople spread the rumour that German troops had landed. The rumour was false, but the bombardment of Scarborough and the nearby towns of Whitby and Hartlepool had killed 122 and wounded 443, the first British civilian deaths by enemy action since 1690. A shocked Holtby said she hoped England would never again 'suffer as she did on that awful December 16th, 1914 – but if she does, may I be there to see it'.[2]

Shell damage to Merryweather's food store in Scarborough after German battlecruisers had bombarded three east coast towns.

She would have been even more horrified if she had known the full story of that traumatic day: that the raid was a deliberate ploy by the five German battlecruisers of Vice-Admiral Frans von Hipper's 2nd Scouting Group to lure the Royal Navy's Grand Fleet on to a recently laid minefield; and, moreover, that the Admiralty knew of the raid in advance, in the form of intercepted signals, yet had chosen to let it go ahead in the hope of destroying Hipper's force. What the Admiralty had not counted on, however, was that the Germans had brought out the whole of their High Seas Fleet, with the bulk of it stationed halfway across the North Sea near the Dogger Bank; whereas it had authorized the use of only part of the Grand Fleet, thus putting its own ships at a qualitative and numerical disadvantage.

Fortunately for the Admiralty, the German fleet commander Admiral Friedrich von Ingenohl lost his nerve when his escorts made contact with British destroyers, assuming they were the van of the Grand Fleet rather than a single squadron of battleships. Mindful of the Kaiser's warning not to risk a general engagement, he ordered his own fleet to turn away to the south-east, thus forfeiting 'Germany's only major opportunity for a decisive naval victory in the entire war'.[3]

This move, in turn, left Hipper vulnerable; but bad visibility, poor British communication and good fortune enabled his ships to avoid the Royal Navy's ambush and return safely to Wilhelmshaven.[4] The official historian was not impressed:

> Two of the most efficient and powerful British squadrons, with an adequate force of scouting vessels, knowing approximately what to expect, and operating in an area strictly limited by the possibilities of the situation, had failed to bring to action an enemy who was acting in close conformity with our appreciation and with whose advanced screen contact had been established.[5]

24 December 1914: 'We marked the goal with our caps' – The Christmas Truce

Late on Christmas Eve, Corporal John Ferguson of the 2nd Seaforth Highlanders was in the forward trenches to the north of Ploegsteert ('Plug Street') Wood in Flanders when his men began singing carols. This caused the Germans opposite to applaud and respond in kind. 'I don't think we were so harmonious as the Germans,' wrote Ferguson, 'they had some fine voices amongst them.'

As the singing died down, a German voice called out: 'Komradd, Onglees Komradd!'

'Hello Fritz!' replied Ferguson. 'Do you want any tobacco?'

'Yes.'

'Come halfways.'

The shouting continued until, at last, a lone German left his trench and was met in no man's land by Ferguson and three others. The corporal recalled:

> We were walking between the trenches. At any other time this would have been suicide; even to show your head above the parapet would have been fatal, but tonight we go unarmed (but a little shaky) out to meet our enemies. 'Make for the light,' he calls, and as we came nearer we saw he had his flash lamp in his hand, putting it in and out to guide us.
>
> We shook hands, wished each other a Merry Xmas, and were soon conversing as if we had known each other for years. We were in front of their wire entanglements and surrounded by Germans – Fritz and I in the centre talking, and Fritz occasionally translating to his friends what I was saying.[1]

German soldiers of the 134th Saxon Regiment meet men of the Royal Warwicks in no man's land during the Christmas Truce of 1914.

A similar scene was taking place at Ploegsteert Wood where the 1st Royal Warwicks had just returned to the front line. This time a sergeant went out to meet the Germans, returning with some cigars and cigarettes (which he had exchanged for two tins of Maconochie's stew and a tin of

Capstan tobacco) and an offer from the Germans not to fire until Boxing Day unless the British did. 'That evening,' recalled Lieutenant Frank Black of the 1st Royal Warwicks, 'we were strolling about outside the trenches as though there was no war going on.'[2]

Most of the Indian Corps had been withdrawn from the front line after heavy fighting in mid-December. But the 1st and 2nd Battalions of the 39th Garhwal Rifles (part of the Meerut Division) were still in shallow trenches to the south of Neuve Chapelle on Christmas Eve, and were reminded of the Hindu festival of Divali when lighted Christmas trees began to appear on the German parapets opposite. No fraternization took place until noon on Christmas Day when the Germans, after much hesitation, climbed out of their trenches. 'Of course we could not shoot them in cold blood like that,' wrote a Captain Berryman of the 2/39th to his mother, 'tho' one or two shots were fired.'[3]

Eventually the Germans and Indians met in no man's land. 'For an hour,' wrote Berryman, 'both sides walked about in the space between the two lines of trenches, talking and laughing, swapping baccy and cigarettes, biscuits, etc . . . You would not believe that we had been fighting for weeks.'[4]

A Major Henderson in the neighbouring 1/39th Garhwal Rifles took a much dimmer view of proceedings when he discovered the 'whole of No Man's Land crowded with our men and the Germans amicably inter-mixed'. He wrote:

> I could distinguish German officers and confabbing with them [Captain] Kenny and [Lieutenant] Welchman . . . For a moment I gazed at the curious sight, and then realized how absolutely wrong and dangerous it was, and decided to stop it. I therefore stood up on the parapet and blew my whistle and signalled and shouted for all to come back. It was amusing to notice that the first to clear off were the Germans. They all bolted like rabbits at the sound of my whistle evidently expecting a ruse, or having a guilty conscience, while our men continued to stand irreso-lutely for a second or two, uncertain of where the whistle had come from and what its meaning was.[5]

The consequences for Captain Kenny were serious. Denied leave by his commanding officer as a punishment, he was killed at the Battle of Neuve Chapelle on 10 March 1915 (as was Welchman), not having seen his mother and relations 'for years'.[6]

Such mean-spirited sanctions for participants in the spontaneous Christmas Truce of 1914 were unusual – probably because so many soldiers were involved. For three days, from Christmas Eve to Boxing Day, unofficial truces affected at least two-thirds of the British front line that, at this stage of the war, stretched from St Eloi in Flanders to La Bassée Canal at Givenchy in northern France. During the afternoon of the 25th, thousands of British and German soldiers were swapping tobacco, food, drink and souvenirs, taking pictures and singing carols. A German soldier who had lived in Suffolk asked a lieutenant in the Scots Guards to post a letter to his girlfriend; a rifleman got a haircut in no man's land from a German who had been his barber on High Holborn before the war. Despite the half-frozen ground, several football matches took place. 'We marked the goals with our caps,' wrote a German lieutenant, Johannes Niemann. 'Teams were quickly established . . . and the Fritzes beat the Tommies 3–2.'[7] Sergeant Clement Barker of the Grenadier Guards wrote to his brother: 'A few of our men went out and brought the dead in (69) and buried them and the next thing [that] happened [was] a football kicked out of our trenches and Germans and English played football.'[8]

There were also some truces in the French and Belgian sectors, mostly initiated by the Germans through messages or song. Yet, with both their countries partly occupied by Germans, these Allies preferred not to mingle with the enemy.

General Smith-Dorrien, commanding the BEF's II Corps, had warned his men in early December of the dangers of slipping into 'a "live and let live" theory of life' which 'destroys the offensive spirit in all ranks'.[9] On the 23rd, Sir John French asked all troops to guard against a possible German attack by maintaining 'special vigilance' during Christmas and New Year. Some heeded his advice. The 2nd Grenadier Guards, for example, having lost a number of men to enemy fire on Christmas Eve, responded to German overtures a day later with a fusillade of bullets. A few Germans were similarly uncooperative. 'Gentlemen,' wrote a Landwehr lieutenant to his British counterparts. 'You asked us yesterday temporarily to suspend hostilities and to become friends during Christmas. Such a proposal in the past would have been accepted with pleasure, but at the present time, when we have clearly recognized England's real character, we refuse to make any such agreement.'[10]

But most were only too happy to extend the hand of temporary friendship, and it was the British and Indian soldier's willingness to do likewise that so irked General Smith-Dorrien and Field Marshal French. 'War to the knife,' commented the former in his diary, 'is the only way to carry on a campaign of this sort.'[11] French agreed, and issued 'immediate orders to prevent any recurrence' of the fraternization, calling 'local commanders to strict account'. Only later did he soften his view, confessing that he might have agreed to an armistice for the day had it been put to him, and asserting that he had always 'attached the utmost importance' to 'chivalry in war'.[12]

Back in Britain, however, the anti-war activist Keir Hardie saw the truce as proof that the common men on both sides had 'no quarrel'. When 'the war is over', he added, 'each will realize that the lies told them by their press and their politicians had been deliberately concocted to mislead them. They will realize . . . that the workers of the world are not "enemies" to each other, but comrades.'[13]

My great-grandfather Captain Markham David's company of Royal Engineers was still working on reserve trenches near Blaringhem in Flanders, and so missed the drama of the Christmas Truce. His diary entry for that day reads: 'We are given a whole holiday from works. I distribute Christmas presents in the morning received from home for the men . . . Service in the afternoon for Church of England in the square playground of the school.'[14] The presents included a Christmas card and an embossed brass box of cigarettes, pipe and tobacco (or another gift for non-smokers) sent from the King and Queen to each soldier of the BEF.

For those New Army volunteers waiting to be despatched to France, this first Christmas of the war was particularly poignant. Some, like nineteen-year-old Second Lieutenant Neil Weir of the 10th Argylls, were unable to get leave and made the best of the holiday in billets with their battalions. 'The men had a huge lunch in a large barn,' wrote Weir in his diary, 'immediately followed by a big tea given by the Skrines [the local vicar and his family], and after that the Officers had their dinner at the Rectory, in which the Major in his best jumper was showered with flour.'[15]

Edward Brittain, having finally gained a commission in the 11th Sherwood Foresters in November, was able to spend the holiday at home. But for his sister Vera Brittain, so used to the 'exuberant house-decorating and present-giving of the prosperous pre-war years', it was 'a strange and chilling experience'. No one could shake off the 'unspoken but haunting consciousness' that it might be the last Christmas they would spend together. Edward tried to lighten the mood by telling his family 'that the British and French armies could drive the Germans back whenever they chose and would have done so weeks ago had they not preferred to wait for the New Armies to come out in the spring'.[16]

Vera knew better and, having spent a few precious hours with her sweetheart Roland Leighton in London after Christmas, confided to her diary: 'I wonder if I shall have found you only to lose you again, or if Time will spare us till it may come about that the greatest word in the world – of which now I can only think and dare not name – shall be used between us.'

The thought of Roland's death was still on her mind when she asked him at dinner on New Year's Eve if he would choose to be killed in action. 'Yes,' he replied, 'I should. I don't want to die, but if I must I should like to die that way.'[17]

PART TWO
1915

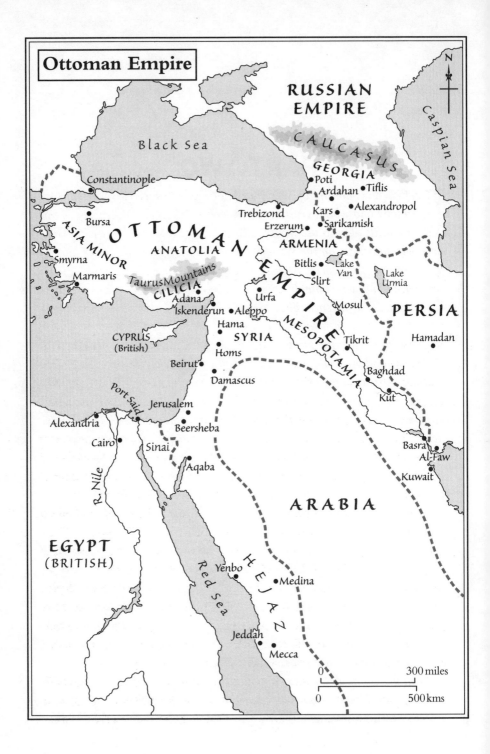

Ottoman Empire

RUSSIAN
EMPIRE

Black Sea

Caspian Sea

C A U C A S U S

GEORGIA

Constantinople

Poti

Ardahan ●Tiflis

Bursa

Trebizond

Kars ●Alexandropol

O T T O M A N

Erzerum ●Sarikamish

ANATOLIA

ASIA MINOR

ARMENIA

Smyrna

Bitlis

Lake
Van

Lake
Urmia

Marmaris

TaurusMountains

CILICIA

Slirt

Adana

Urfa

Mosul

PERSIA

Iskenderun ●Aleppo

E M P I R E

Hama

MESOPOTAMIA

Hamadan

CYPRUS
(British)

SYRIA

Tikrit

Homs

Beirut

Baghdad

Damascus

Kut

Port Said

Jerusalem

Alexandria

Beersheba

Cairo

Basra

Sinai

Al-Faw

R. Nile

Aqaba

Kuwait

EGYPT
(BRITISH)

ARABIA

Red Sea

H E J A Z

Yenbo

●Medina

Jeddah

Mecca

0   300 miles

0   500 kms

The first few months of war had ended unsatisfactorily for all sides. Germany had won a crushing victory over Russia at Tannenberg in late August, but its plan to use the breathing space to defeat the French, British and Belgian armies on the Western Front had been undone a week later by the Miracle of the Marne. All further German attempts to achieve a breakthrough in Flanders, notably at the First Battle of Ypres, had been repulsed by a stout Allied defence. Elsewhere Germany had lost the Chinese treaty port of Tsingtao to an Anglo-Japanese assault (7 November), while most of its warships outside the North Sea had, after initial successes, been sunk by the Royal and Australian navies. In the colonies of German South-West and East Africa, on the other hand, its tiny forces had won unlikely victories. But its political and military leaders knew that the war would be decided on the continent, and that their best hope of avoiding defeat would be to detach Russia from the Entente. Their initial strategy for 1915, therefore, was a reversal of the original Schlieffen plan: now they would go on the defensive in the west – where they had lost the vast majority of their 800,000 casualties since August 1914 – and concentrate their main effort in the east.

A major factor in this change of strategy was the series of defeats suffered by Germany's ally Austria-Hungary against both the Russians and the Serbians, losing Bukovina and much of eastern Galicia to the former, and being twice ejected from Serbian territory (the second time after capturing Belgrade in early December) by the latter. The pressure had been slightly relieved in December when the Austrian Third and Fourth Armies drove the Russians back across the Carpathians. But with total casualties already at 1.25 million, there was still every chance that, without German assistance, Austria-Hungary would not remain a combatant for long.

With this in mind, Germany's leaders had begun to consider the possibility of a negotiated peace – but with one of their enemies rather than a general settlement. This was something none of the Entente governments would consider at this stage of the war, having signed the Pact of London on 5 September 1914 that they would neither negotiate nor make peace independently.

One chink of light for the Central Powers, however, was the decision by the Ottoman Empire to join the war on their side in early November, thus closing the strategic Straits of Constantinople to Entente shipping. 'It is,' declared Asquith on 5 November, 'the Ottoman Government and not we who have rung the death knell of Ottoman dominion not only in Europe but in Asia.'[1] To speed up the process, 4,500 British and Indian troops landed at the head of the Persian Gulf a week later, while Russian soldiers had already invaded eastern Turkey. Visiting the Caucasus front on 30 December, the Russian Tsar appealed for help against Turkey by telling the head of the Armenian Church that 'a most brilliant future awaits the Armenians'.[2] It was a fateful comment that would have disastrous consequences for the many Armenians who still lived in Turkey, and who, henceforth, would be regarded as a Fifth Column.

Russia's casualties were already an appalling 1.8 million – 400,000 killed and almost 500,000 captured – and, with the entry of Turkey into the war, its armies were fighting on three fronts. To relieve the pressure on it it was vital that the other Entente powers took the offensive in 1915.

France was happy to do so. Its 525,000 casualties were the fewest of any continental power and, having narrowly avoided defeat in September, it had one overriding objective for 1915: to clear the invader from French soil, not least because the occupied area of north-eastern France contained the bulk of the country's heavy industry and coalfields. To this end, Joffre agreed with Sir John French at a conference at Chantilly on 27 December to concentrate their offensives in 1915 against the shoulders of the great German salient that stretched from Ypres to Verdun: the Aubers and Vimy Ridges in the north and the Champagne heights in the south (both protected vital German railway lines in the plains behind). The plan, therefore, was for a spring offensive: jointly British and French in Flanders and Artois, and French alone in Champagne.

However, the British government – shaken by the loss of more than 90,000 soldiers on the Western Front, most of them regulars* – had other strategic

---

* Of the British troops who landed in August, one-third were dead, and only nine of eighty-four battalions (of 1,000 men each) had more than 300 effectives by 1 November 1914 (Stevenson, *1914–1918*, p. 92).

objectives: to continue the naval blockade of Germany in the hope of starving the Central Powers of vital resources; to clear enemy forces from German South-West and East Africa; and, in Lloyd George's phrase, to bring 'Germany down by knocking the props from under her'. A landing on Austria-Hungary's Dalmatian coast was considered. But it was soon jettisoned in favour of a 'demonstration against the Turks', a move that would assist a hard-pressed Russia by drawing Ottoman troops from the Caucasus front. The nature of that demonstration had yet to be decided, but Winston Churchill was already convinced that it should take the form of a naval attack on the Turkish forts of the Dardanelles.[3]

24 January 1915: 'A magnificent but dreadful sight' – The Battle of Dogger Bank

At 7 a.m., nearing its rendezvous with British battlecruisers to the north of Dogger Bank in the North Sea, Rear Admiral Tyrwhitt's force of light cruisers and destroyers made contact with the more powerful German 1st and 2nd Scouting Groups and opened fire. A paymaster on the light cruiser HMS *Arethusa* recorded:

> We went to Action Stations, and as I was taking up my position on the rangefinder, firing was reported on the starboard quarter. We could see huge flashes of rippling flame on the horizon and hear the dull boom of firing. It was evident to us that we had just missed the German fleet, but that [the light cruisers] *Aurora* and *Undaunted* and our destroyers had been sighted by them in the growing daylight. At 7.09 am we sighted the smoke of our own battle cruisers and light cruisers ahead. At 7.20 am we all turned to [the south-east] and increased to full speed to chase the enemy who on sight of us made a beeline for Heligoland.[1]

Vice-Admiral Hipper's scouting groups – consisting of three battle-cruisers, an armoured cruiser, four light cruisers and eighteen destroyers – had been sent to Dogger Bank to sink British destroyers and wireless-equipped trawlers. But the Admiralty, forewarned of Hipper's intention by wireless intercepts, had sent an even more powerful battlecruiser force under Vice-Admiral David Beatty to destroy it. Aware, now, that the trap was about to be sprung, Hipper ordered his ships to flee. But they could not match the 26 knots of the three newest British battlecruisers – *Lion*, *Tiger* and *Princess Royal* – who were soon within range. Midshipman Alderson was on Beatty's flagship *Lion*:

> Just before 9 we opened fire with A & B turrets at 22,000 yards. The guns are graduated to 20,000, so the gunlayers aimed at the tops of their funnels. We were gradually closing the enemy. Our first salvo fell 400 yards to the right of the rear ship and short. Our second salvo went over. The enemy replied and their salvoes fell short. Half an hour of this, and then the enemy began to straddle.

As the two fleets steamed south-east in parallel lines, firing at each other, Hipper's flagship *Seydlitz* was hit in her rearmost 11-inch gun turret by a 13½-inch shell from *Lion*, the fire igniting ammunition and incinerating the crew. 'Suddenly *Lion* found the range,' wrote a boy seaman in the battlecruiser *Tiger*, 'and nearly blew *Seydlitz* to Kingdom Come. Her two [rear] turrets went up in a holocaust of flames and smoke . . . We were very thrilled with our success, but our ship's gunnery was not too good. One of our destroyers, seeing that we were not finding the target, signalled to us spotting corrections.'[2]

Over 150 German sailors were killed in the explosion on the *Seydlitz*, but the ship was saved when the executive officer flooded both magazines. Less fortunate was the armoured cruiser *Blücher* that, badly hit, began to lag behind. She was set upon by a number of light cruisers and destroyers, including *Southampton* and *Arethusa*. 'The ship heeled over as the broadsides struck her,' remembered a crew member, 'then righted herself, rocking like a cradle. Gun crews were so destroyed that stokers had to be requisitioned to carry ammunition. Men lay flat for safety. The deck presented a tangled mass of scrap iron.'[3]

Beatty's flagship *Lion*, meanwhile, had been hit below the water line by two shells from the *Derfflinger*. The nine-inch-thick armour plates buckled but did not break, allowing water to flood the engineers' workshop, stop the port engine and cause the ship to list ten degrees. 'So we had bad luck,' wrote the *Lion*'s captain. 'We had given much more than we got.'[4]

It was now 10.45 a.m. The *Lion* had been hit seventeen times and, with only one engine working, was falling behind the other battlecruisers. Convinced he had seen a submarine periscope, Beatty ordered all ships to turn to the north-east, putting them on a course that would cross Hipper's wake. This was a needless manoeuvre. There were no submarines in the area, and even if there had been they were not capable of hitting a battlecruiser moving at 26 knots. Beatty still wanted his captains to 'engage the rear of the enemy', but the signal got confused with the previous one and was read as 'attack the rear of the enemy bearing NE'.[5]

The end result was that the battlecruisers joined the one-sided assault on *Blücher*, leaving Hipper to escape with *Seydlitz* and the rest of his battered ships. Assailed by huge 13-inch shells, the *Blücher* was a 'magnificent but dreadful sight as although burning furiously in many places and struck over and over again, she slowly fired her last remaining gun'.[6]

The *Arethusa* delivered the coup de grâce with two torpedoes. 'These caused frightful havoc,' wrote a British gunner, 'one bursting in the engine-room and the other just below the fore turret, and rapidly caused her to capsize. She was before this a battered wreck on deck, practically all her gun crews were killed, and her officers drove the men from the stoke-hole at their sword-points to man the guns. This was told us by German prisoners aboard, and one or two of them have wounds which they said had been caused by their own officers' swords.'[7]

Dogger Bank was the first Dreadnought battle and, like the attempt to intercept Hipper's battlecruisers a month earlier, had ended unconvincingly for the Royal Navy. Command and communication were blamed, but this ignored the deficiencies in British gunnery. Of the 1,150 heavy shells fired by Beatty's battlecruisers, only six (not including the seventy fired into the hapless *Blücher*) had found their mark, and only one of the 355 fired by *Tiger*. The Royal Navy's response was to concentrate not on accuracy but on rate of fire. 'Ready-use cartridges were kept in the gun turrets and stowed close to the magazine doors,' wrote Hew Strachan. 'Neglect of safety procedures compounded the lack of armour in highlighting the vulnerability of the British battlecruiser when confronted by her own kind.'[8]

The Germans' response was far more comprehensive: they increased the elevation and size of their guns, revised their fire-control arrangements and thickened their deck, turret and magazine armour; they also improved anti-flash precautions to prevent fire reaching ships' magazines, and limited the amount of ready-use ammunition in each gun turret. Yet the essence of the battle, as it had been on 16 December, was Hipper's flight. 'Rather than seek action the Germans were shunning it,' wrote Strachan. 'The effect of such a policy was to consolidate British sea-power, not threaten it.'[9]

25 February 1915: *'The sound of rifle shots would fill the air'*

– The start of the Armenian genocide

The order to disarm all Armenian Christians serving in the Ottoman forces had been signed by the War Minister Enver Pasha. It stated that 'Armenian individuals are absolutely not to be employed in armed service, either in the mobile armies or in the mobile and permanently deployed gendarmerie, nor in service in the retinue or offices of the army headquarters.'[1]

Already some Armenians serving in the Ottoman Third Army on the Caucasus front had been disarmed. But now the process was to be extended to the whole Ottoman armed forces. Reports soon followed that Armenians soldiers were not just being disbanded, but murdered. According to a German missionary, Armenians in labour battalions were killed in March 1915, 'mostly' with knives 'because the ammunition was needed for the foreign enemy'. Henry Morgenthau, the US ambassador to Constantinople, concurred:

> In almost all cases, the procedure was the same. Here and there squads of 50 or 100 men would be taken, bound together in groups of four, and then marched out to a secluded spot a short distance from the village. Suddenly the sound of rifle shots would fill the air, and the Turkish soldiers who had acted as the escort would sullenly return to camp. Those sent to bury the bodies would find them invariably stark naked, for, as usual, the Turks had stolen all their clothes. In cases that came to my attention, the murderers had added a refinement to their victims' sufferings by compelling them to dig their graves before being shot.[2]

These murders, which continued for many months, were soon followed by an even more ominous development: the wholesale deportation of the Armenian civilian population – elderly men, women and children – from the eastern provinces. During these long forced marches towards detention camps in northern Mesopotamia – which one Turkish-born academic, Taner Akçam, has characterized as deliberate genocide by the Ottoman state to provide 'a complete and fundamental elimination' of the Armenian problem – up to a million Armenians lost their lives.[3]

When the news reached Europe in late May that Ottoman Armenians were being killed, the Entente powers issued a joint statement: 'In view of these crimes of Turkey against humanity and civilization, the Allied governments announce publicly to the Sublime Porte that they will hold personally responsible [for] these crimes all members of the Ottoman government and those of their agents who are implicated in such massacres.' Despite various attempts to bring the perpetrators to justice – some by the Turks themselves – no one was punished.[4]

Armenian widows with their children after the forced deportations and murders of early 1915.

Yet most objective historians now acknowledge that the killings were deliberate and state-sanctioned. The question is why? When the Ottoman

Empire entered the war in early November 1914, it contained between 1.5 and 2 million Christian Armenians, almost half living on the Armenian plateau in the north-east of Anatolia (where my own family had resided before they were deported to Persia in the early seventeenth century). Like all Ottoman citizens, Armenian men between the age of twenty and forty-five were conscripted into the military, while those between fifteen and twenty and forty-five to sixty were enlisted in labour battalions or as porters for the army. They were, however, neither trusted nor well treated. Some Armenians, wrote Ambassador Morgenthau, 'had been transformed into road labourers and pack animals'. He added: 'Army supplies of all kinds were loaded on their backs, and, stumbling under the burdens and driven by the whips and bayonets of the Turks, they were forced to drag their weary bodies into the mountains of the Caucasus.'[5]

This victimization was prompted by two factors: the Armenians followed the same Orthodox Christianity (albeit their own earlier version) as the Ottomans' chief foe, the Russians, and were therefore regarded by many Turks as the 'enemy within'; and they had been agitating for self-government for many years, a process that seemed close to fruition in February 1914 when Germany and Russia signed an accord to divide Turkey's eastern provinces.[6] Following the recent loss of Christian provinces in the Balkans, such a partition in the 'very heart of the Turkish homeland' would, to many Muslims, 'have meant not the truncation, but the dissolution of the Turkish state'.[7] Fear of this plan was, according to Taner Akçam, 'a critical factor' in the decision by Enver Pasha and the other Ottoman leaders 'to turn to genocide because the partition would have created an independent Armenian state in Anatolia, destroying the empire'.[8]

Such an option was being considered even before November 1914. But the outbreak of war provided both the pretext and the opportunity to take revenge on the Armenians. The key moment was the costly defeat of Enver Pasha by the Russians at the Battle of Sarikamish in eastern Turkey in early January 1915. Partly to deflect blame from his own incompetence, Enver attributed the defeat to Armenian treachery. This was echoed in many regions as Turkish propaganda referred to an Armenian 'stab in the back'.[9] Random murders began almost immediately, but they intensified after the order to disarm all Armenian soldiers on 25 February.

4 March 1915: *'Just off to see the Germans'*
– Second Lieutenant Hugh Neely leaves for France

Shortly after noon, the telegram she had been dreading was delivered to my grandmother Phyllis Neely at her new school, Convent Oisemont, at Westgate-on-Sea in Kent. It was from her brother Hugh and read: 'Just off to see the Germans. Goodbye. Love Oogles x.'[1]

Around the same time, Jack Neely received a similar telegram from Hugh at his Lancashire boarding school: 'Just off to France for the summer. Goodbye.'[2]

That evening, nervous but excited, Second Lieutenant Hugh Neely set off from London with a batch of reinforcement officers bound for the 1st Suffolks in the Ypres salient. It was a posting he had almost despaired of getting. Only a few weeks earlier, he had written to his mother from the 3rd (Reserve) Battalion at Felixstowe:

> If the man from Hythe returns before the new list is sent to the War Office (some time Saturday) I shall be in my old place near the top – about 2nd – but if he doesn't I shan't be on the list at all till a new list goes up the following Saturday. Rather complicated isn't it? Anyway old mum I hope to get off for a week end next Saturday week that is providing I am not on the list this week.[3]

Also in this letter was the momentous news that his brother Clive had finally been given leave by his firm to return from Kuala Lumpur to serve his country. 'He said he had got his commission from the governor,' wrote Hugh, '& now wants a regiment to go to. I was anxious to get him in here – as altho' I grouse a good bit (!), yet the Suffolks are very warm stuff & we Special Reserve people go straight out to join the Regular Battalions (no buying horses for weeks or guarding railways for us). So I was very surprised & rather annoyed when the Colonel told me he had got his officers booked up for months.'[4]

About the same time, Hugh wrote to Clive (who was due to return in late April) that he was 'now 3rd on the list for draft so I ought not to be long'. He added: 'Well, lad, this is probably the last you will get from me before I go so you might like my opinion as to what to get & where'. The list included uniform and hat from 'Hawkes & Co'; boots from

Manfield; 'cellular' underclothes; a Webley Scott .45 revolver from the regimental quartermasters (cost £3 16s); camp kit from Humphrey & Cook; a 'good Burberry with detachable leather lining'; '2 thin wetter sheets made into a sleeping bag'; an 'extra & strong haversack'; 'heaps of Savoury's heat lozenges'; 'a few medicines' like iodine, zinc ointment and boracic powder; waterproof knee pads 'for kneeling in the wet'; a 'magnetic prismatic compass'; a 'phosphorus watch'; a 'torch and so on'. He added: 'They are all what *I* think are good tips. Well best luck kid. I might be here in 3 months but hope not. Anyway I sincerely hope you get thro' all right & get a good job.'[5]

On 16 February, a week or two later, Hugh wrote to Phyl that his commanding officer had 'promised to see Clive when he comes home, which means he will take him on if Clive likes. It would be rather decent if he joined say in June & you all came up in August.'[6]

In the same letter, Hugh played down the chances of an imminent posting to France: 'The wretched fellow who was to have taken my place in the company, & set me free to go, has gone sick so still I wait & wonder when you will get letters from your brother in the trenches!! Shall feel such a slacker going out when all this lovely weather is over.' He ended it by imploring his sister not to be upset if he left before seeing her. 'They scarcely ever let us know till a few hours before we go,' he wrote, '& then it's off we go straight through London & mother would have to fetch you too, which she wouldn't have time to do. So I will send you a wire when I go, girl, if I don't write again.'

Now he had sent that telegram, but not before writing a heartfelt letter to his parents at 11 a.m. on 4 March:

Darling old Mum & Dad – Just got my orders & no false alarms I'm afraid this time, but there is the usual panic. I have wired you Darling & needless to say I am counting on seeing you both at Liverpool St or Waterloo & probably at both. Well Darling old Mum I don't think we have left much unsaid, anyway we have had plenty of chances haven't we? Try & not worry too much about me & remember always that no news is good news, that every day I shall be thinking of you dear & all of you & praying for you too. But I count on your prayers to bring me back safely to you not so very long hence. Good bye Darling and dear old Dad.

You have both been simply topping to me all my life & never more so during these last months and you won't go unrewarded for it all.

Tell Clive & the others how sorry I am to have missed them. Have wired 'the others'. Best love old Mum to you both & to you all.

May God bless you all and bring us all together again soon.

Ever your loving son Hugh.

P.S. Only this morning I went to Mass (before I knew I was off).[7]

Warned of Hugh's imminent departure by telegram, his parents met him off the train from Folkestone at Liverpool Street Station. They then accompanied him across London for an emotional farewell at Waterloo Station where Hugh and his fellow reinforcements caught the 6.55 p.m. to Southampton. The following morning, after a night crossing, they disembarked in Rouen.[8]

Hugh and the others were bound for the 1st Suffolks, a regular battalion that had been stationed in Khartoum when war broke out. Ordered home in October, it had finally reached France with twenty-seven officers and nearly 1,000 men on 16 January 1915. Much of its time since had been spent in and out of the front-line trenches of the Ypres salient, suffering its first fatality when a Private Nunn was 'shot through the head while cooking his breakfast' in the early morning of 5 February.[9] Many more men were lost in mid-February when the battalion tried to regain a section of lost trench between the Ypres–Comines Canal and a feature known as Hill 60. The failed attack cost the battalion more than 250 killed, wounded and missing, including two captains who had served with the unit in the Boer War.[10] It was, therefore, in dire need of reinforcements like Hugh; but, as was standard practice at the time, he had to spend a couple of weeks training at one of the infantry base depots in Rouen before he was sent forward on 26 March, by which time the battalion had taken over trenches in front of Kemmel.

As Hugh Neely entered the Ypres salient, my great-grandfather Captain Markham David was supervising the construction of new railway sidings at Abbeville to accommodate the huge build-up of the BEF in France that was now under way. By coincidence, however, he and his men had just spent three weeks in the same divisional sector of the Ypres salient as the 1st Suffolks,* working at night to construct a second-line position from Zillebeke reservoir to Elzenwalle. It was difficult work. 'The weather continued to be very bad,' noted the regimental history, 'and trenches rapidly filled with water, and owing to the water-logged state and flatness of the ground, drainage was impossible.' Markham and his officers were expected to reconnoitre and mark out each night's work the day before, exposing themselves to artillery fire.[11] They were glad to leave the salient on 12 March, with only Markham and a small party remaining behind an extra day to hand over stores to their relief.[12]

10 March 1915: *'It was hell let loose'*
– The Battle of Neuve Chapelle

At 7.30 on a cold and misty morning, 276 field guns and howitzers and sixty-six heavy guns opened up on the German front line at Neuve Chapelle, a ruined village south of Ypres in the Artois sector. During the next half-hour, more shells were fired into the German trenches than had been used during the whole of the Boer War. 'It was hell let loose,' wrote Captain Arthur Agius, the Machine-gun Officer of the 3rd Royal Fusiliers; 'the village and the trenches in front of it were blown to bits. The village seemed to melt before our eyes . . . The infantry assault was launched at 8.05. Nearest us on the right were the 2/39 Garhwals. They went trotting over. Suddenly I saw a fellow stop then spin and spin until he fell. Others pushed on . . . It was wonderful to watch the two attacks converge and meet.'[1]

Agius' machine-guns were supporting the assaulting Garhwal Brigade of the Meerut Division on the right, while a simultaneous attack was made by the 8th Division's 23rd Brigade on the left. Within twenty minutes, having overwhelmed the bewildered and shell-shocked defenders, they had captured the village and torn a 1,600-yard breach in the enemy line. An artillery runner, advancing with the second wave, recalled:

---

* The 1st Suffolks was part of the 28th Division's 84th Brigade; while in the Ypres salient, Markham David's No. 2 (Railway) Company, RMRE, came under the orders of the 28th Division's Commandant of Royal Engineers.

The infantry were clearing the houses and I never saw anyone so pleased as these little Gurkhas! They looked as if they were having the time of their lives. There was one that caught my eye . . . He was carrying the face of a German – not his head, just his face, clean sliced off. And he was grinning like mad, this little Gurkha, which was more than you could say for the German prisoners who were being marched back. It must have given *them* a very nasty turn.[2]

The same eyewitness remembered another Gurkha 'driving a bunch of Germans in front of him at bayonet point'. He added: 'There must have been half a dozen of them and they were twice his size!' For this action the second Gurkha, Gane Gurung, was awarded the Indian government's highest award for bravery, the Order of Merit.[3]

The original plan of attack at Neuve Chapelle was for a simultaneous French assault at Vimy Ridge to the south. But General Joffre had postponed the latter on 7 March because the BEF commander refused to take over more of the French line at Ypres, a move that would have released troops for the Artois offensive. Undeterred, Sir John French had authorized Haig, now commanding the expanded BEF's First Army,* to launch an independent operation that, if successful, might lead not only to the capture of the Aubers Ridge behind Neuve Chapelle, but even to a breakthrough into the plain beyond. So hopeful of success did Sir John become that he personally briefed his cavalry commanders on the need to exploit quickly any gap in the German line.[4]

Now, given the initial success of the infantry assault, the use of cavalry was a real possibility. But only if the infantry could follow up their success and widen the breach. That it failed to do. Haig was a frustrated onlooker as his reserve formations took far too long to leapfrog the first wave. This gave the Germans time to bring forward reinforcements and prevent any further gains. A second major assault was launched in the morning of 11 March, but it foundered on a newly dug German trench whose location was not known to Haig's artillerymen. When one colonel was asked by a neighbouring battalion, 'We have *got* to advance. Will you give the order?', he replied: 'No, it

* On 26 December 1914, Haig and Smith-Dorrien had been promoted to full general and given command of the newly constituted First and Second Armies respectively.

is a mere waste of life, impossible to get twenty yards much less two hundred yards.'[5]

A subsequent German counter-attack by the 6th Bavarian Reserve Division on the morning of the 12th (in which Adolf Hitler took part) was stopped in turn with heavy casualties. This prompted further British assaults that made little headway, though two battalions of the 7th Division were able to rush a trench after advancing under the cover of artillery fire. Misled by over-optimistic reports from Sir Henry Rawlinson's IV Corps headquarters, Haig issued the following order at 3.06 p.m.: 'Information indicates that enemy on our front are much demoralized. Indian Corps and IV Corps will push through the barrage of fire regardless of loss, using reserves if required.'[6]

Convinced a breakthrough was imminent, Haig even ordered up the cavalry for the pursuit phase. But the new assaults by IV Corps failed, and those of the Indian Corps were first postponed and then cancelled altogether. The battle was over. A small salient, 2,000 yards by 1,200 yards, had been won at a cost of 11,652 casualties; German losses, thanks chiefly to their costly counter-attack on the 12th, were 8,600.

Haig later blamed Rawlinson for not advancing quickly enough during the morning of the 10th. But the battle had nevertheless demonstrated that the enemy line could be broken with careful preparation. Moreover, wrote a recent Haig biographer, 'many of the factors that had brought this about – such as the achievement of surprise aided by a short "hurricane" artillery bombardment, and infantry moving across No Man's Land under the cover of artillery fire to rush enemy positions – were to be part of the winning formula that in 1918 would help win the war'.[7]

In the short to medium term, however, the battle made future breakthroughs even less likely. It caused the Germans to strengthen their defences by adding more barbed wire and greater depth to their trench systems; while the Allied response was to demand more shells for longer and heavier preliminary bombardments that would, they hoped, destroy the German defences before the infantry took possession of them on a wide front. This over-reliance on artillery would not be properly addressed until the last year of the war.

18 March 1915: *'The day had gone against us'*
– Churchill's attempt to force the Dardanelles

At 10.45 a.m., under a blue sky flecked with the occasional high cloud, seventeen Allied battleships left their anchorages near Tenedos and steamed for the entrance to the Dardanelles. The plan was for the battleships' heavy guns to silence first the Turkish forts at the Narrows, the thinnest point of the channel, and the batteries protecting the five lines of mines at Kephez Bay, three miles below the Narrows. This would allow the accompanying minesweepers to work through the night clearing a 900-yard channel through the Kephez mines. The following day the fleet would continue on to Sari Sighlar Bay from where it could 'batter the forts at the Narrows at short and decisive range'. Once the mines at the Narrows had been cleared, nothing could prevent the fleet from entering the Sea of Marmara, leaving the Turkish capital of Constantinople at its mercy.[1]

That, at least, was the intention. As early as 3 January 1915, Winston Churchill had asked the then naval commander in the eastern Mediterranean, Vice-Admiral Sir Sackville Carden, if he considered 'the forcing of the Dardanelles by ships alone a practicable operation'. The 'importance of results', added the First Lord of the Admiralty, 'would justify severe loss'. Carden's response was cautiously optimistic. 'I do not consider Dardanelles can be rushed,' he wired on 5 January. 'They might be forced by extended operations with large number of ships.'[2]

Despite the obvious caveats in Carden's answer, Churchill took it to mean that the Dardanelles might be 'forced' by the navy alone. He said as much during a meeting of the War Council in London on 5 January, and was enthusiastically backed by Lord Kitchener who thought 'the Dardanelles appeared to be the most suitable objective' for alternative military operations because 'an attack here could be made in co-operation with the Fleet'. If successful, it would open up the sea route to Russia, settle the Near Eastern question (in effect the problem of filling the vacuum left by the gradual disintegration of the Ottoman Empire), and draw in Greece, and possibly Bulgaria and Romania, on the Allied side. Colonel Maurice Hankey, the Secretary of the War Council, believed it might even 'give us the Danube as a line of communication for an army penetrating into the heart of Austria, and bring our sea power to bear in the middle of Europe'.[3]

While the War Council was united in its support for the Dardanelles operation, it disagreed over the means: Churchill thought he could do it without landing a field army on the Gallipoli peninsula; Kitchener was less convinced, and just in case he authorized the concentration of a sizeable force of 75,000 men – comprising the Royal Naval Division (RND), the regular 29th Division and the Australian and New Zealand Corps (Anzac, which had been training in Egypt) – on the nearby island of Lemnos. The RND reached Lemnos in time to participate in the naval operation on the 18th; its task was to land men at the battered forts to destroy their guns.

At first the attack on the 18th went well. The Turkish forts at the entrance to the Dardanelles had been put out of action in an earlier bombardment, which enabled the first line of four Royal Navy battleships – including the super-Dreadnought *Queen Elizabeth* (with 15-inch guns) and the battlecruiser *Inflexible* (part of the force that had destroyed Spee's

The British battleship HMS *Cornwallis* fires during the failed Allied attempt to force the Straits of Constantinople on 18 March 1915.

squadron) – to steam as far as the Eren Kuei Bay from where, just after 11 a.m., they opened up on the forts on either side of the Narrows. Before long their targets had fallen silent and a pall of smoke rose over Çanakkale on the Asian shore.

Keen to press his advantage, Vice-Admiral Sir John de Robeck, commanding Allied ships in the eastern Mediterranean, ordered his second line of French ships to pass through the British line and engage the Narrows' forts at even closer range. But as they did so a number of Allied ships were hit by Turkish fire, including the *Gaulois* (holed below the waterline), *Charlemagne*, *Lord Nelson*, *Agamemnon* and *Inflexible*. Even so, no ships had yet been sunk and Allied casualties were minimal. The Turks, on the other hand, were short of ammunition, with many guns jammed or masked by piles of earth and rubble. 'The situation,' wrote a member of the Turkish General Staff, 'had become very critical.'[4]

At 1.45 p.m., de Robeck instructed the French squadron to retire while he brought up his final line of six British battleships to continue the bombardment. But as the French ships turned towards the Asian shore, disaster struck. 'Suddenly I saw a terrific explosion,' recalled Lieutenant-Commander Henry Kitson on the battleship *Swiftsure*, 'apparently along-side the *Bouvet*. A great sheet of flame & then a cloud of black smoke. I remarked to the Captain who was then alongside me at the standard Compass that one of the French ships had been hit by a big shell & sure enough within a very few seconds this ill-fated ship was listing heavily to starboard.'[5]

In fact the *Bouvet* had struck a mine, part of an unidentified field that had been laid parallel to the shore. 'She was steaming at high speed,' noted Kitson, 'and I can see her bow-wave now gradually increasing as her list increased. Then she was on her beam ends & we could see plainly through a glass [telescope or binoculars] her unfortunate ship's company climbing over the ship's side. Then she was bottom up with her screws in the air & then nothing but a cloud of black smoke & great commotion in the water. It was all over in less than three minutes.'[6]

So quickly did the *Bouvet* sink that only thirty-five of her 674 officers and crew were rescued. One survivor was pulled so deep by the suction that his eardrums burst.

Emboldened by this success, the heavy Turkish guns at the Narrows began firing again. De Robeck's six battleships responded, and before long the forts fell silent. Now it was up to the minesweepers. They cleared three mines; but when the Turks opened up with mobile howitzers they fled.

Just after 4 p.m. the battlecruiser *Inflexible*, already badly damaged by Turkish shells, hit a mine close to the *Bouvet*'s watery grave. 'A terrific explosion,' noted one of her officers, 'ship shuddered and shook, men came up from magazine and said powers were dud . . . Ship had a bad list to starboard & we were making for Rabbit Island or Tenedos, depending on what we could do.'[7]

The next to hit a mine was the pre-Dreadnought *Irresistible*. Without power, she began drifting towards the Asian shore and was an easy target for the Turkish gunners. This prompted the transfer of most of *Irresistible*'s crew to a Royal Navy destroyer. But when *Ocean*, another pre-Dreadnought, moved closer to see if she could tow *Irresistible* she, too, was put out of action. 'We must have been hit by 50 shots,' recalled a young midshipman. 'An 11-inch smashed up the Gunroom. Then, about 5.30, we hit a mine and abandoned ship. Destroyers were quickly alongside, my destroyer was hit, but just got alongside the *Lord Nelson*, where, worse luck, I still am.'[8]

The 'manner', wrote Kitson on the *Swiftsure*, 'in which the captains of those destroyers took their ships alongside' the *Irresistible* and the *Ocean* 'under heavy fire' and rescued their crews was 'splendid'. But with 'the sun now setting and darkness coming on', de Robeck gave the signal 'for all ships to retire'. Kitson added: 'It was borne on me then that the day had gone against us and it seemed we had sustained a disaster.'[9]

Kitson was right. The Allies had lost three capital ships and 700 sailors, with three more ships crippled; the Turks, by contrast, were down only eight of their 176 fixed guns, and 110 casualties.[10] They were low on ammunition, it is true, but not so low they could not continue the fight the following day. More importantly, only one of the ten lines of mines had been partially swept, and the possibility of clearing the rest with the Turks' mobile howitzers fully operational was virtually non-existent. Churchill's gamble had failed and, as de Robeck's cable to the Admiralty of 23 March made clear, any future attempt to capture the Dardanelles would need the help of a field army.[11]

That necessity, according to Kitson, should have been obvious. He wrote later:

It is almost an impossibility for a ship to destroy a modern fort with a reasonable amount of expenditure. We who have seen bombardments and been bombarded ashore, can not fail to have been astonished at the small amount of damage caused by even the largest shells, and unless a shell makes a *direct hit* on a gun it will *not* destroy it or even do it any serious damage . . .

These observations . . . apply with still greater force to moveable batteries of howitzers and it is this great disability of ships to *knock out* shore guns that has undoubtedly been the cause of our failures, both during the Naval bombardment and later.[12]

A day after de Robeck's failure, having heard that he and his men would not be landing to knock out guns, Rupert Brooke wrote from a troopship: 'We did not see the enemy. We did not fire at them; nor they at us. It seemed improbable they saw us. One of B Company . . . was sick on parade. Otherwise, no casualties. A notable battle.'[13]

1 April 1915: *'Like shooting a sitting rabbit'*
– Birth of the fighter plane

On April Fool's Day, 1915, a twenty-six-year-old French pilot called Roland Garros – the first man to fly non-stop across the Mediterranean – took off from a tiny airfield in a Morane-Saulnier Type L monoplane and headed for the German lines. He soon came across a two-seater German Albatros BII reconnaissance plane and astonished the pilot when he headed straight for him. The accepted mode of air combat at the time was for an observer, or occasionally the pilot himself, to take pot-shots at his opponent with a rifle or revolver. Archibald James, an observer (and later pilot) in the Royal Flying Corps, recalled one such 'duel' in early 1915:

Our standard armament was an ordinary service rifle in the cockpit of the observer, who sat in the front seat. As yet we had no conception of the limited effectiveness of small-arms fire in the air. On the first occasion when as an observer I met a German aircraft, it was flying level with us at a range of 500 yards. I had done a good deal of deer stalking in Scotland and was confident of my shooting. I signalled the pilot to a convenient angle to facilitate my aim, put my sights up to 500 and fired six deliberate shots. I was bitterly disappointed at the nil results.[1]

Given that such an outcome was fairly typical, the German Albatros pilot was understandably perplexed, if not particularly alarmed, by Garros' unconventional tactics. What he did not know, however, was that the French pilot's plane was armed with a revolutionary new weapon that, if it worked, would transform air combat: a forward firing machine-gun.

The sticking point had always been the likelihood that such a weapon would destroy the firer's own propeller blades. To solve this problem Garros had wedge-shaped metal deflector plates fitted to his monoplane's propeller, an idea first developed by the plane's designer Raymond Saulnier and adapted by Garros after a chance visit to the Morane-Saulnier factory the previous December. The theory was that most bullets would either miss the propeller or be safely deflected. But would that actually happen? Or would Garros shoot himself down? He was about to find out.

Closing fast on his prey, Garros opened fire and saw the majority of his bullets arc towards the German plane, striking its fuselage and eventually sending it down in flames. The innovation had worked, bar some superficial damage to the propeller, and after Garros had twice repeated the feat during the next fortnight the French began fitting the plates to all similar aircraft. Before long another noted pre-war French aviator, Adolphe Pégoud, was chalking up enough kills to be regarded as the first 'ace' (an accolade given after five victories).[2]

Garros might have got there before Pégoud had he not himself been brought down, probably by ground fire, as he tried to bomb a German train in Flanders on 18 April. A member of the railway defence force remembered:

> We shot at him from a distance of only 100 metres as he flew past. After he had thrown his bomb at the train he tried to escape, switching his engine on again and climbing to about 700 metres through the shots fired by our troops. But suddenly the plane began to sway about in the sky, the engine fell silent, and the pilot began to glide the plane down in the direction of Hulste.[3]

French air ace and pioneer Roland Garros
with his Morane-Saulnier monoplane.

Once on the ground, Garros tried to set fire to his plane to protect its innovations. But he failed,* and the plane's propeller and gun were sent to the nearby Fokker factory where the Dutch-born aircraft designer, Anthony Fokker, was told to replicate it on his own similar monoplane. Fokker went one better by adapting a pre-war patent for a synchronized gun to produce a weapon whose rate of fire was controlled by the turning of the propeller. Now, instead of the odd bullet hitting the propeller blades, all would pass harmlessly through the space between them. A further improvement was the replacement of drum magazines with belt-fed ammunition, thus removing the need for pilots to reload their weapon by hand. The modern fighter plane was born.

* Garros was captured and sent to a prisoner-of-war camp. After several failed attempts, he escaped in February 1918 and returned to front-line flying, enjoying one more confirmed victory on 2 October. Three days later he was shot down and killed near Vouziers in the Ardennes.

It remained only for Fokker to test the innovation, as Garros had tested his on 1 April. Fokker recalled:

> While I was flying around about 6,000 feet high, a Farman two seater biplane . . . appeared out of a cloud 2,000 or 3,000 feet below. That was my opportunity to show what the gun would do, and I dived rapidly toward it. The plane, an observation type with propeller in the rear, was flying leisurely along . . .
>
> Even though they had seen me, they would have had no reason to fear bullets through my propeller. While approaching, I thought of what a deadly accurate stream of lead I could send into the plane. It would be just like shooting a sitting rabbit, because the pilot couldn't shoot back through his pusher propeller* at me.
>
> As the distance between us narrowed the plane grew larger in my sights. My imagination could vision my shots puncturing the gasoline tanks in front of the engine. The tank would catch fire. Even if my bullets failed to kill the pilot and observer, the ship would fall down in flames. I had my finger on the trigger . . .
>
> Suddenly, I decided that the whole job could go to hell. It was too much like 'cold meat' to suit me. I had no stomach for the whole business, nor any wish to kill Frenchmen for Germans. Let them do their own killing![4]

Fokker returned to Douai airfield and told the irate German commander that he 'was through flying over the Front'. Instead four German pilots – two of whom, Oswald Boelcke and Max Immelmann, would win the Pour le Mérite and become national heroes – were chosen to try out the Fokker EI, as the armed plane was known. The first kill was of a British two-seater by Immelmann on 1 August, with Boelcke chalking up his maiden victory on the 19th. It was the start of what came to be known as the 'Fokker Scourge', though at first it was moderated by the German practice of using the new Eindeckers as escorts for two-seater reconnaissance planes. Only later, when the plane's successor EIIs and EIIIs were grouped in special units, would the destructive power of this new technology be fully demonstrated. 'From its early scepticism,'

---

* Sited behind the pilot so that he could not fire to the rear; a tractor propeller was in front of the pilot and impeded his forward field of fire.

noted Fokker, 'headquarters shifted to the wildest enthusiasm for the new weapon.'[5]

24 April 1915: *'We would have followed him anywhere'*
– The Second Battle of Ypres

At dawn, shortly after reaching his battalion's bivouac 'under hedges and in hastily constructed shelters' near Frezenberg in the Ypres salient, Lieutenant-Colonel Wallace of the 1st Suffolks received orders to take command of a scratch brigade – consisting of his own unit, the 12th Londons and the 1st Monmouths – and to place it in a defensive position on a ridge facing north-east. Having issued the necessary instructions to Captain Balders, who had assumed command of the 1st Suffolks, Wallace went back to Verlorenhoek where he had sited his brigade headquarters.[1]

Balders instructed his men to start digging a trench on the ridge astride the Ypres–Zonnebeke road. But they had hardly begun when a staff officer arrived from divisional headquarters with new orders for Balders to 'take the 1st Suffolk and 12th London Regiments and advance northwards, attacking any bodies of the enemy he might meet'. The Germans had 'broken through on the northern side of the Salient', explained the staff officer, and his unit and the 12th Londons were the only battalions that 'stood between the enemy and the town'.[2]

This was the critical moment in what came to be known as the Second Battle of Ypres. The original German plan was for a limited attack at Ypres to disguise the movement of troops to the Eastern Front for the planned Gorlice–Tarnów offensive against the Russians. It was also a chance to experiment with the new gas weapon that had first been used (in the form of tear gas) with minimal effect against the Russians at Bolimov, west of Warsaw, on 31 January. Yet by April the Germans had developed a new poisonous chlorine gas that killed by stimulating over-production of fluid in the lungs, thus drowning the victim; they had also found a way to release it from pressurized cylinders if the wind was favourable.

By 22 April, 6,000 cylinders (containing 160 tons of gas) had been sited opposite Langemarck, north of Ypres, where two French divisions – one Territorial and one Colonial – were holding the line. Next to them was the Canadian Division, the first of the imperial divisions to reach the front, with the rest of the salient held by three regular British divisions, the 5th, 27th and 28th (which included the 1st Suffolks).

The gas was released at 5 p.m., following a heavy bombardment, and soon thousands of Frenchmen were stumbling to the rear, clutching their throats, coughing and turning blue. They left behind an 800-yard gap in the Allied defences, into which the Germans advanced cautiously. Because the attack had been experimental and not tactical, no reserves were available to exploit the breakthrough.

Next day more gas was released on the Canadians who – despite improvising gas masks from cloths soaked in water (chlorine is soluble) – were driven back. As the attacks continued on the 24th, the situation became desperate and reserves were rushed forward. Hence the reason Captain Balders was told to advance with the 1st Suffolks and the 12th Londons.

After double-checking with Lieutenant-Colonel Wallace, Balders ordered his men to down tools and advance on the hamlet of Fortuin. Among them was my great-uncle Second Lieutenant Hugh Neely who, since reaching the battalion in mid-March, had been commanding D Company's 13 Platoon. Four days earlier, as the 1st Suffolks returned to the front line at Ypres, Neely had written in his pay book: 'Just off to windy Trenches. Best love to you all. If I don't come back God bless you all Mother, Dad, Clive, Guy, Phyl, Jack & Dorrie.'[3] That stint in the trenches had ended the night before, and the battalion was acting as brigade reserve when it was sent north to help the Canadians. But as the Suffolks advanced they were shelled from three sides, an indication of how perilous their situation was becoming. Assailed by rifle and machine-gun fire, they stopped to dig in while two companies were sent to help the Canadians on their left. A Private Foreman in Neely's 13 Platoon recalled:

We advanced across open fields under a murderous shrapnel fire at first and when we came nearer rifle and machine gun fire. [Lieutenant Neely] kept the lead and he brought us through to within 500 yards of the enemy.

A ditch ran across the field and Lieutenant Neely told the few of us that were left to get into it and give the Germans as hot a time as we could manage. It was after we had been in the ditch an hour that Mr Neely was hit.[4]

A shrapnel shell had exploded almost at Neely's feet, causing severe wounds to his head, left elbow and chest.[5] His platoon sergeant Pegg – who liked and admired Neely, having served in his company at Felixstowe and shared the 'smooth as well as the rough on the football field, as well as the battle field' – at once gave him two morphine pills to dull the pain, and then dressed his wounds. But the fire was too hot to evacuate Neely, so instead Pegg and a Lance-Corporal Nisbett dug a trench to put him 'out of harm's way until it got dusk'. And all the time, Neely kept asking: 'Do you think I shall pull through? If I don't give my love to Mother and Dorothy.'[6]

For four agonizing hours, Neely was forced to lie in the shallow trench, his life seeping out of him. When darkness finally fell, at 7.30 p.m., Pegg and another soldier helped him back to the makeshift battalion dressing station where he lost consciousness. 'He was quite cheery with me,' remembered Pegg, 'right up to the time that he went to sleep.' Pegg knew that his officer had lost a lot of blood, particularly from his elbow wound, but 'thought he might stand a good chance of pulling through as he was a very strong man'.[7]

Having examined Neely's wounds the battalion medical officer, Lieutenant McNicol, knew he needed expert treatment and sent him back in a motor ambulance to the nearest main dressing station (MDS)* run by the Canadians at Vlamertinghe. But it was a long and tortuous journey along roads clogged with transport and casualties, and Neely did not reach the hospital until 6 a.m. on the 25th. 'I remember his case very well,' wrote the Canadian medical officer who treated him, 'though it was during the night we attended to 855 wounded. He was brought in unconscious . . . and died shortly after we received him.'[8]

---

* Small temporary field hospitals, usually set up in huts or under canvas a few miles from the front line, and run by a mobile unit of the Royal Army Medical Corps known as a field ambulance. The chain of evacuation – depending on the severity of the injuries – was regimental aid post (RAP), advanced or main dressing station, casualty clearing station (CCS), base hospital and general hospital in Britain.

If Neely had survived he would have been sent on to the No. 3 Casualty Clearing Station at the railhead of Poperinghe, nine miles west of Ypres, where thirty-seven-year-old Nurse Edie Appleton from Deal in Kent was working thirteen-hour days. She wrote in her diary: 'Officers and men come in – many so blown to bits that they just come in to die. Most go straight to the theatre for amputation of limb or limbs, or to have their insides – which have been blown out – replaced, and to be made a little more comfortable for the few hours left to them. The big ward is all agonized groans and pleadings and we feel we don't know where to start on the hundreds of things to be done at once.'[9]

Neely was one of 400 casualties sustained by the 1st Suffolks in the ten days of fighting that ended on 28 April.[10] The battalion's heroic advance on the 24th – which cost my great-uncle his life after barely a month at the front – had helped to stem the advance that day and save Ypres, though German attacks would continue to nibble away at the salient until 25 May.

Neely's brief time in action was not unusual. During the first year of the war, one in seven British Army officers were killed, the highest attrition rate of the conflict and more than double that of ordinary soldiers. Officers were also more likely to be wounded, with one in four succumbing to injury from 1 October 1914 to 30 September 1915 (compared to other-rank casualties of just under one in six). The chief burden fell on junior officers – those who actually led soldiers 'over the top' – and being a platoon commander in the infantry like Neely 'was unquestionably the most dangerous job on the Western Front'. One officer wrote: 'I am quite convinced that no subaltern stands a chance of avoiding becoming a casualty out here. He must simply be killed or wounded sooner or later.' Another added: 'Our lives were forfeit and we knew it.'[11]

The news of Hugh Neely's death reached the family home in Bromley on 27 April. 'Deeply regret to inform you,' read the standard War Office telegram, 'that Second Lieutenant H. B. Neely was killed on 25th April. Lord Kitchener expresses his sympathy.'[12] A day later hope flared when a letter arrived for Mrs Neely from one of Hugh's fellow officers, Second Lieutenant Pargeler, stating that although Hugh had been 'rather badly wounded', he had 'every chance of complete recovery'.[13] But it was a false dawn, and confirmation of his death was received on 3 May from

Buckingham Palace. 'Their Majesties,' the message read, 'truly sympathize with you in your sorrow.'[14]

As the awful news spread through the family, two thoughts were uppermost: how did Hugh die, and where was he buried? Desperate to know, his mother wrote to and received letters from a host of his fellow officers and soldiers. On 18 May she opened a note from Captain Rushbrooke, the new temporary commander of the 1st Suffolks (who himself was killed a couple of weeks later), giving the first details of Hugh's fatal wounding. 'He was quite conscious but his stomach caused him a fair amount of pain. At 9 o'clock they got him into the dressing station where Sergeant Pegg last saw him. His last words to Sergeant Pegg were: "If I don't pull thro' give my love to my mother and Dorothy." . . . It will help you to know that your son's loss has been felt by the Officers, NCOs and men who knew him.'[15]

Sergeant Pegg wrote soon afterwards, explaining in detail his dogged but ultimately futile attempt to save Hugh's life. 'I honestly believe,' he noted, 'that it was the wound below his left elbow that caused his death. He had lost too much blood . . . I could not grieve more if he had been my own.' He added: 'I think it was to be that I should be near him [after he was wounded] as we had been such great friends . . . Please accept my deepest sympathy and excuse green envelope and bad writing as I am writing this under fire.'[16]

In late May came word from the Canadian medical authorities that Hugh had died at a field hospital shortly after 6 a.m. on 25 April and had been buried at noon the same day in the Vlamertinghe Military Cemetery. A week or two later Mrs Neely received Hugh's personal effects, including his pay book, two unsent letters, various photos of Dorothy, a leather purse containing twenty-five francs, a prayer book and a silver cigarette case, the latter pair badly damaged by the shell burst that had killed him.[17]

Finally, in late June, arrived a letter from Private Foreman who was himself badly injured on the 25th. He described the events before and after Hugh's fatal wounding. 'His head was bleeding,' wrote Foreman from hospital in New Cleethorpes, 'and the bearers told me afterwards that his chest was badly hurt.' Yet Hugh had 'walked away with the help of two men' and that was the last time Foreman had seen him. 'Your son,' he concluded, 'was respected by the entire company and more so by his platoon who would have followed him anywhere.'[18]

Hugh's sister Phyl found it particularly hard to cope with his death. 'In time you will forget all the sadness of it all,' her brother Guy wrote to her on 20 May, '& have only beautiful memories – but now you must try to do what Hugh would have you do, then later on you will be able to remember that you too did your job, when it was much easier to mope about the place, & be mildly unpleasant & unsociable to all your schoolfriends.' Having recently returned home on leave, Guy mentioned in the same letter that their mother was 'keeping well' and that Clive, who had arrived back from Kuala Lumpur in late April, 'already looks stronger' and was training with the 14th Royal Fusiliers in Oxford if she wanted to 'drop him a line.'[19]

Years later Phyl's younger brother Jack wrote to her: 'It is natural you should have such vivid mental pictures of Hugh's last hours. You were very close to him, his only sister.' Referring to the letters from Pegg and Foreman, Jack agreed that it was 'sad reading, and yet inspiring'. Imagine, he added, 'a mere private writing after he himself had been wounded'. As to the cause of Hugh's death, Jack opined: 'I think our brave brother slowly bled to death. I don't think the doctor at the casualty station could have done anything to have saved him. He was too badly wounded ... The wound in his arm, the bleeding brachial artery, and the bleeding from his ruptured liver would have required immediate and extensive surgery. It is doubtful whether Hugh would have recovered his former wonderful physique.'[20]

But if it was bad enough for a mother to lose a son, and a sister to lose a brother, how much harder must the news of Hugh's death have hit his fiancée Dorothy Averill in Southampton? There is no record of how she coped, or of what became of her. Was she consoled in her grief by the knowledge, passed on by both Captain Rushbrooke and Sergeant Pegg, that Hugh was thinking of her at the end, and wanted her to know that he loved her? Did she recover from her loss to marry another? Or was she destined, like thousands of other young women who lost their future husbands in the war, to live out their lives as spinsters?

When Hugh died, in April 1915, the war was still in its first year. Most of the New Army volunteers had yet to see action, and a significant proportion of them would not do so until 1916. Their idealism and sense of duty was still strong. Hence the upbeat tone of the obituary for Hugh that was printed in the *Guy's Hospital Gazette* on 8 May 1915:

'Dead on the field of honour!' How grand! How terrible, and – how sad! Those of us who have personal recollections of H. B. Neely will read of his death with acute regret, for a finer man, a cleaner sportsman, never entered the hospital . . . In the heavy fighting which took place around Ypres about the end of April, he was one of the many officers who fell in action – brave men who gave their lives cheerfully and willingly for their country. We men of Guy's can realize what a loss he must have been to his men, for he was always a man who thought of others before himself.

An even more intimate eulogy of Hugh appeared a day earlier in his hometown's local paper, the *Bromley District Times*:

Of a bright and cheerful disposition, endowed with robust health and a fine physique, he was a typical specimen of an athletic Englishman, and was beloved by everyone who came within the orbit of his loveable personality.

Lieutenant Neely's last letters were typical of the man: they were full of anxiety for the health and welfare of his men, of his enthusiastic admiration for the way in which they 'stuck it' during the bad weather, of his 'football of sorts' behind the lines and the joy of abundant straw when in billets, of his having been able to receive Holy Communion the Sunday before he died, in a partially ruined church near the billets. Always cheerful and optimistic, full of care for others and forgetfulness of himself, Hugh Neely died as he lived, 'a very perfect knight'.

25 April 1915: *'No one was in charge'*
– Anzac Cove

At 5 a.m., as he steamed past Anzac Cove in the battleship *Queen Elizabeth*, the soldier-poet General Sir Ian Hamilton wrote: 'The day was just breaking over the jagged hills, the sea was glassy smooth. The landing of the lads from the South was in full swing. The shrapnel was bursting over the water. The patter of musketry came creeping out to sea. We are in for it now. The machine guns muttered as though chattering teeth – up to our necks in it now. But would we be out of it? No;

not one of us; not for five hundred years stuffed full of dullness and routine.'[1]

Hamilton was speaking for himself and the romantics under his command. They would not have included, by this time, many members of the 3rd Australian Infantry Brigade who, barely half an hour earlier, had landed on the north coast of the Gallipoli peninsula, opposite the Narrows, in near darkness and without a preliminary barrage. The plan had been to disembark the bulk of the troops on 'Brighton Beach' to the south, where the coastal plan was broader and the terrain not so steep and broken; but the tows lost their way in the darkness and, as they approached the shore a mile further north than intended, they came under fire from Turkish positions. 'It was just breaking dawn,' recalled twenty-four-year-old Lieutenant Ivor Margetts of the 12th Battalion, a teacher from Hobart, 'and as we looked towards the sound of the firing, we were faced by almost perpendicular cliffs about 200 feet above sea level.'[2]

Having landed on the wrong beach, Margetts and his commanding officer, Colonel Clarke, climbed the first ridge on their hands and knees with fifty men, driving a handful of Turks before them. Onwards they advanced to a feature known as the Nek where Clarke was shot and killed as he was writing a note to brigade headquarters. Margetts and the rest of the men took cover, as did another party of the 12th under Captain Joseph Lalor, a professional soldier who had served with the French Foreign Legion. But that option was not available to Captain Eric Tulloch, a brewer from Ballarat in New South Wales, who had reached the Nek with sixty men of the 11th Battalion from a beach even further north. With orders to capture the vital feature of Chunuk Bair, to the north-east of the Nek, Tulloch and his men pushed on through prickly scrub and over a feature called Baby 700 to the inland slopes of Battleship Hill. With their objective directly ahead, they tried to cross the intervening gully but were stopped by machine-gun fire that killed a number of Tulloch's men and caused the rest to crawl. Away to their right, tantalizingly close, was the glinting silver ribbon of the Dardanelles. But Tulloch's attention was focused on a lone tree on the Chunuk Bair from where an officer was directing the Turkish defence. Tulloch fired at him and missed. The officer continued as if nothing had happened. His name was Colonel Mustapha Kemal, commander of the Turkish 19th Division, and his timely

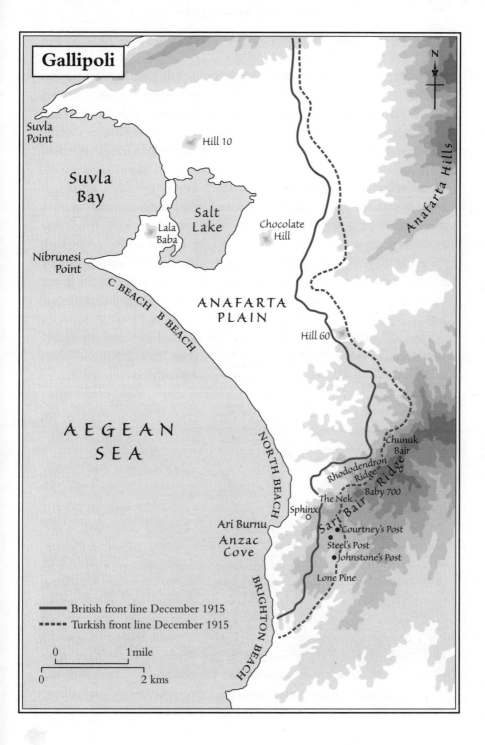

Gallipoli

Suvla Point

Hill 10

Suvla Bay

Salt Lake

Lala Baba

Chocolate Hill

Nibrunesi Point

C BEACH

B BEACH

ANAFARTA PLAIN

Hill 60

AEGEAN SEA

Anafarta Hills

NORTH BEACH

Chunuk Bair

Rhododendron Ridge

Sari Bair Ridge

Baby 700

The Nek

Sphinx

Ari Burnu

Anzac Cove

Courtney's Post

Steel's Post

Johnstone's Post

Lone Pine

BRIGHTON BEACH

N

—— British front line December 1915

▪▪▪▪ Turkish front line December 1915

0   1 mile

0   2 kms

arrival a short while earlier had prevented the original garrison on Chunuk Bair from running away.

As the morning wore on, Kemal's soldiers began to work round Tulloch's flanks. In danger of being cut off, the captain withdrew half his men to Baby 700 and the rest to the Nek. After Lalor had been killed and Tulloch wounded, Baby 700 and the Nek were lost to the Turks, causing the survivors to retreat to a feature known as Russell's Top that would form part of the Anzac front line for the next eight months.

A similar pattern was repeated further south as isolated groups of Australians and New Zealanders were outflanked and eventually overrun. The furthest point was reached by a solicitor from Adelaide called Arthur Blackburn, then serving as a private in the 10th Battalion, who with Corporal Phil Robin, a bank accountant, advanced a little beyond Scrubby Knoll, a peak to the south of Chunuk Bair. He recalled: 'We got to the top of the ridge in safety and there found several other chaps but no-one was in charge. Just at that moment, however, Captain Herbert came up . . . He had decided to entrench there and so sent Phil and me out to watch a valley on his front and flank . . . We stayed out there until driven in by the enemy who were coming out to attack us in force.'[3]

Dead, wounded and exhausted Australian soldiers on the beach at Anzac Cove during the Gallipoli landings of 25 April 1915.

At eleven that evening, by which time 2,000 of the 15,000 Anzacs ashore were casualties, and none of their objectives had been gained, the corps commander General Birdwood wrote to Hamilton:

> Both my divisional generals and brigadiers have represented to me that they fear their men are thoroughly demoralized by shrapnel fire to which they have been subjected all day after exhausting and gallant work in morning. Numbers have dribbled back from firing line and cannot be collected in this difficult country. Even New Zealand Brigade which has been only recently engaged lost heavily and is to some extent demoralized. If troops are subjected to shell fire again tomorrow there is likely to be a fiasco as I have no fresh troops with which to replace those in firing line. I know my representation is most serious but if we are to re-embark it must be done at once.

Having consulted the senior naval officer, Vice-Admiral Thursby, Hamilton sent the following reply:

> Your news is indeed serious. But there is nothing for it but to dig yourselves right in and stick it out. It would take at least two days to re-embark you . . . [General] Hunter-Weston, despite his heavy losses [at the simultaneous landing that day at Cape Helles], will be advancing tomorrow which should divert pressure from you. Make a personal appeal to your men and Godley's* to make a supreme effort to hold their ground . . . You have got through a difficult business, now you only have to dig, dig, dig, until you are safe.[4]

The prospect of an Allied victory at Gallipoli had prompted the signing of two secret treaties. The first, on 20 March, was an agreement between Britain and Russia to divide the Ottoman and Persian Empires into spheres of influence: Britain would control Mesopotamia, Palestine and central Persia; while Russia annexed Constantinople and the Bosphorus, more than half of Turkey-in-Europe, and the European and Asian shores of the Dardanelles, including the Gallipoli peninsula. Britain had fought the Crimean War to prevent Russia from capturing the Turkish capital; now it was fighting the Turks to give Russia what it wanted.[5]

---

* British-born Major-General Alexander Godley was commanding the composite Australian and New Zealand Division.

The second treaty was signed by Italy and the Entente powers in London a day after the landings at Anzac Cove and Cape Helles, by which time tens of thousands of Allied troops were ashore and the possibility of capturing the Dardanelles still seemed good. In return for fighting on the Allied side, Italy was promised significant territorial gains from a defeated Austria-Hungary and Turkey, including the South Tyrol, the Istrian peninsula, northern Dalmatia, colonies in North Africa and a 'sphere of influence' in Anatolia.[6]

One man, however, did not live long enough to influence the Gallipoli campaign: the poet-soldier Rupert Brooke. He died of blood poisoning – probably from an infected mosquito bite – on 23 April, St George's Day, and was buried in an olive grove on the island of Skyros. His final and arguably best war sonnet, 'The Soldier', published a few weeks earlier to popular acclaim in *New Numbers*, would serve as a fitting if self-obsessed epitaph:

> If I should die, think only this of me:
>> That there's some corner of a foreign field
> That is for ever England. There shall be
>> In that rich earth a richer dust concealed;
> A dust whom England bore, shaped, made aware,
>> Gave, once, her flowers to love, her ways to roam,
> A body of England's, breathing English air,
>> Washed by the rivers, blest by suns of home.

28 April 1915: *'With mourning hearts we stand united here'*
– The International Congress of Women

'It is unthinkable,' railed the pro-war suffragette leader Emmeline Pankhurst in the *Sunday Pictorial*, 'that English-women should meet German women to discuss terms of peace while the husbands, sons and brothers of those women are . . . murdering our men on the seas and who have committed the awful horrors of the war in Belgium and elsewhere.'[1]

Pankhurst was referring to the International Congress of Women – often referred to as the Women's Peace Congress – that was opened in an ornate hall in The Hague's Zoological and Botanical Gardens on 28 April 1915 as the Second Battle of Ypres raged in neighbouring Belgium. The brainchild of Aletta Jacobs, the first Dutch woman to be admitted to university, the congress's stated aim was to bring together an international assembly of women to exert moral pressure on the governments of belligerent countries to find ways to end the war.

'With mourning hearts we stand united here,' declared Jacobs in her opening address. 'We grieve for many brave young men who have lost their lives on the battlefield before attaining their full manhood; we mourn with the poor mothers bereft of their sons; with the thousands of young widows and fatherless children, and we feel that we can no longer endure in this twentieth century of civilization that government should tolerate brute force as the only solution of international disputes.'[2]

Nodding in sad agreement were more than 1,100 women's rights activists from twelve countries, including Germany, Austria-Hungary, Italy, Poland, Belgium and the United States – all of them dedicated to the cause of peace. They included Lida Gustava Heymann, one of twenty-eight delegates from Germany who were arrested on their return; two future Nobel Peace Prize winners from the United States, Jane Addams and Emily G. Balch; and Emmeline Pethick Lawrence, a former honorary treasurer of the militant Women's Social and Political Union (or WSPU, the movement set up by Emmeline and Christabel Pankhurst in 1903 to demand women's suffrage), who was one of only three British delegates (none of whom came directly from Britain).

Having debated various forms of non-violent conflict resolution, the congress concluded on 1 May by calling for a process of continuous mediation, without armistice, until peace could be restored among the warring nations. It also announced the foundation of the Women's International League for Peace and Freedom (WILPF), an organization that would influence US President Woodrow Wilson's famous Fourteen Points in 1918 and one that still exists today.

There were no French delegates at the congress. They had been prevented from attending by their government, as had women from Russia, Serbia and Japan. All of the 180 or so British-based delegates – including Sylvia Pankhurst, Emmeline's pacifist daughter, and Charlotte

Despard, the feminist and socialist reforming sister of Field Marshal Sir John French – were prevented from travelling by Reginald McKenna, the Home Secretary, who would give passports (another wartime innovation) only to twenty 'women of discretion', and even that group was stymied by the temporary cancellation of ferry services between Britain and Holland.[3]

It was a rare moment of accord between Emmeline Pankhurst and the Liberal government. She had gone to prison in 1913 for supporting a suffragette attempt to blow up the house of David Lloyd George, the Chancellor of the Exchequer. When war broke out she was living with her daughter Christabel in exile in France, having recently fled there to avoid another stint behind bars, and many in government had assumed the suffragette leaders would oppose Britain's belligerent status. But they did not. As Christabel put it, they could not be 'pacifists at any price';

Suffragette leader Emmeline Pankhurst making an open-air speech.

their country was at war and they were bound to support it.[4] Emmeline at once ordered all WSPU activity to halt; the government responded by freeing imprisoned suffragettes and offering an amnesty to those guilty of offences.

A few weeks later, having returned to Britain, Emmeline and Christabel held a large WSPU rally in London on 'The Great Need of Vigorous National Defence against the German Peril'. Militant women, Christabel told the adoring crowd, should now put their efforts into arousing militancy in men. When someone shouted 'Votes for women!', she responded, 'We cannot discuss that now.'[5] Instead she urged her listeners to emulate their French sisters who, 'while all the able-bodied men are at the front, are able to keep the country going, to get in the harvest, to carry on the industries'. When the war ended in victory, she prophesied, women who were paying their share of the price of victory would insist on being brought into 'equal partnership as enfranchised citizens of this country'.[6]

Listening in the audience was Christabel's socialist sister Sylvia, one of the few suffragettes willing to condemn the war. 'I listened to her with grief,' she wrote, 'and resolved to write and speak more urgently for peace.' In her newspaper *Woman's Dreadnought*, Sylvia proposed a thousand-strong 'Women's Peace Expeditionary Force' to march into no man's land between the rival armies. She was one of only a hundred British women who signed an open Christmas letter to their German and Austrian counterparts, urging peace and stressing that 'our very anguish unites us'.[7]

Her mother and sister, meanwhile, did everything they could to support the war effort. Christabel went on a six-month lecture tour to the United States, aimed at persuading the Americans to join the Allies; Emmeline spoke to crowds across Britain, telling a cheering Plymouth audience that 'to give one's life for one's country, for a great cause, is a splendid thing'.[8]

Emmeline had nothing but contempt for her daughter's pacifism, telling her she was 'ashamed to know where you ... stand'.[9] Her own position was firm and unflinching. On 16 April 1915, less than a fortnight before the start of the Women's Peace Congress, she and Christabel relaunched *The Suffragette* newspaper (suspended since August 1914) with a new name, *Britannia,* and a leading article that claimed it was 'a thousand times more the duty of militant Suffragettes to fight the Kaiser for the sake of liberty than it was to fight anti-Suffrage Governments'.

As a sop to the hardliners, the paper would soon publish a list of men's jobs now open to women: railway clerk, ticket collector, stationmaster, tram conductor, grocer's assistant, motor-van driver, lift attendant, post-girl, news-girl, munitions and armament worker, sheep-dipper, bank clerk, signaller and many others.[10] The implication was clear: the war was changing the role of women in society and their inability to vote, the major impediment to sex equality, could not be maintained for long.

1 May 1915: *'We had to wrench our skirts from their clinging hands'*
– The Gorlice–Tarnów offensive

The first that British nurse Florence Farmborough, aged twenty-seven, knew of the offensive was when she was woken before dawn by shrapnel bullets clattering down on the roof of the Russian field hospital she was attached to at Gorlice in the Carpathians.[1] It was the start of a huge 1,600-gun Austro-German bombardment,* the largest yet attempted on the Eastern Front, which lasted for four hours and fired more than 700,000 shells (some filled with gas). When the barrage was over, 350,000 German and Austro-Hungarian troops advanced against 220,000 Russians manning shallow trenches in a formerly quiet sector of the front.[2]

Working before the war as governess to the children of a Moscow heart surgeon, the Buckinghamshire-born Farmborough had volunteered in August 1914 to train as a nurse in a private military hospital, later transferring to the No. 10 Mobile Field Hospital at Gorlice. She was part of a medical 'flying detachment' – consisting of an officer, an NCO, two doctors, a medical assistant, eight nurses (four female) and thirty ambulancemen – that had set up an improvised hospital in a deserted house, 'scrubbing it clean, painting it and setting up both an operating theatre

---

* The Austro-Germans had massed 1,270 field guns against the Russians' 675, and 430 heavy guns and mortars to the Russians' four (Stevenson, *1914–1918*, p. 154).

and a pharmacy'.[3] On hearing the first explosions on 1 May, she leaped out of bed – fully dressed, fortunately, because an attack had long been forecast – and stared through the rattling window at the great lightning flashes from enemy guns on the horizon.

Soon the casualties arrived. 'At first we could cope,' wrote Farmborough in her diary. 'Then we were overwhelmed by their numbers. They came in their hundreds, from all directions; some able to walk, others crawling, dragging themselves along the ground . . . Those who could walk were sent on immediately without attention. "The base hospitals will attend to you," we told them; "Go! Go! Quickly!" The groans and cries of the wounded were pitiful to hear.'[4]

The following morning, after another ferocious bombardment, the order came for hospital personnel to abandon their equipment and the wounded, and join the general retreat. 'A dreadful feeling of dismay and bewilderment took possession of us,' recorded Farmborough. 'There *must* be some mistake! But there was no mistake, we had to obey; we had to go. "*Skoro! Skoro!*" (Quickly) shouted familiar voices . . . "The Germans are outside the town."'[5]

Farmborough grabbed her coat and rucksack, and ran outside. 'Those who could walk, got up and followed us,' she recorded,

> running, hopping, limping by our sides. The badly crippled crawled after us; all begging, beseeching us not to abandon them in their need. And, on the road, there were others, many others; some of them lying down in the dust, exhausted . . . We had to wrench our skirts from their clinging hands. Then their prayers were intermingled with curses; and, far behind them, we could hear the curses repeated by those of our brothers whom we had left to their fate. The gathering darkness accentuated the panic and misery.[6]

The attack at Gorlice–Tarnów was the main German offensive of 1915, in line with the OHL's new strategy of concentrating its military effort in the east. An earlier assault – the winter battle of the Marsurian Lakes (7–21 February) – had cleared East Prussian soil of invaders and inflicted 200,000 Russian casualties, but there was no repeat of the Tannenberg encirclement and the Germans themselves lost many men. Further south the Austro-Hungarians failed to relieve the besieged fortress of Przemśyl in Galicia, which surrendered with its garrison of 117,000 in March (a disaster that reduced the normally stoic Emperor Franz Joseph to tears), and Russian counter-attacks reached the Carpathian passes and threatened the Hungarian plains beyond.[7]

With Austria-Hungary on its knees, and threatening a separate peace, the Germans had to act. A new army, the Eleventh, was formed under General August von Mackensen – by detaching a regiment from each of Germany's Western Front divisions, and replacing it with more machine-guns – and sent south to assist the Austrians. The main aim of the Austro-German attack at Gorlice–Tarnów, therefore, was to keep Austria in the war and recover lost territory. It achieved both. What it was not designed to do, however, was to defeat Russia so badly that it would not want to make terms. Falkenhayn's strategy at this juncture was to split the Entente. 'Military pressure was necessary to make the Russians negotiate,' wrote David Stevenson, 'but it should neither humiliate them nor conquer territory that might obstruct compromise.'[8]

The spearhead of the Austro-German attack on 1 May was pointed at the junction of two Russian army corps. Within two days, as Farmborough so graphically describes, Russian resistance had crumbled, allowing Mackensen's men to advance eight miles and capture Gorlice. Tarnów fell five days later, and by the end of June the attackers had retaken the fortress of Przemśyl and driven the Russians from the Carpathian passes, capturing almost 290,000 prisoners and 2,000 guns.

Now was the time to negotiate, 'with the Russian army in flight and the Russian fortresses falling like a pack of cards', and Bethmann Hollweg duly put out peace feelers.[9] Only when they were rebuffed was Mackensen told to continue his advance into Russian territory, while Hindenburg and Ludendorff attacked south from East Prussia. By September the Austro-German pincer attack had overrun the whole of Russian Poland and Lithuania, pushing the front back more than 300 miles. The casualties on both sides were huge: the Russians lost 1.4 million; the Central Powers more than a million. But, as Falkenhayn had feared, these enormous German gains had made peace more elusive than ever. 'Victory,' wrote Stevenson, 'made the German annexationists eager to detach Poland from Russia permanently, while defeat made Nicholas II no readier to talk.'[10]

7 May 1915: *'By heavens, they've done it'*
– The sinking of the *Lusitania*

Oliver Bernard, a young British theatrical designer, was taking a post-lunch stroll on the deck of the luxury Cunard liner *Lusitania* when he saw to starboard what appeared to be the 'tail of a fish' in a sea so still it looked like an 'opaque sheet of polished indigo'. Convinced the object was a submarine periscope, he stared hard until he picked up 'the fast-lengthening track of a newly launched torpedo, itself a streak of froth'.

He stared open mouthed as an American woman beside him asked: 'This isn't a torpedo is it?'

Bernard felt sick, unable to answer. It was left to a broad-shouldered American male to state the obvious: 'By heavens, they've done it.'

Seconds later the torpedo hit the side of the ship below the bridge, causing a 'slight shock through the deck' and then a 'terrific explosion'. An immense column of water rose sixty feet above the deck, followed by an eruption of debris. Then came a 'sullen rumble in the bowels of the liner' and a second, even louder explosion. Others watched in horror as 'bits of wood, iron and cinders were blown up through funnels and fell down' on the roof of the Verandah Café and the smoking room at the aft end of the Boat Deck.[1]

Warned seconds before the impact by a shout from the starboard look-out, Captain William ('Bowler Bill') Turner, a fifty-eight-year-old veteran of more than four decades at sea, had raced up the narrow steps from his cabin to the bridge in time to see the bubbles from the torpedo as it hurtled towards the ship. Choking and temporarily blinded by coal dust, Turner ordered the helmsman to turn 'hard-a-starboard!' and make for the nearby Irish coast. He tried but the ship would not respond. Its steering mechanism had locked.[2]

Next Turner tried to slow the ship's speed so that lifeboats could be launched. But his order for the engine room to make 'full speed astern' was in vain. The steam pressure had dropped from 195 pounds to 50, and the engines were useless. The *Lusitania* was running under its own momentum as water poured through the gigantic hole in its side.

Such an attack on a British-owned liner was inevitable once the

Germans had declared unrestricted submarine warfare on hostile shipping on 4 February 1915, adding two weeks later that the waters round Britain, bar a small stretch north of Scotland, was a war zone in which all enemy ships 'would be destroyed even if it is not possible to avoid thereby the dangers which threaten the crews and passengers'. Even neutral ships, continued the announcement, might be hard to identify and sunk as a result (a reference to the practice of British ships flying 'neutral' flags to fool the Germans).[3]

The policy was the brainchild of Admiral von Tirpitz, the Chief of the German Naval Staff, who saw it as the most effective way to counter the British blockade of the German coast. Yet it worried others in the German government, particularly Bethmann Hollweg, because it overturned established maritime law and custom that exempted non-military ships from unprovoked attack, allowing only that they could be stopped and searched to establish their identity and the nature of their cargo. If neutral, they should be allowed to continue; but, either way, proper provision had to be made for the safety of the ship's passengers and crew.

Tirpitz rejected these archaic 'Cruiser Rules' on two grounds: to comply with them would make submarines highly vulnerable to attack while their crew searched a suspicious vessel; and many hostile ships, the *Lusitania* included,* were using fake neutral flags to fool the Germans.

The response of US President Woodrow Wilson to Germany's declaration was unequivocal: it violated the rights of neutral countries and Germany would be held to 'strict accountability' for any loss of American life.[4] But the Germans were unconcerned, sinking a British passenger-cargo ship, the SS *Falaba*, off southern Ireland on 28 March 1915, with an American mining engineer among the fatalities.

On 1 May, the day the *Lusitania* left Pier 54 in Manhattan on its final voyage, the German Embassy in Washington took out an advertisement in the *New York Times* to remind 'Travellers intending to embark on the Atlantic voyage' that 'vessels flying the flag of Great Britain, or any of her allies, are liable to destruction' in the war zone 'adjacent to the British Isles', and that any travellers who crossed by such means did so 'at their own risk'.[5] Most of the 1,250 passengers booked on the *Lusitania* ignored

---

* The *Lusitania* had flown the American flag as she neared the Irish coast during a voyage from New York to Liverpool in late January 1915.

the threat, trusting on the ship's maximum speed of 21 knots to get them through safely.*

With the German position abundantly clear, the Admiralty had issued secret guidelines to merchant skippers: to 'avoid headlands, near which submarines routinely lurked and found their best hunting'; to steer 'a midchannel course'; to operate at 'full speed'; and to zig-zag rather than sail in a straight line. For various reasons, Captain Turner ignored all these guidelines as the *Lusitania* skirted the south coast of Ireland on 7 May.[6]

He knew that danger lurked. On 6 May the *U-20*, commanded by Leutnant Walther Schweiger, had torpedoed two medium-sized merchant ships, the *Candidate* and the *Centurion*. That evening, Turner received the wireless message: 'Submarines active off south coast of Ireland.' Five further Admiralty warnings were sent that night and the following day, culminating in the last at 12.40 p.m. on the 7th.[7]

Part of the reason for Turner's overconfidence was that he expected a naval escort, telling his passengers on the evening of 6 May that they would soon 'be securely in the care of the Royal Navy'.[8] At 10 a.m. on the 7th, having slowed for fog, he ordered the speed back up to 18 knots. But this was still 3 knots less than his ship was capable of, even with one of four engine rooms out of commission (to save coal). The method behind this madness was Turner's plan to sail through the Irish Sea during the hours of darkness, timing his arrival at the Mersey Bar to catch the early tide. That way he could steam straight over the Bar without waiting for a pilot, thus reducing the danger of attack in an area known to be infested with submarines.[9] Yet by minimizing the risk to his ship near Liverpool, he increased it as he steamed past Ireland.

But arguably the truly fatal decision that Turner took on the 7th was to order the fixing of *Lusitania*'s exact position – a laborious process that took two hours and necessitated a steady course, constant speed and proximity to land – in case the weather deteriorated again.[10] This explains why, when the *U-20* attacked it at 2.10 p.m., the *Lusitania* was neither zig-zagging, at top speed nor in mid-channel.

Watching through his periscope, Leutnant Schweiger remembered 'an unusually heavy detonation' as the torpedo struck, followed by a 'very strong explosion cloud'. He wrote in his diary:

* Prior to this, no ship travelling at more than 14 knots had been torpedoed.

The ship stops immediately and quickly heels to starboard, at the same time diving deeper in the bows. She has the appearance of being about to capsize. Great confusion on board, boats being cleared and part lowered to water. They must have lost their heads. Many boats crowded come down bow first or stern first in the water, and immediately fill and sink.

. . . Submerge to twenty-four metres and go to sea. I could not have fired a second torpedo into this throng of humanity attempting to save themselves.[11]

Front page of the *New York Times* on 8 May 1915, the day after a German submarine had sunk the luxury Cunard liner *Lusitania*.

The *Lusitania* sank in just eighteen minutes, taking 1,198 of its 1,959 passengers and crew with it. Among the dead were 128 Americans and ninety-four children (including thirty-five out of thirty-nine babies), causing British newspapers to condemn 'The Hun's Most Ghastly Crime' and the sinking as the latest in a 'long and terrible list' of unprincipled acts of war. Anti-German rioting broke out in British and American cities, with property worth £40,000 destroyed in Liverpool alone. The most keenly awaited response, however, was from President Woodrow

Wilson who, on 13 May, reminded the German government of the principle of 'strict accountability' and that it had been warned not to kill American citizens. The note added: 'no warning that an unlawful and inhumane act will be committed can possibly be accepted as an excuse or palliation of that act' or abate 'the responsibility for its commission'.[12]

Alarmed by the international condemnation of the sinking, the Kaiser's government apologized for the loss of American life and ordered its submarines not to sink neutral shipping or passenger liners. But this would not last, partly because the German press and public opinion were so incensed by the British blockade. 'The sinking of the giant English steamship', wrote the *Kölnische Volkszeitung*, 'is a success of moral significance which is still greater than material success. With joyful pride we contemplate this latest deed of our Navy. It will not be the last. The English wish to abandon the German people to death by starvation. We are more humane. We simply sank an English ship with passengers, who, at their own risk and responsibility, entered the zone of operations.'[13]

Despite the provocation of the sinking, Woodrow Wilson was determined to preserve the United States' neutrality. But not all his fellow countrymen agreed. Former President Theodore Roosevelt, for example, was convinced that a better-armed Britain could have deterred Germany in 1914, and warned in a 1915 book that 'what befell Antwerp and Brussels will surely some day befall New York [and] San Francisco' if adequate preparations were not made for America's defence. If the nations of Europe wanted peace, and America's help in securing it, he added, 'it will be because they have fought as long as they will or can. It will not be because they regard us as having set a spiritual example to them by sitting idle, uttering cheap platitudes, and picking up their trade, while they have poured out their blood in support of the ideals in which, with all their hearts and souls, they believe.'[14]

14 May 1915: *'We had not sufficient high explosive'*
– The shell crisis

As Britons opened their copies of the *The Times* at breakfast, they were shocked by the headline: 'Need for shells: British attacks checked:

Limited supply the cause: A lesson from France'. The article beneath, by the military correspondent Colonel Repington, blamed the recent failure of the BEF's Aubers Ridge offensive of 9 May on the type and quantity of artillery shells. Repington wrote:

> We found the enemy much more strongly posted than we expected. We had not sufficient high explosive to level his parapets to the ground after the French practice, and when our infantry gallantly stormed the trenches, as they did in both attacks, they found a garrison undismayed, many entanglements still intact, and Maxims on all sides ready to pour in streams of bullets. We could not maintain ourselves in the trenches won, and our reserves were not thrown in because the conditions for success in an assault were not present.
>
> The attacks were well-planned and valiantly conducted. The infantry did splendidly, but the conditions were too hard. The want of an unlimited supply of high explosive was a fatal bar to our success.[1]

Repington was not one of the five civilian journalists who, thanks to an agreement between the Cabinet and GHQ in France, had just been given permission to report from the front under close supervision. Instead he had used his friendship with Sir John French to arrange a number of unofficial visits to GHQ in France, the first in late November 1914. This provocative article was the result of his most recent visit a week earlier when French had quite deliberately given him information about the lack of explosives that he knew would harm the government in general, and Lord Kitchener in particular.

The origin of the feud between French and Kitchener went back to the previous August when the BEF commander, not without reason, had suspected the War Secretary of withholding troops and interfering with operations. Nor had French forgotten the humiliation of Kitchener's arrival in France on 1 September to order the BEF back into the fighting line; or Kitchener's decision in August 1914 to appoint Horace Smith-Dorrien to command II Corps, a man French despised and had recently been sacked* for his 'pessimistic attitude' during the Second Battle of Ypres.[2]

---

* Smith-Dorrien was formally relieved of the command of Second Army on 6 May 1915. His replacement was General Sir Herbert Plumer.

The final straw for French, however, was a breakfast meeting with Kitchener on 31 March. 'He told me,' recalled the BEF commander, 'that he considered Joffre and I were "on trial" – that if we showed within the next month or 5 weeks that we really could make "substantial advances" and "break the German line" he would – so far as he was concerned – always back us up with all the troops he could send. But if we failed it would be essential that the government should look for some other theatre of operations.'[3]

This was not an idle threat. The planning for a landing at Gallipoli was already under way, and the inevitable division of limited military resources would infuriate French for months to come. He claimed later to have taken Kitchener's warning on the chin. 'I told him,' wrote French, 'that I thought he had put the matter very fairly and I was content to accept what he said.'[4] Yet it is hard not to conclude that French's unofficial briefing of Repington after the failure at Aubers Ridge was an attempt to get his retaliation in first.

Repington, moreover, was a willing accomplice. He wrote later:

I had been able, during my frequent visits to France, to ascertain how lamentably short we were of high-explosive shells for our field artillery in particular ... we were also short of heavy guns of all calibres, in which the enemy enormously outnumbered us, and of shells for those which we possessed, we were short of trench mortars, of maxims, of almost all the necessary instruments and materials for trench warfare; and the trouble was that Lord Kitchener did not comprehend the importance of artillery in war, took no effective measure to increase our supplies of it, and concealed the truth of the situation from his colleagues in the Cabinet.[5]

Was this criticism justified? Not entirely. Given the unprecedented scale of the conflict, it was bound to take time for each side's peacetime armaments industry to adjust. Each of the combatants, moreover, had its own limits to production: Germany lacked the necessary raw materials to make cordite (the vital propellant for bullets and shells) and explosives; Austria-Hungary was hampered by a lack of rail transport and rail infrastructure; Britain had a manpower shortage and a paucity of acetone (the key component for making cordite); and France had to make up for the loss of much of its industrial heartland to the advancing Germans.

Britain, in particular, needed to invest in new machinery, retrain labour and step up explosives production, 'for which the denial of German chemicals proved a crucial bottleneck'.[6] To speed up the process, Kitchener had reorganized the (albeit small) state munitions industry, warned the private sector to regard armaments supply in terms of years rather than months, and secured the support of the labour force. Yet, at the same time, he and the War Office had stuck 'mainly to its list of approved companies' and let them 'compete with one another for raw materials, workers and machinery'. The end result was that the companies 'contracted for more than they could deliver, and by June 1915 the shortfalls were 12 per cent for rifles, 19 per cent for artillery pieces, 55 per cent for machine-guns, and 92 per cent for high explosive shells'.[7]

In other words, French and Repington had a case: by the spring of 1915, Kitchener and the War Office were not providing the BEF with adequate munitions, particularly high-explosive shells that were needed to destroy strong defences. Why then did French not complain more vociferously in the weeks leading up to the Aubers Ridge attack? Instead,

Lloyd George inspects munition girls.

on 2 May, he assured Kitchener that 'the ammunition will be all right', a claim the War Secretary passed on to Asquith.[8]

It was only after the loss of 11,500 men during the First Army's failed attack on Aubers Ridge on 9 May, with his job on the line, that French decided to go for Kitchener's jugular by briefing Repington. He showed him documents that proved the supply of shells and other weapons were far less than the War Office had promised (and sent staff officers with the same information to brief Lloyd George, and the opposition leaders Arthur Balfour and Bonar Law, in London). A furious Repington was 'determined to expose the truth to the public no matter at what cost', and sent off his famous despatch by telegram on 12 May. The key line about the lack of high-explosive shells being 'a fatal bar to our success' was, he admitted later, his own concoction and 'not suggested by Sir John French'. His only regret was that the army censor, General Macdonough, chose to remove all reference to the casualties suffered by Repington's old corps, the Rifle Brigade, as well as his remarks 'about the want of heavy guns, howitzers, trench mortars, maxims, and rifle grenades'.[9]

French and Repington knew exactly what they were doing, as did Lord Northcliffe, the proprietor of *The Times* and a harsh critic of Kitchener, who wrote a leading article on 14 May accusing the government of failing 'to organize adequately our national resources'.[10] Only a few weeks earlier, in a speech at Newcastle, Asquith had insisted that the supply of ammunition was equal to the army's needs, an assurance he had been given by Kitchener.[11] By casting doubt on the competence and honesty of both the Prime Minister and the War Secretary, therefore, Repington's article and Northcliffe's leader were bound to have severe political repercussions. Even so the government might have survived had the 'shell crisis' not coincided with the resignation of the First Sea Lord, Jackie Fisher, over Churchill's handling of the Dardanelles campaign (in particular the failed attempt to force the seaway with ships alone).

The end result was the fall of the Liberal Cabinet and the formation of a coalition government with Asquith staying on as Prime Minister, Kitchener as War Secretary (thanks to his popular support, and much to French and Repington's disappointment) and Balfour replacing Churchill as First Lord of the Admiralty. But the most significant change of all was the creation of a Ministry of Munitions, entirely separate from the War Office, with David Lloyd George as its first chief. This ministry was to transform shell production: from 2.3 million units in the first six months of 1915 to 14 million in the same period of the following year, and an incredible 35.4 million in the last six months of 1916, 'though (as in France), higher totals were offset by mediocre quality control'. The new Vickers machine-gun was also being produced in much greater numbers – from 109 in March 1915 to 1,000 in November 1916 – as were higher-calibre artillery pieces.[12]

The ends had justified the means, but Repington paid the price when he was banned from visiting the BEF in France until March 1916.[13]

31 May 1915: *'Only a few houses will be struck'*
– London burning

Sylvia Pankhurst was writing in her room in the former East End pub that she and her suffragette friends Mrs Payne and Norah Smyth had converted into a nursery for the poor when the late-evening quiet was broken by an 'ominous grinding . . . growing in volume . . . throbbing, pulsating, filling the air with its sound'. It was, she concluded, 'an air raid!'[1] Then Mrs Payne appeared in her doorway, 'her face ineffably tender', recalled Sylvia:

> 'Miss Pankhurst,' she said, her arms outstretched, 'come down to us! Let us keep together . . .'
>
> 'No use to worry; only a few houses will be struck among the thousands,' I rallied her gently, feeling detached from it all – and faraway. The thought of the bombs crashing down on the densely populated city was appalling – yet for our household I had not the least shade of apprehension – and for myself Life had no great claim. I was only a member of the salvage corps,* saving and succouring as I might amid this wreckage.[2]

---

* A voluntary corps, first set up by insurance companies in the eighteenth century, to attend fires, with the Fire Brigade, and protect goods from water damage and the effects of fire-fighting as much as to rescue them from the fire.

Meanwhile, up on the flat roof of the same building, 438 Old Ford Road, Norah Smyth watched aghast as bombs, incendiaries and grenades – 120 in total, weighing more than 3,000 pounds – were dropped on the East End by a marauding Zeppelin,* a giant airship, 500 feet long, held aloft by huge bags of hydrogen within its light alloy frame, and flying at 10,000 feet, a height most British planes took more than fifty minutes to reach. The Zeppelin over London was the *LZ 38*, commanded by Erich Linnarz, one of the new P-class models that had already attacked Ipswich, Southend, Dover and Ramsgate. Twice Royal Naval Air Service planes had tried to shoot it down; but on both occasions the Zeppelin either outclimbed its enemy or was already too high to intercept.

This occasion was no different. At first Smyth stood her ground as incendiaries – a simple metal canister, filled with thermite, tar and benzol, and wrapped in tarred rope – started fires all around her. Only when bomb shrapnel came uncomfortably close did she go indoors. The damage and casualties were relatively light: seven buildings were destroyed at an estimated cost of £19,000; and seven people (including an infant boy) were killed and thirty-five injured.[3] The main effect was psychological: a reminder, if Britons needed one, that in this new and unrestricted form of total warfare, nowhere and no one was safe.

To prevent accusations of barbarism, Kaiser Wilhelm II had initially banned raids on London in particular, and historic and government buildings in general. Instead the attacks were to concentrate on military and industrial sites on the east coast and around the Thames estuary. But this directive was relaxed in May 1915 to any location east of the Tower of London, particularly the docks, and collateral damage was inevitable.

'The lesson to be drawn from the visit of the Zeppelins to London,' warned a leader in *The Times*, 'is a very old one. It is simply that the Germans mean to prosecute the war with every resource at their disposal, legitimate and illegitimate . . . Their principal object is extremely simple

---

* Named after its inventor, Count Ferdinand von Zeppelin, who got the idea from the French use of observation balloons during the Franco-Prussian War of 1870–1. The first Zeppelin, *LZ 1*, flew over Lake Constance in 1900. Ten years later the German airline DELAG began the first commercial flights in Zeppelins, ferrying over 34,000 passengers by the outbreak of war.

and thoroughly German. They wish to kill as many people and to destroy as much property as they possibly can. They have succeeded very poorly in their object so far, but that will not deter them from trying again.'4

London's chief problem was the weakness of its air defences. Of the fifteen planes sent up to intercept the *LZ 38*, only one made fleeting visual contact and no shots were fired. There were a number of 1-pounder pom-pom anti-aircraft guns sited in London, particularly near the docks, but they were of 'very little value', according to the Ministry of Munitions' official history, which added: 'There was no shrapnel available for them, and the shell provided for them would not burst on aeroplane fabric but fell back to earth as solid projectiles . . . They were of no use except at a much lower elevation than a Zeppelin attacking London was likely to keep.'5

A London news vendor announces the destruction of two Zeppelins during a raid in November 1916.

Only with the introduction in 1916 of bigger anti-aircraft guns, more searchlights and incendiary bullets did the Zeppelins become vulnerable. Before then pilots like Sub-Lieutenant Rex Warneford of the Royal Naval Air Service (RNAS) had to use extraordinary courage and ingenuity to bring them down. In the early hours of 7 June 1915, flying a French Morane-Parasol monoplane, Warneford was en route to bomb the Zeppelin sheds at Berchem-Sainte-Agathe, Belgium, when he spotted a lone airship, *RZ 37*, returning from a failed mission to London. He tried shooting at it with a carbine, his only weapon, but was driven off by the Zeppelin's machine-guns. So instead he tracked it for two hours, climbing to a height of 11,000 feet where breathing was difficult. When the Zeppelin began its descent, near Brussels, Warneford dived after it and dropped his 20-pound bombs from an advantage of 200 feet. He recalled: 'Whilst releasing the last, there was an explosion which lifted my machine and turned it over. The aeroplane was out of control for a short period, went into a nose dive, but control was regained. I then saw the Zeppelin was on the ground in flames.'[6]

Still with no power, however, Warneford was forced to land behind enemy lines to make repairs to his broken fuel line. He did so before he was discovered and, 'after considerable difficulty', managed to restart his engine and head in a south-westerly direction. But he lost his way and had to borrow petrol from a French aerodrome before he reached his own base at 10.30 in the morning.[7]

For this extraordinary feat, Warneford was awarded the Victoria Cross and the French Légion d'Honneur. He died on 17 June, shortly after receiving the latter, in a flying accident near Paris.

By the end of the war, air raids on Britain – by Zeppelins and, later, by German bombers – had killed 1,400 people and wounded a further 3,400.[8] One of the most destructive over London was by two Zeppelins on 7/8 September 1915, witnessed by the novelist D. H. Lawrence, who wrote to a friend:

> Then we saw the Zeppelin above us, just ahead, amid a gleaming of clouds: high up, like a bright golden finger, quite small . . . Then there were flashes near the ground – and the shaking noise. It was like Milton – then there was war in heaven . . . I cannot get over it, that the moon is not Queen of the sky by night, and the stars the lesser lights. It seems the Zeppelin is in the zenith of the night, golden like a moon, having taken control of the sky; and the bursting shells are the lesser lights.[9]

7 August 1915: *'It was simply murder'*
– The Nek

At 4.23 a.m., seven minutes ahead of schedule, the artillery bombardment ceased and an eerie quiet fell over the narrow patch of no man's land, barely 100 yards wide and 150 deep, that separated the men of the dismounted Australian Light Horse from the forward Turkish trench on the Nek.*

The attack on the Nek was part of a wider offensive at Gallipoli – a new landing at Suvla Bay to coincide with an Anzac assault on the Sari Bair ridge – that was designed to break the stalemate that had lasted since the initial landings on 25 April. The plan was for the first line of 150 men from the 8th Light Horse to storm the trenches at the Nek with bayonets and bombs, while a second line from the same unit swept on past the first and took the lower trenches of Baby 700. Two further lines, from the 10th Light Horse, would then drive deeper into the Turkish positions and consolidate their gains with picks and shovels. And all the while the Turks would be assailed from behind by New Zealand troops who, after a long flank march, were supposed to have captured the Chunuk Bair the night before.[1]

As things turned out, the New Zealanders were still 500 yards from their objective at 4.30 a.m. on the 7th and in no position to assist the Australian Light Horse. But the attack was ordered to go ahead by Major-General Alexander Godley, a Kiwi commanding the Australian and New Zealand Division, because it would draw enemy reserves from the main attack.†

At exactly 4.30 a.m., Lieutenant-Colonel Alexander White of the 8th Light Horse shouted 'Go!' and led the 150 men of the first wave out of their trench. They were met by a storm of fire from Turkish rifles and machine-guns, described by Charles Bean, the Australian war

---

* The same feature that had been won and lost by Anzac troops on their first day at Gallipoli, 25 April 1915.
† He was also influenced by the success of another diversionary attack by the 1st Australian Division at Lone Pine on 6 August, a brutal struggle in the elaborate network of roofed Turkish trenches that cost the Antipodeans 2,000 casualties. Seven Australians were awarded the Victoria Cross, two posthumously.

correspondent, as 'one continuous roaring tempest'.[2] White covered ten yards before he was killed and, incredibly, four Australians made it as far as the Turkish trench. But most were hit within a few paces of their parapet. 'I got mine shortly after I got over the bank,' recalled Sergeant Cliff Pinnock, 'and it felt like a million ton hammer falling on my shoulder. However I managed to crawl back and got it temporarily fixed up till they carried me to the Base Hospital. I was really awfully lucky as the bullet went in just below the shoulder blade round by my throat and came out just a tiny way from my spine very low down on my back . . . It was simply murder.'[3]

It took less than thirty seconds for the Turkish machine-guns to destroy the first line. The next wave, under the circumstances, should not have been sent. Something similar had just happened at nearby Quinn's Post where a follow-up attack was cancelled by the commanding officer of the 1st Light Horse after forty-nine of fifty men had been shot down in the first wave. Unfortunately White, the 8th's commander, was already dead.

The second line went two minutes after the first, though Turkish bullets were still thudding into bodies on the Australian parapet. The result was the same. Hit in the shoulder, Captain George Gore was lucky to fall near a Turkish corpse and a fold in the ground. They shielded him until he could crawl to safety. Few of his soldiers were as fortunate. In under three minutes, the 8th Light Horse had ceased to exist, losing 234 out of 300 men (with 154 killed).[4]

Due to charge next were the West Australians of the 10th Light Horse. Unlike their comrades from Victoria in the 8th – particularly the men of the first line who had gone over the top with high hopes – they knew they could not reach the Turkish trenches. Major Tom Todd, in charge of the third line, said as much to his regimental commander, Lieutenant-Colonel Noel Brazier, who decided to take the matter up with the brigade commander Frederic Hughes at 4.40 a.m. But Hughes was absent from brigade headquarters, having left for an observation post, and Brazier was forced to appeal to the brigade major, Lieutenant-Colonel John 'Bull' Antill. Described by one historian as a 'martinet and a bully',[5] Antill was furious with Brazier for querying the order and responded by saying a red-and-yellow marker flag had been seen in the Turkish trench. 'Push on!' he insisted, without referring the matter to either Hughes or Godley.[6]

Brazier returned to the 10th's trench, now filled with the dead and dying from previous waves, and said: 'I am sorry, lads, but the order is to go.' Men shook hands, knowing they would not meet again. 'Goodbye cobber,' said Trooper Harold Rush to a mate, 'God bless you.' (The words adorn his headstone in the nearby Walker's Ridge Cemetery.)[7]

At 4.45 a.m., the first wave of men from the 10th were mown down as they left their trench. Among them were two brothers: Gresley Harper, a barrister; and Wilfred, a farmer, last seen 'running forward like a schoolboy in a foot race'. Wilfred was the model for the doomed sprinter Archie Hamilton in Peter Weir's film *Gallipoli*.[8]

Todd survived the charge and sent back a message saying he was pinned down and needed instructions. Brazier relayed the message to Antill, hoping to stop any more slaughter. But the brigade major was adamant. 'Push on!' he repeated.

Brazier ignored him and sought out Hughes, telling the brigade commander that the attacks were 'murder'.

Hughes responded, 'Try Bully Beef sap,' a suggestion that an attack from another direction might be more successful.[9]

But before Brazier could halt the attacks at the Nek, the men on the right of the fourth line thought they had been ordered to move and left the trenches. As Sergeant W. L. Sanderson ran forward he could see the Turks standing two deep in the front trench. He was saved when he tripped on a bush near the Turkish trench, bringing him down behind a dead Turk. Just ahead, on the parapet, lay two Australians he thought were the Harper brothers. After thirty minutes, by now with flesh wounds from shrapnel, Sanderson began crawling back to his own lines. He came across a survivor from the 8th Light Horse smoking a cigarette, and together they tried to drag back a lieutenant whose hip had been blown away by one of his own bombs. They ignored his pleas to leave him, and got him safely back to the Australian trench where he promptly died. 'About 50 yards of the line,' recalled Sanderson, 'had not a man in it except the dead and wounded – no one was manning it.'[10]

Beyond the trench, on a piece of ground the size of three tennis courts, lay the broken fragments of two regiments of light horse. 'At first here and there a man raised his arm to the sky, or tried to drink from his waterbottle,' wrote war correspondent Charles Bean. 'But as the sun of that burning day climbed higher, such movement ceased. Over the whole summit the figures lay still in the quivering heat.'[11]

Of the 500 or so men who charged at the Nek, almost half were killed.[12] Such a high death toll is almost unprecedented. On the first day of the Somme, by comparison, the fatalities were one in five; at the infamous Charge of the Light Brigade, in 1854, the death rate was under 16 per cent. History has rightly condemned the action at the Nek as tragic and unnecessary, particularly the last three charges. For many Australians – thanks to Peter Weir's 1981 film *Gallipoli* – it is seen as a vital moment in their struggle for national identity: a tale of heroic young colonials sent needlessly to their deaths by incompetent and vindictive British officers who were hoping to distract the Turks from the landings at nearby Suvla. The truth, of course, was very different. 'The scale of the tragedy at the Nek,' acknowledged L. A. Carlyon in his masterly *Gallipoli*, 'was mostly the work of two Australian incompetents, Hughes and Antill. Hughes was the brigade commander and he didn't command; Antill wasn't the brigade commander and he did. Responsibility rattled Hughes and, either consciously or unconsciously, he walked away from it. Antill behaved as he always did, like a bull strung up in barbed wire.'[13]

8 August 1915: *'Golden opportunities are being lost'*
– Suvla Bay

Shortly before noon, two men stepped ashore at the Suvla Bay beach-head: Colonel Aspinall, a member of Sir Ian Hamilton's staff, who had been sent from Imbros to report on the progress of the Suvla landings and government representative Colonel Maurice Hankey MP who had travelled from London to witness the last throw of the Gallipoli dice. 'A peaceful scene greeted us,' recalled Hankey.

> Hardly any shells. No Turks. Very occasional musketry. Bathing parties round the shore. There really seemed to be no realization of the overwhelming necessity for a rapid offensive, of the tremendous issues depending on the next few hours. One staff officer told me how splendidly the troops were behaving, and showed me the position where they

were entrenching! Another remarked sententiously that it was impossible to attack an entrenched position without a strong artillery, and this was not yet available . . .

What distressed me even more was the whole attitude of the [11th] Division. The staff of the division and corps were settling themselves in dug-outs. The pioneers, who should have been making rough roads for the advance of the artillery and supply wagons soon to be landed, were engaged on a great entrenchment . . . 'to protect headquarters'. It looked as though this accursed trench warfare in France had sunk so deep into our military system that all idea of the offensive had been killed.[1]

Hankey added: 'I was filled with dismay, as was the General Staff man [Aspinall] whom I accompanied.'[2]

Aspinall had good reason to be worried. As the architect of the Suvla plan – a landing at Suvla Bay by two New Army divisions, the 10th and 11th, to coincide with an assault further south on the Sari Bair ridge by the Anzac troops and a third New Army division, the 13th – he knew the vital importance of capturing the high ground beyond the bay before the Turks brought up reserves. The troops at Suvla had landed at dawn on the 7th, a full thirty hours earlier, and yet most of their key objectives – including the Tekke Tepe Ridge, Chocolate Hill, Green Hill and 'W' Hills, all of which should have been secured by the end of the first day at the latest – were still not in British hands.

Part of the reason for this tardiness was the watering down of the Suvla plan on 29 July: no longer were the troops expected to take much of the high ground by dawn; instead they would 'gain possession of these hills at an early period of your attack', and only if that did not interfere with their main objective which was 'to secure Suvla Bay as a base'.[3] But that cannot excuse the utter passivity of the commanders ashore. Despairing of this, Aspinall and Hankey dashed off to speak to Lieutenant-General the Hon. Sir Frederick Stopford, the sixty-one-year-old commander of IX Corps (which included the 10th and 11th Divisions), who had sprained his ankle and was directing operations off the coast in the sloop *Jonquil*. 'Well Aspinall,' grinned Stopford as they shook hands, 'the men have done splendidly and been magnificent.'

'But they haven't reached the hills, sir,' replied a nonplussed Aspinall.

'No, but they are ashore.'[4]

Trying not to lose his temper, Aspinall stressed the importance of an immediate advance. But Stopford was implacable: until the men were rested, and more guns and supplies had been landed, it was impossible to move. He had every intention, he added, of ordering a fresh advance on the 9th. Argument was useless, so Aspinall left for the naval flagship and sent the following signal to Hamilton: 'Just been ashore, where I found all quiet. No rifle fire, no artillery fire, and apparently no Turks. IX Corps resting. Feel confident that golden opportunities are being lost and look upon situation as serious.'[5]

Perhaps stung by Aspinall's vehemence, Stopford finally went ashore at 4 p.m. and ordered Hammersley, the commander of the 11th Division, to 'attack at once'. An hour and a half later, back on the *Jonquil*, he issued orders for a simultaneous advance to capture the heights all round Suvla. But he left the timing to Hammersley who, to fit in with a pre-planned attack on 'W' Hills, scheduled the general advance for the morning of the 9th.[6]

Alerted by the weak tone of Stopford's orders, Sir Ian Hamilton reached the *Jonquil* at 6.30 p.m. and told the corps commander that Tekke Tepe Ridge had to be taken that night as it would be the first point of contact with Turkish reinforcements. Stopford replied that the 11th Division needed another night's rest before attacking. Beside himself with rage, Hamilton went to see Hammersley who reeled out the usual excuses: the troops were scattered, the terrain was difficult and no reconnaissance had been made. Only when Hamilton insisted did he agree to order one brigade to attack that night. After much unnecessary delay, its vanguard reached the top of the ridge at the same time as a Turkish reserve division and was driven back.[7]

A general attack, supported by the newly arrived 53rd (Welsh) Division, was put in later that morning and continued throughout the day. It achieved nothing now that the Turks, well entrenched on the high ground, had been strongly reinforced. Stopford, meanwhile, spent the day not directing the battle but supervising the building of shell-proof huts for himself and his staff. 'He was absorbed in the work,' wrote Hamilton after going ashore on the 9th, 'and he said it would be well to make a thorough job of the dug-outs as we should probably be here for a very long time.'[8]

While Stopford fiddled at Suvla, opportunities were also being lost at the Anzac beachhead. The plan had been to take the Sari Bair ridge during the night of 6/7 August before linking up with Stopford's troops. At first all went well with the two covering forces – the left made up of two New Army battalions of the 13th Division and the right of dismounted New Zealander horse – showing verve and courage to clear the foothills before dawn. The way was now open for both assaulting columns: but the two brigades on the left – the 29th Indian and John Monash's 4th Australian Brigade – got lost; while on the right Brigadier-General Francis Johnston, commanding the New Zealand Infantry Brigade, paused for his whole force to concentrate before sending it up the Chunuk Bair feature, then held by just twenty Turkish infantrymen protecting a gun battery. 'He sat for hours in absolute silence,' wrote Johnston's brigade major, 'he was frequently barely coherent and his judgement and mind were obviously clouded.'[9]

This fatal delay gave the Turks, under the German Colonel Hans Kannengiesser, just enough time to reinforce Chunuk Bair so that when the New Zealanders did attack, at 10.30 a.m. (six hours behind schedule), they were easily repulsed with heavy casualties. 'Thus passed,' wrote the Australian war correspondent Charles Bean, 'by far the best chance of winning a great campaign.'[10]

Chunuk Bair was finally captured by the New Zealanders, after an artillery bombardment, in the morning of 8 August. At around the same time a mixed column of Gurkhas, Warwicks and South Lancashire men – including a young captain of the Warwicks called Bill Slim (who would become a field marshal and Britain's finest general of the Second World War) – gained a toehold on the neighbouring peak of Hill Q. The following day, in one of the great actions of the campaign, Major Allanson's Gurkhas stormed Hill Q's saddle. But Monash's Australians had failed to capture Hill 971, and on 10 August the Turks retook Chunuk Bair with a devastating counter-attack that destroyed the two New Army battalions – the 6th Loyal North Lancs and 5th Warwicks – that had relieved the New Zealanders the night before. 'The North Lancashire men were simply overwhelmed in their shallow trenches by sheer weight of numbers,' noted Hamilton's despatch, 'while the Wilts, who were caught in the open, were literally almost annihilated.' The North Lancs, alone, lost its colonel and 492 men, most missing presumed killed.[11]

The moment was now past; there would be no break-out. Two costly beachheads had merely become three. The lack of resolve by Stopford and his senior commanders on the 8th had proved fatal. Eight days later, Stopford was relieved of his command; he would never command troops in the field again and retired in 1920.

25 September 1915: *'There seemed to be nothing ahead of us'*
– The Battle of Loos

At 5 a.m., Sir Douglas Haig walked out of his First Army HQ near Loos in northern France to test the wind. It was 'almost a calm', he noted in his diary, so his ADC Lieutenant-Colonel Alan Fletcher 'lit a cigarette and the smoke drifted in puffs towards the northeast', the direction of the German lines. Still Haig was uncertain, fearing that the chlorine gas they were about to release 'would simply hang about *our* trenches!'[1] At 5.15 he telephoned Sir Hubert Gough, commanding I Corps (attacking on the left), and asked if it was too late to reduce the frontage of the assault.[2] When Gough said yes, a visibly upset Haig gave the order to 'Carry on'. He wrote: 'I went to the top of our lookout tower. The wind came gently from the southwest and by 5.40 had increased slightly. The leaves of the poplar gently rustled. This seemed satisfactory.'[3]

At 5.50 a.m. the gas canisters were opened and Lieutenant-General Sir Henry Rawlinson, commanding IV Corps (attacking on the right), remembered a 'huge cloud of white and yellow gas [that] rose from our trenches to a height between 200 and 300 feet and floated quietly away towards the enemy lines'.[4] At 6.30 the whistles blew and the men of six divisions, the largest British attacking force to date, climbed out of their trenches. Only on the left, where the 2nd Division went over the top, did the gas hang around in no man's land and in places blow back on the attackers. Elsewhere the gas did its work, allowing the five divisions to capture most of the German front line and, in places, part of the second line at least a mile to its rear.

Corporal Frank Moylan of the 1/7th London Regiment, part of the Territorial 47th Division attacking on the right, reached a second line that was deserted. 'Where we were the gas blew over the Germans,' he recalled, 'and that may have driven them out.' Exploring a deep dug-out, Moylan was surprised when a wounded German grabbed him in the dark. He had been peppered with fragments from a bomb and was 'calling for his mother and for water'. Moylan helped the German out of the dug-out and was shocked to see civilians leaving Loos village to his left. 'There was a whole bunch of them, at least a dozen, maybe more.'[5]

Loos had been taken by the Jocks of the 15th (Scottish) Division, as had a vital tactical feature known as Hill 70 a mile to the village's rear. Helping to guide the Scotsmen through the village was Emilienne Moreau, the seventeen-year-old daughter of a grocer, who was dubbed the 'Heroine of Loos'. She later told two Black Watch officers that when the gas attack began she had been 'standing in the loft near her home, which was 200

A French newspaper announces the award of the
Croix de Guerre to Emilienne Moreau.

yards behind the German line, with a handkerchief and a basin of water, which was all she had as a gas mask'. Suddenly she saw 'some enormous men, with gas masks on and a tube coming out of their mouths, a Glengarry on their heads with tails behind, and wearing the kilt'. She rushed to tell her mother who exclaimed: 'The seven devils from hell have been loosed and we'll all die.'[6]

But Moreau saw the advancing Scots as rescuers, and once they were in the village she 'went out and made them stop before they got into booby traps, and came under the fire of machine guns, placed on top of a slag heap behind the village'. She eventually 'got hold of a young officer who spoke a little French, and pointed out where the machine guns were, and also told him how he could move through the village in safety through tunnels and trenches'. She used grenades to help clear a German dug-out, and shot two machine-gunners through a wooden door with a revolver. After the village had been captured she set up a first-aid post in her house and 'helped to tend the wounded'.[7] For these extraordinary feats of courage she was awarded the French Croix de Guerre and the Croix de Combattant, the British Military Medal, the Royal Red Cross and the Venerable Order of St John of Jerusalem.*

To the north of Loos another New Army formation, Neil Weir's 9th (Scottish) Division, had captured a stretch of the German front-line trench, including the infamous Hohenzollern Redoubt, and a slag heap beyond called Fosse 8. Neil Weir, who was now the Bombing Officer of the 10th Argylls, recalled:

> We extended in a line and advanced in rushes as we were under fire from the top of the Hohenzollern Redoubt, although our infantry had passed beyond the place. I remember chucking my water bottle to the first man that I had ever seen dying . . . We took refuge in a trench called Fosse Alley, and found the rest of the Battalion.
>
> Fosse Alley was a dreadful place. It was really a Boche Communication Trench with no parapet or firing step. Here we discovered that, although our infantry had gone ahead, the right of Fosse Alley was held by the

---

* During the Second World War Moreau was a leading figure in the French Resistance. In 1944, having narrowly avoided capture in Lyons, she fled to Britain but returned that September to sit in the Assemblée Consultative. She was awarded the title Compagnon de la Libération and made a Chevalier of the Légion d'Honneur.

Boche. The Gordons even got as far as Haisnes [beyond the German second line], but from here the line bent back to pit No. 8 and Cité St Elie.[8]

Other divisions, notably the regular 1st and 7th, were less successful. But major incursions had been made and at 7 a.m., keen to exploit them, Haig ordered forward his reserves from the 3rd Cavalry Division and asked Sir John French to have the 21st and 24th Infantry Divisions of the New Army's XI Corps 'ready to advance in support'. He repeated this request at 8.45 a.m. But these divisions were so far back they did not reach the original British front line till 6 p.m. on the 25th, too late to attack that day. Haig was still pleased with the progress made. 'The day has been a very satisfactory one on the whole,' he wrote in his diary. 'We have captured 8,000 yards of German front, and advanced in places 2 miles from our old front line. This is the largest advance made on the Western Front since this kind of warfare started.'[9]

But German counter-attacks negated some of the gains that night, and when the 21st and 24th Divisions attacked the following morning they were badly mauled, the German defenders standing on the parapets of their trenches to fire into them with rifles and machine-guns. More than half of the 15,000 infantrymen who went over the top were killed or wounded. At 1 p.m. Haig was told the divisions 'had broken and were coming back in great disorder'.[10] He eventually plugged the gap with the Guards Division, but the opportunity for a decisive breakthrough – if it had ever existed – was long past.

The origin of the battle lay in the agreement reached at the first inter-Allied conference – held at Marshal Joffre's headquarters at Chantilly on 7 July, and attended by representatives of the French, British, Belgian, Serb, Russian and Italian armies – that the Allies would keep up the pressure on the Central Powers by launching a co-ordinated offensive on all fronts. Lloyd George, Minister of Munitions, had been keen to delay these attacks until the following spring when more guns and shells would be available. But he bowed to pressure from General Joffre, the French Commander-in-Chief, who was desperate to liberate northern France (which contained most of the country's heavy industry, including its coalfields) from German occupation. Joffre also had the backing of Sir John French, who needed to take the initiative to prove that the war could be won on the Western Front.

Joffre's plan was for the French to strike the shoulders of the great German salient at Vimy Ridge and (their major effort) in Champagne, with Haig's British First Army supporting the Vimy effort by advancing across the coalfields of Loos, south of Lille. The line Mons–Namur, across the Belgian frontier, was their final objective. Haig had wanted to try again at Festubert,* to the north, because the ground around Loos was too flat and exposed, with good cover for the defenders in the form of miners' cottages, slag heaps and winding gear. Sir John French agreed, using the lack of ammunition as an additional excuse. But when Joffre insisted on the Loos attack, Haig gambled all on the first British use of chlorine gas, noting in his diary on the morning of the attack: 'What a risk I must run of gas blowing back upon our dense masses of troops.'[11]

Postponed twice (from the end of August to 8 September, and from then to 25 September), the attack at Loos was against a German defensive system of two lines, three miles wide, with concrete machine-gun posts in between. It was a difficult nut to crack, and Sir John French, commanding the BEF, hoped for steady but unspectacular gains. Haig, despite his earlier misgivings, was now more optimistic that his assaulting divisions would make a sufficient breach in the enemy lines for his operational reserve to advance into open country. He was, he told his wife three days before the attack, 'pretty confident of some success' and that by October he hoped the BEF 'may be a good distance on the road to Brussels'.[12] Some of this optimism must have trickled down to regimental officers like Weir who thought it would be 'the attack that would end the war, that Division after Division would break through after we had made the gap in the Boche defences' and that 'we went into that fight with the firm belief that it was to be the end of Germany'.[13]

They were to be disappointed. After three days in action – during the last of which Weir's divisional commander George Thesiger was killed by shellfire (one of three major-generals to die at Loos) – the 9th Division was relieved and taken out of the line. Weir commented in his diary: 'What a show. Few instructions, little ammunition or bombs, next to no support from the artillery. No system of looking after the

* The first offensive (including the first night attack of the war), from 15 to 27 May, had made modest gains at a cost of 16,000 casualties.

wounded. And practically no food. No wonder we lost the ground we had won and lost so many in casualties.' Weir was one of just nine unwounded officers in the battalion. His B Company was left with twenty-five effectives.[14]

Attack and counter-attack continued at Loos for another day, but any chance of a comprehensive victory had vanished. The French operations in Champagne and Artois had also failed, and Joffre temporarily halted the offensive. It was renewed at Loos on 13/14 October; but in spite of some careful preparations, the attack on the Hohenzollern Redoubt (which the Germans had recaptured) was a total failure and Haig blamed the commander of the Territorial 46th (North Midland) Division, Major-General the Hon. E. J. Montagu-Stuart-Wortley, for using 'up his reserves before they were really required'.[15]

The battle had gained for the BEF nothing more than a narrow salient two miles deep, at a cost of 16,000 dead and a further 25,000 wounded. Total German casualties at Loos were 25,000.[16] And yet, for a fleeting moment on the 25th, it had seemed to some who fought that day as if the battle was won. Richard Hilton, a Forward Observation Officer, recalled:

> Most of us who reached the crest of Hill 70, and survived, were firmly convinced that we had broken through . . . There seemed to be nothing ahead of us, but an unoccupied and incomplete trench system. The only two things that prevented our advancing into the suburbs of Lens were, firstly, the exhaustion of the 'Jocks' themselves (for they had undergone a bellyfull of marching and fighting that day) and, secondly, the flanking fire of numerous German machine-guns, which swept that bare hill from some factory buildings in Cité St. Auguste to the south of us. All that we needed was more artillery ammunition to blast those clearly located machine-guns, plus some fresh infantry to take over from the weary and depleted 'Jocks'. But, alas, neither ammunition nor reinforcements were immediately available, and the great opportunity passed.[17]

Among the soldiers killed at Loos was Second Lieutenant John Kipling of the Irish Guards, only son of Rudyard Kipling, whose body was never recovered. His heartbroken and embittered father wrote the poem 'The Children' in his memory:

That flesh we had nursed from the first in all cleanness was given
To corruption unveiled and assailed by the malice of Heaven –
By the heart-shaking jests of Decay where it lolled in the wires –
To be blanched or gay-painted by fumes – to be cindered by fires –
To be senselessly tossed and retossed in stale mutilation
From crater to crater. For that we shall take expiation.
But who shall return us our children?

Another poet whose early enthusiasm for the war had given way to disillusionment was Roland Leighton. He had arrived in France in late March 1915, having transferred from the Norfolks to the 7th Worcesters, and barely a month later was writing to his sweetheart Vera Brittain of the nerve-shattering experience of shellfire: 'horror piled on horror till one feels that the world can scarcely go on any longer'.[18] By now engaged to Brittain ('for three years or the duration of the war'),* he described shortly before Loos the horror of seeing 'the fleshless, blackened bones of simple men who poured out their red, sweet wine of youth unknowing, for nothing more tangible than Honour or their Country's Glory or another's Lust of Power'. He added:

> Let him who thinks war is a glorious, golden thing . . . but look at a little pile of sodden grey rags that cover half a skull and shin-bone and what might have been its ribs . . . and let him realize how grand and glorious a thing it is to have distilled all Youth and Joy and Life into a foetid heap of hideous putrescence! Who is there who has known and seen who can say that Victory is worth the death of even one of these?[19]

8 October 1915: *'The whole city was in retreat'*
– The fall of Belgrade

After three days of bombardment from river, land and air, the inhabitants of Belgrade woke to the terrifying news that Austro-German

---

* Brittain, by this time, had left Oxford after one year's study, joined the Voluntary Aid Detachment (VAD) and was about to start work as a nurse in the 1st London General Hospital in Camberwell.

forces had crossed the Sava and Danube rivers and were closing in on the city from both east and west. Among the foreign nationals who feared capture was a brilliant twenty-year-old Irish-born scholar called Theobald Butler who had interrupted his studies at Oxford to work as a volunteer orderly at a Red Cross hospital in Belgrade. Unlike Roland Leighton, Neil Weir and many other undergraduates, Butler had opted to serve as a non-combatant rather than a soldier because he feared he 'might be sent to fight his own [Irish] countrymen'.[1]

'By the morning of the 8th,' recalled Butler,

> it was pretty clear we must either evacuate our hospital or be taken prisoners. The Serbian Government had invested the chief doctor of the American hospital, Dr Ryan, with full powers as Consul, and he had told us that he would send stretcher-bearers to remove our patients when it became absolutely necessary for us to depart. There was still some faint hope that the city might be saved, as drafts of Serbian troops were pouring in; but they were wholly inadequate to meet the immense numbers of the enemy who now occupied the quays and lower part of the town.[2]

In the afternoon, Butler went out to try and find a wagon to transport some of the hospital's medical stores; but all were in use. As he made his way back empty-handed, he passed a 'fairly continuous stream' of refugees heading south, including 'several old women' who warned him with 'unmistakeable gestures not to go back into the town'. He ignored them, and helped to carry back some wounded civilians and gendarmes for treatment.[3]

At 6 p.m., the promised stretcher-bearers arrived to transport the patients to the American hospital where, in theory, they would be safe. Soon after Dr Ryan himself appeared to say it was imperative that all the staff left immediately. 'We had only one cart,' recalled Butler, 'which could hold little more than two heavy boxes containing provisions in case of need, so that we were compelled to leave behind everything beyond what we could carry.'[4]

As they were setting off, a grocers near by was destroyed by a shell. Street fighting was already under way, and Serbian troops were building a barricade at the bottom of the main street. Butler wrote:

A few minutes later we found ourselves among an immense throng of refugees; the whole city, one might say, [was] in retreat, moving along the one road that could lead them to safety. The spectacle was the most melancholy I have ever witnessed. One saw old women struggling along as best they could under heavy burdens, and usually there were crying children following along behind them. There were wounded soldiers, too, in groups of three or four, often supporting each other for the order had been given that every wounded man who could walk must do so, as it was feared that the only remaining hospital, the American, might become overcrowded.[5]

It was pitch black, raining and the sides of the road were clogged with mud. With most of the wealthier inhabitants moving in carts or bullock wagons, those on foot were regularly 'swept aside into the ditch' to let troops pass. Moving at such a snail's pace, it took Butler and his companions 'several hours' to cover the six miles to the Torlak heights. There they found most of the refugees camped round roadside fires, 'pitiably cold and wet'. Yet no one was complaining and 'all displayed', wrote Butler, 'that heroic spirit of endurance which is characteristic of every Serbian, and which has led their army to offer almost superhuman resistance to the overpowering forces of their enemies'.[6]

Butler was fortunate to miss the worst rigours of the retreat when he and his fellow hospital workers were given a lift in a British Naval Mission lorry to Mladnovatz, and from there they took trains south to Greece and safety. But his praise of Serbian fortitude was justified. None of the Entente powers could have predicted in August 1914 that Serbia would long withstand the military might of a vengeful Austria-Hungary. Yet it had, and for more than a year. What made this latest assault so destructive was that it was multinational, multi-pronged and involved armies twice as strong as their typhus-ravaged Serb opponents.

It began on 5 October when German and Austro-Hungarian forces invaded Serbia, later capturing Belgrade (on 9 October) and advancing down the Morava valley into the heart of the country; while on 12 October Bulgaria became the latest country to join the seemingly ascendant Central Powers when it invaded Serbia from the east with the intention of annexing the southern Serb region of Macedonia.

Though French troops had already landed at Salonika in neutral Greece to assist the Serbs* – and were joined by reinforcements from France and Britain while the attack on Serbia was under way – they were too little, too late. On 5 November, Bulgarian forces captured the vital rail link of Niš in central Serbia. But the Serbian Army fought on and, despite being hampered by tens of thousands of refugees, made its way back to Kosovo, and then, having abandoned its heavy weapons and vehicles, began the tortuous crossing of the mountains to Albania and Montenegro. 'People who shared in the retreat', stated a wartime history of Serbia, 'tell a confused story of cold, hunger, gorgeous scenery, Albanian ambushes, of paths covered with the carcases of horses, and men dying at the wayside. We hear of the Ministers of Russia and Great Britain lying on straw next to the Serbian Foreign Minister . . . of the King [Peter], lying on a stretcher, drawn by four bullocks, sharing the difficulties of the road with the common soldier.'[7]

Ox-drawn artillery and transport of the Serbian Army during its tortuous retreat to Albania in the autumn of 1915.

---

* A deployment that did not have the permission of the Greek government, prompting Falkenhayn, the Chief of the German General Staff, to describe it as a 'serious breach of international law, which deprived the Entente even of ostensible justification for any further outcry against the march through Belgium' ('The Fall of Serbia' in Horne (ed.), *Source Records of the Great War*, III, p. 363).

More than 20,000 people died of hunger, exposure and disease on the retreat through the mountains. But 260,000 Serbs – mostly soldiers – survived the epic three-week march to reach the Adriatic coast in early December. From there, in one of the largest sea evacuations in history, they were taken in Italian, French and British steamers to the island of Corfu. Meanwhile the 20,000 Austrian prisoners they had dragged along with them were interned in Italy.[8]

The loss of Serbia, however, was a strategic disaster for the Entente: it removed, at a stroke, the Serbian Army from the fray and allowed Austria to concentrate its forces against Russia and Italy; and it completed the direct rail link from Berlin to Baghdad, thus enabling the Central Powers to send vital supplies and munitions (particularly heavy artillery) to Turkey. The Gallipoli campaign, as a result, was all but doomed.

12 October 1915: *'She was killed immediately'*
– The execution of Edith Cavell

As dawn was breaking, a car drove through the Gothic gatehouse of the Saint-Gilles military prison in Brussels and a man in German uniform got out. He was the prison's Lutheran chaplain, Pasteur Le Seur, and had come to offer solace to the British nurse Edith Cavell on the day of her execution.[1]

'In the cell,' recalled Le Seur,

a flickering gas-flame was burning. Two large bouquets of withered flowers, which had been standing there for ten weeks, awakened the impression of a vault. The condemned lady had packed all her little property with the greatest care in a handbag.

I accompanied her through the long corridors of the great prison. The Belgian prison officials stood there and greeted her silently with the highest respect. She returned their greetings silently. Then we boarded the motor-car which awaited us in the yard.[2]

Moments later, into a second car climbed a Catholic priest and Philippe Baucq, a thirty-five-year-old Flemish architect, who, like Miss Cavell, was due to be shot that day for helping Allied prisoners to escape to neutral Holland. The cars took them to the Belgian rifle range known as the Tir National where they found a full company of German soldiers on parade, and nearby various military and civilian officials. Le Seur wrote:

> We clergymen led the condemned persons to the front. The company presented their rifles, and the sentence was about to be read aloud in German and in French, when M. Baucq called out with a clear voice in French: 'Comrades, in the presence of death we are all comrades.' He was not allowed to say anything more. The sentence was read out, and then the clergymen were permitted to have a last word . . . I took Miss Cavell's hand and only said (of course in English) the words: 'The Grace of our Lord Jesus Christ and the love of God and the Communion of the Holy Ghost be with you for ever. Amen.'

Miss Cavell responded by squeezing Le Seur's hand and asking him to pass on to the Reverend Stirling Gahan, the Irish-born Anglican chaplain in Brussels, her belief that her soul was 'safe' and that she was 'glad to die' for her country.[3]

Born on 4 December 1865, the daughter of a Norfolk parson, Edith Cavell had worked as a governess in England and Belgium before retraining as a nurse at the age of thirty. After various posts in Britain – including a spell as assistant matron of the Shoreditch Infirmary, where she pioneered the practice of post-discharge follow-up visits – she returned to Brussels in 1907 to take charge of Dr Antoine Depage's* pioneer training school for lay nurses, the Ecole Belge d'Infirmières Diplômées (the Belgian School of Registered Nurses), in the rue de la Culture. By 1912, the school was providing nurses for a variety of hospitals, communal schools and kindergartens.

Edith was visiting her mother in Norfolk when Germany declared war on Russia on 1 August 1914. Unwilling to abandon her school and her mission, she set off at once for Brussels and arrived on 3 August, the day before German troops violated Belgium's neutrality. Her first act was to send her German probationers home, impressing on the remaining nurses

---

* Depage's wife Marie drowned when the *Lusitania* was torpedoed on 7 May 1915. She was returning from a successful mission to the United States to raise funds for her husband's Ocean hospital at La Panne on the Belgian coast.

that their duty was to care for wounded soldiers of all nationalities. The school provided nurses for the Red Cross Hospital in the Palais Royal and German casualties were treated like everyone else. But after Brussels fell to the Germans on 20 August, most of the British nurses were repatriated and only Edith, her chief assistant Miss Wilkins, her goddaughter Pauline Randall and a nurse called Grace Jemmett remained at the school.

Despite the warning on German posters that anyone helping to hide an Allied soldier would be severely punished, Edith sheltered two British fugitives – Colonel Dudley Boger of the 1st Cheshires and a Sergeant Harry Meakin – at the school for two weeks in November 1914 before finding guides to take them to neutral Holland.* Soon, with the assistance of the Prince and Princess de Croÿ (cousins of the Belgian King) who lived in a château near Mons, an underground escape route was established. Fugitive Allied soldiers were taken first to the Croÿs' château, where they were given food and medical treatment, and then on to safe houses in Brussels (including Edith's school). When the time was right, guides organized by Philippe Baucq led them to the safety of the Dutch border.

By June 1915, with Belgium crawling with German-paid informers and agents provacateurs, Edith and others in the network discussed the increasing danger of betrayal. But Edith was of the view that if 'we are arrested we shall be punished in any case, whether we have done much or little'. So it made sense to continue as before 'and save as many as possible of these unfortunate men'.[4]

But Edith suspected that the escape network's good fortune could not last, and on 6 July 1915, after various close shaves, she wrote to her mother: 'Do not forget if anything *very* serious should happen you could probably send me a *message* thro' the American Ambassador in London (not a letter). All is quiet here as usual. We are only a small number so many being at the front nursing the Belgian soldiers.'[5]

On 31 July, having spent months amassing evidence from spies who had passed through the network, the German military police in Brussels arrested Baucq and an associate. Edith was picked up six days later and, told by her German interrogators that her friends had already confessed, she admitted everything. Part of her deposition read:

---

* Meakin got back to England; Boger was arrested before he left Brussels and spent the remainder of the conflict as a prisoner of war.

I lay particular stress on the fact that of all the soldiers English or French lodged with me two or three only were wounded and in these cases the wounds were slight and already beginning to heal.

I acknowledge that between November 1914 and July 1915 I have received into my house, cared for, and provided with funds to help them to reach the front and join the Allied Army:

(1) French and English soldiers in civilian clothes, separated from the ranks, amongst whom was an English colonel.
(2) French and Belgians eligible for military service who desired to get to the front.[6]

This was not entirely accurate. At least twelve of the soldiers were severely wounded; and one of them, Colonel Boger, did not escape. But as the transcript of Edith's interrogation was written in German, she had no way of checking it.

For ten weeks Edith was held incommunicado* in her tiny prison cell – barely twelve feet by eight, and sparsely furnished with a folding bed, a basin and a bucket for a toilet – in the Saint-Gilles fortress while her family, the Foreign Office and the American Legation in Brussels tried to find out why she was being held. On 24 August, for example, her brother-in-law Dr Longworth Wainwright wrote to Sir Edward Grey at the Foreign Office in London: 'I have news through Dutch sources that my wife's sister, a Miss Edith Cavell, has been arrested in Brussels and I can get no news as to what has happened to her since August 5.'[7]

Grey duly asked the American Ambassador in London to make inquiries in Brussels as to the reason for Miss Cavell's arrest, which he did by cable on 27 August.[8] But it was not until 21 September that Brand Whitlock, the American minister in Brussels (and sometime novelist), replied that Edith Cavell had 'admitted having hidden in her house English and French soldiers and has facilitated the departure of Belgian soldiers to the front, furnishing them money and guides to enable them to cross the Dutch frontier'. The Legation would, he added, do its best to see that she got a 'fair trial'. But in the light of Edith's confession, senior Foreign Office mandarins were not hopeful of the outcome. 'I'm afraid it is likely

---

* Apart from half an hour's exercise each day in the prison yard, she was kept in solitary confinement.

British matron Edith Cavell with her dogs
in Brussels in 1914.

to go hard with Miss Cavell,' wrote the Under-Secretary of State, Sir Horace Rowland, on 1 October. 'I'm afraid we are powerless.'[9]

The trial of Edith and thirty-four others, including Philippe Baucq and the Princess de Croÿ, began in the Senate Room of Parliament House on 7 October. Bizarrely, though none was a German citizen, they were charged under paragraph 34 of the German military penal code, which defined as treason to the Fatherland various crimes such as 'conducting soldiers to the enemy'.[10] Edith denied the charge of treason, claiming that her motive was not to aid Germany's enemies but rather 'to help those men who asked for my help to reach the frontier' and freedom, and that some had written letters thanking her for this.[11] Her lawyer Sadi Kirschen – a Brussels attorney who spoke to her for the first time on the opening day of the trial – did his best by saying she had acted only out of compassion for others, and to save the lives of people she thought were in danger.[12] But the court was implacable and found Edith and twenty-five others guilty of treason. The only question was whether it would impose the ultimate sanction.

'Miss Cavell's trial has been completed,' wrote Whitlock to the Foreign

Office on 11 October, 'and the German prosecutor has asked for sentence of death penalty against her. I have some hope that the court martial may decline to pass the rigorous sentence proposed.'[13] This was wishful thinking and later that day, having heard the grim news that Edith and three others would be shot, American and Spanish diplomats went to see the head of the German political department in Brussels, Baron von der Lancken, to plead for Cavell's life. Lancken referred the matter to General von Sauberzweig, the military governor, who rejected the appeal for clemency on the grounds that Cavell's immediate execution was necessary to protect German troops. When the diplomats heard this, they pleaded with Lancken to telephone the Kaiser and seek his personal intervention. But Lancken refused. 'I am not a personal friend of my sovereign like you,' he sarcastically told the Spanish minister, the Marquis de Villobar. The last chance to save Edith had slipped away.[14]

That evening, thanks to the intercession of Pasteur Le Seur, the Anglican chaplain Stirling Gahan was allowed into Edith's cell to give her Holy Communion. He found her 'perfectly calm and resigned', and grateful for the previous 'ten weeks' quiet before the end'. While she wanted her friends 'to know that she willingly gave her life for her country', she insisted she felt 'no hatred or bitterness' towards the Germans. 'They have,' she declared, 'all been very kind to me here. But this I would say, standing as I do in view of God and eternity, I realize that patriotism is not enough.'

When their time was up, Gahan rose and said goodbye.

Edith smiled. 'We shall meet again.'[15]

Next morning, she showed similar composure as Pasteur Le Seur led her forward to the execution post at the Tir National. Only after she had been loosely bound, and a blindfold was raised to her eyes, did she begin to cry.

Seconds later, on the German officer's command, two squads of eight men fired simultaneous salvoes from a distance of just six paces. 'The two condemned persons sank to the ground without a sound,' wrote Le Seur, adding:

My eyes were fixed exclusively on Miss Cavell, and what they now saw was terrible. With a face streaming with blood – one shot had gone through her forehead – Miss Cavell had sunk down forwards, but three times she raised herself up without a sound, with her hands stretched upwards. I ran forward with the medical man, Dr Benn, to her. He was doubtless right when he stated that these were only reflex movements . . . The bullet-holes, as large as a fist in the back, proved, in addition, that without any doubt she was killed immediately.[16]

This last comment by Le Seur was in response to false reports in British and American newspapers that the firing squad had deliberately fired wide of Edith who then fainted and was shot by a German officer while she lay on the ground. The *New York Tribune*, for example, included a drawing of a tall, spiked-helmet-wearing officer standing over a prostrate and bleeding Cavell, a smoking revolver in his hand. The caption read: 'GOTT MIT UNS' ('God is with us').[17]

But the truth was bad enough, and by martyring Edith Cavell the Germans handed another propaganda victory (and one eagerly seized upon by pro-war Americans) to the Allies. Sir Horace Rowland said as much when he wrote on 14 October: 'I had hoped the Germans wouldn't go beyond imprisoning her in Germany. Their action in this matter is part and parcel of their policy of frightfulness and also I venture to think a sign of weakness.'[18]

22 November 1915: *'Trenches filled with dead and dying'*
– The Battle of Ctesiphon

It was still dark as the four columns of Major-General Sir Charles Townshend's 6th (Poona) Division moved forward in echelon, with muffled wheels and a ban on lights, towards their jumping-off points in the barren desert. With his final objective of Baghdad just twenty-two miles distant, and a string of victories behind him, Townshend might have approached this battle with confidence. He did not because he knew the odds were against him: directly ahead of his troops, nestled in a loop of the Tigris River, was the ancient town of Ctesiphon (site of a famous Roman victory over the Persians in AD 530); and to reach it they would have to fight their way through two lines of Turkish trenches and redoubts, the first of which was protected in the centre by a forty-foot-high wall (the relic of an ancient fortified city), and the whole manned by 18,000 troops and fifty-two guns. Townshend, by contrast, had fewer than 8,000 men available for the assault, many of whom were sick, undernourished and battle weary after three months of almost constant marching and combat.[1]

The foray into Mesopotamia had begun with the occupation of Basra in November 1914 by Indian Expeditionary Force D, made up of a single infantry division (the 6th) that was sent from the sub-continent even before Turkey entered the war. The ostensible reason was to protect the Anglo-Persian Oil Company's wells at Abadan in southern Persia (a vital source of fuel for the oil-powered ships of the Royal Navy); but even more pressing was the need to 'strengthen' the Indian government's hand 'in contacts with the local Arab rulers, many of whom were restive against the Ottomans, and to safeguard British interests if the Gulf descended into disorder'.[2]

From April 1915, when the ambitious Sir John Nixon took command of all troops in Mesopotamia, the Indian government (and, in retrospect, the India Office in London) authorized Force D to make successive advances up the River Tigris to Kut-al-Amara. Hard-fought victories were won against the Turks at Shaiba in April, Qurna in May, Amara in June and, finally, at Kut-al-Amara in late September. But even before this last action Townshend (commander of Force D since the Battle of Shaiba) had worried that his force was becoming overextended and vulnerable. 'You may afford to have reverses and retreat in France, perhaps,' he told his wife, 'but not in the East and keep any prestige. Imagine a retreat from Baghdad and the consequent rising of the Arabs of the whole country behind us, to say nothing of the Persians and Afghans.'[3]

After the success at Kut – a bold plan of attack that narrowly failed to trap the Ottoman Army – and the pursuit to Aziziyeh, 102 river miles (sixty land miles) upriver and less than sixty from Baghdad, Townshend was even less inclined to continue the advance. 'I do not want you to send [reinforcements] up here,' he wrote to Nixon's staff on 3 October, 'because I do not approve of holding on at Aziziyeh.' He added: 'We ought to come back; we are too far ahead.'[4]

Nixon's headquarters, however, thought differently. The occupation of

Baghdad would be strategically decisive, argued his staff in August 1915, as it would require the Turks to 'draw their resources from a great distance'. If the enemy 'is beaten 100 miles in advance of Baghdad', added the paper optimistically, 'the 6th Division might be able in certain circumstances to enter that City practically unopposed'.[5] Nixon backed up this opinion in October by informing Townshend that a continued advance towards Baghdad 'will have a demoralizing effect on the Turks and a corresponding good effect on the political situation in this portion of Asia'.[6]

But Townshend was adamant. 'On military grounds,' he wrote to Nixon, 'we should consolidate our position at Kut.' And if the government wanted Baghdad to be taken for political reasons, it was 'absolutely necessary that the advance from Kut should be carried out methodically by two divisions'.[7]

Nixon thought only cavalry reinforcements were necessary, and that once Townshend had them there was 'every probability of catching and smashing the enemy at Ctesiphon'. If, on the other hand, the 6th Division withdrew to Kut this would encourage the Turks and the Arab tribes. This was not an opinion shared by the General Staff at the War Office in London, which condemned the move to Baghdad with the forces available as a 'dangerous operation'. But, crucially, Nixon's strategy received the support of the Indian government and ultimately the Cabinet. Edward Grey, in particular, was mindful of the looming need to evacuate Gallipoli and the consequent damage to British prestige; and saw Mesopotamia as a chance to 'score a notable success'.[8] The capture of Baghdad would, he hoped, encourage the Arab tribes to enter the war on the Allied side.

With the decision made, Townshend began his advance from Aziziyeh on 14 November, and a week later put the final touches to his assault on the Turkish position at Ctesiphon. From aerial reconnaissance reports he had noted the weakness of the Ottoman defences – the fact that the trenches (the second of which was unfinished) were two miles apart, that there were no communication trenches between them, and that the ground to the north was flat desert with low scrub, ideal for a flanking attack – and had planned accordingly. 'I hoped to paralyse,' he wrote later, 'a great part of the forces of the enemy, entrenched along a large extent of the front, by the use of an inferior fraction of my troops, disguising its weakness by boldness of action and ruse, while I hit the hammer blow on the enemy's flank and rear with my Principal Mass.'[9]

Of his four attacking columns, only one (C) would fix the enemy in their position. The job of Column A, the strongest, was to capture the northernmost redoubt of the front line, known as Vital Point (or VP); Column B would exploit this success by rolling up the line from the north; and the Flying Column, made up of a mixture of cavalry and infantry, would sweep round to the Turkish rear to cut off the line of retreat. The plan was necessarily ambitious because only a battle of annihilation would enable Townshend's small, exhausted and undersupplied force of 8,000 men to hold Baghdad after it had captured it.[10]

The fatal flaw in the plan, however, was that it assumed fewer defenders than were actually present. This was partly the fault of Nixon's staff who, not wishing to discourage a battle, deliberately gave Townshend the lower end of their 13,000–23,000 estimate of enemy troops (when in fact the upper figure was more accurate); and partly down to bad luck when a reconnaissance flight that had spotted Turkish reinforcements was brought down by engine failure and the pilot captured by Arab irregulars on 21 November.[11]

The battle opened at dawn with shells fired from Townshend's tiny naval flotilla on the Tigris, and from the guns of Brigadier-General Hoghton's Column C. 'At day break the Battery opened fire at 5,000 yards,' recorded Sergeant William Groves of the Royal Field Artillery. 'Infantry commenced to advance.'[12]

Hoghton's men were held up short of the Turkish trenches. But further north Brigadier-General Delamain's Column A – spearheaded by the 1st Dorsets and a battalion of Gurkhas – had captured the VP and were pursuing the beaten Turks towards their second line. To exploit the breakthrough, Townshend ordered Hoghton's column to disengage and march north. But as it did so it was 'heavily enfiladed by having to pass for nearly a mile at a distance of a few hundred yards in front of the Turkish trenches', and 'only the lucky got through'.[13] Groves recalled: 'Our section came under a terrific oblique rifle and shell fire. We stopped firing but the Turks were bent on destroying us.'[14]

Meanwhile Delamain's men had broken into the Turks' second line of trenches where they were joined by elements of Column B. But when the

Turkish infantry launching a counter-attack in Mesopotamia.

Turkish commander, Colonel Nureddin, sent forward his reserves – notably the tough Anatolians of the 51st Division – it was all the Anglo-Indian troops could do to hang on. 'It was about 3 o'clock in the afternoon that the Turks counter-attacked so strongly,' wrote an artillery officer in his diary. 'The 82nd and ourselves were sent forward to try and stop it. I think we managed to do so, for a time anyway, but it was a very *warm* time. Then they attacked from another quarter and drove our infantry in and we had to limber up and get out as quickly as we could under a most beastly hot fire.'[15]

Elsewhere the Flying Column had been stopped in its tracks and, thanks to heavy fire from both banks of the Tigris, the naval flotilla was not able to offer its usual artillery support. 'Now the plain became dotted with hundreds of our troops walking slowly back towards V.P.,' wrote Townshend. 'It soon became apparent that a retirement was taking place, though no orders had been given for one.' He put it down to the loss of white officers: with no one 'to keep them in hand', hordes of Indian sepoys were 'streaming towards the rear'.[16]

With threats and curses the retreating troops were rallied at the VP where, according to Sergeant Groves, the 'carnage' was 'awful'. He added: 'Terrible stench of blood. Trenches filled with dead and dying lying on top of one another. Dead in thousands as well as hundreds of animals . . .

Night spent quiet apart from snipers. Wounded being brought in all night. Rations issued: 1 loaf – 3 men. Nothing else.'[17]

Townshend's first instinct was to order a renewal of the assault the following day. But when he realized the extent of his casualties – with most of the columns down to fewer than 1,000 men, half their original strength – he chose to remain on the defensive. 'If I live a hundred years,' he wrote later, 'I shall not forget that night bivouac at V.P. amongst hundreds of wounded.'[18]

Nureddin launched repeated counter-attacks during the late afternoon and evening of the 23rd, but could not break through. 'Infantry held Turks,' noted Sergeant Groves, whose section of guns was down to its last ten rounds. 'Suspense terrible. Almost 1/3rd of our force casualties by this time.'[19]

Turkish losses were even higher – 6,000 – and the following morning Colonel Nureddin authorized a withdrawal to Baghdad. Left in possession of the field, it seemed to Townshend that he had won a 'great victory'. But with almost half his force killed or wounded he knew a further advance was senseless. Once his 3,500 wounded had been evacuated back to the nearest river transport – an agonizing ordeal in iron-framed spring-less carts – he gave the order to retreat.[20]

Harried all the way by the Turks, the exhausted remnants of the 6th Division finally reached Kut during the morning of 3 December. Despite the horrors of the retreat, noted a gunner in the 86th Heavy Regiment, they 'were in high praise of their leader', and to all 'it seemed a marvel how he had extricated them'.[21] But Townshend's decision to turn Kut into an armed camp while he waited for reinforcements was, in retrospect, a fatal error. Two days later the Turks completed the encirclement of the town and the epic siege of Kut was under way.

1 December 1915: *'I am on the move now'*
– Reinforcements reach Gallipoli

It was not a good time for my great-uncle, Second Lieutenant Clive Neely, to arrive at Suvla Bay. The worst of the fighting may have been over, but for much of the previous week the Gallipoli peninsula had been battered by some of the fiercest storms in memory.

They began on 26 November with hurricane-force winds that 'howled and hammered, sweeping away piers, dashing small vessels into matchwood, uprooting trees, tearing the flimsy roofs from dug-outs, lashing whirlwinds of stinging sand against the bare limbs of the miserable soldiers still clad in thin khaki drill'.[1] Then torrents of rain flooded dug-outs and trenches, particularly those held in flat ground to the right of Chocolate Hill at Suvla by the 6th Loyal North Lancashires,* the battalion so badly cut up at Chunuk Bair and the destination for my great-uncle and his draft of reinforcements.

The 6th Loyals had a number of men drowned in the inundated trenches, but what came next was even worse. 'For nearly two days and nights snow descended in whirling blizzards,' noted the regimental history, 'and two days and nights of bitter frost succeeded the snow. The surface of the pools and trenches froze thick. The sentries and outposts in the advanced trenches could not pull the trigger of their rifles for cold. Few can realize the suffering of those days.'[2]

Despite the death of his brother at Second Ypres in April, Clive Neely had left for Gallipoli in high spirits. 'Well old girl,' he had written to his sister Phyllis from Seaford Camp near Brighton on 10 November, 'I am on the move now and have been pitched over here with a few officers to take out a draft of Lancashire men to the Mediterranean. I do not know when we are going but I think very soon and it looks as though it would be service.'[3] A week or so later, he wrote from his troopship:

Dear old Phyll – Here I am you see actually on the way to it. We don't know exactly where and I can't give you any details of the journey because you see we might lose the war if I did! However I can let you know that I am very comfortable on board – absolutely calm sea, bright warm sun such as rejoices my heart and I spend my day just as I did last spring when I came through here sitting in it.[4]

The arrival of Clive and his Lancashire reinforcements at Suvla on 1 December brought the strength of the 6th Loyal North Lancs up to fifteen officers and 619 NCOs and men.[5] But Clive's first taste of action would

* Part of the 28th Brigade of the 13th Division.

not last long because the decision to abandon the campaign had already been as good as taken. The beginning of the end was a London meeting of the Dardanelles Committee* on 11 October to consider two documents: a report by the disgraced General Stopford on why his landings at Suvla had failed; and a letter from the Australian war correspondent Keith Murdoch† to his Prime Minister that violently criticized General Hamilton's handling of the campaign. Stopford's report – described by one historian as 'a farrago of half-truths and downright lies'[6] – was also scathing of Hamilton, and the end result was that the committee decided to sack him.

Before abandoning the campaign entirely, however, they chose to send General Sir Charles Monro out to Gallipoli to investigate. Monro arrived at Imbros on 28 October and spent the next few days touring the three beach-heads with their 'crazy piers', 'kicking mules' and jostling crowds 'within range of the enemy guns'. 'It's just like *Alice in Wonderland*,' he remarked to one staff officer, 'curiouser and curiouser'.[7] He cabled back to Kitchener: 'We merely hold the fringe of the shore,' while the Turks have 'all the advantages of position and power of observation of our movements'. His advice, before leaving for Egypt and Salonika,‡ was to evacuate the troops – though 40 per cent of them might be lost in the process, he warned.[8]

Unconvinced by Monro's advice, Kitchener put the less pessimistic General Birdwood in command and went out to see for himself in mid-November. But he soon came to the same conclusion. 'The country,' he cabled to Asquith on the 15th, 'is much more difficult than I imagined, and the Turkish positions . . . are natural fortresses.'[9] Kitchener toyed with the idea of saving face by a new landing in southern Turkey; but when it was vetoed by the Cabinet he agreed to an immediate evacuation of Anzac and Suvla, with Helles retained 'for the present'.

It began on 8 December and ended twelve days later, by which time 83,048 troops, 4,695 horses and mules, 1,718 vehicles and 186 heavy guns

---

* Set up in June 1915, the Dardanelles Committee was at this stage of the conflict the closest thing the British government had to a War Cabinet.
† Father of the media mogul Rupert Murdoch.
‡ Where the French and British had opened a new front to assist the Serbians in mid-October 1915, following the entry of Bulgaria into the war on the Central Powers' side a week earlier.

Supplies and building material abandoned on 'W' Beach at Cape Helles
during the final evacuation from Gallipoli in January 1916.

had been rescued from the two beachheads.[10] Clive Neely was among the
last of the soldiers to be shipped from Suvla to Mudros on 20 December.
He had spent less than three weeks at Gallipoli, but it was still enough
time for a fellow reinforcement officer (Second Lieutenant J. C. Stokoe
of the Manchesters) to be killed by shellfire.[11]

If Clive wrote letters from Gallipoli, none survives. But an impression
of his first experience of war can be gained from the diary of another
reinforcement, Private Ned Roe (a ten-year veteran, wounded at Second
Ypres), who joined the 6th East Lancs in the same 38th Brigade in trenches
on Chocolate Hill in early December. He wrote on the 7th:

> The Turkish positions were pointed out to me at 8.00 am this morning.
> They hold every commanding spur, ridge and mountain. Their field
> guns command the beaches . . . Truly the Turk is master of this graveyard.
> Members of the Alpine club in mountaineering rig-out could, with no
> little difficulty, scale the mountains confronting us, but the half-starved
> dysenteric army that opposes the Turks today, in full war kit and in face
> of determined opposition, would never achieve the impossible. The 6th

South Lancs and Gurkhas who breasted the crest of Sari Bair in August must have been 'super-men' indeed.

At 10.00 am the Turks welcomed us new arrivals with a hurricane bombardment by their field artillery. It lasted twenty minutes and 'KOd' four of my draft.[12]

The low point of the twenty-nine-year-old Roe's brief and unpleasant experience of Gallipoli was his inclusion on a firing party to execute a young private of the 6th East Lancs, Harry Salter, who had twice deserted his battalion and joined the Anzacs. Roe and his comrades were unconvinced by the charge. 'Our position in comparison to the position that the Anzacs held,' wrote Roe, 'was as heaven compared to hell. He therefore did not seek safety; he absconded because his life was made a hell by the CSM of my Company.'[13]

Of the execution itself, Roe recorded: 'He was marched from a dugout about 80 yards away, to a kind of disused quarry where the final scene was enacted. A clergyman preceded the doomed youth and his escort, reading prayers for the dying (the mockery of it all). The doomed youth was tied up to a stake, his grave already dug. His last request was, "Don't blindfold me."'[14]

Among the last to leave Suvla Bay on 18 December, Roe was shocked by the quantity of abandoned supplies:

There are about one million pounds worth of stores that cannot be taken away, so the dumps are thrown open to the troops and the Navy . . . We loaded our valises and sandbags to their full capacity with all kinds of preserved eatables and 'smokables' . . . It is a disgrace the amount of stores that will have to be destroyed by fire owing to the evacuation. These stores could have been very well issued to the famished, half-starved troops months before.[15]

The last Allied soldier was evacuated from V Beach on Cape Helles in the early hours of 9 January 1915. Contrary to Monro's fears, hardly a man was lost in the operation. Even so, the total Allied casualties at Gallipoli were 140,000, with more than 42,000 killed (11,000 of whom were Anzacs); Turkish losses, surprisingly for a defending force, were even greater: 251,000, including 86,000 dead.[16]

A lengthy inquiry concluded that the difficulties of the operation had been underestimated, as had the fighting ability of the Turks. It largely exonerated individual commanders like General Hamilton. Prime Minister Asquith was less forgiving. At a private dinner party in July 1916, he agreed with Lord Crewe, the former Secretary of State for India, that 'the failure of the Dardanelles expedition was entirely the failure of one man: Ian Hamilton'.[17]

But, for Australians and New Zealanders, their role in the campaign was – and still is – remembered with pride. 'They had fought as well as any "British" troops,' wrote L. A. Carlyon, 'and in the grottoes of Lone Pine and on Chunuk Bair they had done things that were imperishable.'[18]

Boxing Day 1915: *'The message was not from Roland'*
– News from France

Vera Brittain woke early in the Grand Hotel at Brighton, excited by the prospect of spending the next six days of leave with her fiancé Roland Leighton. Having not seen him since August, she had been delighted to hear in early December that he hoped to be back from the front around New Year's Eve. 'I knew that my own chance of some extra off-duty time would be better after Christmas than before,' she wrote, 'and the world brightened with the suddenness of an electric light going up in a dark room.'[1]

There was a brief moment of concern a few days later when Vera was told by the matron of her hospital in Camberwell that all the VADs were expected to take their week's leave immediately. But when she explained the circumstances of Roland's return, adding that she had seen him only once during the nine months he had been at the front, the matron relented. 'Certainly nurse,' she replied, 'I'll postpone your leave.'[2]

Vera 'nearly fell over a chair from excess of gratitude' as she 'stumbled out of her office', and immediately went off duty to give Roland the good news. 'To think that I can *really* look forward now to the end of this month!' she wrote. 'If only you are safe till then.'[3]

On her next half-day off duty, she went to Gorringe's department store in Buckingham Palace Road to spend 'what was left from two months' pay', and the pocket-money given by her 'forgiving father', on new clothes for Roland's visit, including a 'black taffeta dinner-dress with scarlet and mauve velvet flowers tucked into the waist'. With her parents staying at the Grand Hotel in Brighton, and Roland's in a cottage at nearby Hassocks, it seemed to Vera that the stage was 'perfectly set' for their reunion.[4]

Roland's next letter confirmed his leave dates from 24 to 31 December, and that he would land on Christmas Day. Vera was ecstatic and, as the days ticked by, two delightful possibilities played on her mind: that Roland would suggest they get married immediately, rather than wait; and, if that happened, that she would become pregnant. 'Oh, God!' her half-articulate thoughts would run, 'do let us get married and do let me have a baby – something that is Roland's very own, something of himself to remember him by if he goes.'[5]

Returning to the practicalities of Roland's return, Vera hoped to meet him off the boat-train at Victoria. But on discovering that the only Christmas Day train arrived at 7.30 in the evening, she decided not to risk missing Roland 'in the winter blackness of a wartime terminus', and went straight to Brighton to wait for him there instead. She recalled:

> All day I waited there for a telephone message or a telegram, sitting drowsily in the lounge of the Grand Hotel, or walking up and down the promenade, watching the grey sea tossing rough with white surf-crested waves, and wondering still what kind of crossing he had had or was having.
>
> When, by ten o'clock at night, no news had come, I concluded that the complications of telegraph and telephone on a combined Sunday and Christmas Day had made communication impossible. So, unable to fight sleep any longer after a night and a day of wakefulness, I went to bed a little disappointed, but still unperturbed.[6]

Meanwhile Roland's family, staying at their cottage in nearby Hassocks, kept an even longer vigil by sitting up 'till nearly midnight over their Christmas dinner in the hope that he would join them'.

Next morning, as Vera was putting the final touches to the pastel-blue crêpe-de-Chine blouse she had bought to impress Roland, a maid informed her that she was wanted on the telephone. 'Believing that I was at last to hear the voice for which I had waited for twenty-four hours,' she remembered, 'I dashed joyously into the corridor. But the message was not from Roland but from [his sister] Clare; it was not to say that he had arrived home that morning, but to tell me that he had died of wounds at a Casualty Clearing Station on December 23rd.'[7]

It would take a heartbroken Vera many weeks to learn the truth. But after writing to and receiving letters back from his colonel, his fellow officers, the Catholic padre who had buried him, and his soldier-servant, she was able to piece together 'the details of his end – so painful, so unnecessary, so grimly devoid of that heroic limelight which Roland had always regarded as ample compensation for those who were slain'.[8]

As night fell on 22 December, Roland's battalion, the 7th Worcesters, were about to take over a stretch of the front line that had been left dirty and dilapidated by the previous occupants. Roland's platoon was given the job of repairing the inadequate wire in front of the trenches, and before taking the wiring party out 'he went to inspect the place himself, using a concealed path which led to No Man's Land through a gap in the hedge, because the communication trench was flooded'. Unfortunately 'the use of an alternative path was known to the Germans' who had 'trained a machine-gun on the gap, and were accustomed to fire a few volleys whenever the troops facing them showed signs of activity'. Yet the previous battalion had made no mention of this habit to the 7th Worcesters during the relief.[9]

With the moon nearly full, the path through the hedge was clearly visible to the Germans barely a hundred yards distant. 'As soon as Roland reached the gap,' wrote his bereaved fiancé, 'the usual volley was fired. Almost the first shot struck him in the stomach, penetrating his body, and he fell on his face, gesticulating wildly, in full view of the company. At the risk of their lives, the company commander and a sergeant rushed out and carried him back to the trench. Twenty minutes afterwards the doctor at the dressing-station put an end to his agony with a large dose of morphia, and from that moment Roland ceased – and ceased for ever – to be Roland.'[10]

He died the following day after a 'complicated abdominal operation' at the Casualty Clearing Station at Louvencourt. The bullet that struck him had damaged his spine and, had he lived, would have paralysed him from the waist downwards. As it was he regained consciousness only long enough to be given Extreme Unction from a Jesuit padre who had received him into the Catholic Church in the early summer of 1915. 'At eleven o'clock that night,' wrote Brittain, 'Uppingham's record prize-winner, whose whole nature fitted him for the spectacular drama of a great battle, died forlornly in a hospital bed.'[11]

Vera found it hard to understand why he had risked venturing into no man's land on a moonlit night when his leave was imminent. But hardest of all to bear was the 'growing certainty that he had left no message for us to remember'. For weeks after his death she waited in vain for word that he had been thinking of her in his last hours. None came. 'I knew I had learnt all there was to know,' she wrote, 'and that in his last hour I had been quite forgotten.'[12]

A month later, still tormented with grief, Vera went to stay with Roland's family in Sussex. 'I had arrived,' she wrote,

> to find his mother and sister standing in helpless distress in the midst of his returned kit, which was lying, just opened, all over the floor. The garments sent back included the outfit that he had been wearing when he was hit. I wondered, and I wonder still, why it was thought necessary to return such relics – the tunic torn back and front by the bullet, the khaki vest dark and stiff with blood, and a pair of blood-stained breeches slit open at the top by someone obviously in a violent hurry. Those gruesome rags made me realize, as I had never realized before, all that France really meant.[13]

She wrote to her brother Edward: 'Everything was damp and worn and simply caked with mud. And I was glad that neither you nor Victor nor anyone who may some day go to the front was there to see. If you had been, you would have been overwhelmed by the horror of war without its glory. For though he had only worn the things when living, the smell of those clothes was the smell of graveyards and the Dead . . . There was his cap, bent in and shapeless out of recognition – the soft cap he wore rakishly on the back of his head – with the badge thickly coated with mud. He must have fallen on top of it, or perhaps the people who fetched him in trampled on it.'[14]

Only later, having made the decision to serve with the VAD in France, did Vera draw strength from Roland's death. 'If ever I do face danger and suffering,' she wrote, 'it will be because I have learnt through him that love is supreme, that love is stronger than death and the fear of death.'[15]

PART THREE
1916

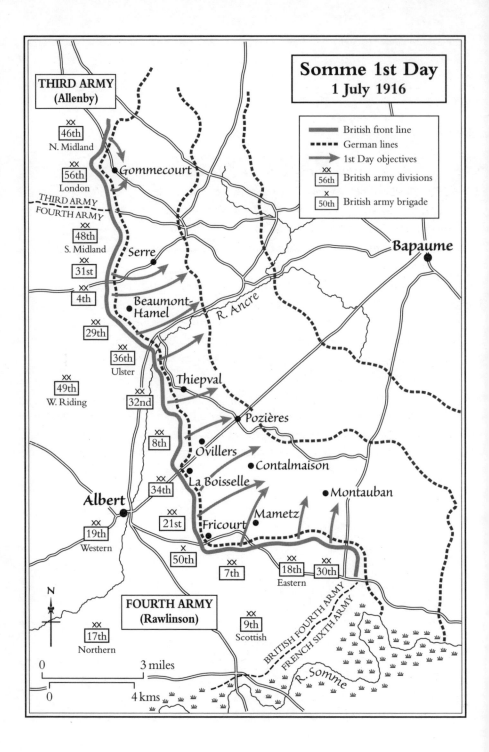

*B*y the close of 1915, the Central Powers had the upper hand: they had conquered Serbia and Russian Poland, and were still in possession of most of Belgium and the key industrial area of north-east France. They had, moreover, acquired a new ally – Bulgaria – and opened up a direct route of supply between central Europe and the Near East, thus denying Russia its own outlet to the Mediterranean.

Yet General von Falkenhayn, the Chief of the German General Staff, felt that time was running out, and that Germany's economy and public morale could not endure more than another year of war. Further advances into Russia would, he thought, be counter-productive because they would require more garrison troops and longer lines of communication. Instead he pinned his hopes for victory in 1916 on twin efforts against the western powers: an 'intensified' submarine campaign to disrupt Allied commerce, with Allied merchant ships in the war zone and armed merchantmen liable to be sunk without warning, and only liners and neutrals to be spared; and a major offensive against French forces defending Verdun and its ring of forts.[1]

The intention of the Verdun offensive, explained General von Falkenhayn in a memorandum to the Kaiser of 15 December 1915, was to wear down the French Army and break the spirit of the civilian population. 'If we succeeded in opening the eyes of her people to the fact that in a military sense they have nothing much to hope for, that breaking point would be reached, and England's best sword knocked out of her hand.' By defending Verdun to the last, argued Falkenhayn, 'the forces of France will bleed to death', irrespective of the outcome. As for Russia intervening, he did not believe that was possible. 'Even if we cannot expect a revolution in grand style,' wrote Falkenhayn, 'we are entitled to believe that Russia's internal troubles will compel her to give in within a relatively short period.' To that end, a million roubles were paid to the Russian Jewish Bolshevik Alexander Helphand on 26 December 1915 to spread anti-war propaganda throughout Russia.[2]

The Entente, by contrast, had made little progress during 1915 (though it, too, had acquired an important ally in the form of Italy). Apart from some early gains by Russia in the Carpathians (and soon to be wiped out by the huge Austro-German counter-offensive at Gorlice–Tarnów in May), their major offensives – on the Western Front, at the Isonzo river,* at Gallipoli and in Mesopotamia – had all failed to achieve their objectives. The Battle of Loos, in particular, had caused recrimination among British generals and politicians and eventually cost Sir John French his job. Blamed for taking too long to release the operational reserve by his subordinates (including Sir Douglas Haig), by King George V (a friend of Haig's and undoubtedly biased in his favour) and ultimately by the government, French was replaced by Haig as Commander-in-Chief of the BEF on 19 December. Haig saw Loos as a 'great opportunity missed . . . all we wanted was some Reserves at hand to reap the fruits of victory and open the road for our Cavalry to gallop through!' French was, he believed, 'solely to blame for the mishandling of the reserves'. Tellingly he also felt that the battles of 1915 had exhausted the Germans, and was optimistic about the future.[3]

So too was Britain's new Chief of the Imperial General Staff, Sir William ('Wully') Robertson, a tough, straight-talking former private who insisted on acting as the government's sole strategic adviser, thus marginalizing Kitchener. Robertson agreed with Haig that the war could be won only on the Western Front, and shared the optimism of the French Commander-in-Chief General Joffre that, despite the setbacks of 1915, the underlying balance was moving towards the Entente, given its superior manpower and expanding production. They just needed staying power and co-ordination.[4]

The second item had been high on the agenda of the Allied conference at Chantilly on 6 December 1915 when senior Entente commanders agreed to the demand by Joffre for synchronized offensives on the Western, Eastern and Italian fronts at some date after March 1916. If, on the other hand, the Central Powers attacked one ally, the others would assist it.[5] The conference was a personal victory for Joffre, who had dismissed the failed Gallipoli campaign of 1915 as a sideshow diverting resources from the main effort on the continent.

---

* In the four battles of the Isonzo, between 24 May and 30 November 1915, the Italians lost 62,000 killed and 170,000 sick and wounded (Stevenson, *1914–1918*, pp. 158–9).

A mere army commander at the time, Haig missed the Chantilly Conference. But in late December, soon after his promotion, he met up with Joffre to discuss the location and timing of the main British offensive in 1916. Haig preferred an attack in Flanders that would strike at the main railway junctions beyond and prevent a strategic withdrawal. But with the instructions of Lord Kitchener ringing in his ears – that the 'closest co-operation between the French and the British as a united Army must be the governing policy' (albeit with the caveat that his command 'is an independent one, and that you will in no case come under the orders of any Allied General further than the necessary co-operation with our Allies above referred to') – he was forced to yield to Joffre's request for a joint effort on the River Somme in Picardy.[6] *The offensive was tentatively set for the summer, though Joffre was keen for the BEF to launch preliminary attacks to exhaust Germany's reserves in the spring.*

26 January 1916: *'War is a game that is played with a smile'*

– A Cabinet minister at the front

'Rest assured,' wrote Winston Churchill to his wife, 'there will be no part of the line from the Alps to the sea better guarded. It will be watched with the vigilance that mobilized the Fleet.' He was referring to the 1,000-yard section of the front line that his new command, the 6th Royal Scots Fusiliers, had just taken over at Ploegsteert Wood (or 'Plug Street' Wood as the British troops called it) in Flanders.[1]

After his sacking as First Lord of the Admiralty in May 1915, Churchill had retained a seat in both the Cabinet – as Chancellor of the Duchy of Lancaster – and on the Dardanelles Committee (in effect, the War Council). But he could not prevent the Cabinet from distancing itself from his Gallipoli venture – a failure that would, according to his wife, haunt him 'for the rest of his life'[2] – and resigned from government in November 1915 when he was excluded from the new Cabinet War Committee, the successor to the Dardanelles Committee. With no effective role to play in the conduct of war, he offered his services to the military and arrived in France on 18 November.

Promised a brigade by Sir John French, Churchill was first attached to the 2nd Grenadier Guards near Neuve Chapelle to familiarize himself with trench warfare. 'Filth and rubbish everywhere,' he wrote to his wife Clementine, 'graves built into the defences & scattered about promiscuously, feet and clothing breaking through the soil, water & muck on all sides.' And yet, he added, 'amid these surroundings, aided by wet & cold & every minor discomfort, I have found happiness & content such as I have not known for many months.'[3]

He spent his forty-first birthday, 30 November, under shellfire and was proud that it 'has not caused me any sense of anxiety or apprehension, nor does the approach of a shell quicken my pulse, or try my nerves or make me about to bob as do so many'.[4] While he ignored shells his fertile mind was devising schemes to break the deadlock on the Western Front, ideas he circulated at General Headquarters in early December in a memorandum called 'Variants of the Offensive'. They included the use of the tank – a new secret weapon that he had helped develop while at the Admiralty – in mass attacks to overcome barbed wire, machine-guns and trenches; infantry advancing behind armoured shields; and digging siege trenches towards the enemy front line (a throwback to the siege warfare of the eighteenth century). He also recognized in the paper that the Allies would prevail in a long war of attrition. 'After all,' he wrote, 'it is the enemy's *army* we are fighting, and not the enemy's *position*.'[5]

Sir John French kept his promise to promote Churchill (a nominal major) to brigadier-general, notifying him on 10 December that he would command the 56th Brigade of 19th Division. But Asquith refused to give his consent. 'The appointment might cause some criticism,' he wrote to Sir John, '& should not therefore be made. Perhaps you might give him a battalion.'[6]

It was left to Sir Douglas Haig, the new BEF commander, to confirm Churchill's appointment as lieutenant-colonel of the 6th Royal Scots Fusiliers, part of the 9th (Scottish) Division that had done so well at Loos. Churchill joined his new battalion near Meteren on 5 January 1916, causing Captain Neil Weir of the neighbouring 10th Argylls to inform his mother: 'Winston Churchill is now commanding our next Battalion – which is curious.'[7]

Like Weir, the men who would serve under Churchill were not

Former Cabinet minister Winston Churchill
with French general Marie Emile Fayolle
(right) in late 1915.

convinced of his credentials. But he soon won them over with his determination to restore morale and smartness to the battalion, informing his
officers at one meeting that he was declaring war on lice, that bane of
the trenches. 'He improved us greatly,' remarked one captain. 'Meantime
he improved on us.'[8]

Churchill's final briefing to his officers, before the battalion took over
the front-line trenches at 'Plug Street' Wood on 26 January, was typical
of his idiosyncratic but useful advice:

> Don't be careless about yourselves – on the other hand not too careful.
> Keep a special pair of boots to sleep in and only get them muddy in a
> real emergency. Use alcohol in moderation . . . Live well but do not flaunt
> it. Laugh a little, & teach your men to laugh – great good humour under
> fire – war is a game that is played with a smile. If you can't smile grin.
> If you can't grin keep out of the way till you can.[9]

For the next three months the 6th Royal Fusiliers rotated in and out of the front line at 'Plug Street', losing a fifth of its strength – fifteen killed and 123 wounded – to snipers and shellfire. Ensconced in battalion head-quarters, a brick farmhouse 500 yards from the forward trenches, Churchill was a little safer than most. But he made regular visits to the forward companies – three times a day, according to one officer – and 'was always in the closest touch with every piece of work that was going on'.[10]

He was lucky to survive a direct hit on his headquarters, the shell exploding in the room next door and covering him and his staff with dust, and later was caught in the open as shells landed ever closer. 'One could calculate more or less where the next one would come,' Churchill informed his wife,

> and I said, 'the next one will hit the [ruined] convent'. Sure enough just as we got abreast of it, the shell arrived with a screech and a roar and tremendous bang and showers of bricks and clouds of smoke and all the soldiers jumped and scurried . . . I do not mind noise as some very brave people do. But I felt – twenty yards more to the left and no more tangles to unravel, no more anxieties to face, no more hatreds and injustice to encounter . . . a good ending to a chequered life, a final gift – unvalued – to an ungrateful country.[11]

Churchill even led raids into no man's land, 'a nerve-wracking experi-ence' for one lieutenant who remembered his colonel's 'loud, gruff voice' and likened him to a 'baby elephant'. The subaltern added: 'He never ducked when a bullet went past with its loud crack. He used to say after watching me duck: "It's no damn use ducking; the bullet has gone a long way past you by now."'[12]

By late March 1916, having learned that a vacant brigade command would not be given to him, Churchill told Clementine that he was ready to resume 'political and Parlt. Duties wh[ich] are incompatible with holding a military command'. The exact timing was determined by the news, at the end of April, that the 6th and 7th Battalions of the Royal Scots Fusiliers would be merged, putting one lieutenant-colonel out of a job. As Churchill was the junior of the two, it was bound to be him. He was given permission to return to London, taking his leave from the battalion on 7 May 1916. Many were sad to see him go. 'I have never known an officer take such pains to inspire confidence,' wrote one captain, 'or to gain confidence.' Another added that 'no more popular officer ever commanded troops' and that he had left behind men 'who are proud of having served in the Great War under the leadership of one who is beyond question a great man'.[13]

27 January 1916: *'This vital measure'*
– Conscription is introduced in Britain

'If we owe a great debt to the Government for their firmness and skill in carrying this vital measure into effect,' wrote Colonel Repington of *The Times* in the wake of the Military Service Act being passed by the House of Lords, 'we certainly owe much to the good sense and patriotism of Labour which has realized that there is no other means of reinforcing our heroes at the front adequately except by the passage of the Bill into law.'[1]

Thus did *The Times* greet the introduction of national conscription for the first time in British history. Lord Kitchener had wanted such a law in August 1914, but had been overruled by his Cabinet colleagues on the grounds that compulsory military service would be hugely unpopular. Yet by the end of 1915 – in the wake of Kitchener's acceptance at the Calais conference in July of a seventy-division target for the BEF, the heavy losses suffered by the New Armies at Loos and the commitment made at Chantilly for a major offensive in 1916 – it had become clear that too few men were volunteering for military service, and that some form of coercion would have to be introduced. An additional but not insignificant factor was the determination of Lloyd George, Minister of Munitions, to protect the skilled workers of the munitions industry from military service by introducing a law that exempted those with jobs vital to the war effort.[2]

Already a National Registration Act had been passed in July 1915 to require all men and women between the ages of sixteen and sixty-five to report their name and occupation. This was followed by the 'Derby scheme' of October–December 1915, overseen by Lord Derby as Director of Recruiting, which invited men of military age to 'attest' their willingness to service. The failure of the 'Derby scheme' may have been anticipated; either way it led swiftly to the passing of the Military Service Act in January 1916.[3] The chief opponents of the act were the Labour Party and the TUC who feared it would lead on to compulsory civilian labour and the end of trade-union bargaining power. But without Liberal support, they could not prevent a comfortable House of Commons majority in favour of the new legislation.

The Act provided for the conscription of all British (but not Irish) men who, as of 15 August 1915, were aged eighteen to forty, unmarried or widowers without dependants, though there were numerous exemptions (to be administered by a tribunal system) that included war work, hardship due to family or business commitments or ill health, and conscientious objection to the 'undertaking of combatant service'.[4]

Neither the provisions nor the timing, however, were enough to satisfy fully *The Times* military correspondent. 'At the best,' wrote Repington, 'and if Lord Derby's estimates work out in practice, we may get 1,400,000 men this year, but this will not do more than enable us to complete our existing divisions, and maintain them in the field until the autumn, given that the war preserves its present general character, and that no one of the Great Powers of the Alliance is struck down.'[5]

In his opinion, the act should have been passed in early 1915, and 'the months now ahead of us should have been devoted to the creation of 30 new divisions, so that we might have possessed this coming summer a large strategic reserve fit to throw into the scales of war at the decisive point and at the decisive hour'. But this would be possible only with a 'stronger dose of compulsion, a greater restriction of the lists of reserved trades, and a preliminary determination that trade should take second place to victory. If not, the responsibility will rest with the Government, and with it alone'.[6]

Repington's fears were soon realized as the initial monthly enlistments under conscription were half those of the voluntary scheme. Finally in May 1916 – under pressure from the press, the War Office (in the shape of the CIGS, General Sir William Robertson), Lloyd George and the Unionist leaders – Asquith agreed to a second Military Service Act that extended compulsion to married men (though Irishmen were still exempted). But even this extra source of manpower did not compensate for the large number of exemptions – from 1 March 1916 to 31 March 1917, for example, almost 780,000 men were excused conscription – and, incredibly, there were fewer soldiers recruited in 1916 with conscription than in 1915 without it.[7]

16 February 1916: *'No other race of human beings . . . could have performed this feat'*
– The fall of Erzerum

For five days Morgan Philips Price, the Harrow- and Cambridge-educated war correspondent of the *Manchester Guardian*, had witnessed the impossible as white-clad Russian soldiers defied snow, freezing temperatures and a fierce Ottoman opposition to edge ever closer to the eastern Turkish stronghold of Erzerum, the gateway to Anatolia. 'The Russian troops,' reported Philips Price, 'had to cross mountain ranges with deep snowdrifts at 10,000 feet, and go for at least three days cut off from supplies of food, with nothing but the few crusts of bread they could carry with them. No other race of human beings, except those accustomed to the cold of sub-arctic climates like that of Russia, could have performed this feat.'[1]

The Russian advance on Erzerum, and from there to Constantinople, had been planned for spring 1916. But the Allied evacuation of Gallipoli in January, releasing 50,000 Turkish veterans for service in the east, had convinced Grand Duke Nicholas, the Russian commander in the Caucasus, that he had to strike before Enver Pasha could bring forward reinforcements – even in winter. Prior to the attack the Russian Black Sea fleet had sunk most of the Turkish transports used to bring men and munitions to Erzerum via the port of Trabizond. Thereafter everything had to travel overland from Constantinople, the last 500 miles over snow-bound roads and mountain passes. The Russians, by contrast, could bring supplies by rail to Sarikamash, just eighty miles from Erzerum.[2]

The Russian plan was for 80,000 troops to converge on Erzerum and its protective ring of a dozen forts from three directions: north, south and east. One of their commanders, General Prejevalsky, had served as a military attaché at Erzerum and from walks and pony rides knew the stronghold's strengths and weaknesses. It was he who suggested targeting only the forts critical to the town's defence; this would avoid a dispersal of effort, but also leave the attackers vulnerable to fire from the untouched forts.[3]

The assault began on 11 February and, at first, took the Turks by surprise. The first fort, Dolan-gyoz, fell on the 12th, but thereafter the

Ottoman defence stiffened. Every fort was protected by a network of snow-trenches, invisible to the naked eye at more than a hundred yards, while they all had plentiful supplies of water to turn their approach slopes into sheets of ice.

The Russian response was to attack the towering fort of Chaban-dede – one of the keys to Erzerum – at night. Philips Price, a thirty-one-year-old former Parliamentary candidate for the Liberal Party, recorded:

> The Russian soldiers were clad in white coats, so that in the darkness and against the slopes they were invisible. Silently creeping up the rocky slopes to the fort, they got to within 250 yards of it before the Turkish searchlights discovered them. At once from the Uzun Ahmet and Chaban-dede forts a murderous cross-fire was poured upon them, which in two hours caused them to lose one third of their number.

One battalion managed to reach the cliffs below Chaban-dede where they were safe from the fort's guns, but not from those in the neighbouring fort that 'could still rake their lines'. They withdrew to await reinforcements who were at that moment struggling across the 10,000-foot Kargar-bazar pass in a snowstorm that would cause more than 2,000 fatalities from frostbite.

Advancing again after dark on the 13th, the soldiers of the Russian Derbent Regiment placed their coats on the deep snow before them to prevent sinking up to their necks. Despite this painfully slow progress, they were soon in a position to attack. 'The Turks, suspecting nothing,' wrote Philips Price, 'were lying in their snow trenches, their attention chiefly concerned on how to prevent themselves from freezing to death. At last daylight began to break upon this arctic scene, and through scuds of snow broken by the icy wind, the Turks saw a chain of dark forms closing in on them. They could hardly believe their eyes, for it seemed to them impossible that a human army with rifles and ammunition could cross the country that lay in front of them.' In danger of being cut off, the Turkish defenders 'hastily left their trenches and retreated as fast as the drifts would allow them across the Olugli snow-field till they reached the fort'.[4]

Even so, the Derbent Regiment had 'not yet broken the Turkish cordon that united the forts' and was still vulnerable to counter-attack unless it was supported by troops of the 4th Division and 2nd Turkestans whose task was to pierce the plateau between forts Chaban-dede and Tufta. 'The critical moment for the Russians had arrived,' noted Philips Price. 'Would these forces unite and press their attack together? Or had one of them failed and been overwhelmed in the snow-fields or defiles?'[5]

The answer came at 1 p.m. on 14 February when the guns of the 2nd Turkestans joined in a barrage that the 4th Division had begun an hour earlier. As the two forces advanced the Turks withdrew from the Grobovoye Heights into Fort Tufta. 'In another half-hour,' recorded Philips Price, 'the Turkestans appeared upon the sky-line; and here, on this desolate Grobovoye height, at this historic moment, they greeted their brothers of the 4th Division. The gap in the Russian line was filled; the mountains and snow-fields had been overcome, and it was now only a question of a few hours before the Turks would be overcome too.'[6]

With their cordon pierced, the Turks began to abandon fort after fort, their men fleeing across the Erzerum plain. The Russians set off in pursuit. But thanks to poor communications they failed to capture more than a single Turkish division, the 34th, though most of the enemy artillery was taken.[7] In the morning of 16 February, escorted by a regiment of Cossacks, General Prejevalsky entered the town of Erzerum to find the enemy gone, many of the buildings on fire and the streets strewn with corpses. A day later Philips Price and three Russian journalists made the same journey in a transport wagon. 'We saw many signs of the Turkish retreat,' wrote Philips Price, 'as we continued our way. Through the snow on the road-side protruded a number of objects, camels' humps, horses' legs, buffa-loes' horns, and men's faces, with fezzes and little black beards, smiling at us the smile of death, their countenances frozen as hard as the snow around them. That was all that was left of the "Drang nach Osten" ["Drive to the East"] in this part of the world.'[8]

As they crossed the last neck of rising ground before descending to the Erzerum plain they could hear 'the rumble of artillery' and through glasses could 'make out detachments of retreating Turks fighting rearguard actions'. Philips Price wrote:

Before long the famous Kars Gate of Erzerum, with its pyramidal Seljuk tomb, became visible. We drove through tunnels and fortress mounds, past rickety old Turkish sentry-boxes with the Star and Crescent painted on them, inhabited not by black-eyed, thick-nosed [Turks], but by round-faced men with grey eyes and flaxen hair . . . In the streets were men wearing baggy trousers, and with fezzes on their heads. The Turks with their characteristic fatalism were going about their business, as if nothing had happened. 'Allah has given Erzerum to the Uruss [Russians]. Allah gives and takes away, and Allah is great.'[9]

In John Buchan's classic spy novel, *Greenmantle*, the fall of Erzerum is brought about when a stolen staff map with details of the Turkish defences is smuggled out of the besieged city to Russian headquarters. Something similar may actually have happened. T. E. Lawrence, then working with military intelligence in Cairo, told his biographer after the war that he had secretly 'put the Grand Duke Nicholas in touch with certain disaffected Arab officers in Erzerum'. As Buchan had good contacts within the British Cabinet and War Office at this time, he may well have heard rumours that the Erzerum garrison had been betrayed from within. Certainly Lawrence told the poet Robert Graves that '*Greenmantle* has more than a flavour of truth.'[10]

The significance of Erzerum's capture in Asia was profound. 'Every bazaar from Shiraz to Samarkand, from Konia to Duldja,' wrote Philips Price, 'began talking of the great Urus . . . Russian military prestige in the East had fallen very low since the Sary-Kamish battle and Enver Pasha's advance into the Caucasus in December 1914. But the Dardanelles expedition had . . . afforded the Russians the necessary respite to prepare for their attack on Erzerum, which in its turn saved the British from being driven completely out of Mesopotamia.'[11]

It also brought an end to the Central Powers' dreams of extending their dominion to Asia. 'The thunder of the Russian guns before Erzerum,' noted Philips Price, 'told the Central Powers that whatever they were or might be in Europe, they could never be masters in Asia, for their centre of gravity was too far to the West to allow them to be lords of two continents.' For Russia, on the other hand, the political importance of the victory was immense: 'It established her finally on the Armenian plateau, and completed a process which had begun in the Trans-Caucasus more than a century before'.[12]

21 February 1916: *'A tempest growing ever stronger'*
– The Germans attack at Verdun

The first shot of the war's longest battle was fired before dawn by a German 15-inch naval gun at Loison. It landed twenty miles away at Verdun, striking a corner of the cathedral, and was the start of an unprecedented eight-hour bombardment, during which 1,220 guns – half of them howitzers or heavy pieces – fired two million shells into a quiet eight-mile sector of the French front.[1]

Corporal Stéphane, forty-six years old, whose battalion of Chasseurs was defending trenches in the Bois de Caures, seven miles north of Verdun, remembered 'a storm, a hurricane, a tempest growing every stronger, where it was raining nothing but paving stones'.[2] At midday* there was a pause, prompting Stéphane and his comrades to emerge from their dug-outs to oppose the expected attack. But this was a ruse: once the Germans had discovered which parts of the line were still defended, they targeted them with heavy mortar fire.[3] Of an original garrison of 1,300 men, the majority of Stéphane's Chasseurs were killed or injured by the bombardment. 'Of five *poilus*,'† wrote another French corporal, 'two have been buried alive under their shelter, two are wounded to some extent or other, and the fifth is waiting.'[4]

At 4 p.m., after a final twenty-minute crescendo of fire, German company commanders cried 'Los!' and their eager men – wearing white brassards for recognition, and each possessing a large-scale sketch of the defences opposite – surged out of their trenches and into no man's land. Most moved in small groups, making skilful use of the wooded and hilly terrain, a deliberate tactic to probe for weaknesses in the French defences. Only on the second day of the battle, 22 February, would the full weight of the German attack be felt.[5]

That, at least, was the plan. But in the centre of the German attack, opposite the Bois de Caures, corps commander General von Zwehl disobeyed orders by sending his stormtroopers in hard on the heels of the fighting patrols. Before long, using a dastardly new weapon called a

---

* All times are French; German time was + 1 hour.
† *Poilu* was an informal term for a French infantryman meaning, literally, 'hairy one'.

flamethrower, they had captured the whole of the trench system in the Bois d'Haumont, to the left front of the Bois de Caures, and were infiltrating between the forward companies of Stéphane's battered Chasseurs. Zwehl's men had prised open the first, vital crack in the French defences.[6]

The objective of this first major German offensive of 1916 was neither to break through into open country nor – probably – to capture Verdun itself (though Crown Prince Wilhelm, commanding the German Fifth Army, would proclaim the latter as his aim). Fighting on two extended fronts, Chief of Staff von Falkenhayn could spare only nine divisions for what was, in effect, a limited operation to take Verdun's protective ring of forts on the heights east of the Meuse. Once they were secure, his troops would be able to use artillery to destroy both the town and the inevitable French counter-attacks. If the British tried to intervene by launching a relief attack, they too would suffer huge casualties.[7] The attack at Verdun was designed, therefore, to provoke an aggressive response that would bleed the Allies white. It was attrition by stealth.

Early German gains were impressive. By the end of the fourth day, 24 February, they had broken through the original trench lines, advanced three miles and captured 10,000 French soldiers, sixty-five artillery pieces

German infantry use grenades and flamethrowers during an attack at Verdun.

and seventy-five machine-guns.[8] Among the captives was a Lieutenant-Colonel Bernard whose battalion had been shelled out of the village of Samogneux by its own artillery. Taken before the Kaiser, who had moved closer to the front to witness the historic and seemingly inevitable fall of the famous fortress, he declared confidently: 'You will never enter Verdun!'[9]

But not all French troops were so defiant. Most of one North African division, composed of tough white *colons* and fierce African tribesmen, broke and fled in the face of relentless German attacks. When shouts failed to stop them, 'a section of [French] machine guns fired at the backs of the fleeing men, who fell like flies'.[10]

The greatest coup of the battle, however, took place on 25 February when the 24th Brandenburg Grenadiers captured Fort Douaumont, five miles north-east of Verdun and the keystone of the town's defences. Ignoring their orders to stop short of the fort, Sergeant Kunze and a small section of pioneers penetrated the outer defences and, forming a human pyramid, got into the fort through a gun embrasure. Kunze and his section, supported by three officers and fewer than a hundred men, were able to capture the fort without support because the original garrison of 500 infantrymen had been dispersed in 1915, as had many of the lighter guns, and only fifty reserve artillerymen remained. It was an incredible combination of boldness and luck, celebrated by the ringing of German church bells and portrayed in one German newspaper as heralding the 'FALL OF FRANCE'. Two of the officers were awarded the Pour le Mérite – while the third, the most deserving, got nothing. Kunze was also overlooked. Only after the war was the record put straight.[11]

With its defences collapsing, Joffre and his staff at Grand Quartier Général (French headquarters) considered Verdun a lost cause, not least because all reinforcements and supplies had to use a single road later dubbed the *voie sacrée*. Joffre was about to order the town's evacuation when the French Prime Minister, Aristide Briand, made a late-night dash to Chantilly. Convinced that national morale and his government's survival were at stake, Briand ordered Joffre to hold Verdun at all costs.[12] Joffre, in turn, appointed General Philippe Pétain, commanding the French Second Army, to revitalize the defence.

When Pétain was finally located, in the early hours of 25 February, he was spending the night with his mistress (and later wife) in the Hôtel

Terminus near the Gare du Nord. Told he was expected at Chantilly at eight the following morning, he advised the waiting staff officer to get a room and they would leave at 7 a.m.[13]

Such calmness under pressure would serve Pétain well at Verdun. He set up his headquarters at Souilly, south of Verdun, on 26 February, and at once issued orders for three lines of defence: one to blunt the enemy's attacks, but not to be held at all costs; a principal 'line of resistance' from which no withdrawal was possible; and a third line to launch counter-attacks from. He also insisted that the French heavy artillery was concentrated under a central command, so that it could be deployed where and when needed; and he solved the supply and morale problems by widening the *voie sacrée* and decreeing that all units were regularly rotated out of Verdun.[14]

Thanks to Pétain, the line of resistance held and the Germans never did conquer all the heights east of the Meuse, though they continued to attack on both sides of the river for much of March. Among the French soldiers captured during a failed assault on Fort Vaux on 2 March was Captain Charles de Gaulle,* wounded in the thigh by a bayonet. Finally, on 9 April, the Germans breached a section of the line of resistance when they captured the height of Mort Homme to the west of the Meuse. But inspired by Pétain's exhortation, 'Courage! On les aura!' ('Courage! We'll have them!'), his troops won back Mort Homme after a succession of costly counter-attacks.[15] Falkenhayn had his battle of attrition: but it was costing his own army as many casualties as the French.

Pétain summed up the effect of the battle on his young soldiers:

> As I stood on the steps of the Town Hall of Souilly, my post of command, which was excellently situated at the crossing of the roads leading to the front, I singled them out for my most affectionate consideration as they moved up into the line with their units . . . But the discouragement with which they returned! – either singly, maimed or wounded, or in the ranks of their companies thinned by their losses. Their eyes stared into space as if transfixed by a vision of terror. In their gait and their attitudes they betrayed utter exhaustion. Horrible memories made them quail. When I questioned them, they scarcely answered.[16]

---

* De Gaulle became the leader of Free French Forces in the Second World War and was President of France from 1959 to 1969.

9 April 1916: *'Men fell by the dozen'*
– The Kut relief force attacks at Sannaiyat

At 4 a.m. the men of the New Army's 13th Division, lying on the desert in a line of platoons, were woken and told to prepare for battle. 'Every man shivered as if he had a dose of ague,' recalled Private Ned Roe. 'We were wet to the skin with the heavy dew. No three tablespoons of rum to warm us up.'[1]

At zero hour, 4.30 a.m., the order 'Advance' was whispered by the platoon officers and three full brigades moved noiselessly and with the 'utmost regularity' towards the three trenches of the Turkish position at Sannaiyat, the second last obstacle between the Mesopotamia Expeditionary Force (MEF) and the relief of Kut.[2] Leading the centre of the line was my great-uncle Clive Neely's battalion, the 6th Loyal North Lancashires, still smarting from its losses to 'friendly' fire at the Hanna defile, four days earlier, when the whole division had advanced too quickly and was caught by its own artillery barrage, the men 'sent to Kingdom Come in bundles of eight by our howitzers and river monitors'.[3]

After its evacuation from Suvla Bay in December 1915, the 13th Division had spent a month on Lemnos, followed by three weeks in Egypt guarding the Suez Canal. But with the failure of the 3rd and 7th Divisions of the Indian Corps – recently arrived in Mesopotamia from the Western Front – to break through the Turkish defences at Hanna and relieve Kut in January 1916, the decision was taken to reinforce them with an all-British division, the 13th.

The three brigades of the 13th Division – the 38th (including the 6th Loyal North Lancs), 39th and 40th – arrived at Basra in early March and were sent up the Tigris in barges lashed to small river steamers. 'Our company disembarks at Sheikh Saad,'* wrote Private Roe of the 6th East Lancs (part of the same brigade, the 38th, as my great-uncle), in his diary on 14 March, 'and joined the Battalion, which arrived on the 13th. The [Tigris] Corps Commander [General Gorringe] rushes troops to the advance base, but nobody seems to see the commissariat or hospital

---

* Sheikh Saad was just twenty-six miles from besieged Kut as the crow flies, but twice that distance by river.

arrangements of such. The Turks in the last Balkan war were about in the same state of chaos.'[4]

Having moved up to Orah camp in late March, Roe added:

This country is very flat indeed and affords no cover for advancing infantry. Marshes, nullahs and irrigation canals form serious obstacles to advancing infantry and particularly cavalry.

[There are] swarms of flies whose feelers and other aids to locomotion, when not in flight, are coated with adhesive layers of 'Tom Tickler's Plum and Apple Jam'. They give us no peace during the day, and night is hell without a mosquito net as millions of mosquitoes and sand flies (both armour piercing) give us their undivided attentions.[5]

Before the attack at Hanna on 5 April, the divisional commander, Major-General Sir Francis Maude, told his men that 'all that was necessary was a bayonet rush, a mighty British cheer, and we were through to starving Townshend in Kut'. Roe noted: 'We discussed the General after dismissal and came to the conclusion he was a born optimist. We sincerely hope, although we do not believe, that the Turkish defences and defenders will collapse like the walls of Jericho.'[6]

In the event, the attack on the 5th – my great-uncle Clive's first experience of battle – did not meet any resistance because the Turks had already withdrawn to their next defensive position at Fallahiya. But this did not stop the officers of Roe's 6th East Lancs from 'losing their heads and, instead of obeying orders by remaining for the stipulated twenty minutes in the captured Turkish trenches, [they] flourished their revolvers and yelled, "Come on boys, we've got them on the run. We won't stop until we get to Kut."' The consequence, wrote Roe, was that 'we made a dive for the first line in the enemy's second position and of course came under the fire of our own artillery'.[7]

Once past the Hanna trenches, the 13th Division was ordered to capture the next Turkish position at Fallahiya, four miles upriver. The night assault began at 7.30 p.m. that day, after a brief artillery bombardment, with the 6th Loyal North Lancs spearheading the 38th Brigade. Roe recorded:

The Turks kept up a heavy machine gun and rifle fire on the advancing Infantry and men were falling fast. The tendency to close up (only natural

I suppose) could not be controlled when under such a heavy fire and we found ourselves on the heels of the Regiment in front and got intermixed. 'Twas the longest 1000 yards I ever 'goose-stepped'. When the leading battalion (the North Lancs I believe) got to within charging distance they 'let themselves go'. The Turks fought their machine guns to the last and conveniently retired along well-constructed communications trenches under cover of darkness.[8]

Then followed an episode of black farce as the attacking battalions, unaware of the Turks' departure, threw bombs at and fired on each other for more than an hour until the whistles blew and order was restored. 'Of course everyone stood up (except those who could not),' recorded Roe bleakly, 'and congratulated each other on another empty victory – no prisoners, no machine guns captured.'[9] The division's casualties on 5 April were 'not far short of 2,000', with the 6th Loyal North Lancs losing six officers and ninety-one men.[10]

Three days later, after the 'gallant, broken, and patched-up battalions' of the Indian 7th Division had failed to take the next Turkish position at Sannaiyat,[11] the 13th Division was ordered to resume the attack the following day. 'We are going to make a surprise attack on the key to Kut (the Sannaiyat position) at dawn in the morning,' announced Private Roe's platoon commander.

> We are going to attack en masse on a frontage estimated at 3500 yards. The Turkish position is flanked on the right by the Tigris and on the left by the Suwaikiya Marsh; therefore a flank attack is out of the question. It must be a frontal attack. There will be no artillery preparation as an artillery bombardment preceding the infantry attack would put the Turks on their guard and the element of surprise would be nullified or lost.[12]

Roe and his comrades were unimpressed. 'A light hearted venture indeed,' he notes in his diary, 'undertaken without the slightest consideration for the defensive power of machine guns, backed up by a well entrenched and stubborn enemy who well knows that Townshend cannot hold out [at Kut] much longer.'[13]

The division attacked before dawn with my great-uncle's 6th Loyal North Lancs spearheading the centre brigade. As he left no written record,

I can only speculate how this pre-war accountant, just turned thirty, must have felt as he led his platoon forward across 1,000 yards of flat, open ground. According to a watching General Maude the advance was orderly and quiet.[14] Roe, who was acting section commander (in charge of ten men), remembered it differently:

> The Divisional line at 200 yards lost all semblance of alignment, shoulder to shoulder in some places and 6 yards between files in other places (the loops or bends in the Tigris were to a certain extent responsible for this). It was a hopeless task trying to keep the 20 yards distance between lines . . . The front line bulged in the centre, receded and bulged again; the flanks in turn . . . lost ground, causing the centre to halt until they came into alignment.[15]

Shortly afterwards, with Clive Neely and the leading line within 100 yards of the front trench, a single Mauser shot rang out, followed by a single Very light, and then more flares. It was, wrote Roe, 'like one man pressing a switch'. He added:

> By their ghastly flares their position was revealed to us and we to them. The Turks were shoulder to shoulder in the trench. Machine guns were embedded on the parados, as also were Turks in the kneeling and standing positions. Before the flares expired their shrapnel was on us good and hard. A cyclone of bullets from machine guns and rifles battered and tore great gaps in the closely packed lines. Men fell by the dozen. You could hear the continual thud of bullets as they came into contact with human bodies. Men bayoneted each other when falling dead or wounded.[16]

A horrified General Maude noted in his diary: 'Second line lay down while first line pushed on. Consequently first line, which did splendidly, got into Turks' trenches in a good many places – North Lancs, King's Own, Welsh Fusiliers and Wilts especially. But being unsupported by second line had to give way.'[17]

Was Clive Neely among the soldiers of the 6th Loyal North Lancs who broke into the Turkish trench, before fierce hand-to-hand fighting and a lack of support forced them out again? We will never know, but I would like to think that an eldest son like him, used to taking responsibility for four younger siblings, would have at least tried to do his duty.

Fortunately – and unlike ten officers and 151 men of his battalion* – he came through the battle unscathed, and made it back to the trench the survivors of the division were hastily digging halfway along the plain. 'We held on tenaciously where we were all day,' noted Maude, 'the troops scratching holes in the ground and digging themselves in as best they could.'[18]

Not all the spectators of the battle were as generous. A Major J. D. Crowdy of the Tigris Corps intelligence staff, for example, thought a large part of the division panicked when the Turks opened fire and withdrew without orders. It was, he wrote, 'very depressing – now we know that the 13th Division is a wash-out'.[19]

This was, perhaps, a little harsh. Shortly after he was wounded in the left arm, Private Roe 'distinctly heard a cultivated and authoritative command given in front and thrice repeated: "Retire, retire you damned fools, retire".' But even he concedes that the survivors 'did not need telling'. For a time Roe lay still among hundreds of other casualties as bombs burst around him and machine-gun bullets flew inches over his head. He decided to move when he saw the Turks leave their trenches and begin to loot the dead and wounded, using their rifle butts on any who resisted. He wrote:

> I arose and doubled back 50 yards, stumbled and fell, [and] repeated the process again. This time I can hear bullets whizzing about me . . . I make for the left, that is the Suwaikya Marsh flank, as if I carry straight on I'll get shot by our own men, who no doubt by now have formed some sort of line. Can't double any more, so I have to walk. Dead and dying all over the line of attack.[20]

Roe took temporary refuge in a small hastily constructed trench where he found 'four badly scared and juvenile Warwicks' who helped to dress his wound. From the trench he could see 'a number of wounded crawling painfully back by inches'. Helping them were two officers. 'They brought several wounded in,' he recorded, 'and appeared to be dressing others. They bore a charmed life, whoever they were.'[21]

---

* The official casualty figures for the 6th Loyal North Lancs at Sannaiyat were seven killed, eighty-five wounded and 169 missing (Wylly, *The Loyal North Lancashire Regiment*, p. 243).

It was only when Roe reached the safety of the advanced dressing station that he learned the identity of the two brave officers: a Roman Catholic padre called Father Lanehan, and the Church of England padre of the 6th Loyal North Lancs, thirty-two-year-old Reverend William Addison. 'Two of the bravest men in Messpot,' remarked a wounded sergeant they had brought in.[22]

The adjutant of the 6th North Lancs, himself injured, wrote that Addison gave 'unceasing attention to the wounded throughout the whole morning under incessant fire on perfectly flat ground within 400 yards of the Turks'.[23] For his extraordinary courage at Sannaiyat, Addison became only the second padre to be awarded the Victoria Cross.* His citation read: 'He carried a wounded man to the cover of a trench, and assisted several others to the same cover, after binding up their wounds under heavy rifle and machine gun fire. In addition to these unaided efforts, by his splendid example and utter disregard of personal danger, he encouraged the stretcher-bearers to go forward under heavy fire and collected the wounded.'[24]

Addison's bravery aside, the attack had been an unmitigated failure, and at a cost of 1,807 casualties.[25] When word reached the besieged and starving defenders of Kut – where the hospitals were 'full to overflowing' and 'dogs, cats and other animals were eaten with relish' – it cast a pall of depression over the garrison. With only enough food to last to the end of the month, time was running out.[26]

24 April 1916: *'Women began to shriek and cry'*
– The Easter Rising

At 11.50 a.m. on Easter Monday, a force of 150 Irish rebels – led by the military committee of the Irish Republican Brotherhood† – set off from their assembly point in Beresford Place to the General Post Office

---

* The first, the Reverend James Adams, was awarded his VC for saving men during the 2nd Anglo-Afghan War of 1878–80.
† A secret oath-bound organization dedicated to the establishment of an 'independent democratic republic' of Ireland during the late nineteenth and early twentieth centuries.

(GPO) on Sackville Street in central Dublin. It was an eclectic mixture of units from the Irish Volunteers* and the Irish Citizen Army,† 'some inadequately armed', and included both men and women.[1]

Bystanders and policemen assumed the march was yet another rowdy but essentially peaceful protest against the London Parliament's decision in August 1914 to suspend the introduction of Home Rule for Ireland for the duration of the war. But events soon took a more serious turn when the rebels reached the front of the Imperial Hotel on Sackville Street and Michael Connolly, head of the Citizen Army, ordered them to wheel left and charge the GPO. At first the staff and bank-holiday customers inside were more baffled than scared by the appearance of armed rebels. They quickly left, however, when threatened with violence.[2]

As word spread that the GPO had been 'stormed', other Volunteers arrived singly and in groups to join their comrades, swelling the garrison to around 400. Not all remained in the GPO; some were sent out to occupy buildings on both sides of Sackville Street, including the Imperial Hotel, Clery's department store and the shops facing O'Connell Bridge.[3]

Elsewhere, another 800 rebels from the 1st–4th Battalions of the Irish–Volunteers and the Citizen Army took over other key buildings in Dublin, including the South Dublin Union, the Four Courts, Jacob's Factory, Harcourt Street Station and the College of Surgeons, in or near which they began to construct sandbag barriers and roadblocks. But the GPO on Sackville Street was the headquarters of the rebellion, a fact made clear to all by the hanging of various republican flags, including the green, white and orange tricolour (designed on the French model, and first introduced in 1848 by the would-be revolutionaries of the Irish Confederation).[4]

The key symbolic moment was the proclamation of an Irish Republic by Patrick Pearse, the Irish Volunteer Director of Organization, from the front of the GPO at noon. Listening was a small and largely unenthusiastic crowd. 'The few cheers that greeted this epochal announcement,'

---

* A military organization created in 1913 by Irish nationalists to counteract the Ulster Volunteer Force (formed a year earlier by Protestants to oppose Home Rule by force).
† A Dublin-based militia force, created by the Transport Workers' Union to protect workers' demonstrations from police and army violence.

wrote Diarmuid Lynch, another IRB leader present, 'furnished an index of the denationalized state of Ireland after the era of Parliamentarianism.'[5]

Addressed to 'Irishmen and Irishwomen' in 'the name of God and of the dead generations', and signed by Pearse, Connolly and five other members of the self-proclaimed Provisional Government, the document insisted that Ireland 'through us, summons her children to her flag and strikes for her freedom'. The republic was, it added, a 'sovereign independent state' that guaranteed 'religious and civil liberty, equal rights and opportunities to all its citizens'.[6]

Exactly which roles the seven members of the Provisional Government – only five of whom were in the GPO – had been assigned was unclear. Pearse was said to be both Commander-in-Chief of the Army of the Republic and President of the government, a sort of Generalissimo, though the widow of another IRB leader, Tom Clarke, later claimed that he had been appointed political supremo. Undoubtedly the most active rebel chief was Connolly who, as leader of the Citizen Army and *de facto* commander of all republican forces in Dublin, at once began dictating a stream of orders while his faithful secretary, Winifred Carney, typed them up.

The first casualty was an elderly Dubliner who was shot by the Citizen Army as he tried to rescue his commandeered lorry from a barricade near the Shelbourne Hotel. The effect, according to one onlooker, was 'awful'. He added: 'Women began to shriek and cry and kneel down to pray in the street, and the *vivandières* [young female republicans with haversacks of food] with the rebels began crying and screaming and wringing their hands, to be told by the rebels to go home.'[7] The Citizen Army then set about digging slit trenches in St Stephen's Green, instead of taking up positions in the tall buildings that overlooked the barricades – an omission that would cost them dearly when British troops did just that under the cover of darkness.

A number of other tactical errors were made by the rebels: notably the failure to occupy large, easily defended and centrally located buildings like Trinity College, the Bank of Ireland and Dublin Castle (the seat of British power). The greatest obstacle to their hopes of success, however, was the last-minute postponement of the rebellion for twenty-four hours, thus reducing the numbers involved from an estimated 5,000 to a little over 1,000.

The rising had been fixed for Easter Sunday. But various mishaps intervened, the first of which was the arrest of the republican sympathizer and former British diplomat Sir Roger Casement on Good Friday. Casement had just arrived by U-boat from Germany – commanded, as it happened, by the former torpedo officer from the infamous *U-20* – to help co-ordinate the arrival of a shipment of arms for the rebels. But he missed his rendezvous on 20 April with the ship carrying the weapons – the SMS *Libau*, disguised as the Norwegian steamer *Aud* – and was captured the following day near Tralee.

A day later, Saturday 22 April, the *Libau/Aud* was intercepted off the south coast by two Royal Navy sloops and escorted to Queenstown. Realizing there was no escape, the German skipper scuttled his ship and sent the much needed arms – including 20,000 rifles, many of them Russian-made Lebels captured at Tannenberg – to the bottom.

Even more momentous, however, was the attempt by Eoin MacNeill, Chief of Staff of the Irish Volunteers (but an opponent of precipitate military action, and therefore not involved in the planning), to stop the rising when he finally learned of Pearse and Connolly's intentions on the 22nd. He did this by countermanding all orders for Easter Sunday, so that 'no parades, marches, or other movements of the Irish Volunteers will take place'. Pearse and the military committee's response was to confirm the cancellation of the planned 'manoeuvres', then to reschedule them for midday on Easter Monday. But in the confusion many Dublin Volunteers failed to turn up, while outside the city the response was virtually non-existent (not least because a number of them, including 1,000 in Cork, unaware of the counter-order, had assembled as planned on Easter Sunday).[8]

'Our plans were so perfect,' cried Tom Clarke on hearing of MacNeill's order, 'and now everything is spoiled.' Pearse agreed, noting in his final communiqué that the 'fatal countermanding order' had prevented the original plans from being realized.[9] Could they have worked without MacNeill's intervention? Not according to historian Maureen Wall, who carried out a detailed examination of the situation in the provinces where, she argues, the plans were so sketchy they could not have been affected by the countermand. 'Absolute secrecy,' wrote Wall, 'maintained by a tiny group of men, who were relying on the unquestioning obedience of the members of a nationwide revolutionary organization, was bound to defeat their object of bringing about a revolution, except in Dublin where these men were, in fact, in a position to control events.'[10] But other historians disagree. 'It seems clear enough,' opined Charles Townshend, 'that the "countermand" had dramatic effects.'[11]

In Dublin, on 24 April, the most obvious 'dramatic effect' of MacNeill's intervention was to reduce the number of armed rebels available to Pearse and Connolly. This, in turn, made it easier for the British military to regain control. Yet its initial response was slow and haphazard. The General Officer Commanding (GOC) Irish Command, Major-General Friend, was visiting London; and of the 120 officers and 2,265 British soldiers in the four principal barracks in Dublin, only 400 were in a state of 'immediate readiness'.[12]

The first clash took place in Sackville Street at 1.15 p.m. when a cavalry patrol, sent out to investigate a report of rioting, was driven off by rebel rifle fire, losing three killed and one wounded. Elsewhere the British infantry – all from Irish regiments, including the Royal Dublin Fusiliers – advanced on rebel positions with more caution. Their chief priority was to secure positions from where they could launch attacks, notably Dublin Castle (which would have fallen to the rebels had they been bolder), Trinity College and the Shelbourne Hotel. By nightfall they had sizeable garrisons in all three locations, and 2,600 reinforcements, under the command of Brigadier-General W. H. M. Lowe, were on their way from the Curragh and Belfast (they arrived early on the 25th).[13]

Two more infantry brigades from Kitchener's 59th (North Midland) Division arrived from England during the evening of Tuesday 25 April. But they were mostly young recruits, many of whom had never fired a rifle, and when one brigade (the 178th), advanced into Dublin on the 26th they were badly cut up by the outposts of the 3rd Irish Volunteers in Northumberland Road and Mount Street. Eventually the superior weight of British fire told, and by the time the rebel position in Clanwilliam House was assaulted, it had become a 'perfect inferno', its curtains shredded, ornaments smashed and 'almost every square foot of the walls inside was studded with bullets'.[14]

But such battles were few. In most cases the rebel garrisons had to sit tight while British troops manoeuvred ever closer, blasting their positions with artillery and machine-gun fire. One British officer, who arrived with the new Commander-in-Chief, General Sir John Maxwell, on Friday 28

April, 'found Dublin like a "blazing furnace" – the whole of Sackville Street was on fire & the buildings along & at the back of Eden Quay – there was vigorous musketry fire going on on both flanks, fortunately not at us!'[15]

The burned-out ruin of the General Post Office in Sackville Street, Dublin, after the Easter Rising of April 1916.

That same day, with Connolly badly wounded and the GPO burning furiously, Pearse gave the order to abandon the building. By Saturday 29 April the situation was hopeless. 'We were simply in a ring of steel,' remembered one rebel officer with military experience, 'from which there were only two avenues of escape – death or surrender.' Regarding surrender as 'hateful', the officer preferred fighting to the last man, as did many of the rebels.[16] Pearse disagreed. His men were exhausted, hungry and disorientated from near-constant shellfire. By surrendering he hoped to save their lives, and to prevent more civilians from dying (already 220 had been killed in the crossfire, and many more wounded).[17]

When Pearse was brought before Maxwell during the afternoon of the

29th, he was refused terms and told the rebels must 'throw themselves on our mercy'. Yet Maxwell held out the possibility that the British government would 'exercise clemency for the rank & file', and said a 'great deal would depend on the celerity of the general surrender'. Pearse duly drafted a general order (signed at 3.45 p.m.) to the 'Commandants of the various districts in the city and Country . . . to lay down arms' so as 'to prevent the further slaughter of Dublin citizens, and in the hope of saving the lives of our followers now surrounded and hopelessly outnumbered'. Countersigned by Connolly – by now receiving treatment at the Red Cross post in Dublin Castle – the order officially ended the rebellion, though some garrisons south of the River Liffey did not lay down their weapons until the evening of Sunday the 30th.[18]

More than twice as many police and British soldiers as rebels lost their lives in the rising: 134 to 64.[19] Yet the British military, after a hesitant start, did well to contain the rebellion so quickly. 'Within twenty hours,' wrote Charles Townshend, 'it could already be said that the military challenge had been neutralized. Within forty-eight hours the rebellion was consigned to an increasingly hopeless "last stand".'[20]

Pearse got his wish when most of the rank-and-file rebels were given sentences of penal servitude. But he, Connolly and another thirteen prominent rebels were found guilty of 'waging war against His Majesty the King, with the intention and for the purpose of assisting the enemy', and were shot in batches from 3 May.[21] The effect of these judicial killings was to create both martyrs and a wave of support for the republican movement. 'What is poisoning the mind of Ireland, and rapidly poisoning it,' the Irish nationalist MP John Dillon told the House of Commons on 11 May, 'is the secrecy of these trials and the continuance of these executions.' Thousands of Dubliners, he added, 'who ten days ago were bitterly opposed to the whole Sinn Fein movement and the rebellion, are now becoming infuriated against the Government.'[22]

Asquith took note and the executions came to an end. The only rebel leader to escape the firing squad was Eamon de Valera, commanding the 3rd Irish Volunteers, probably because he was an American citizen.*

---

* De Valera spent the rest of the war in British jails, opposed the treaty that created the Irish Free State in 1922, and later became both Prime Minister and President of the Irish Republic (Eire).

29 April 1916: *'A shattering and humiliating experience'*
– The fall of Kut

'The dismal 29th,' wrote Artilleryman Sergeant William Groves of the day Kut was surrendered to the Turks after a 147-day siege. He added:

> We first emptied all ammunition that was left. Destroyed rifles, revolvers, glasses, instruments and all kinds of gear, harness etc. At about 8 a.m. we commenced to blow the guns up.* We first put gun-cotton in the breech end which absolutely destroyed it. In some cases the breech was blown a matter of 200 yards or more. Then a charge was placed in [the] muzzle end which buckled the whole piece . . . After wrecking the whole position and making it practically uninhabitable we packed as much kit as we could comfortably carry, ate our ration of horsemeat and waited for the Turks to come.[1]

The Turkish soldiers marched into the British 'entrenched camp' at Kut at midday, their commander Halil Pasha (the uncle of Enver Pasha) making straight for the 6th Division's headquarters where Major-General Sir Charles Townshend handed him his pistol and sword. Halil graciously handed them back, saying 'they are as much yours as they ever were'. Townshend was, he announced, 'the honoured guest of the Turkish nation' and his troops would be interned somewhere with 'a good climate near the sea'. The general still hoped his men would be offered parole, telling them in his final communiqué the night before that he would travel to Constantinople and 'get you exchanged at once'. His last message to the Tigris Corps was sent at 1 p.m. on the 29th: 'To all ships and stations from Kut. Goodbye and good luck to all.'[2]

Townshend's last hope of relief had ended a week earlier with the narrow failure of the third attempt – this time by the Indian 7th Division – to break through the Turkish lines at Sannaiyat. From that point on, wrote Sergeant Groves, it 'became quite obvious that the relief force could not win its way through in time to relieve us as our rations were only enough to last until the end of the month. We were then on 3 oz. bread per day.'[3]

---

* Thirty-eight field guns and four howitzers were destroyed in under an hour.

Many Indian troops, having refused to eat horsemeat since its issue in February, were on their last legs. 'Poor devils,' wrote an officer of the 76th Punjabis, 'I don't know how they live . . . yet it is their own fault.'[4] Conditions generally in the besieged camp had been unbearable for some time. 'Many buried every day,' noted Sergeant Groves in early April. 'Men looking thin and wan. Animals fed on date wood only. Simply skin and bones. Nothing to be bought so had to exist on rations. Time hanging terribly. Weather beginning to get very hot. Flies and lice in swarms. Men praying for the end.'[5]

Since late January, some supplies – flour, newspapers, gramophone needles and even fishing nets – had been dropped by planes (the first time an air resupply was attempted), but they could not hope to keep up with the garrison's requirements.[6] A last desperate attempt was made to send 240 tons of supplies up the Tigris on the steamboat *Julna*. It ended when a Turkish shell put the boat's boiler out of commission on the 25th.

'So we have failed,' wrote Brigadier Theodore Fraser of the relief efforts that had cost the Tigris Corps 23,000 men, twice the number besieged in Kut. In the opinion of Fraser, commanding a brigade of the Indian 3rd Division, 'Kut could have been relieved by a good – or even a respectable general.' Instead Gorringe ('damn him!') had 'thrown away' the troops 'in driblets' and 'disregarded' every 'principle of war'.[7]

In March, when Halil Pasha had first offered to discuss surrender terms, Townshend had urged the commander in Mesopotamia, General Sir Percy Lake, to accept while he could still negotiate from a position of strength. He hoped his division, he told Lake, would be 'allowed to march out through the Turkish lines with its arms, artillery and pouch ammunition and join you'. But Lake, backed by India and London, did not agree; he thought the Turks were tottering and the relief force was bound to get through.[8]

Even after Gorringe's final defeat on the 22nd, Townshend was hopeful that Halil would let his troops leave Kut. 'The Turks cannot feed my force,' he told Lake, and 'they have not enough ships to take it to Baghdad'. If it was forced to march, he warned, 'the force would all die, both from weakness and Arab bullets'.[9] Claiming sickness 'in body and in mind', he asked Lake to conduct the surrender negotiations. But the latter refused and instead gave the poisoned chalice to a small group of intelligence officers who had been brought over from Cairo for a quite separate task: to help foment an anti-Turk Arab revolt. Leading the group was Aubrey Herbert MP, already a veteran of Mons and Gallipoli, and a young archaeologist called T. E. Lawrence, soon to be famous as 'Lawrence of Arabia'.[10]

General Sir Charles Townshend, commanding the 6th Indian Division, at Kut-al-Amara in Mesopotamia.

In the morning of 27 April, before Herbert and Lawrence could reach Kut, Townshend met Halil and was told that 'unconditional surrender followed by captivity was the only option'. He offered £1 million and the garrison's guns in return for the 6th Division's freedom; but Halil made no promises, simply agreeing to consult Enver Pasha. The latter's reply was typically ruthless: if Townshend gave up 'everything in Kut', he – and he alone – would be allowed to 'go whither he will' on parole. On 28 April, aware the offer was unacceptable, Townshend encouraged Lake to increase the bribe to £2 million. Lake agreed to consult London, and said that Herbert and Lawrence would try to talk to Halil the following day; in the meantime Townshend should start the destruction of his supplies and equipment.[11]

He did just that, having sent the troops a final communiqué that he had come to terms with the Turkish Commander-in-Chief (which he had not) and would surrender the following day. 'All that day,' wrote Sergeant Groves on the 28th, 'we were kept busy destroying ammunition and spare parts. During [the] night of the 28th we threw all tools and ammunition and spare fittings into [the] river.'[12]

Herbert, Lawrence and Colonel Beach (Lake's intelligence chief) did not speak to Halil Pasha in his camp until the afternoon of 29 April, by which time Townshend had already surrendered. With few bargaining chips, they could only get Halil to agree to the release of 500 sick and wounded, in return for the same number of fit Turkish prisoners; but when Halil asked for ships to take Townshend and his men to Baghdad, 'otherwise they would have to march, which would be hard on them', Beach refused. Halil brought the meeting to a close with a yawn, saying he 'had much work to do'.[13]

Thus passed the last opportunity to save Townshend's command. Despite Halil's assurances, Sergeant Groves must have guessed their likely fate as the Turks marched into Kut on the 29th. 'A more ragged dirty or slovenly crowd could not be imagined,' he wrote. 'When they saw us they growled "Ingles" and drew a greasy finger across their throats . . . As soon as the Turkish troops were let loose in Kut they immediately started to loot us of what small articles of value we had such as rings, watches, pipes etc.'[14]

For Private Harold Wheeler of the 1/4th Hampshires, the surrender was a 'shattering and humiliating experience'.[15] He was among the 2,869 British officers and men taken prisoner; a further 7,192 Indian officers and men were captured, along with 3,248 Indian camp followers, bringing the total to more than 13,300.[16] As Townshend had feared, it was more men than the Turks could cope with. That much was obvious when the captives arrived at Shumrun, a few miles upriver, and found no shelter and an inadequate daily ration of 'three black biscuits' – as 'hard as bricks and had to be soaked in water' – per day. 'Hundreds were taken sick through eating these hard biscuits,' recalled Sergeant Groves, 'and a large percentage of those admitted to hospital died.'[17]

It was the start of a gruesome ordeal as the ordinary soldiers, already weakened by the privations of a long siege, were force-marched northwards to prisoner-of-war and work camps in northern Iraq and Anatolia.* 'We were hustled along like animals,' wrote Sergeant Groves of 9 May. 'The guards would often gallop through the ranks, scatter us, and then round us up with whips and butts of rifles. At every halt many men had to fall sick unable to walk owing to wounds caused by blows. These men were left at different villages and never heard of again.'[18]

More than 1,750 British and 2,500 Indian soldiers died on the march or in the appalling conditions of the POW camps.[19] Meanwhile their former commander General Townshend, whom they cheered as he took his tearful leave of the 6th Division, travelled in relative comfort to Constantinople where, in a large house on the island of Prinkipo, he saw out the war as a pampered guest of the Turkish government.

Ned Roe, recovering from his wound in a hospital at Basra, wrote of the surrender at Kut: 'It is all the more disheartening when one dwells on the futile and bloody sacrifices made by the relief force who fought their way to within almost a stone's throw of Kut.'[20]

My great-uncle Clive Neely probably felt as Roe did. But he never put his frustrations down on paper – or if he did the letters have been lost – and was soon too ill to do so. Like hundreds of others in the Tigris Corps that spring and summer, he was struck down with illness – in his case jaundice – and died in a field hospital in Sheikh Saad on 20 June 1916. His former commanding officer, Captain W. F. Cragg, wrote to the Neely family three days later: 'I myself, when I was commanding the regiment, thought so highly of his abilities that I sent his name in for promotion and he would doubtless have very soon got his captaincy as well.' He added a few months later: 'I am sure I must have told you what a splendid soldier he was and of his devotion to duty.'[21]

Clive never got his promotion, though it is reasonable to assume that Cragg's high opinion of him was formed during the actions at Hanna, Falahiyah and Sannaiyat in early April 1916 when the 6th Loyal North Lancs lost a quarter of its men. Either way, a second Neely brother had paid the ultimate price.

* The officers, by contrast, were taken to Baghdad by boat.

31 May 1916: 'Were we celebrating a glorious naval victory or lamenting an ignominious defeat?'
– Battle of Jutland

At 2.15 p.m., as Vice-Admiral Sir David Beatty's Battle Cruiser Force began its turn to the north-east to rendezvous with the main body of the Grand Fleet, the light cruiser HMS *Galatea* spotted an unidentified merchant ship and, accompanied by three escorts, went to investigate.

As they closed on the merchant ship, a Danish tramp steamer, they saw two German torpedo boats – part of Admiral Hipper's force of battlecruisers – on a similar mission. 'Urgent,' read the *Galatea*'s wireless message to the rest of Beatty's fleet. 'Two cruisers [sic], probably hostile, in sight bearing ESE, course unknown.'[1] Minutes later *Galatea* and the light cruiser *Phaeton* opened fire on the torpedo boats with their 6-inch guns, the first shots in the greatest naval engagement in history.

It had never been the intention of Vice-Admiral Reinhard Scheer, commander of the German High Seas Fleet since February 1916, to take on the British Grand Fleet in a single titanic action. Scheer's strategy – endorsed by the Kaiser – was to use submarine and air attacks, and surface-ship raids on British shipping and the east coast, to lure part of the Grand Fleet to its destruction. Only once the two fleets had reached parity would he consider risking a major battle. The British approach was bolder. Commanding the Grand Fleet, Admiral Lord Jellicoe was keen for Beatty's battlecruisers to draw part or all of the High Seas Fleet on to his more powerful force. This was exactly what happened at Jutland on 31 May, but not in the way the British had planned.

Thanks to the codebreakers in Room 40 of the Admiralty, Jellicoe had advance warning that the High Seas Fleet was coming out on 31 May, and his and Beatty's 151 ships* were at sea a full two and a half hours *before* the Germans. But because the Admiralty feared the Germans might try to 'rush the Dover Straits', they refused to let the powerful Harwich Force join Jellicoe, as had been arranged.

A more serious error was the message sent to Jellicoe at 12.48 p.m.

---

* The Grand Fleet at Jutland was made up of twenty-eight battleships, nine battle cruisers, eight armoured cruisers, twenty-six light cruisers, seventy-eight destroyers, a minelayer and a seaplane carrier.

that there was 'no definite news of the enemy' and that 'Directionals place [Scheer's] flagship in Jade [its home port] at 11.10 am GMT'. This had been sent because Captain Jackson, Director of Naval Operations, had mistakenly assumed that Scheer had yet to put to sea because his call sign was still in harbour. In fact he always left his call sign in harbour when he weighed anchor, a ruse familiar to the staff in Room 40. Had Jackson asked them, he would have been told that Scheer was 'at sea'. The consequences were twofold: Jellicoe assumed there was no hurry and, slowing to conserve fuel, was further from Beatty than he needed to be when the latter sighted Hipper's battlecruisers; and the sudden appearance of German capital ships, so soon after the Admiralty had insisted they were still in harbour, made both Jellicoe and Beatty mistrustful of Room 40 intelligence (with unfortunate consequences later in the battle).[2]

No sooner had Beatty received *Galatea's* message than he ordered his battlecruisers to turn about and make for the enemy. The main concern of Walter Cowan, captain of the battlecruiser *Princess Royal*, was that the attached squadron of battleships under Rear Admiral Hugh Evan-Thomas was closest to the enemy and would get all the glory. 'That damned 5th B.S. [Battle Squadron],' exclaimed Cowan, 'is going to take the bread out of our mouths.' He recalled:

> They were the nearest and seemed to have the inside turn had they at once gone the shortest way at them to close the range, but I believe their Admiral expected a signal from D.B. [Beatty] and there was just that pause, and then the way they led round put them rather a long way astern of us with the result that instead of being able to join us in battering away at their Battle Cruisers at the head of their Battle line they got rather heavily hammered by the German Battleships.[3]

Thanks to Evan-Thomas's lack of initiative, Beatty would begin the fight without four modern Queen Elizabeth-class battleships, the world's fastest and most heavily armed Dreadnoughts (with 15-inch guns).

Spotting Hipper's battlecruisers at 3.35 p.m., Beatty raced to intercept them, convinced that Scheer's battleships were still in port. They were, in fact, steaming sixty miles to the south-east of Hipper who promptly steered towards them to lead Beatty to his destruction. Jellicoe, meanwhile, was under the impression that *Galatea's* sighting was a light cruiser and that all the heavy German ships were still in port. He only increased his speed, and ordered Admiral Hood's faster 3rd Battle Cruiser Squadron to join Beatty with all haste, after he had received a signal from Beatty's flagship *Lion* at 4 p.m. that five German battlecruisers were in view.

Scheer was also slow to react. Informed by Hipper of Beatty's presence, and assuming that Jellicoe was not in the vicinity, he ordered his battleships to make 17 knots, the top speed that his slowest-moving squadron of pre-Dreadnought Deutschland-class ships could manage.* He, also, would arrive too late to influence the fight between the battlecruisers.

Hipper's ships opened fire first, and with superior rangefinders – which magnified the target twenty-three times – the advantage of a leeward position (thus helping the gunsmoke to clear), and a westering sun which silhouetted the British battlecruisers, they soon found their targets. Before long *Lion* and *Princess Royal* had been hit twice, and *Tiger* four times. The next shell blew the roof off *Lion's* midships turret, killing everyone inside and igniting cordite charges in the loading cages. A mortally wounded Royal Marine major saved the ship by flooding the magazine; but twenty minutes later some smouldering fragments ignited charges in the supply hoist, killing all seventy men in the turret magazine and shell-rooms.[4]

Soon after *Lion* had been crippled, *Indefatigable* was struck by a salvo near its after turret, with one shell detonating deep within the vessel. She was already sinking by her stern when two more shots hit her forecastle and forward turret. After a brief delay, the ship exploded, sending smoke and debris 200 feet into the air. Of *Indefatigable's* 1,019 officers and crew, only two were rescued.[5]

Finally Evan-Thomas's battleships arrived and, working in pairs, opened fire with their 15-inch guns on the battlecruisers *Moltke* and *Von der Tann* at 19,000 yards, scoring several hits. But the German counter-fire was equally effective and the battlecruiser *Queen Mary* was the next to succumb to multiple hits. Captain Cowan of the neighbouring *Princess Royal* recalled: 'Our Signal Boatswain snapped out to me, "Something has happened to *Queen Mary*, sir". I looked round and saw a billow of soft white smoke and her stern sliding beneath the water, and a Destroyer

---

* Scheer's decision to bring this outdated squadron with him was one of four key errors he made this day, any of which could have cost him his whole fleet.

dashing in to the pool of oil to try and pick up some of them.'[6] There were eight survivors out of a crew of 1,266.[7]

Despite being outnumbered and outgunned (particularly since the arrival of Evan-Thomas's battleships), Hipper's five battlecruisers had scored considerably more hits – forty-four to seventeen – and had sunk two ships. But they had also suffered significant damage – the *Von der Tann*, for example, had two turrets out of action – and Hipper was relieved to hear at 4.30 p.m. that Scheer's sixteen Dreadnoughts were 'in sight'.[8]

A few minutes later, Beatty was astonished to receive the following signal from the light cruiser HMS *Southampton* (one of the ships that had helped to sink the *Blücher* at Dogger Bank): 'Have sighted enemy battlefleet SE. Enemy's course north. My position is 56° 34′ N 6° 20′ E.' Aware that he was hugely outnumbered, Beatty at once ordered his ships to turn back towards his own battlefleet. Once again Evan-Thomas's reaction was too slow and his flagship *Barham* was hit as it turned. For more than thirty minutes, Evan-Thomas's 5th Battle Squadron fled north-west with salvoes falling all around it. Both *Malaya* and *Warspite* were struck by multiple shells – with one starting a fire on the former that killed 102 officers and men – but so solid was their construction that neither sank nor slowed enough to be caught by the German battleships.[9]

Their flight was assisted by the heroics of two of Beatty's destroyers, *Nestor* and *Nicator*, who disobeyed the recall signal and turned to attack the High Seas Fleet. 'It was an amazing sight,' recalled Torpedoman Thorne of the *Nicator*, 'five battle cruisers followed by twelve battle ships firing every possible gun. Commander Bingham suddenly changed course followed by the *Nicator*, and made for the German battleships to "attack with remaining torpedoes", both having two each. Only a miracle could save us from the intense fire of the German ships, but we came through unharmed.'[10]

At a range of 3,000 yards, the destroyers selected a battleship each and fired their torpedoes. Both missed, and as the destroyers tried to flee the *Nestor* was hit by a large shell and stopped in its tracks. The *Nicator* turned to help but was ordered away by the stricken ship's captain, Commander the Hon. Barry Bingham. 'We raced away from *Nestor* with sad hearts,' wrote Thorne, 'and got clear.'[11] Pulverized by German shells, the defenceless *Nestor* was sunk, as was the destroyer *Nomad* that had been crippled earlier. Bingham was rescued from the sea by a German torpedo boat and spent the rest of the war in captivity, latterly in the infamous Holzminden POW camp. His consolation was the award of the Victoria Cross.[12]

As Beatty closed with Jellicoe, he changed course to NNE to mask the approach of the Grand Fleet. Scheer should have asked himself why Beatty had put himself at greater risk by diverting from the direct course home, but he did not. Convinced that Jellicoe was nowhere in the vicinity, he continued his blind pursuit of Beatty.

At 5.50 p.m. the Grand Fleet sighted Beatty's battered battlecruisers and, still unaware of the exact position of Scheer's ships, Jellicoe hesitated before ordering his battleships to deploy into line of battle by forming single line ahead on the port wing column, with *King George V* leading, a manoeuvre that took them momentarily away from the High Seas Fleet. It was a slow and laborious process, and the cause of much confusion. 'We in the 5th Battle Squadron,' wrote an officer on the *Malaya*, 'took station in the rear of the 1st Battle Squadron. In doing so we must have been going too fast, for we ran up on to the last ship of the line and were actually overlapping each other, thus presenting an excellent target to the Huns, who were extremely quick in taking advantage of it.'[13]

Beatty's ships cut the corner of the deploying Grand Fleet, to protect it from the approaching Germans, and were astonished to see Rear Admiral Sir Robert Arbuthnot's First Cruiser Squadron, led by his flagship *Defence*, heading past them towards the disabled German light cruiser *Wiesbaden*. 'It was just what one reckoned of his form,' noted Captain Cowan on the *Princess Royal*, 'to fly straight at their throats, regardless of any odds.' But Arbuthnot soon paid for his rashness when '3 quick salvoes' struck *Defence* 'one after another and down she went'.[14] Also sunk by German battleships were *Warrior* and *Black Prince*, with only the *Duke of Edinburgh* escaping. Arbuthnot had 'vastly exceeded his instructions', wrote my great-uncle Midshipman Charles David* of the armoured

---

* Charles David was the seventeen-year-old son of Major Markham David of the Royal Monmouthshire Royal Engineers. A cadet at Dartmouth when war broke out, he and the rest of his 'Drake' term of seventy boys were at once distributed among the ships of the fleet. By the summer of 1916 more than a third of this 'band of "children" sent so gaily to sea in 1914' had been killed (David, *Seventy Years*, p. 22).

cruiser HMS *Shannon*. 'His job was to beat off light forces – cruisers and destroyers – and scout for the German Fleet, reporting back to the C.-in-C. But he got too far ahead.'[15]

German battlecruiser *Derfflinger* fires a broadside during the
Battle of Jutland on 31 May 1916.

Next to go was the battlecruiser *Invincible*, conqueror of the *Scharnhorst* and *Gneisenau*, and the flagship for Rear Admiral Horace Hood's detached squadron that had come from Scapa Flow. The *Invincible* opened fire on the German battlecruisers and hit *Lützow* and *Derfflinger* (the former later sank). But five ships returned fire, with one shell exploding inside a gun turret and, thanks to inadequate anti-flash precautions, igniting the magazine below. Hood's flagship was blown in half. 'It was shallow water there,' remembered Cowan, 'and as we roared close past her the two ragged ends of her rested on the bottom and her two sharp ends were leaning together like the beginning of a card house and one man climbing out of the wreckage of the control top.'[16] She took the forty-five-year-old Hood, a rising star of the Royal Navy, and 1,026 officers and men with her. Only six survived.[17]

But the rest of the Grand Fleet, having crossed the enemy's 'T', was now in a hugely advantageous position. Scheer's first intimation that he was facing the whole Grand Fleet was when six miles of the horizon burst into flame as twenty-four heavy ships opened fire. Greatly outgunned, 150 miles from home and handicapped by his slower-moving pre-Dreadnoughts, Scheer knew his only hope was the onset of darkness. Playing for time he ordered his fleet to turn 180° while a flotilla of destroyers laid a smokescreen.

The light was failing and, fearful of a mass torpedo attack, Jellicoe chose not to follow through the smoke. Instead he ordered the Grand Fleet to steam on a south-easterly course to cut off the German line of retreat to Wilhelmshaven. As the battleships began their pursuit, the *Marlborough* was hit and disabled by a torpedo, possibly fired from the stricken *Wiesbaden*. Twice Scheer changed direction and tried to charge through Jellicoe's battle line, and twice he was forced to turn about, protected by another smokescreen and a mass torpedo-boat attack. Jellicoe's response, as he had warned it would be, was to turn away from the torpedo attack. He thus wasted a perfect opportunity to destroy the German High Seas Fleet.

Yet all was not yet lost. Jellicoe was still positioned between Scheer and his home base and there was every chance that he might finish the job in the morning. There was even time, before nightfall, for one more battlecruiser engagement in which *Seydlitz* and *Derrflinger* suffered yet more hits before fleeing to the west. This was another chance for Jellicoe to engage the High Seas Fleet, but he was wary of fighting at night and chose to alter course, keeping himself between the Germans and their home port.[18]

That night there were a number of cruiser and destroyer contacts between the two fleets. But British ships failed to report these actions, and Jellicoe was 'in the dark' as Scheer sailed his vessels behind the faster-moving Grand Fleet. Room 40 of the Admiralty knew from decrypts that Scheer was heading for home by the Horns Reef, and some of this information was sent on to Jellicoe by Vice-Admiral Sir Henry Oliver, Chief of the Admiralty War Staff. Mindful of the egregious mistake that Oliver's deputy Captain Jackson had made the day before, however, Jellicoe chose to disbelieve this intelligence and Scheer was allowed to escape.[19]

Midshipman David remembered the intense feeling of 'anti-climax' as they returned to Scapa Flow.[20] 'It was,' wrote Captain Cowan, 'a bitter disappointment for us in the Battle Cruisers. We had found the enemy, fought them, and led them into the jaws of our main Fleet and had lost 3 out of our 9 Battle Cruisers with near to 4,000 men in doing so.'[21] A total of fifteen British ships – three battlecruisers, four armoured cruisers and eight destroyers – and 6,094 sailors were lost at Jutland. German losses were lighter: one battlecruiser, a pre-Dreadnought, four light cruisers and five destroyers, with 2,551 sailors.[22]

Though Scheer had made a number of errors that could have cost him his fleet, the actual fighting indicated that German ships were superior in a number of areas: German gunnery was more accurate thanks to 'better training, superior range-finders, and more effective armour-piercing shells with delayed action fuses, while the British were less well armoured and had fewer watertight bulkheads'. Even so, Jellicoe would almost certainly have sunk more capital ships had he 'pursued Scheer more vigorously after the latter's first about turn and had he not turned away after the second'.[23] Yet he was probably right to claim that his chief priority was not to lose the battle, and therefore hand Germany the strategic advantage. Instead he kept it for Britain. 'The central fact remains,' wrote David Stevenson, 'that Scheer failed in his strategic aim of annihilating Beatty's battlecruisers and equalizing the balance between the two fleets, thus ending up no better placed than before to attack the British Isles or shipping in the Channel, send out his cruisers as commerce raiders, or break the Allied blockade.'[24] Midshipman Charles David agreed. 'Never again did the "High Seas Fleet" proceed to sea except to surrender,' he wrote later, 'and in that way the Battle of Jutland was decisive.'[25]

And yet it was because of the significant disparity in losses that many German newspapers hailed the battle as a victory, and some Britons agreed. 'Well the Navy have caught it in the neck this time,' wrote Captain Neil Weir from the trenches on 5 June. 'It is no good being so cocksure.'[26] Vera Brittain in London, meanwhile, was perplexed by the press coverage. 'Were we celebrating a glorious naval victory or lamenting an ignominious defeat?' she wrote later. 'We hardly knew; and each fresh edition of the newspapers obscured rather than illuminated this really quite important distinction. The one indisputable fact was that hundreds of young men, many of them midshipmen only just in their teens, had gone down without hope of rescue or understanding of the issues to a cold, anonymous grave.'[27]

On 11 June, after attending a service at St Paul's Cathedral at which a hymn of Thanksgiving was sung for Britain's 'moral' victory, Brittain wrote to her brother Edward: 'We couldn't do more than that if we had given the German navy a smashing blow, instead of having ended the battle in a draw which we say was a victory to us, and they say was a victory to them.'[28]

4 June 1916: *'The ceaseless torrent poured westward'*
– The Brusilov offensive

The sheer scale of Russia's dawn offensive against multiple sectors of the southern Austro-Hungarian front – from the River Styr to the Bukovina – was unprecedented. In just a matter of hours, 1,938 guns delivered a concentrated barrage of high explosive and gas shells that shattered the Austrian defences and silenced their guns. 'Apart from the bombardment's destruction of wire and obstacles,' admitted an Austrian inquiry, 'the entire zone of battle was covered by a huge, thick cloud of dust and smoke, often mixed with heavy explosive gases, which prevented men from seeing, made breathing difficult, and allowed the Russians to come over the ruined wire obstacles in thick waves into our trenches.'[1]

At the Austro-Hungarian town of Czernowitz in the Bukovina, twenty miles behind the front line, the day was meant to be one of celebration. A resident recalled:

> The town was beflagged as 'an Imperial Eagle in Iron' was unveiled at the Rathaus 'in memory of the time of Russian invasion' [in 1914]. The wide town-square was filled with people, and General von Planzer-Baltin himself was expected. But then in the afternoon, whilst the artillery fire in the north, in the direction of Okna and Dobronovste, was getting louder and louder, a dispatch-rider arrived with the following message, which was read out to the expectant crowds in the square: 'His Excellency General von Planzer-Baltin is prevented from taking part in the festivities to-day, and gives notice of his absence.'[2]

By nightfall on the first day of the offensive the Russians had captured 26,000 prisoners. Florence Farmborough, the British nurse now serving with a Russian mobile field hospital in the southern sector of the attack, recalled: 'The 9th Army had broken through the Austrian defences against a strongly fortified Line stretching for more than 16 versts [about twenty-five miles] and our cavalry had advanced some 25 versts into Austrian territory; over 10,000 prisoners had been taken and 25 guns captured . . . We could scarcely believe our ears! Could it really be true?'[3]

Within two days Brusilov's offensive had torn a breach in the Austrian line twenty miles wide and seventy miles deep. 'Events crowded on events,' wrote General von Cramon, the German liaison officer with Austrian forces.

On the northern wing the positions west of Rovno were lost . . . Our reserves had been used up with astonishing rapidity, but ineffectually. The ceaseless torrent poured westwards. Lutsk with its notorious bridge-head fell. The Russian stood on the western bank of the Styr, and before him were only the shattered remnants of divisions.

On the southern wing a Russian attack pierced the front between the Dniester and the Pruth; whereupon one part withdrew to the west, the other crossed the Pruth. In the centre of the front the Army of the South alone maintained its ground.

. . . On June 7th the Austrian Headquarters declared that the situation could not be maintained with the help of Austro-Hungarian troops alone.[4]

Already it was the most successful Entente offensive since the Marne in 1914, and as the attacks continued through the summer more ground was won. How was this possible? Only a year earlier, Austro-German forces had driven the demoralized Russians out of Austria-Hungary and captured most of Russian Poland and Lithuania. What had produced this remarkable turnaround? The answer was a combination of Russian ingenuity and Austrian complacency.

The broad-front offensive was the brainchild of General Alexei Brusilov, commanding the four armies of the South-West Front, who was able to take advantage of a recent increase in the number of front-line troops – from 1.7 million to 2 million – and a marked improvement in their equipment. 'Rifles were supplied,' recalled Brusilov, 'of various types perhaps, but anyhow with a sufficiency of cartridges; while the ammunition for the artillery, especially the light guns, arrived in abundance. The number of our machine-guns increased, and every unit had its bombers, armed with hand-grenades and bombs. The men were in excellent spirits.'[5]

When Brusilov took over the South-West Front in early April 1916 (he had formerly commanded the Tenth Army), he was told by his predecessor that the troops 'were quite unfit to undertake any sort of offensive, and that the only object to set oneself was to save South-West Russia from further invasion by the enemy'.[6] Brusilov disagreed, and told the Tsar so during the latter's visit to his front on 9 April. His men were 'full of mettle', he said, 'and would be ready to take the offensive by the middle of May'. He repeated these points at the next Council of War, chaired by the Tsar at Mogilev on 14 April, and argued for a simultaneous attack by all three army groups on the Eastern Front so that the enemy could not use his superior 'railway system to move his troops from point to point as he pleases'. The other army group commanders – Generals Evert (West Front) and Kuropatkin (North-West Front) – were much less optimistic, not least because they both faced German formations, and said they were prepared to attack but 'could not guarantee success'. Thus it was agreed that all fronts would be ready to advance 'before the end of May'.[7]

Brusilov's tactics were unorthodox. Without numerical superiority or adequate heavy artillery, he ordered all four of his armies to start preparing for an assault so that the enemy 'would be unable to mass all his forces at one point'. He decided to use his northerly Eighth Army to make the main blow in the direction of Lutsk and Kovel because an attack here would give the 'best support' to General Evert's attack. 'Further,' he wrote, 'I attached great importance to the success of the Ninth Army on the frontier of Rumania, which was hesitating to join the Allies. The Seventh and Eleventh Armies were, to my mind, of secondary importance. I had allotted my reserves and material on this basis.'[8]

To prepare for the offensive, Brusilov ordered a meticulous reconnaissance of the Austro-German trench system (including the drawing of large-scale maps and aerial photography), had extra trenches dug to house his assault troops and quietly moved artillery into position. Meanwhile the Austrians had weakened their defences – a fact not lost on Brusilov – by moving six of their best divisions to the Italian front to take part in a major offensive in the Trentino region of the Alps known as the

Strafexpedition ('punishment attack') that, when it was launched on 15 May, drove the Italians back fourteen miles to the edge of the Asiago Plateau. The response of the panicked Italian high command was to urge the Russians to launch their own offensive as soon as possible. The Stavka agreed to this request, and ordered Brusilov to attack alone on 4 June; Evert would not be ready until the 14th.[9]

Russian soldiers advance during the Brusilov offensive of June 1916.

So successful was Brusilov's offensive that by 9 June, just five days in, he had captured 72,000 prisoners, ninety-four guns, 167 machine-guns, fifty-three trench mortars and minenwerfers (mobile mortars), 'and a vast quantity of miscellaneous military booty'. Yet that same day he was told by General Alexeez, the Chief of the Russian General Staff, that Evert would not now be ready to attack until the 18th. Though 'exasperated beyond measure', Brusilov continued his own assaults and on 13 June the southern Eleventh Army was closing in on Czernowitz.[10] A Polish-born landowner recalled:

Suddenly the [artillery] fire stopped and the expert ear could catch the rattling of machine-guns. The decisive attack had begun. All a-strain, we were awaiting news. Some soldiers appeared round the corner of the road, slightly wounded. Then a panic began. Someone had come from a neighbouring village reporting that he had seen Cossacks. Soon refugees from the villages outside were streaming through the town. General confusion. Children were crying, women sobbing . . .

We had to go. As I was mounting the carriage I perceived in the distance, near the wood on the hill, a few horsemen with long lances – Cossacks from Kuban. They were slowly emerging from the forest and approaching the town. 'Drive ahead!' I shouted to the coachman.[11]

At first Falkenhayn, the Chief of the German General Staff, had been loth to help the Austro-Hungarians by moving reinforcements from the Western Front where the battle for Verdun was still raging. But on 8 June, at a meeting with his Austrian counterpart General Franz Conrad von Hötzendorf in Berlin, he agreed to release several divisions for a counter-attack in the direction of Kovel in the north of the threatened sector. Joined by Austrian reinforcements from the Italian Front, these extra German troops succeeded 'in compressing somewhat the Russian offensive circle west of Lutsk'.[12]

Evert's West Front finally launched its much postponed and ill-prepared assault on 3 July, but it was easily beaten off. Brusilov was furious. 'Had there been any other Supreme Commander-in-Chief [than the Tsar],' he wrote later, 'Evert would have been removed from his post, after such a display of indecision . . . while Kuropatkin would never have obtained employment in the field. But, under the then existing regime, there was no sort of responsibility in the army.'[13]

Brusilov was left to fight on alone, and though he made some headway near the Styr river, north-west of Rovno, he was unable to capture Lutsk. 'Little by little,' wrote Brusilov, 'reinforcements reached me from the other idle fronts, but the enemy lost no time; having more rapid means of transport available, the number of his troops increased at a far higher rate than mine.'[14]

Further south Brusilov's armies continued the advance, and by 12 August his offensive had yielded an incredible 378,000 prisoners, 496 guns, 144 machine-guns and 367 trench mortars and minenwerfers. But as more German divisions arrived – fifteen by mid-September – the defence stiffened and progress became slower and more costly. 'I continued to fight,' wrote Brusilov, 'but already at a lower pressure, trying to spare my men as far as possible, and only to the extent necessary to pin down in front of me as many troops as possible, and thus indirectly assist our French and Italian allies.'[15]

By the time the fighting petered out in October, Brusilov's armies had reached but not taken the passes of the Carpathians. They had inflicted more than a million casualties on the Austro-Hungarian Army – roughly half its strength on the Eastern Front – and had suffered a similar number in doing so. But their achievements were notable: they had advanced the front line from thirty to sixty miles; forced General Conrad von Hötzendorf to abandon his initially successful Trentino offensive, and Falkenhayn to suspend the attacks at Verdun; and encouraged Romania to join the Entente.[16]

Brusilov deserved the hundreds of admiring telegrams that arrived from 'every class of Russian society', including one from the Grand Duke Nicholas his former Commander-in-Chief. It stated: 'I congratulate, kiss, embrace, and bless you.' The Tsar, by contrast, sent 'a few cold, insipid words of thanks'. Brusilov was mortified. 'Such impressions are never effaced,' he wrote, 'and I shall carry them with me to the grave.'[17]

5 June 1916: *'It began yesterday at Medina'*
– The Arab Revolt

In the early morning of 6 June a Royal Navy warship anchored off a deserted beach near the Red Sea port of Jeddah, and a Briton in a white linen suit was rowed ashore. His name was Ronald Storrs, the thirty-four-year-old head of the Arab Bureau in Cairo, and he brought with him two strongboxes that each contained £5,000 in gold, two cartons of cigarettes and a sack of anti-Ottoman newspapers.[1]

Carried with his baggage across the last few yards of surf by Arab slaves, Storrs was led inside a dark tent on the shoreline where he was welcomed by a chubby youth who was 'evidently attempting to encourage the growth of a somewhat backward beard'. The youth was Zeid, the youngest son of Emir Ibn Ali Hussein, the Grand Sharif of Mecca and Guardian of the Holy Places,* who had an agreement with the British to lead an Arab Revolt against the Ottomans in return for Arab independence after the war.[2]

---

* One of 800 men from two families, the Aoun and the Zeid, who claim direct descent from the Prophet Muhammad.

Handed a list of requests by Zeid that included £70,000 in cash, Storrs said that no more money would be paid until he knew the revolt had begun. 'I am then happy to be able to announce to you,' replied Zeid, 'that it began yesterday at Medina.'[3]

Taking Zeid at his word, Storrs handed over the gold, cigarettes and newspapers, and even added his own gold watch as a gesture of friendship. He then invited Zeid and his cousin Shakir on to the British warship, and while they were shown 'the wireless, which appeared to fascinate them, the guns, the Captain's bathroom and other wonders of the deep', Storrs composed a telegram to his political masters in Cairo:

> Rising began yesterday Monday at Medina but as all communications in Hijaz are cut no news. Other towns to rise on Saturday. Arabs hope to induce 800 Turks at Jeddah, 1,000 at Mecca, and 1,200 at Taif to surrender; otherwise they will kill them . . . Please dispatch immediately 50,000 pounds now definitely promised but not payable until revolt satisfactorily ascertained to have begun.[4]

The rising had begun, but it was not going well. The walled town of Medina had recently been reinforced by thousands of Turkish troops and was easy to defend. Against it, and its protective chain of outlying concrete forts, bristling with artillery and machine-guns, the Arabs attacked with camel-mounted tribesmen, led by Ali, Sharif Hussein's eldest son. The attack was a failure, as was an attempt by Ali's brother Feisal to sever the railway north of Medina, causing both brothers to retire to a safe distance from the town.

On 10 June another brother, Abdullah, failed to capture the garrison town of Taif in the mountains of the Hijaz, though he did prevent Turkish troops from reinforcing the garrison at Mecca, also under attack by forces under Sharif Hussein himself. Hussein had fired the first shot at Mecca from the window of his palace towards the Turkish barracks opposite, finally prompted into rebellion not by promises of British gold or an independent Arabia, but rather by the fear that the Turks were about to depose him as Emir (or Governor) of Mecca. Hussein had long been playing a double game with both the British and the Ottomans, hoping 'to remain neutral and collect bribes from both sides'.[5] To that end he had come to an agreement with both to raise the tribes to fight the other, the deal with the Turks sweetened by a payment of £50,000. Yet earlier, in July 1915, he had promised Sir Henry McMahon, the British High Commissioner in Cairo, that 100,000 Arab soldiers of the Ottoman Army would desert to his standard when he proclaimed a revolt.[6]

In return for Arab friendship, said Hussein, Britain would have to recognize 'the independence of the Arab countries' under Ottoman control, including the entire Arabian peninsula (bar Aden, then a British dependency), Israel, Jordan, Iraq, Lebanon and Syria, and even a strip of southern Turkey. This was more than McMahon had the inclination or authority to concede, so he procrastinated by telling Hussein that it was too early to discuss the future of land still under Ottoman control. But when it became clear to the British government in November 1915 that Hussein was thinking of throwing in his hand with the Ottoman Sultan who, in his role as Caliph of all Muslims (and at Germany's request), had proclaimed a holy war against the Allies a year earlier, they ordered McMahon to give the Sharif 'cordial assurances' of Arab independence, and that the boundaries would be discussed at a later date. McMahon did just that, but specifically excluded two vital areas: the head of the Persian Gulf, then occupied by troops of the Indian Army; and the coastal region of Syria (including the towns of Damascus, Homs, Aleppo and Hama), on the grounds that the French might object.[7]

Hussein refused to accept the loss of the Syrian coast, but agreed to resolve the dispute after the war.* Meanwhile the Arab revolt, he promised the British, would begin as soon as an opportunity presented itself.[8] That might never have happened had Hussein not learned in April 1916 from Jemal Pasha, Governor of Syria, that a crack Ottoman force of 3,500 men, accompanied by a German mission, was about to march through the Hejaz to the tip of the Arabian peninsula where it planned to establish a telegraph station. Fearing that the Turkish authorities had got wind of his negotiations with the British, and would use the force to arrest

---

* Unbeknown to Hussein, the British government made a secret deal with the French in the spring of 1916 – known as the Sykes–Picot Agreement after its negotiators – to divide the future Arab 'confederation' into northern and southern areas under French and British protection respectively. It also reserved certain key areas for direct control: the Syrian coast and part of Anatolia for France; and the head of the Persian Gulf for the British; Palestine meanwhile, at Russia's insistence, would be internationally administered.

and hang him en route (the fate of many other anti-Ottoman Arab plot-
ters in Syria), Hussein was forced to act.[9]

His first move was to offer the Turks a deal. The message, Jemal
recalled, was as follows: 'If you want me to remain quiet, you must
recognize my independence in the whole of the Hijaz – from Tabuk to
Mecca – and create me hereditary prince there. You must also drop the
prosecution of the guilty Arabs and proclaim a general amnesty for Syria
and Iraq.'[10] When Enver Pasha refused point blank, and the Arab nation-
alists were duly hanged in Damascus on 6 May, Hussein gave orders for
the revolt to begin in early June.

By the end of June, with the Turkish garrison in Mecca still holding
out, the British landed explosives, 3,000 rifles, six machine-guns, 1.2
million rounds of ammunition, 600 tons of food and a battery of mountain guns manned by Egyptian artillerymen (so as not to offend Muslim
sensibilities) at Jeddah. These supplies, particularly the guns, helped to
tip the balance at Mecca and the Turkish garrison surrendered to
Hussein's forces on 10 July. That same day the British War Committee
agreed to pay Hussein £125,000 a month to meet the costs of the rebellion.[11] But in Cairo it was decided that money, arms and Muslim gunners
were not enough: Medina was still holding out and the Turks were
beginning to probe south towards Mecca; to prevent the flow of Turkish
arms and troops to Medina it was vital to cut the Hijaz railway line. To
that end Ronald Storrs and another intelligence officer, T. E. ('Ned')
Lawrence, were sent from Cairo to advise Hussein and direct operations
in October 1916.

A small man with short blond hair and electric-blue eyes, the twenty-
eight-year-old Lawrence had graduated with a First in History from
Oxford in 1910 before working as an archaeologist in Syria. In January
1914 he and his mentor D. G. Hogarth were used by the British Army as
an archaeological smokescreen for a military survey of the Negev Desert,
across which an Ottoman army would have to pass en route for Egypt.
When war broke out, Lawrence – thanks to his fluent Arabic and intimate
knowledge of the Middle East – was assigned to intelligence work in
Cairo. But having failed to buy the release of the British troops captured
at Kut in April 1916, he was treading water in the map section of the
Intelligence Department when Storrs selected him for the Hijaz expedition. He was the perfect man for the job, having earlier written to Hogarth

about the tribesmen in Syria: 'I want to pull them all together, & to roll up Syria by way of the Hijaz in the name of the Sharif.'[12]

By February 1916, Lawrence was convinced that a rebellion in Mecca would have the same effect as the papal schism of the fourteenth century:

> If we can arrange that this political change shall be a violent one, we will have abolished the threat of Islam, by dividing it against itself, in its very heart. There will then be a Khalifa in Turkey [the Sultan] and a Khalifa in Arabia [Sharif Hussein], in theological warfare, and Islam will be as little formidable as the Papacy when Popes lived in Avignon.[13]

15 June 1916: *'You and I will be burnt at the stake'*
– The Boulogne 'Absolutists'

Shortly before 5 p.m., in a camp overlooking Boulogne, four British 'Absolutists' – hardcore Conscientious Objectors (COs) – were taken under guard from the field punishment barracks to the parade ground where a thousand members of the Non-Combatant Corps and Labour Battalions had formed three sides of a hollow square. In the centre of the square stood the camp adjutant with a sheaf of papers containing the verdict and sentence of the trial of the four men that had finished a week earlier. The first to be called forward was a Quaker bank clerk from north London. With churning stomach, he ambled to the centre of the square, refusing to march.[1]

'Private Howard Marten,' said the adjutant loudly, 'you have been found guilty by a court martial of refusing to obey a lawful order when on active service.' There was a deliberate pause. 'The sentence is death by shooting.'

Marten seemed resigned, as if the awful news was something he had both expected and prepared for. It was even a moment for black humour as one of the other three Absolutists, whose objection to military service was not religious (like Marten's) but political, said to another: 'If they shoot Quakers you and I will be burned at the stake.' He was told by the guard to hold his tongue.

After an extended pause, giving the news time to sink in, the adjutant continued: 'The sentence has been confirmed by the Commander-in-Chief, but afterwards was commuted by him to one of penal servitude for ten years.'[2]

Marten at once had visions of Dartmoor Prison and 'cells, bolts, bars and gangs of stone-breakers'. But there was also huge relief that he would live.[3]

A similar feeling washed through a young Methodist second lieutenant of the York and Lancasters, Phil Brocklesby, standing with a group of spectators. His elder brother Bert had been tried on the same charge and was likely to receive a similar sentence. 'My heart relaxed,' he recalled, 'my tension disappeared.'[4]

The news that the first four death sentences had been commuted did not take long to reach Bert Brocklesby and the other Absolutists in the field punishment barracks. 'We felt relieved and very hopeful we should get the same,' remembered Bert. '"Ten years" held no terrors for us.'[5]

One of them, twenty-one-year-old Quaker Harry Stanton, also felt vindicated. 'Slowly we came to realize,' he wrote, 'that a great, perhaps a decisive victory had been gained. Once and for all, we hoped, the government had been brought to face the question of its ultimate treatment of COs and had decided not to shoot them.'[6]

When the Military Service Act was passed on 27 January 1916, it specifically included in its list of exemptions conscientious objection to the 'undertaking of combatant service'.[7] In practical terms, this meant that many thousands of COs were excused front-line duty if they agreed to join Labour Battalions and the newly created Non-Combatant Corps. But for Absolutists the very act of wearing a uniform and contributing in any way to the war effort was contrary to their religious and political beliefs, and they did everything they could to resist.

Bert Brocklesby was twenty-five years old in August 1914. The son of a South Yorkshire grocer and sometime Methodist lay preacher, he had been raised in a family of strict believers and retained a strong personal faith in Divine Will. Having trained as a teacher at the Methodists' College in Westminster, he was working at a school in his hometown of Conisborough, and had recently got engaged to a local girl, when Kitchener made his appeal for volunteers. Two of his brothers – George and Phil – answered the call. Bert refused. 'God had not put me on earth,' he wrote, 'to go destroying his own children.'[8]

After conscription was introduced in 1916 – by which time George and Phil had both become officers – Bert went before a tribunal and said it was 'better to be killed than kill anyone else'.[9] He had anticipated the compulsory call-up by joining the No Conscription Fellowship, set up by Clifford Allen and Fenner Brockway in December 1914, and was duly exempted from active service and ordered to join the Non-Combatant Corps. But again he refused. For him it was still the army under another name. He was arrested in May 1916 and imprisoned with other Absolutists in a tiny cell in Richmond Castle. They were typically non-conformists – Jehovah's Witnesses, Methodists and Quakers – and came from lower-middle-class and working-class backgrounds: there were two ironstone miners, a decorator, a shopkeeper and a clerk from Rowntree's factory in York. A 'mixture of threats, punishments and blandishments' was used to encourage Bert and the others to join the NCC. But when none agreed, the army lost patience.[10]

In mid-May, after receiving reports from the Adjutant-General and the army's Director of Personal Services, Kitchener informed the Cabinet: 'There is reason to believe that if men find that objection on religious or other grounds has the effect of removing them from danger, a very large number will endeavour to take advantage of this means of escaping.'[11]

This was an exaggerated fear. The total number of British COs during the war – 16,300 – was less than two-thirds of a per cent of those conscripted.* Yet, at the outset, the War Office feared the figure would be much greater and was determined to make an example of those who refused even non-combatant work. It was for this reason that in late May 1916 forty-nine† of the most recalcitrant COs – including Bert Brocklesby – were sent from prisons in Richmond and along the south coast to France where acts of disobedience on active service could be punished by execution.

When they refused orders to drill in France, some were given Field Punishment No. 1, otherwise known as 'crucifixion', whereby the offender

---

* Of those 16,300, more than a third served at least some time in prison during the war (including the philosopher Bertrand Russell, grandson of a duke, who was jailed for five months in 1918). The hard core of Absolutists numbered 1,300.

† Of the forty-nine Absolutists sent to France, thirty-five were tried in one block and fourteen in another. Brocklesby was part of the first block.

was tied to a gun wheel or, if that was not available, a rope stretched between two posts so that the arms were spreadeagled. It could last for up to twenty-eight days and, according to one of the Absolutists, was an 'exquisite torture' for the shorter men 'who were virtually hanging by the wrists'.[12]

As the Absolutists continued to ignore military authority, a court martial was inevitable. The first took place in a shed in Boulogne in early June, and involved the four alleged ringleaders Howard Marten, Harry Scullard, Jack Foister and Jonathan Ring. The court gave an 'attentive hearing' to his statement, said Marten, but it all took less than an hour and a half. Some of the later trials were over in fifteen minutes. Bert Brocklesby recalled: 'The president was clearly at a loss to understand my line of defence, which was to show that I had consistently disobeyed all military orders from the start. He said, "You seem to be making your case twice as bad as it need be." This struck me as being really funny and I almost laughed out loud; as though the penalty would be to be shot twice.'[13]

All found guilty and sentenced to death, their reprieve was the result of two appeals to the Prime Minister. The first was by Gilbert Murray, Regius Professor of Classics at Oxford University (and a former tutor of Asquith's), who told the premier that the army had shipped some Absolutists to France with a view to shooting them. 'Abominable,' responded Asquith, before assuring Murray that no executions would be authorized.[14]

The second, on 11 May 1916, took the form of a delegation to Downing Street by three men and one woman: Liberal MP Philip Morrell, Labour MP Philip Snowden, the philosopher Bertrand Russell and Catherine Marshall of the No Conscription Fellowship. At the meeting Asquith agreed to give directions to Sir Douglas Haig, commanding the BEF, 'that no conscientious objector in France is to be shot for refusal to obey orders'. If any court martial imposed the death penalty, he added, it would not be confirmed. And so it proved. 'But for Asquith,' wrote Russell, 'a number of them would have been shot.'[15]

The man who bore ultimate responsibility for sending the COs to France was Lord Kitchener, the War Secretary. Though a late convert to conscription, he was determined to keep the number of COs to a minimum by making their sanctions as harsh as possible. Did he consider executions? Almost certainly, yet he was also sufficiently concerned to ask a churchman to go to France in early June to see if the COs were being fairly treated and to inquire if they would accept alternative service.[16]

Whatever Kitchener's true intentions were, they died with him on 5 June when the cruiser HMS *Hampshire*, the ship that was taking him to Russia, hit a German mine and sank in the icy North Sea. The backbone of Britain's war effort was no more, and the public felt his loss keenly. 'The words "KITCHENER DROWNED",' wrote Vera Brittain,

> seemed more startling, more dreadful, than the tidings of Jutland; their incredibility may still be measured by the rumours, which so long persisted, that he was not dead . . . [and] would return in his own good time to deliver the final blow of the War.
>
> For a few moments during that day, almost everyone in England must have dropped his occupation to stare, blank and incredulous, into the shocked eyes of his neighbour . . . So great had been the authority over our imagination of that half-legendary figure, that we felt as dismayed as though the ship of state had foundered in the raging North Sea.[17]

1 July 1916: 'Not a man wavered, broke ranks or attempted to come back'
– First day of the Somme: The BEF perspective

Just hours before the start of the biggest British offensive of the war, General Sir Douglas Haig noted in his diary: 'With God's help, I feel hopeful for tomorrow. The men are in splendid spirits: several have said that they have never been so instructed and informed of the nature of the operation before them. The wire has never been so well cut, nor the artillery preparation so thorough.'[1]

This confidence was also noted by Captain Kenelm Dormer whose detachment of Irish Guards had helped to lay light railways 'right up to the Royal Field Artillery Batteries', numbering one thousand guns of every calibre, that were concentrated 'in an area of about a mile wide, so when they opened fire, we had no sleep practically until they stopped'. He noted: 'At 10.30 p.m. on the night before the battle, the Brigade that was billeted next to me marched off by platoons past my Mess Hut, and I was very much impressed with the wonderful spirits of the men, especially as a number of them had only had a few weeks training.'[2]

But as the heavily laden and helmeted* assault troops – all 100,000 of them – shuffled forward in the darkness through packed communication trenches to their jumping-off points, accidents were inevitable. One of the most dramatic took place in a short narrow assembly trench in Thiepval Wood, opposite the powerful Schwaben Redoubt that was the objective of the 36th (Ulster) Division. Preparing grenades for the attack was twenty-year-old Private Billy McFadzean – a tall, well-built linen apprentice and keen rugby player from County Armagh – and a section of bombers from the 14th Royal Irish Rifles (Belfast Young Citizens battalion). As Billy placed the primed bombs in a box on the parados, a tremor knocked two to the trench floor and released their pins. While his mates stared in horror, knowing that in four seconds the bombs would explode and cause carnage in the packed trench, McFadzean acted without hesitation. Throwing himself forward on to the grenades, he absorbed most of the double blast with his body, thereby sacrificing his own life to save his comrades.† No braver or more selfless act would be committed that day.[3]

A short time later, at 6.25 a.m., the British artillery began the same intense bombardment they had been firing for the past week. It normally lasted for eighty minutes; today it would stop fifteen minutes early at 7.30 a.m., zero hour for the attack, in the hope that the German defenders would still be cowering in their dug-outs as the troops surged across no man's land.

Second Lieutenant Phil Brocklesby, brother of Bert (the recently reprieved Conscientious Objector), was with his platoon of Barnsley Pals‡ in a reserve trench opposite the village of Serre, due to go over the top in the second wave, when with ten minutes to go he heard German

---

* British troops were first issued with the Brodie steel helmet in the first half of 1916, but this was its debut in a major offensive. Designed with a wide brim to protect the head and shoulders from shrapnel balls, it reduced head injuries by up to 75 per cent. The French had been wearing the Adrian helmet since mid-1915.

† McFadzean was awarded a posthumous VC, the first member of the Ulster Division to be given that honour.

‡ Officially known as the 13th York and Lancasters, part of the 31st Division.

machine-guns open up. 'Even in our trench about 800 yards behind the front line,' he recalled, 'the bullets just seemed to be skating over the parapet . . . and one of my men said to me, "We haven't got to go over in that, Sir?" "Yes we have," I replied, but I had visions of half of us being toppled back into the trench as soon as we tried to get out.'[4]

At 7.30 a.m., as the British barrage lifted and a deathly quiet fell over the battlefield, whistles blew and the vanguard of the assaulting battalions climbed out of their trenches, or rose from their prone positions in no man's land, to begin the attack. Spearheading the advance of Brocklesby's brigade were the Accrington Pals (officially the 11th East Lancs), tasked with capturing the German front line and the village of Serre beyond. But German machine-guns and artillery were quickly in action and a signaller lance-corporal, watching the advance, remembered his comrades being 'mown down like meadow grass' as they tried to reach the German trenches. He added: 'I felt sick at the sight of this carnage and remember weeping. We did actually see a flag signalling near the village of Serre, but this lasted only a few seconds and the signals were unintelligible.'[5]

As the Accrington Pals began their doomed attack, Brocklesby and the Barnsley Pals rose from their cover in support. 'I rushed up a trench ladder shouting, "Come on lads, now for it,"' he recalled. 'I was surprised I wasn't hit, so I ran along the top of the trench giving a hand to pull my heavily laden men out.'[6] Burdened with almost seventy pounds of kit – including a rifle, bayonet, 150 rounds of ammunition, two Mills bombs, a pick or spade, two sandbags and a haversack with two days' rations – they had been instructed to move at a methodical pace of no more than fifty yards a minute, and not to run until within twenty yards of the enemy trench. But Brocklesby was losing men before he had even crossed the British front line. When he reached it he found it full of dead and dying Sheffield Pals, some with 'limbs blown off, and faces burned black' from a direct hit by a heavy shell.[7] Brocklesby and the surviving Barnsley Pals pressed on towards the German front line but were beaten back. A second attempt was ordered, but then cancelled. The brigade commander had seen enough. He reported:

The brigade advanced in line after line, dressed as if on parade, and not a man shirked going through the extremely heavy barrage, or facing the machine gun and rifle fire that finally wiped them out. He saw the lines that advanced in such admirable order melting away under the fire. Yet not a man wavered, broke ranks, or attempted to come back. He has never seen, indeed never could have imagined, such a magnificent display of gallantry, discipline and determination.[8]

Yet the brigade had achieved little, and the pattern was repeated across much of the sixteen-mile front that the British attacked on 1 July.

The agreement to launch a major Anglo-French offensive on the Somme in July – with the BEF committing twenty-five divisions and the French forty, a total of a million men – had been made at a meeting between Haig and Joffre on 14 February 1916.[9] The decision was supported by the new CIGS, Sir William Robertson, though less enthusiastically by the War Council which, despite the failure at Gallipoli, was reluctant to acknowledge the primacy of the Western Front.[10]

The strategy began to unravel, however, after the Germans attacked at Verdun on 21 February. As France fed more and more troops into the meatgrinder, Joffre was forced to appeal to Haig not only to take over more of the front line but also to bring forward the date of the Somme offensive to late June, and to do most of the fighting. Haig preferred to wait until August when his New Army troops would be better trained, more heavy artillery would be available, and maybe the first tanks as well. But Joffre was adamant that the French needed help before then, and Haig reluctantly agreed to give it. 'Ultimately,' wrote Haig's biographer Gary Sheffield, 'the BEF fought on the Somme because of the demands of coalition warfare.'[11]

Haig anticipated a battle that would unfold in stages, possibly over a prolonged period. It would be a 'step by step' attack with each 'bound forward by the Infantry' dependent 'on the area which has been prepared by the Artillery'.[12] On 30 June his intelligence chief, Brigadier-General Charteris, had written: 'We do not expect any great advance, or any great place of arms to fall. We are fighting primarily to wear down the German armies and the German nation, to interfere with their plans, gain some valuable position and generally to prepare for the great decisive offensive which must come sooner or later.'[13] If, however, the attack broke through the first two German lines on 1 July, the cavalry would be committed in a more ambitious role. As Gary Sheffield put it: 'Hoping for a major triumph, perhaps he expected something less dramatic, planning for various degrees of success.'[14]

In any event, Haig's plan was watered down by General Sir Henry Rawlinson – commanding the Fourth Army that would undertake the burden of the attacks – who preferred limited advances to capture the high ground, followed by a pause to repulse German counter-attacks. The eventual plan was 'an unhappy compromise'.[15] The principal attack would be by Rawlinson's nine divisions on a ten-mile front from Montauban in the south up to the River Ancre, a tributary of the Somme. At the same time three more of the Fourth Army's divisions would secure its left flank on a three-mile front north of Ancre. A little further north, and partly as a diversion, two of Lieutenant-General Sir Edmund Allenby's Third Army divisions would attempt to eliminate the awkward German salient at Gommecourt. Meanwhile six French divisions would attack in the sector between Montauban and the Somme.

If all went well, Lieutenant-General Sir Hubert Gough's Reserve Army (redesignated the Fifth Army during the battle) of three cavalry divisions would push through the gap and take the town of Bapaume, nine miles behind enemy lines, before turning north into open country. Then Rawlinson's infantry would roll up the German trench line by heading in the same direction, while the French would secure the right flank and prevent German reserves intervening from the south.

Delayed for two days by rain, the battle was finally launched on 1 July after a seven-day bombardment in which 1,500 British field guns, howitzers and heavy mortars – one for every seventeen yards of front – fired more than 1.5 million shells (more than had been used in the whole first year of war). Yet artillery observation was hampered by five days of low cloud and drizzle. The result, according to Captain James Marshall-Cornwall, Haig's intelligence officer, was that the guns failed to 'pinpoint the machine-gun posts opposite them' and 'to cut the wire'.[16] It did not help that many of the shells had faulty fuses and failed to explode. 'They didn't all burn the right length,' wrote Marshall-Cornwall, 'and, I'm afraid, a lot of the half-trained gunners of the New Army divisions didn't set the fuses exactly accurate.'[17]

Despite these failures, fourteen British and six French divisions went over the top at 7.30 a.m. on 1 July, the established practice of attacking at dawn having been sacrificed in favour of better artillery observation.

The results were disappointing. The attack at Gommecourt by two Third Army divisions was, after initial gains, repulsed with heavy casualties. Immediately to the right, in the northern half of the Fourth Army's front, the assaults on the villages of Serre, Beaumont-Hamel and Thiepval were also unsuccessful. The Royal Newfoundland Regiment, the only Dominion unit to advance on the first day, lost 684 of its 758 men (a casualty rate of 90 per cent) at Beaumont-Hamel.[18]

Soldiers of the 1st Lancashire Fusiliers fix bayonets prior to their failed attack at Beaumont-Hamel on 1 July 1916. The officer in the foreground (right) is wearing an ordinary soldier's uniform to be less conspicuous.

The sole success in this sector was by the Ulstermen of Billy McFadzean's 36th Division who managed to capture not only the first two German trenches north of Thiepval, but also the powerful Schwaben Redoubt – a triangle of trenches, machine-gun nests and dug-outs up to 600 yards long and 200 deep – that dominated the hillside beyond. It was during the fierce fighting for the redoubt that the division earned its second VC of the day when Captain Eric Bell of the 9th Royal Inniskilling Fusiliers, attached to a Light Trench Mortar, took on and killed a German machine-gunner, threw mortar bombs at the enemy and repulsed a counter-attack with a rifle. He was killed 'rallying and reorganizing infantry parties which had lost their officers'. By mid-morning the whole of the Schwaben was in the 36th's hands and 500 Germans had been taken prisoner (some of whom were killed before they could reach the POW cages). But as no gains were made on either side of the Schwaben, the Germans were able to counter-attack it from three sides and by evening the surviving Ulstermen had been driven back to the old German front line.

Just below the old Roman Road that bisected the battlefield, the 34th Division was easily repulsed as it attempted to capture the ruined village of La Boisselle. The divisional commander had ordered all three of his brigades to advance at the same time, causing the Tyneside Irish to start from support trenches a mile to the rear. Most were hit as they descended a slope towards the British front line. The brigadier and two battalion commanders were wounded, a third killed. 'Militarily,' noted historian John Keegan, 'the advance had achieved nothing. Most of the bodies lay on territory British before the battle had begun.'[19]

The greatest gains were made by the four divisions on the extreme right of the British line – the 21st, 7th, 18th and 30th – who took advantage of their proximity to the excellent French artillery and the fact that their own artillery lifts were well timed, enabling them to advance with a reasonable amount of protection.* Between them they captured two villages – Mametz and Montauban – and a three-mile stretch of the German front line. As the French had taken all their objectives in a similar-sized sector between Montauban and the River Somme, this meant the Allies were now in possession of six miles of the forward German trenches to a depth of a mile.

But nowhere had the German second line of trenches been breached, let alone the third. The cost was a staggering 57,470 casualties (with 19,240 killed and 35,493 wounded), just under half the number of men engaged. This was more than the British had lost or would lose in the Crimean, Boer and Korean Wars combined. French casualties were just 1,590, most lightly wounded, emphasizing the superiority of their battle tactics at this

---

* This recent innovation was known as the 'creeping barrage' and involved timed lifts of artillery fire, usually fifty or a hundred yards every few minutes, so that it moved forward slowly, keeping pace with the infantry.

stage of the war. German losses were 8,200 (with more than a quarter taken prisoner). It was, and still is, the bloodiest day in the British Army's history.[20]

1 July 1916: *'Only isolated parties got as far as the wire'*
– First day of the Somme: The German perspective

I t was still dark when a German eavesdropper in a listening station south of La Boisselle intercepted a message from General Sir Henry Rawlinson to the men of the British Fourth Army. It read:

> In wishing all ranks good luck, the Army Commander desires to impress on all infantry units the supreme importance of helping one another and holding on tight to every yard of ground gained. The accurate and sustained fire of the artillery during the bombardment should greatly assist the task of the infantry.[1]

Sent from Rawlinson's headquarters at Querrieu to all units in the Fourth Army, the message should have been delivered by hand. But fearing it might not reach the forward units in time because of the crush in the trenches, a harassed staff officer of the 34th Division had rung it through by field telephone though he knew the Germans might be listening. They were, with the result that the troops of General Fritz von Below's Second Army were put on immediate notice to expect a general offensive that day.

But it was still a matter of luck and timing as to which German front-line units would be overrun: were their protective belts of barbed wire still intact after seven days of shelling? And even if they were, when should they leave the shelter of their deep dug-outs? Too early and they would be caught by the British barrage; too late and the British assault troops would be on top of them.

The men of the German 55th Reserve Regiment (part of the crack 2nd Guard Reserve Division), guarding the northern face of the Gommecourt salient on the extreme left of the British attack, timed their exit from the shelters perfectly thanks to First Lieutenant Count von Matuschka. As the British barrage lifted at 7.30 a.m., he hurried his men to their firesteps where they were relieved to discover most of their wire still intact and crowds of enemy troops from the 46th (North Midland) Division bunching danger-ously in the gaps. After half an hour of unequal slaughter, the British survivors began to withdraw and the attack, in this sector at least, was over.[*2]

On the southern face of the salient, however, a second battalion of the 55th had less success in repulsing an attack by the British 56th (London) Division, arguably the finest Territorial formation on the Western Front with a high proportion of well-educated men from London's commercial classes. Here the defenders were handicapped by an unusually effective British bombardment which had cut wire, levelled trenches and blocked the exits of dug-outs. It had also combined with morning fog to reduce visibility. 'The sunlight became grey and feeble,' wrote a defender, '. . . our eyes searched to the west but encountered nothing but a single bank of smoke and fog, twitching here and there with flashes.'[3]

Before the Germans could man their defences, the Londoners had emerged from a newly dug trench in no man's land and were upon them. 'By 9 a.m. we had taken our final objective,' recalled a major in the 1st London Scottish, 'although the German trenches were so badly smashed up, we didn't really know where we were. From my company of 150 men there were only thirty-five who were not wounded. That final trench was, then, the safest in the countryside, for our own guns were not firing on it, nor were the Germans; they were not sure whether their own men had been ousted or not.'[4]

The foremost troops of the 56th Division, men from the Queen's Westminster Rifles, were just yards from their projected meeting point with the North Midlanders to the rear of Gommecourt village when the Germans counter-attacked and drove them back. By early afternoon Major Tauscher had brought up the III (Reserve) Battalion of the 55th Regiment to seal off the British breakthrough and, assisted by troops and artillery from the neighbouring German 52nd Division, which was not attacked that day, they gradually regained their regiment's lost ground. By the time two battalions of the British 168th Brigade attacked across no man's land at 4 p.m., the Germans were back in possession of their front-line trench and the assault was easily repulsed. By their skilful and

---

* The divisional commander Major-General Montagu-Stuart-Wortley (the same man who had failed at Loos), bravely refused to renew the attack in the afternoon despite pressure from his corps commander, Lieutenant-General Sir Thomas Snow.

energetic counter-attacks, they had killed and wounded almost two-thirds of the 5,000 Londoners who went over the top. The 46th Division's losses, by contrast, were 1,352.[5]

A little to the south, where the Magdeburgers of the 66th Regiment were holding the line to the front and north of Serre, a defender recalled: 'We were under an extraordinarily heavy fire, and suffered accordingly, but the troops holding the sectors of trench under attack stood along the fire-steps of the parapet and awaited the enemy with rifles and machine-guns. The waves of assaulting troops came under the concerted fire from all our weapons, and only isolated parties got as far as the wire.'[6]

They were firing into the front and flank of the two forward battalions of the British 94th Brigade, the Sheffield and Accrington Pals, a few of whom made it as far as Serre itself. 'The British succeeded in making their way through a zone of wrecked wire and trenches,' noted a soldier of the German 169th Regiment, 'and a number of dugouts which had collapsed under the impact of heavy mortars bombs, and they broke into our position where flanks of our 4th and 3rd Companies adjoined. Major Berthold ordered a counter-attack on the part of our I Battalion, and such British as had penetrated our position were driven out again.' The remains of Accrington Pals were found in Serre after the Germans abandoned the village in 1917.

Holding Hawthorn Ridge, the objective of the left brigade of the Regular British 29th Division, were the Württemburgers of the 119th Reserve Regiment. They had had a double warning that an attack was imminent – both from Rawlinson's intercepted message and from a British deserter from the 2nd Royal Fusiliers (a Russian-born Jew called Joseph Lippmann) – but nothing had prepared them for the detonation of a 40,000-pound British mine beneath the ridge at 7.20 a.m., ten minutes before Zero Hour. 'A great blue flame shot into the sky,' noted a watching Lancashire Fusilier, 'carrying with it hundreds of tons of bricks and stones and great chunks of earth mixed with wood and wire and fragments of sandbags. The great mine had gone up.'[7]

To German eyes 'the ground became all white as if it had been snowing, and a gigantic crater forty or fifty metres wide and twenty deep gaped on the hill'. Most of a platoon of the 119th Reserve's 9th Company had been killed in the explosion, enabling two platoons of the attacking 2nd Royal Fusiliers to establish themselves on the far lip of the crater. But when their comrades in the 1st Lancashire Fusiliers and 1st Dublin Fusiliers tried to link up with them at 7.30 a.m., they were shot down as they crossed no man's land. A few Lancastrians 'reached as far as the third German trench', according to a British POW, but there they 'lost contact' with the troops on their right and were 'surrounded'.[8]

Back at the crater, meanwhile, the unsupported platoons of the Royal Fusiliers were counter-attacked by men of the 9th and 11th Companies of the 119th Reserve and eventually forced to surrender. 'Private Schneider of the *Landsturm*,'* wrote a comrade,

> noticed that a number of the British, who had appeared to be dead, were now raising their heads. He spoke perfect English, and called out to them to come into the German trenches. After some hesitation a number of the unwounded soldiers carried in their first lieutenant, who had been badly hit. When the other wounded saw that their comrades were being treated well, they lifted their hands in supplication and asked for help. Men of our 9th Company went out to them, and together with a number of wounded British . . . they retrieved thirty-six casualties, five of them officers. Orders of some consequence were found on the regimental adjutant.[9]

Further south, at Thiepval village, the German 99th Regiment had little difficulty thwarting an attack by men of the 16th Lancashire Fusiliers and 16th Northumberland Fusiliers. A German soldier recalled:

> The British believed it would just be a question of harvesting the fruits of their seven-day bombardment and wiping out or taking prisoner such troops as had survived. They were sorely deceived! When their protecting smoke dispersed a murderous fire spewed against them from foxholes, shell-holes and what was left of the trenches. The gaunt and dust-covered shapes of our soldiers, some of them in shirt sleeves, hastened out of their collapsing cellars and ploughed up shelters. Seized by an indescribable lust for battle they stood, kneeled or lay flat as best enabled them to send a murderous massed fire into the continuous ranks of the British . . . Before long the leaderless masses of the British began to come to a halt. Their hesitations were converted into consternation, and finally into a panic-stricken flight.[10]

At the southern end of the German front attacked by the British, however, it was a different story. Defending the village of Montauban

* A German reserve force, similar to the British Territorials.

and its approaches – the target of the British 18th and 30th Divisions – were two battalions of the 23rd Reserve Regiment, three more of the 109th Reserve Regiment and one of the Bavarian 6th Reserve. But all had been badly mauled by the effective British bombardment that, by 1 July, had knocked out their supporting heavy artillery, torn great gaps in the wire and wrecked the trenches. As a result the British advanced steadily against feeble opposition and by 10.05 a.m. the 17th Manchesters had fought their way into Montauban where, according to one soldier captured by the Germans, 'some extremely precious hours were lost' because the officers 'had no idea . . . how to exploit the opportunity'.[11]

By nightfall the defending German regiments had all but ceased to exist. 'It was a pitifully small remnant,' wrote the official history of the 109th Reserve Regiment, 'which the regimental commander [Lieutenant-Colonel von Baumbach] was able to gather about him in the evening.' The Bavarian 6th Reserve Regiment was even harder hit, with just 500 survivors from the original 3,500. Its commander noted: 'They, for the most part, were men who had not taken part in the battle. There remained also two regimental officers and a few stragglers, who turned up the

Kaiser Wilhelm II (right) with German infantry commanders
on the Western Front.

following day. All the rest are dead, wounded or missing: only a small fraction fell as prisoners into the enemy's hands. The regimental and battalion staffs were all captured in their dugouts.'[12]

Given the disparity in casualties across the whole frontage of the attack, and the relatively small amount of ground gained by the British, the German commanders were right to regard the first day of fighting on the Somme as something of a victory. But they also realized that the longer-term effect of the offensive might not be disadvantageous to the Allies. Falkenhayn and his staff at OHL had been planning an offensive to the north; that was now abandoned, as were all further attacks at Verdun from 11 July (thus achieving one of the main British objectives for the Somme attack, viz. to relieve the pressure on the French at Verdun).

The German press, moreover, saw the offensive as part of a dangerous concerted effort by the Entente. 'For the first time since the commence-ment of the war,' acknowledged the *Kölnische Volkszeitung* on 4 July, 'unity of action on the fronts of the Quadruple Alliance has become a fact, on which our enemies can congratulate themselves. We have got to face a Russian, an Italian and a Franco-English offensive at the same time . . . Although we are supremely confident, the present hour is of very great significance, and perhaps decisive.'[13]

The German Army drew solace from the intelligence gleaned from 170 British POWs that the attack had failed completely on the left wing because of five main causes: reinforcements arrived 'too late . . . or not at all'; the German wire was 'in many places in astonishingly good condition'; the Germans put up 'an unexpectedly strong resistance in their first and second trenches'; the fire from German machine-guns was so effective that a 'breakthrough was unthinkable'; and, most encouraging of all for the Germans, the British junior officers had shown a complete 'lack of leadership' after their men had penetrated the German lines.[14]

Yet while German intelligence acknowledged, in the aftermath of 1 July 1916, that 'French soldiers are better trained and more skilful than the British', and showed 'more independence' when their officers were killed,[15] it also accepted that the British would not allow their huge first-day casu-alties to derail their offensive. 'We can be pretty sure,' stated an intelligence report of 4 July, 'that they will continue to pursue their aim by new attacks, perhaps backed up by even more artillery and ammunition . . . The British have invested too many hopes in the success of this attack for them to be deflected from their course by an initial failure.'[16]

The Germans also had to contend with the French who, on 2 July, made significant gains south of the Somme. That same day, to stop the rot, Falkenhayn rushed to the Second Army headquarters at Saint-Quentin and sacked a corps commander and Below's chief of staff, General Grünert, replacing the latter with Colonel Fritz von Lossberg, a defensive specialist. Falkenhayn also promised reinforcements in the shape of four infantry divisions and thirty-eight heavy artillery batteries (many taken from Verdun). But there were to be no more withdrawals. If a foot of ground was lost, Falkenhayn told Below, it was to be retaken by an immediate counter-attack, 'even to the use of the last man'. Below's 3 July order of the day read:

> The decisive issue of the war depends on the victory of the Second Army on the Somme. We must win this battle in spite of the enemy's temporary superiority in artillery and infantry . . . For the present the important thing is to hold our current positions at any cost and to improve them by local counter-attacks. I forbid the evacuation of trenches . . . The enemy should have to carve his way over heaps of corpses.[17]

1 July 1916: 'An atmosphere of tense expectation'
– First day of the Somme: The Home perspective

Vera Brittain and her friend Betty, a fellow nurse, spent the afternoon of the battle at a performance of Brahms' Requiem in Southwark Cathedral. She remembered:

> In the cool darkness of the Cathedral, so quieting after the dusty, reeking streets of Camberwell, we listened, with aching eyes, to the solemn words in their lovely, poignant setting . . .
>
> When the organ had throbbed away into silence, we came out from the dim, melodious peace to hear the shouting of raucous voices, and to see newspaper boys with huge posters running excitedly up and down

the pavement. Involuntarily I clutched Betty's arm, for the posters ran: 'GREAT BRITISH OFFENSIVE BEGINS'.

A boy thrust a *Star* into my hand, and shivering with cold in the hot sunshine, I made myself read it.

Under the headline 'FRONT LINE BROKEN OVER 16 MILES', Brittain discovered that the attack had begun at 7.30 that morning on a twenty-mile front north of the Somme, and that 'the British troops have already occupied the German front lines'.[1]

She was particularly alarmed by the news because she knew her brother Edward's battalion had been due to play a prominent part in the attack. A few days earlier, using their pre-agreed code, he had written: 'I am sure you will be interested to hear that we have quite a lot of celery growing near our present position . . . It is ripening quickly although it is being somewhat delayed by this cold and wet weather, and . . . I expect it will be ready in under a week.' ('The celery is ripe' was the obscure phrase they had chosen to indicate the imminence of a major attack).[2]

She also knew that many casualties were expected because, towards the end of June, her hospital in Camberwell was cleared of convalescents and told to 'prepare for a great rush of wounded'. She wrote later: 'The sickening, restless apprehension of those days reminded me of the week before Loos . . . Hour after hour, as the convalescents departed, we added to the long rows of waiting beds, so sinister in their white, expectant emptiness.'[3]

On 30 June, having received a brief pencil-written note from Edward, bidding her 'adieu', she replied: 'There seems to be an atmosphere of tense expectation about all the world, and a sense of anguished fore-knowledge of the sacrifice that is to be made . . . Adieu, then, if it must be. But I still prefer to say, and believe, what I said before at Piccadilly Circus – "Au Revoir."'[4]

A day later, having read the first accounts of the battle, Brittain relied on the 'mechanical habit of work' to get her through the evening. 'For the whole of my conscious mind,' she wrote, 'resolved itself into one speculation: Was Edward still in the world, or not?' For the next three days she 'lived and worked in hourly dread of a telegram', not helped by the news, on Monday 3 July, that 'the first rush of wounded was on its way to Camberwell'.[5]

On 4 July, shortly before the usual 9.30 a.m. 'break' for biscuits and apron-changing, Brittain heard the 'Fall In' herald the arrival of the first ambulances. 'On my way to the dining-hall,' she recalled,

> I went – as I had gone at every available opportunity for the past three days – to the V.A.D. sitting room to take another fearful glance at the letter-rack, and there, high above the other letters, I saw a crushed pencil-scrawled envelope addressed in Edward's handwriting. In a panic of relief – for at least he couldn't be dead – I pulled it down, but even then I could hardly open it, for the paper was so thin and my fingers shook so.
>
> The little note was dated July 1st, and the written words were faint and uneven. 'DEAR VERA,' it said, 'I was wounded in the action this morning in left arm and right thigh not seriously. Hope to come to England. EDWARD.'[6]

For a moment the 'empty room spun round'; then Brittain remembered 'the waiting ambulances and the Sister's injunction to "hurry back"', and the fact that her parents would not get a letter in Macclesfield for another twenty-four hours. Determined to relieve their 'cruel anxiety', and 'regardless of the indignant glances of Sisters who knew that V.A.D.s were only allowed to run in cases of haemorrhage or fire', she 'dashed like a young hare down the stone corridor to the telephone' and asked her uncle at the National Provincial Bank 'to wire to the family'.[7]

This time fortune had shone on the Brittains: Edward had narrowly survived the costliest day in the British Army's history. Other families were not so lucky, particularly those with friends and relations in the same Pals battalion. 'When the news came through it was terrible,' remembered seventeen-year-old Edith Storey from Sheffield. 'Several of the boys I went to Sunday School with had joined the Sheffield Pals. We'd grown up together and they'd all joined together as a crowd . . . Dad came in and said he had something very sad to tell me. They'd all been killed on the Somme. I was devastated.'[8]

At Methil, on the east coast of Scotland, the villagers crowded round the grocer's shop window when the Somme casualty lists were first put up. 'As people read them,' recalled Maud Cox, the then six-year-old

British nurse Vera Brittain remembered the 'sickening,
restless apprehension' as she waited for news.

daughter of the grocer, 'they shouted out to friends, who were too far
away to see, "You're all right, your lad's not on it." Then you'd hear
somebody start to cry. I remember one time going outside and there was
a woman . . . rolling on the pavement and screaming her head off.' She
had six children, with barely a year between them, and had just found
out her husband was dead.[9]

Such was the unprecedented number of casualties on 1 July 1916 – more
soldiers were killed in a single day than had been during the first four
months of the war – that some families were hit by multiple deaths. A
widow called Lydia Ayre lost both sons and both nephews, all officers
(three in the Royal Newfoundland Regiment and one in the 8th Suffolks).
'By their death,' reported one newspaper, 'Mrs Ayre has lost every member
of her family.'[10] Mary Donaldson of Ballyloughlan in County Down had
three sons: Samuel (aged twenty-one), James (twenty-three) and John
(twenty-six). All had volunteered to join the 13th Royal Irish Rifles (County
Down), had been posted to the same company (B), and had died within
yards of each other on 1 July. A similar fate befell another three brothers

from Ulster, Privates Andrew, David and Robert Hobbs of the 9th Royal Irish Fusiliers; a fourth brother, Herbert, was wounded in the same attack at Thiepval but survived.[11]

Unlike the families of officers, who were informed of their fate by telegram, the Donaldsons and Hobbses received from the postman a plain buff-coloured envelope with the letters OHMS (On His Majesty's Service) on the outside. Opening it with trembling hands, they found Army Form B104-82B which read: 'It is my painful duty to inform you that a report has been received from the War Office notifying the death of —'. It added (in a recent refinement), a paragraph expressing the 'sympathy' of 'Their Gracious Majesties the King and Queen' as well as the 'regret' of the Army Council.[12]

More fortunate relatives would have opened Army Forms B104-80 and later 81, covering non-fatal wounds, and B104-83 that notified kin of soldiers missing in action. Many of the latter, however, were never found and the families were left in limbo. 'My brother had only been in France fighting on the Somme for a matter of weeks when we heard he was missing,' recalled Londoner Joyce Crow, then aged eight. 'And that was the awfulness, not knowing . . . You felt you were letting your brother down if you doubted he was alive, because there was always hope, however small.' A year or two later came final confirmation in the shape of Army Form 82A: '. . . no further news having been received relative to — the Army Council have been regretfully constrained to conclude that he is dead.' The bodies of more than 40 per cent of British fatalities in the Great War have no known grave.[13]

A day after hearing that her brother had been wounded in the 1 July offensive, Vera Brittain was preparing dressing-trays in a ward full of 'acute surgical cases' when she was hailed by a panting VAD: 'I say, *Do* you know your brother's in J ward?'

'*What?*' replied Brittain, almost dropping the dressing bowls. 'Edward in J?'

'Honestly, he is. I've just been washing him. Sorry I can't stop – only got permission to come over and tell you.'

With the blessing of the Matron, and 'half-dazed with surging emotions', she rushed over to J ward to see him. 'Half way down the ward,' she wrote, a blue pyjama-clad arm began to wave, and the next moment I was beside his bed. For a minute or two we gazed at each other in tremulous silence. One of his sleeves, I saw, was empty and the arm beneath it stiff and bandaged, but I noticed with relief . . . that the outer bandage was spotless . . . He seemed . . . gayer and happier than he had been all through his leave. The relief of having the great dread faced and creditably over was uppermost in his mind just then;* it was only later, as he gradually remembered all he had been through on July 1st, that [his friends] Victor and Geoffrey and I realised that the Battle of the Somme had profoundly changed him and added ten years to his age.[14]

The first day of the battle had also, thanks to the crippling losses suffered by Kitchener's battalions, swept away the young men of whole communities. Gone for ever was the patriotic enthusiasm of August 1914, leaving only a dogged determination to continue the fight, and a weary lament for lost youth. 'By 1916,' wrote Vera Brittain, 'the optimistic ideals of earlier years had all but disappeared from the title-page of my ingenious journal.' They were replaced by a four-line verse by Paul Verlaine that, in Brittain's opinion, perfectly encapsulated 'the heavy sense of having lived so long and been through so much that descended upon the boys and girls of my generation after a year or two of war':

> Qu'as tu fait, ô toi que voilà
> Pleurant sans cesse,
> Dis, qu'as tu fait, toi que voilà
> De ta jeunesse?[15]
> (What have you done, O you over there
> Constantly crying,
> Tell me what you have done, you over there
> With your youth?)

---

* 'For conspicuous gallantry and leadership' on 1 July, continuing to lead his men until he was wounded a second time, Second Lieutenant Edward Brittain of the 11th Sherwood Foresters was awarded the Military Cross (*The Times*, 21 October 1916).

14 July 1916: *'The best day we have had this war'*
– The assault on Bazentin Ridge

U nder the cover of darkness, the kilted Highlanders of the 10th Argylls left the front-line trench near Bernafay Wood and crept into no man's land where the battalion adjutant had laid out white tape to mark the jumping-off point for the various platoons. 'Unfortunately the Boche was shelling No Man's Land hard,' recalled Captain Neil Weir, commanding B Company, 'and naturally we had some casualties. I thought that the men's groans would give our positions away, but the Boche didn't seem to suspect anything.'[1]

His four platoons were lined up, one behind the other, on the right of the battalion's two-company front. Their objective was 'to capture and consolidate the line from the cross roads' in the nearby village of Longueval 'to a point called Piccadilly about 200 yards to the left'. But first they had to remain undetected in no man's land until dawn when a brief five-minute hurricane bombardment would herald the start of the second major British 'push' on the Somme. Weir recalled:

> It was a dreadful and damp wait but as the dawn came so our guns started until they reached a tremendous intensity and at a real outburst from the 18 pounders just behind us, we knew that it was time for us to go forward and raising ourselves from our cramped positions we moved first at a walk and then broke into a double over the 400 yards that separated us from our friend the Boche.
>
> . . . We could see little for smoke caused by the explosion of our shells and mortars. The noise too was terrific and yet I could distinctly hear the 'tap-tap' of the Boche machine guns away to our right. In such circumstances men get out of all control and consequently my two front platoons dashed on towards their objective meeting with little opposition. Unfortunately we were too quick for the gunners who had not lifted, and so these keen men dashed into their own barrage. This did not help matters so we came back 50 yards or so and got back into some kind of formation.
>
> We then advanced once more and reached the cross roads at Longueval at the same time as the Black Watch on our right.[2]

Amid the euphoria of the 9th (Scottish) Division's successful advance, Weir was shocked when men from two neighbouring battalions, the 8th Black Watch and 7th Seaforths, 'hauled some 50 odd Boche prisoners out of a deep dug-out and setting them out in the square were about to shoot them wholesale' until the Argylls intervened. 'Luckily we were able to stop it,' noted Weir, 'as assuredly they would have shot them. The Boche doubled down towards our back lines – willingly!'[3]

It was now barely 5 a.m., the attack having started in darkness at 3.25 a.m., and with his platoons well dug in and his company headquarters established in a large dug-out ('evidently an old Boche Headquarters') in the centre of the village, Weir went off to make contact with battalion headquarters. He found Colonel Tweedie and his adjutant, Captain Stevenson, 'in a big shell hole' in nearby Clarges Street. Both were suffering from minor wounds – Tweedie was 'very deaf' from a bomb explosion, and Stevenson had been hit in the finger – but the worst casualties were in A Company which had advanced on Weir's left. With its ranks severely depleted and only one officer still standing, it had been relieved by C Company in the new front line.[4]

The road that separated C Company from Weir's position was, recalled the latter, 'a perfect death trap as the Boche had snipers and a machine gun playing down the road. Consequently all were cautioned not to cross the road. However poor Dickerson [Officer Commanding No. 6 Platoon] was killed in crossing at the double and we buried him just near our redoubt.' Weir had now lost two officers and his company sergeant major killed, and a sergeant wounded.[5]

The 'chief excitement in the afternoon' was the break-out of eight Germans from a concealed dug-out just behind Weir's headquarters. They assailed No. 7 Platoon with bombs, 'were soon surrounded' and, having 'put up a sturdy fight', were 'all killed'. Weir's diary for the day concluded:

Now if all had gone well, the 27th Brigade should have right wheeled and occupied the North East of the village in front of us. This they failed to do as the Boche had got back into some strong points up there although my bombers had cleared them out in the morning. The 27th Brigade spent all the day trying to clear and reach their objective but failed to do so. Thus 'B' Company were holding the front line in a very disadvantageous position . . . The Boche were very quiet. What were they up to?[6]

The answer, according to a recent history of the battle from the German perspective, is that the forty-six separate British attacks on the Somme from 2 to 13 July – capturing La Boisselle, Contalmaison and Mametz Wood at a cost of 25,000 men – had caused Falkenhayn's troops to lose the initiative and remain 'constantly off balance'.[7] Falkenhayn acknowledged the crisis when he appointed General Max von Gallwitz as the new commander of the unified Somme front from 14 July. But it would take time for him to co-ordinate a response to this latest attack, the largest since the first day of the battle.

The British plan on 14 July was for two corps to attack the German second position between Longueval and Bazentin-le-Petit. Using eighteen times the weight of shell delivered on the 1st, the bombardment began on 11 July and continued for three days. 'The whole horizon,' noted a British observer, 'seemed to be bursting shells in front of us, and behind us flashing guns.'[8]

Four divisions were assigned to the assault: the 21st and 7th of XV Corps on the left, and the 3rd and 9th of XIII Corps on the right, with the 18th Division supporting the attack by clearing Trône Woods. The task of Weir's brigade, the 26th, was to take Waterlot Farm and the lower part of the village of Longueval while its sister brigades, the 27th and South African, took upper Longueval and Delville Wood respectively.

At General Rawlinson's insistence – and much against Haig's better judgement – the attack began before dawn, after a brief hurricane bombardment, with the assaulting troops protected by a 'creeping' barrage of high-explosive shells that lifted fifty yards every one and a half minutes to give the Germans no time to man their machine-guns before the enemy was upon them. By mid-morning more than 6,000 yards of the German second position – including the villages of Bazentin-le-Petit, Bazentin-le-Grand and part of Longueval and Delville Wood – were in British hands.

Much has been written of the lost opportunity to make further progress beyond Bazentin-le-Petit to the Pozières–Combles Ridge, dominated by High Wood. Led to believe by an early reconnaissance report that the wood

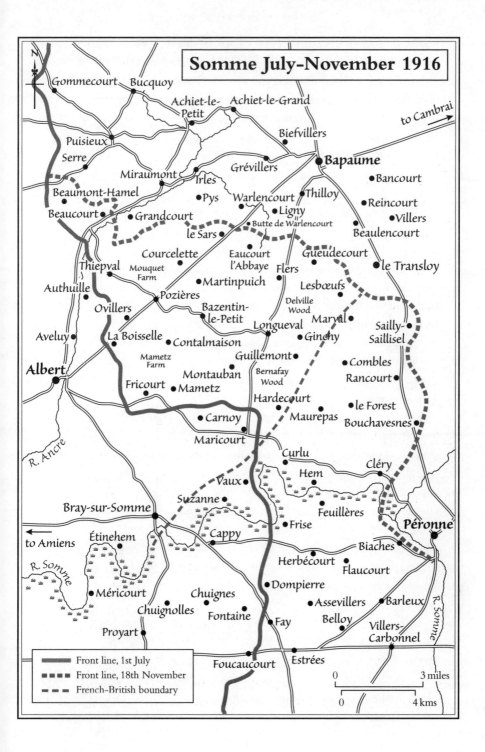

Somme July–November 1916

N

to Cambrai

Gommecourt · Bucquoy
Achiet-le-Petit · Achiet-le-Grand
Biefvillers
Puisieux
Serre
Miraumont · Irles · Grévillers · **Bapaume**
Beaumont-Hamel · Pys · Warlencourt · Thilloy · Bancourt
Beaucourt · Grandcourt · Ligny · Reincourt
le Sars · Butte de Warlencourt · Villers
Courcelette · Eaucourt · Gueudecourt · Beaulencourt
Thiepval · Mouquet Farm · l'Abbaye · Flers · le Transloy
Authuille · Martinpuich · Lesbœufs
Ovillers · Pozières · Bazentin-le-Petit · Delville Wood · Marval
Aveluy · La Boisselle · Longueval · Ginchy · Sailly-Saillisel
La Boisselle · Contalmaison
Mametz Farm · Guillemont · Combles
Albert · Montauban · Bernafay Wood · Rancourt
Fricourt · Mametz · Hardecourt · le Forest
Carnoy · Maurepas · Bouchavesnes
Maricourt
Curly · Cléry
R. Ancre · Vaux · Hem
Suzanne · Feuillères · **Péronne**
Bray-sur-Somme · Cappy · Frise
Étinehem · Biaches
to Amiens · Herbécourt · Flaucourt
R. Somme · Méricourt · Dompierre
Chuignes · Asseviller · Barleux
Chuignolles · Fontaine · Belloy
Proyart · Fay · Villers-Carbonnel
Foucaucourt · Estrées

	Front line, 1st July
	Front line, 18th November
	French-British boundary

0   3 miles
0   4 kms

was undefended, the commander of 7th Division asked for permission to occupy it with infantry. This was refused because it was the task of the 2nd Indian Cavalry Division to exploit any breakthrough. By 9.30 a.m., having been delayed by congested roads and unfamiliar ground, the leading cavalry brigade was ready to advance from the old British front line. But it was held there because the situation ahead was unclear. Eventually an infantry brigade was ordered to occupy the wood with cavalry support, but it took so long to move forward that the attack did not begin until 7 p.m. Even then the British found Germans dug in along the rear edge of the wood – where they had been all day – and so went to ground facing them. 'It would have been suicidal,' noted the historian William Philpott, 'to push through woodland against a defended trench line.'[9]

However, two squadrons of supporting cavalry from the 7th Dragoon Guards and Deccan Horse did manage to penetrate between two German battalions to the right of High Wood, killing or capturing more than a hundred in open cornfields before dismounting to hold their ground with rifles and machine-guns. They had lost eight dead and fewer than 100 wounded in this effective little action, causing Haig to comment: 'All the cavalry are much heartened by this episode and think that their time is soon coming.'[10]

Meanwhile, on XIII Corps' front, a series of determined counter-attacks by a fresh German division, the 7th, had prevented Weir's 9th Division from completing the capture of either Longueval or Delville Wood. Yet overall the operation was judged a great success, with General Foch congratulating Haig on his troops' fine performance.[11] They had, at a cost of 9,000 men, broken through the second German position, the last of the heavily wired defensive systems that they had had to face on 1 July (though, in the interim, the German third position had been made as, if not more, formidable). Haig himself described 14 July as the 'best day we have had this war',[12] no small endorsement in the context of almost two years of combat.

Later that month the attacks on the Somme continued with imperial troops (Australians and South Africans) taking Pozières and Delville Wood. The battle for the wood – 'a thick tangle of trees, chiefly oak and birch, with dense hazel thickets intersected by grassy rides' – was particularly brutal. 'We moved forward through an orchard in single file, led by the platoon officer,' remembered Hugh Boustead of the 1st South

African Brigade. 'Smith, the Second Lieutenant, got through, but the next seven who followed him were shot dead in a circle of a few yards, picked off by clean shooting without a murmur.'[13]

For six days (15–20 July) the South Africans were shelled from three sides, at a rate of up to 400 shells per minute, and faced constant German counter-attacks. Boustead was wounded on the fifth day and remembers feeling only relief that now he would 'get some sleep'.[14] His comrades held on, but when they were relieved only 143 of the original brigade of 3,153 were unscathed.[15]

By 31 July, the Germans had lost 160,000 men; the British and French more than 200,000. Yet the line had moved barely three miles since 1 July. North of the Ancre, or along half the original front, it had scarcely moved at all.[16] Even so, the first month of the battle was to prove the German supremo Falkenhayn's undoing. Coming so soon after the disappointments of Verdun and the Brusilov offensive, the break-ins on the Somme (both French and British) cost Falkenhayn his remaining military and political support. In August, shortly after Romania had joined the Entente, he was sacked as chief of the Oberkommando des Heere, or Army High Command, and replaced by Paul von Hindenburg, one of the two heroes of Tannenberg; the other, Erich Ludendorff, was appointed Chief Quartermaster-General (nominally Hindenburg's deputy, but in practice they formed a highly effective partnership).

15 September 1916: *'It was a phantasmagoric vision'*
– The tank attack at Flers

'There was a fresh morning breeze which eased our cramped limbs,' wrote a Bavarian soldier in a trench near High Wood on the Somme, 'but the waiting, the perpetual tension and the uncertainty had left us exhausted. We had just set about getting something to eat when all at once a thousand-voiced throaty scream came at us from the sky, and a long chain of flashing impacts announced that the *Trommelfeuer* [bombardment] had returned.'[1]

For three days the trenches of the German second and third positions between Flers and Courcelette, a front of 9,000 yards, had been the target of more than 1,500 British guns. Now, as morning dawned and the bombardment began anew, the Germans were anticipating an attack – but not the means by which it was carried out.

The clues were there. By early August, some German units on the Somme knew that the British possessed armoured 'land cruisers' that could be used to attack trenches. The intelligence claimed they were 'very hard to hit and distinguish', admitted a German POW, 'and only a 15 cm direct hit was of any use in destroying them'. Yet no specific warning reached the front-line troops. Instead, wrote a Bavarian lieutenant, they could hear from the British lines 'a most peculiar gurgling, scraping and grinding, as if from engines of some kind. We had never heard anything quite so sinister, inexplicable or noisy.' Their best assumption was that the British were using engines to dig tunnels.[2] They would soon discover the truth.

As early as October 1914 a visionary officer of the Royal Engineers, Colonel Ernest Swinton, had proposed the construction of an 'armoured vehicle immune against bullets, which should be capable of destroying machine guns and of ploughing a way through wire'. He imagined it to have tracks, or 'caterpillars', similar to those in use on agricultural vehicles since the turn of the century. The idea was taken up by his superior, Maurice Hankey, and presented to the War Cabinet on Boxing Day 1914 as a machine-gun-armed, caterpillar-track-driven, armoured vehicle capable of crushing barbed wire and providing support for advancing infantry. This paper caught the eye of Winston Churchill, then First Lord of the Admiralty, who in February 1915 established the Admiralty Landships Committee to develop the idea. The first prototype 'Little Willie' – the brainchild of William Tritton, managing director of the agricultural machinery manufacturer Foster's, and a motor-vehicle designer called Lieutenant Walter Wilson RNVR – was ready by December 1915. A month later a larger and gun-equipped version, 'Mother', had been produced, and by September a fleet of forty-nine similar Mark I 'tanks', as they had been named to fool the Germans, were in France ready for action.[3]

The tank crews were mostly motor enthusiasts like William Dawson, a twenty-seven-year-old from Boston in Lincolnshire, who had joined the Motor Machine Gun Service in February 1916 after answering an advertisement in the *Motor Cycle* magazine. Shortly after training began at Bisley, Dawson and his fellow recruits were asked if they would volunteer for a 'new secret service'. He remembered: 'No details could be given except that it was connected with motoring. This, of course, was the bait and we all volunteered.'[4]

In May 1916, by which time they had trained only on machine-guns and 6-pounders, the recruits were told they would henceforth be known as the Heavy Section, Machine Gun Corps (the precursor to the Tank Corps). This outraged some who thought it a downgrade, causing a staff officer (possibly Swinton) to explain 'that the new project was so very very secret that he could give no details, but that it was most important and . . . we should get all the motoring we could ever wish for'.[5]

Those who stayed were moved to a secret camp and training ground on Lord Iveagh's estate near Thetford in Norfolk. Its perimeter, wrote Dawson, was 'guarded day and night by 500 or more reservists fully armed with rifles and ammunition'. Inside they constructed trenches and dug large holes, the purpose of which was about to become clear. Dawson recalled: 'Early one morning, just after daylight, we were awakened by a rumbling and rattling . . . In great excitement everybody rushed out of their tents, just as they had slept, and there they were, the first of the tanks, passing our tents to the practice ground which we had prepared.' The tanks were the prototypes 'Little Willie' and 'Mother', the latter the template for all Mark I battle tanks. 'We immediately started to learn its mechanism and engine,' wrote Dawson, 'and commenced driving it round the course of three to four feet high obstructions, shell and mine craters which we had made.'[6]

Soon after the appearance of 'Little Willie' and 'Mother', armour-plated battle tanks began to arrive. There were two types: the 'male', mounted with two 6-pounder guns and three Hotchkiss machine-guns; and the slightly narrower 'female', armed with four Vickers machine-guns. Both were twenty-six feet long, travelled at two miles per hour and carried a crew of eight. The name 'tank', according to Dawson, was a deliberate ploy to fool German spies. When they were shipped to France they were described as mobile Russian water tanks, and marked as such. 'It is doubtless through this,' wrote Dawson, 'that such extraordinary machines acquired such a nondescript name which has continued ever since.'[7]

The culmination of Dawson's training was a full demonstration in front of a crowd of VIPs – among them King George V, Sir Douglas

Haig, Winston Churchill, Lloyd George and even one or two French generals – over a practice battlefield that included German and British front lines, no man's land, communication trenches, barbed wire, shell-holes, mine craters, dug-outs and machine-gun emplacements. Dawson recalled: 'With trenches so splendidly built and strong, with new sandbags all so very symmetrical and true as for an exhibition, and everything being dry, every tank made a good show. It was all so different from what we were to be faced with in our first battle actions.'[8]

Haig was later criticized for using his new secret weapon prematurely. With fewer than fifty tanks at his disposal on 15 September, thanks to production bottlenecks, he had been advised by both Lloyd George and Asquith to wait until he had enough for a massed attack. Yet Haig felt that the Germans were close to cracking on the Somme, and that to speed up the process he must use every weapon available.[9] There was also the danger that the Germans would find out about the tank and, in Brigadier-General Charteris's words, devise 'a suitable reply'.[10]

The primary objective of the Battle of Flers–Courcelette – launched

A British Mark I tank – C19 – prior to the first armoured action in history at Flers–Courcelette on 15 September 1915.

in conjunction with a French attack on both sides of the Somme – was to complete the capture of the German second position and, if all went well, to push through the third to Bapaume. Rawlinson was keen to do this in stages, not least because the last German defensive line was beyond the reach of most of his artillery; but Haig insisted on an all-out attack by three corps – III, XV and XIV – using nine fresh and retrained divisions, with three tired infantry and five cavalry divisions in reserve. Reserve Army's Canadian Corps would support the left flank by assaulting Courcelette.[11] Haig has been criticized for planning a decisive breakthrough at Flers–Courcelette in which all-arms would help to roll up the German defensive line, allowing British armies further north to join in the rout. But, as William Philpott has argued, Haig would have been more remiss if the attack on 15 September had succeeded and he had not had a follow-up plan in place.[12]

With only forty-nine tanks available, they were spread across the battlefield and assigned particular German strongpoints as their objectives. Their job was to crush wire, neutralize machine-gun posts and protect infantry. They were supported by 1,563 artillery pieces (406 of heavy and medium calibre) firing high-explosive shells to cut wire, gas shells (never before used by the British) to neutralize German guns, long-range interdiction and a creeping shrapnel barrage – at a slower speed and a greater concentration than formerly.

The most successful attack was in the centre where the tanks of D Company had been ordered to help the 41st Division capture the village of Flers behind the German third position. Three tanks – D9, D14 and D17, commanded by Second Lieutenants Hatton, Court and Hastie – were told 'not to deviate, but to make straight for Flers'. Hatton recalled: 'Court in D14 started. Before he had gone two or three hundred yards he attempted to cross a disused support trench, and as he crossed it, the tank – weighing twenty-eight tons – crumbled the parapet beneath him, and the tail of his tank disappeared into the trench.'[13]

In attempting to tow D14 out, Hatton got the sponson on the side of his tank tangled with one on Court's, immobilizing both. They climbed on to their tanks to watch the battle. 'The last I saw of Hastie,' recalled Hatton, 'he was headed in a straight line for Flers.'[14]

As Second Lieutenant Stuart Hastie, a twenty-seven-year-old graduate of Edinburgh University, slowly negotiated the shell-pocked road to Flers, a mile beyond the German front line, he could see the houses shrouded 'in smoke from the barrage which had come down on top of it'. D17's steering gear had been hit early in the attack, so the driver kept the tank in a straight line 'by putting on the brake on each track alternately'. Having crossed the Flers Trench, the last obstacle before the village, D17's engine began 'to knock very badly', but on they went. Hastie recalled:

> We made our way up the main street, during which time my gunners had several shots at various people who were underneath the eaves, or even in the windows of some of the cottages. We went on down through the high street, as far as the first right angle bend . . . At this point, we had to make up our minds what to do. The engine was really in such a shocking condition, that it was liable to let us down at any moment . . . I could see no signs of the British army coming up behind me, so I slewed the tank round with great difficulty on the brakes, and came back to Flers Trench, and turned the tank to face the Germans again.[15]

An artillery observer in the Royal Flying Corps had spotted Hastie as he made his way through the village, and his report reached the British press as 'a tank is walking up the High Street of Flers with the British infantry cheering behind'.[16] In truth the infantry of 41st Division were lagging behind and, according to a lieutenant of the East Surreys, those 'laughing Tommies' were actually a group of Germans with chattering teeth'.[17]

Minutes after meeting British infantry digging in at the southern end of the village, Hastie's tank was hit by artillery fire and abandoned.* But D17 was not the only tank to reach Flers. Four others crossed the Flers Trench, which had been abandoned by panicked troops of the 9th Bavarian Reserve Regiment, and strafed the village from its western flank, helping to knock out strongpoints and disrupt a German counter-attack.[18]

Two more tanks – D6 and D5 – got well beyond Flers. D6 helped men of the 26th Royal Fusiliers advance up the east side of the village, destroyed a battery on a rise to the north-east, and was finally knocked out by artillery fire as it approached the Gird Trench in front of Guedecourt. Its commander, Reginald Legge, was mortally wounded by rifle fire and only three crew escaped. Further to the east, D5 took advantage of a hidden valley to surprise an artillery detachment and reach Gird Trench,

---

* For his actions that day Hastie was awarded the Military Cross.

the furthest advance that day. With no infantry support, it turned back and was hit and abandoned south-east of Flers.[19]

Elsewhere the tank/infantry co-operation was less successful. Tanks arrived late on both sides of the 41st Division, causing the infantry of the 14th and New Zealand Divisions to advance into heavy machine-gun fire until the German panic in the centre spread right and left. Both divisions came up on either side of Flers, escorted by their remaining tanks, but were stopped from reaching their final objective by German artillery firing over open sights.

In XIV Corps' sector, to the south, most of the supporting tanks failed to arrive and the three attacking divisions – the Guards, 6th and 56th – were badly cut up by machine-guns which should have been knocked out by artillery fire and armour. The Guards pressed on regardless, driving the 7th Bavarian Regiment before them, and eventually reached a trench close to their objective of Lesbœufs before a counter-attack drove them back to an intermediate position. Raymond Asquith, a brilliant scholar and the Prime Minister's eldest son, was killed in this attack;* two future Cabinet ministers, Harold Macmillan and Harry Crookshank, were badly wounded.[20]

William Dawson's tank, C20, was tasked with supporting the 6th Division in its attack on the Quadilateral Redoubt. He recorded: 'The briefing and instructions regarding objectives were quite inadequate and there was little or no co-operation between the infantry and the tanks. We reached a point which we believed was our objective and after a while as our petrol was getting low, we had to return some distance where we were joined by the other tank in our section. Both it and ourselves came up against machine gun fire with armour piercing bullets† and whilst we had a few holes I counted upwards of 40 in the other tank.'[21]

On the left, III Corps captured High Wood (two months after British troops had reported it empty of defenders) and Martinpuich village, though not without severe casualties – some caused by one tank shooting

---

* Asquith's death prompted his heartbroken father to write: 'Whatever pride I had in the past, and whatever hope I had for the future – by much the largest part of both was invested in him. Now all that has gone. It will take me a few days more to get back my bearings' (Asquith, *Memories and Reflections*, II, p. 158).
† Intended for use against snipers' shields.

at infantry as they entered the wood. Even more successful was the Reserve Army's assault on Courcelette, with the 2nd Canadian Division securing the village in the afternoon. 'It was a phantasmagoric vision,' wrote a German defender on seeing his first tank, 'this giant in the light of dawn, its nose rearing up from a shell-hole, then lurching on, slowly – no doubt – but with a horrid sense of purpose.'[22]

By now the situation behind the front was chaotic, according to the future German Chancellor Franz von Papen (an operations officer of the 4th Guards Division) who 'hurriedly collected batmen, cooks, orderlies and clerks from our own divisional headquarters and from a few neighbouring formations, and with them produced signs of activity as if fresh reserves had arrived'. He added: 'In fact there was not a single reserve company for scores of miles behind us. A complete tactical break-through, the achievement of which the enemy dreamed, had taken place, although they did not seem to realize it.'[23]

Four thousand yards of the German third position had been captured at a cost of 29,000 casualties (equivalent to the losses on 1 July). But, as Papen suggests, Haig and his generals never knew how close they were to a general breakthrough and so kept the cavalry in reserve. The tanks had made a very real contribution to the success of the day. 'Certainly some of the Tanks have done marvels!' noted Haig in his diary, 'and have enabled our attack to progress at a surprisingly fast pace.'[24] But of the twenty-seven that reached the German front line, only three were serviceable the following day. The rest had succumbed to artillery fire, mechanical breakdown and uneven ground.[25]

24 October 1916: 'I have only one man left!'
– The French recover Fort Douaumont

A thick autumnal mist coated the Meuse hills above Verdun, as it had on the first day of the battle eight months earlier. For the previous four days, 650 French guns (half of them heavies) had fired 250,000 shells into the Fort Douaumont sector that the Germans had held since their bloodless coup de main on 25 February. The heavier pieces included two

400mm railway guns that had a longer range and greater penetrating power than even the Germans' Krupp 'Big Berthas'.[1]

The architect of this bombardment was a rising star of the French Army, artillerist General Robert Nivelle, fifty-eight years old, who had taken over day-to-day control of the battle in April when Pétain was promoted to command Army Group Centre. A month later Nivelle had made his first attempt to recapture Douaumont, using the 5th Division commanded by his right-hand man General Mangin (known to his men as 'the Butcher'). Though Mangin's troops managed to penetrate the superstructure, they were eventually driven off with heavy losses, and Nivelle was criticized for launching an attack without adequate artillery preparation and on too narrow a front.[2]

This time, to avoid a repetition, Mangin (now a corps commander) would use three divisions in the first line, followed by three more, with two in reserve. And when the attack went in, it would be protected by Nivelle's meticulously planned creeping barrage: the infantry advancing at a steady 100 yards in four minutes, 70 yards behind the field gun barrage and 150 yards from the heavy shells; and with telephone lines laid in trenches six feet deep to ensure constant communication between the infantry and the guns.[3]

Nivelle's last refinement was a ruse. On the afternoon of 22 October the guns fell silent and cheers ran along the French front line as if an attack was imminent. The German field guns, hitherto silent, began their counter-barrage on an empty no man's land, thus giving their positions away to the French medium 155mm guns who responded with suppressing fire. It continued for a day and a half, by which time only ninety of the Germans' original 158 batteries were still in action.[4]

Even more damage was done when the railway guns opened up on Douaumont Fort at noon on 23 October, their giant shells smashing through eight feet of concrete to wreak havoc in the interior. Gun casement after casement was destroyed, causing the fort commandant, Major Rosendahl, to evacuate the upper works. Then a shell penetrated through to an arms store in the heart of the fort, its detonation filling the corridors with fumes and flames. With large quantities of heavy French shells stored near by, Rosendahl feared a catastrophic explosion and ordered the fort's garrison to evacuate. All had left by nightfall, bar two soldiers manning the gallery in the distant north-west corner of the fort that had received the least attention from the French 400s. They were not told of the withdrawal and remained at their posts.[5]

At 7 a.m. on 24 October, a Hauptmann Prollius of the German Artillery entered the fort with a small squad of signallers and runners. Discovering the fires in the Pioneer Depot still burning, but no longer a danger to the store of shells, he decided to defend the fort with his two dozen men until reinforcements arrived. Before they could, the sound of bugles was heard from the French trenches. The attack was under way.[6]

Aided by their training on a battlefield replica, and by the lack of an immediate German counter-barrage (the remaining guns took twelve minutes to respond), the French assault troops were in the German front line before the defenders could react. The bastions of Fleury and Ouvrage de Thiaumont were captured within minutes, allowing the African troops of General Guyot de Salins' 38th Division to surge into the Ravin de la Dame where they secured a battalion commander and his staff. Another senior officer was taken in his underpants, and a French listening post intercepted the following message from a German commander: 'I have only one man left, all the others have run away.'[7]

At first Major Nicolai's Régiment Infanterie Coloniale de Maroc, the illustrious unit tasked with storming Fort Douaumont, got lost in the fog. But when it lifted for a moment, revealing the great dome of the fort in a patch of sunshine, Nicolai sent his men forward. With minimal opposition, they were quickly on to the glacis, from where engineers and skirmishers forced their way inside. For more than an hour a handful of defenders stalled the attack; but eventually they succumbed to French flamethrowers, grenades and bullets. It was not until that evening, however, that two French privates found Prollius, four officers and twenty-four men hiding in a cellar. Douaumont Fort was French once more. That it had been captured and then recaptured almost undefended was, as one French officer commented, 'a singular fate for a fort which during eight months had been the key to a field of battle watered with the blood of hundreds of thousands of men'.[8]

France rejoiced, and Nivelle's men redoubled their effort to recover more lost ground, retaking Fort Vaux (lost in early June) on 2 November and Louvermont and Bezonvaux on 15 December (an action in which Nicolai, promoted lieutenant-colonel and decorated with the Légion d'Honneur for his work on 24 October, was killed by a sniper). The terrible eight-month battle, the longest of the war, was finally over. It had

French soldiers at the entrance to Fort Douaumont after it was retaken from
the Germans on 24 October.

consumed more than a quarter of a million lives, with double that number
wounded. The French Army, thanks to its costly counter-offensives, had
suffered the lion's share of casualties: 400,000 to the Germans' 355,000.
It had also experienced the first ominous rumblings of discontent: when
President Poincaré arrived at Verdun in December to award gallantry
medals, he had stones thrown at his car by soldiers shouting 'Embusqués'
(shirkers); someone scrawled 'Chemin de l'Abbatoir' (Slaughterhouse
Way) on the road out of the town; and a whole division, bound for the
final offensive, began bleating like sheep.[9]

The meatgrinder that was Verdun had left the French Army close to
breaking point, and would cost General Joseph Joffre, the hero of the
Marne, his job as Commander-in-Chief. Joffre was blamed for neglecting
Verdun's defences and allowing the initial German breakthrough; for the
relative failure of his much heralded Anglo-French offensive on the
Somme; and also for refusing to reinforce the hard-pressed Romanian
Army in the autumn of 1916, thus contributing to the latter's rapid defeat
by Austro-German and Turkish forces. On 27 December, to sweeten the

pill of his sacking, Joffre was made a marshal of France and the government's 'technical military adviser' (a hollow post he soon resigned from).[10]

His replacement was not Foch or General Noël Edouard de Castelnau (Joffre's chief of staff), the obvious choices, or even Pétain, the hero of the early Verdun fighting. Instead it was the relatively junior Nivelle who, following the recapture of Fort Douaumont, was seen by most Allied politicians as the 'saviour' they had long sought. Tall, charming, cultured and eloquent, Nivelle had an almost hypnotic allure. Even Lloyd George, generally mistrustful of generals, was disarmed by Nivelle's perfect English (his mother was British) and steely self-confidence. It was, after all, Nivelle and not Pétain who had coined the famous Verdun promise: 'Ils ne passeront pas!' ('They will not pass!').[11] Now as Commander-in-Chief he used a new mantra: 'Our method has proved itself. Victory is certain, I give you my assurance.'[12]

But, despite Nivelle's late victories, no one could claim outright success at Verdun. 'The campaign of 1916,' wrote the future Chancellor Prince Max of Baden, 'ended in bitter disillusionment all round. We and our enemies had shed our best blood in streams, and neither we nor they had come one step nearer to victory. The word "deadlock" was on every lip.'[13]

The French Army was indeed 'bled white' by the fighting, as Falkenhayn had intended; but the German Army had also been badly weakened and was, by 1917, in no fit state to take advantage. Crown Prince Wilhelm, the German commander at Verdun, wrote: 'The Mill on the Meuse ground to powder the hearts as well as the bodies of the troops.'[14]

Typical of the carnage was the summit of the Mort Homme, described by a French sergeant in the winter of 1917 as resembling in places 'a rubbish dump in which there had been accumulated shreds of cloth, smashed weapons, shattered helmets, rotting rations, bleached bones and putrescent flesh'.[15]

18 November 1916: *'It was snowing hard and freezing'*
– The last day on the Somme

Long before dawn, the men of the 7th East Kents had to struggle through atrocious weather and cloying mud to be in position for the final attack of the four-month Somme offensive. 'It was snowing hard and freezing, and pitch dark,' recalled Private Rueben Smith. 'We were guided by the star shells from the firing line. It was impossible to follow the trench and too risky to get in it. I did get in it once and got stuck up to my waist in mud and ice-cold water.'[1]

Shortly before Zero Hour, 6.10 a.m., the British guns began a carefully targeted twenty-minute hurricane bombardment. 'It was the weirdest awe-inspiring sight I have ever seen – words fail,' wrote a medical officer. 'The guns' flashes were wonderful – sometimes battery fire – at others almost as quick as machine-gun fire . . . Overhead was the dull swish and clanking of our heavy shells. No Hun shells came over in reply.'[2]

As the guns lifted, the spearhead battalions of Private Smith's 55th Brigade advanced towards Desire Trench in front of Grandcourt on the Ancre river. Soon afterwards, according to Smith, 'a runner came back breathless and excited saying we had taken the trench'. But that was only partially true because in places the Germans had abandoned the front line and dug themselves in behind, filling the empty trench with barbed wire. Smith wrote: 'Some of our men fell into this trap in the dark, others lost their way and were surrounded and captured without a fight. The East Surreys on our left and the West Kents on our right were in the same predicament.'[3] Eventually, after more men had been sent forward, Desire Trench was secured and a communications trench dug back to the original British front line.

By the end of the day the troops of General Gough's Fifth Army had achieved mixed results: the three divisions of II Corps – from left to right the 19th, 18th and 4th Canadian – had secured most of Desire Trench and pushed the line closer to Grandcourt and the Ancre (though not quite as far as intended); north of the river the 32nd and 37th Divisions of V Corps had also made small gains beyond Beaumont-Hamel and Beaucourt – both of which had been captured during the first two days of the Battle of the Ancre, 13/14 November – yet the village of Serre, the rock on which the Pals battalions of the 31st Division had foundered on 1 July, remained in German hands.

This final battle on the Somme was part of Haig's more realistic strategy: to improve his tactical position before the winter, and to wear out the enemy. Despite some disquiet among politicians at home, Asquith was still broadly supportive of the offensive, telling Haig on a visit to

France in early September that 'he and the Government are well pleased with the way the operations have been conducted here, and he is anxious to help me in every way possible'.[4]

This was not entirely true. On a separate trip to the continent in mid-September Lloyd George, War Secretary since Kitchener's death, had asked General Foch 'why the British who had gained no more [ground] than the French, if as much, had suffered such heavy casualties!' He also asked Foch for his opinion of British generalship – an implicit criticism of Haig who, when he found out, was understandably furious. 'I would not have believed,' he noted in his diary, 'that a British Minister could have been so ungentlemanly as to go to a foreigner and put such questions regarding his own subordinates.'[5]

In truth Lloyd George's concern was not that the strategy of attrition was wrong; rather that it was being pursued prematurely before the Allies were adequately resourced. 'By next year,' he confided to Repington in July 1916, 'we should have a lot more men and guns, and the Russians the same; we should begin breaking the Germans down.'[6]

Haig was keen to start the process in 1916 and, since the introduction of tanks at Flers in mid-September, had authorized a series of mini-offensives on the Somme. At Morval on 25 September, for example, a well-planned and executed attack by General Horne's XV Corps had captured a single trench system. At the same time General Gough's Reserve Army (soon renamed the Fifth Army) took positions that had held out for two months: Mouquet Farm and Thiepval. On 29 September, encouraged by these successes and convinced that German reserves were almost exhausted, he ordered the Third, Reserve and Fourth Armies to plan ever more ambitious operations. Rawlinson, commanding the Fourth Army, was told to carry the Le Transloy line as the first phase in a push towards Cambrai, twenty miles away. The attack failed.

When a new attempt was ordered in early November, Lieutenant-General Lord 'Fatty' Cavan, the commander of XIV Corps, complained to Rawlinson that it had 'no chance of succeeding'. Cavan added: 'No one who has not visited the front trenches can really know the state of exhaustion to which the men are reduced. The conditions are far worse than in the First Battle of Ypres, and my General and Staff Officers agree that they are the worst they have seen, owing to the enormous distance of the carry of all munitions, food, water and ammunition.'[7]

This argument cut no ice with Haig, not least because he was under pressure from the French to keep attacking. 'Foch laid great stress,' noted Haig in his diary on 4 November, 'on the dangerously exposed position in which his troops would be north and northeast of Sailly Saillisal [sic] if we did not also press on, and asked me to give him a date when I would put in the attack with my Fifth Army.'[8] So the attack by XIV Corps went ahead as planned, and foundered as its commander had anticipated. But Cavan's complaint did prompt the despatch of a staff officer from GHQ, Major the Viscount Gort (the future field marshal and commander of the BEF in 1939–40), to investigate conditions at the front. Gort concluded that the Fourth Army's failure to advance was more down to 'physical exhaustion owing to mud and water which the men had been standing in and the resultant reduction in morale', than it was to the strength of German defences.[9] It was Gort's report, backed up by Rawlinson's assertion that his divisions were exhausted and needed a lengthy break from offensive operations, which finally prompted Haig to bring the fighting on the Somme to a close. But not before one last push by Gough's Fifth Army on the Ancre, the last day of which was 18 November.

In four and a half months of fighting, the furthest point of the Allied advance was at Lesbœufs, seven miles from the front line of 1 July. The British has lost a scarcely credible 420,000 men (131,000 killed), the French 204,000 and the Germans between 450,000 and 600,000.[10] In his despatch of 23 December 1916 – entitled 'The Opening of the Wearing-Out Battle' – Haig implied that he had never sought a decisive engagement (which was not true, though he had accepted the possibility that he might have to settle for attrition). Instead he claimed to have achieved his 'main objects': 'Verdun had been relieved; the main German forces had been held on the Western front; and the enemy's strength had been very considerably worn down.'[11]

Was Haig justified in making these claims? Most recent British scholars of the war think that he was. 'The Somme,' wrote Gary Sheffield, 'did bring about some tangible results. The Allied offensive indeed tipped the balance in favour of the French at Verdun where the battle had become stalemated. It put paid to a key plank of Falkenhayn's strategy, a counter-offensive to destroy what was left of Allied armies after they had been shattered by their own relief offensives.'[12]

In the opinion of William Philpott the battle ended in a 'pyrrhic victory' for the Allies 'that nevertheless reversed the fortunes of war; and a genuine moral victory in adversity over circumstances, the elements, and the enemy'. He added: 'It was the military turning point of the war . . . although two further years of hard fighting were necessary to assert Anglo-French superiority on the battlefield and deliver the *coup de grâce*.'[13]

Even Erich Ludendorff, co-commander of the German Army after August 1916, acknowledged the negative effect the Somme had had on Germany's prospects of ultimate victory. '[The leadership] had to bear in mind,' he wrote in retrospect, 'that the enemy's great superiority in men and material would be even more painfully felt in 1917 than in 1916. They had to face the danger that "Somme fighting" would soon break out at various points on our fronts, and that even our troops would not be able to withstand such attacks indefinitely, especially if the enemy gave us no time for rest and for the accumulation of material.'[14]

Grave of an unknown British soldier, Thiepval, Autumn 1916.

This type of grand strategic calculation, however, was of little concern to the families of the million or so casualties of the Somme, or, for that matter, to the surviving soldiers who had fought in such appalling conditions. An officer of the 63rd (Royal Naval) Division, a veteran of Gallipoli, could hardly believe his eyes when he reached the battlefield in autumn 1916: 'The Somme area was a God-forsaken battleground created by earnest staff officers now slightly hysterical about their still incomplete labours. An atmosphere of over-elaborated brusque inefficiency pervaded the hinterland of slaughter. Too many men, too many officers, far too many generals . . . and endless seas of mud.'[15]

But even the newcomers became quickly inured to the horror all around them. 'We are using the dead bodies of Fritz to step on in the trenches to get out of the mud,' wrote a Canadian private. 'We don't take any more notice of a dead person now than we do of a rat.'[16]

23 November 1916: *'The Englishman could not help falling'*
– A duel in the clouds

At 1 p.m. Major Lanoe Hawker VC DSO, Britain's first air ace, took off from Bertangles Aerodrome in northern France on a routine patrol with two of his squadron's senior pilots, Captain Jock Andrews and Lieutenant Bob Saundby. They were flying single-seater Airco DH2 biplanes, powered by rear-mounted rotary engines and armed with a forward-firing Lewis gun whose double drum magazine, ring gun sight and mounting Hawker had himself helped to design.[*1]

A twenty-five-year-old native of Hampshire, Hawker had originally joined the Royal Engineers as a regular; but such was his fascination with aeroplanes that he learned to fly at his own expense, receiving Aviator's Certificate No. 435 from the Royal Aero Club in March 1913. Transferring to the Royal Flying Corps a few days before Britain entered the war, he

---

* A noted innovator, Hawker had also introduced thigh-length sheepskin boots, known as 'fug-boots', to combat the risk of frostbite at high altitude.

was posted to France in October 1914 as a captain with No. 6 Squadron, flying Henri Farmans. But it was in a Bristol Scout that he managed the incredible feat of downing three German planes in a day in July 1915, thus earning a Victoria Cross.[2]

This was a period of the war when a single 'victory' was unusual, and the RFC had yet to emulate the German aircraft-designer Anthony Fokker by introducing a workable synchronizer gear that allowed machine-guns to fire 'through' the forward-mounted propellers of tractor planes like the Bristol. Instead Hawker's Bristol was armed with a Lewis gun that, to avoid the propeller, could only fire forward of his left side at a 45-degree angle.[3]

Promoted major in early 1916, Hawker was given the task of forming and commanding the RFC's first single-seater fighter squadron, No. 24. Inspired by Hawker's simple tactical philosophy of 'Attack Everything', 24 Squadron had helped to counter the scourge of the German Fokker Eindecker and later, during the Battle of the Somme, had shot down seventy enemy planes at a cost of just twelve of its own. This was in stark contrast to the general ratio of losses during the battle that, thanks to RFC commander Hugh Trenchard's determination to win air superiority over the front line at any cost, was weighted heavily *against* the RFC. In September 1916, for example, the Germans destroyed 127 British and French machines for the loss of just twenty-seven.[4]

By mid-1916, aware of the dangers, Trenchard had banned squadron commanders from operational flying. Typically Hawker ignored the veto and continued to make occasional offensive patrols and reconnaissance flights over the German lines. But they were becoming more dangerous as 24 Squadron's plane, the DH2, struggled to match the performance and speed of new German fighters like the Halberstadt DII and the even more advanced Albatros DI and DII. Hawker, moreover, was dangerously exhausted after two years of constant combat.[5]

A brief stint of leave in early November, during which he became engaged to his sweetheart Beatrice, seemed to rejuvenate Hawker. He expected to serve another two to three months in France before promotion to lieutenant-colonel and a cosy staff job. In the meantime it was business as usual, which was why he chose to accompany two of his senior pilots on a patrol over the German lines on 23 November.[6]

Flying 9,000 feet above Bapaume the trio spotted two slow-moving

German two-seaters below, described by Captain Andrews as 'a few fat Huns'.[7] Andrews was about to attack, but paused when he spotted a host of Albatros DIIs above him. Hawker, unaware of them, dived past his flight commander to get at the two-seaters, followed by one of the German scouts. Thus began a swirling dogfight as the remaining planes engaged each other. Andrews managed to drive off Hawker's original attacker before his plane was shot up and he was forced to limp home. Saundby's engine was also hit, and as he glided to safety he could see Hawker in a circling fight with another Albatros at 3,000 feet. Knowing Hawker's extraordinary flying ability (which had yielded him nine kills, the most by an RFC pilot to this date), Saundby was not overly concerned. But he might have been if he had known the identity of Hawker's assailant: Leutnant Manfred Freiherr* von Richthofen of the Imperial German Air Force's Jasta 2.[8]

A protégé of the German ace Oswald Boelcke – killed in a collision with one of his own planes a month earlier – Richthofen had already downed ten Allied planes in less than three months as a Jasta pilot. With Max Immelmann also dead, shot down by a British two-seater in June 1916, Richthofen had assumed the mantle of Germany's deadliest airman.

Born into the Silesian aristocracy in May 1892, Richthofen had emulated his cavalryman father by joining the 1st Uhlans (a reconnaissance regiment armed with lances) in 1911. He served with the Uhlans on the Eastern Front, capturing Kalisch in Russian Poland in August 1914, and was then transferred to the west where he took part in the invasion of France. But once the war of movement was over, he lost interest in the cavalry and in May 1915 wangled a transfer to the nascent 'Flying Service'. 'My greatest wish,' he wrote later, 'was fulfilled.'[9]

Richthofen spent the first year of his air service as an observer and pilot of two-seater planes, initially on the Eastern Front during the Gorlice–Tarnów offensive, and later in Belgium and France (though he returned briefly to Russia in June 1916 to help stem the Brusilov offensive). In late August 1916, still in Russia, he was invited by Oswald Boelcke to join Jagdstaffeln (or Jasta) 2, one of the new elite 'hunting squadrons' that were being formed on the Western Front to wrest control of the air back from the Allies. Each Jasta was equipped with the latest single-seater

* A rank of German or Austrian nobility, equivalent to a British baron.

fighters, namely the D-type Albatros and Halberstadt, both armed with twin machine-guns that fired through the propeller arc, and flown by selected pilots.

It was in his new Albatros DII that Richthofen shot down his first British plane, a large two-seater bomber, killing both the pilot and the observer, near Cambrai on 17 September 1916. During the next two months, inspired by his commander Boelcke whose own 'bag of machines increased from twenty to forty' in the weeks before his death, Richthofen's number of kills rose quickly into double figures. 'The spirit of our leader animated all his pupils,' he wrote later. 'We trusted him blindly. There was no possibility that one of us would be left behind . . . Animated by that spirit we gaily diminished the number of our enemies.'[10]

With Boelcke gone, Richthofen became Jasta 2's leading pilot. His memory of his fight with Lanoe Hawker on 23 November is that he was 'blithely flying to give chase' when he 'noticed three Englishmen who also had apparently gone a-hunting'. One of them, Hawker, tried to get on

On 23 November 1916 an extraordinary aerial duel took place between Major Lanoe Hawker VC DSO, Britain's first air ace (left), and Leutnant Manfred Freiherr von Richthofen, Germany's foremost pilot.

his tail and even managed a few shots before Richthofen shook him off. Thus began the circling fight as each of these highly skilled pilots tried to get 'behind and above the other'. It was quickly clear to Richthofen that his opponent was no beginner, and that his agile DH2 'turned beautifully'. Yet Hawker could not manoeuvre indefinitely because, thanks to the prevailing wind, each turn was taking him further into German territory and sooner or later a shortage of fuel would cause him to flee. Not that he appeared concerned when, during one turn, he 'merrily waved' to Richthofen, as if to say 'Well, how do you do?'[11]

But eventually, using his extra climbing speed, Richthofen got behind Hawker, causing the latter to break off and head for the British lines. 'When he had come down to about 300 feet,' recalled Richthofen, 'he tried to escape by flying in a zig-zag course . . . That was my favourite moment. I followed him at an altitude of from 250 feet to 150 feet, firing all the time. The Englishman could not help falling. But the jamming of my gun nearly robbed me of my success.'[12]

Hawker was just seconds from the front lines, and safety, when one of the last bullets fired by Richthofen hit him in the back of the head, killing him instantly. His plane crashed in German territory 200 yards east of Luisenhof Farm, south of Bapaume, enabling Richthofen to recover Hawker's Lewis gun as a trophy. 'It ornaments,' he wrote, 'the entrance of my dwelling.'[13]

Richthofen was even more delighted when he discovered later that the airman he had bested on 23 November 1916 was none other than 'the English Immelmann'.[14]

12 December 1916: 'A basis for the restoration of a lasting peace'

– Germany proposes peace talks

Barely a month after his re-election for a second term, US President Woodrow Wilson was fine-tuning an appeal for the belligerents to hold peace talks when the Germans pre-empted him with an offer of their own. It arrived in the form of a note from Theobald von Bethmann

Hollweg, the German Chancellor, to Joseph Grew, the secretary of the US Embassy, for onward transmittance to the leaders of the Entente.

Coming just days after the fall of Bucharest to German, Austrian and Bulgarian forces, the note stressed that the four Central Powers, though on the verge of victory, were prepared to discuss a negotiated peace. The note made no specific proposals, but instead stressed 'that the propositions which they would bring forward and which would aim to assure the existence, honor, and free development of their peoples, would be such as to serve as a basis for the restoration of a lasting peace'. Should their offer be rejected, the note continued, they would fight on to a 'victorious end' while 'solemnly disclaiming any responsibility before mankind and history' for the slaughter which followed.[1]

In truth, following the military setbacks of 1916 – notably the fall of Erzerum, the grinding attrition of Verdun and the Somme, and the gains made by the Russians during the Brusilov offensive – the Central Powers in general, and Germany in particular, could see no likelihood of ultimate victory by December 1916 and wanted to negotiate an armistice before their position became any weaker. Bethmann was clearly hoping that Wilson would bring forward his own peace proposals, giving Germany 'two irons in the fire'. What he failed to understand, however, was that by linking the two initiatives he deprived Wilson of that 'unembarrassed neutrality' which he needed 'to secure a fair hearing from the Allies'.[2]

Yet, though disturbed by its timing, Wilson reacted positively to the German initiative. He informed Grew that the US government would 'very cheerfully' transmit the note, and that it 'welcomed this expression of the willingness of the Imperial German Government to discuss terms of peace'. To the ambassadors who would communicate the note to the various Allies he referred to the offer as 'a very welcome surprise because it seems to . . . promise at least a beginning of interchanges of view'.[3]

Wilson knew, of course, that the Allied governments were in a difficult position with dwindling resources, rising war costs and the first rumbling of political discontent in Russia. He hoped that his intervention would encourage those who yearned for a moderate peace based on international co-operation; instead it merely strengthened the Allies' determination to fight on.

In Britain, where Lloyd George – a conspicuous success as Minister of Munitions and War Secretary – had recently replaced the ageing and demoralized Asquith as Prime Minister, the response to the German note was unenthusiastic. On 18 December, in line with the London Pact of 1914, the newly created five-man War Cabinet agreed to consult the other Allies before making an official statement. But all ministers accepted, as Lloyd George's biographer put it, 'that to negotiate peace at a time of weakness would be the equivalent of surrender'. A day later, in his first speech to the House of Commons as premier, Lloyd George dismissed the German offer with a quote by Abraham Lincoln. When the war began, he said, 'we accepted this was for an object and a worthy object and [it] will end when that object is attained. Under God, I hope it will never end until that time.'[4]

If this resort to Lincoln's battle cry was chiefly directed at Wilson, it did not have the desired effect because the following day, 20 December, the US President asked the Allied governments to state their peace terms. In attempting to be even-handed, Wilson gravely offended the Entente powers by his ludicrous assertion that both sides had the same essential war aim, namely 'to make the rights and privileges of weak peoples and small states as secure against aggression and denial in future as the rights and privileges of the great and powerful states now at war'.

He added that he was not offering mediation or proposing peace, but simply expressing the hope that his request might begin a dialogue and lead to a conference. The United States, he explained, had an 'intimate interest' in ending the war, lest the conflict continue for so long that a durable peace would become impossible, the position of neutrals 'be rendered altogether intolerable', and 'more than all, an injury done to civilization itself which can never be atoned for or repaired'.[5] Yet perhaps the most offensive phrase in his note was the claim that America was 'too proud to fight'.[6]

The bemused reaction of the British public was neatly summed up by Bill Bervon, a thirty-five-year-old senior executive at the National Provincial Bank, in a letter to his niece Vera Brittain (then serving with the VAD in Malta):

> The German peace inquiries have left us quite cold; they were so evidently an attempt to get a German (in the strongest sense of the word) peace. But today President Wilson has stepped boldly into the arena and had the consummate effrontery to tell us that both sides are evidently fighting

for the protection of small States (what price Belgium and Serbia?) and therefore the Allies should try to discuss terms with Germany. The newspaper comments are amusing and very instructive* and even the American papers in some cases have taken Mr Wilson to task pretty severely.[7]

With battles being fought on their soil, the French were particularly outraged by Wilson's offer and wanted to snub him. But at meetings between British and French ministers on 26 and 27 December it was agreed that the Allies could not afford to alienate America: they relied on it for arms and loans, and hoped that one day Congress would see sense and declare war on the Allied side. So Britain and France issued a joint response, demanding the evacuation of all occupied territories and the return of Alsace-Lorraine to France. The purpose of any peace negotiations, they added, would be 'the rescue of Europe from the brutal encroachment of Prussian militarism'.[8]

The use of such language, of course, was designed to strangle the prospect of a negotiated peace at birth. Any last lingering hopes for a peace conference, however, were dispelled when the German government refused to state its terms in advance. To enter on Germany's invitation, Lloyd George told the House of Commons, 'without any knowledge of the proposals she proposes to make, into a conference, is to put our heads into a noose with the rope in the hands of Germany'.[9]

The effect of Germany's rebuff was to 'deepen American suspicions of Germany's war aims and of the genuineness of her desire for a better world order'. But no one in Britain was surprised, and the whole affair had served only to increase the Prime Minister's popularity and to harden the public's support for the war. 'Lloyd George is quite marvellous,' wrote Bill Bervon to his niece Vera, '. . . and one almost feels afraid when one realises to what an extent the Nation is leaning upon the energy and brains of one man through this awful crisis.' He added:

We are up against it with a vengeance this time but there is no panic and we are all prepared to carry the thing through and damn the

---

* The *Morning Post*, for example, thought Wilson's Olympian detachment 'reminiscent of the attitude of the antique gods'; while *The Times* pronounced him sincere but sadly deluded (Stannard Baker, *Woodrow Wilson*, VI, pp. 400–1).

consequences . . . I feel a worm, of course, and quite naturally, but when I look on and watch my fellow men and women carrying on and doing it with grim determination but withal everlasting cheerfulness and modesty, I cannot help feeling a very proud worm. It is something to know from what a nation one is bred.[10]

PART FOUR
1917

*S*uperficially, at least, the Central Powers were still marginally in the ascendant by the close of 1916. They had overwhelmed Romania – giving them possession of five enemy capitals* at a time when the Allies held none – fought the British and French to a standstill on the Somme, bled the French Army white at Verdun and made some ground against Italy in the Alps. They had 'ended the year controlling more European territory than at the beginning, and having survived the Chantilly onslaught'.[1]

Yet they had also suffered major setbacks, with Austro-German forces conceding a large chunk of territory to Russia during the Brusilov offensive, Turkey losing the key fortress of Erzerum to the same foe, and the epic but inconclusive naval Battle of Jutland ending in strategic defeat for the Imperial German Navy. German forces, moreover, were exhausted from their own huge sacrifices on the Western Front, and their leaders rightly feared that the Allies' superiority in men and matériel would become even more marked in 1917. This conviction that outright victory was probably beyond them was the reason Germany's leaders considered a negotiated peace in December 1916; but the idea quickly ran out of steam when the Allies, determined to punish the Central Powers for starting the war, demanded the restoration of Alsace-Lorraine to France and the evacuation of all occupied territories as a starting point for negotiations.

The replacement of Falkenhayn, Chief of the German General Staff, with the dual team of Hindenburg and Ludendorff had, however, given more vigour and cunning to their country's war strategy. The duo ended the costly German offensives at Verdun, and on the Somme introduced a more elastic defence with a thinner front line and more counter-attack troops and artillery in reserve.

* Brussels, Warsaw, Belgrade, Cetinje (Montenegro) and now Bucharest.

But by diverting more of Germany's economic resources to the war effort*
the new Generalissimos caused chaos. The country had actually begun the
war with an industrial advantage over both Britain and France – chiefly
because it led the way in steel production, and in many branches of chemicals and engineering. But shortages of vital raw materials – particularly
cotton, camphor, pyrites and saltpetre – meant it could not expand its
production at the same rate, and only 8.9 million shells were made in 1915.
The following year saw a near fourfold increase to 36 million shells, thanks
to the efforts of the KRA (the wartime raw-materials department) that
commandeered stockpiles, allocated distribution and, most importantly,
oversaw the chemical industry's production of synthetic substitutes. Much of
the good work was undone, however, by the Generalissimos' introduction
of the poorly thought-out and ineptly administered Hindenburg Programme
in the summer of 1916. Designed to increase the production of all armaments
(but particularly key weapons like artillery pieces, machine-guns and trench
mortars that could compensate for the expected shortage of men), it ultimately
had the opposite effect by draining the army of a million men, bringing on
a major transportation crisis and intensifying the shortage of coal.

Hindenburg and Ludendorff's strategy for 1917, meanwhile, was essentially
defensive on all land fronts. They refused, for example, to send extra divisions so that Austria could launch a fresh attack on the Trentino front in
the spring; and they anticipated a new Allied offensive on the Western Front
by withdrawing in February to a new 300-mile-long pre-prepared defensive
position known as the Hindenburg Line. It not only restored the tactical
advantages they had lost at the Somme, but also shortened the line by thirty
miles, thus releasing ten divisions. When combined with unit reorganizations
– in effect reducing the size of a division, but not its area of operations –
and an early call-up of the 1897 class of conscripts, this enabled the creation
of a 1.3 million-strong strategic reserve. In a sign of desperation, however,
the German leadership pinned their remaining hopes of winning the war
on a resumption of unrestricted submarine warfare. Knowing it would almost
certainly lead to war with the United States, they gambled on their U-boats
bringing Britain to its knees before American forces could tip the balance.

---

* In a conscious inversion of the dictum by the great Prussian military theorist Carl von
Clausewitz that war was an extension of policy by other means, Ludendorff advocated
the subordination of politics to warfare, a concept known as total war.

The Allied strategy, by contrast, was more of the same. At a Chantilly conference in mid-November 1916, it was unanimously agreed 'that the Western theatre is the main one, and that the resources employed in the other theatres should be reduced to the smallest possible' (a signal victory for Joffre and Haig); 'that all the Allies will press the Enemy throughout the winter', weather permitting; that 'if one of the Allies is attacked, the others will at once take the offensive to relieve the pressure', and with this in mind were 'to complete their offensive preparations early next year'; and that if the 'Enemy leaves the initiative to the Allies, the date of the general offensive will be settled later'.[2] In a separate conference with his army commanders on 18 November, Haig explained the thinking behind this strategy as the need to avoid another surprise like Verdun, while at the same time preventing the enemy 'from recovering from his demoralised condition by methodical pressure'.[3]

Not all the Allies, however, were either willing or able to apply this pressure. The reputation and confidence of the Italian Commander-in-Chief, Luigi Cadorna, had been severely shaken by the Austrian Strafexpedition and, though his army would grow to 2.2 million in 1917, he was fearful of another Austrian attack and loth to take the initiative. When it was proposed by Lloyd George at a conference in Rome on 2 January 1917 that the other Allies would supply heavy artillery for an Italian offensive towards Trieste, Cadorna also demanded four Anglo-French corps, and the right to use them to defend the Trentino if Austria attacked first. In any event he would not move until 1 May.[4]

The Russians hoped to resume the offensive in Brusilov's sector, but their army was still reeling from the huge number of men it had lost in 1916 and its logistical organization was beginning to disintegrate. At a further inter-Allied conference at Petrograd* in February they declared they had fewer reserves than a year earlier and would also not be ready to attack until May.[5]

Even the British and French leaders – following the fall of Asquith and Joffre in December 1916 – were far from united in their support for the Chantilly strategy. Lloyd George was unconvinced by British generalship on the Western Front, and had long supported attacks on other fronts like Salonika, Mesopotamia and Egypt to keep up the pressure on Turkey and divert German attention from France and Flanders. But he was overruled at Chantilly – 'crushed' in Haig's words[6] – and then charmed into

---

* The Russian capital had been renamed Petrograd in 1914 because its former name of St Petersburg was thought to be too Germanic.

compliance by the new French Commander-in-Chief, Nivelle, after they had met first at the Rome conference and then again in London where the French general, at Lloyd George's invitation, addressed the British War Cabinet. All were impressed by Nivelle's 'vigour, strength and energy', and relieved that his plan of attack did not require a major British effort.[7] *The war, he told them, could be won by a single deadly blow; and it would be delivered not on the Somme, as Joffre and Haig had agreed at Chantilly, but instead against the 'shoulders' of the great German salient in a mirror image of the September 1915 offensive: a preliminary Franco-British attack near Arras, followed by the main effort by the French along the Chemin des Dames in Champagne.*[8]

Despite the fact that Nivelle's plan met none of his objectives – which were principally to reinforce fronts outside Europe – Lloyd George gave it his blessing: partly because it promised a reduction in British casualties, but chiefly because he believed that, unlike Haig, the new French Commander-in-Chief knew what he was doing. 'Nivelle,' he wrote, 'has proved himself to be a Man at Verdun, & when you get a Man who has proved himself why, you back the Man!'[9]

To underline this faith in Nivelle on the one hand and his lack of confidence in Haig on the other, Lloyd George agreed to place his British field marshal* under the command of the less senior French general for the duration of the offensive. Haig never forgot or forgave this humiliation, telling King George V: 'It is indeed a calamity for the country to have such a man at the head of affairs in this time of great crisis.'[10]

With relations between the British premier and his senior commander close to breaking point at the start of the year, it did not augur well for the Allies' chances of ending the war in 1917.

17 January 1917: *'D'you want to bring America into the war?'*
– Intercepting the Zimmermann Telegram

At 10.30 a.m. Rear Admiral William 'Blinker' Hall, the forty-six-year-old hook-nosed and balding Director of the Naval Intelligence

---

* Haig had been promoted to field marshal in late December 1916.

Division,* was working through the usual 'morning docket of papers' in his office in the Old Admiralty building in Whitehall when one of his star codebreakers, an Old Etonian and former RNAS pilot called Nigel de Grey, entered the room. 'D.I.D.,' said de Grey, scarcely able to conceal his excitement, 'd'you want to bring America into the war?'

'Yes, my boy,' replied Hall. 'Why?'

De Grey explained: 'I've got something here which – well, it's a rather astonishing message which might do the trick if we can use it. It isn't very clear, I'm afraid, but I'm sure I've got most of the important points right. It's from the German Foreign Office to [Johann Heinrich von] Bernstorff [the German ambassador in Washington].'

De Grey then handed to Hall the partially decoded message that he and the other cryptanalysts had translated from German – which the director did not read – into English. The key parts read:

16th Jan. 1917

Most secret for Your Excellency's exclusive personal information and to be handed on to the Imperial Minister in (?Mexico) . . .

We propose to begin on the 1st of February unrestricted submarine warfare. In doing so however we shall endeavour to keep America neutral.

(?? If we should) not (succeed in so doing) we propose to (?Mexico) an alliance upon the following basis. (joint) conduct of the war. (joint) conclusion of peace.

Your Excellency should (for the present) inform the President secretly (that we expect) war with the U.S.A. (possibly) (A sentence in which Japan is mentioned) and at the same time to negotiate between us & Japan.

(. . . please tell the President) that . . . our submarines . . . will compel England to peace in a few months.[1]

Though much of the original telegram from Arthur Zimmermann, the German Foreign Secretary, to Bernstorff had yet to be deciphered, the fragment laid before Hall on 17 January contained enough bombshells to justify de Grey's excitement. They included the imminence of unrestricted submarine warfare; the possibility of a German–Mexican alliance

---

* Hall was described by one contemporary as looking 'like a demonic Mr Punch in uniform' (Boghardt, *The Zimmermann Telegram*, p. 83).

against the United States; and evidence of Germany's intention to lure Japan away from the Allies.[2]

Hall knew that his standing orders required him to share such explosive material with the Admiralty and the Foreign Office so that the government could respond appropriately.[3] But this 'duty' was outweighed, in his mind, by the pressing need to protect his sources, in this case the fact that his cryptanalysts in Room 40 were routinely intercepting and reading diplomatic cables from both neutral and enemy states. They had discovered the top-secret Zimmermann telegram embedded in diplomatic traffic between the American Embassy in Berlin and the State Department in Washington (a favour the Americans had earlier granted Germany without imagining that it could be used against them).

As all this was bound to come out if the United States was told the true story of how Hall had come by his intelligence – causing not only a major diplomatic row but also the changing of the State Department's codes – he chose not to inform his government (which was also unaware of his illegal activities) or the Americans until he had found a separate copy of the telegram and his staff had completed the decoding.[4] 'This,' he told de Grey, 'is a case where standing orders must be suspended. All copies of this message, both those in cipher and your own transcripts, are to be brought straight to me. Nothing is to be put on the files. This may be a very big thing, possibly the biggest thing of the war. For the present not a soul outside this room is to be told anything at all.'[5]

Hall knew from the partial decrypt that Bernstorff would forward a copy of the telegram to his counterpart in Mexico City, Heinrich von Eckardt. He also knew from experience that Bernstorff would use a more vulnerable code to communicate with Eckardt, because the latter did not have access to the German Foreign Office's most sophisticated codebook (0075). All he needed to do, therefore, was get a copy of Bernstorff's telegram to Eckardt and his staff would be able to crack it in its entirety. He would then be in a position to share it with the Americans without admitting that he was reading their cables. 'In short,' wrote historian Thomas Boghardt, 'this ruse would enable him to conceal British eavesdropping operations from the Americans as well as afford Room 40 continued access to U.S. diplomatic messages.'[6]

If, on the other hand, the US responded to Germany's public declaration of unrestricted submarine warfare by joining the Allies, Hall would never need to make the telegram public. Of course this second scenario ran the risk that Germany's scheme to encourage Mexico to attack the United States might bear fruit; yet Hall felt it was a gamble worth taking.

Arthur Zimmermann, the author of the telegram, had been Germany's Foreign Secretary only since the resignation of the moderate Gottlieb von Jagow in November 1916. Bright and articulate, the son of an East Prussian innkeeper, Zimmermann had done well in the less prestigious consular service of the Foreign Office before transferring to the diplomatic section where his middle-class origins probably prevented his earlier promotion to the top job. 'One should never,' remarked the Kaiser in 1912, 'make the scullion chef.'[7]

War broke down these social barriers, and by late 1916 the hardworking, jovial and unpretentious Zimmermann was the obvious choice to replace Jagow. He took charge in the Wilhelmstrasse at a time when the debate over the use of unrestricted submarine warfare was entering its final phase. In favour of using this 'miracle weapon' – certain, said its supporters, to bring Britain to its knees in a matter of months – were the naval and army chiefs; more cautious were Bethmann, the Chancellor, and some of the Foreign Office's senior diplomats, including Bernstorff. At first Zimmermann opposed a policy he knew would provoke America. But when the military leaders won the Kaiser's support at a conference in Pless on 9 January 1917 – threatening to have Bethmann replaced if he did not acquiesce – Zimmermann bowed to the inevitable.[8]

It was during the Foreign Office's frantic attempts to prepare its embassies for the announcement of unrestricted submarine warfare on 1 February that a member of Zimmermann's staff – Hans Arthur von Kemnitz – reminded his chief of an earlier offer from Mexico for an alliance against the United States. 'I suggested,' he wrote later, 'that we now accept this proposal in principle, and simultaneously tell the Mexicans that this offer would be significantly more valuable if they succeeded, in view of their 10-years-old, intimate relations with Japan, to interest the latter in this issue.' Though Kemnitz did not hold out much hope that this initiative would succeed, he still felt it was his 'duty to leave no stone unturned in order to ameliorate our desperate military situation through diplomatic means'. Zimmermann agreed and Kemnitz was told to draft the telegram.[9]

The final draft, with minor amendments by senior officials, was author-ized by Zimmermann on 13 January. It read:

Berlin, 13 January 1917.
Minister von Eckardt
Mexico

Most secret. Decipher yourself.

We intend to begin on the first of February unrestricted submarine warfare. We shall endeavour to keep America neutral.

In the event of this not succeeding, we propose to Mexico an alliance on the following basis: Conduct war jointly. Conclude peace jointly. Substantial financial support and consent on our part for Mexico to reconquer lost territory in Texas, New Mexico, Arizona. The settlement in detail is left to your Excellency.

Your Excellency will present to the President [of Mexico, Venustiano Carranza] the above most secretly *as soon as the outbreak of war with the United States is certain*, and add the suggestion that he should, on his own initiative, invite Japan to immediate adherence, and at the same time mediate between Japan and ourselves.

Please call the President's attention to the fact that ruthless employ-ment of our submarines now offers the prospect of compelling England in a few months to make peace.[10]

The telegram was given oral clearance by Ludendorff, but not by Chancellor Bethmann who heard of its contents only *after* it had been despatched on 16 January as part of a much longer top-secret telegram to Bernstorff. Before the war such telegrams would have been sent via Germany's transatlantic submarine cables. But after the Royal Navy severed these cables in 1914, other means were required. They included sending encrypted messages in the diplomatic traffic of friendly neutral powers like Sweden and, in this instance, the United States. The right to piggyback on American diplomatic cables – from Berlin to Washington, via Copenhagen and London – had been granted to the Germans by Woodrow Wilson in late 1914 as a way of ensuring a reliable means of communication between the two governments. 'Trusting in the Germans' good faith,' wrote Thomas Boghardt, 'the Americans accepted numerous encrypted messages without being knowledgeable of their actual content.'[11]

The American ambassador to Berlin, James Gerard, duly sent off the Zimmermann Telegram as part of his own lengthy message to the State Department on 16 January. A day later the gist of the message was in the hands of 'Blinker' Hall, the chief of British naval intelligence, who decided to wait on events.

13 February 1917: 'A haggard look came into her eyes'
– The arrest of a dancer

Police Commissioner Albert Priolet knocked loudly on the door of Room 131 in the Elysée Palace Hotel in Paris. The door was opened by a tall, handsome woman wearing an expensive lace-trimmed dressing gown. Are you Madame Zelle-MacLeod, otherwise known as the dancer Mata Hari? asked Priolet. When the women said yes, he explained that he had a warrant for her arrest on charges of attempted espionage, complicity and passing intelligence to the enemy.[1]

While a shaken Mata Hari got dressed, Priolet and his five subordinates ransacked the room, looking for incriminating evidence. They found nothing, though a number of documents – including her Dutch passport, a travel permit to Vittel in the War Zone and some money – were carefully placed in sealed bags. Mata Hari was then taken to the Palace of Justice where she was interrogated by the Third Council of War's investigating magistrate Pierre Bouchardon. Did she understand the charges against her? Yes, she replied, but there had been a mistake. 'I am innocent. Someone is playing with me – French counter-espionage, since I am in its service, and I have only acted on instructions.'[2]

Waiving the right to a lawyer, Mata Hari insisted she had done nothing wrong. With the interview over, she rose from her seat as if expecting to be released. But Bouchardon soon disabused her. '[When I told her she was to stay in Saint-Lazare prison],' he recalled, 'she turned to me, a haggard look came into her eyes, which were dumb with fear.'[3]

Born Margaretha Geertruida Zelle at Leeuwarden in northern Holland on 7 August 1876, the daughter of a prosperous haberdasher, she had enjoyed an early childhood of privilege and comfort. But this all changed in 1889 with her father's bankruptcy and, a year later, the break-up of her parents' marriage (her mother died soon afterwards). In 1895, at the age of seventeen, she met and married Rudolf MacLeod* of Dutch-Scottish descent, a thirty-nine-year-old infantry captain and veteran of the brutal Aceh War in Sumatra, part of the Dutch East Indies.[4]

By 1898 they had two children – Norman-John and Jeanne Louise – and were living in Sumatra where Rudolf, now a major, was garrison commander at Medan. But his drinking and jealous rages were beginning to take their toll on the marriage and the final straw was the death of their son, possibly from cholera, in June 1899.

They returned to Holland in 1902 and separated not long afterwards, Rudolf taking custody of their daughter Jeanne. Destitute and alone, Margaretha travelled to Paris where she struggled to earn a living as, variously, an artist's model, an actress and almost certainly a prostitute. But a second visit in 1904 was more successful: she worked first as a circus rider and then as a dancer, devising a series of nearly naked 'sacred dances' that she claimed to have learned in the East Indies. Parisians were entranced. A British journalist wrote:

> The door opened. A tall dark figure glided in. Her arms were folded upon her breast beneath a mass of flowers . . . She was enshrouded in various veils of delicate hues, symbolizing beauty, youth, love, chastity, voluptuousness and passion.
>
> The first notes of a plaintive weird melody were sounded and with slow, undulating, tiger-like movements she advanced towards the God . . . Then the movements became more and more intense, more feverish, more eager. She first threw flowers and then divested herself, one by one, of the veils, implying that, as a sacrifice, she gave beauty, youth, love, etc.; and finally worked to a state of frenzy, unclasped her belt and fell in a swoon at Siva's† feet.[5]

---

* Margaretha had answered MacLeod's ad in the *News of the Day*, stating that an 'Officer on home leave from Dutch East Indies would like to meet a girl of pleasant character – object matrimony'. Within six days they were married (Shipman, *Femme Fatale*, p. 38).
† Shiva, the Hindu god of destruction and transformation.

Within a year she had changed her stage name from 'Lady Gresha MacLeod' to 'Mata Hari' (Indonesian for 'Sun' or literally 'Eye of the Day'), acquired as a manager the top impresario Gabriel Astruc – whose clients included Diaghilev's *Ballets Russes*, the dancer Nijinsky and the composer Stravinsky – and was performing for huge fees to audiences across Europe.

She also acquired a string of lovers, among them the industrialist Emile Guimet, the diplomat Jules Cambon and a rich young German officer called Alfred Kiepert who established her in an apartment in Berlin. By the time her dancing career began to decline in 1912, she had had affairs with high-ranking military officers, politicians and businessmen from across Europe. She was also an excellent linguist, fluent in Dutch, French, German, Russian and English, and an obvious target for intelligence services when war broke out in 1914.

Having returned from Berlin to neutral Holland, she was living in The Hague in the summer of 1915 when Karl Kroemer, the German honorary consul, approached her. Would she agree to spy for Germany for 20,000 francs? he asked. Initially doubtful, she eventually said yes because, as she admitted later, she was bored and tired of wartime shortages of food and coal. Yet at no time did she give Kroemer any information worth having – at least that is what she claimed under interrogation.[6] It was probably now, according to the *Historical Dictionary of German Intelligence*, that she received from her lover Kroemer the codename 'H21'.

Arriving at Folkestone on 3 December, en route to Dieppe, Mata Hari was questioned by British police. She claimed she was on her way to her home in Paris 'for the purpose of selling her effects and to sign professional contracts which might be for [dancing] engagements in South America'. During a second interrogation by a Captain Dillon of the counter-intelligence service MO5, she contradicted herself by saying that 'her object in going to France was to sell her home and then return to The Hague to take up residence there'. But nothing was found in her luggage to incriminate her and, despite their suspicions, MO5 let her proceed to France.[7]

They did, however, inform the French authorities of their suspicions; and on 9 December 1915 an MO5 circular was distributed to port officers and the British military authorities in France saying Madame

The Dutch-born exotic dancer and spy, Mata Hari.

Zelle, professionally known as 'Mata Hari', was 'not to be allowed to return to the United Kingdom'. If she did, noted a second circular despatched in February 1916, she was 'to be arrested and sent to Scotland Yard'.[8] This was in response to a report by Richard Tinsley, a British intelligence agent in Holland, that Mata Hari was alleged to have been paid 15,000 francs by the German Embassy, and was suspected of 'having gone to France on an important mission that will profit the Germans'.[9]

Having spent just three months in France – during which time she resumed her love affair with the diplomat Henri de Marguérie – Mata Hari returned to Holland via Spain and Portugal. Yet she was back in France by the summer of 1916, and in August was recruited as a double agent by Captain George Ladoux, the head of the Deuxième Bureau (French military intelligence). Ladoux knew of British suspicions that she was spying for Germany, but had no definite proof. 'To get this,' he wrote later, 'it was necessary to gain her confidence and to propose to her a mission on behalf of France.'[10]

Mata Hari, for her part, was again short of money and was enticed by the promise of great riches if she brought back vital intelligence for the French. Her attempt to travel to occupied Belgium via Holland, however, was cut short at the English port of Falmouth on 14 November when, ironically, she was arrested on suspicion of being another German spy, Clara Benedix. Taken to Scotland Yard in London, she was questioned for three days by Sir Basil Thomson, the head of Special Branch, who was eventually satisfied that 'she was not identical with Clara Benedix'. She had told him her true identity, and that she was working for French intelligence.[11] When he checked with the Deuxième Bureau in France, Thomson received the reply that Ladoux 'has suspected her for some time, and pretended to employ her, in order, if possible, to obtain definite proof that she is working for the Germans'.[12] This convinced Thomson not to let her proceed to Holland and on 1 December, after a brief stay at the Savoy Hotel in London, she was put on board the Spain-bound SS *Araguaga* at Liverpool.

Her arrest in Paris in February 1917 was precipitated by the interception of messages from Major Kalle, the German military attaché in Madrid, describing the helpful activities of a German spy, codenamed H21. The first, dated 13 December, notified Berlin that 'Agent H21 . . . has arrived here. She has pretended to accept offers of service for French intelligence and to carry out trips to Belgium for the head of the service.' It then related the story of her arrest in Falmouth and her intention to reach Holland via Paris and Switzerland; and ended with a promise to forward her 'very complete' reports by letter or telegram.[13]

Was Mata Hari agent 'H21'? Yes according to Jefferson Adams, author of the recently published *Historical Dictionary of German Intelligence*. Adams added: 'Lacking a clearly defined set of instructions from either France or Germany, Mata Hari began to work on her own initiative. One of her major new acquaintances was the German military consul in Madrid, Arnold von Kalle, with whom she exchanged pieces of information.' But it was another double agent, 'Marthe Richer (alias Marthe Richard, or Agent 32 on the German list)', who obtained for the French 'high-level intelligence – including the code used by Kalle to communicate with

[Kroemer] in the Hague'. It was this code that gave Ladoux and the Deuxième Bureau 'concrete proof that Mara Hari was on the payroll of the Germans'.[14]

Armed with this seemingly irrefutable evidence of her guilt, Ladoux ordered Mata Hari's arrest.*

19 February 1917: *'Texas and Arizona? Why not Illinois and New York?'*
– America learns of the Zimmermann Telegram

Ned Bell, the Harvard-educated second secretary at the US Embassy, arrived at the Old Admiralty Building in Whitehall for what he assumed would be a routine meeting with Rear Admiral 'Blinker' Hall, Britain's naval intelligence chief. As a member of the State Department's secret service, the Bureau of Secret Intelligence (BSI), Bell was in regular contact with Hall and other members of British intelligence. He was wholly unprepared, therefore, to be handed a fully decrypted copy of the Zimmermann Telegram.†

Bell read the transcript with a mixture of incredulity and anger. 'Mexico to "reconquer lost territory"!' he exclaimed. 'Texas and Arizona? Why not Illinois and New York while they were about it?'

So extraordinary were the main points of the telegram – Germany's offer of an alliance with Mexico against America, help to recover Mexico's former territories and a potential tripartite alliance with Japan – that for a moment Bell doubted its authenticity. But Hall quickly reassured him, adding that he had decided on his own initiative to share this explosive information with America because the Foreign Office had not

---

* The two-month delay in arresting Mata Hari may be accounted for by the fact that the German diplomatic code used to send messages from Madrid to Berlin was the same one – 0075 – that British cryptanalysts in Room 40 cracked in January 1917 to enable them to read the Zimmermann Telegram. It was probably thanks to the British, therefore, that the contents of the Mata Hari cables were known to the French.

† Not the original copy from Zimmermann to Ambassador von Bernstorff in Washington but rather Bernstorff's relayed telegram to Heinrich von Eckardt in Mexico City.

yet decided what to do with it. Under the circumstances, asked Hall, would he and Ambassador Page be prepared to keep quiet about the telegram until Arthur Balfour, the British Foreign Secretary, 'has made a decision'?[1]

Bell agreed to 'sit tight . . . for as long as you say',[2] but Hall must have known that he and Walter Page were duty bound to inform Washington. In other words Hall had made the decision to share this information with a foreign power without any authority from his own government. Why did he do this?

The answer lies in Woodrow Wilson's firm but restrained response to Germany's declaration of unrestricted warfare on 1 February, advance warning of which had been given the day before by Zimmermann to James Gerard, US ambassador in Berlin. 'But as you will see,' added an optimistic Zimmermann, 'everything will be all right. America will do nothing, for President Wilson is for peace and nothing else.'[3]

The German Foreign Secretary was half right. On 3 February Wilson severed diplomatic relations with Germany in protest at the resumption of unrestricted submarine warfare, but stopped short of declaring war. That, he told Congress, would have to wait until 'overt acts' by submarines had proven beyond doubt that Germany's intentions were hostile.[4] This meant, of course, the sinking of an American ship; as long as the Germans steered clear of US vessels, American intervention could be postponed indefinitely.

Disappointed by Wilson's response, Hall decided to force the issue by making the Zimmermann Telegram public. But first he had to inform his own government of its existence – which he did on 5 February – and, at the same time, find a copy from a separate source to show the Americans. This was obtained from the telegraph office in Mexico City and decoded in London by de Grey on 19 February. There is a colourful myth, repeated in a number of histories, that the British were able to crack the less sophisticated German code used for messages from Washington to Central and South America – and known as 13040 – because they had captured the cipher in the baggage of arch-spy Wilhelm Wassmuss, the German 'Lawrence of Arabia', in Persia. Hall himself is said to have discovered it after a hunch caused him to search Wassmuss's belongings once they reached London.[5]

According to the best recent book on the subject by Thomas Boghardt, however, 'the British broke 13040 not by means of a fanciful cloak-and-dagger operation, but through tedious, painstaking cryptanalysis'. By 1917, Room 40 was 'routinely and quickly' decoding 13040 messages, which is why de Grey was able to produce a complete transcript of the Zimmermann Telegram found in Mexico City on the day he received it: 19 February.[6]

It was only now that Hall felt able to show the telegram – and a full transcript at that – to intelligence agent Bell. He did so without first gaining the permission of the Foreign Office because he suspected that it might drag its feet and wanted to present his government with a fait accompli. The plan worked: Balfour gave his consent retrospectively; and the Americans believed Hall's claim that the telegram had been intercepted in Mexico City and decoded by means of a captured German codebook (hence the origin of the Wassmuss myth).[7]

Wilson read the text of the telegram with 'much indignation' on 25 February, and four days later, after the BSI had obtained a separate copy for verification from the Western Union cable office in Washington, it was published in the American press. From this point onwards, wrote the American Secretary of State Robert Lansing, 'the United States' entry into the war was assured'.[8]

15 March 1917:* *'The people will not understand it'*
– Tsar Nicholas II abdicates

Nicholas was in his study on the imperial train at Pskov, 180 miles south-west of Petrograd – Soviet revolutionaries having prevented him from reaching the capital the day before – when the Northern Front commander General Ruzsky entered his carriage at 10 a.m.

Ruzsky handed the Tsar a transcript of a conversation he had just had with Mikhail Rodzianko, the President of the Duma (or Russian parliament), via an early telex machine known as the Hughes Apparatus. So

---

* According to the Russian Julian calendar, which was thirteen days behind the western Gregorian calendar, the Tsar abdicated on 2 March. Hence the political upheaval, which had begun in Petrograd a week earlier, was (and still is) known as the February Revolution.

serious was the disorder in the capital, said Rodzianko, that only the Tsar's abdication would be enough to satisfy the crowds.[1]

The trouble had begun on 22 January when 150,000 workers had marched through the capital – an act mirrored by tens of thousands in other cities – in protest at food shortages, with a few sporting banners 'Down with the war' and 'Down with autocracy'. This had been followed up, on 8 March, by another large-scale demonstration by women textile workers and metal workers from the war industries. Within two days more than 200,000 Petrograd workers were on strike. This prompted the German-born Tsarina Alexandra, a granddaughter of Queen Victoria, to write to her husband from the royal palace at Tsarskoe Selo near Petrograd: 'It's a hooligan movement . . . But this will all pass & quieten down.'[2]

It did not, and the point of no return was on 10 March when Nicholas, then at military headquarters at Mogilev, ordered the Petrograd garrison commander to use force to 'put down the disorders by tomorrow'.[3] Next day, after scores of protesting workers had been shot on the Tsar's instructions, the Pavlovsky Regiment mutinied and killed some policemen. It was eventually disarmed and arrested, the ringleaders imprisoned in the Peter and Paul Fortress. But more regiments disobeyed orders to fire on demonstrators on the 12th, and by nightfall the majority of the Petrograd garrison had gone over to the protesters. It was this defection, wrote historian Orlando Figes, 'that turned the disorders of the previous four days into a full-scale revolution'.[4]

When Nicholas received the news that evening at Mogilev, he ordered the new chief of the Petrograd Military District, General Ivanov, to march into the capital and crush the rebellion. He himself set out by train for Tsarskoe Selo to be with his wife and children, but was held up at Pskov on 14 March because the line beyond was in the hands of revolutionaries.[5] At Petrograd, meanwhile, Ivanov's counter-rebellion failed when some of his troops fraternized with the revolutionaries, and on his own authority General Alexeev, the temporary Commander-in-Chief of the Russian Army, ordered a halt to further military operations. He did this because Rodzianko had convinced him that the leaders of the Duma would form the new Russian government, rather than the left-wing intellectuals of the Petrograd Soviet's Provisional Executive Committee – Mensheviks, Bolsheviks and Socialist

Revolutionaries (SRs) – who had set up a rival power base in the capital. Having stayed Ivanov's hand, Alexeev cabled the Tsar at Pskov, begging him to let the Duma form a government and restore order. 'A revolution throughout Russia,' warned the general, 'would mean a disgraceful termination of the war. One cannot ask the army to fight while there is a revolution in the rear.'[6]

By the morning of 15 March, however, Rodzianko had persuaded both Alexeev and Ruzsky that Nicholas had to go. When the Tsar received this shattering news at Pskov, in the form of the Rodzianko/Ruzsky transcript, he rose from his seat and stared out of the carriage window in silence. Returning to his desk, he said he been 'born for misfortune', adding: 'If it is necessary that I should abdicate for the good of Russia, then I am ready for it. But I am afraid that the people will not understand it.'[7]

A few minutes later a telegram arrived from Alexeev, confirming Rodzianko's opinion that Nicholas had to step down in favour of his son to save the army, the war, the nation and the dynasty. Still Nicholas procrastinated, preferring to wait for the opinions of the individual army commanders before he made his decision. They arrived after lunch, and all agreed with Alexeev. Brusilov insisted that it was the only way to restore order in the rear and continue the war. Grand Duke Nicholas begged his nephew 'on his knees' to relinquish the crown. At last the Tsar buckled: 'I have made up my mind. I have decided to abdicate from the throne in favour of my son Alexei.' Crossing himself, he withdrew to his cabin.[8]

Nicholas II had never wanted to become Tsar. A young man of moderate intelligence who knew 'nothing of the business of ruling', he would happily have lived his life as a Guards officer or country gentleman.[9] But since the early death of his larger-than-life father Alexander III from kidney disease in 1894, propelling him to the throne at the age of twenty-six, he had stuck to his coronation oath to uphold and pass on his autocratic powers to his son with, in Orlando Figes' words, a 'dogged narrow-mindedness, as if he was terrified that God (or his wife) would punish him if he failed to rule like Ivan the Terrible'. Figes added: 'For twenty-two years he had ignored the lessons of history, as well as the pleadings of countless advisers, which all pointed to the fact that the only way to save his throne was to grant a government accountable to the

Former Tsar Nicholas II of Russia under house arrest at
Tsarskoe Selo near Petrograd after his abdication.

people. His motive was always the same: his "conscience" forbade him to
do it.'[10]

By early 1917, however, the pressure for some form of constitutional
reform had become irresistible as food became scarcer and living standards
plummeted. Worst hit was the capital Petrograd, the country's industrial
powerhouse, whose population had grown by a third to 2.4 million since
1914 as the war industries expanded. To feed its citizens, Petrograd required
12,000 wagonloads of supplies a month; in January 1917 just over half that
number arrived. That month an agent of the Tsar's secret police, the Okhrana,
reported: 'Children are starving in the most literal sense of the word. A
revolution if it takes place will be spontaneous, quite likely a hunger riot.'[11]

It was also in January that Grand Duke Paul had pleaded with his
nephew to grant a constitution and cede executive powers to a Duma
ministry. Nicholas refused: 'I took an oath for Autocracy on the day of
my coronation and I must remit this oath in its integrity to my son.'[12]
Within two months his intransigence had caused not only his downfall

but also that of his dynasty. He abdicated on 15 March in favour of his brother Grand Duke Michael, believing his son Alexei's haemophilia would prevent him from ruling; but a day later, on the advice of the leaders of the new Provisional Government (who feared a civil war), Michael refused the crown and more than 300 years of Romanov rule were brought to a close.

Most soldiers and civilians rejoiced. Red flags were raised in the trenches; parades were held to celebrate. It was one in the morning when word reached the town of Yefremov in Tula province, but church bells were soon ringing in celebration. 'Lights were lit in all the houses,' recalled a resident. 'The streets filled with people . . . Strangers, weeping openly, embraced each other. The solemn, exultant whistling of locomotives could be heard from the direction of the station. Somewhere down one street there began, first quietly, then steadily louder, the singing of the Marseillaise.'[13]

The fear in Britain and France was that a Russian revolution would presage the break-up of the Entente. When this failed to materialize, and the Provisional Government assured its western allies it would continue to fight, many Britons applauded the advent of democratic government. 'Now the curtain is raised again,' wrote Bill Bervon to his niece Vera Brittain after the news blackout from Petrograd, 'we find this most wonderful upheaval has taken place with comparatively no bloodshed and certainly no interruption of war operations.'[14]

2 April 1917: *'The world must be made safe for democracy'*
– Woodrow Wilson's war speech

It was not until early evening that word reached the White House that Congress would receive President Woodrow Wilson at 8.30 p.m. Since early morning the streets of Washington had been packed with people hoping to hear Wilson's speech, or at least get a glimpse of him as he made his way to the Capitol. But by the time the grim-faced President finally left the White House with a cavalry escort at 8.20 p.m, the onset of darkness and persistent rain had thinned the crowds and dampened their enthusiasm.

The same could not be said for his audience in the Capitol, its famous white dome illuminated by lights from below. As he entered the House of Representatives – filled with congressmen, senators, justices of the Supreme Court, diplomats and Cabinet officials, many wearing or carrying little flags – the chamber rose and gave him a rapturous welcome. The applause continued as Wilson crossed the floor to the rostrum in front of the Speaker's desk, and only ended as he stood there impatiently, shuffling the papers of his speech.[1]

At last, with the room deathly quiet, Wilson rested his right arm on the high green-covered desk and started to speak in a voice husky with emotion.[2] He began by explaining that he had called the Congress into extraordinary session 'because there are serious, very serious, choices of policy to be made, and made immediately'. They had come about because of the 'extraordinary announcement' by the Imperial German Government to, as of 1 February, 'put aside all restraints of law or of humanity and use its submarines to sink every vessel that sought to approach either the ports of Great Britain and Ireland or the western coasts of Europe of any of the ports controlled by the enemies of Germany within the Mediterranean'.[3]

Such a policy had seemed to be the object of Germany's leaders earlier in the war, he continued, 'but since April of last year the Imperial Government had somewhat restrained the commanders of its undersea craft, in conformity with its promise, then given to us, that passenger boats should not be sunk and that due warning would be given to all other vessels'. Though the results were 'haphazard', a 'certain degree of restraint was observed'. The new policy, however, had 'swept every restriction aside'. Wilson added:

> Vessels of every kind, whatever their flag, their character, their cargo, their destination, their errand, have been ruthlessly sent to the bottom without warning and without thought of help or mercy for those on board, the vessels of friendly neutrals along with those of belligerents. Even hospital ships and ships carrying relief to the sorely bereaved and stricken people of Belgium . . . have been sunk with the same reckless lack of compassion or of principle.[4]

He noted that the German government had 'swept aside' the right of free passage on the seaways – a right only gradually and painfully cemented into international law – 'because it had no weapons which it could use at sea except these, which it is impossible to employ, as it is employing them, without throwing to the wind all scruples of humanity'.[5]

His greatest regret, he said, was not 'the loss of property involved, immense and serious as that is', but rather the 'wanton and wholesale destruction of the lives of noncombatants, men, women and children, engaged in pursuits which have always, even in the darkest periods of modern history, been deemed innocent and legitimate'. Property could be paid for, he added, 'the lives of peaceful and innocent people cannot be'.[6]

He characterized Germany's new U-boat campaign as 'warfare against mankind'. Every nation had to decide how to meet its challenge, he declared, but the choice for the United States had to be made without 'excited feeling' and with no desire for revenge. Instead the sole aim should be the 'vindication of right, of human right, of which we are only a single champion'. One option, which he himself had considered, was armed neutrality. Yet now he believed it would be 'worse than ineffectual' and 'likely only to produce what it was meant to prevent' by drawing the United States into the war 'without either the rights or the effectiveness of belligerents'. He continued: 'There is one choice we cannot make, we are incapable of making; we will not choose the path of submission and suffer the most sacred rights of our nation and our people to be ignored or violated.'[7]

On hearing the word 'submission', reported the *New York Times*, Chief Justice Edward White 'dropped the big soft hat he had been holding, raised his hands high in the air, and brought them together with a heart-felt bang; and House, Senate, and galleries followed him with a roar like a storm'.[8] This affirmation seemed to calm Wilson and as he reached the crux of his address his voice was 'vibrant and firm':[9]

> With a profound sense of the solemn and even tragical character of the step I am taking and of the grave responsibilities which it involves, but in unhesitating obedience to what I deem my constitutional duty, I advise that the Congress declare the recent course of the Imperial German Government to be in fact nothing less than war against the government

and people of the United States; that it formally accept the status of belligerent which has been thrust upon it; and that it take immediate steps not only to put the country in a more thorough state of defence, but also to exert all its power and employ all its resources to bring the government of the German Empire to terms and end the war.[10]

This would involve, he said, 'the immediate full equipment of the navy', particularly the 'best means of dealing with the enemy's submarines', the raising of an army of 'at least 500,000 men' on the principle of 'universal liability to service' (in other words national conscription), and 'the utmost practicable cooperation in counsel and action with the governments now at war with Germany'. He added: 'They are in the field, and we should help them in every way to be effective there.'[11]

The remainder of his speech was an attempt to claim for America and all other democratic nations the moral high ground: 'Our object . . . is to vindicate the principles of peace and justice in the life of the world as against selfish autocratic power and to set up amongst the really free and self-governed peoples of the world such a concert of purpose and of action as will henceforth insure the observance of those principles.'[12]

America's enemy was, in this sense, not the German people but their government. 'Only free peoples,' Wilson said, 'can hold their purpose and their honor steady to a common end and prefer the interests of mankind to any narrow interest of their own.' The recent revolution in Russia had come at a good time for the President because it enabled him to hold up the new Provisional Government as a shining beacon for the rest of the world. 'The great, generous Russian people,' he told Congress, 'have been added in all their naïve majesty and might to the forces that are fighting for freedom in the world, for justice, and for peace. Here is a fit partner for a League of Honor.'[13]

Prussian autocracy, on the other hand, had proven itself singularly untrustworthy and a 'natural foe to liberty' by its conduct in the war, its subversive activities in the United States, its intrigues and its plots. 'That it means to stir up enemies against us at our very doors,' said Wilson, 'the intercepted Zimmermann note to the German Minister at Mexico City is eloquent evidence.'[14]

America's task, as a result, was to fight 'for the rights of nations great and small and the privilege of men everywhere to choose their way of life and of obedience'.[15] His next passage is arguably the speech's most memorable:

> The world must be made safe for democracy. Its peace must be planted upon the tested foundations of political liberty. We have no selfish ends to serve. We desire no conquest, no dominion. We seek no indemnities for ourselves, no material compensation for the sacrifices we shall freely make. We are but one of the champions of the rights of mankind. We shall be satisfied when those rights have been made as secure as the faith and the freedom of nations can make them.[16]

It was, he confessed in his closing words, 'a fearful thing to lead this great, peaceful people into war, into the most terrible and disastrous of all wars, civilization itself seeming to be in the balance'. But the 'right is more precious than peace, and we shall fight for the things which we have always carried nearest our hearts'. He concluded: 'To such a task we can dedicate our lives and our fortunes, everything that we are and everything we have, with the pride of those who know that the day has come when America is privileged to spend her blood and her might for the principles that gave her birth and happiness and the peace which she has treasured. God helping her, she can do no other.'[17]

For a moment there was silence, as Congress digested the gravity of his words. Then, almost as one, the audience broke into deafening applause, with only a few anti-war diehards standing aloof. Leaving the chamber Wilson was stopped by Senator Henry Cabot Lodge of Massachusetts, a former opponent of the war, who shook him warmly by the hand. 'Mr President,' said Lodge, 'you have expressed in the loftiest manner possible the sentiments of the American people.'[18]

Most of his colleagues agreed, with the Senate passing Wilson's war resolution by 82 votes to 6 on 4 April, and the House of Representatives following suit by 373 votes to 50 in the early hours of the 6th. At 1.18 p.m. on 6 April, Wilson signed Congress's joint resolution and a state of war with Germany was formally declared.[19]

More than a month had elapsed since the publication of the Zimmermann Telegram, and more than two months since Germany's declaration of unrestricted submarine warfare. It had taken that long for Wilson and many of his countrymen to overcome their doubts about intervention, a process undoubtedly helped when U-boats sank four

American ships – the *Algonquin*, the *City of Memphis*, the *Vigilancia* and the *Illinois* – in a week in mid-March. A day after the last sinking, Wilson's entire Cabinet advised him to declare war.[20]

9 April 1917: *'Everything was smashed in'*
– The Canadians at Vimy Ridge

At 3.25 a.m., under the cover of darkness, the assault brigades of the 2nd Canadian Division left the shelter of the tunnels under Neuville-Saint-Vaast and moved to their jumping-off points in the trenches below Vimy Ridge, the objective of no fewer than three previous French attacks. The Canadians were confident, however, that after months of training and detailed planning this assault would be different. 'Nothing was left to chance and nothing kept secret,' noted a major of the 20th Battalion. 'We were all very tired and muddy,' wrote a Canadian signaller, 'but in good spirits as we were to go over all right and for most of us this was to be the first time.'[1]

Composed almost entirely of wartime volunteers, the 2nd Canadian Division had arrived in France in late 1915, but did not fight its first major action until the following spring when it lost 1,400 men in a botched attempt to consolidate the hard-won St Eloi Craters at the southern end of the Ypres salient. These blunders saw Lieutenant-General Edwin Alderson replaced as commander of the Canadian Corps by another British officer, Lieutenant-General Sir Julian Byng, in late May 1916. Byng admired the Canadians for their 'fighting qualities' and 'high morale', but thought them undisciplined and poorly trained.[2] Further setbacks – such as the failure of the 1st Division to capture the Regina Trench at Thiepval on the Somme – seemed to confirm his low opinion of Canadian troops. But it began to rise after the 2nd Division's successful attack on Courcelette on 15 September 1916, and improved still further during the intensive training for the Vimy Ridge attack in early 1917.

All four infantry divisions of the Canadian Corps were assigned to the Vimy operation. But, as Byng acknowledged in late March, 'the

French women sell oranges to Canadian soldiers on the march.

sector of the 2nd Canadian Division . . . is likely to have the heaviest fighting'. Here lay the villages of Les Tilleuls, Thélus and Farbus, several woods and a height known as Hill 135. The division was attacking on a front of 1,400 yards, expanding to 2,000 yards by the final objective – the Brown Line – which was located more than 2,500 yards from the British forward trench. Because the distance was so great, the 4th and 5th Canadian Brigades were assigned to capture the first three German trench systems – the front line, the Zwischen Stellung (the Red Line) and the Turko Graben (the Black Line) – while the 6th Canadian Brigade moved through them to take Thélus and the Blue and Brown Lines beyond; an attached British brigade, the 13th, would assist in the latter operation.[3]

So difficult was the 2nd Canadian Division's task that it had been assigned eight British tanks* – specifically to destroy barbed wire near Thélus – and no fewer than 183 field guns, howitzers and trench mortars, with additional heavy artillery support from three heavy and six medium howitzer batteries.[4] In all there were 963 heavy guns for a front of

* The only tanks assigned to the Canadian Corps on 9 April 1917.

fourteen miles, or one for every twenty-one yards; as opposed to 455, or one per fifty-seven yards, for the first day of the Somme.[5]

At 5.30 a.m. on 9 April, these guns opened fire on the German front line for three minutes, before adjusting their sights and making the first of forty-six carefully timed lifts. 'Looking towards the Hun trenches,' noted Second Lieutenant R. Lewis MM of the 25th (Nova Scotia) Battalion, a former mate on a Newfoundland steamboat, 'it appeared as if the whole line was afire. It was a grand and impressive sight.'[6]

At the same time whistles blew and the assaulting battalions climbed out of their trenches and moved steadily through sleet and light snow towards the German trenches, keeping 'well close to the protective barrage, as they had been instructed in their pre-battle training'.[7] Within eleven minutes, the leading waves of riflemen and rifle grenadiers, followed by Lewis gunners and bombers, had overrun the battered German front-line trench and captured the support line beyond. Advancing with a support battalion of the 5th Brigade, on the left of the division front, was Lieutenant Lewis of the 25th:

> The gallant pipers leading the 25th could be seen but it was impossible with the din to hear what they were playing. Gradually we advanced our ground – nothing but holes filled with mud and water to make the going very difficult. At last we reached the German line which had been taken by the 24th and 26th Battalion. We jumped into what was left of the trench and waited until the set time to move forward. Looking at the Hun trench one could easily see what good work the gunners were doing. Everything was smashed in; dugouts were gone and many of the enemy in them.[8]

Up ahead the advance was slowing as the opposition grew. 'Enemy machine guns by this time were sweeping the front,' noted a 5th Brigade summary, 'and were subdued only after sharp encounters, sometimes by rifle brigades . . . sometimes by counter machine-gun fire . . . sometimes by bombing with Mills grenades . . . and again by straight driving bayonet attacks in which many of the men participated.'[9]

On the 4th Brigade's front, a machine-gun held up the 18th (West Ontario) Battalion for a time, causing heavy casualties, until it was eventually overcome by a twenty-five-year-old lance-sergeant called Ellis Sifton who charged it alone, killing all the crew. He then held off a German counter-attack with his bayonet and clubbed rifle until help arrived; but soon afterwards fell mortally wounded. He was awarded a posthumous Victoria Cross, his valour saving 'many lives' and contributing 'largely to the success of the operation'.[10]

With the Black Line secure, the second stage of the attack was begun at 6.45 a.m. by the follow-up battalions. 'By this time,' recalled Lieutenant Lewis, 'the Boche realized that he had no small attack to deal with and his artillery, helped with many machine guns, started causing us many casualties . . . Major Delancy [the commanding officer] was killed and also R.S.M. Hinchcliffe. We could see our boys for miles advancing with confidence and determination. The Hun shells and bullets were coming swift but that did not stay the Canadians.'[11] By 7.15 a.m. Lewis and his Nova Scotians had taken the Turko Graben trench (the Red Line), two 77mm field guns, eight machine-guns, six trench mortars and scores of prisoners, at a cost of 253 casualties, including Major Delancy.[12]

None of the eight tanks assigned to the third phase of the attack made it much past the German support line, all breaking down or wallowing in the thick mud. The men of the 6th Canadian Brigade, meanwhile, saw many wounded as they advanced to their jumping-off point in the Red Line, 'some screaming to the skies, some lying silently, some begging for help, some struggling to keep from drowning in craters, the field swarming with stretcher-bearers trying to keep up with the casualties'.[13] They and men of the British 13th Brigade began their attack at 9.35 a.m., protected once again by a precise creeping barrage that lifted 100 yards every three minutes. Within ninety minutes they had taken Thélus and the Blue Line, though a similar time elapsed before they were ready to begin their assault on the final objective, the Brown Line, which stretched along the eastern sections of two woods.

Despite desperate German resistance – with gunners 'firing their guns point blank and using machine guns, rifles and revolvers' – the 2nd Canadian Division had secured all its objectives by 2.30 p.m. In congratulating his troops on their 'magnificent success', the GOC Major-General Burstall noted that the division 'had penetrated the enemy's defences to a depth of 2 miles' and captured 'some 1,500 prisoners and probably 15 guns in addition to Machine Guns and Trench Mortars'.[14]

The other Canadian divisions had enjoyed similar success – though the 4th suffered heavy casualties and would not take its final objectives until 12 April – and by nightfall the Vimy Ridge was, to all intents and purposes, in Allied hands. Further south General Allenby's Third Army had also made deep inroads into the German position near Monchy-le-Preux, with the 4th and 9th (Scottish) Divisions advancing four miles and another New Army division, the 12th, capturing German guns in Battery Valley.[15] General Humbert's Third French Army had supported the attack to the south.

The first day of what came to be known as the Battle of Arras was an unqualified success and Field Marshal Haig was delighted. 'Your Majesty will be pleased to hear,' he wrote to George V, 'that I found the troops everywhere in the most splendid spirits . . . [The] fact that the Army was *advancing* made everyone happy! . . . Our success is already the largest obtained on this front in *one* day.'[16]

Haig had never wanted to attack at Arras in 1917. His preference was for a continuation of the Somme attack, followed by a switch to Flanders to capture the Belgian coast. But since Joffre's replacement by Nivelle in December 1916, he had been forced by Lloyd George to conform to the new French Commander-in-Chief's plan to force a decisive breakthrough by attacking in Champagne while British and French forces pinned German reserves in the Arras–Somme area.

In order to achieve this, Haig had to keep on attacking, and this resulted in an attritional struggle with huge losses on both sides. By the time the Arras offensive finally ended on 17 May, British and Empire casualties were more than 159,000 – a daily rate of 4,076 that was higher than for any other major battle (including the Somme).[17] Among the casualties were two of Vera Brittain's closest friends: Victor Richardson (the 'third musketeer')* and Geoffrey Thurlow. Richardson was blinded near Arras on 9 April, and Thurlow killed two weeks later at Monchy-le-Preux. Vera's brother Edward, recovered from his Somme wound, wrote to her from Brocton Camp: 'Dear child, there is no more to say; we have

---

* On hearing of Richardson's serious injury, Vera returned from Malta to care for and, she hoped, eventually marry him. But he died two weeks after her arrival in June 1917. Edward wrote to her: 'I suppose it is better to have had such splendid friends as those three [Richardson, Thurlow and Roland Leighton] were rather than not to have had any particular friends at all, but yet, now that all are gone, it seems that whatever was of value in life has tumbled down like a house of cards' (Brittain, *Testament of Youth*, p. 360).

lost almost all there was to lose and what have we gained? Truly as you say has patriotism worn very very threadbare.'[18]

Recent historians have been more upbeat about the battle's outcome.

'The first day of the Arras offensive,' wrote Gary Sheffield, 'demonstrated that given careful preparation and staff work, massed artillery and well-trained and motivated infantry, the BEF was capable of capturing strong positions. The second and subsequent days of the battle, however, were to show that while since July 1916 the BEF had learned how to break *into* an enemy position, it had yet to master the art of breaking *out* and fighting a mobile battle.'[19]

By mid-April, Haig had kept his side of the bargain. Now it was the turn of the French.

16 April 1917: *'You won't find any Germans in front of you'*
– The first day of the Nivelle offensive

At 6 a.m. the whistles blew and infantrymen from twenty-four French divisions left their trenches in a blizzard and advanced towards the Chemin des Dames in Champagne, a twenty-five-mile ridge that for eight days had been saturated by more than eleven million shells. The intention behind the offensive – the brainchild of the new French Commander-in-Chief, Robert Nivelle – was to use 'violence, brutality and rapidity' to 'erupt' through to the third and fourth German lines in a single day. This they would manage, insisted Nivelle, by using the same tactics he had employed at Douaumont: a huge bombardment by 5,300 guns, followed by a carefully timed creeping barrage. So convinced was Nivelle that the guns had done their work that, shortly before the attack, he assured one of his army commanders: 'You won't find any Germans in front of you.'[1]

General Mangin of the French Sixth Army, the formation that would do most of the attacking, was just as bullish. 'I am ready,' he had told his men as they prepared to attack; 'the day after tomorrow my headquarters will be at Laon.'[2] Such certainty seems to have convinced the *poilus*. 'This offensive?' wrote Georges Bonnamy of the 131st Infantry. 'It's got to be our final effort, the end to all our suffering; it's got to bring a quick victory and put the enemy to rout. Everyone's talking about it and we're all confident . . . Everything's been carefully planned and any problems anticipated.'[3]

At first, with the French infantry encountering little opposition as they advanced up to half a mile in driving rain and sleet, it seemed as if their commanders' confidence was justified. What they could not know, however, was that this absence of defenders in the front line was deliberate. Having captured vital documents in raids on French trenches in February, the Germans knew an attack was planned and, moreover, had learned from Nivelle's two previous assaults at Verdun – in October and December 1916 – and adapted their tactics accordingly by introducing an 'elastic' defence in depth. 'Had we held to the stiff defence which had hitherto been the rule,' wrote Crown Prince Wilhelm, the German commander at Verdun, 'I am firmly convinced that we should not have come through the great defensive battles of 1917.'[4]

The sector chosen by Nivelle for his attack on 16 April could not have been more formidable: the Chemin des Dames ridge was 600 feet high, with a road running along the flat plateau from Fort Malmaison to Craonne; below it flowed the Aisne, fifty yards wide, with the French army packed into a bridgehead twelve miles wide between the river and the ridge. The ground on the right bank of the river was flat and marshy, rising as it neared the ridge to slopes and plateaux covered in thickets and small woods that offered excellent defensive cover.

To this naturally strong position the Germans had added their new system of defence in depth. The immediate front had been largely abandoned, with only poisoned wells and booby-traps left behind. Half a mile back, however, was a network of wire-concealed machine-gun nests and, even more formidable, subterranean concrete machine-gun posts with their roofs only a few inches above the ground. With interlocking fields of fire, these strongpoints dominated the killing-ground ahead. Much further back were placed the German artillery batteries and, beyond the reach of most French guns, the counter-attack divisions. 'The whole,' wrote French Army historian Anthony Clayton, 'comprised a trap within which the French could advance, expending manpower and energy, then enter a reverse slope zone where artillery could not provide support, only to meet, finally and when exhausted, fresh German reserves.'[5]

It was a trap that worked all too well. The preliminary bombardment had failed to destroy the subterranean machine-gun bunkers, and as the French *poilus* began to climb the slopes of the ridge they were cut down in their thousands. 'I went over the top,' wrote a soldier of the 25th Infantry. 'I ran, I shouted, I hit, I can't remember who or where. I crossed the wire, jumped over holes, crawled through shell craters still stinking of explosives, men were falling, cut in half as they ran; shouts and gasps were half muffled by the sweeping surge of gunfire.'[6]

A corporal of the 1st Infantry remembered: 'What disappointment! What slaughter! . . . The machine-guns stopped us dead. Within ten or fifteen minutes the company had been cut to pieces; among the dead, many veterans of Verdun and the Somme.'[7]

Held up, the attackers lost the support of their precisely timed creeping barrage and were easy prey for the German reserve units arriving from the rear. The Tirailleurs Marocains of Mangin's Sixth Army – attacking on the left of the line – was one of only a few units to reach its objective on the Chemin des Dames before it was forced back. Less impressive was a unit of Tirailleurs Sénégalais that broke and fled after being decimated by machine-gun fire,[8] though in their defence these black colonial troops were badly officered and poorly armed with out-of-date rifles and machetes.[9]

On the Fifth Army's front, to the right of the main attack, 132 Schneider tanks were used for the first time to help capture the village of Berry-au-Bac. But hampered by poorly trained and inexperienced crews, and deployed in a tactical role as close infantry support rather than as a shock weapon in their own right, the tanks made little headway against trenches serving as anti-tank ditches and artillery fire directed from aircraft or observation points. Tank corporal Jean-François Perette recorded: 'A deafening din fills the tank, the 75[mm gun] thunders, the two machine-guns spit continuously . . . Then the inevitable happens . . . A flash of lightning and a roar of thunder! I'm thrown to the base of the central pit, knocked out, dead! Yet, after a few moments of unconsciousness, I realize I'm still alive.'[10]

Other crews were not so fortunate. 'The tank on the left suddenly becomes an inferno,' recalled officer Charles Chenu. 'In front of it is the shell which set it alight. Two torches get out, two torches making a mad, frantic dash towards the rear, two torches which twist, which roll on the ground . . . A tank burns on the right; another one, behind. And on our left, it looks as if someone is setting our line of steel alight like a row of floodlights.'[11]

In all, fifty-seven Schneiders were destroyed; a further nineteen broke down or got bogged in the marshy ground. Only the group commanded by Major Louis Bossut crossed the German trenches; but as the accompanying infantry were unable to keep up, most were forced back to their start line. Bossut was killed.[12]

By the end of this disastrous first day's fighting, the French had suffered an appalling 100,000 casualties, with almost 25,000 dead (both figures significantly higher than the record British losses on 1 July 1916). Nivelle had predicted 10,000 wounded, and the medical authorities had catered for an extra 5,000. In the event, more than 75,000 men required treatment, causing the evacuation system to break down.[13] 'We had to go as far as the canal,' noted a soldier of the 8th Cuirassiers. '. . . There were at least 400 seriously wounded men on the banks. The chief MO [medical officer] was fuming. Although this attack had been planned a long time, no provision had been made for the evacuation of the wounded.'[14]

Conditions in a field hospital near Prouilly were chaotic, remembered René Naegelen of the 172nd Infantry:

> Stretchers cover the courtyard and the surrounding area. Greatcoats are thrown over immobile bodies, and the stretcher-bearers look for the gleam of rank braid under the dried mud. We'll bandage those, we'll do the others later. But the medical officers are overworked; there are too many wounded and not enough doctors. The walking wounded crowd around, demanding attention, pushing in front of their comrades moaning on stretchers. Blood-soaked linen is deftly removed, despite the cries of pain, [and] bottles of ether empty quickly, spreading their atrocious odour of suffering; soiled dressings pile up . . . And still the ambulances keep arriving.[15]

Amid this chaos, the morale of the *poilu* collapsed. '[The wounded men] were not the men the nurses expected, were used to,' noted Captain Edward Spears, the British liaison officer to the French Tenth Army, 'mangled but gallant, and very courteous. These men were broken in spirit as well as body; not a laugh among them, not a smile of greeting.

They were discouraged as French wounded had never been discouraged before. "It's all up," they said, "we can't do it, we shall never do it."[16]

Yet the fighting continued on the 17th, with the Fifth Army altering its axis of attack to the north-east so that it could link up with the assault by the neighbouring Fourth Army in the Monronvillers Hills. Both advances were driven back with heavy casualties. Further west the Sixth Army won a foothold on the ridge when it captured the villages of Condé, Vailly and Cerny. But over the next few days many of these gains were negated by German counter-attacks.

On 19 April the War Minister Paul Painlevé, who had initially argued for more limited attacks, tried and failed to persuade Nivelle to halt the offensive. Four days later, worried by mounting casualties and a slump in morale, President Poincaré forbade any more attacks on the Chemin des Dames, and soon extended this veto to Fifth Army attempts to capture Fort Brimont to the south-east of the ridge. Nivelle protested, blaming Mangin (who was sacked on 29 April), and was allowed to resume smaller-scale attacks that did manage to clear part of the Chemin des Dames and reopen the Reims–Soissons railway line. But the government had already lost faith in Nivelle and, as a prelude to his supercession, Pétain was appointed Chief of the Army General Staff (or senior military adviser to the government) on 29 April.

Pétain's influence was felt at an inter-Allied conference in Paris on 4 May – attended by, among others, Lloyd George, General Robertson and Field Marshal Haig, Alexandre Ribot (the new French Prime Minister), Painlevé and Nivelle – at which it was agreed that a 'breakthrough' operation on the Western Front was no longer feasible.[17] Instead the Allies would resume the strategy of attrition by continuing 'the offensive to the full extent of our power', but with the British Army playing the major role and the French confined to 'attacking vigorously to wear out and retain the Enemy on their front' – in other words, to prevent the Germans from reinforcing other fronts.[18] Lloyd George's preference was for a future offensive against the Belgian ports to stop their use as a base for German submarines.[19] But, he told the conference, he was no strategist and would give Haig 'full power to attack where and when' he 'thought best'.[20]

Eleven days later Pétain's ascendancy was complete when he replaced Nivelle as Commander-in-Chief, with Foch becoming Chief of the Army

General Staff. But Pétain was under no illusions as to the French Army's weaknesses: it had reserves of barely 35,000 men and, he told Haig on 3 May, would shrink through wastage at the rate of a division a month 'unless the Americans can be induced to send over men to enlist';[21] and, even more seriously, a combination of dreadful living conditions and the horrors of Verdun and the failed Nivelle offensive had reduced morale to such a level that a significant proportion of French soldiers were in open mutiny.[22]

29 April 1917: *'They have ruined the heart of the French soldier'*
– The start of the French mutinies

It began in a miserable rest camp near Soissons when the *poilus* of the 2nd/18th Regiment were ordered back into battle. Having lost more than half their comrades on 16 April, the disastrous first day of the Chemin des Dames offensive, they had been told their next front-line duty would be in a quiet sector in Alsace. It was a lie, and when the truth became known the whole battalion refused to parade prior to marching. Instead the men went on a drunken rampage, shouting that they were fed up with the war and wanted nothing further to do with it.[1]

Next morning, having sobered up, the men were all present for roll call. But their indiscipline had not been forgotten and, before the battalion began its march to the front, the suspected ringleaders were pulled from the ranks and court-martialled. Six were sentenced to death and subsequently shot; a further eight were given ten years' imprisonment with hard labour. Moreover their CO, Major Lavall, was demoted to captain and other officers replaced.[2]

As word of the 'mutiny' spread, there were more outbreaks of indiscipline on the Chemin des Dames, both from those already in the line and from others in reserve. By 20 May it was clear that a general mutiny had broken out in the armies in the battle zone. General Maistre, the new commander of Sixth Army, postponed an attack because he could not trust the men 'to leave the trenches'. When he asked for replacements,

General Franchet d'Espèrey (the army group commander) promised five divisions but said they were 'in a wretched state of morale'. On 26 May four battalions of the 158th Infantry Division refused orders to move to the front. Instead soldiers stormed railway stations, demanding trains to take them home. When some did reach Paris on leave they wrecked the terminals, hoping to prevent their return.[3]

Pétain's immediate response was to issue a directive to the generals commanding armies on the Western Front. The balance of forces at that time, he told them, did not allow for the possibility of a breakthrough. All efforts should therefore be directed to wearing down the enemy with smaller-scale attacks and minimum losses. 'To secure such attrition,' he wrote, 'it is wholly unnecessary to mount huge attacks with distant objectives.' Instead they should seek to achieve limited gains by the use of heavy artillery support, surprise and a rapid change of the point of attack to keep the enemy off balance. It was an attempt to deal with at least one of the mutineers' chief grievances: costly and fruitless large-scale attacks.[4]

But Pétain knew that other factors were at play. 'The real problem,' wrote his biographer Charles Williams, 'lay in the way the men of the line infantry were treated. Their trenches were little more than rivers of mud, urine and excrement. Their food was cold and maggot-ridden; their "rest areas" behind the front were squalid and rat-infested; the army medical service could not cope with the diseases, let alone the wounded . . . Above all, they were infuriated at being denied the proper entitlement to home leave.'[5]

Pétain at once set about tackling the latter issue by making seven days' leave compulsory for every four months of service, without exception. More trains were earmarked for this purpose, and reception facilities at the Paris terminals were overhauled. While poor service conditions were factors he could do something about, he told Painlevé in a memorandum of 29 May, others were beyond his control. They included the discontent sowed by newspapers and parliamentary deputies when they criticized the conduct of military operations.[6] There had also been, as he recognized later, the 'launching and exploitation of a pacifist propaganda campaign' in the winter of 1916–17, with soldiers in the trenches bombarded by 'antimilitarist leaflets'.[7]

This movement had gained traction because of the rising cost of living:

Disgruntled French soldiers leaving the battle zone.

in Paris food prices rose 92 per cent between July 1914 and July 1917, while real wages fell 10 per cent. An Interior Ministry survey in June 1917 found morale good in three departments, fairly good in thirty, indifferent in twenty-nine and bad in eight; in those regions with low morale, the influence of soldiers on leave was cited as a factor.[8] Yet Pétain was convinced that the soldiers became 'politicized' only when they felt let down by their generals, specifically Nivelle and Mangin. Restoring discipline was therefore a matter of restoring appropriate leadership.[9]

But all this took time to implement, allowing the virus to spread. On 1 June, the protests took a more sinister turn when two regiments of the 41st Division went on the rampage, waving red flags and singing the 'Internationale'. The men of a separate regiment, the 162nd, which had also suffered badly in the recent offensive, began to stone their headquarters when they heard rumours of a return to the front. A witness recorded:

Officers positioned in the front row tried to intervene. No good came of it since all they did was start a fight. Some of the hotheads pounced on them. Suddenly there was a bright light: it was a Ruggieri smoke pot, intended to set fire to the floorboards. That produced a stampede for the exit. Outside a crowd had grown, shouting and gesturing. There were cries of 'Down with war!' 'Rest and leave!' 'Death to shirkers!' 'Death to officers and NCOs!' 'To Paris! To Paris!' . . . A good thousand soldiers had gathered.[10]

At an emergency Cabinet meeting on 3 June, War Minister Painlevé reported that only two divisions between Paris and the Chemin des Dames front could be 'absolutely and wholly relied on'. The most that Pétain was prepared to admit to Haig, at a meeting on 7 June, was that some rebels had been shot and the disorder was well in hand.[11]

This was far from the truth. In all there were 250 separate incidents of disobedience, involving up to 40,000 men in sixty-eight divisions, more than half the total. Nine divisions were classified as 'very seriously affected', and a further five 'profoundly affected'.[12] One of the worst was the 5th Division where, according to a study by the American historian Leonard Smith, soldiers mixed calls for more regular leave and better food with appeals for peace and an end to the butchery. 'Once links to the home front were guaranteed by leave reform,' wrote Smith, 'soldiers could give up their demand for an immediate peace.' It was the soldiers' perception of themselves as citizens rather than subjects, argued Smith, that 'opened the door to tacit negotiations with Pétain', and the latter's use of a combination of 'repression, reforms, and proportionality' was what 'he and French soldiers could persuade each other to accept'.[13]

The repression came in the form of an instruction, on 1 June, that all armies had the power to summon *conseils de guerre* without reference to higher authority; this was followed on 9 June by an order from Painlevé abolishing the right of convicted soldiers to have their sentences reviewed (in either a civil court or, in the case of the death penalty, by the President himself). The result was a total of 554 men sentenced to death by *conseils de guerre*, of whom forty-nine were actually shot. A further 1,400 were sentenced to deportation and forced labour.[14] 'I set about suppressing serious cases of indiscipline with the utmost urgency,' explained Pétain to his army commanders on 18 June. 'I will maintain the repression firmly, but without forgetting that it applies to soldiers who have been in the trenches with us for three years and who are our soldiers.'[15]

Reforms were chiefly to conditions of service. Once they had been improved – with better food, more regular leave and, most importantly, no more futile attacks – the loyalty of the French Army in the Great War was never again in doubt. But while it would happily hold its ground, and even carry out limited attacks, it could not be trusted to mount a major offensive. Henceforth the chief burden of defeating the Germans on the Western Front would be left to the British and, when they arrived, the Americans. 'Pétain had purified the unhealthy atmosphere,' noted Sergeant Boasson, a veteran of Verdun and the Nivelle offensive. 'But it will be difficult for him to wipe out the impression of defiance which now rests in the heart of the soldier towards those whom he should have considered his leaders, his guides, his protectors, his paternal friends . . . They have ruined the heart of the French soldier.'[16]

29 April 1917: 'We attacked them by a rush'
– The Red Baron's deadliest day

'The weather was glorious. We were ready for starting,' remembered Rittmeister* Manfred von Richthofen. 'I had as a visitor a gentleman who had never seen a fight in the air or anything resembling it and he had just assured me that it would tremendously interest him to witness an aerial battle.'[1]

So before taking off from Douai airfield with five members of Jasta 11, the fighter formation he had commanded since January 1917, Richthofen gave the visitor a telescope to watch the drama unfold. It was a beautiful late-spring day and the bright colours of the Jasta's planes – the latest Albatros DIIIs, faster and more agile than anything the British could put in the air – were easy to spot against the clear blue sky, none more so than Richthofen's red Albatros which had caused the British to dub him 'le diable

---

* Richthofen had been promoted to the rank of *Rittmeister* (captain of cavalry, his original corps) in early April 1917.

rouge' and later 'the Red Baron'.* Richthofen was accompanied that day by some of his best pilots, including his brother Lothar, Karl Schäfer, Kurt Wolff and Bruno Loerzer. He himself was at the peak of his powers, having shot down more than thirty enemy planes since the turn of the year, giving him a total of forty-eight (the highest score for a living ace).[2]

At 6,000 feet Richthofen spotted five British planes coming towards him. 'We attacked them by a rush,' he recalled, 'as if we were cavalry and the hostile squadron lay destroyed on the ground. None of our men was even wounded. Of our enemies three had plunged to the ground and two had come down in flames.'[3]

The Jasta was using classic Richthofen tactics: simple, direct and deadly. 'I dive out of the sun,' he explained, 'taking into consideration the wind direction. Whoever reaches the enemy first has the privilege to shoot. The whole flight goes down with him. So-called "cover" at great altitude is a cloak for cowardice. If the first attacker has gun trouble, then it is the turn of the second, or the third and so on; two must never fire at the same time.' Like Boelcke, his late mentor, Richthofen preferred to close within fifty metres of his prey before opening fire. 'One does not need to be a clever pilot,' he wrote, 'or a crack shot, one only needs the courage to fly in close to the enemy.' This, he felt, was the 'secret of aerial victory' – and, as usual, it worked on 29 April.[4]

Three of his Jasta's five British victims were flying French-made Spads of 19 Squadron, sent to scout for Richthofen. They were led by Major Hubert Harvey-Kelly, the first British pilot to land on French soil in 1914, who earlier that month had described the current crop of German pilots as 'floating meat'. This overconfidence cost him his life, and added to Wolff's growing total; meanwhile Richthofen accounted for a young second lieutenant called Richard Applin, and his brother the remaining Spad flown by W. N. Hamilton. Of the trio, only Hamilton survived. The fate of the other two non-Spad pilots is unclear.[5]

On arriving back in Douai in time for a 'decent breakfast', Richthofen asked the visitor his impression of the fight. He was surprised by the response. Richthofen wrote: 'He had imagined that the affair would look

---

* Richthofen had begun by painting sections of his aircraft red, partly to discourage friendly fire, and his pilots did likewise as a sign of squadron unity. But they also applied other colours, prompting the British to refer to the Jasta as the 'Flying Circus'.

quite different, that it would be far more dramatic. He thought the whole encounter had looked quite harmless until suddenly some machines came falling down looking like rockets. I have gradually become accustomed to seeing [this], but I must say it impressed me very deeply when I saw the first Englishman fall and I have often seen the event again in my dreams.'[6]

The day's fighting, however, was far from over. Having wolfed down their breakfast, Richthofen and his men took off in their rearmed planes and shot down a further eight planes, giving a total of thirteen for the day. The star pilot, wrote the Red Baron, was 'Lieutenant Wolff, a delicate-looking little fellow in whom nobody could have suspected a redoubtable hero.* My brother destroyed two, Schäfer two, Festner two and I three.' That evening, Richthofen was asked by one of the downed British pilots if there was any truth in the rumour that the red Albatros was piloted by a girl, 'a kind of Jeanne d'Arc'. The Briton was 'intensely surprised' when Richthofen assured him 'that the supposed girl was standing in front of him'. He was 'convinced that only a girl could sit in the extravagantly painted machine'.[7]

The thirteen planes shot down by Richthofen's Jasta 11 on 29 April 1917 were the climax to a disastrous month for the Royal Flying Corps that became known as 'Bloody April'. It lost a total of 245 planes, 211 aircrew killed or missing, and a further 108 taken prisoner; German losses were 119 machines.[8] This disparity was caused by Trenchard's determination to continue to take the fight to the Germans at a time when British planes were markedly inferior. He admitted as much when he told Haig that various new types of plane – the Bristol Fighter, the SE5 and the Sopwith Camel – would not be available in any significant number until after the Arras offensive. 'Our fighting machines,' wrote Haig, 'will almost certainly be inferior in number and quite certainly in performance to those of the enemy.'[9]

Haig was right about quality but not about quantity. On the Arras front alone the RFC had 365 aircraft in twenty-five squadrons, almost double the number available to the Germans. But most of the German planes were scouts, vastly superior to the British aircraft in speed, climb and armament. Trenchard was forced to rely on numbers to bridge the

* Kurt Wolff was just twenty-two years old when he was shot down and killed in September 1917. He had thirty-three 'kills'.

quality gap during the Battle of Arras, and his crews paid the price.[10]

In an attempt to justify the heavy RFC losses since the turn of the year, Major-General Sir David Henderson, head of Military Aeronautics at the War Office, pointed out that the German retirement to the Hindenburg Line had increased the flying time for the RFC; and that its positive record of reconnaissance, artillery co-operation, contact patrols and tactical bombing had to be set against the German Air Force's primary and defensive role of shooting down British machines.[11] But many in Britain were unconvinced that Trenchard's tactics were working when the life expectancy of a newly arrived pilot was just seventeen days. 'Is the work being done, even in wartime,' asked Manchester MP William Joynson-Hicks, 'at too great a sacrifice?'[12]

Some pilots thought so. Describing Trenchard's policy as 'aerial attrition', Harold Balfour wondered whether a little more subtlety might have saved lives and produced the same results. Others applauded the RFC chief. 'The essential point,' wrote Jack Slessor, a 5th Squadron flight commander, 'is that the requirements of the army in reconnaissance, photography and artillery cooperation must always be met.' Another added: 'It makes me wild to see articles in the papers running down our Flying Corps on account of the casualties. If you only knew the work we do compared with the Hun, you would realise how ridiculous this is.'[13]

Help, however, was at hand. With the arrival over the coming months of Bristol Fighters and Sopwith Camels – the latter 'difficult to handle but superbly manoeuvrable' – the RFC had 'aeroplanes that could outfly and outshoot the Albatroses'. The 'crisis of April passed', wrote air historian Patrick Bishop, 'and the tide turned towards increasing Allied dominance of the air'.[14]

25 May 1917: *'I saw dead animals and people lying everywhere'*
– Death from above

In the late afternoon of a beautiful spring day, ten-year-old Win Reynolds was in the garden of her home in Folkestone, waiting for her aunt to take her shopping, when she heard the drone of aeroplanes. 'They were flying at a height where you could see the pilots,' she recalled, 'and thinking they were ours, I began to wave. I should think there were twenty-five planes in all flying about, very low. Other people came out and waved, as did my grandparents, there was no bother at all. We'd never seen aircraft like these before.'[1]

A few minutes later a lady spotted the planes near Earl's Avenue in Folkestone:

I stopped to watch their graceful antics [she wrote], and thought to myself, 'Now at last we are up and doing,' fondly imagining they were our own machines. I walked leisurely on, and as I was crossing Earl's Avenue I noticed a woman coming towards me carrying a basket. I had hardly time to reach the gate of the house I meant to visit when a bomb fell behind me, killing the woman I had just seen, and falling on the ground I had just walked over.[2]

Terrified that her daughter's school might be hit, she ran down Grimston Gardens over broken glass that 'crackled and broke under one's feet'. She added: 'In Grimston Gardens Tennis Courts a bomb had made a hole twenty-five feet across. I breathed once more when I found all the girls [in the school] well and safe.' She discovered later that other residents of Folkestone had not been so lucky:

[The enemy] dropped their final lot of bombs on Tontine Street, the poorer part of town near the harbour, where crowds of women were doing their week-end shopping. I was told afterwards by a medical man that it resembled a battlefield – a gruesome mass of severed heads, arms and legs mixed up with the wreckage of houses and broken windows. Doctors and ambulance men did their utmost to alleviate the suffering, and in a very short time every available bed in the hospital was filled. The exact number killed was not known until some time afterwards, but including several casualties at Shorncliffe Camp it amounted to several hundreds and a large number of horses.[3]

Caught up in the horrific carnage in Tontine Street was Win Reynolds, the young girl who had seen the planes from her garden. After the first bomb exploded she was dragged into the nearest shop and taken into the cellar. But she had only been there a few seconds when a lady with two blonde girls, both about five, decided to leave to 'see that her husband was safe'. Reynolds recalled: 'Well, as she left the shop a bomb fell on Stokes [greengrocers] and she got killed along with the two children with her . . . [She] was supposed to have been picked up with the two children's hands, one in each of her hands, and the children blown to pieces.'[4]

One of the first on the scene was John Pannett, a fourteen-year-old tobacconists' assistant. 'I ran along the street as fast as I could,' he remembered, 'and when I got to the point of the impact I saw dead animals and people lying everywhere, a terrible sight. All the gas was blowing out of a fractured main, six or seven feet in the air, and then I saw a lady, Mrs Sheridan . . . standing with a huge hole in her leg. Hardly anyone to my mind was moving.'[5] By the time Win Reynolds emerged from the cellar, 'there was just confusion and ever such a lot of screaming', including the 'horrifying, uncanny sound' of a horse neighing in pain. It had just delivered a wagonload of potatoes to Stokes and had been caught in the blast.[6]

Schoolgirl mourners look down into the freshly dug grave of one of the twenty-five child fatalities of the Folkestone air raid of 25 May 1917.

In all, 159 bombs were dropped in or near Folkestone, killing ninety-five people (including thirty women and twenty-five children) and injuring 192. The German plane responsible was the new Gotha IV, a twin-engined biplane with a three-man crew, a flight distance of 400 miles and a bomb payload of 1,100 pounds. It was designed to fly in formation and deliver wave after wave of devastating bombing raids that would eventually, the German leadership hoped, demoralize the British population and encourage its politicians to sue for peace. The strategy was aided by Britain's flimsy air defence, the result of a recent reduction in the number of fighter squadrons available for home defence so that more pilots could be sent to fight on the continent; and an order given to anti-aircraft batteries that, to husband resources, only those on the coast were to fire on enemy planes.[7]

The attack on Folkestone by twenty-three Gothas of Kampfgeschwader 3 – a special squadron formed to carry out strategic bombing – was the first of its kind over mainland Britain. Its intended target was London, but low-lying cloud – and not the scrambled fighters of the Home Defence Squadron – forced the German commander to look for an alternative. He chose the major Channel port of Folkestone and, having first bombed nearby Shorncliffe Camp, full of Canadians about to be shipped to France, released the rest of his 100-pound ordnance over the railway station and the docks.[8]

This latest example of 'Hun barbarity' was doubly shocking to residents of a port that, before the war, had sent fishermen and a lifeboat to rescue crewmen and recover bodies from a stricken German ship. 'So we thought,' recalled Win Reynolds, 'wherever they bomb, it won't be here, not after what we had done for them, saving a lot of sailors.'[9]

Folkestone and many other coastal and inland towns now installed klaxons to warn their residents of an impending air attack. Home defence squadrons were assigned better planes, and more of them. But Gothas still got through, launching one attack on London on 13 June 1917 that killed 162 people and injured 432 (the highest number of casualties inflicted by a single raid). After March 1918, the air raids tailed off as the Germans devoted all their resources to winning the war on the Western Front. There had, nevertheless, been a total of fifty-three Zeppelin and fifty-seven aeroplane raids on Britain, killing 1,413 people and injuring 3,407. The figures seem tiny when compared to the losses caused by

German air attacks during the Second World War: the 'Blitz' of London alone claimed 43,000 lives by mid-1941.[10] Yet their significance was in their novelty. Never before had civilians been considered a legitimate target of warring European nations; never again would non-combatants assume they were safe from enemy attack.

'You expect soldiers to fight and you expect some to be killed,' commented Win Reynolds, 'but you don't expect poor people going about their daily business, queuing for something to eat. The grown-ups hated them worst and their expression used to be there's only one good German and that's a dead one.'[11]

7 June 1917: *'The earth seemed to tear apart'*
– Messines Ridge

'It was an appalling moment,' recalled Second Lieutenant Jim Todd of the 11th West Yorkshires. 'We all had the feeling, "It's not going!" And then a most remarkable thing happened. The ground on which I was lying started to go up and down like an earthquake. It lasted for seconds and then, suddenly in front of us, the Hill 60 mine went up.'[1]

The mine was one of twenty-one that British tunnellers – most of them miners from Northumberland, Durham and South Wales in civilian life – had spent the previous five months digging under the German-held Messines–Wyschaete Ridge, just to the south of the Ypres salient. Placed in big chambers deep under the German positions, the mines contained almost 500 tons of ammonal explosive, the wire of their firing mechanisms fed back through tunnels – the longest of which stretched 2,000 feet – to detonators in the front line.[2] Nineteen-year-old Jimmy Naylor, a gunner officer attached to brigade staff, was standing next to one such detonator:

> Our plunger was in a dug-out, and the colonel and I were actually standing outside the dug-out because we both knew what was going to happen and we wanted to see as much as we could. The earth seemed to tear apart, and there was this enormous explosion right in front of us. It was an extraordinary sight. The whole ground went up and came back down again. It was like a huge mushroom.[3]

It was 3.10 a.m., shortly before dawn, and nineteen of the twenty-one mines had exploded on a nine-mile front,* the prelude to an infantry attack by nine British and imperial divisions, including New Zealanders transferred from Gallipoli. The assault was designed as a prelude to an even bigger offensive in the Ypres salient that Haig had been hoping to launch since early 1916, but which had been postponed because of the need to co-operate with the French (first on the Somme and then at Arras). The rationale for the Ypres offensive was that a relatively modest advance of twelve miles would allow the British to capture the vital communications junction of Roulers, which in turn would paralyse German logistics in Flanders and put the coast within striking distance. With German submarines operating from the Belgian coast, this was a strategic prize worth winning.[4]

But first Haig wanted to capture the Messines Ridge, guarding the southern flank of the Ypres salient, as part of the new Allied strategy agreed in early May to 'wear down and exhaust the Enemy by attacking by surprise as far as possible at points where not expected'.[5] His initial hope had been that his First, Third and Fifth Armies would 'simulate a continuance' of the Arras battle, mounting strictly limited attacks that would distract attention from the preparations for Messines. But these armies soon ran out of resources and the French were in no position to make their promised contribution, leaving Messines as a stand-alone operation. The detailed planning was left to General Sir Herbert Plumer, commanding the Second Army, with Haig optimistically insisting on the contingency of a cavalry advance towards Courtrai and Roulers in the event of a spectacular German collapse.[6]

So thorough were Plumer's preparations – including the digging of jumping-off and assembly trenches by night and camouflaging them by day – and so effective the preliminary bombardment (which was begun on 30 May by 2,266 guns, or one for every seven yards of front), that when the mines were blown on 7 June the 80,000 attacking infantrymen had the easiest task to advance under a protective creeping barrage and

---

* So powerful was the explosion that it was felt as far away as London, with Vera Brittain recalling 'a strange early morning shock like an earthquake' (Brittain, *Testament of Youth*, p. 356). Of the two mines that failed to explode, one was deliberately detonated in 1955. The other is still 'live'.

The edge of one of nineteen huge craters – this one 125 yards in diameter and more than 50 deep – caused by the detonation of British mines under the German front line at the Messines–Wyschaete Ridge in Flanders on 7 June 1917.

capture the shattered German trenches on the ridge.

Ten thousand German soldiers were killed outright or buried alive in the massive explosions, one of which – at Spanbroekmolen in the centre of the ridge – left a crater 430 feet in diameter. Thousands more were stunned or dazed, and 7,354 taken prisoner. 'They didn't seem to have any wits about them,' recalled Rifleman Tom Cantlon of the 21st King's Royal Rifle Corps, attacking near St Eloi. 'We didn't even have to bother to take them prisoner ... We just saw them coming at us through the smoke, running towards us like jellies. They didn't know where they were. You just jerked your thumb backwards and they ran off towards our lines – and on we went.'[7]

The future Prime Minister Anthony Eden, then a young officer in Cantlon's battalion, remembered the 'screams of the imprisoned Germans in the crater' to their front. 'We could do nothing for them,' he wrote, 'for we had at all costs to keep up with our barrage.' Only one of his men was killed, a 'trusted' young rifleman who went ahead to knock out a German position. When Eden found him 'spread-eagled on the ground, mortally wounded and already unconscious', he was 'overwhelmed for the moment with bitter sadness'. He explained: 'Perhaps it was the helpless position in which his body lay, the sudden and pathetic waste of a young life, a boy determined to do his duty.'[8]

Further north, having skirted the immense craters on Hill 60, the men of the 11th West Yorkshires had the task of securing the old German front line. Second Lieutenant Jim Todd recalled:

> We found a lot of German pillboxes up there and had to clear them out. There were quite a few Germans in them and we'd shout into them to come out; if they didn't, then we chucked a bomb in. They came out fast enough then! It was eight or nine in the morning before we got properly dug in and by then the Germans had started a counter-barrage, so we were having some casualties.[9]

The toughest opposition was faced by the New Zealand Division, opposite the village of Messines to the south of the ridge, where the German counter-barrage was particularly effective. 'It was a case of shell-hole to shell-hole,' recorded Bert Stokes, a gunner from Wellington, 'as the enemy shells were beginning to stream over . . . We reached our destination and ran a wire to a shell-hole where we decided to stop. It was as good a place as any. The "Dinks" (New Zealand Rifle Brigade) were holding our front line in Unbearable Trench about a hundred yards ahead of us. This trench had been our first objective and the boys were digging in for all they knew. We were now about 800 yards past Messines on our right.'[10]

The furthest advance was achieved by two tanks that made it as far as a farmhouse strongpoint, five miles beyond their start point. Corporal Nick Lee of the *Revenge* recalled:

> We went left and *Iron Rations* went right and we started attacking the farmhouse from both sides. Well, after about half a dozen shells we hit something flammable . . . perhaps some petrol cans or small-arms ammunition. Flames started belching out of one of the windows and to our absolute amazement we suddenly saw all these Jerries streaming out of the back door . . . Very few of them made it to the wood. When the

resistance had finished we turned away. We were getting low on ammunition and low on petrol too.[11]

Everywhere the attacking troops had reached their final objectives and the ridge was in Allied hands for the first time since November 1914. A delighted Haig wrote in his diary:

> The explosion of the mines was highly successful . . . Altogether nearly *one million* pounds of explosives were used! The 'Tunnelling Companies' concerned deserve high praise for their endurance and perseverance for they fought the Enemy continuously underground all these many months!
>
> Soon after 4 p.m. I visited General Plumer at his HQ at Cassel, and congratulated him on his success. The old man deserves the highest praise for he has patiently defended the Ypres salient for 2½ years . . .
>
> The operations today are probably the most successful I have yet undertaken . . . Our losses are reported to be very small. *Under* 11,000 for the 9 divisions which attacked.[12]

But Haig's hopes of exploiting this success were dashed by Plumer's unwillingness to keep attacking until he had redeployed his artillery. Haig duly handed over operational control to Gough, the Fifth Army commander, who advised against any more assaults on 14 June because they would simply create 'a very exposed and difficult salient'.[13]

28 June 1917: 'We lacked not only the training, but the organisation'
– The doughboys arrive in France

Corporal Clarence Mahan, a former mechanic from Shelby County in Texas, was just twenty-three years old when he disembarked at Saint-Nazaire with the first contingent of 14,000 US troops – or 'doughboys'*

---

* The derivation of the name 'doughboy' is disputed: some claim it was because the US soldiers were paid ten times as much as their French colleagues and so were loaded with 'dough'; others that it dated back to a time when the infantry wore spherical buttons resembling dumplings (Mead, *The Doughboys*, pp. 66–7).

– to reach France. Escorted by warships, the journey in three transports had been long and uncomfortable. 'We were packed in the ship like sardines in a can,' recalled Mahan. 'The carpenters made bunks four high. The bottom man was almost on the floor while the top man was practically against the ceiling. I drew the second bunk.[1]

Mahan and his comrades in the 2nd/16th Infantry were part of the American Expeditionary Force (AEF)'s 1st Infantry Division, a regular formation of professional soldiers. Hardly any of them, however, were veterans: Mahan had joined up after the US had entered the war; fewer than half the company commanders had more than six months' experience; and two-thirds of the rank and file were half-trained raw recruits. Their commander, Major-General Robert Lee Bullard, recalled:

> Most of them expected to join in the fighting without delay. So little real comprehension had any of us of the conditions we were facing! It was to be months before any of us would see the front. We had not upon landing, we later found out to our chagrin, anything but a willingness to fight. We lacked not only the training, but the organisation; and even for the infantry, the body of the army, we lacked the kind of arms with which we were later to face the enemy.[2]

This was hardly surprising. In April 1917, when President Wilson committed the United States to war with Germany, the regular army consisted of just 5,000 officers and 120,000 men, few of whom had fired a shot in anger; the only other military force was the part-time National Guard, consisting of 80,000 poorly trained men. Yet within three weeks of the passing of the Selective Service Act – committing all males between the ages of twenty-one and thirty (later extended to between eighteen and thirty-five) to military service – almost ten million young men had presented themselves for registration. Of that number, 800,000 were deferred because they were doing essential war work, while 687,000 were selected by national lottery to form the first batch of military recruits. Eventually more than 2.8 million men were inducted by the local draft boards. They formed the bulk of the new National Army (77 per cent), with the balance made up of regulars (13 per cent) and National Guardsmen (10 per cent).[3]

The inevitable weakness of such a rapidly expanded army was, of course, its lack of experienced and competent officers and NCOs. The problem was partially solved by the setting up of a national network of officer-training camps (OTCs), the first 43,000 candidates of which were admitted in May 1917. But the provision of staff for these camps meant that fewer than half the original regulars were available to fight in France.[4]

The typical enlisted doughboy was a 'white man in his early twenties, having little education and no previous military experience'. If he 'was lucky, he received six months' training in the United States and then two months' in France'. Many 'were relatively recent immigrants with naturalized status, and spoke or read very little English'. There were large numbers of black American soldiers, though none was permitted to serve in the same unit as whites, and only a few black regiments

General John 'Black Jack' Pershing, commander of the American Expeditionary Force, arriving in France on 13 June 1917.

fought on the Western Front (and not for lack of trying). 'Marginalized, despised, poorly led and inadequately trained,' wrote Gary Mead in *The Doughboys*, 'only two black combat divisions were raised and sent to France, the 92nd and 93rd. Only the 92nd saw service alongside white American divisions. Most of those black Americans who enlisted were shepherded towards the Service of Supply (SOS), the logistics branch of the AEF, where they were generally shovelled into the worst kinds of brutalizing labour.'[5]

The man chosen to command the AEF was fifty-six-year-old Major-General John 'Black Jack' Pershing, a tall and broad-shouldered bull of a man who made up with his combat experience what he lacked in seniority. Of German Alsatian descent – his paternal grandfather's name was Poersching – he was not gifted academically and had passed out thirtieth of his class at West Point in 1886. Instead his strong work ethic, willingness to learn and powers of organization had enabled him to reach the rank of brigadier-general by the age of forty-five (passing over the heads of 862 more senior officers in the process). He was undoubtedly helped by the patronage of President Theodore ('Teddy') Roosevelt, who had become a good friend, and of his father-in-law, the Wyoming Republican senator Francis E. Warren.[6]

His first major command was to lead 15,000 soldiers on a punitive expedition against the Mexican bandit 'Pancho' Villa in 1915; it was a mission that, while politically ill-considered, he conducted with 'skill and courage' by taking his men 400 miles into Mexico, 'wounding Villa and scattering his bandits' before pulling back. His professional gain, however, came at a huge personal loss: while still in Mexico, Pershing received the tragic news that his wife and three daughters had been killed in a San Francisco house fire.[7] The widower's chief attraction for President Wilson was that, unlike some of his contemporaries, he was unswervingly loyal to his political superiors.

When Pershing arrived in France with his staff on 13 June, he carried orders instructing him to maintain a distinct and separate US army. He was welcomed with open arms by the hard-pressed French who, with a large proportion of their army still paralysed by indiscipline, were hoping the Americans would fill the breach. Yet they reckoned without the inexperience of the American troops, their complete ignorance of industrial warfare, and their inadequate supplies of artillery and munitions (a problem that would last until the end of the war), machine-guns, tanks and motor transport.[8]

At his first meeting with Pétain on 16 June, Pershing agreed that when strong enough the AEF would hold a sector of the front to the east of the Argonne Forest in Lorraine. It was the ideal location: it was quiet, and it would not require the AEF to guard either Paris or the Channel ports; yet a successful offensive here would, wrote Pershing, threaten 'the invasion of rich German territory in the Moselle Valley and the Saar Basin', have 'a decisive effect in forcing a withdrawal of German troops from northern France', and help to achieve Wilson's aim of bringing the war to a swift conclusion.[9] But first the new arrivals needed instruction in trench warfare and, following a welcome parade in Paris on 4 July (at which Pershing won over the French by kneeling to kiss Napoleon Bonaparte's sword), Mahan and his comrades in the US 1st Division were sent to a base at Gondrecourt, near the Argonne front, where for two months they were tutored by elite French troops.

While his men trained, Pershing and his staff worked hard to prepare the ground for an army that by 1918, they hoped, would have increased in size to one million men and twenty divisions, with room for a further expansion to three million men and 100 divisions by the end of 1919. He also took his senior staff officers to meet Haig at GHQ. 'I had a talk with General Pershing before and also after dinner,' Haig noted in his diary on 20 July.

> I was much struck with his quiet gentlemanly bearing – so unusual for an American. Most anxious to learn, and fully realizes the greatness of the task before him. He has already begun to realize that the French are a broken reed.
>
> His AG [Adjutant-General] and CGS [Chief of General Staff] are men of less quality, and are hardly 'soldiers' in our sense of the term, and all quite ignorant of the problems of modern war. The CGS is a kindly soft looking fellow with a face of a Punchinello. The AG having served long in Manila and other hot places, seems less alert mentally than the others.[10]

The BEF commander was more impressed by Pershing's aide-de-camp, a thirty-one-year-old captain from California who had finished fifth in the modern pentathlon at the Stockholm Olympics in 1912. 'The ADC,' wrote Haig, 'is a fire-eater, and longs for the fray.'[11] His name was George S. Patton.

1 July 1917:* *'To vanquish is our desire'*
– Russia's last throw of the dice

Just hours before the soldiers of the Russian Eleventh Army began their assault on the Austro-Hungarian Second Army near the Strypa river, the Commander-in-Chief Alexei Brusilov sent them a message of encouragement. 'He who advances vanquishes, but he who awaits the attack of the enemy perishes ingloriously. To vanquish is our desire.'[1]

For the previous two days, 900 guns had pounded the Austrian positions on a thirteen-mile front. 'Never before,' wrote General Anton Deniken, Brusilov's chief of staff, 'had I had the good fortune to fight with great numerical superiority in bayonets and materials. Never before had success seemed more assured.'[2] At dawn the Russian guns ceased fire and Alexander Kerensky, War Minister and the driving force behind the offensive, held his breath as he and Brusilov looked through binoculars from the Eleventh Army's observation post. Would the soldiers actually leave their trenches? Kerensky wondered. He soon got his answer as a few specks appeared in no man's land, followed by more and then a general horde of advancing troops.[3]

The focus of the attack was the Czech 19th Division that, prior to the battle, had been persuaded by a battalion of former Czech prisoners of war to surrender en masse. It now did so, with 3,000 men laying down their arms and leaving a huge hole in the Austrian defences.[4] Elsewhere the resistance to the attack was minimal: the Zoraisky Regiment captured the village of Prosovce and the 4th Finnish Division, supported by the Czech Brigade (former Austrian prisoners of war who had agreed to fight for Russia), took the heights of Zborov and Korshiduv. By nightfall on 1 July the Seventh Army had captured nearly 18,000 prisoners, twenty-one guns and sixteen machine-guns.[5]

* 18 June 1917, using the Russian Julian calendar.

At the inter-Allied conference at Petrograd in February 1917, the Russians had agreed to launch their major offensive on the Eastern Front in the spring. But after the February Revolution it was clear to General Alexeev, then Commander-in-Chief, that that date would have to be postponed: 'the roads were still covered in ice; horses and fodder were in short supply; the reserve units were falling apart; military discipline was breaking down; and the [Petrograd] Soviet, which controlled all the essential levers of power, was still reluctant to support anything beyond a purely defensive strategy'.[6]

Yet most of the military commanders were agreed that an offensive in the summer was necessary to pre-empt a German attack and, they hoped, compel the government to tackle indiscipline in the army, particularly the appearance of soldiers' committees in the wake of the Petrograd Soviet's Army Order No. 1 in March (forcing officers to coexist with them or risk arrest). The generals found support in the Provisional Government which, though it urgently 'desired an end to the war', refused to negotiate separately. 'In order to achieve a general peace,' wrote David Stevenson, 'it believed it must persuade its allies to reduce their war aims, and that as a precondition it must restore its credibility by proving to them that Russia was indispensable.'[7] In other words, it launched the offensive to make a general settlement possible.

Kerensky chose General Brusilov to replace Alexeev and direct the offensive because of the latter's optimism. 'I needed men who believed that the Russian army was not ruined,' explained Kerensky. 'I had no use for people who could not genuinely accept the *fait accompli* of the Revolution, or who doubted that we could rebuild the army's morale in the new psychological atmosphere.'[8] Brusilov – the hero of the 1916 campaign – had been one of the first Tsarist generals to throw in his lot with the revolution, supporting the soldiers' committees in the belief that they would help to restore esprit de corps. But as the date for the offensive approached he began to have second thoughts. On the Northern Front he visited a division that had driven out its officers and was threatening to go home. 'When I arrived at their camp,' he recalled,

> I demanded to speak to a delegation of the soldiers: it would have been dangerous to appear before the whole crowd ... I asked them which party they belonged to, and they replied that before they had been

Socialist Revolutionaries, but that now they supported the Bolsheviks.* 'What do you want?' I asked then. 'Land and freedom,' they all cried. 'And what else?' The answer was simple: 'Nothing else.' When I asked them what they wanted now, they said they did not want to fight any more and pleaded to be allowed to go home in order to share out the land their fellow villagers had taken from the squires.[9]

Officially more than 170,000 Russian soldiers deserted during this period, though the true figure was much higher. Some stormed trains heading to the rear; others lived as bandits. When they were not abandoning their posts, they were fraternizing with the enemy. On the front of the Seventh Army, for example, a German scout persuaded the troops to observe an unofficial armistice that lasted until the offensive. Brusilov warned Kerensky that troops were refusing to move up to the front, mutinies were on the increase and a number of unreliable units had been disbanded. But Kerensky would not listen. 'He paid not the slightest attention to my words,' wrote Brusilov, 'and from that moment on I realized that my own authority as the Commander-in-Chief was quite irrelevant.'[10]

The plan was to launch consecutive attacks by three armies – the Eleventh, Seventh and Eighth – across 120 miles of the South-Western Front with Lemberg as the objective. Nominally the Russians had a numerical advantage of forty-eight divisions and 1,350 guns (including 370 heavy calibre) to the Austro-Germans' twenty-six divisions and 988 guns (with only sixty heavies).[11] But that would depend on how many Russian units were prepared to fight.

In the event the Eleventh Army made excellent progress on 1 July and, for a couple of days at least, Kerensky's optimism seemed justified. But on 4 July, when the Seventh Army – the largest of the three – began its offensive against the German Südarmee it found that the enemy had abandoned the forward trenches and stiffened its defences to the rear. Against these the advance foundered, and even some of the abandoned trenches could not be held against counter-attacks.

---

* The Bolsheviks were the only revolutionaries who supported an immediate end to the war. Both the SRs and Mensheviks had, in the form of the Petrograd Soviet, endorsed the offensive in the hope of strengthening Russia's bargaining position before peace talks.

War Minister Alexander Kerensky (under the 'X') meets front-line troops
prior to the last Russian offensive of the war in July 1917.

Three days later the Russian Eighth Army attacked in the south and
even the Eleventh's gains were eclipsed: a seven-mile advance was achieved
on the first day; Halicz fell on the 10th, severing the rail link between
Lemberg and Stanislau; and by 15 July the Austro-Hungarian Third Army
had withdrawn to the left bank of the Stryi river in Galicia. In just over
a week the Eighth Army had taken 10,000 soldiers and eighty guns and
established a salient fifty-five miles wide and forty deep.[12]

But when the Austro-Germans counter-attacked on 19 July, using four
divisions sent from the Western Front, Russian resistance swiftly collapsed.
At one point, according to Brusilov, the 607th Mlynovsky Regiment 'left
their trenches voluntarily and retired, with the result that the neighbouring
units had to retire also'. He added: 'Our failure is explained to a considerable degree by the fact that under the influence of the extremists
(Bolsheviks) several detachments, having received the command to support
the attacked detachments, held meetings and discussed the advisability of
obeying the order . . . The efforts of the commanders and committees to
arouse the men to the fulfilment of their commands were fruitless.'[13]

Within six days the Austro-Germans had driven all three Russian armies back more than twenty-five miles, retaking Stanislav and capturing Tarnopol. By 4 August, by which time their supply lines were overextended and their soldiers exhausted, the Central Powers' soldiers had captured Cernowitz (in Russian hands since the Brusilov offensive) and reached the border of Romania. They had advanced ninety miles in two weeks.

The failed offensive – Russia's last of the war – cost Brusilov his job (he was succeeded by General Kornilov) and convinced Kerensky, who had replaced Prince Lvov as Prime Minister on 20 July after the failure of a Bolshevik coup d'état,* that a negotiated peace was the only way to save the tottering Russian Empire.

2 July 1917: *'They shoot a lot and hit a little'*
– The Battle for Aqaba

As dawn broke, Captain T. E. Lawrence and his Arab allies – led by the chiefs Sharif Nasir and Auda abu Tayi – were sitting astride the Jabal al Batra ridge in southern Syria. Directly to the south, glowing green and gold in the early morning light, was the Quwayrah plain; and beyond that the Wadi Itm gorge leading down to the port of Aqaba at the head of the Red Sea. But their immediate target was the Turkish battalion holding the pass below them at Abu al Assal.[1]

Once it was light Auda's Bedouin tribesmen – whose loyalty Lawrence had bought for £10,000 in gold – began to snipe at the Turks in their exposed position. They were hoping, wrote Lawrence, to 'provoke' their foes to charge up the hill. But the Turks would not be drawn and, as the morning wore on, the Arabs began to wilt in temperatures hotter than Lawrence had known in Arabia. He recalled:

> Some even of the tough tribesmen broke down under the cruelty of the sun, and crawled or had to be thrown under rocks to recover in

---

* Prompting Vladimir Ilich Lenin, the leader of the rising, to flee to Finland. In April 1917, after the Tsar's downfall, Lenin had returned to Petrograd from exile in Switzerland, courtesy of a 'sealed train' provided by the Germans who felt his pacifist stance would best serve their interests.

their shade. We ran up and down to supply our lack of numbers by mobility . . . Our rifles grew so hot with sun and shooting that they seared our hands; and we had to be grudging of our rounds, considering every shot and spending great pains to make it sure . . . We consoled ourselves with knowledge that the enemy's enclosed valley would be hotter than our open hills.[2]

Shortly after noon, feigning sunstroke, an exhausted Lawrence crawled into a hollow where he tried to slake his thirst in a trickle of muddy water. He was joined by Sharif Nasir, the brother of the Emir of Medina, who was 'panting like a winded animal, with his cracked and bleeding lips shrunk apart in his distress'. When Auda found them he was unimpressed. 'All talk and no work?' he asked. Lawrence's tart response was that Auda's men were useless: 'They shoot a lot and hit a little.'[3]

This infuriated Auda, who tore off his headdress and ran back up the hill, shouting at his men to get their horses. By the time Lawrence and Nasir had mounted their camels and joined the remaining 400 camel men in a slight depression, just out of sight of the Turks, Auda and his horsemen had begun their charge. Lawrence wrote:

> We kicked our camels furiously to the edge, to see our fifty horsemen coming down the last slope into the main valley like a run-away, at full gallop, shooting from the saddle. As we watched, two or three went down, but the rest thundered forward at marvellous speed, and the Turkish infantry, huddled together under the cliff ready to cut their desperate way out towards Maan, in the first dusk began to sway in and out, and finally broke before the rush, adding their flight to Auda's charge.[4]

This gave Lawrence, Nasir and the camel men the chance to take the retreating Turks in the flank. They 'fired a few shots', remembered Lawrence, 'but mostly only shrieked and turned to run'. As Lawrence led the charge, firing at the fleeing enemy with his pistol, his camel tripped and sent him flying over its head, the impact driving 'all power and feeling out of me'. Coming to his senses, he realized he had accidentally shot the beast in the back of its head. The battle, however, was won: at a cost of two killed and one wounded, the Arabs had taken 160 prisoners (including the wounded Turkish commander) and a further 300 'dead and dying' Turks lay 'scattered over the open valleys'.[5]

Auda, miraculously, had survived a Turkish volley that killed his mare, shattered his field glasses, pierced his pistol holster and cut his sword scabbard to ribbons. He put his good fortune down to the purchase, thirteen years earlier, of a small Koran for £120. Lawrence was unconvinced, noting that 'the book was a Glasgow reproduction, costing eighteen pence'.[6]

Having learned from a shaken Turkish prisoner that nearby Maan, a stop on the strategically vital Damascus-to-Medina railway, was held by only two companies of troops, Lawrence considered heading there next. But Nasir and Auda persuaded him to stick to the original scheme to capture Aqaba, arguing that they had 'no supports, no regulars, no guns, no base nearer than Wejh, no communications, no money even, for our gold was exhausted'.[7]

They pushed on south the next day – many of the Bedouin tribesmen wearing Turkish uniforms – and used local tribesmen to capture the outposts of Quwayrah and Kethera on 3 and 4 August respectively. The last fort of Khadra, at the mouth of the Wadi Itm, surrendered two days later after protracted negotiations. 'We mounted our camels,' recalled

Camel-mounted Arab allies of Captain T. E. Lawrence ('of Arabia') on campaign in 1917.

Lawrence, 'and raced through a driving sand-storm down to Aqaba, only four miles further, and splashed into the sea, on July the sixth, just two months after setting out from Wejh.'[8]

That same day, escorted by a small band of tribesmen, Lawrence set off across the Turkish-held Sinai peninsula to report the fall of Aqaba to the British authorities in Egypt. His arrival at the Suez Canal in Arab dress caused a sensation, particularly at the British military headquarters where General 'Bull' Allenby had just arrived from the Western Front to take command. True to form, Lawrence took all the credit for the successful Aqaba campaign, exaggerating his own role and belittling that of Auda and Nasir. What was not in doubt, however, was the effect the capture of Aqaba had on breathing new life into an Arab rebellion that 'had hitherto been bottled up in the Arabian peninsula by the Turkish garrison at Medina'.[9] All attempts to take Medina by force had failed, and would continue to fail, prompting this latest strategy to bypass the bottleneck by raising the tribes in northern Arabia and striking towards the coast from Bair. Feisal ibn Hussein, son of the Sharif of Mecca (the leader of the rebellion), was in overall command; but Lawrence, Nasir and particularly Auda had directed the Aqaba operation, with results that were far reaching. 'Now the Royal Navy could transport Arabian tribesmen to Palestine,' wrote David Fromkin, 'and thus, for the first time, Hussein's forces could reach a battlefield on which the British–Turkish war was actually to be fought, for Lawrence persuaded Allenby that Arab irregulars could assist British forces in the coming Palestine and Syria operations.'[10]

31 July 1917: *'A fine day's work'*
– The opening of the Third Battle of Ypres

Lieutenant Jim Annan of the 1/9th Royal Scots had just moved his platoon on to a temporary bridge over the Yser Canal, on the left of the Ypres salient, when a shell landed on the exact spot he had just vacated, destroying an ambulance full of wounded. He hurried his men forward towards Minty Farm, a German strongpoint half a mile to his front, which had already been captured by the 4th Gordons. 'They took it with the bayonet, like wild things,' he remembered, 'and when we got to it the dead were lying all around. Germans, grey against the mud, all mixed up with dead Gordons lying there in their kilts.'[1]

Elsewhere in the centre and left of the Ypres salient the attacking troops also made good progress. William Dawson, the veteran of armoured actions at Flers–Courcelette and Arras, was tasked with driving his Mark IV tank up the Ypres–Passchendaele Road towards the German second line at Frezenberg. He recorded:

> By careful observation of the ground ahead and steering accordingly we made what could be called good progress in spite of the fact that the battlefield was a total mass of shell holes, great and small, smashed trenches and almost a quagmire owing to it being so low and almost no drainage. We were soon in front of the infantry and heading for the enemy second line and Frezenberg. Our guns had already been in action but as we neared these points we were being hit by heavy machine gun fire. The 6 pdr guns however began to have a great effect on the Frezenberg stronghold, silencing the enemy machine guns and helping to overcome the strongpoint.

But the next wave of tanks did not get much further as 'the ground', wrote Dawson, 'became even worse – if that was possible – and they were stuck in mud or ditched or knocked out'. With no possibility of moving forward, and running low on ammunition and fuel, Dawson's tank returned to its lines, one of only two to do so.[2]

Further south, where the Fifth Army's objective was the Gheluvelt plateau, the German resistance was stiffer and the progress less impressive. Hooge Château, Haig's headquarters in November 1914, was recaptured in the first rush. But as men of the 8th Division moved towards the second German line at Westhoek they and their supporting tanks were held up just short. Commanding a tank in a section of four – part of the second wave of attackers – was twenty-one-year-old Lieutenant N. M. Dillon. As the section approached the start line in darkness, Dillon was asked by his captain to lead the tanks on foot because he 'knew the way better than the rest'. So Dillon did so, walking ahead 'while my tank waddled over shell-holes & trenches with the other three following'.[3]

On reaching the original front line, just before Hooge village, he noticed the German trenches 'had been smashed almost out of recognition by our gun-fire & here and there a dead German could be seen'. Up ahead, in the gap between Château and Sanctuary Woods, the tanks came 'under direct fire from the German batteries, anti tank guns & machine guns'. Both Westhoek and Glencorse Wood should, by this time, have been captured by the first wave; but they were still held by Germans and Dillon could 'distinctly see the flashes of the Bosch machine-guns, whose gunners had climbed the trees'.[4]

Dillon was still on foot, preferring the open to the 'stifling interior of a tank under shell-fire', and was 'dodging, as best I could, from one side of my tank to the other as the machine guns fired from various directions'. It was now that he directed the fire of his tank's 6-pounder against a concrete machine-gun emplacement, the fifth shot entering the embrasure and knocking it out. But further progress was no longer possible. 'The ground was getting worse & worse,' wrote Dillon, '& soon became impassable . . . Everything was now a hopeless mess up, the shelling was very heavy, our infantry on our right were falling back & could be seen digging in feverishly.'[5]

Just short of Windhoek village, Dillon's tank got bogged down in a huge crater. Finally, at around midday, he and his crew decided to abandon the tank and return to the British lines. 'A very weary & dirty crowd we looked as we made the best of our way back,' he wrote, 'with a walk of about 4 miles in front of us, during which we lay down & slept about six times . . . So ended a most unfortunate day.'[6]

What came to be known as the Third Battle of Ypres had for Haig – as he told his army commanders on 14 June – two main objectives: 'wearing out the Enemy' and 'securing the Belgian coast and connecting with the Dutch frontier'. To achieve both he envisaged three phases: capturing the Passchendaele ridge; advancing towards Roulers 'so as to take coast defences in the rear'; and 'an amphibious landing combined with an attack along the coast from Nieuport'. But 'if effectives or guns inadequate', he admitted, 'it may be necessary to call a halt after No. 1 is gained!'[7]

In his post-war memoir, Lloyd George accused Haig of misleading the government about the scale and nature of the new Ypres offensive. There is some truth to this. Called to London to present his plans to the War

Cabinet, Haig followed 'Wully' Robertson's advice to use language that was 'moderate and cautious'. He spoke of a phased attack that would grind down the enemy and avoid a 'tremendous offensive involving heavy losses'. His true intention was more ambitious.

Lloyd George's belief, as he made clear at the same War Cabinet meeting on 19 June, was that the 'decisive moment of the war would be 1918', and that until then Britain ought to husband its forces and 'do little or nothing, except support Italy with guns and gunners (300 batteries were indicated)'. But Haig won the day by 'strongly' asserting that 'Germany was nearer her end than they seemed to think, that *now* was the favourable moment [for pressing her], and that everything possible should be done to take advantage of it by concentrating on the Western Front *all* available resources.' Germany was, he added, 'within 6 months of the total exhaustion of her available manpower'.[8]

Haig's case was undoubtedly helped on 20 June when Admiral Jellicoe, the First Sea Lord, told the War Cabinet that so serious were the losses of merchant ships to German submarines that 'it would be impossible for Great Britain to continue the war in 1918'.[9] Though few agreed – believing instead that Britain had adequate food reserves – it made them more amenable to Haig's efforts to clear the Belgian coast of submarine bases and, ideally, to end the war in 1917. Britain's war leaders were also mindful of the political situation in France, 'where strikes and ministerial instability had revived the spectre of a separate peace'.[10] On 25 June, therefore, the War Cabinet gave Haig the green light to continue with his 'preparations' for the offensive.[11] The only caveat, made by the War Policy Committee* in mid-July, was that 'on no account' should the battle replicate the Somme with 'protracted, costly and indecisive operations'.[12] Yet that is exactly what happened.

Much of the blame must rest with Haig and his unfortunate choice of General Gough and his Fifth Army to spearhead the offensive. Haig had considered plans put forward by Plumer and Rawlinson, commanding the Second and Fourth Armies respectively, but regarded both as too cautious. Gough, on the other hand, thought a first day's infantry advance of 4,000–5,000 yards was possible. Haig's advice to Gough was that a

---

* A committee established by the War Cabinet in June 1917 to weigh up Britain's strategic options in light of the crises in Russia and France.

step-by-step offensive, biting off 3,000 yards every two to three days, would be enough to smash up German reserves and keep the enemy off balance. He also urged Gough, on 28 June, to limit the advance north 'until our right flank has really been secured on the [Passchendaele] ridge'. But this was counsel, not a direct order, and Gough ignored it.[13]

The gains made by the nine attacking British divisions and six French (placed under Haig's orders by Pétain) on 31 July 1917, the first day of the battle, were relatively impressive: eighteen square miles for the loss of 27,000 men; compared to 3.5 square miles for more than twice the casualties on 1 July 1916. Haig noted in his diary: 'This was a fine day's work. Gough thinks that he has taken over 5000 prisoners and 60 guns or more. The ground is thick with dead Germans killed mostly by our artillery.'[14]

Yet, as David Stevenson has noted, the gains were well short of the day's objectives, 'despite advancing on a shorter front than in the previous year with air superiority and forty-eight tanks, and after firing four times as many shells'.[15]

9 September 1917: *'The Red Cap must have lost his head'*
– The Etaples Mutiny

It began, innocuously enough, with the arrest of a Kiwi gunner, A. J. Healy, as he tried to return to camp from the nearby town of Etaples that was out of bounds to troops. 'It was the practice,' recalled Healy's son, 'for those who wished to visit the township to walk across the estuary or river mouth at low tide, do their thing and return accordingly. However in my father's case the tide came in, in the interval, and to avoid to avoid being charged as a deserter he returned across the bridge [over the railway] . . . was apprehended by the "Red Caps"* and placed in an adjoining cell or lock up.'[1]

The arrest was witnessed by a group of soldiers milling around the

---

* The nickname for Military Policemen (MPs) because of the red bands they wore round their caps.

recreation huts near the bridge and 'some feeling was shown against the police'. By 4 p.m. a threatening crowd had begun to form, augmented by soldiers leaving the camp cinema. Told that the prisoner had already been released from the guardroom, one vocal New Zealander demanded to see his empty cell. As he was being shown it, the crowd outside spilled on to the bridge and an altercation broke out between an Australian soldier and an MP called Private H. Reeve, an ex-boxer with a reputation as a bully. A Scots soldier recalled:

[The] Red Cap tried to move [the Australian] away without any result so he brought force into it and that started something that others joined in till the Red Cap must have lost his head and started using his gun. He wounded one or two but hit our post Corporal (an innocent minding his own business and passing by) in the head, he I believe died later; I knew him and a grand and good-living chap he was.[2]

The shooting of the popular Scots corporal, W. B. Wood of the 4th Gordons, and a Frenchwoman on the far side of the bridge (she survived), enraged the crowd and caused the MPs to beat a hasty retreat to their huts on the railway embankment under a hail of stones. When the Assistant Provost Marshal, the officer in charge of MPs, appeared on his horse he also became a target.[3]

By now the crowd had swelled to 4,000 strong as word of the disturbance spread to the huts and tents of the various Infantry Base Depots that were located on rising ground to the east of the railway. As most of the MPs had now fled into Etaples – a small coastal town a dozen miles south of Boulogne – part of the crowd pursued them, and by 7.30 p.m. more than a thousand soldiers were milling round the town. A group of officers, six deep, had tried to stop them from crossing the bridge but, according to the camp adjutant Captain Guinness, 'the men swept them aside'. He added: 'They swarmed into town, raided the office of the Base Commandant, pulled him out of his chair and carried him on their shoulders through the town.'[4]

Many gathered outside the Sévigné Café where they thought two policemen were hiding. Second Lieutenant Randolph Grey, sent with a picquet of fifty men from the New Zealand Base Depot to restore order, remembered:

The Maoris were making things pretty hot. We found several hundred with a big sprinkling of Scotties clamouring outside . . . Some twenty English officers were guarding the door, and were being badly hustled. A Colonel was trying in a wildly excited manner to calm the mob. I pushed my way in with the intention of telling him I could help with the Maoris. He must have been blind with excitement because he raised his stick to strike me. A big husky Maori rushed in and grabbed him, and bawled at him, 'You . . . hit a New Zealand officer, I . . . will kill you!' This brought the Colonel to his senses a bit, and he told me to do what I could with our men. Liquor had inflamed them, and as you know, the Maori is an ugly customer when he gets a few in. But they have great respect for their officers, and when the Scotties moved away after the Colonel promised them full justice, our fellows followed. Two redcaps who very foolishly showed themselves were badly hustled, but the excitement soon cooled down.[5]

By 10 p.m. the town was clear of troops and the camp was quiet.

Next day, however, despite the beefing up of picquets on the bridge, soldiers again broke through them and held meetings in Etaples in the afternoon. At one a committee of six was elected, chaired by a corporal of the Northumberland Fusiliers. Some soldiers tried to stop traffic, others headed for the detention camp to the north. This last group was intercepted by the Base Commandant, Brigadier-General A. Graham Thompson, and his staff, and persuaded to return. Other bands were deterred from entering the field punishment barracks and the railway station where they thought the police were hiding.[6]

On the 11th, the authorities asked GHQ for troops to quell the disturbances and a battalion of the Honourable Artillery Company – made up chiefly of men from the middle and lower-middle classes – was ordered to Etaples. But it would not arrive until 12 September and in the meantime the disorder continued. Again the mob invaded the town and a group of 100 marched part of the way to nearby Paris Plages before Major Cruickshank, the Railway Transport Officer, brought them back. 'None of the picquets,' noted the disgusted Base Commandant, 'made any determined effort to prevent these men.'[7]

A more serious incident took place at 9.15 p.m. when a crowd of eighty men, carrying sticks tied with red rags and noticeboards torn from the camps, approached a 200-strong armed picquet on the bridge that led to Paris Plages. Captain E. F. Wilkinson of the 1/8th West Yorkshires, commanding the picquet, recalled:

> These men pushed through, the picquet practically standing on one side ... Officers who stood out were also pushed aside. The picquet was absolutely unreliable at that moment so I called the officers together and made them fall their men in by Regts. I then addressed the picquet & whilst I was doing so [Corporal Jesse Short of the 24th Northumberland Fusiliers] ... came back from the crowd of men who had just broken through & told the men they were not to listen to me. 'What you want to do to the Bugger is to put a stone round his neck & throw him into the river.'[8]

Instead they helped Wilkinson to arrest Short, who was later tried by a field general court martial, found guilty of exhorting soldiers to mutiny and sentenced to death. Despite a good disciplinary record, Short had his sentence confirmed by Field Marshal Haig and was shot on 4 October 1917.[9]

The disturbances at Etaples finally petered out on 14 September after more reinforcements had arrived and sixty men had been arrested in the town. Writing many years later Captain Guinness, the camp adjutant, remembered as the 'chief cause of discontent' the fact that veterans had to undergo 'the same strenuous training as the drafts of recruits arriving from home'. Guinness also referred to the lack of familiarity between officers and men: 'It should be realized that each Infantry Base Depot was commanded by an elderly retired officer who had an adjutant to help him. The remaining officers, like the men, were either reinforcements from home, or had been sent down the line on account of ill-health, and therefore did not know them.'[10]

In a detailed analysis of the 'mutiny', Douglas Gill and Gloden Dallas referred to the 'particular hatred' directed towards the Military Police who had not seen active service and who were trying to impose 'the disciplinary standard of the glass house'. They also noted the prominent role played by Anzac soldiers – who had a tendency to be 'contemptuous of the narrow discipline to which British troops subscribed, and [who] were led by officers who had invariably first shown their qualities as privates in the ranks' – and their close relationship with the Scottish troops 'who gave the mutiny its force'. There was also the inevitable factor of low morale after three years of seemingly futile offensives.[11]

To prevent a repeat, all the MPs and most of the camp officers were replaced, and the notorious system of training at the 'Bull Ring'* was abandoned; henceforth reinforcements passing through Etaples would complete their instruction at the front. It was inevitable, given the numbers of soldiers involved, that rumours of the 'mutiny' would spread through the army. But no details reached the press and the so-called 'Battle of Eetapps' would remain, in the words of Vera Brittain (who was nursing in one of the six base hospitals that ringed the camp), 'wrapped in a fog which the years have deepened, for we were not allowed to mention it in our letters home, and it appears, not unnaturally, to have been omitted from standard histories by patriotic authors'.[12]

While the disorders continued, Brittain and her fellow nurses were 'shut up within our hospitals' and left, as she tartly put it, 'to meditate on the effect of three years of war upon the splendid morale of our noble troops'. She added:

> As though the ceaseless convoys [from the front] did not provide us with sufficient occupation, numerous drunken and dilapidated warriors from the village battle were sent to such spare beds as we had for slight repairs. They were euphemistically known as 'local sick'.[13]

15 October 1917: *'She lay prone, motionless'*
– Mata Hari's execution

It was still dark when a convoy of black cars drew up next to the muddy fields of the Caponnière, the ground used by the French cavalry for field exercise at Vincennes near Paris. Out stepped a handsome middle-aged woman in a long black velvet cloak edged with fur, black kid gloves and fashionable ankleboots. Her unwashed grey hair was hidden by a jauntily angled three-corner black felt hat.[1]

---

* The pejorative name given to the training area at Etaples by disgruntled British soldiers who had passed through it.

She was led towards a stake in the ground, facing which was a firing squad of twelve men from the 4th Regiment of Zouaves, grizzled French settlers from Algeria and Tunisia in khaki uniforms and red fezzes, commanded by Sub-Officer Petoy of the 23rd Dragoons. Refusing to be tied to the stake, she also declined the offer of a blindfold. 'That is not necessary,' she said.[2]

The chief military recorder, Captain Thibaut, then read out the sentence: 'By the order of the Third Council of War, the woman Zelle has been condemned to death for espionage.'

She stood unmoved, awaiting her fate. 'By God,' muttered Petoy. 'This lady knows how to die.'

He lifted his sabre and the men shouldered their rifles. 'En joue!' ('Aim!') he shouted. Then finally, after a pause, he dropped his sabre. 'Feu!'[3]

As the shots rang out, 'the woman Zelle' fell. 'Slowly, inertly,' recalled British reporter Henry Wales, an eyewitness, 'she settled to her knees, her head up always, and without the slightest change of expression on her face. For the fraction of a second it seemed she tottered there, on her knees, gazing intently at those who had taken her life. Then she fell backward, bending at the waist, with her legs doubled up beneath her. She lay prone, motionless, with her face turned towards the sky.'[4]

Petoy delivered the coup de grâce by drawing his revolver, placing it next to her left temple and pulling the trigger. Mata Hari, once the most famous exotic dancer in Europe, was dead.[5]

Following her arrest in February, she had done her best to stave off the inevitable by denying she had ever spied for Germany. She tried to explain her contact with Major Kalle, the German military attaché in Madrid, by saying she had seduced him to get intelligence for France. Though this might well have been true – she was eminently capable of playing one side off against the other – it was not the whole story.

Bouchardon, the investigating magistrate, meanwhile, was carrying out his interrogations without the benefit of the intercepted Madrid telegrams because the Deuxième Bureau wanted to conceal the fact that it had broken Germany's diplomatic codes. Only if he regarded these proofs 'of a particularly secret nature' as 'indispensable' to his interrogation, Ladoux told Bouchardon, should he 'ask for permission from the Minister of War who alone could authorize their release'.[6]

By late April, however, Bouchardon had failed to elicit a confession and Ladoux decided on his own authority to hand over transcripts of the telegrams on the condition that their existence was not made public. When Bouchardon questioned Mata Hari about them on 1 May, she continued her denials. But on 21 May, after three miserable months in solitary confinement, she was ready to confess. She said she had been recruited as a spy by Karl Kroemer, the German honorary consul, in the autumn of 1915. She had chosen not to mention this to Ladoux because she had never done anything for Kroemer, and thought it sensible not to raise the matter. As for Kalle, she had turned to him only after Ladoux had abandoned her following her arrest at Falmouth and return to Spain. She insisted that all she told Kalle was that the French had tried to recruit her; she then offered him some useless information cobbled together from newspaper reports. He had paid her, in return, 3,500 pesetas.[7]

Though Mata Hari had left much unsaid, her admission that she had accepted money from the Germans was enough to condemn her. She was tried *in camera* by a military court on 24 and 25 July, found guilty of espionage and 'assisting' the enemy and sentenced to death. [8] On 14 October, after President Poincaré had rejected her appeal for clemency, her lawyer made a last attempt to save his client by suggesting to the Military Commandant of Paris that she was pregnant and, moreover, could be useful to France if exchanged for a general captured by the Germans. It failed, and the following day she was executed.[9]

24 October 1917: *'Eviva Germania!'*
– The Italian collapse at Caporetto

At 2 a.m. the Austro-German artillery opened up on sixty miles of the Italian Isonzo front, north of the Adriatic coast. Around the mountain villages of Tolmino and Caporetto, the focal point of the attack by the German Fourteenth Army, no fewer than 1,800 heavy guns and mortars were used to fire high-explosive and gas shells in the initial two-and-a-half-hour bombardment. This caused the lively Italian counter-fire to die away and, after a pause, a fresh barrage began against Italian headquarters, ammunition dumps, approach roads and artillery positions. Finally, at 7 a.m., shrouded by mist and rain, the infantry attacked.[1]

The offensive had been planned as a response to Italian gains in the eleventh battle of the Isonzo in August – including the capture of Gorizia and the high plateau of Bainsizza – that threatened the Austrian port of Trieste, now just thirty miles from the front line. Despite low morale among his troops, not helped by opposition to the war from the Socialist Party, the Italian Commander-in-Chief General Cadorna was determined to keep attacking on the Isonzo and in September 1917 had managed to persuade the British and French to lend him 200 heavy artillery pieces. Though this attack had been cancelled, and many of the guns returned, the Austrians were not aware of this. 'It became questionable,' wrote General von Cramon, German liaison officer to the Austro-Hungarian Army, 'whether Trieste could be held in the event of another Italian attack.' Attack, therefore, was seen as the best mode of defence.[2]

Previously no German troops had been used on this front because the Austrians, for political reasons, had insisted on tackling the Italians alone. But with Trieste in danger these objections were cast aside and it was eventually agreed that seven German divisions – forming, with three Austrian divisions, the German Fourteenth Army – would participate in a joint attack that would, if successful, roll up the Isonzo front from the north after a breakthrough in the region of Tolmino in the Julian Alps.[3]

The main assault was delivered by the Fourteenth Army, under General Otto von Below, while supporting attacks were made north and south by the Austrian Tenth, Second and First Armies. Their intention was to drive the Italian Second and Third Armies back behind the River Tagliamento, thirty miles to the rear.[4]

Initially, thanks to clever Austrian ruses – including the despatch of several German storm battalions to the Tyrolean front – Cadorna believed the attack would take place further west in the Trentino region north of Lake Garda. But by early October his intelligence had identified thirty-five of the fifty-three German and Austrian divisions on the Isonzo front. Facing them were the thirty-four divisions of his Second and Third Armies. Clearly the attack would be here.[5]

The commander of Cadorna's Second Army, General Capello, was keen to advance from the Bainsizza plateau so that he could take the attacking enemy in the flank. He had, as a result, concentrated all his reserves there and left nothing to support his left wing. When Cadorna refused to authorize this operation, Capello was sick in bed and neglected to alter his troop dispositions. Eventually Cadorna realized that the line around and to the north of Caporetto was held by just two battalions per mile, instead of eight elsewhere, and ordered a division to move up from the south. But it was still in transit when the attack – delayed from the 15th because of bad weather – finally began on 24 October.[6]

An Italian gun position at the Cividale Pass captured by Austro-German forces during the Battle of Caporetto.

The most spectacular breakthrough was made, not surprisingly, in the thinly guarded Caporetto sector. Having made a breach in the Italian line and taken Caporetto, the German 12th Division wheeled right and moved north some five miles behind the Italian 46th and 43rd Divisions that were still holding out. Then it wheeled right again, into the rear of the Italian 19th Division that was being attacked frontally by Austrian troops. The result was the 19th's complete destruction, leaving a huge gap in the Italian front. Finally the 12th Division turned west and by nightfall had advanced more than fifteen miles and taken 15,000 prisoners and 100 guns. 'The conduct of the 12th Division, both as regards leaders and men, is worthy of a place in the book of fame,' wrote General von Cramon. 'The resolution required to march straight through the enemy's front, regardless of the exposure of one's flanks, is not readily appreciated by everyone.'[7]

Slightly less spectacular advances were made by the 12th's neighbouring formations, the 50th Austrian Division and the German Alpine Corps, and by General Krauss's I Corps further north. More modest progress was made to the south by the remaining two corps of the Fourteenth Army, while below them the Austrian Second Army was counter-attacked and driven back to its start line. Overall, however, the day had yielded immense gains.[8]

Next day, as the Austro-Germans continued their advance, a number of Italian units began to flee in disorder back to the Tagliamento; others, notably the crack Alpini, obeyed orders and held their ground. But it was only a matter of time before they were outflanked and forced to surrender. In one such action a young German *Oberleutnant* called Erwin Rommel, commanding a detachment of the Württemberg Gebirgsbattalion (Mountain Battalion), captured twelve officers and 500 men.[9]

By the end of the second day, 25 October, the Italian Second Army was in total disarray – much of it self-inflicted. 'Reserves moving up prepared to do their duty were greeted with yells of "Blacklegs"', according to one account of the battle. 'Krauss's troops encountered Italian units in formed bodies marching into captivity, calling out: *"Eviva la Austria!"* and *"A Roma!"* This picture of complete demoralization certainly did not apply to all troops, but it had made deep inroads.'[10]

On the 26th Monte Maggiore was taken by the German Alpine Corps, as were the peaks of Kuk and Matajur to the west of Tolmino. Rommel was instrumental in both the latter actions, at one point walking towards an enormous group of Italians, waving a handkerchief and calling upon them to surrender. When he was just 150 yards from them, they threw down their arms and surrendered. 'In an instant I was surrounded,' he recalled, '"*Eviva Germania!*" sounded from a thousand throats. An Italian officer who hesitated to surrender was shot down by his own troops.' Rommel had captured 1,500 men of the veteran Salerno Brigade. By the end of the day his total haul since the start of the offensive was 150 officers, 9,000 men and 150 guns.[11] He should have been awarded the

Pour le Mérite that had been promised by General von Below to the first officer on Mount Matajur. Instead it went to a brother officer, Ferdinand Schörner,* though Rommel got his own Blue Max at the close of the campaign.[12]

By 27 October the German Fourteenth Army had advanced more than fifteen miles, though the Austrian Second had managed just four. With the whole of his north-east front in danger of collapsing, Cadorna ordered a withdrawal behind the Tagliamento. His official communiqué a day later read:

> A violent attack and feeble resistance of detachments of the Second Army permitted Austro-German forces to pierce our left wing on the Julian front . . . The bravery displayed by our soldiers in so many memorable battles fought and won in the past two and a half years gives our Supreme Command a pledge that this time, too, the army to which the honour and safety of the country are entrusted will know how to fulfil its duty.[13]

It did not. To give the Third Army, still largely intact, time to get away the Second Army was ordered to hold an intermediate line on the River Torre until the 29th. But its demoralized units could provide only piecemeal resistance and German troops were soon across the Torre and driving towards Cadorna's headquarters at Udine. Now began the race for the Tagliamento, during which the Second Army all but disintegrated.[14] 'Mainly between Udine and Tagliamento,' wrote George Trevelyan, head of the British Red Cross in Italy, 'they gave way at length to the war-weariness which had so long been at strife with their valour and patriotism, flung away their rifles wholesale, and passed round the word, "*Andiamo a casa*" (We're going home).'[15]

The Italians won the race – chiefly thanks to the enemy's exhaustion and supply difficulties – but at a cost of 180,000 troops and 1,500 guns. On 31 October, and for the next two days, the Austro-Germans tried without success to cross the Tagliamento, their original objective. It

---

* Schörner became a committed Nazi general and was infamous for his brutality on the Eastern Front during the Second World War. He was named as Commander-in-Chief of the German Army (with the rank of field marshal) in Hitler's 'Last Testament' in early May 1945, and was later imprisoned in both Russia and Germany for war crimes. He died in 1973.

seemed as if the Italians would hang on, and Cadorna told the French and British he would no longer need the twenty divisions he had asked for; the six they had already begun to send would suffice.[16]

But during the night of 2 November the German 55th Division secured a bridgehead near Cornino, north-west of Udine, and a day later Cadorna ordered a further withdrawal to the River Piave. The Allies agreed to send more troops – a total of six French and five British divisions – but on condition that the Commander-in-Chief was sacked. On 7 November, having just issued an Order of the Day for his men to 'die and not to yield' on the Piave, Cadorna was replaced by General Armando Díaz.[17]

Various Austro-German attempts were made to force the Piave, and small footholds were gained (including one by Rommel's detachment, which captured Langarone on 10 November), but overall the operation was a failure. The Austro-German lines of supply were so strung out, and transport so scarce, that there were not enough guns, boats or bridging supplies to make a crossing possible. With winter closing in, the Austrians decided to postpone further offensives until the following spring.[18]

The Caporetto offensive was a major defeat for the Italians. In just two weeks the Austro-Germans had forced them back fifty miles and captured 3,000 guns and vast amounts of equipment. They had, in addition, inflicted more than 325,000 casualties, almost 90 per cent of whom were taken prisoner, thus emphasizing the moral collapse of the Italian Second Army. A further 300,000 Italian deserters (*sbandati*) were put in cages and eventually reallocated to different units.[19]

2 November 1917: *'I knew that this was a great event'*
– The Balfour Declaration

The declaration – written in the form of a letter from British Foreign Secretary Arthur Balfour to Lord Rothschild, a leading Zionist – ran only to a single, albeit lengthy, sentence. Yet it would become one of the most controversial documents of the twentieth century. It read:

His Majesty's Government view with favour the establishment in Palestine of a National Home for the Jewish people, and will use their best endeavours to facilitate the achievement of this object, it being clearly understood that nothing shall be done which may prejudice the civil and religious rights of the existing non-Jewish communities in Palestine or the rights and political status enjoyed by Jews in any other country.[1]

The significance of the declaration is that it was the first time in history a major power had endorsed the Zionists' hopes for a separate homeland in Palestine; moreover that power, Britain, was in a position to put its words into action because at that very moment its troops, led by General Allenby, were poised to drive the Turks out of Palestine.

When Dr Chaim Weizmann, the celebrated Russian-born scientist and a man who had worked tirelessly for this moment, was informed by Sir Mark Sykes* that 'it's a boy!', meaning the Imperial War Cabinet had just approved the final draft of the declaration, he was torn. 'Well,' he wrote later, 'I did not like the boy at first. He was not the one I had expected. But I knew that this was a great event. I telephoned my wife.'[2]

Balfour had earlier asked Weizmann to whom the declaration should be addressed. 'I suggested Lord Rothschild rather than myself,' recalled Weizmann, 'though I was President of the English Zionist Federation.'[3] This was typical of Weizmann's modesty – but also a canny move. Though well known in government circles for his vital war work, Weizmann was neither British-born nor a public figure; Rothschild, on the other hand, was the head of the famous banking family and the uncrowned king of British Jewry. At a time when a number of prominent British Jews were opposed to a Jewish homeland on the grounds that it would undermine their own nationality, Rothschild was a useful flagbearer for the British Zionist movement. But it was Weizmann's close relationship with Balfour (and, to a lesser extent, Lloyd George) that had made the declaration possible.

The two could not have been more different. The son of a Jewish timber merchant from a small Belorussian town, Weizmann had embraced Zionism as a boy and left Russia to study science in Germany and Switzerland, before teaching chemistry at Manchester University; Balfour was an Eton-educated patrician, romantic and foppish, who had succeeded

---

* A politician, traveller and expert on the Middle East, Sykes was the co-author of the 1916 Sykes–Picot Agreement.

his uncle Robert Cecil, Lord Salisbury, as Tory Prime Minister on the latter's death in 1902.[4]

They had first met in a Manchester hotel room in 1906, three years after Balfour had suggested Uganda as a possible homeland for Jews (an offer Weizmann rejected). Now Balfour was out of office and interested to meet one of the opponents of his scheme. He sat, according to Weizmann, 'in his usual pose, his legs stretched out in front of him, an imperturbable expression on his face'. Weizmann explained to him that Zionism was not a practical movement but a spiritual one. 'I pointed out,' he recalled, 'that nothing but a deep religious conviction expressed in modern political terms could keep the movement alive, and that this conviction had to be based on Palestine and on Palestine alone.'

To illustrate his point, he asked Balfour if he would accept Paris instead of London. 'But Dr Weizmann,' replied Balfour, 'we have London.'

'That is true. But we had Jerusalem when London was a marsh.'

When asked if there were many Jews who thought as he did, Weizmann said he spoke for 'millions of Jews whom you will never see and who cannot speak for themselves'.

'It that is so,' commented Balfour, 'you will one day be a force.'[5]

For many years Balfour was in no position to help the Zionists. The Tories lost the 1906 general election and Balfour spent the next nine years in the political wilderness, resigning the leadership of the Conservative and Unionist Party in 1911. But war would transform his political fortunes, as it would the aspirations of Weizmann and the Zionists.

Weizmann became indispensable to the British government after he had demonstrated, in early 1915, how his new anaerobic fermentation process could convert 100 tons of grain into 12 tons of acetone, the key solvent in the manufacture of cordite explosive that, at this stage of the war, was in desperately short supply. 'Well, Dr Weizmann,' Winston Churchill, then First Lord of the Admiralty, had asked at their first meeting, 'we need thirty thousand tons of acetone. Can you make it?' The answer was yes, if he had the resources.[6]

The government provided them by commandeering brewing and distillery equipment, and by building factories to utilize the new process in Dorset and Norfolk. Together they produced more than 90,000 gallons of acetone a year, though this figure fell when unrestricted submarine warfare reduced the supply of North American maize in 1917. Eventually acetone production was moved to Canada and the United States, but it still utilized Weizmann's process.

Weizmann's vital war work was a factor in the Cabinet's support for the Balfour Declaration in 1917, but not the only one. Just as important was the fact that a number of key ministers – notably Lloyd George, Balfour and Churchill* – were instinctively sympathetic towards the Zionist cause. 'I was taught more in school about the history of the Jews than about my own land,' confessed Lloyd George, the former radical reformer who had mutated during the war into a romantic imperialist.[7]

It was Lloyd George who reintroduced Weizmann to Balfour in 1915, by which time the latter had replaced Churchill as First Lord of the Admiralty. 'You know,' said Balfour, 'when the guns stop firing you may get your Jerusalem. It's a great cause you're working for. You must come again and again.' They began to meet regularly for evening walks around Whitehall, discussing how a Jewish homeland could serve the interests of historical justice and British power.[8]

It hugely helped Weizmann's cause, of course, that Lloyd George became Prime Minister and Balfour Foreign Secretary in December 1916. But to sway their Cabinet colleagues they needed an argument based on power politics rather than sentiment. The first pieces of the jigsaw fell into place in the spring of 1917 when the Russian Tsar was overthrown and the United States entered the war. This prompted Balfour to tell his fellow ministers that 'the vast majority of Jews in Russia and America now appear favourable to Zionism', and that if Britain could make a pro-Zionist declaration 'we should be able to carry on extremely useful propaganda both in Russia and America'.[9]

Such an announcement became even more pressing after Jemal Pasha, the brutal Turkish ruler of Syria and Palestine, met German Zionists in Berlin in August 1917, and it became clear that the Germans were preparing a Zionist declaration of their own. These issues of high state, 'not Weizmann's charm, were the real reasons that Britain embraced Zionism', wrote Simon Sebag Montefiore in *Jerusalem*.[10]

First, however, Lloyd George and Balfour had to overcome opposition from senior ministers like Lord Curzon, former Viceroy of India, who queried what was 'to become of the [Arab] people of the country'; and

---

* Churchill returned to government as Minister of Munitions in July 1917.

from 'Assimilationist' British Jews like Edwin Montagu, Indian Secretary, who argued that a Jewish homeland would increase anti-Semitism and make him and others unwelcome in the country of their birth.[11]

Montagu's impassioned anti-Zionist speech to the War Cabinet on 4 October was the reason the original text – drafted by Weizmann and Lord Rothschild, and agreed in principle by Lloyd George and Balfour – was watered down. In place of 'His Majesty's Government' (HMG) accepting 'the principle of recognizing Palestine as the National Home of the Jewish people and the right of the Jewish people to build up its national life in Palestine under a protectorate', there was now simply HMG 'view with favour the establishment in Palestine of a National Home for the Jewish People'; and instead of HMG 'regard as essential for the realization of this principle the grant of internal autonomy to the Jewish nationality in Palestine' and 'freedom of immigration', the final text stated that 'nothing shall be done which may prejudice the civil and religious rights of the existing non-Jewish communities in Palestine or the rights and political status enjoyed by Jews in any other country'.[12]

Weizmann later wondered whether he and the Zionists should have 'stood by our guns'. But on reflection he felt that the threat from the Assimilationists meant they had been right to accept the altered wording, and that the declaration, 'emasculated as it was', was still a 'tremendous event in exilic Jewish history'.[13]

The final hurdle was cleared when Britain's French and American allies – the former with a strategic interest in Palestine, the latter with an influential Jewish population – gave their grudging approval to the draft letter and, following the War Cabinet's decision, the Balfour Declaration was announced to the world on 9 November. It had, at a stroke, unilaterally revised the Sykes–Picot Agreement, which had allotted part of Palestine to the French, and was the first crucial step on Israel's long and controversial road to nationhood. Lloyd George wrote later:

> It was not [the Imperial War Cabinet's] idea that a Jewish State should be set up immediately by the Peace Treaty without reference to the wishes of the majority of the inhabitants. On the other hand, it was contemplated that when the time arrived for according representative institutions to Palestine, if the Jews had meanwhile responded to the

opportunity afforded them and had become a definite majority of the inhabitants, then Palestine would thus become a Jewish Commonwealth.[14]

The British newspapers were even more bullish. 'Palestine for the Jews', read the headline in *The Times*. 'It is no idle dream,' said the *Observer*, 'that by the close of another generation the new Zion may become a State.'[15]

As if to confirm this, Gaza fell to Allenby's forces on 7 November, two days before the declaration was made public, and the road to Jerusalem was open.

6 November 1917: *'A very important success'*
– The Canadians take Passchendaele

'I had an open view of the whole Ypres salient,' recalled Pastor van Wallaghem at Dickebusch, 'and the fireworks in the semi-dark over the whole of the front from Wytschaete right up to Vrijbosch was [sic] really awe-inspiring. Several thousand cannons spewed their murderous fire over the fighting troops.'[1]

Wallaghem was witnessing the preliminary bombardment to the final attack of the Third Battle of Ypres. By the time he had returned to his presbytery from celebrating mass, fifteen miles away the men of the Canadian Corps were entering the shattered village of Passchendaele. Corporal H. C. Baker of the 28th (North-West) Battalion recalled:

> The buildings had been pounded and mixed with the earth, and the shell-exploded bodies were so thickly strewn that a fellow couldn't step without stepping on corruption. Our opponents were fighting a rearguard action which resulted in a massacre for both sides. Our boys were falling like ninepins, but it was even worse for them. If they stood to surrender they were mown down by their own machine-gun fire aimed from their rear at us; if they leap-frogged back they were caught in our barrage . . .
>
> They started to counter-attack. Our SOS flared up: our artillery thundered and sent a screening barrage over our heads; machine-guns and rifles blazed; the earth and the air quivered. Hades was let loose all over again.[2]

The fight went on all day and, but the Canadians held on. 'Three times during the night they shelled us heavily,' wrote Private Le Brun of the 16th Canadian Machine Gun Company, 'and we had to keep on spraying bullets into the darkness to keep them from advancing. The night was alive with bullets. By morning, of our team of six, only my buddy Tombes and I were left. Then came the burst that got Tombes . . . His blood and brains, pieces of skull and lumps of hair, spattered all over the front of my greatcoat and gas-mask . . . It was a terrible feeling to be the only one left.'[3]

Field Marshal Haig was delighted with the gains made by the Canadians. 'The operations were completely successful,' he noted in his diary. 'Passchendaele was taken, as also were Mosselmarkt and Goudberg. The whole position had been most methodically fortified. Yet our troops succeeded in capturing *all* their objectives early in the day with small loss – "under 700 men"! . . . Today was a very important success.'[4] Passchendaele was less than five miles from the jumping-off point on 31 July, and yet it had taken Haig's troops ninety-nine days to get there.

It did not help that the fighting in Flanders was on a 'clay coastal plain with a high water table, where lines of concrete pillboxes formed the core of the defence system, supported by converging artillery on the Gheluvelt plateau and Passchendaele ridge'; nor that after Messines Ludendorff had appointed General Lossberg, the defensive specialist, as chief of staff to the German Fourth Army holding this sector. Lossberg ordered two more lines of defence – making five in total – and insisted that the British were held as far forward as possible by outposts occupying shellholes, machine-guns and field guns supplied by light railways. Further back were stationed counter-attack (*Eingreif*) divisions, armed with new light machine-guns and organized into small infiltration groups (*Gruppen*). The Germans also had a new weapon – mustard gas – that caused painful blistering to the skin and temporary blindness, and hampered the advance. But their final advantage was rain, with five inches falling in August (double the normal rainfall): the result was that planes could not observe, tanks could not advance, weapons jammed and guns could not be moved.[5]

Gough, the general directing the battle, captured Pilckem Ridge on 31 July but not the Gheluvelt plateau. The weather then postponed oper-ations until 16 August when a second general offensive took the village of Langemarck, a loss Ludendorff described as 'another great blow'.[6] At the end of the month, recognizing that his appointment of Gough had been a mistake, Haig transferred the responsibility for capturing the vital Gheluvelt plateau to General Plumer's Second Army. Plumer, a more prudent commander, planned a series of limited assaults to take advantage of the drier weather in September. 'The attack,' wrote Gary Sheffield, 'would be in four phases, with a six days pause between each to allow guns and supplies to be brought forward. Each infantry assault of a maximum 1,500 yards would be conducted under the cover of an artillery barrage, with fresh troops at hand to deal with the inevitable German counterattacks. The advance would be in three bounds, with pauses for mopping up, consolidation and the bringing up of reserves. By restricting the length of each bound the infantry would stay within range of their own artillery and machine-guns ... This model would transform the fortunes of the British army in the Third Battle of Ypres.'[7]

In these three actions – Menin Road (20 September), Polygon Wood (26 September) and Broodseinde (4 October) – Plumer largely achieved his limited objectives, breaking through the German defences on each occasion and beating off counter-attacks. At Broodseinde his Anzac troops inflicted heavy casualties in the forward trenches, where the Germans had been preparing an assault of their own, and took 5,000 prisoners, a clear sign of demoralization.

Believing the Germans near to collapse, Haig ordered Plumer to continue his attacks. The latter did so, but left shorter intervals between each assault and less time to relocate his guns. He was further hampered by the return of heavy rain, and two attacks towards Passchendaele ridge – on 9 and 12 October – were bloody failures. Haig should now have halted; but he was determined to capture the Passchendaele ridge before the winter, to set up a renewed offensive in the spring, and more attacks were ordered. The man tasked with this final objective was Lieutenant-General Sir Arthur Currie, a former estate agent who was now commanding the Canadian Corps. Having made a personal reconnaissance, Currie told Haig it could not be done, speaking in such vehement terms that, had he been a British officer, he would probably have been sacked. Instead Haig replied softly: 'Some day I will tell you why, but Passchendaele must be taken.'[8]

In successive bounds – 26 October, and 6 and 10 November – the Canadians finally took the bulk of the Passchendaele ridge at a cost of

Stretcher-bearers carrying a wounded man across the shattered, waterlogged terrain at Passchendaele, November 1917.

12,000 casualties. Only now – with the battlefield 'a wilderness of brimming shellholes, perilous duckboards, shattered forests, and obliterated villages' – did Haig agree to call off the offensive. The British had lost 275,000 men; the Germans around 225,000.[9]

Historians are divided over the merits of the battle. Gary Sheffield, Haig's biographer, acknowledged that 'Roulers and the coast, ambitiously marked as objectives on GHQ's maps back in the summer, remained as far away as ever.' Yet in Sheffield's opinion it was reasonable to seek objectives that were actually achieved a year later. Haig's mistake was to choose 'the thrusting Gough over the cautious Plumer' to lead off the battle, 'although the decision was not inherently unreasonable in the light of Allenby's near-success at the beginning of Arras'.[10]

David Stevenson, author of *1914–1918*, is not so generous. 'By December Haig was preparing for a defensive battle in 1918,' he wrote, 'and the offensive had left him worse placed to fight it. The capture of Passchendaele left the British less exposed to German gunfire and in command of most of the ridge, but the salient was deeper and more angular than in July and Haig admitted to Robertson [Chief of the Imperial General Staff] that it would be untenable.' Nor does Stevenson believe that the battle improved the British Army's battle tactics. 'The BEF's effectiveness improved considerably in 1917,' he wrote, 'but not at Ypres.'[11]

Even Sheffield conceded that the battle, by eating into scarce troop reserves, had 'eroded Haig's future liberty of action' and, even more significantly, dealt a heavy blow to British morale, 'not a mortal blow, but serious nonetheless'. He added: 'Collectively, the men of Haig's army were pushed close to the abyss; but they did not topple into it.'[12]

Ironically, the Third Battle of Ypres – one of the grimmest of the war – was my own great-grandfather Major Markham David's finest hour. He had enjoyed a welcome break from the Western Front in early 1916 when he returned to England to take command of the newly formed No. 6 (Siege) Company of the Royal Monmouth Royal Engineers, consisting largely of men who had enlisted in 1915 and 1916, and recovered casualties from other companies. When he went back to France with his new command in May 1916, preparations for the Battle of the Somme 'were in full swing' and No. 6 Company was given the distinctly unglamorous task of building new hutted camps, hospitals and base installations in the area around Calais and Etaples. 'This was no doubt work of the greatest importance,' stated the regimental history, 'but for a new Company just arrived from home, this breaking down into widely separated detachments was a misfortune. The Company lost cohesion and the company spirit – subaltern officers had too many masters – and the Company Commander and Company Headquarters more or less faded from the picture.'[13]

My great-grandfather must have been relieved, therefore, when in early 1917 he was given command of No. 4 (Siege) Company, a unit that had served in the Ypres salient as corps sappers since the first year of the war. It finally left the salient in early September 1917, having seen action both at Messines and during the early stages of the Third Battle of Ypres.[14] On 7 November my great-grandfather was mentioned in a despatch from Field Marshal Haig for 'gallant and distinguished services in the Field'; and the following January was gazetted a member of the Distinguished Service Order.*[15] Exactly where and when he performed the deeds that

---

* After the Victoria Cross, the highest gallantry award available for British officers.

led to these awards is a mystery. Given the timing of the awards, the mention in despatches was probably for his leadership at Messines where, according to the regimental history, the company 'greatly distinguished itself'. The DSO, however, was almost certainly won during the first day of Third Ypres when No. 4 Company supported the attack of the 41st Division on both sides of the Comines Canal. I was always told by my father – Markham's grandson – that the DSO had been awarded for supervising the building of a bridge under fire. This seems to be confirmed by Markham's eldest son Charles, then a young naval officer on the destroyer HMS *Vanessa*, who wrote: 'I understand [the DSO] was for keeping his men working steadily under heavy fire . . . but I was never able to confirm it in detail.'[16]

7 November 1917:* 'Go where you ought to go – into the dustbin of history!'
– The Bolshevik coup

The plan for the coup was straightforward enough. The Bolshevik-dominated Military Revolutionary Committee (MRC) – which only days earlier, posing as an '*ad hoc* body of revolutionary defence', had superseded the authority of the Provisional Government inside the Petrograd garrison – would first seize control of the Mariinsky Palace and disperse the deputies of the pre-parliament. It would then demand the surrender of the ministers of the Provisional Government who were meeting in the Winter Palace and, if they refused, storm it with garrison soldiers, Red Guards and Kronstadt sailors on a signal from the Peter and Paul Fortress and the cruiser *Aurora* that was moored near the Nikolaevsky Bridge.[1]

If everything went smoothly, the MRC hoped to have completed its operations by midday so that Vladimir Ilich Lenin, the Bolshevik leader, could present the Second All-Russian Congress of Soviets, meeting that

---

* Or 25 October 1917, according to the Julian calendar then used by the Russians, hence the expression 'October Revolution'.

afternoon in the great hall of the Smolny Institute, with a fait accompli. The first part of the plan – the dispersal of the deputies at the Mariinsky Palace – was accomplished at noon. But the coup then descended into farce as the Kronstadt sailors were late to appear and no suitable cannon could be found to fire the signal from the Peter and Paul Fortress. Even the simple task of hoisting a red lantern to the top of the fortress's flagpole defeated the Bolshevik commissar, Blagonravov, who got lost looking for one.[2]

At 3 p.m. Lenin, infuriated by the delays, took the calculated risk of telling a packed meeting of the Petrograd Soviet that the coup had taken place and the Provisional Government had been arrested. 'This day,' he declared, 'we have paid our debt to the international proletariat, and struck a terrible blow at the war, a terrible body-blow at all the imperialists.'[3] His deputy Leon Trotsky, a member of the MRC and the architect of the coup, then told the congress that telegrams had been sent to the front announcing the victorious insurrection, but that no reply had yet come and he feared a counter-revolution. 'You are anticipating the will of the All-Russian Congress of Soviets,' shouted one moderate delegate. To which Trotsky replied: 'The will of the All-Russian Congress of Soviets has been anticipated by the rising of the Petrograd workers and soldiers!'[4]

Back at the Winter Palace, meanwhile, the ministers of the Provisional Government were still holding out. Their leader Kerensky, however, was not with them. Having summoned loyal troops from the Northern Front the night before, he had set out at 11 a.m. to find them in a car borrowed from the American Consulate and flying the Stars and Stripes. When his ministers had got over the shock of his departure they made plans to defend the palace, appointing the engineer Palchinsky as *de facto* commander. Palchinsky had 3,000 soldiers at his disposal, including two companies of Cossacks, young officer cadets from the military schools and even 200 women from the Shock Battalion of Death. But few could be relied on and many entrances were left unguarded, allowing Bolshevik spies and foreign press to come and go as they pleased.[5] John Reed, an American journalist, remembered the chaos inside the palace:

> On both sides of the parquetted floor lay rows of dirty mattresses and blankets, upon which occasional soldiers were stretched out; everywhere

was a litter of cigarette-butts, bits of bread, cloth, and empty bottles with expensive French labels. More and more soldiers, with the red shoulder-straps of the *yunker*-schools, moved about in a stale atmosphere of tobacco-smoke and unwashed humanity. One had a bottle of burgundy, evidently filched from the cellars of the Palace . . . The place was a huge barrack, and had been for weeks, from the look of the floor and walls. Machine guns were mounted on window-sills, rifles stacked between the mattresses.[6]

As the day wore on, most of these half-hearted soldiers left their posts to search for food; by 6.50 p.m., when the MRC finally delivered its ultimatum, only 300 were left. Despite the weakness of their position the ministers refused to surrender, assuming the Bolsheviks would not dare to overthrow them by force. They were wrong, though another three hours elapsed before the first blank shot was fired from the cruiser *Aurora*. This caused the terrified ministers to hide under their dinner table – they had been enjoying a meal of borscht, steamed fish and artichokes – and many of the remaining cadets to leave their posts. After a short pause, Blagonravov ordered the real firing to begin from the fortress, the cruiser and the Palace Square, though most rounds fell short.[7]

Around the same time the All-Russian Congress of Soviets finally opened in the great hall at Smolny with the Bolsheviks the largest single group – numbering around 300 of the 670 delegates – and able, with the support of the Left SRs, to push through any motion they chose. When, after hours of discussion, a number of SR and Menshevik delegates left the hall in protest at the violence, Trotsky declared: 'Here no compromise is possible. To those who have left and to those who tell us to do this we say: You are miserable bankrupts, your role is played out; go where you ought to go – into the dustbin of history!'[8]

At the Winter Palace, meanwhile, the soldiers and Red Guards had finally summoned up enough courage to enter the near-defenceless building. 'Carried along by the eager wave of men,' recalled John Reed, an eyewitness,

we were swept into the right hand entrance, opening into a great bare vaulted room, the cellar of the East wing, from which issued a maze of corridors and staircases. A number of huge packing cases stood about, and upon these the Red Guards and soldiers fell furiously, battering them open with the butts of their rifles, and pulling out carpets, curtains, linen, porcelain plates, glassware . . . The looting was just beginning when somebody cried, 'Comrades! Don't touch anything! This is the property of the People!' . . . Roughly and hastily the things were crammed back in their cases, and self-appointed sentinels stood guard. It was all utterly spontaneous.[9]

Soon afterwards, Reed saw the ministers of the Provisional Government being taken from the palace to the Peter and Paul Fortress. 'First came Kishkin,' he wrote, 'his face drawn and pale, then Rutenberg, looking sullenly at the floor; Terestchenko was next, glancing sharply around; he stared at us with cold fixity . . . They passed in silence.'[10]

Only later, having been rescued from a suspicious mob by a commissar of the MRC, did Reed think to ask about the Women's Battalion. 'Oh the women!' laughed the commissar. 'They were all huddled up in a back room. We had a terrible time deciding what to do with them – many were in hysterics, and so on. So finally we marched them up to the Finland station and put them on a train.'[11]

The final act of the Bolshevik coup took place at 5 a.m. when the All-Russian Congress of Soviets passed Lenin's Manifesto 'To All Workers, Soldiers, and Peasants', in which he declared the Provisional Government deposed and all power transferred to the Bolshevik-dominated Soviet. The manifesto added: 'The Soviet authority will at once propose an immediate democratic peace to all nations, and an immediate truce on all fronts. It will assure the free transfer of landlord, crown and monastery lands to the Land Committees, defend the soldiers' rights, enforcing a complete democratisation of the Army, establish workers' control over production.'[12]

The Bolsheviks' control over the whole of Russia would take another three years of bloody civil war to establish. But by toppling the Provisional Government they ensured that Russia would withdraw from the war at the earliest opportunity, and a one-month armistice with the Germans and Austro-Hungarians was eventually agreed on 2 December. 'The bulk of the remaining troops,' wrote David Stevenson, 'departed en masse to return to their homes and to take part in the agrarian revolution. Having on the whole hung together through the upheavals since March, the army finally disintegrated.'[13]

9 December 1917: *'The most famous city in the world . . . has fallen to the British Army'*
– The capture of Jerusalem

Two Cockney privates were foraging for eggs in a valley three miles north of Jerusalem when they saw a crowd approaching. At its head was a man on horseback, clutching a makeshift white flag (actually a bedsheet tied to a broom handle), who introduced himself as Hussein Husseini, Mayor of Jerusalem. The Turks and Germans had gone north to Jericho and Nablus, explained the mayor, and he wanted to surrender the keys to the Holy City. Incredibly the privates refused to accept them: they suspected a ruse and, in any case, their officer was waiting for his breakfast.[1]

So the mayor and his cavalcade trudged on, and were next stopped at gunpoint by two British sergeants. 'Hey,' one asked, 'don't any of you Johnnies speak English?' Husseini spoke it fluently, but preferred to use it on Britons of a more senior rank. Two British artillery officers seemed more promising, but they were too busy with their guns to engage in ceremonial and passed the mayor and his followers up the line.[2] 'None of these felt themselves equal to so historic an occasion,' wrote Archibald Wavell, the future Viceroy of India who was serving on General Allenby's staff.[3] Only when Husseini encountered Major-General John Shea, commanding the 160th Division, outside the Tower of David was he at last able to hand over the keys to the city. Shea accepted the surrender in the name of General Allenby, who was talking to Major T. E. Lawrence in his tent at Jaffa when the news reached him later that day. He at once made plans for a ceremonial entry into the holy city, inviting Lawrence to join him.[4]

General Sir Edmund Allenby's Palestine campaign had, thus far, gone like clockwork. Two previous efforts to breach the Turkish defensive lines at Gaza had failed. But Allenby not only had more men in his Egyptian Expeditionary Force (EEF) than his predecessors – seven infantry divisions and three cavalry division, giving him a numerical advantage over the Turks of 2:1 – he was also willing to try different tactics. So on 31 October, when the third battle opened, he launched a flank attack on Beersheba, which fell to Australian troops two days later. Gaza followed on 7 October and Jaffa on the 16th.[5]

Mayor of Jerusalem Hussein Husseini (fourth from right with walking stick) tries and fails to surrender the keys to the Holy City to two British sergeants, F. H. Hurcomb (centre) and James Sedgwick (left).

This caused fury at Turkish headquarters in Damascus where Jemal Pasha, the Governor of Syria, ordered the deportation of Jerusalem's Christian priests and Jews, and the dynamiting of Christian buildings, including St Saviour's Monastery. Fortunately for these ethnic minorities, the Germans were now in control of Jerusalem and their commander Field Marshal von Falkenhayn, the former head of OHL, was persuaded by subordinates to ignore Jemal's instructions.[6]

Another German officer, the Roman Catholic Colonel von Papen, had less success when he begged Falkenhayn to evacuate Jerusalem, a city of 'no strategic value', before it came under direct attack and the Germans were blamed. Papen knew that Allenby had just captured nearby Nabi Samuel and feared headlines such as 'Huns Blamed for Razing Holy City!' But Falkenhayn was adamant: 'I lost Verdun and now you ask me to evacuate the city which is the cynosure of the world's attention. Impossible!'[7]

A combination of Turkish and German diplomatic pressure brought Falkenhayn round, however, and he moved his headquarters to Nablus as refugees poured out of Jerusalem. On 8 December the Ottoman governor, Izzat Bey, gave his writ of surrender to the mayor and left for Jericho in a carriage borrowed from the American Colony. That night the remaining Ottoman and German troops evacuated the city, the last Turk leaving St Stephen's Gate at 7 a.m. on the 9th.[8] Thus ended more than seven centuries of Muslim rule.*

British Prime Minister Lloyd George was overjoyed. 'The capture of Jerusalem,' he proclaimed, 'has made a most profound impression throughout the civilized world. The most famous city in the world, after centuries of strife and vain struggle, has fallen into the hands of the British army, never to be restored to those who so successfully held it against the embattled hosts of Christendom. The name of every hill thrills with sacred memories.'[9]

British officials were determined, however, that Allenby's entrance into the holy city would be suitably humble. Robertson, the CIGS, advised him that 'it would be of considerable political importance if you, on officially entering the city, dismount at the city gate and enter on foot. German Emperor rode in and the saying went round "a better man than he walked".'[10]

Allenby did as he was told on 11 December – a 'brilliant day', cold and sunny – walking through the Jaffa Gate to be met, according to one of his officers, by the 'indescribable smell of Jerusalem', a 'mixture of spices and sweet herbs, strange eastern cooking and dried fruits, camels and native garments and open drains'. He then read out a brief proclamation to the large crowds, pledging to uphold religious freedom. 'Great

---

* Jerusalem had been under Muslim control since the Crusaders surrendered it to the Saracen leader Saladin in 1187.

enthusiasm – real or feigned – was shown,' he remembered.[11] His final act was to receive the keys to the city from Husseini, commenting untactfully: 'The Crusades have now ended.'[12] Among the general's large retinue was T. E. Lawrence, who had swapped his flowing Arab robes for the uniform of a British major. For Lawrence the simple ceremony at the Jaffa Gate was 'the supreme moment of the war'; and though he still regarded Jerusalem as 'a squalid town', he left it 'shamefaced with triumph' and in awe of the 'mastering spirit of the place'.[13]

Allenby's Palestine campaign had by this point cost the British 18,000 men (and the Turks 25,000), a small price when set against the losses at Third Ypres. During a celebration picnic lunch at General Shea's headquarters, the French envoy Picot made a brazen bid for his country to share Jerusalem's rule. 'Tomorrow, my dear General,' he told Allenby, 'I will take the necessary steps to set up civil government in this town.'

The room fell silent. 'Salad, chicken mayonnaise and foie gras sandwiches hung in our wet mouths unmunched,' recalled Lawrence, 'while we turned to Allenby and gaped. Even he seemed for the moment at a loss. We began to fear that the idol might betray a frailty. But his face grew red: he swallowed, his chin coming forward (in the way we loved), whilst he said, grimly, "In the military zone the only authority is that of the Commander-in-Chief – myself."'[14]

PART FIVE
1918

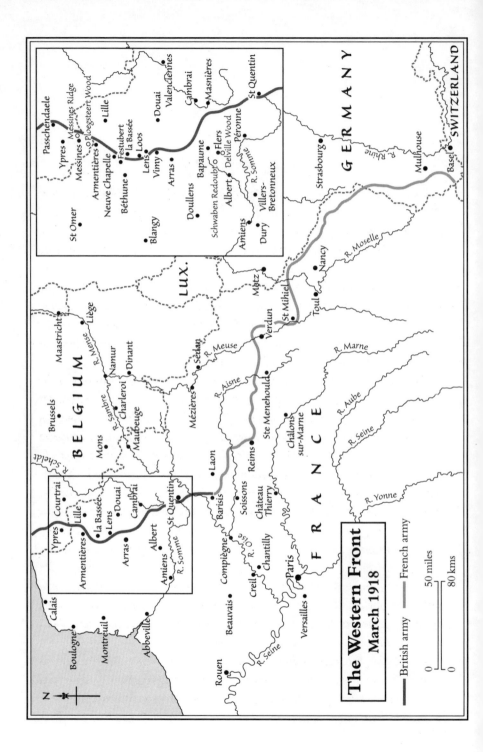

The Western Front
March 1918

British army ——— French army

0   50 miles
0   80 kms

A year that had promised much for the Entente had ended with their overall strategy in tatters and the Central Powers poised, for the first time in two years, to attack on the Western Front. Despite the early success of the BEF's operations at Arras, Messines and Third Ypres, there was no breakthrough and the latter offensive, in particular, was continued in appalling conditions for a month longer than it should have been. Far more serious for the long-term prospects of the Allies, however, was the collapse in French Army morale in the spring of 1917, following the disastrous Nivelle offensive, a dangerous situation that was redeemed only by Pétain's promise that there would be no more futile attacks.

The entry of the United States into the war in April 1917 was one of the few causes that year for Entente celebration. The Americans' immediate contribution was primarily maritime, financial and diplomatic, though it had plans for a huge army to be ready to fight in France by the summer of 1918. But in the short to medium term its entry was more than counterbalanced by Russia's departure, following the Bolshevik-inspired October Revolution. With Russia out of the war, the Central Powers were at last free from a war on two fronts, and could transfer the bulk of their troops to the west in the hope of landing a knock-out blow before the United States could bring its immense economic and military power to bear. 'Owing to the breakdown of Russia,' wrote German Quartermaster-General Erich Ludendorff, 'the military situation was more favourable to us at New Year, 1918, than one could ever have expected. As in 1914 and 1915, we could think of deciding the war by an attack on land. Numerically we had never been so strong in comparison with our enemies.'[1]

Even before the second Russian Revolution in November 1917, the Central Powers' fortunes had begun to revive as the application of new artillery and infantry tactics brought marked gains on the Eastern and Italian fronts. They benefited, in particular, from Lieutenant-Colonel Georg Bruchmüller's *development of predicted shooting, whereby bombardments dispensed with prior registration and relied instead on aerial or photographic reconnaissance to plot targets. Bruchmüller's system aimed not to destroy the defence but rather to incapacitate it by a sudden hurricane bombardment in depth. It was used in the successful attack at Riga in Russia on 1 September 1917, and later at Caporetto. The method was not unique to the Germans – and was mirrored by similar developments in Allied artillery – but it became even more potent when combined with new German 'stormtroop' tactics that used a thin skirmishing line, backed up by squads with mortars, flame-throwers and machine-guns, to push rapidly through enemy positions, bypassing strongpoints that could be dealt with later.*

Such tactics were used at Cambrai in late November, and helped to negate the gains made by the BEF on the first day. This was the first major tank attack of the war – with 216 Mark IVs used in the initial assault, and 476 overall – and benefited from the British version of predicted artillery fire to achieve total surprise on 20 November. By 9 a.m. the breach in the German front line was five miles wide, and at the end of the first day the British had advanced up to six miles, capturing 4,000 prisoners and 100 guns. But the short November days gave the British little time to consolidate, while the defenders received seven reinforcement divisions in twenty-four hours. On 30 November, after more British assaults, the Germans launched a twenty-division counter-attack, the largest against British troops since 1915, using stormtroop tactics to all but wipe out the British salient. The final British position – after both sides had lost 44,000 men – was in some places behind its 20 November start line.

Haig reflected on the diplomatic and military setbacks of the year, and the heavy burden being shouldered by the British, when he told his army commanders on 7 December: 'We expected at the time [of Messines] help from Russia, Italy and France! In reality the British Army has had to bear the brunt of it all. I added that we might well be proud of the achievements of the Armies this year and I thanked them one and all for their help and support.'[2] The point of the conference was to reorganize the BEF's defensive line in the light of Russia's withdrawal from the war, the availability of as many as thirty extra German divisions on the Western Front, and the near exhaustion of British reserves. The BEF had suffered nearly 800,000 casualties from January to November 1917, and in October the new Director of National Service, Auckland Geddes, had said the home economy could spare no more men. This, in turn, prompted the War Cabinet to predict in late November that Britain would need to continue fighting into 1919. Haig was still keen to resume the offensive in Flanders, if only to pre-empt a German attack, but the politicians were far from enthusiastic and soldier morale was also a concern.[3]

The only bright spots for the British in a year of disappointments were the capture of Baghdad and Jerusalem by respectively Generals Maude and Allenby (in March and December 1917), and the use of convoys to defeat Germany's unrestricted U-boat campaign. The submarines took their biggest toll of British shipping in April when more than 540,000 tons were sunk, up from 153,000 tons in January. 'The chances of an ocean-going steamer leaving the United Kingdom and returning safely fell to one in four,' wrote David Stevenson, 'the losses far exceeded replacement building, and if they had continued at this rate Britain would indeed have had to sue for peace before the year ended.'[4] *They were saved by the introduction of the convoy system, a Napoleonic Wars' stratagem that sailed merchant ships in organized groups with a warship escort. At first the Royal Navy was sceptical, but it came round after the US had entered the war (and made its destroyers available) and Allied shipping had lost a record number of ships in the last two weeks of April. The first convoy sailed from Britain on 10 May, and by June there were eight every eight days. The results were extraordinary: of 5,090 merchant ships convoyed in 1917, only sixty-three were sunk. 'The U-boats were Germany's answer to the checkmating of its surface fleet,' noted Stevenson, 'but convoying checkmated them in their turn.'*[5]

Having failed to force Britain to its knees, Germany and its allies were suffering their own economic freefall. Ottoman expenditure had quadrupled since the start of the war, but revenue rose by barely a fifth, resulting in currency depreciation and soaring inflation. Some of the provinces – ravaged by a collapse of trade and by the influx of thousands of refugees – were close to famine. In Austria-Hungary a lack of raw materials and an inadequate railway system were causing the seizure of heavy industry, with coal output halving and many steel firms closing for the winter. The production of arms fell accordingly: the output of machine-guns, for example, dropped from 1,900 to 350 pieces a month between October 1917 and February 1918. Even though fighting on the Russian and Balkan fronts had virtually ceased, most Austrian Army units were at two-thirds of regulation strength and 'could now do little more than wait passively' for the war to end.[6]

In Germany, too, the economy was in a downward spiral of rising prices, falling output and monetary depreciation. The tightening of the Allied blockade after the Americans entered the war had made vital raw materials needed for armaments – including non-ferrous metals, sulphur and glycerine – even scarcer. And yet by early 1918 the Hindenburg Programme had enabled Germany's armed forces to stockpile vast amounts of munitions, 'and neither shells nor infantry and artillery weapons' were in short supply 'until the final stages of the war'.[7]

The scene was now set for the war's final act. Germany had gambled everything on unrestricted submarine warfare in 1917, hoping to starve Britain into submission; it failed, and brought the United States into the war as a consequence. And yet on land, where Germany had planned to remain on the defensive, it and its allies ended 1917 with the strategic initiative. It was now a race against time for the Central Powers: to win the war in 1918 before the Americans arrived in force; and before their own creaking economies collapsed. 'I felt obliged,' wrote Ludendorff, 'to count on the new American formations beginning to arrive in the spring of 1918. In what numbers they would appear could not be foreseen; but it might be taken as certain that they would balance the loss of Russia; further, the relative strengths would be more in our favour in the spring than in the late summer and autumn, unless indeed we had by then gained a great victory.'

8 January 1918: 'A world . . . fit and safe to live in'
– Woodrow Wilson's Fourteen Points

'We entered this war,' declared President Woodrow Wilson in his most important speech to the US Congress since 2 April 1917,

because violations of right had occurred which touched us to the quick and made the life of our own people impossible unless they were corrected and the world secure once for all against their recurrence. What we demand in this war, therefore, is nothing peculiar to ourselves. It is that the world be made fit and safe to live in; and particularly that it be made safe for every peace-loving nation which, like our own, wishes to live its own life, determine its own institutions, be assured of justice and fair dealing by the other peoples of the world as against force and selfish aggression.[1]

He therefore wished to set out a programme for world peace, as he saw it, in Fourteen Points. As he read through them, it would quickly have occurred to his audience that Points I to IV and XIV simply restated general principles that Wilson had outlined in earlier speeches: open covenants of peace and diplomacy; absolute freedom of navigation in peace and war; the removal of economic barriers and the establishment of equality of trade; the reduction of national armaments to the 'lowest point consistent with domestic safety'; and the creation of a 'general association of nations' for the purpose of 'affording mutual guarantees of political independence and territorial integrity to great and small states alike' (the future League of Nations).[2]

More noteworthy was Wilson's qualified support for Allied territorial aims. Belgium 'must be evacuated and restored' (Point VII), while 'an independent Polish state should be erected' with 'free and secure access to the sea' (Point XIII). Point IX, on the other hand, challenged the extensive territorial gains promised to Italy in the Treaty of London by stating that the 'readjustment' of Italy's frontiers 'should be effected along clearly recognizable lines of nationality'; and though Point VIII stated that all French territory had to be 'freed and the invaded portions restored', there was no mention of France's ambitions in the Rhineland, and the reference to Alsace-Lorraine was deliberately ambiguous ('the wrong done to France by Prussia in 1871 . . . should be righted').[3]

There was, at this stage, no mention of national self-determination because Wilson was still hopeful of detaching Austria-Hungary and Turkey from Germany and, moreover, did not want to alienate the Entente. Points X and XII, therefore, talked of autonomy but not independence for the subject peoples of the Austro-Hungarian and Ottoman Empires. On the colonial question there was a fudge: there would be, stated Point V, a 'free, open-minded, and absolutely impartial adjustment of all colonial claims', but only if the 'interests of the population concerned' had 'equal weight with the equitable claims' of the colonial government. In practice, therefore, Germany was likely to lose its colonies and France and Britain would not.[4]

The remaining points – addressed chiefly to the Central Powers – called for the 'evacuation of all Russian territory' so that Russia could be given 'an unhampered and unembarrassed opportunity for the independent determination of her own political development' (Point VI); and also for Romania, Serbia and Montenegro to be evacuated and all 'occupied territories restored', with Serbia granted the additional benefit of 'free and secure access to the sea' (Point XI).[5]

In brief, the Fourteen Points called for an equitable peace that would leave the Central Powers with most of their territory intact, obliged to restore all invaded countries but not to suffer financial indemnity or even disarmament. They represented, in that sense, a relatively generous offer of peace (and certainly more generous than the one eventually imposed by the victorious Allies at the 1919 Paris peace conferences). But Wilson did not have – and would not get – the full backing of his Allies for a programme that clashed with their own war aims; nor was Germany, with its own hopes of an imminent military victory, yet prepared to consider a peace that would strip it not only of the huge gains it was about to wring out of Bolshevik Russia, but also of its colonies and probably Alsace-Lorraine and part of Silesia as well.

Wilson knew all this, yet he was determined to offer his own 'truncated and sanitized version of coalition objectives'.[6] The timing of the speech was in response to recent events in Russia, in particular the armistices with the Central Powers and the start of peace negotiations at Brest-Litovsk: he wanted to appeal to the Bolsheviks (and, as a peace treaty had not yet been agreed, hopefully keep them in the war), to the opposition groups in the Central Powers, and to socialists and progressives in the Entente countries, many of whom were supportive of the Bolsheviks. He was also encouraging his allies to reduce war aims that had been made public when the Bolsheviks published, in the wake of the October Revolution, the details of the secret treaties between Tsarist Russia and the other members of the Entente. At first Wilson had tried direct negotiation with the Allies, sending his envoy Colonel House to warn them that the American people would not fight for their 'selfish aims'. All the Allies would concede, however, was a commitment to reassess their war aims when Russia acquired a 'stable government'. It was this failure to secure a collective agreement that had prompted Wilson to issue unilaterally his Fourteen Points, consulting neither the Allies nor even his own Cabinet (though Secretary of State Lansing offered some advice).[7]

The response of the Allies was lukewarm – with Lloyd George and Georges Clemenceau (French Prime Minister since November 1917) giving Wilson's speech a non-committal welcome – but no Entente government 'revised its war aims as a consequence or felt bound by the American programme, the British and French continuing to stand by the Turkish partition agreements and the Italians by the London treaty'. Wilson seemed to have more success with the Central Powers: Count Georg von Hertling, German Chancellor since September 1917, accepted the Fourteen Points in principle but made no specific concessions; whereas Count Czernin, the Austrian premier, thought they might form the basis for peace negotiations.[8]

Duly encouraged, Wilson issued his follow-up 'Four Principles' on 11 February, a carefully worded commitment to self-determination: that territorial settlements 'must be made in the interests and for the benefit of the populations concerned'; and that 'all well-defined national aspirations' should be satisfied as long as they do not cause international conflict.[9] These qualifications left room for manoeuvre, and in February and March Austrian envoys met British, French and American officials. But their discussions foundered on Austria's unwillingness to negotiate a peace separate from Germany. The Dual Monarchy's leaders had probably calculated that a successful German spring offensive, rather than a negotiated peace, was their best hope of emerging from the war with their territory intact.[10]

6 February 1918: *'An unadvertised triumph'*
– Women get the vote

When the climactic moment finally came, some women hardly noticed. 'Remembering the eager feminism of my pre-war girlhood,' wrote Vera Brittain, 'and the effervescent fierceness with which I was to wage post-war literary battles in the cause of women, it seems incredible to me now that I should have gone back to hospital completely unaware that, only a few days before my leave began, the Representation of the People Bill, which gave votes to women over thirty, had been passed by the House of Lords.' She added:

I had been equally ignorant of its passage through the Commons the previous June, when my thoughts were occupied with Victor's death and the daylight air-raid, but my indifference to the fact that, on February 6th, 1918, women suffrage became a part of English law only reflected the changed attitude of the war-absorbed Pankhursts themselves. With an incongruous irony seldom equalled in the history of revolutions, the spectacular pageant of the women's movement, vital and colourful with adventure, with initiative, with sacrificial emotion, crept to its quiet, unadvertised triumph in the deepest night of wartime depression.[1]

The pro-war stance of the suffragette leaders Emmeline and Christabel Pankhurst to which Brittain referred was, of course, only part of the reason that Lloyd George's government had sponsored the bill. A far more compelling argument – though not unconnected – was the vital role that women had played in supporting Britain's war effort, a contribution mirrored across Europe. 'By 1917,' wrote David Stevenson, '40 per cent of the British Expeditionary Force were married men, and in Continental armies the ratio was higher. All over Europe women not only managed families but also took over businesses and farms or filled jobs their partners had vacated. Their role in sustaining morale and patriotism was vital, and they directly supported the armed forces.'[2]

A British poster linking women's support for the war effort with female suffrage.

They did this in various ways: by serving, like Brittain, as nurses; from 1917 as uniformed auxiliaries in the WAAC (Women's Army Auxiliary Corps), WRNS (Women's Royal Naval Service) and WRAF (Women's Royal Air Force) which eventually had more than 90,000 members between them; and by making armaments. By April 1918 more than 750,000 women were working for the Munitions Ministry, producing more than nine-tenths of its shells. Their contribution was 'beyond all praise', the Munitions Minister Winston Churchill told the House of Commons. 'They constituted today an additional reserve in labour-power without which we could not carry on.'[3]

In her memoir *Unshackled*, Christabel Pankhurst hinted at other factors influencing the government: 'War conditions had shattered the electoral register and Parliament must attend to the franchise before it could be re-elected.'[4] What she meant was that some form of franchise reform was inevitable given the huge sacrifices on the battlefield made by men as young as eighteen (and even younger if they had lied about their age). As things stood, only male householders over the age of twenty-one could vote (the result of the Third Reform Act in 1884); but that still left 40 per cent of adult men unenfranchised. Clearly this was an unacceptable state of affairs for men who had fought and died for King and Empire; but if more men were enfranchised then it was only right that women, who had also played their part, got the vote. This was the conclusion reached by the Speaker's Conference on Electoral Reform – attended by members of all parties – which proposed in January 1917 an end to the property qualification and virtually universal male suffrage, votes for women over thirty years of age and general elections held on a single day.[5]

Inevitably some diehard Tory Cabinet ministers opposed the measure. But Lloyd George won them over by making clear to the doubters that he was 'not going to be dragged at the heel of the Tory reactionaries who supported them'. He recalled: 'I impressed them enormously and swung them round . . . Not a bad start for a renegade Radical in a Tory camp.'[6] Even former Prime Minister Herbert Asquith, an inveterate opponent of women's suffrage, was convinced. 'Some of my friends may think,' he told the House of Commons, 'my eyes . . . have at last been opened to the truth.'[7]

Christabel Pankhurst put the collective change of heart down to a fear of the suffragette movement. 'The franchise could not be touched without giving votes to women,' she wrote, 'because Mrs [Emmeline] Pankhurst and her Suffragettes would resume militancy as soon as the war was ended, and no Government could arrest and imprison women who, in the country's danger, had set aside their campaign to help the national cause.'[8]

In the event many former opponents in the House of Lords – including Lord Curzon, the president of the National League for Opposing Women Suffrage – chose not to contest the bill and it passed by 134 votes to 71. By extending the vote to almost all men over twenty-one and women over thirty who met minimum property qualifications, the Representation of the People Act increased the electorate from 7.7 million in 1912 to 21.4 million when the next general election was held in December 1918. Women now made up 43 per cent of the electorate – a figure skewed by the enormous number of men killed in the war – and it was partly a determination to keep them from dominating the ballot that the minimum age of thirty was settled upon. The Pankhursts had deliberately held aloof from such negotiations at the Speaker's Conference, believing 'that a certain detachment on our part', wrote Christabel, 'would give more effect to the potential, post-war militancy which it was the aim of political leaders to avert'. She added: 'We therefore left it to others to discuss such points as the differential age limit for women voters, designed to prevent them from becoming at once an electoral majority.'[9]

But age limit or no, Parliament's concession of women's right to vote was a major landmark in British constitutional history and the culmination of almost fifty years of campaigning by the Pankhurst family.* 'The vision of its pioneers,' noted Christabel, 'the persistence of those who followed them during the long middle period, the sacrifice of the militants, had been rewarded. Women at last were citizens and voters.'[10]

The bar against women sitting in Parliament was removed in November 1918 with the Eligibility of Women Act. The first woman to be elected – in the December general election – was the Sinn Fein candidate Constance Markiewicz; but she chose not to take her seat, preferring to attend the Dáil Éireann in Dublin. Instead it was left to Nancy Astor to

---

* It was Emmeline's husband, Dr Richard Pankhurst, who had drafted the first women's suffrage bill which was introduced to Parliament in 1870 but blocked by the Liberal Prime Minister William Gladstone.

become the first woman to sit at Westminster on 1 December 1919. Equal voting rights with men were finally conceded in 1928 by the Representation of the People (Equal Franchise) Act.

3 March 1918: *'Our conditions are hard and severe'*
– The German diktat at Brest-Litovsk

At five in the afternoon, in the fortress serving as the German Army's headquarters at Brest-Litovsk, the Russian delegation led by G. V. Chicherin, the Commissar for Foreign Affairs, signed a peace treaty with Germany that would reduce Russia, in economic and territorial terms, 'to a status on a par with seventeenth-century Muscovy'.[1]

By the terms of the treaty, the Bolsheviks agreed to give up all claims to 'European' Russia, including the Baltic provinces, Poland, White Russia (now Belarus), Finland, Bessarabia, the Ukraine and the Caucasus. This made up a third of its pre-war population (fifty-five million people), a third of its agricultural land, more than half its industry and nine-tenths of its coalfields – 'almost all the territory, in fact,' wrote Martin Gilbert, 'that had been added to the Tsarist dominions since the reign of Peter the Great more than two hundred years earlier'.[2]

In addition, Russia lost all its naval bases in the Baltic bar Kronstadt; its Black Sea fleet was to be disarmed and detained; and the territory in eastern Turkey that it had captured in 1916, including the fortress of Erzerum, was returned to the Ottomans.* How had it come to this?

The initial Bolshevik stance in the Brest-Litovsk negotiations had been to play for time in the hope that copycat revolutions would break out in Berlin and Vienna. Trotsky's hard bargaining caused the talks to break down over Christmas 1917 as the Germans refused to return the occupied territories of Courland, Lithuania and Poland. But Ludendorff and Hindenburg, the German military chiefs, soon got wise to Trotsky's procrastination; and the Bolsheviks' bargaining position was fatally undermined

---

* Armenian soldiers tried to prevent this but were defeated by Ottoman troops moving eastward.

on 9 February when Germany signed a separate deal with Ukrainian nation-alists, effectively turning Ukraine into a German protectorate, and opening the way for German and Austrian troops to occupy the country.

By now the Bolsheviks' Central Committee was split between three factions: Bukharin's, the largest, which saw the resumption of hostilities with Germany as the best hope of sparking a revolution in the West; Trotsky's, the next largest, which thought procrastination was still the best option (summed up by its leader's slogan 'Neither war nor peace'); and Lenin's, the smallest, which was convinced that a peace treaty with Germany was inevitable and for the sake of the revolution in Russia it was better to sign it sooner rather than later. 'There is no doubt that it will be a shameful peace,' acknowledged Lenin in January 1918, 'but if we embark on a war, our government will be swept away.'[3]

But with only five supporters on the Central Committee (including a tough Georgian called Josef Stalin), Lenin was forced to ally himself with Trotsky's faction and the negotiations continued. Matters were finally brought to a head on 10 February when the Kaiser, at the prompting of his military chiefs (who were desperate to transfer divisions to the Western Front for the spring offensive), issued the Russians an ultimatum to sign the peace treaty or face a resumption of hostilities. Trotsky refused, and on 18 February the Germans advanced with fifty-two divisions, occupying Dvinsk in the north and Lutsk in the south.[4]

That evening, as news of the German advance into the Ukraine reached Petrograd, Lenin finally persuaded Trotsky and the Central Committee to agree to the enemy's terms. A telegram to this effect was at once despatched to General Hoffmann, the German commander in the east. But Hoffmann played for time by insisting that the Russian acceptance had to be in writing. Meanwhile his troops continued to advance, taking Minsk and 9,000 prisoners on 20 February. 'The Russian army is more rotten than I had supposed,' noted Hoffmann in his diary. 'There is no fight left in them. Yesterday one lieutenant with six men took six hundred Cossacks prisoner.'[5]

Two days later he added: 'This is the most comical war I have ever known. We put a handful of infantrymen with machine guns and one gun on a train and push them off to the next station; they take it, make prisoners of the Bolsheviks, pick up a few more troops and go on. This proceeding has, at any rate, the charm of novelty.' In just five days the Germans had advanced 150 miles.[6]

The Russian delegation is welcomed by German officials to the peace
talks at Brest-Litovsk.

On 23 February, Berlin rejected Lenin and Trotsky's note and imposed
even harsher terms for peace. They included a demand for all the territory the Germans had occupied during the war, including the conquests
of the last five days. Despite this, Lenin urged the Central Committee to
accept. 'Only a blind man,' he declared, 'or men infatuated by phrases can
fail to see that the policy of a revolutionary war without an army is water
in the bourgeois mill . . . Their knees are on our chest, and our position
is hopeless. This peace must be accepted as a respite enabling us to prepare
a decisive resistance to the bourgeoisie and the imperialists.'[7] In other
words, Russia's territorial integrity was to be sacrificed while the Bolsheviks
took on the counter-revolutionaries who – led by the former Tsarist
commanders Kolchak, Yudenich and Deniken – would soon be flexing
their muscles in southern, northern and eastern Russia, the first chapter
in a bitter civil war that would rage until 1920.

Reluctantly, Trotsky and a majority of the Central Committee agreed
with Lenin, and their decision to accept the new German terms was
transmitted to Berlin on 24 February. After the treaty had been signed a

week later, a young German *Leutnant* of artillery, Herbert Sulzbach, noted in his diary:

> Our conditions are hard and severe, but our quite exceptional victories entitle us to demand these, since our troops are nearly in Petersburg [Petrograd], and further over on the southern front, Kiev has been occupied, while in the last week we have captured the following men and items of equipment: 6,800 officers, 54,000 men, 2,400 guns, 5,000 machine-guns, 8,000 railway trucks, 8,000 locomotives, 128,000 rifles and 2 million rounds of artillery ammunition. Yes, there is still some justice left, and the state which was first to start mass murder in 1914 has now, with all its missions, been finally overthrown.[8]

The reaction in Russia could not have been more different. The treaty 'is not being recognized by patriotic Russians', wrote the British nurse Florence Farmborough, living with friends in Moscow, 'and countless Russians are horrified to hear about it'. She added: 'There is, of course, overpowering relief that soldiers' lives are no longer in danger; on the other hand, peace has been brought at a heavy price, namely dishonour to their country and disloyalty to their allies.'[9]

21 March 1918: *'Only a few of the enemy had survived the storm'*

– The opening of *die Kaiserschlact* ('the Kaiser's battle')

'The darkness begins to lift, very, very slowly,' recorded Leutnant Herbert Sulzbach of the German 63rd Field Artillery, stationed in the ruins of the Saint-Quentin suburbs. 'We stand at the guns with our gas masks round our necks, and the time until 4.40 crawls round at a dreadfully slow pace. At last we're there, and with a crash our barrage begins from thousands and thousands . . . of gun barrels and mortars, a barrage that sounds as if the world were coming to an end.'[1]

Almost half the German artillery pieces on the Western Front – 6,608 guns, more than a third of them 5.9-inch heavies – had opened up over fifty miles of the British front between Arras and the River Oise. Also in action were more than 3,500 mortars, capable of firing bombs of 100 kilos. It would be the most concentrated barrage of the war, firing 1,160,000 shells in just five hours; at the Somme, by contrast, the British had fired 1,500,000 shells in seven days.[2]

A young British second lieutenant in the 22nd Northumberland Fusiliers recalled the moment the barrage began: 'I was going round inspecting the posts and just happened to be standing on the fire-step, with my head just over the parapet, looking out over No Man's Land. Then I saw this colossal flash of light. As far as I could see from left to right was lit up by it . . . I just managed to hear the gunfire itself before the explosions as the shells arrived all around us.'[3]

As the storm of steel descended, the British infantry in the front line took what cover they could. Some were in dug-outs, safe from all but a direct hit by a heavy shell, though the walls shook and dry earth kept trickling through the joints in the roof timbers. But many were in open trenches, huddled into corners and crammed into scrape holes in the walls. The shells exploding all around them were like 'millions of sauce-pans all boiling together', recalled one soldier. Then they realized to their horror that many contained gas – chlorine, phosgene, lachrymatory (tear) and, particularly in the Flesquières salient,* mustard gas. Even those lucky enough to get their gas masks on in time were severely debilitated: breathing was difficult through the primitive filters and visibility restricted by the poor eyepieces.[4]

At 9.40 a.m., the guns lifted to targets behind the British front line and the stormtroops of thirty-two German divisions began to advance. They were greatly assisted by a dense fog. 'The infantry commander shouts "*Drauf*" and we rush forward,' recalled one German pioneer armed with explosives. 'But where is the expected enemy fire! There is hardly any . . . Then we reached the barbed wire, our objective. But there was nothing for us to do. The wire was completely destroyed. There wasn't really any trench left, just craters and craters . . . Only a few of the enemy had survived the storm; some were wounded. They stood with hands up. There was no need to tell them; they got the message – "to the rear".'[5]

The German artillery and mortars had done their job: most of the

* Ground gained during the Cambrai offensive in November 1917.

wire had been blown away and the front-line trenches were largely cratered ruins. Hardly surprising, therefore, that in many places the British had deliberately evacuated the forward trench, often without orders. The few soldiers left were either dead and wounded or so shocked and gassed as to be incapable of offering any serious resistance. 'It would not be an exaggeration,' wrote historian Martin Middlebrook, 'to say that nine-tenths of the British front-line trench or outposts fell without much of a fight.'[6]

Using the same stormtroop tactics that had worked so well in the counter-attack at Cambrai, the Germans concentrated on punching holes in certain sectors, leaving isolated pockets to be dealt with later. Some defenders fought bravely, others quickly surrendered. Only a few got back to the next line of trenches. Within an hour the Germans were in possession of almost all fifty miles of the British front line they had targeted. The only exceptions were the Flesquières salient, which had not been attacked, and a few scattered outposts.

Why were the British so incapable of meeting an attack they knew was coming? The answer lies partly in the extra manpower the Germans had enjoyed since transferring divisions from the Eastern Front, giving them a numerical advantage in the West of 191 divisions to the Allies' 169. Their plan was to use these extra troops in a series of huge spring offensives, the first – codenamed Operation Michael – against a large sector of the British front where the ground was drier than further north and the defenders weaker: twenty-six British infantry and three cavalry divisions faced an attack by seventy-six German divisions, with thirty-two in the first wave.[7] Once a breakthrough had been achieved, the German troops would begin to roll up the British front from the south, while a second attack was launched just to the south of the Ypres salient in Flanders. The bulk of the BEF would either be destroyed piecemeal or driven back to the Channel ports.

Field Marshal Haig had been expecting a German offensive since the turn of the year, and to counteract it he ordered his troops to construct a system of defence in depth – not dissimilar to the one the Germans had been using since 1917. In February he correctly predicted an initial attack in late March between Lens and the Oise, followed by an assault in April near Ypres. He was also advised, in the wake of Riga, to expect the Germans to use a surprise bombardment and infiltration tactics.[8]

A British officer and his men keep a sharp lookout for attacking Germans
during the Michael offensive of March 1918.

The BEF troops, however, were not used to fighting defensively and
the 'elastic' system that Haig created was a poor imitation of its German
counterpart. It comprised three zones: the Forward Zone, comprising
outposts rather than a continuous line, which was to be held to the last
man and in greater strength than the German equivalent; the Battle Zone,
with defensive redoubts sited in the best tactical position and far enough
back – 2,000–3,000 yards from the Forward Zone and the same distance
in depth – to avoid being destroyed in the initial attack; and finally the
Rear Zone (or Corps Line), a further four to eight miles back, but many
of these defences had yet to be completed. The British Third and Fifth
Armies (on whom the main blow would fall), for example, had hardly
begun their Rear Zones and '84 per cent of their battalions were within
3,000 yards of the front line (and therefore more exposed to bombardment)

against a maximum of 50 per cent under the German system, while relatively few troops were available to relieve the "redoubts" in the Battle Zone.'[9]

Of the four armies* that made up the BEF in March 1918, the Fifth Army – commanded by Lieutenant-General Sir Hubert Gough (the man who had performed so poorly at Third Ypres) – was by far the weakest. It had just twelve infantry and three cavalry divisions to defend a front of forty-two miles; the Third Army, by comparison, had fourteen divisions for just twenty-eight miles of front, while the two British armies further north were of similar strength. Haig had deliberately concentrated his resources in the centre and north of his line because he feared a German breakthrough there would cut his armies in two and/or sever his communications with the Channel ports. 'Of course, I am uneasy,' he told an officer querying the length of the Fifth Army's front, 'but where else can I afford to bend without risk of losing the war!'[10]

In the unlikely event that the Fifth Army was attacked, Haig had instructed Gough to stand firm for as long as he could, and only if severely pressed to conduct a fighting retreat along the line of the Somme. The French, in any case, had agreed to provide six divisions in an emergency. Haig knew an offensive was imminent – noting in his diary on 18 March that 'we must expect an attack at short notice, and make our plans accordingly' – yet he was still confident enough to approve special leave for 88,000 troops.[11]

By 19 March Haig's intelligence staff predicted an attack on the British Third and Fifth Armies on the 20th or 21st after a short bombardment using a high proportion of gas shells. Yet GHQ still refused Gough's request to move two reserve divisions closer to the front. A despondent Gough replied: 'I shall fight them in my Battle Zone as long as we can hold them there. Good night. Good night.'[12]

In the event, not even the more formidable defences of the Battle Zone could stem the tide on 21 March. By late afternoon the Germans had made spectacular gains. Of the four British divisions above the Flesquières salient, three had been pushed back to the rear of their Battle Zones, and the fourth would be forced to withdraw that evening. Though the salient

---

* The original Second Army, under Plumer, served in Italy from November 1917 to March 1918 as part of the Allied reinforcements sent after the Battle of Caporetto.

itself had not been attacked, its four divisions were 'in the air' and also bound to retire. From the salient down to the Somme Canal in front of Saint-Quentin, a distance of nineteen miles, only a single division had been forced out of its Battle Zone, the 16th; the other five were either still holding the front of their Battle Zones or had halted the Germans within them.

It was south of here, on a stretch of the front taken over from the French only eight weeks earlier, that the real disaster occurred. All three divisions – the 36th, 14th and 18th – had been all but driven from their Battle Zones and large gaps existed between the few battalions that remained. A major cause of this collapse was the tendency for British troops to surrender or fall back after the briefest of fights. 'When the Jerries came towards our line in large numbers,' wrote one private, 'they were firing from the hip and I thought, "Tosh. Do what some of the others are doing. Hop it back." So I did. I was not alone.'[13]

The effect of such retreats, according to Martin Middlebrook, 'was that, right from the beginning of the battle, there developed an attitude of uncertainty about the flanks, a tendency for men in good defensive positions to look over their shoulders and wonder if they too ought not to be moving back'.[14] By midnight, the Germans had taken 98½ square miles of ground, all but nineteen from the hapless Fifth Army. (On the Somme in 1916, the British and French had taken 140 days to capture the same area.) That night, the British would tactically withdraw from a further forty square miles of ground to prevent many units from being encircled.[15]

The best estimate of German and British losses is roughly 39,000 for each side,* though the former lost more killed: 10,900 to 7,500. The most telling statistic, however, was the number of British prisoners: 21,000, or more than half the total.[16] This meant that the vast majority of British casualties were lost to the army for the duration of the war, whereas many of Germany's 28,000 wounded would return to active service. Haig tried to put a gloss on the day's fighting by sending a message of congratulation to the Third and Fifth Armies. 'Having regard,' he wrote in his

---

* The total casualties of 78,000 were the highest for a single day's fighting on the Western Front, though more lives were lost at the Somme on 1 July 1916 (Middlebrook, *The Kaiser's Battle*, p. 322).

diary, 'to the great strength of the attack . . . and the determined manner in which the attack was everywhere pressed, I consider that the result of the day is highly creditable to the British troops.'[17]

It did not seem that way to British nurse Vera Brittain when the first casualties reached her base hospital at Etaples on 22 March. She remembered 'gazing, half hypnotised, at the dishevelled beds, the stretchers on the floor, the scattered boots and piles of muddy khaki, the brown blankets turned back from smashed limbs bound to splints by filthy blood-stained bandages. Beneath each stinking wad of cotton wool and gauze an obscene horror waited for me – and all the equipment that I had for attacking it in this ex-medical ward was one pair of forceps.'[18]

In truth the day had been a disaster for the British Army, in terms both of ground lost and of men taken prisoner. 'Morale wasn't high,' confessed a lieutenant in the Manchester Regiment. 'If we'd had the guts we'd had eighteen months earlier, the Germans would never have knocked a hole in the line as they did that time. I heard later that most of the battalion became prisoners without putting up much of a fight.'[19]

4 April 1918: *'They won't come any further'*
– Operation Michael runs out of steam

The objective of the attack by fifteen German divisions south of the River Somme was to cut the Allies' vital north–south trunk railway: either by capturing the railway junction of Amiens; or, failing that, by taking the high ground near the small town of Villers-Bretonneux from where the city could be targeted by long-range artillery fire.

Defending Villers-Bretonneux – formerly a prosperous manufacturing town just ten miles to the east of Amiens – was the British 14th Division that had performed so poorly on 21 March. 'Our division,' recalled Second Lieutenant Walter Harris, 'tired after its March battles, was in no mood to fight and for the first time I saw British troops retreating in disorder and individually leaving their trench without orders; for the first and only time I saw a British officer holding his own men with his revolver. I happened to be in a support trench, and all these men crowded into our trench for a time, but very soon, as the enemy attack developed, we were retiring again.'[1]

Separated from his unit, the 9th Rifle Brigade, Harris stumbled into an Australian headquarters and reported the loss of the front-line trenches. 'They won't come any further,' an Anzac officer assured him, 'only over my dead body.'[2]

The staff officer was part of the Australian Corps that had been ordered to replace the 'blown' British divisions guarding Villers-Bretonneux. By now all the inhabitants of the town had fled, bar one woman and her children who were encouraged to stay by an Australian soldier. 'You needn't go, Ma,' he told her, 'the Aussies are here. Best stay where you are.'[3] The soldier was as good as his word as he and his comrades, two battalions of the Australian 9th Brigade, first held and then pushed back the German advance. Next day, 5 April, the Germans widened their attack to the north of the Somme river. When it made only negligible gains, Ludendorff called off the offensive.

After the spectacular gains of the first day – 21 March – the Germans had maintained their attack's momentum; by the 23rd they had torn a forty-mile gap into open country. That same day the first French troops arrived to assist the British, as the 88,000 BEF troops on leave and the mobile reserve were rushed across the Channel. But when Haig asked Pétain for more French divisions to cover Amiens, he was refused. Fearing a separate attack in Champagne, Pétain's priority was to keep the French Army intact and only then to maintain contact with the British. His instructions, he told Haig on 24 March, were to protect Paris even if it meant exposing the BEF's right flank.[4]

On 26 March, to get more French divisions north of the Somme, Haig agreed to place himself under the orders of a French generalissimo. At a meeting of senior Allied politicians and generals at Doullens, it was agreed that General Foch would take responsibility 'for the co-ordination of the action of the Allied armies on the Western Front', while Haig and Pétain retained responsibility for the tactical direction of their armies. Doullens is often cited as a key moment in the campaign, the point at which Allied co-operation made a German victory impossible. In truth the German offensive was already starting to run out of steam and Doullens' significance was more symbolic than practical.[5]

By the time the two-week offensive was closed down on 5 April, the

Germans had captured (or destroyed) 1,200 square miles of territory, 1,300 artillery pieces, 200 tanks, 2,000 machine-guns and 400 aircraft, as well as taking 90,000 prisoners of war. They had killed or wounded a further 212,000 Allied soldiers (the majority British), losing 239,000 of their own men in the process.[6] To incur fewer total losses (including prisoners of war) than the enemy when attacking was unprecedented on the Western Front, and it underlines the scale of the German achievement during the Michael offensive. For the British the setback – described by the influential Repington as 'the worst defeat in the history of the Army' – was to cost General Gough his job (he was replaced as Fifth Army commander by General Rawlinson in late March) and cause Haig to offer his resignation in early April. It was not accepted. 'The politicians,' wrote Gary Sheffield, 'thought Haig was a poor general but there was no one better.'[7]

Some British historians have, with the benefit of hindsight, condemned Michael as a grave strategic error. 'Ludendorff had intended to win the war outright,' wrote Peter Hart, 'before the Americans could join the fray, by breaking through the British lines and rolling them up to the north . . . In reality all that had been gained was a 40-mile deep salient bulging uncomfortably into the Allied lines.'[8]

In fact Michael was the start of a series of co-ordinated hammer blows on the Western Front that were designed, in Hindenburg's words, to shake 'the enemy building by closely sequenced partial blows' until it 'collapses'.[9] While failing to achieve a decisive breakthrough, it had caused immense material damage and its effect on the morale of the BEF in particular was serious. All would depend on how the British responded to the next offensive (Georgette) about to be launched on the River Lys in Flanders. What is not in doubt, however, is that some Britons, in the dark days after 21 March, were contemplating the awful possibility of defeat. British nurse Vera Brittain recalled:

> Each convoy of men that we took in – to be dispatched, a few hours later, to England after a hasty wash and change of dressing, or to the cemetery after a laying-out too hurried to be reverent – gave way to a discouragement that none of us had met with in a great battle before.
>
> 'There's only a handful of us, Sister, and there seem to be thousands of them!' was the perpetual cry . . . Day after day, while civilian refugees

fled panic-stricken into Etaples . . . and the wounded, often unattended, came down in anything that would carry them – returning lorries, A.S.C. [Army Service Corps] ambulances and even cattle-trucks – some fresh enemy conquest was incredulously whispered . . . One after another, Péronne, Bapaume, Beaumont Hamel, were gone, and on March 27th Albert itself was taken. Even Paris, we learnt, had been shelled by a long-range gun from seventy-five miles away.[10]

The low point for Brittain came on 4 April when rumours reached Etaples that the 'Germans are in the suburbs of Amiens!' She remembered: 'We were already becoming a Casualty Clearing Station, with only the advance units at Abbeville between ourselves and the line; how much longer should we be able to remain where we were? How long until we too fled before the grey uniforms advancing down the road from Camiers? This horror . . . monstrous, undreamed of, incredible . . . this was defeat.'[11]

That same day the German advance was stopped by the Australians at Villers-Bretonneux and 'defeat' postponed; but for how long?

21 April 1918: *'He was hunched in the cockpit aiming over his guns'*
– The Red Baron's last flight

Rittmeister Manfred Freiherr von Richthofen – the German air ace better known as the Red Baron – was in good spirits as he and the men of Jasta 11 took off in two flights from Cappy airfield in the Somme valley. A day earlier Richthofen had shot down two British Sopwith Camels – his seventy-ninth and eightieth victories – and was looking forward to a period of leave which he planned to spend hunting in the Black Forest. 'Everything was prepared,' recalled Leutnant Richard Wenzl, who flew with him that day, 'even sleeping car reservations had been obtained in case the lack of flying weather remained.'[1]

So relaxed had been Richthofen that morning that while the Jasta waited for fog to clear he initiated a bout of horseplay by tipping over stretchers that two of his pilots were napping in. They retaliated by tying a wheel chock to the tail of Richthofen's dog Moritz. Wenzl remembered:

'One jump and the poor beast succumbed to his fate and ran with the chock in circles. I photographed the moment twice. They are the last photos of the Old Master.'[2]

Moments later a gaggle of British planes overflew Cappy airfield, prompting Richthofen and his pilots to race for their Fokker Dr.I triplanes.* The Jasta took off in two flights of five planes – Richthofen leading one – and proceeded towards the front lines where they joined a flight of Jasta 5 Albatroses in a dogfight with a similar number of Sopwith Camels 'with red snouts' from the RAF's 209 Squadron.† 'There was a massive twisting and turning,' wrote Wenzl, 'as often happened in recent days. Most [of the new men] did not come down far because everyone was ready to shoot. Only the "aces" got down into it.'[3]

Among the aces was Leutnant Hans Joachim Wolff – Richthofen's wingman – whose tally had been growing steadily since he had shot down his first victim John McCudden, brother of famous British ace James, a month earlier. Wolff recalled:

> While Oberleutnant Karjus and I fought against two or three Camels, suddenly I saw [Richthofen's] red machine near me, as he fired at a Camel that first went into a spin, then slipped away in a steep dive towards the west. We had a rather strong east wind and Herr Rittmeister had not taken that into account. As I now had clear air around me, I got closer to the Camel and shot it down . . . I looked for Herr Rittmeister and saw that he was at extremely low altitude over the Somme near Corbie, and instinctively shook my head and wondered why [he] was following an opponent so far over the other side.[4]

The unfortunate pilot in Richthofen's sights was Lieutenant Wilfrid May, a twenty-two-year-old Canadian rookie who had fought his first air combat only a day earlier. 'The enemy were coming at me from all sides,' he recalled. 'I seemed to be missing some of them by inches . . .

---

* Richthofen's all-red Fokker triplane is the aircraft most commonly associated with him; yet he gained only nineteen of his eighty kills in this model, having switched to it after he was shot down and badly wounded in his previous aircraft, an Albatros DV, in July 1917.

† On 1 April 1918, the RFC had amalgamated with the RNAS to create a third service known as the Royal Air Force (RAF).

Through lack of experience I held my guns open too long, one jammed and then the other. I could not clear them, so I spun out of the mess and headed west into the sun for home . . . The first thing I knew I was being fired on from the rear. I could not fight back unfortunately, so all I could do was to try to dodge my attacker. I noticed it was a red Triplane, but if I had realised it was Richthofen I would probably have passed out on the spot.'[5]

May continued 'dodging and spinning', falling from around 12,000 feet to hedge height in a desperate attempt to shake off his pursuer – but to no avail. 'Richthofen was firing at me continually,' he noted, 'the only thing that saved me was my poor flying. I didn't know what I was doing myself and I do not suppose that Richthofen could figure out what I was going to do.'

It was during the long pursuit that Captain Roy Brown, a Canadian friend of May's and the seasoned commander of 209 Squadron's A Flight (with nine victories to his credit), dived steeply on to the Red Baron's tail and fired 'a long burst into him'. Brown later claimed that it was this burst that brought Richthofen down. In fact Richthofen continued chasing May long after Brown had pulled out of his vertical swoop.[6]

As they sped up the Somme valley from Sailly-le-Sec to Vaux-sur-Somme, passing low over the lines of the Australian 5th Division, May was convinced his time was up: 'I went round a curve in the river just near Corbie. Richthofen beat me to it and came over the hill. At that point I was a sitting duck. I was too low down between the banks to make a turn away from him. I felt that he had me cold, and I was in such a state of mind at this time that I had to restrain myself from pushing my stick forward into the river as I knew that I had had it.'[7]

Unbeknown to May, Richthofen's plane had already been hit by bullets fired by an Australian Lewis gunner, Robert Buie, who was protecting an artillery battery on Morlancourt Ridge. Buie wrote later:

> I can still remember seeing Richthofen clearly. His helmet covered most of his head and face and he was hunched in the cockpit aiming over his guns at the lead plane. It seemed that with every burst he leaned forward in his cockpit as though concentrating very intently on his fire. Certainly he was not aware of his dangerous position or of the close position of our guns. At 200 yards, with the peep sight directly on Richthofen's body

I began firing with steady bursts. His plane was bearing frontal and just a little to the right of me and after 20 rounds I knew that the bullets were striking the right side and front of the machine, for I clearly saw fragments . . . Then just before my last shots finished at a range of 40 yards Richthofen's guns stopped abruptly. The thought flashed through my mind – I've hit him! – and immediately I noticed a change in engine sound as the red triplane passed over our gun position at less than 50 feet and still a little to my right.[8]

Richthofen now turned sharply to the left, breaking off the engagement with May, and reversed his course back to the German lines. This gave another Australian machine-gunner, Sergeant Cedric Popkin – who had fired at the Red Baron shortly before he reached the ridge – the chance to open up again. 'I don't think that I was firing so long the second time as the first. I would be firing about half to three quarters of a minute each time.'[9]

Seconds later the triplane crash-landed in a ploughed field near the Corbie-to-Bray road, its undercarriage collapsing in the heavy soil. Australian troops pulled Richthofen from the wreckage but he was dead, killed by a single bullet through the heart. His only other injuries were a fractured jaw and two broken front teeth caused when he collided with his gun butts on impact. The question remains: who killed him?

A rudimentary post-mortem at Poulainville aerodrome, home of No. 3 Squadron of the Australian Flying Corps, concluded that the fatal bullet had entered the right side of Richthofen's back at the level of the ninth rib, passed through the chest and exited about two inches higher by the left nipple. He had, therefore, been shot from behind, slightly from below and to the right.[10] This would seem to rule out Brown who was diving from above when he fired his burst at the Red Baron, as would the fact that Richthofen kept on flying for a few minutes after Brown's attack, whereas a shot to the heart would have left him conscious and capable of flying for thirty seconds at most.

Buie, also, could not have killed him because all his shots were from the front. The man responsible, therefore, was probably Popkin. 'It was . . . when the triplane was flying away from Popkin,' wrote Australian Dr Geoffrey Miller, author of a detailed investigation into Richthofen's death, 'that he opened fire with his Vickers gun for a second time . . . [There] is no doubt that he could have inflicted a bullet wound that entered Richthofen from below, from the side and slightly behind, just as was found at the post-mortem examination. Neither Captain Brown nor Gunner Buie could have inflicted such a wound.'[11]

Richthofen was buried in Bertangles Cemetery with full military honours on 22 April. Ten days later, a date that would have been the Red Baron's twenty-sixth birthday, members of his family, senior military officers and the Kaiserin Auguste Victoria attended a memorial service in the Garrison Church at Potsdam. General von Hoeppner, commander of the German Air Force, assured the Red Baron's mother that her son was not the victim of an enemy pilot. 'Manfred had taken a chance hit from the ground,' he explained, adding: 'We have no replacement for your son in the whole Air Force.'[12]

With eighty confirmed kills, Richthofen had the highest tally of any pilot during the war. The top Allied ace was Frenchmen René Fonck with seventy-five, followed by Billy Bishop, a Canadian who flew for the RFC and RAF, with seventy-two. Both survived the war. But Richthofen – the Red Baron – is the name remembered today: the subject of countless books and films who lives on in Jagdgeschwader 71 'Richthofen', a squadron in the modern German Luftwaffe. In 1918, the response of Allied pilots to news of the Red Baron's death was chiefly one of relief. 'I read a book called *The Red Air Fighter* by von Richthofen,' wrote one British pilot. 'It strikes me that it is a good thing he is dead!'[13]

25 April 1918: *'The men remained petrified in their holes'* – The battle for Mont Kemmel

For the French troops dug in on Mont Kemmel, a 500-feet-high feature in the flat wasteland south-west of Ypres, the German bombardment that opened at 2.30 a.m. was worse than anything they had experienced at Verdun. 'For more than four hours,' recalled Captain Pinçon of the 99th Infantry, 'it was impossible to take off our gas-masks. The men remained petrified in their holes, under a deluge of iron, fire and poison, half-smothered, suffocating, overwhelmed by the noise and the concussions in ground and air, their vision blurred behind the misted lenses of their masks.'[1] Gas shells neutralized the French artillery support and, when the attack began at 6 a.m., thick fog made it impossible to identify the attacking stormtroopers until it was too late.[2]

Among the assaulting troops was Unteroffizier Frederick Meisel of the German 371st Infantry. 'Suddenly our artillery fire stopped,' he recalled.

> An awful silence followed the terrific noise. A whistle shrilled, bayonets were fixed. Another whistle signalled the descent into the valley. Not a sound, not a rifle shot could be heard from the opposite side. Crossing the valley we stopped to readjust ourselves and began the climb to the hill before us. Now we discovered why it had been so quiet, for over this territory lay the silence of death. The shell holes were filled with ghastly and bloody messes; freshly built trenches had caved in burying the occupants. Stumbling over mutilated bodies we reached the summit.[3]

By 7.10 a.m., Mont Kemmel had fallen to the German Alpine Division and more than 6,000 dazed Frenchmen were prisoners. Their countrymen responded by firing gas shells and launching a fierce counter-attack to retake the height, but it was driven off. 'Through the damp glasses of my [gas] mask,' wrote Meisel, 'I saw dim outlines of men appear and when they approached more closely I could distinguish French uniforms and dully blinking bayonets. Gruen threw himself behind the machine gun and I instinctively pointed the barrel . . . into the mist towards the advancing enemy . . . Flames spurted from the barrel of the guns and I saw the Frenchmen plunge headlong into the grass.'[4]

Four days later another surprise attack captured a second height in the 'Belgian Alps' – Scherpenberg – but that was the final gain of the second of the Germans' spring offensives – codenamed Georgette – that had been launched on the River Lys in Flanders on 9 April. Involving fewer troops than originally planned (because of the high losses incurred during Michael), Georgette had thrown twelve assault divisions (with a further fifteen in reserve) against six British and two Portuguese divisions on a twenty-mile front. But the main focus of the attack was a six-mile sector held by a single Portuguese division which General Horne, the First Army commander, had neither relieved nor reinforced despite warnings that it was vulnerable. Though British troops held up the attack to the south with machine-gun outposts and a traditional trench line, the

Portuguese broke and fled, forcing the 40th Division to the north to join the retreat. By nightfall the Germans had taken 100 guns and advanced five miles to the line of the River Lys, though a shaky British line still contained the eighteen-mile-wide incursion.[5]

But fresh attacks to the north the following day captured the important railway junction of Armentières and part of the Messines Ridge from the British Second Army. On 11 April the Germans advanced to within five miles of Hazebrouck, an even more important 'choke point' on the BEF's railway system. 'Put simply,' wrote Gary Sheffield, 'if Hazebrouck was lost the BEF would find it difficult to fight . . . It could even have led to the capture of some of the Channel ports, and the eventual collapse of the Anglo-French alliance in mutual recrimination as the British troops were evacuated by sea.'[6]

That same day, to hearten his outnumbered troops, Haig issued a 'Special Order of the Day' to all ranks. It read:

Three weeks ago to-day the enemy began his terrific attacks against us on a fifty-mile front. His objects are to separate us from the French, to take the Channel Ports and destroy the British Army.

In spite of throwing already 106 Divisions into the battle and enduring the most reckless sacrifice of human life, he has as yet made little progress towards his goals.

We owe this to the determined fighting and self-sacrifice of our troops. Words fail me to express the admiration which I feel for the splendid resistance offered by all ranks . . .

Many amongst us now are tired. To those I would say that Victory will belong to the side which holds out the longest. The French Army is moving rapidly and in great force to our support.

There is no course open to us but to fight it out. Every position must be held to the last man: there must be no retirement. With our backs to the wall and believing in the justice of our cause each one of us must fight on to the end. The safety of our homes and the Freedom of mankind alike depend upon the conduct of each one of us at this critical moment.[7]

Vera Brittain saw Haig's call to arms as she 'stumbled up to the Sisters' quarters for lunch', convinced by yet another 'dizzying rush of wounded from the new German offensive' that she 'could not go on'. After reading it on the noticeboard, she knew that 'I should go on, whether I could or not.' She recalled: 'There was a braver spirit in the hospital that afternoon, and though we only referred briefly and brusquely to Haig's message, each one of us had made up her mind that, though enemy airmen blew up our huts and the Germans advanced from Abbeville, so long as wounded men remained in Etaples, there would be "no retirement".'[8]

Though Brittain could not know it at the time, the worst of the crisis was over as French, Australian and British reinforcements were helping to stabilize the line. The Passchendaele ridge was relinquished on 13 April – thus yielding in four days what the British had taken three months to capture in 1917 – and by the end of the month, thanks to German advances further south, the Second Army had withdrawn from the whole Ypres salient. But Hazebrouck remained under British control (ably defended by the 1st Australian Division) and while more German efforts were made to break through in Flanders on 17 and 25 April, the latter capturing Mont Kemmel, the Allied line held. Georgette was called off by Ludendorff on 30 April, having failed to achieve its strategic objectives, though it had inflicted more casualties than it had cost: 112,000 Allies to 86,000 Germans.[9]

More importantly the Germans still held the strategic initiative. With many fewer reserve divisions, wrote David Stevenson, the Allies 'remained at a disadvantage and could not tell where Ludendorff would strike next'.[10]

27 May 1918: *'I've never seen anything like it'*
– The Germans attack in Champagne

At 1.30 a.m., the Germans began the most concentrated artillery bombardment of the war when 5,263 guns and 1,233 trench mortars opened up on a twenty-four-mile sector of the Chemin des Dames ridge* in Champagne, firing more than two million shells in just three hours, and drenching the French defences with gas and high explosive to a depth of eight miles.[1] 'I've never seen anything like it,' wrote a French

---

* Having repulsed Nivelle's attack on the ridge in April 1917, the Germans had relinquished the Chemin des Dames after Pétain's Malmaison offensive the following October.

survivor of the 135th Infantry to his parents. 'What a dreadful – in the true sense of the word – bombardment.'

> The poor [33rd] division. You should see what it's like now, there's nothing left. As for the regiment, while we've been in the line 2,000 men have been reduced to just over 200. So you can see what kind of a storm these swine unleashed upon us. There are just ten men left from our poor machine-gun company, and it's still not over. We haven't been relieved as yet, we have to wait until the reinforcements arrive.[2]

By 9 a.m. the thirty-six assault divisions of the German Seventh Army had wrested the crest of the ridge from the eleven divisions (three of them British and sent to the sector for a rest) of General Denis Duchêne's French Sixth Army. By mid-morning the German spearheads had reached the River Aisne, where they captured eighty bridges intact. Duchêne had prepared their demolition, but delayed giving the order because he 'feared cutting off supplies to the forward troops and underestimated the speed of the collapse'. That afternoon the Germans overran the French second position between the Rivers Aisne and Vesle, and by nightfall had crossed the latter obstacle, their advance assisted by lorries bringing forward reinforcements and artillery.[3]

German soldiers attack an enemy position with mortars and hand grenades during the spring offensives of 1918.

In a single day they had torn a twenty-five-mile-wide gap in the Allied line and advanced up to twelve miles, a gain even more spectacular than on the first day of Operation Michael. And all that was left to face the twenty-five German divisions ready to attack the following day was a thin screen of French and British units, the equivalent of just seven and a half broken-up divisions (the remnants of Duchêne's original force of sixteen divisions, with five originally in reserve).[4]

Already the operation – codenamed Blücher (after the famous nine-teenth-century Prussian commander) – had exceeded German expectations. It had been planned as a limited offensive to draw French reinforcements away from the north where OHL hoped to land a fatal blow in the form of a renewed attack south of Ypres known as Operation Hagen. The Chemin des Dames was chosen as the site of the attack because it would threaten Paris and, though a formidable obstacle (rising 400 feet above the River Ailette on the German side of the front), was one of the most thinly garri-soned sectors of the French line. Even so the Germans left nothing to chance by quadrupling their divisions in this sector from eight to thirty-six; concealing the extra troops and their equipment (including river pontoons) by day and moving only at night; issuing their infantry with more light machine-guns, rifle grenades and anti-tank rifles; and ordering troops spotted by aircraft to change direction away from the front.[5]

Their preparations were greatly aided, however, by French incompe-tence. Pétain suspected that another offensive was imminent – and had ordered day and night aerial reconnaissance to find out where – but during May GQG lost track of more than forty-five German reserve divisions and, anticipating that the attack would be north of the River Oise, Foch refused to move divisions down from Flanders (and instead ordered Haig and General Marie Emile Fayolle, commanding the huge French Army Group Reserve, to prepare counter-attacks). There were many indications from prisoners and deserters that an attack on the Chemin des Dames was imminent, and local British commanders reported the registration of German guns. Haig was even more specific when he warned GQG on 26 May that an attack on the ridge was likely, but General Duchêne brushed these warnings aside, as he did one from the Americans. Only later on the 26th was Sixth Army headquarters finally convinced by its own inter-rogation reports that an offensive would be launched the following day. But by then it was too late to alter the troop dispositions.[6]

It did not help that Duchêne, an irascible character with a martinet's reputation, had disregarded Pétain's instructions for a German-style defence in depth. Pétain wanted him to concentrate the bulk of the defenders in the second line and beyond the enemy bombardment, thus using the first line as a means of slowing the enemy assault before the reserves counter-attacked. But Duchêne saw this as needlessly sacrificing French territory, particularly in an area relatively close to Paris, and chose to defend his forward line north of the Aisne. Partly to avoid a clash with Foch and Clemenceau (who both agreed with Duchêne that his tactics were too cautious), Pétain acquiesced. He later excused himself by saying he was loth to relieve a commander when an attack was imminent, and knew, moreover, that Duchêne's second position was incomplete.[7]

When the blow fell, therefore, it achieved almost complete surprise against a lop-sided French defensive system that had too many forces in the forward line and not enough in reserve. Once the initial breakthrough had been made, it was almost impossible to seal off.

The aim of the attack was to redistribute Allied reserves by seizing the Chemin des Dames and, ideally, the heights south of the Vesle river. The latter objective had been reached by 2 p.m. on 28 May when OHL, keen to take advantage of French disarray, set a new line of Soissons to Reims, and later Compiègne to Dormans and Epernay, expanding the target area to the south, west and east. On the 29th the Marne became the new objective, with Paris tantalizingly close. 'Ludendorff,' wrote David Stevenson, 'was succumbing to mission creep, exploiting success while losing sight of his larger goals, and this time irretrievably.'[8]

The railway centre of Soissons fell on the 29th, by which time the Germans had taken 50,000 prisoners. A day later Pétain, fearing the loss of his entire eastern sector from the Chemin des Dames to the Swiss border, instructed General de Castelnau to draw up plans for the evacuation of his army group. On 31 May – after a French counter-attack had failed to dent the western side of the rapidly growing German pocket – the Commander-in-Chief advised Clemenceau to evacuate the government from Paris. In the days of panic that followed, more than a million inhabitants fled the city.[9]

So worried was Haig by Foch's movement of French, American and British reserves south to stem the German advance that he made a formal protest on 4 June 'against troops leaving my Command until the bulk of the reserves of Prince Rupprecht's Armies [opposite the BEF] had become involved in the battle'. He noted in his diary how the British troops on the Marne – five divisions of IX Corps – 'are being used up to the last man in order to give the French courage and fight!'[10] Fearful that a French collapse would trap the BEF (as it was to do in 1940), Sir Henry Wilson, Robertson's successor as CIGS, contemplated abandoning the Channel ports and retreating behind the Somme. He also drew up contingency plans for a maritime evacuation, a subject that was discussed by the British Cabinet.[11] But Lloyd George and Haig were firmly opposed to a withdrawal, as were the army commanders, and their decision was made easier by the fact that the German attack was losing momentum.

Munitions were in short supply and some German troops were keener to loot than fight. The Allies, meanwhile, had gained air superiority, hampering German attempts to capture Reims. Pétain's strategy was to hold a line of natural barriers from the Villers-Cotterêts forest to the Marne and Reims. It worked. On 2 June, twenty-five French divisions and two US divisions counter-attacked, the Americans eventually clearing Belleau Wood on the 6th in a celebrated action that cost them 10,000 casualties.[12]

By then the danger was over. On 4 June, Ludendorff had halted major operations in favour of minor assaults. Only later would he and Hindenburg admit the offensive had gone on too long. Though the Germans had again lost fewer men than their opponents – 105,370 to 127,337 – they were casualties they could not replace. The Allies, on the other hand, were being reinforced by more than 200,000 US troops a month, a transfusion of men and matériel that made victory all but certain. 'The junction [*la soudure*] will take place,' promised Pétain, 'it is imminent, and we will have no more to fear.'[13]

28 May 1918: '*Will the Americans really fight?*'
– The doughboys attack at Cantigny

'The ground was pounded to dust by our shells,' recalled American artillery Captain Raymond Austin. 'All that was visible was the heavy smoke hanging over Cantigny and the ridge.' At 6.45 a.m., after a bombardment lasting just an hour, the guns delivered a curtain of fire in no man's land that 'moved forward at a rate just fast enough for the infantry to keep up with it at a walk'. Austin added:

> At the same time as the barrage left the line of departure (our front line trenches) the infantry suddenly appeared on the slope of the ridge close behind . . . a long brown line with bayonets glistening in the sun . . . They walked steadily along behind our barrage accompanied by the tanks which buzzed along with smoke coming out of their exhausts and their guns. As the line reached the crest and was silhouetted in the morning sun . . . it looked like a long picket fence.[1]

Attacking uphill and weighed down with equipment – each carrying '220 rounds of ammunition, three sandbags, two hand grenades, one rifle grenade, two water canteens, two iron rations . . . two cakes of chocolate as emergency rations, plus one lemon and wads of chewing gum as thirst quenchers' – the doughboys of the American 1st Division could do little more than walk. Fortunately the supporting French heavy guns and mortars had done their job and German resistance was slight. By 7 a.m. the village and 250 prisoners had been captured at a cost of fifty casualties.[2]

But as the Americans pushed beyond the village – sited on a ridge at the apex of what had been a three-mile deep German salient, the furthest point gained during the Michael offensive – they were shot from behind by defenders emerging from deep dug-outs and cellars. Then the German counter-barrage began – huge shells raising 'a cloud of yellow smoke' – and was followed in the afternoon by wave after wave of counter-attacks. All were repulsed, with Major Theodore Roosevelt, son of the former President, helping to plug one gap when he courageously led his battalion across the fields in front of Cantigny.[3]

By the following morning the 28th Infantry Regiment – the unit tasked with taking the village – had lost 30 per cent of its men, while the remainder were exhausted. 'Some of our companies were practically annihilated,' recalled Captain Austin, 'and others held on without budging an inch, with their officers dead. In the last two counter-attacks the Boches brought up tanks as a sort of final resort and we caught the tanks in our barrage and they never even reached our front lines. In 72 hours I had six hours' sleep, which was getting off easy.'[4]

Despite the loss of 1,300 men – 199 killed – the 26th Infantry held on and Cantigny remained in Allied hands, much to the delight of General

Bullard, the divisional commander. 'Cantigny was,' he wrote, 'the first serious fight made by American troops in France, and it was greeted enthusiastically as a wonderful success . . . Hundreds greater had preceded and would follow it in the mighty war. But Cantigny was, nevertheless, one of the most important engagements of the war in its import to our war-wearied and sorely tried Allies. To both friend and foe it said, "Americans will both fight and stick." '[5]

At a time when the British and French were under extreme pressure from German attacks – the third of the great spring offensives (codenamed Blücher) had begun the day before Cantigny against the French on the Marne – an American success, however small, was extremely welcome. By March 1918, only 251,000 doughboys had reached France: the first seven divisions were in the front line under French supervision; the rest were now being tutored by British formations. Their losses, up to this point, were just 136 killed in action; far more – 641 – had died of disease.[6]

This slow build-up infuriated the Allies who pleaded with General Pershing, the AEF commander, to add his troops piecemeal to their armies. He refused. 'We all desire the same thing,' he told a meeting of the Supreme War Council* on 2 May, 'but our means of attaining it are different from yours. America declared war independently of the Allies and she must face it as soon as possible with a powerful army . . . The morale of our soldiers depends upon their fighting under our own flag.'[7]

During the emergency of March 1918, the British had offered to make ships available to transport 120,000 American troops a month, but only if they were front-line infantrymen and machine-gunners. The US government agreed and the monthly figure for troops landing in France rose from 64,000 in March to more than 200,000 for May to October (peaking at 280,000 in August).[8]

But even these extra troops could not mollify Lloyd George, who in June 1918, frustrated by Pershing's intransigence, described the AEF as the 'worst disappointment' of the war.[9] But, if anything, Cantigny convinced the AEF commander that he was right to keep his troops under American control until they were ready to fight as an independent army within the Allied command structure. 'I am certainly,' he declared,

* The Versailles-based central command that had been created in November 1917 at Lloyd George's suggestion to co-ordinate Allied strategy.

banging his fist on the table, 'going to jump down the throat of the next person who asks me, "Will the Americans really fight?"'[10]

15 June 1918: *'The position was critical'*
– The Asiago Plateau

At 3 a.m., Captain Edward Brittain of the 11th Sherwood Foresters was on 'trench duty' with his servant in his battalion's forward position at the edge of a forest on the Asiago Plateau when Austrian guns opposite began a huge bombardment. 'We managed to get back to our [Company] Headquarters safely,' recalled the servant.[1]

But Brittain knew that his under-strength company was far too weak to resist a determined attack. He had fewer than 100 men to hold 900 yards of the forward trench – the right sector of the battalion's front – and to provide a platoon for night picquet and outpost duty. The neighbouring D Company, under Captain Frith, was in a similar position. Their numbers, moreover, were much reduced by the intensive artillery fire, and when the assault began at 6.45 a.m. the left of Brittain's forward trench was quickly overwhelmed. 'Seeing that the position was critical', and that he was the company's only unwounded officer, Brittain led a counter-attack with his headquarters staff and some soldiers loaned by the neighbouring French 24th Division that succeeded 'in driving the enemy out again'. Brittain then set about reorganizing the defence of the trench, forming a flank with the troops available.[2]

The Austrian attack on the Asiago Plateau west of the River Piave was part of a wider offensive that was timed to coincide with the Germans' Operation Gneisenau on the Western Front. Authorized by Emperor Karl (who had succeeded Franz Joseph in 1916) to reassert the Austrians' military independence, the offensive was a compromise between the plans of Field Marshal Conrad von Hötzendorf,* who wanted to launch the main assault on the Asiago, and General Boroević, who argued that a

---

* Since March 1917, when he was replaced as the Austrian Chief of Staff by General Arz von Straussenburg, Field Marshal Conrad had been commanding the South Tyrolean Army Group.

breakthrough on the Piave would threaten Venice and potentially knock the Italians out of the war. Both attacks were authorized and, as a consequence, both were too weak. The Austrians enjoyed a slight manpower advantage in the Italian theatre – sixty-five infantry divisions and twelve cavalry divisions to the Allies' fifty-six (including three British and three French) – but had fewer guns and half as many aircraft.[3]

In the event the results of the simultaneous attacks on 15 June were mixed. Several bridgeheads were established on the Piave and more than 100,000 Austrians reached the west bank. But heavy rain and British bombers destroyed the Austrians' pontoon bridges, and Italian counter-attacks forced Boroević's men to withdraw.[4] Conrad's attack on the Asiago Plateau, where Allied forces 'occupied undulating and thickly forested ground with a steep downward slope only three miles behind them', was stopped in the centre of the Allied line by two French divisions by counter-fire alone.[5] The British 23rd and 48th Divisions to their left, on the other hand, were taken by surprise and their forward trenches breached in a number of places. But determined counter-attacks, like the one led by Edward Brittain, had regained all the lost ground by the morning of the 16th. In the Italian sector, to the right of the French, the Austrians broke through to a depth of more than a mile towards the escarpment and it took five days of hard fighting to restore the line.

A week after it had started, the offensive was over. It had cost 150,000 casualties (Allied losses were 80,000) and achieved nothing. 'This unsuccessful attack,' wrote Ludendorff, 'was extremely painful to me. I could no longer hope that relief on the Western Front might be secured in Italy itself.'[6]

The first official news of the offensive was printed in British papers on Sunday 16 June. Edward Brittain's sister Vera, back in London to look after her sick mother, read an account in the *Observer* – headlined 'ITALIAN FRONT ABLAZE' – that revived all her old fears for her brother's safety. She felt 'afraid' and 'suddenly cold in spite of the warm June sunlight that streamed through the dining-room window'. But with no means of discovering if he was even involved, she practised 'that concealment of fear which the long years of war had instilled, thrusting it inward until one's subconscious became a regular prison-house of apprehensions and inhibitions which were later to take revenge'.[7]

A couple of days later Vera was dismayed to discover from press reports that Edward's battalion had fought in the battle. 'After that,' she wrote, 'I made no pretence of doing anything but wander restlessly round Kensington or up and down the flat . . . Somehow I couldn't bring myself even to wrap up the *Spectator* and *Saturday Review* that I sent every week to Italy, and they remained in my bedroom, silent yet eloquent witnesses to the dread which my father and I . . . refused to put into words.'[8]

By the following Saturday they had still heard nothing. As word of casualties rarely took this long to reach Britain, Vera began to hope that there was 'no news to come'. She was taking afternoon tea with her father, and had just announced her intention to send Edward's papers after all, when 'there came the sudden loud clattering at the front-door knocker that always meant a telegram'.

> For a moment [she wrote later] I thought that my legs would not carry me, but they behaved quite normally as I got up and went to the door. I knew what was in the telegram – I had known for a week – but because the persistent hopefulness of the human heart refuses to allow intuitive certainty to persuade the reason of what it knows, I opened and read it in a tearing anguish of suspense.

It stated: 'Regret to inform you Captain E. H. Brittain M.C. killed in action Italy June 15th.'

That night, after her father had gone to bed, a distraught Vera 'crept into the dining-room to be alone with Edward's portrait'. She remembered:

> Carefully closing the door, I turned on the light and looked at the pale, pictured face, so dignified, so steadfast, so tragically mature. He had been through so much – far, far more than those beloved friends who had died at an earlier stage of the interminable War, leaving him alone to mourn their loss. Fate might have allowed him the little sorry compensation of survival, the chance to make his lovely music in honour of their memory . . .
>
> And suddenly, as I remembered all the dear afternoons and evenings when I had followed him on the piano as he played his violin, the sad, searching eyes of the portrait were more than I could bear, and falling on my knees before it I began to cry 'Edward! Oh, Edward!' in dazed repetition, as though my persistent crying and calling would somehow bring him back.[9]

In the weeks ahead, Vera's sole concern was to discover the details of her beloved brother's death. Three letters – from his company second-in-command, his servant and a Red Cross acquaintance – confirmed to Vera 'that Edward's part in withstanding the Austrian offensive had been just what we might have expected from his coolness and fortitude on the Somme'. The 'most direct and vivid' testimony came from his servant, who explained how Captain Brittain, after successfully leading the counter-attack, 'was keeping a sharp look out on the enemy' when he was 'shot through the Head by an enemy sniper' and 'only lived a few minutes'. The letter ended: 'Captain Brittain was a very gallant officer who feared nothing.'[10]

No less welcome was another acquaintance's report of a conversation she had heard in a railway carriage between men of the 11th Sherwood Foresters. One of them had mentioned 'a real good officer, a slim dark chap ... and a regular *nut*'. He added: 'You'd have thought that he hadn't an ounce of ginger in him, but Lord! miss, he didn't know what fear was.' The soldier gave the officer's name as 'Brittain' and said he had deserved the VC for pushing back the enemy 'by sheer force' in that 'do' on the plateau.[11]

Such praise, however, was scant consolation for the loss of a brother. 'I had never believed,' wrote Brittain later, 'that I could actually go on living without that lovely companionship which had been at my service since childhood ... Yet here I was, in a world emptied of that unfailing consolation, most persistently, most unwillingly alive.' She was alive enough to unpack his possessions when they returned from Italy, and to find among them 'unopened and unread' the newly published war-poets' anthology *The Muse in Arms*, on the fly-leaf of which was her own poem eulogizing his courage, that she had sent to Edward a few weeks earlier. 'I knew then that he had died without even being aware of my last endeavour to show him how deeply I loved and admired him.'[12]

1 July 1918: *'What I saw there I will never forget'*
– The Chilwell explosion

Eight-year-old Bert Smith was playing cricket after school on the recreation ground of his village near Nottingham when he felt 'an almighty bang' on the back of his neck. 'It seemed to push me forward,' he remembered. 'I turned round to look and there was this huge . . . black cloud of smoke from ground level right to the heavens above. It seemed to be rolling and everybody . . . was looking at it with their mouths wide open. There were two old boys sitting under a tree and one said, "That's Chilwell gone up." The other replied, "And I bet some bugger's done it as well, sabotage."'[1]

As the aftershock of the explosion – heard more than thirty miles away – shook the leaves off nearby trees, Smith and his friends went to 'have a look'. He wrote later:

> We got as far as Beeston and we couldn't get no farther on account of the people milling around the streets. So I sat down on the edge of the pavement and I could see a wagon coming. It must have been one from the factory, and when it got level with me, only two feet away, there was a smell of burning rag. I looked and this wagon was piled up with . . . half naked, blackened bodies and the arms and legs were hanging over the side. I noticed there was blood trickling out of the back of the wagon. Then another wagon came, same again. I felt like I had a nest of rats inside my belly . . . One of the kids said, 'Come on Bert, let's go home.' So I did. But what I saw there I will never forget if I live to be as old as Methuselah.[2]

The corpses that young Bert Smith had the misfortune to see were just some of the 134 victims of the most deadly munitions explosion of the war, caused by the ignition of eight tons of amatol, a mixture of TNT and ammonium nitrate, at the No. 6 National Shell Filling Factory at Chilwell in Nottinghamshire. Many of the fatalities were so badly disfigured they could not be identified. Body parts were thrown hundreds of feet into the air and lay strewn across the fields surrounding the giant munitions complex, the biggest in the country. A further 250 workers were wounded.[3]

In the wake of the 'shell crisis' in 1915, the sleepy village of Chilwell on the outskirts of Nottingham had been chosen as the site for a new shell-filling factory because it had good road and rail links, was shielded from the surrounding area by hills, and was roughly halfway between the shell manufacturers in the north and the embarkation ports in the south. Located as it was in an area where women had long worked in local textile factories, the vast majority of its employees were female.[4]

Munition workers painting ordnance at the No. 6 National Shell Filling
Factory at Chilwell, Nottinghamshire, before the accidental explosion.

The factory opened on New Year's Day 1916 and within a year had
filled more than a 1.25 million heavy shells – chiefly 60-pounders up to
huge 15-inch shells – with lyddite and amatol high explosive. As the war's
consumption of heavy ordnance grew ever more voracious, Chilwell took
on more employees until, by July 1918, more than 10,000 were clocking
on daily. As well as artillery shells, they were filling naval mines, depth
charges and aerial bombs. By the end of the war the factory had filled
more than half the country's total output of heavy shells – a total of
nineteen million, weighing an incredible 1.1 million tons.

The hours were long, the pay poor and the labour monotonous for
the young, mostly working-class women in munitions factories like
Chilwell. 'I was six months on night work,' recalled Jennie Johnson from
Newcastle, 'from six o'clock at night to six in the morning. Then I had
to walk home. In the winter I'd go up in the dark and come home in the
dark . . . You didn't do anything apart from work. It was a miserable
existence, it wasn't worth having.'[5]

For some the knowledge that they were making lethal weapons was a concern. 'We had relations out there,' explained one woman, 'and we were glad to make the munitions, but we also had to think about the ones that were going to be on the end of it, you see. They were youngsters just coming up in life like I was, sixteen or seventeen . . . That made me feel sad sometimes.' Others, particularly those who had lost relations or partners in the fighting, were more sanguine. 'It made me very bitter towards the Germans,' wrote Essex girl Gladys Hayhoe, 'and it made me work that bit harder.'[6]

The skin and hair of many of the women filling shells at Chilwell – and elsewhere – went yellow thanks to lyddite poisoning, hence their nickname 'canary girls'. Other symptoms included chest pains, nausea and skin irritations, resulting in workers at Chilwell being given masks and improvements made to ventilation. Yet many fell seriously ill – a total of 349 across the country, of whom 109 died.[7]

The other major hazard for workers in munitions factories – where thousands of tons of TNT were stored – was a sudden explosion. One of the most serious incidents prior to Chilwell was a blast at Silvertown munitions factory in east London on 19 January 1917 that was heard fifty miles away in Cambridge. More than fifty tons of TNT exploded, killing seventy-three and injuring more than 400 (100 seriously). Even more destructive was the combustion of 200 tons of TNT at the gunpowder mill at Faversham in Kent after some empty sacks caught fire on 2 April 1916. As it was a Sunday, no women were at work and all 115 fatalities were men and boys, including the whole of the Works Fire Brigade.

The speed with which the Chilwell factory recovered from the disaster was astonishing. A day later its employees returned to work and by the end of the month had achieved their highest weekly production. Winston Churchill, Minister of Munitions, sent the following message:

> Please accept my sincere sympathy with you all in the misfortune that has overtaken your fine Factory and in the loss of valuable lives. Those who have perished have died at their stations on the field of duty and those who have lost their dear ones should fortify themselves with this thought: the courage and spirit shown by all concerned, both men and women, command our admiration, and the decision to which

you have all come to carry on without a break is worthy of the spirit which animates our soldiers in the field. I trust the injured are receiving every care.[8]

The exact cause of the explosion has never been explained. Lord Chetwynd, the founder of the factory, allegedly told the police that he thought it was sabotage and even named the culprit. But no one was prosecuted and it is more likely that lax safety standards on an unseasonably warm day were to blame.

The extent of the damage and loss of life was kept from the public, as was the location of a plant so vital to the war effort. Most papers confined themselves to a short statement: '60 feared dead in Midlands factory explosion'. Only after the war had ended did more details emerge. *The Times* reported on 18 November 1918: 'The band of the National Shell Filling Factory at Chilwell, Notts – the munitions factory where a disastrous explosion took place last July and where many deeds of heroism were performed, as a result of which the factory earned the title "V.C." – visited London on Saturday. The bandsmen drove from St Pancras to Buckingham Palace, where they played in the quadrangle.'

The term 'VC Factory' was unofficial. In July 1918 F. G. Kellaway, the Parliamentary Secretary to the Minister of Munitions, had suggested to the House of Commons that Chilwell be awarded the Victoria Cross in recognition of the heroism shown that day, much as the citadel at Verdun had been given the Croix de la Légion d'Honneur by the French government. Though the award was never made, the name stuck. For some bereaved families, however, this was little consolation. 'My father had been wounded in the war and came back,' a young girl, the middle of seven children, recalled years later. 'He went to work at Chilwell. He was sent to his death and the family were left to fend for themselves. It tore us apart and only later in life did I find my brothers and sisters. If there's a war now I hope the families of any casualties are looked after a lot better than we were.'[9]

18 July 1918:* *'The presidium . . . has sentenced you to be shot'*
– The Romanov executions

At 1.30 a.m. Dr Evgeny Botkin, the Tsar's personal physician, was woken by the insistent ringing of the bell at the entrance to the Romanovs' sitting room, situated on the second floor of the large Ipatiev House that had served as the imperial family's prison since their arrival at Ekaterinburg in the Urals in late April 1918. Opening the double-doors, Botkin was confronted by Commandant Yakov Yurovsky, a tall dapper Bolshevik with high cheekbones and a well-trimmed beard, who had assumed responsibility for guarding the Romanovs only two weeks earlier.[1]

What's the matter? asked a bleary-eyed Botkin. The reply from Yurovsky – a former political exile who had risen from soldier deputy to executive member of the regional Soviet and justice commissar for the Cheka secret police – was disingenuous. There was a danger, he said, that the forces of the approaching White Russians might at any moment launch an artillery attack on the city that would threaten the upper floor of the house. It was therefore necessary for Botkin to wake the Tsar and his family and take them down into the basement for their own safety.[2]

An unsuspecting Botkin agreed and after a lengthy delay, time used by the Romanovs and their few remaining servants to wash and dress, the family appeared on the landing all 'neat and tidy'. The Tsar was first, carrying his thirteen-year-old haemophiliac son Tsarevich Alexei, both dressed in their military tunics and forage caps. Next came the pale and thin Tsaritsa Alexandra, leaning on a walking stick; her four daughters – Grand Duchesses Olga, Tatiana, Maria and Anastasia – wearing plain white blouses and skirts, carrying pillows and small bags; and lastly Botkin and three servants, including the maid Demidova with two cushions that contained the Tsaritsa's jewels.[3]

Accompanied by Yurovsky, his young assistant Grigory Nikulin and two guards, the Romanovs made their way down the steep internal staircase and out of a door into a small courtyard where they re-entered

---

* In February 1918 the Bolshevik rulers of Russia had switched from the Julian to the Gregorian calendar, thus adding thirteen days to their former date.

the house by an adjacent entrance. They were then led down twenty-three steps – one for every year of Nicholas II's reign – to the basement and into an empty storeroom lit by a single naked lightbulb. Unsuspecting, the three youngest grand duchesses were smiling and happy; only twenty-two-year-old Olga, the eldest, and her mother were grim-faced, the latter immediately asking for chairs. She needed one because of her sciatica, she explained, as did the invalid Alexei. Yurovsky at once sent a guard to fetch two chairs, while Nikulin muttered under his breath: 'The heir wanted to die in a chair. Very well then, let him have one.'[4]

Once the chairs had been brought, the Tsaritsa sat on one near the barred window and Alexei was placed on another to her right with the Tsar by his side. Then Yukovsky placed the rest of the family and servants behind the two chairs as if they were posing for a photograph, a profession the ardent Bolshevik had once practised. They would have to wait here, he told them, until a truck arrived to take them to safety. He, Nikulin and the guards then left the room.[5]

Half an hour later – as the engine of a Fiat truck was gunned outside – Yurovsky and Nikulin re-entered the storeroom with seven members of the Cheka crowding behind them. 'Well here we all are,' said the Tsar stepping forward, confident that the truck had come to take them to safety. 'What are you going to do now?'[6]

Ignoring him, Yurovsky asked everyone to stand – which they all did apart from the Tsarevich – and then read from a sheet of paper he was holding in his left hand. 'In view of the fact that your relatives in Europe continue their assault on Soviet Russia,' he announced in a loud clear voice, 'the presidium of the Ural Regional Soviet has sentenced you to be shot . . .'[7]

The Tsar was horrified. Turning to his family, he stuttered: 'What? What?'

Botkin was incredulous. 'So you're not taking us anywhere?' he asked.

'I don't understand,' added the Tsar. 'Read it again.'

Yurovsky continued: '. . . in view of the fact that the Czechoslovaks are threatening the red capital of the Urals – Ekaterinburg – and in view of the fact that the crowned executioner might escape the people's court, the presidium of the Regional Soviet, fulfilling the will of the Revolution, has decreed that the former Tsar Nicholas Romanov, guilty of countless bloody crimes against the people, should be shot . . .'[8]

Amid cries of shock and protest, the Tsaritsa and Olga crossed themselves as Yurovsky pulled out a Colt pistol from his pocket, took a pace forward and shot the Tsar in the chest. Others did the same, the bullets tearing through Nicholas's flesh and spattering his family with blood and tissue. As the Tsar fell, an inebriated Bolshevik commissar called Petr Ermakov turned his German Mauser pistol on the Tsaritsa, shooting her in the left temple.[9]

Many of the other victims fell to the floor, either shot by bullets that had missed the Tsar and Tsaritsa or desperate to find a way out. More shots were fired until finally Yurovsky ordered a halt, he and his men staggering from a room now filled with gunsmoke and dust from shattered plaster. But groans and cries told Yurovsky that not all were dead and he and Ermakov re-entered the charnel house – its floor sticky with blood – to finish off the wounded.* The last to die were Anastasia,† Alexei and the maid Demidova, the first two shot after Ermakov had failed to kill them with an eight-inch bayonet.[10]

The road that led to the brutal murder of the Romanovs was long, circuitous and far from inevitable. For the first five months after the Tsar's abdication, the imperial family had remained under house arrest at the Alexander Palace in Tsarskoe Selo where, free from the cares of office and living the life of a country gentleman (albeit one confined to his estate), Nicholas II 'seemed generally to be very good tempered and appeared to enjoy his new manner of life'.[11] But in mid-August, with the political temperature rising in Petrograd, Kerensky moved the imperial family to the relative backwater of Tobolsk in Siberia. The original intention of the Provisional Government had been to take up the offer of George V, the Tsar's cousin, and send Nicholas and his family to England. But the Petrograd Soviet vetoed the idea, arguing that the former Tsar should be incarcerated in the Peter and Paul Fortress, and George V's offer was in any case withdrawn to appease the Labour Party.[12]

---

* The killers later claimed that many bullets had deflected off the layers of jewels sewn into the girls' bodices (Rappaport, *Ekaterinburg*, p. 191).
† Several women later claimed to be Anastasia who, they said, had survived the killings. The most notorious was Anna Anderson, who died in 1984. But seven bodies found at two graves near Ekaterinburg, in 1991 and 2008, have been positively identified by DNA testing as the royal couple and their five children.

Tsar Nicholas II and his family celebrate 300 years
of Romanov rule at the Kremlin in 1913.

At Tobolsk the imperial family lived in comparative comfort, billeted
in the former governor's house and cared for by thirty-three courtiers
and servants. But Lenin's successful Bolshevik coup in Petrograd in
November 1917 meant a hardening of political battle lines and a less
benign approach to the Romanovs. By early 1918 their guards were
becoming ruder, their luxuries scarcer and their movements more
restricted.

In early April 1918, the Central Committee sent a commissar to bring
Nicholas and his family back to Moscow – the Russian capital since
March – where Trotsky was planning a great show trial with himself as
chief prosecutor. But en route they were diverted to Ekaterinburg at the
request of militant Bolsheviks from the regional Soviet who had guaranteed their safety (an assurance they had no intention of keeping). The
order to execute the Romanovs, however, came ultimately from Moscow.[13]

On 16 July, with White Russians of the Czech Legion – former prisoners of war – closing in on Ekaterinburg (they would capture it on 25 July), the local party boss Goloshchekin asked Moscow for permission to carry out an immediate execution of the family; it was given the same day by Lenin and Yakov Sverdlov, Chairman of the Central Committee, because, as the latter explained to Trotsky, 'Ilich [Lenin] thought that we should not leave the Whites a live banner [to rally round], especially under the present difficult circumstances.'[14]

But there were other reasons for Moscow's decision: party leaders had begun to doubt the logic of a show trial that presupposed the *possibility* of the Tsar's innocence, and therefore undermined the moral legitimacy of the revolution; and they concluded that it was more important to eliminate him as a rival source of legitimacy than to prove his guilt. As Orlando Figes put it: 'Nicholas had to die so that Soviet power could live.'[15]

24 July 1918: *'The night air, how good it was'*
– Escape from Holzminden

At 10.15 p.m., shortly after the German guards had made their last check of barrack block Kaserne B, three officers left their rooms, climbed through a hole in the attic and made their way down into the basement of the neighbouring orderlies' quarters where the tunnel entrance was located. The first officer into the tunnel was Lieutenant Walter Butler, the 'break-out man', whose job was to remove the last few feet of earth. As Butler crawled 'along the hole for the last time', he noted 'all the old familiar ups and downs', and bumped his head 'against the same old stones'. Reaching the face, he knelt in the pit they had dug to take the remaining spoil and began to loosen the earth above him with a large bread knife. 'The earth,' he recalled, 'fell into my hair, eyes and ears, and down my neck.'[1]

By 11 p.m. Butler had cut a small hole through to the surface. It was raining but the guards' arc lights 'made it look very light outside'. Peering through the hole, he was relieved to see that he had come up beyond a row of beans that screened the exit from a sentry standing near the outer perimeter wall, barely forty yards away. At 11.40 p.m., having made the hole wide enough to pass through, he pushed his kit ahead of him, crawled out of the tunnel – 'the night air, how good it was' – and paused for thirty seconds so that a watching orderly could see him and warn the next batch of escapers. The German sentry was hidden in the shadow of the wall, but his cough gave away his rough location. Is he looking my way? wondered Butler. It was impossible to tell, so he took a risk and began crawling towards a tall crop of rye beyond the row of beans.[2]

Joined in the rye a short while later by his two 'travelling companions' – Captain William Langren and Lieutenant Andrew Clouston, the latter a 'big, coarse-featured and red-faced' Canadian with 'beetling brows and a dark mustache' – the trio made their way down to the banks of the nearby River Weser where they found four wooden hurdles and used them to ferry their kit and clothes across while they swam alongside. It was now 2 a.m. and, as they dressed, Butler thought he heard the faint sound of a shot. Fearing that the tunnel had been discovered, they donned their rucksacks and set off on a north-west compass bearing for the Dutch frontier, a distance of seventy-five miles.[3]

Holzminden prisoner-of-war camp had been in use for less than a year. Situated in Lower Saxony, sixty miles south-west of Hanover, it had been built in 1913 as a cavalry barracks. But a combination of the reduced need for horsemen on the industrial battlefield and a steady increase in the number of Allied prisoners had caused the barracks to be converted in 1917 to an *Offizier Gefangenenlager* (prison camp for officers), with the first British captives arriving that September. The largest such camp in Germany, it eventually held more than 560 officers and a further 160 other ranks or 'orderlies' who would act as the officers' servants and perform other menial task. They were housed in two four-storey stone-built *Kasernen* – barrack blocks – with steeply pitched roofs. Both blocks, however, were partitioned internally: the west wing of Kaserne A formed the Kommandantur, the area reserved for German officers and camp personnel; while the east wing of Kaserne B contained the orderlies.[4]

Camp facilities were poor: the bath house had not even been started in September 1917 and there were only three cookers to feed all the prisoners and more than a 100 German staff. The food, moreover, was basic and in short supply – black bread and turnip soup – and before Red Cross parcels started to arrive most of the inmates lost weight dramatically (though, to be fair, most of Germany was suffering from food shortages at this stage of the war). When the camp was full, up to fourteen officers were crammed into a room twenty-two feet by fourteen (rooms for orderlies were even more crowded); they lay on mattresses stuffed with wood shavings, covered by one sheet that was changed once a month (if they were lucky) and two blankets that were never changed.[5]

These Spartan conditions were deliberate: Holzminden had been set up as a *Strafe* (punishment) camp for inveterate escapees and quickly gained notoriety for its harshness and impregnability, the inmates dubbing it 'Hellminden'. For most of its existence the camp at Holzminden was run by Hauptmann Karl Niemeyer, a thick-set florid-faced man with close-cropped grey hair and 'grey mustachios with the usual Kaiser twirl', who had lived in Milwaukee, Wisconsin, for seventeen years before the war. He spoke English with a strong American accent and had picked up 'a good deal of . . . bar-room slang'. Because of this he was nicknamed 'Milwaukee Bill' by the prisoners who revelled in his error-strewn grammar. 'You think I do not understand the English, but I do,' he was fond of saying. 'I know damn all about you.'[6]

But for all Niemeyer's eccentricity, he soon acquired a reputation as a vindictive martinet who 'succeeded', wrote the camp adjutant Captain Hugh Durnford, 'in impregnating the entire camp with an atmosphere of acute discontent and jumpiness'. Durnford added: 'Holzminden might have been from the start a happy camp. The air was good, the view was good, the buildings were waterproof, the water supply was good. Only the Commandant was vile.'[7]

One prisoner given a particularly rough ride by Niemeyer was Lieutenant William Leefe Robinson VC, famous for destroying the first Zeppelin over Britain in September 1916. Sent to Holzminden after he was shot down and wounded by a pilot of the Red Baron's Jasta 11 in April 1918, Robinson tried to escape but was quickly recaptured. Thereafter Niemeyer singled him out for special treatment, placing him in the 'most uncomfortable room in the camp', causing him 'to answer to a special appel two or three times a day', and forbidding him to enter Kaserne B.[8]

Small wonder that many officers were keen to escape Holzminden, and numerous attempts were made to cut through the wire or simply walk out of the main gate in disguise. All failed to reach the safety of neutral Holland, despite the assistance of disaffected members of Niemeyer's staff who, in return for food from the British officers' Red

Cross parcels, handed over useful contraband and intelligence. The latter included official documents from the Kommandantur, provided by a female typist who had fallen in love with an Australian pilot, Captain Peter Lyon, and who communicated with him by dropping notes on a weighted string.[9]

The officers who came up with the idea of tunnelling from the foot of the staircase in the orderlies' quarters of Kaserne B, the closest point to the perimeter wire, were two Canadians called Colquhoun and Moysey. When they were transferred soon after they had begun work in October 1917, British officers took over. Only fifteen were involved in digging the tunnel. They worked in three-man shifts: one man digging with improvised tools; another dragging the soil back on pans tied to rope and stacking it in sacks in the basement; and the third working the makeshift bellows, made from wood, leather and biscuit boxes.[10]

At an almost glacial pace the tunnel – 'merely a rat hole', just sixteen inches wide by twelve high, and so narrow that the diggers had to wriggle rather than crawl along it – extended out from Kaserne B until, by mid-December, it was fifteen yards in length and just beyond the outer perimeter.[11] Though tempted to risk an escape, the tunnellers resisted because Niemeyer had just 'put a sentry at the outside corner of the building, effectually covering the spot'. The guard would easily spot an escaper who emerged into the open. So reluctantly the tunnellers agreed on a new plan: to extend the tunnel to a field of rye fifty yards beyond the perimeter that would give the escapers cover.[12]

It was a Herculean task. As the tunnel grew longer, bed boards were used to strengthen it and prevent roof falls; and excess soil was carried in the tunnellers' pockets and emptied in the attic. Yet by late June 1918 the tunnel was still an estimated eight or nine yards short of the rye and, with harvest time approaching, time was running out. 'To carry on into the rye,' wrote Captain Durnford, 'would take at least three weeks' hard work, by which time the rye would probably have been cut and the only cover afforded would be the darkness of the night. But about three or four yards nearer than the rye was a row of beans, and it was decided to make a last effort to reach these and to trust to luck and the darkness to carry the party across the bare space between.'[13]

Finally, on 24 July, the tunnel was thought to have reached the row of beans:

It was over 60 yards in length [wrote Durnford] and it took nine months to complete. It was dug, except for one brief period, in the hours of daylight between morning and evening appel, and its workers, in order to reach and return from the scene of their labours, ran the daily risk of being identified by the German sentries. Much of it was dug through layers of stones; all of it was dug with appliances that a miner would have scorned.[14]

Following Butler, Langren and Clouston through the tunnel were the other ten 'diggers': Captain Gray and Lieutenants Blain, Kennard, Mardock (RNAS), Lawrence (RNAS), Wainright (Royal Navy), Macleod, Morris, Robertson and Paddison. Then an hour elapsed, to give the tunnellers the best chance to get away, before Lieutenant-Colonel Charles Rathbone, the Senior British Officer, and Lieutenant Bausfield and Captain Lyon, both of whom had played supporting roles, entered the tunnel at 12.30 a.m. on 25 July. This trio was followed by a 'supplementary working-party of six', men who had assisted by scouting and digging in the building. The last of this group, James Bennett, was clear of the tunnel by 1.15 a.m,

The dug-out tunnel used by twenty-nine
British officers to escape from Holzminden
prisoner-of-war camp on 24 July 1918.

at which point there was another hiatus of an hour before the first of the sixty men on the extra list, known as 'the ruck', was led to the tunnel entrance.[15]

Various mishaps slowed the process – including one man who lost his nerve and had to be hauled backwards by his heels – but by 4.30 a.m. the number of men safely through had reached twenty-nine. As the thirtieth, an officer called Lee, tried to push his pack over the debris that had accumulated at the foot of the final slope, he caused a roof-fall. The tunnel was blocked. Despite 'groans, curses and cries of encouragement' from those waiting behind, there was nothing to be done.[16]

The last two men in the tunnel – Lee and a Captain Jack Shaw – were finally extricated at around 6.30 a.m. But instead of returning through the attic to their beds to await the first roll call at 9 a.m., they left the orderlies' quarters by the recently unlocked main entrance and ran straight into Hauptmann Niemeyer on a morning tour of inspection. As he was questioning them, some irate farmers appeared at the postern gate with news of tracks through their rye. When Niemeyer discovered the tunnel entrance, he posted a guard over it and returned to the Kommandantur to report the break-out. One question remained: how many? When Niemeyer discovered the truth, his 'jaw dropped' and he suddenly 'became grey and looked very old'. He then began shouting and 'gesticulating in such a furious way' that the prisoners watching from the two *Kasernen* broke into howls of laughter.[17]

Ten of the twenty-nine escapees reached the safety of neutral Holland using fake papers, stolen and homemade compasses, and maps provided by an Australian orderly, Private Dick Cash. They were: Gray, Blain, Kennard, Bennett and Bousfield of the tunnellers, and Rathbone, Purves, Tullis, Campbell-Martin and Wilmer Leggatt of the others. Most walked all the way, hiding by day and moving by night. The exception was Colonel Rathbone, a fluent German speaker, who first walked east to Göttingen where he boarded a train for Aachen, via Frankfurt and Cassel. Reaching the Dutch border after just five days on the run, he sent Niemeyer a telegram: 'HAVING LOVELY TIME STOP IF I EVER FIND YOU IN LONDON WILL BREAK YOUR NECK STOP.'[18]

The other nine crossed the border between 1 and 6 August 1918, and the whole group returned to Britain together on the 15th. They were rewarded with steps in rank and gallantry medals. Rathbone, for example, was given a Bar to his DSO. Blain, Gray and Kennard were invited to dine at Windsor Castle with the King who was anxious to hear of their exploits. In both the number of initial escapees* and those who reached safety, it was the greatest escape of the war.[19]

8 August 1918: *'The black day of the German Army'*
– Battle of Amiens

'Early on August 8th,' wrote General Erich Ludendorff, 'in a dense fog, rendered still thicker by artificial means, the English, mainly with Australian and Canadian divisions, and the French attacked between Albert and Moreuil with strong squadrons of tanks, but otherwise no great superiority. Between the Somme and the Luce they penetrated deep into our positions. The divisions in line at that point allowed themselves to be completely overwhelmed. Divisional staffs were surprised in their headquarters by enemy tanks.' It was, he noted, 'the black day of the German Army in the history of this war'.[1]

A major factor in the success of the attack was the Allies' meticulous artillery fire which, like Bruchmüller's system, aimed to neutralize counter-fire rather than destroy defences: the heavy guns targeted the German batteries with phosgene and gas, while field guns protected the infantry with a creeping barrage. 'Every gun shot together and the thing was off,' recalled Gunner Bertie Cox of the 14th Brigade, Royal Field Artillery.

> I never heard anything like it in my life, neither had anyone else, as it was about the biggest show that has ever been staged on the Western Front. Several times I could not hear my own gunfire, and for half the series, I laid and fired the gun myself. After three hours, I was practically deaf. We fired our first shot at 4.20 a.m. at 800 yards and in three hours

---

* Of the nineteen who did not make it, the unluckiest were Lieutenant Paddison and Second Lieutenant A. T. Shipwright, both captured within a mile of the Dutch border. After four to six weeks in solitary confinement, all nineteen were found guilty of mutiny and 'conspiring to destroy Imperial Government property', and sentenced to six months' imprisonment. The end of the war intervened. (Hanson, *Escape from Germany*, pp. 230–6.)

the enemy was out of our range (6,500 yards). Within ten minutes of the start, the tanks, by the hundreds, and cavalry, by the thousands, were passing our guns. It made an awful pretty picture to see the tanks and cavalry looming up in the mist, over the crest, just about dawn. The field guns began to pass us at a gallop, too, not to mention the infantry.[2]

A crewman of one of the 552 British Mark V and Whippet* tanks to attack that day – representing the entire Tanks Corps fleet – was Private Charles Rowland. 'It was 4.20 a.m., time to move,' he recalled, 'and all of a sudden, a mist fell over the area, which pleased us but did not help the navigator. But it did not last long and we were on our way to the first line, with all the machine guns firing. Slowly moving towards that, we found that the barrage had not killed all the enemy troops, but what was left were coming out with their hands up. But it was the Canadians' job to see to them, and we started to crawl into and out of the trenches, being bumped here and there, sideways, all over the place.'[3]

By mid-morning Rowland was through all three lines of the German Forward Zone: 'What a sight met the eye: as far as we could see, tanks moving forward, infantry behind, taking shelter from them, hundreds of field guns following. The whole lot looked as if it was on parade.'[4] A few tanks in Rowland's 14th Battalion were now destroyed by concealed German guns that had been missed by counter-battery fire; but most crewmen had to contend only with ditching, mechanical trouble, small-arms fire and the suffocating atmosphere inside the steel monsters. 'You could hardly put a foot down for spent shell cases,' wrote Rowland, 'and could hardly breathe for the fumes of the engine, which was red hot by now, steam from the boiling water, and even the oil in the return tank boiling over. Sweat was pouring out of us and we kept having a swig of water out of a petrol tin, when there was a chance, and the cordite fumes from the 6-pounders was nearly choking us.'[5]

So rapid was the advance by the tanks, cavalry and infantry in the Australian and Canadian sectors – in the centre and on the right of the BEF attack – that a German ammunition train was surprised as it entered Harbonnières station. Struck by 6-pounder tank shells, 'it burst into one

---

* Light tanks that could reach a speed of 8mph.

great sheet of flame reaching to a height of not less than 150 feet', recalled Captain Henry Smeddle, commanding a section of specially elongated Mark Vs. He added: 'Needless to say that train was stopped. It was followed by another, a passenger train rushing up fresh troops; this was running on another rail and ran right into our lines – it was captured complete with personnel.'[6]

By nightfall the Canadian and Australian Corps had gained nearly all their objectives. Less successful was the British III Corps, attacking north of the River Somme, which was held up on its first objective and failed to take the Chilpilly Spur. There were reasons for this: the divisions of III Corps had suffered badly in earlier fighting and were largely made up of recent drafts from home; two of them had been weakened by a local German attack on 6/7 August; and the ground they were attacking was intersected by gullies and spurs that precluded the use of many supporting tanks and greatly aided the defence.[7]

Even so, the gains made that day by Rawlinson's Fourth Army were spectacular: an advance of eight miles on a ten-mile front – the furthest advance on the Western Front in one day since 1914 – with the French mirroring this success to the south. Even more extraordinary was the imbalance in casualties: the BEF lost 9,000 men; the Germans 27,000 (including 12,000 POWs) and 450 guns.[8]

How – given the relative success of the German spring offensives – did this sudden turnaround occur? Part of the answer lies in the war-weariness of the enemy. After the Blücher offensive, the Germans launched two more in Champagne – Operations Gneisenau (9–11 June) and Friedens-sturm (15–17 July), the latter known to the French as the Second Battle of the Marne – but both were stopped after modest gains by determined French–US counter-attacks. By the time the Marne battle ended on 4 August, the Allies had driven the Germans back to the Aisne (thereby snuffing out most of the Champagne bulge) and had re-established the vital railway link between Paris and Châlons-sur-Marne. Ludendorff suffered a mini-nervous breakdown during this setback and, arguably, never properly recovered his poise. On 2 August he ordered his commanders to adopt the strategic defensive, hoping to return soon to the attack. He never did so.[9]

The spring offensives had cost the Germans a million men and severely depleted their stockpile of munitions; they would soon lose another million men to Spanish Influenza. Meanwhile the Allies were growing steadily stronger. By 20 July there were almost 1.9 million American soldiers on French soil. Between April and July the number of French fighter aircraft rose from 797 to 1,070, while the army took delivery of 500 Renault light tanks. This extra firepower tipped the balance in the fighting on the Marne.[10]

Foch acknowledged that a 'turning point' had been reached in a memorandum – largely the work of his chief of staff, Maxime Weygand – that he distributed to Haig, Pétain and Pershing at a meeting at his headquarters on 24 July: the Allies now had the advantage and to keep it they needed to deliver a series of sharp surprise attacks, each with a specific objective, and to halt them before the enemy brought in reserves. He did not expect victory until 1919, but the sooner the better.[11]

The Battle of Amiens was the first major British contribution to this new strategy. Rawlinson's orders were to advance six miles to the Outer Amiens Defence Line, an old French defensive position that lay on the edge of the old Somme battlefield. If the attack went well he was to continue on to Chaulnes and, ideally, to Ham on the Somme.[12] He was using fewer troops than he had on 1 July 1916 – probably no more than half the 100,000 soldiers who attacked that day – but they were far better trained and, more importantly, enjoyed a huge advantage in firepower. As well as many more tanks, the Allies had four times as many aircraft as the defending Germans, more heavy guns, eight times as many Lewis guns per battalion than in 1916, eight trench mortars instead of two, and sixteen grenade-firing rifles. Moreover 'they faced dispirited German units that had recently arrived in the lines, knew their positions only poorly, and were outnumbered two to one'.[13]

Haig was understandably delighted with the day's results. 'Who would have believed this possible even 2 months ago?' he wrote to his wife. 'How much easier it is to attack, than to stand and await an enemy's attack!'[14] A major factor in the day's success was Haig's insistence on the use of horsemen. 'Without the rapid advance of the Cavalry,' he wrote later, 'the effect of the surprise attack on the 8th would have been much less and very probably the Amiens outer defence line would not have been gained either so soon or so cheaply.'[15]

With a less effective artillery bombardment and fewer tanks available, the BEF's advance slowed on 9 August, though the Canadians still gained four miles. By the end of 11 August the Fourth Army was just short of Chaulnes, at which point Rawlinson requested a halt in operations. Foch was reluctant to grant more than a brief pause, but Haig stood his ground. It was an important moment. 'The Allies,' wrote David Stevenson, 'would no longer batter away along the same sector beyond the point of diminishing returns. The secret of success lay not only in new technology and good preparation, but also in a willingness to halt while the going was good before starting again elsewhere.'[16]

With total losses of 75,000 men (50,000 captured) during the four-day battle – compared to French and British losses of 22,000 men each – Ludendorff acknowledged that 'the [morale] of the German Army was no longer what it had been'.[17] On 13 August, with this in mind, he told Hindenburg and the Chancellor Count von Hertling that 'it was no longer possible to force the enemy to sue for peace by an offensive'. The only alternative was a negotiated settlement. A day later the Kaiser seemed to agree with this assessment and instructed Paul von Hintze, the Foreign Secretary, 'to open up peace negotiations, if possible, through the medium of the Queen of Netherlands'.[18]

19 September 1918: *'Ninety-four squadrons . . . hurrying forward relentlessly'*
– Battle of Megiddo

Shortly after 1 a.m., a single Handley Page O/400 heavy bomber of the RAF's Palestine Brigade dropped its sixteen 112-pound bombs on the telephone exchange and railway station at Al-Afuleh, thus severing communications between General Liman von Sanders, commanding Turkish troops in Palestine, and his armies on the front line. Other British bombers targeted Messudieh railway junction, the headquarters of the Ottoman Seventh Army and the telephone exchange at Nablus.[1]

At 4.30 a.m., the 385 guns of the British XXI Corps opened up on two Turkish divisions defending a stretch of the front that extended fifteen miles inland from the coast north of Jaffa. After a twenty-minute hurricane bombardment, the guns lifted to a creeping barrage to protect the

British and Indian troops who surged from their trenches. Within minutes, faced with only minimal opposition, they were over the sandy ridge that contained the Ottoman front-line trench and heading for the enemy's unwired second and third positions. By mid-morning the entire defensive system had fallen to XXI Corps, and three cavalry divisions of the Desert Mounted Corps – mainly Australians and Indians, and equipped with machine-guns, horse artillery and Hotchkiss rifles – were advancing north up the coast with no Turkish reserves to stop them. A cavalry officer wrote:

> From 10.00 hours onwards, a hostile aeroplane observer, if one had been available, flying over the Plain of Sharon would have seen a remarkable sight – ninety-four squadrons, disposed in great breadth and in great depth, hurrying forward relentlessly on a decisive mission – a mission of which all cavalry soldiers have dreamed, but in which few have been privileged to partake.[2]

Early on the 20th the Allied horsemen reached the passes between the plains of Sharon and Esdraelon, thus sealing off the means of escape for the retreating Turkish Eighth Army. Later that day they captured Al-Afuleh, Beisan and Nazareth (narrowly missing Liman von Sanders) and, according to their Commander-in-Chief General Allenby, 'were collecting the disorganized masses of enemy troops and transport as they arrived from the south'. Allenby added: 'All avenues of escape open to the enemy, except the fords across the Jordan between Beisan and Jisr-ed-Dameer, were thus closed.'[3]

It was across these fords and into the Jordan valley that Mustafa Kemal's Seventh Army tried to escape during the night of 20/21 September. But the retreating army was spotted and attacked by the RAF in a defile west of the Jordan. Trapped by the steep sides of the defile, the column was easy prey for the waves of bombers and fighters that passed over every three minutes. The operation was planned to last for five hours, but it was all over in sixty minutes. British cavalry later found a six-mile stretch of charred and smouldering wreckage, including eighty-seven guns, fifty-five motor-lorries, four motorcars, 837 four-wheeled wagons and scores of water-carts and field kitchens. 'The RAF lost four killed,' commented T. E. Lawrence. 'The Turks lost a corps.'[4]

By the evening of 21 September the British had taken 25,000 prisoners, most from the destroyed Turkish Eighth Army, while the Seventh was fragmented and scattered, and the Fourth retreating north from the Jordan crossings on foot as the railway line to Damascus had been cut by the Northern Arab Army (NAA) under Emir Feisal, with T. E. Lawrence in attendance. In a letter to his wife, Allenby wrote: 'I, myself, am almost aghast at the extent of the victory.' But to Sir Henry Wilson, the CIGS, he was more self-assured. 'Everything went according to plan, without a hitch,' he wrote, adding that the Indian battalions 'did grandly, in spite of their newness and short training'.[5]

Allenby's insouciance was also in evidence when Lawrence visited his headquarters in Ramleh on 21 September. 'There I found the great man unmoved,' wrote Lawrence, 'except for the light in his eye as [Allenby's chief of staff General Louis] Bols bustled in every fifteen minutes, with news of some wider success. Allenby had been so sure, before he started, that to him the result was almost boredom: but no general, however, scientific, could see his intricate plan carried out over an enormous field in every particular with complete success, and not know an inward gladness: especially when he felt it (as he must have felt it) a reward of the breadth and judgement which made him conceive such unorthodox movements.'[6]

What, then, was Allenby's plan? And why had it taken him so long to advance north from Jerusalem? His original intention had been to attack in the spring. But this was forestalled by the Ludendorff offensive on the Western Front which necessitated the transfer to France of twenty-three infantry battalions, nine regiments of yeomanry horse and supporting units of machine-guns and artillery. In return Allenby was given fifty-four Indian Army battalions, many of them raw recruits with few signallers or Lewis gunners. So worried was he that the necessary halt for training would harm British prestige in Egypt – where, he wrote, 'we are surrounded by an alien and unfriendly people' – that he even asked the War Office for Japanese divisions. They were refused.[7]

But the Turkish armies defending northern Palestine were also weakened during the first half of 1918 – as the best Ottoman troops were sent to former Russian Transcaucasia to take advantage of the Bolshevik Revolution – and by September the EEF enjoyed a numerical advantage of 2:1. Allenby's estimate of his combat strength was 57,000 infantry, 12,000 cavalry and 540 guns; that of the Turks 26,000, 3,000 and 370 respectively. His force was supplemented, moreover, by Feisal's NAA – 5,000 or so strong – which was operating in the interior.[8]

His plan was the reverse of that used to break through to Jerusalem: then he misled the Turks into thinking he would attack by the sea at Gaza, and instead turned their flank inland at Beersheba; now he would feint in the interior and make his main attack on the coast, using cavalry to sever the Turks' lines of communication. Meanwhile the NAA would complete the encirclement by raiding the railway hub of Deraa and leading a local Arab revolt.[9]

The plan was assisted by German commander Liman von Sanders' insistence on packing the forward Turkish trenches with troops – the opposite approach to the Western Front's defence in depth – so that once the lines were pierced there was little to stop a rapid advance. Allenby also made sure that his advantage in troops in the crucial zone running fifteen miles inland from the sea was almost 3:1 in infantry and guns and 9:1 in cavalry. He used deception measures such as deploying dummy horses and old tanks in the Jordan sector inland, while all movement of troops and munitions near the coast was done at night. The RAF, moreover, enjoyed complete air superiority in Palestine – with 100 planes to the Germans' fifteen – and was able to prevent any enemy overflights while it, in turn, took more than 42,000 photos of the area north of the start line. By mid-September all was ready. 'I do not think,' Allenby told Sir Henry Wilson, 'that the Turks have, so far, any inkling of my plan.' He was right.[10]

After the success of the first three days of the attack, Allenby ordered a pause. But the pursuit continued on 26 September, and during the next five days Feisal's NAA and Indian cavalry captured the bulk of the Turkish Fourth Army (though one Turkish column guilty of killing Arab non-combatants was slaughtered by the enraged NAA). Late on 30 September, with Allenby's blessing, Feisal's Arab irregulars entered Damascus.* Lawrence followed in his Rolls-Royce next morning. 'The way was packed

---

* By the time Allenby's troops reached Aleppo in northern Syria on 29 October, thereby cutting the rail link between Constantinople and Turkish forces in Mesopotamia, the EEF had captured 75,000 prisoners (including 3,700 Germans and Austrians) from a total force of 104,000, and 360 guns. British casualties were 5,666 (Stevenson, *With our Backs to the Wall*, pp. 153–4).

with people,' he recalled, 'lined solid on the side-walks, in the road, at the windows and on the balconies or house-tops. Many were crying, a few cheered faintly, some bolder ones cried our names: but mostly they looked and looked, joy shining in their eyes. A movement like a long sigh from gate to heart of the city, marked our course.'[11]

27 September 1918: *'The old trench warfare was a thing of the past'*
– Piercing the Hindenburg Line

There was to be no preliminary bombardment to warn the Germans that an attack was imminent. Instead, at 5.20 a.m., the massed British guns opened fire on twelve miles of the northern extension of the German Hindenburg Line near Cambrai, using a combination of 50 per cent shrapnel shell, 40 per cent high explosive and 10 per cent smoke to neutralize the defenders and obscure the assault. It was still dark when, ten minutes later, the barrage moved forward and British and Dominion troops surged towards the German positions.

The first obstacle faced by Private Stan Colbeck of the 4th Canadian Division was the unfinished and largely dry Canal du Nord – 120 feet wide and with revetted banks up to ten feet high – that the Germans had cleverly integrated into their defensive system. 'We had to carry scaling ladders as the canal was very deep where we crossed over. Myself and a pal named Brown, we carried the ladder so we were the first up and had gone a little way [beyond the canal] when a shell exploded right behind us. It hit us like a giant fist in the small of the back. I thought I was blown in two. I was all numb. I asked Brown if he was okay. He said he thought so! The screams behind us I will never forget. Brown and I were fine, but that shell wiped out our whole section.'[1]

The plans drawn up by General Currie, commanding the First Army's Canadian Corps, were for his two spearhead divisions, the 1st and the 4th, to cross the canal on a relatively narrow frontage of 2,700 yards and pierce the actual Canal du Nord Line 300 yards beyond. There they would then be joined on either side by the British 11th and 3rd Canadian Divisions for the assault on the remaining two defensive systems, the Marquion and Marcoing Lines (including the villages of Marquion and Bourlon, and Bourlon Woods), by which time the frontage of attack would have extended to 9,500 yards.[2]

Royal Engineers bridging the Canal du Nord near Moeuvres in late September 1918.

The key to Currie's attack – which, because of the terrain and priorities elsewhere, had little tank and aircraft support – was an exceptionally accurate creeping barrage from guns and machine-guns to protect the infantry, and a vigorous counter-battery fire to suppress the German guns. This worked, as did the plan for Canadian engineers to bridge the canal as quickly as possible so that more troops, vehicles and guns could join in the advance. By mid-morning the defenders of the 1st Prussian Guards Reserve Division and the 3rd German Naval Division had been overwhelmed, the survivors either captured or in retreat. Resistance stiffened through the day, particularly at Bourlon Wood, but by nightfall the Canadians had achieved all of their objectives.[3]

Meanwhile other First Army troops had carried out diversionary attacks to the north, to distract German artillery fire, while to the south three corps of Byng's Third Army had assaulted the Hindenburg Line proper (where, in places, the canal was *behind* the first defensive line). The furthest advance was made by Lieutenant-General Aylmer Haldane's VI Corps, comprised of the regular 2nd, 3rd and Guards Divisions. A second lieutenant in the Coldstream Guards recalled:

> Imagine the problem of crossing a dry canal fixed with barbed wire, entailing scrambling down a 20-foot sloping brick wall, fighting through the wire and climbing up the other side with machine guns not more than 30 yards away! Was it surprising the troops hesitated? But the company commander, Captain Cyril Frisby, didn't hesitate! He ... immediately called for volunteers, leapt up himself and slid down the bank followed by three equally brave men. Somehow they got through the wire and up the other side – the gunners surrendered.[4]

Major Deneys Reitz,* second-in-command of the 1st Royal Scots Fusiliers (part of 3rd Division) remembered his men 'clubbing and bayoneting' as they fought to capture the first German trench. When it was taken, he noticed that 'every few yards along the parapet stood a machine gun, and in addition there were many trench mortars and anti-tank rifles'. The trench, moreover, 'was full of dead and wounded Germans and beside every machine gun lay its crew, smitten down by the hurricane of artillery barrage'. British casualties were also heavy, and 'in one small area' Reitz 'counted over a hundred officers and men lying in all manner of attitudes ... some still hugging their rifles, others horribly torn by shells'.[5]

Eventually support battalions moved through 1 RSF to continue the attack and by 8 p.m., noted Reitz, 'practically every British battery had moved up and along the lip of the Hindenburg Line the guns stood in an unbroken line firing as fast as they could load'. He added: 'On this day the British had blasted their way through the Hindenburg Line into the open country beyond, and from there onward the evil of the old trench warfare was a thing of the past.'[6]

This was a slight exaggeration. The attack had indeed pierced the

* During the Anglo-Boer War of 1899–1902, the South-African born Reitz had fought *against* the British.

Hindenburg Line (or at least its northern extension), creating a breach twelve miles wide and up to six deep. It had, moreover, yielded 16,000 prisoners and 200 guns. But the German defence in this sector would stiffen over the coming days and the Canadian Corps, in particular, suffered heavy casualties as it inched towards Cambrai (the city falling on 9 October).[7]

The real significance of the battle was in its wider context. Since the success of the Battle of Amiens, the Allies had used a succession of carefully planned attacks to drive the Germans out of territory they had occupied since March. By early September OHL had reluctantly withdrawn its troops to the Hindenburg Line, its last prepared position. But still the Allies attacked, reluctant to give the Germans any breathing space to shorten their line further and build up reserves. In mid-September, for example, Pershing's AEF pinched out the 200-square-mile Saint-Mihiel salient in Lorraine in the United States' first major operation of the war.

Far more ambitious, however, was Foch's plan for a series of co-ordinated offensives in late September – the first in the west since April 1917 – with the aim of piercing the final German line of defences, entering open country, 'cutting off the Noyon bulge and driving towards the trunk railway between Cambrai, St-Quentin, Mézières, and Sedan'. At first Foch wanted the attacks to diverge, with the main effort made from Saint-Mihiel towards the German border. But Haig persuaded him that the attacks would have more effect, and would be mutually supporting, if they converged.[8] 'Foch was very pleased with what the British Army has done,' Haig noted in his diary after a meeting with the Generalissimo on 29 August. 'As regards future plans he is "in full agreement with me".'[9]

Less supportive were the British politicians. 'Just a word of caution,' wrote Sir Henry Wilson, CIGS, to Haig on 1 September. '. . . I know the War Cabinet would become anxious if we received heavy punishment in attacking the Hindenburg Line WITHOUT SUCCESS.' Haig was disgusted. 'The object of the telegram,' he noted in his diary, 'is, no doubt, to save the Prime Minister . . . in case of failure. So I read it to mean I can attack the Hindenburg Line if I think it right to do so . . . If my attack is successful I will remain on as C-in-C. If we fail, and our losses are excessive, I can hope for no mercy! I wrote to Henry Wilson in reply. What a wretched lot of weaklings we have in high places at the present time!'[10]

Fortunately for Haig the four co-ordinated Allied offensives at the end of September were largely successful, with the laurels going to the BEF. The first attack, by the Americans and French at Meuse–Argonne on 26 September, made good early progress before stalling. The same could be said of the British First and Third Armies' assault across the Canal du Nord a day later, though this first breach in the vaunted Hindenburg Line was a tremendously significant moment. On the 28th, a group of Allied armies under King Albert of the Belgians (including Plumer's British Second Army) advanced up to eight miles in Flanders, overrunning the salient and the area to the south, and capturing most of the ridge line (including Passchendaele which fell to the Belgians). But further significant progress was prevented by heavy rain.

It was the last attack on 29 September – by Rawlinson's British Fourth Army along the Saint-Quentin Canal – that was the most successful. Aided by the earlier capture of detailed plans of the defensive system, a massive preliminary bombardment (that landed 126 shells per minute for eight hours on every 500 yards of the German position), and morning fog that obscured the assaulting troops, it drove straight through the German defences.[11] Despite the presence of Australian troops, who did very well, the laurels went to the county regiments of the 46th (North Midland) Division* which stormed across the canal, taking '4000 prisoners and 40 guns'.[12] By 5 October, despite rain slowing the follow-up attacks, the British were through the last reserve defences of the Hindenburg Line and into unfortified ground.[13]

Just as momentous was the news that the Bulgarians, in the wake of their defeat by General Franchet d'Espèrey's Franco-Serbian force, had signed a ceasefire in the Balkans on 29 September (and later agreed to all the Allied terms for peace).† Foch knew it was the beginning of the end, telling Haig on 30 September 'that the Germans cannot much longer resist our attacks against their whole front and that "soon they will crack"'.[14]

He was right. Already the news from the Balkans – combined with the unprecedented Allied successes on the Western Front – had convinced a demoralized Ludendorff that it was now in Germany's interest to seek

---

* The 46th Division had come a long way from its poor showing at Loos, an improvement that underlines the advances made in the BEF's tactical training since 1916.
† They required the Bulgarians to demobilize, evacuate Greece and Serbia, and allow the Allies to occupy their territory as a base for future operations.

an immediate ceasefire. He quickly enlisted the support of Hindenburg, the Kaiser, Foreign Secretary von Hintze and Prince Max of Baden (a liberal who succeeded Hertling as Chancellor on 3 October), and during the night of 4/5 October a brief note was sent to President Wilson: it asked him to make arrangements for an armistice, and for peace negotiations to begin on the basis of his Fourteen Points.[15]

9 November 1918: *'Long live the German Republic!'*
– The Kaiser abdicates

At 8.30 a.m., after a sleepless night, a hollow-eyed and gaunt Field Marshal von Hindenburg entered the office of his deputy, Chief Quartermaster-General Wilhelm Groener,* and told him that the Kaiser should not only abdicate at once, but also leave the country for his own safety. Groener was shocked: not because he disagreed – he had been coming round to that way of thinking – but because until now the field marshal had always insisted that Wilhelm II should keep his throne.[1]

There was, however, no time to discuss the issue further as a crucial meeting of army officers was scheduled for 9 a.m. in the dining room of the Hôtel Britannique, OHL's headquarters·in the picturesque Belgian town of Spa. A day earlier, with news of a left-wing revolution spreading across Germany, Hindenburg had summoned fifty senior officers to Spa to discuss the workability of the Kaiser's scheme to march on Berlin and restore order after a ceasefire. The thirty-nine officers who had made it in time for the meeting, however, were unaware of the reason for their summons and probably assumed it was to discuss the Armistice.[2]

Hindenburg began the meeting by summing up the political situation in Germany and stressing that, since the mutiny of the navy and the setting up of a sailor's council at Kiel on 4 November ('Red Monday'), the revolution had spread to Berlin and most of the Germany's provincial capitals, including Munich and Cologne on the Rhine. The Kaiser's

---

* Groener had replaced Ludendorff as Chief Quartermaster-General after the latter's sacking by the Kaiser on 26 October.

solution, he told them, was for the army to march on Berlin, a move that would take at least two or three weeks now that the rebels controlled most of the key railway junctions. Such a march would, moreover, present almost insuperable supply difficulties and would be opposed by Bolshevik revolutionaries along the way. When Hindenburg had finished speaking there was no response, just shocked silence.[3]

Due to meet the Kaiser at his Spa residence Villa Fraineuse, Hindenburg and Groener left the officers to consider two questions: 'Would it be possible for the Kaiser to regain control of Germany by force of arms, at the head of his troops?' 'Would the troops march against the Bolshevists in Germany?'

Arriving at the Villa Fraineuse, Hindenburg and Groener were shown into the garden room where the Kaiser was reading telegrams from Prince Max of Baden, the Chancellor, announcing the deposition of various German monarchs, including the King of Bavaria. Turning to his visitors, he asked what progress the army had made with his plan to march on Berlin. Hindenburg tried to bring up the subject of abdication but could not find the words. Instead, with tears in his eyes and in 'a voice choked with sorrow', he offered to resign. The Kaiser went pale and walked to the fireplace where logs were burning. Shivering slightly, he turned and said he wanted 'to look into the matter first'. Then he invited his Chief Quartermaster-General to speak.[4]

A Württemburger with a background in economic management and logistics – and who had earlier been sacked as head of the Kriegsamt* because Ludendorff thought him too sympathetic to workers' demands – Groener was less emotionally attached to the Hohenzollern dynasty than Prussian officers like Hindenburg. Without mentioning abdication, he told the Kaiser that a march on Berlin was out of the question. It was no longer a matter simply of suppressing an insurrection; instead, if the Kaiser tried to lead his troops back into Germany through a Rhineland already in rebel hands, it would spark a civil war. Some of the garrison troops had already gone over to the rebels and the army as a whole could no longer be trusted. This was, added Groener, not only his opinion but that of the field marshal and most of the army's senior commanders.[5]

---

* The Kriegsamt (or War Office) had been set up by Ludendorff and Hindenburg in 1916 to oversee the German war economy.

The implication was clear. But General Count von der Schulenburg, Crown Prince Wilhelm's chief of staff who had arrived at Spa that morning, disagreed with Groener's assessment. The troops just needed rest, said Schulenburg, and in a week or ten days would be ready to restore order city by city. If the rebels tried to cut off the army's supplies the country would rise in protest. This argument reinvigorated the Kaiser who wanted to send troops to recapture the nearest cities, including Cologne. But Groener was adamant. 'Sire,' he said, 'you no longer have an army. The army will return to Germany as an organised force under the orders of its generals, but not under those of your Majesty. The army is no longer with your Majesty.'[6]

Outraged, the Kaiser demanded evidence in writing from the army commanders. Was not Schulenburg's view proof that others thought differently? he asked. Groener shrugged. 'I have other information.' When Hindenburg then agreed broadly with his deputy's assessment, the Kaiser angrily adjourned the meeting with the words: 'Interrogate all the army commanders as to the morale of the army. If they tell me that the army is no longer with me I am ready to go; but not before.'[7]

The sequence of events that led so rapidly to discussions about an armistice, revolution in Germany and calls for the Kaiser's abdication had begun with Ludendorff's acknowledgement on 28 September that the war was lost. As soon as this became public, in the form of the note sent to President Wilson on the night of 4/5 October, Germany's allies quickly lost heart and its citizens decided that enough was enough. The decision to request a ceasefire, wrote David Stevenson, 'was by no means tantamount to a decision to *accept* one, and yet it started an avalanche, so fracturing military and civilian morale and the Central Powers' cohesion that within weeks the Germans had to accept whatever conditions were dictated to them'.[8]

In late October, after a month-long exchange of notes between Berlin and Washington, Prince Max's government accepted Wilson's various demands: that peace would be negotiated on the basis of his Fourteen Points and subsequent speeches; that torpedo attacks on passenger ships would end; that future German governments and the high command would be responsible to the Reichstag (thus reducing the Kaiser's role to that of a constitutional monarch); and that the terms of the ceasefire would render Germany militarily incapable of resuming the conflict.[9]

These harsh terms were too much for Ludendorff who had recovered from his loss of nerve and wanted to continue the war into 1919 to improve Germany's bargaining position. But he and Hindenburg went too far on 26 October when they repudiated the government's acceptance of Wilson's Third (and final) Note and, after a furious confrontation with the Kaiser, Ludendorff was sacked and the field marshal brought into line. Not only was the Hindenburg/Ludendorff partnership broken – they would never speak again – but so too was OHL's veto over German foreign policy.[10]

It was naval opposition to the peace process, however, that was to provoke revolution at home. Without consulting the Kaiser, naval chiefs ordered the High Seas Fleet to ready itself for a final clash with the Royal Navy. Fearing – with good reason – that an armistice would result in the loss of their vessels to Britain, Admiral Scheer (now head of SKL, the Naval Warfare Directorate) and his chief of staff Magnus von Levetzow preferred the destruction of the fleet to dishonourable surrenders. But when rumours circulated that the fleet was to be sent on a suicide mission, disobedience spread among its sailors and the operation was postponed. This did not prevent outright mutiny at Kiel on 4 November when, after a mass arrest of suspected ringleaders and the death of many civilian protesters, sailors broke into the rifle stores and took over their ships. The local garrison mutinied in sympathy and, after a Soviet-style soldiers' and sailors' council had been elected, the anti-government revolt was under way.[11]

While their domestic support ebbed away, the Kaiser and his government also had to contend with the loss of Germany's allies: Turkey, with its northern flank exposed by the defection of Bulgaria, signed an armistice with the Allies on 30 October; and Austria-Hungary, badly defeated by Italy at the Battle of Vittorio and rocked by mass desertions and internal rebellion, followed suit four days later. Undermined from within and without, Germany was on the brink of political and military collapse even before the Kaiser's conference of 9 November. What sealed his fate that day, however, was the refusal of the Berlin garrison (including the Kaiser's own palace guard) to act against a huge public demonstration that had been orchestrated by independent socialists of the USPD.

Even before the mutiny in Berlin, Prince Max's office had made a number of telephone calls to Spa, insisting that the Kaiser's abdication was necessary to save Berlin from revolution. With no definite response, and the enormous crowd closing in on the Chancellery, Max took the matter into his own hands. He issued a press release to the Wolff telegraph agency that announced the Kaiser's immediate abdication as both Emperor of Germany and King of Prussia. Wilhelm II's son, the Crown Prince, would also stand down, though the possibility of a regent for Wilhelm II's grandsons was left open. As for Max himself, he would resign as Chancellor in favour of Friedrich Ebert, the leader of the SPD. The news was on the streets of Berlin by lunchtime.[12]

Meanwhile at Spa the Kaiser had received the results of the officers' poll at OHL headquarters. 'The troops remain loyal to His Majesty,' reported a staff colonel, 'but they are tired and indifferent and want nothing except rest and peace. At the present moment they would not march against Germany, even with Your Majesty at their head. They would not march against Bolshevism. They want one thing only – an armistice at the earliest possible moment.'[13]

It was this decisive statement that finally convinced the Kaiser that resignation was his only option. But encouraged by Schulenburg and Crown Prince Wilhelm, who had just arrived at Spa, he told his officials to prepare a document of abdication as Emperor of Germany but not as King of Prussia. It was after he had signed it, and the text was being telephoned through to Berlin at 2 p.m., that word came back of Prince Max's fait accompli. 'It's a betrayal,' raged the Kaiser. 'A shameless, disgraceful betrayal!' But there was nothing to be done. After briefly considering a last stand at the Villa Fraineuse, the Kaiser bowed to Hindenburg's advice and early on 10 November left for exile in Holland.[14]

By then even the possibility of one of his grandsons ascending the throne had vanished, thanks to the precipitate action of Philipp Scheidemann, a rabble-rousing SPD deputy, on 9 November. Scheidemann had been having lunch with Ebert, the new Chancellor, in the Reichstag restaurant when they were informed that the Bolshevist Karl Liebknecht, a former member of the SPD, was about to declare a republic from the balcony of the Kaiser's palace at the other end of the Unter den Linden. A large crowd had gathered to hear him; another, of similar size, was waiting outside the Reichstag for the SPD leaders to speak. Scheidemann volunteered. Aware that the future of Germany was in the balance, and that if he did not seize the initiative the Bolshevists would, he told the red-flag-waving crowd: 'Workers and soldiers ... the cursed war is at an end ... the people have triumphed ... Prince Max of Baden has handed over his office as chancellor to Ebert. Our friend will form a workers' government ... miracles have happened ... the old and rotten has broken down ... long live the new! Long live the German republic!'[15]

Ebert was furious when he learned the truth. Scheidemann had no right, he yelled, to declare a republic; that was for the forthcoming constituent assembly to decide. But he knew, too, that the damage had been done. After 500 years on the thrones of Prussia and Germany, the Hohenzollern dynasty was no more.[16]

11 November 1918: *'VICTORY! VICTORY! VICTORY!'*
– The Armistice

It was still dark as the German ceasefire delegates trudged once more over duckboards to meet their Allied counterparts in Marshal Foch's dining car – carriage 2419D of the Compagnie Internationale des Wagon-Lits – in a railway siding of the Compiègne Forest, north of Paris. On one side of the large conference table sat Foch and Admiral Sir Rosslyn Wemyss, Britain's First Sea Lord and the Allies' naval representative at the talks, flanked by their deputies General Maxime Weygand and Rear Admiral George Hope; on the other Matthias Erzberger of the Catholic Centre Party, the head of the German delegation (described by Wemyss as a 'common looking man' and a 'typical German bourgeois'), with Captain Ernst Vanselow, Count Alfred von Oberndorff and Major-General Detlev von Winterfeldt ('a horrid looking man, with a cruel face'), representing respectively the German navy, Foreign Ministry and army.[1]

The talks had opened on 8 November when Weygand presented the German delegation with the Allied terms. The thirty-four clauses included: all occupied lands to be given up, including Alsace-Lorraine; all cash and gold reserves to be returned to their original owners; all German territory west of the Rhine, and some bridgeheads on the east bank to a depth of thirty kilometres, to be occupied by the Allies; the Treaty of Brest-Litovsk to be annulled; reparations to be paid for war damage; most capital ships and 160 submarines to be interned in a neutral port; and the Allied blockade of German ports to continue until a peace treaty had been signed. In addition the Germans had fourteen days to withdraw back across the Rhine and hand over 5,000 locomotives, 150,000 railway carriages, 10,000 lorries, 2,000 aircraft, 30,000 machine-guns and most of their heavy artillery.[2]

Though shocked by the severity of the terms, Erzberger had requested an immediate armistice so that the German army could be used to prevent a Bolshevist revolution at home. But Foch was adamant: there would be no armistice until all the Allied terms had been met. The Germans had, he added, seventy-two hours to make up their minds. When Erzberger requested an additional twenty-four hours, pointing out that both the OHL at Spa and Prince Max's government in Berlin would have to be consulted, Foch refused. The deadline was 11 a.m. on Monday 11 November: take it or leave it.[3]

There had then been a pause in negotiations as a copy of the terms – too detailed to send by coded message – was taken across the lines by hand (a journey made longer still when for half a day the German front-line troops refused safe passage). Finally, late on 10 November, the new Chancellor Ebert (or 'People's Commissar' as he now styled himself to appease the far left) sent his reply by radio message: 'The German Government accepts the conditions of the Armistice communicated to it on 8 November.'[4]

It was followed soon afterwards by a much longer message from Hindenburg that raised certain objections. They included a fear that the German economy would collapse if the specified number of lorries and railway carriages were handed to the Allies; that the Germans no longer had the number of aircraft the Allies were demanding; that the food blockade needed to be lifted at once to prevent starvation; that they required some of their weapons to tackle the Bolshevist revolutionaries; and that their troops should be allowed to march back to Germany via a corner of Holland to save time. Erzberger was to fight hard for these concessions, insisted Hindenburg, but if the Allies objected he was to agree to the Armistice regardless.[5]

Armed at last with these instructions, Erzberger requested the final session of talks to begin at 2 a.m. on the 11th, hence the early-morning trek to Foch's dining car. Over the next three hours the German delegation did manage to wring out of Foch some minor concessions: he would settle for 25,000 machine-guns (not 30,000); 1,700 planes (not 2,000); 5,000 lorries (not 10,000), and delivered over a longer time-frame. The German Army would be given six more days to retreat behind the Rhine, and the size of the neutral bridgeheads beyond was reduced from thirty kilometres to ten so that German soldiers could control the vital Ruhr industries. As for the naval blockade, Wemyss would only to refer the matter to his government and was prepared to 'consider supplying Germany with food, to the degree considered necessary'.[6]

Finally, at 5.12 a.m., the delegates reached agreement and the ceasefire document was signed (two of the Germans, Winterfeldt and Vanselow, weeping as they did so). The Armistice would come into force at 11 a.m. on 11 November – six hours after the official time of agreement – thus ending a war now in its 1,560th day. Erzberger's parting shot was to read out a prepared statement: 'The German people, which held off a world of enemies for fifty months, will preserve their liberty and unity despite every kind of violence. A nation of seventy million people suffers, but it does not die.'

'Très bien,' was Foch's terse response. The carriage then emptied without a handshake, all sides keen to spread the word.[7]

It came too late for twenty-five-year-old Private George Ellison of the 5th Royal Irish Lancers, the last British casualty of the war, killed by a sniper a few minutes before 11 a.m. as his unit advanced into Saint-Denis, a few miles to the north-east of Mons where it had all begun for the BEF more than four years earlier; and also for Private Henry Gunther, a German-American bank clerk from Baltimore, struck in the head by a machine-gun bullet as he charged a German-held ridge near Ville-devant-Chaumont in Lorraine – possibly in a last desperate attempt to win back the sergeant stripes he had forfeited for advising a friend not to enlist. Gunther died at 10.59 a.m.[8]

For defeated German soldiers like gunner Leutnant Herbert Sulzbach, serving with his battery close to the Belgian border, the news of the armistice was bittersweet. 'The war is over,' he wrote. '. . . How we looked forward to *this* moment; how we used to picture it as the most splendid event of our lives; and here we are now, humbled, our souls torn and bleeding, and know that we've surrendered. Germany has surrendered to the Entente!'[9]

The blow was even greater for Gefreiter Adolf Hitler, recovering in a military hospital in Pomerania from the effects of a British mustard-gas attack a month earlier. 'As my eyes once again went dark,' he remembered in *Mein Kampf*, 'I fumbled and felt my way back to the dormitory, threw myself on the bed, and buried my burning head in the pillow and the duvet. I had not cried since the day I had stood at my mother's grave. Now I couldn't do anything else.'[10]

For the Allies, on the other hand, the armistice was cause for wild celebrations. 'We came back to [Le] Tréport just minutes after the news broke there,' recalled Sister Edith Appleton, 'and in less than an hour the whole place had gone stark mad, with flags of all nations flying everywhere and sirens blowing. All the bands turned out and processed along the camp, with convalescent patients and oddments of French following. Ambulances bedecked with flags and streamers . . . carried about 16 inside and as many as could manage to stay up on the roof. Then they paraded solemnly round and round the roads, the men cheering, shouting and waving flags.'[11]

Soldiers of the US 64th Regiment celebrate news of the armistice on 11 November 1918.

Back in Britain, remembered my great-uncle Charles David (then serving on the destroyer HMS *Vivacious* in the Firth of Forth), the people went 'mad' when they heard the news: 'Never in all history can rejoicing so utterly spontaneous have gripped an entire nation. It was as if all the bottled up emotions of 4½ years had been suddenly let loose, and without orders or promptings from anyone an entire population "downed tools" and swarmed into the streets of the cities, towns and villages. They cheered, they sang, they laughed, and they wept. They grabbed complete strangers and kissed them and danced in the streets for hours on end.' He and his shipmates celebrated with a double ration of rum and later went ashore to Bo'ness where an immense crowd 'was singing and milling around, too happy to care what they did next. The war was over. It was all that mattered.'[12]

Paris, too, had exploded with joy. 'Here and there little excited groups gathered,' wrote Alison Strahan, a Canadian in the American Red Cross, 'then a mob came down the Avenue de l'Opéra [and] developed into a procession. At its head marched Latin Quarter students . . . carrying the flags of the Allied countries. They were followed by soldiers, sailors, midinettes [shopgirls], members of the Red Cross, YMCA, civilians and soldiers . . . In front of the Opéra the procession seemed to hesitate for a moment, then with one accord they broke into "La Marseillaise". It was like a match to a bonfire, now we were a seething crowd celebrating VICTORY! VICTORY! VICTORY!'[13]

There were humorous exchanges among the troops. 'Finie la guerre!' shouted a French *poilu* to Americans of the 80th (Blue Ridge) Division. 'Well for lawd's sake,' came the reply, 'don't start another one unless you can finish it yourself!'[14]

Most Allied combatants felt a mixture of joy and relief, and were looking forward to seeing loved ones. 'We laughed and yelled and whooped it up till about midnight,' wrote nineteen-year-old Private Arthur Yensen of the US 7th Engineers Train. 'Good times have come at last! We'll soon turn in our mules and go home where we can eat sugar, sleep in beds, get rid of cooties [lice], ditch our wrap leggings, see our folks, chase around with girls, and maybe rate a little importance since we've been to war!'[15]

The chief concern for British lieutenant Richard Dixon was that the horror and discomfort of trench life were finally over:

There was a future ahead of me. Something I had not imagined for some years. No more slaughter, no more maiming, no more mud and blood, and no more killing and disembowelling of horses and mules – which was what I found most difficult to bear. No more of those hopeless dawns with the rain chilling the spirits, no more crouching in inadequate dugouts scooped out of trench walls, no more dodging of snipers' bullets, no more of that terrible shell-fire. No more shovelling up of men's bodies and dumping them into sand-bags; no more cries of 'Stretcher-bear-ER!', and no more of those beastly gas-masks and the odious smell of pear drops which was deadly to the lungs, and no more writing of those dreadfully difficult letters to the next-of-kin of the dead.[16]

For those like Vera Brittain who were still grieving for loved ones, however, the Armistice produced conflicting emotions. During the evening of the 11th, having detached herself from her fellow VAD revellers, Brittain 'walked slowly up Whitehall' with her 'heart sinking in cold dismay'. She wrote:

Already this was a different world from the one that I had known during four life-long years, a world in which people would be light-hearted and forgetful, in which themselves and their careers and amusements would blot out political ideals and great national issues. And in that brightly lit, alien world I should have no part. All those with whom I had really been intimate were gone; not one remained to share with me the heights and the depths of my memories . . . For the first time I realized . . . how completely everything that had made up my life had vanished with Edward and Roland, with Victor and Geoffrey. The war was over; a new age was beginning; but the dead were dead and would never return.[17]

EPILOGUE

At 8 a.m. on Thursday 11 November 1920 – the second anniversary of the Armistice – a plain oak coffin, topped with a frayed Union Jack, steel helmet and bayonet, was taken from its purple-draped funeral coach at Victoria Station and placed on a Royal Horse Artillery gun-carriage for the procession to Westminster Abbey. Preceded by the massed bands of the four regiments of foot guards playing Chopin's Funeral March, the horse-drawn gun carriage moved slowly through 'the western arch of the station into the kindly sunshine of a mellow day'. Alongside it marched twelve distinguished pall-bearers – senior officers from all services including Air Marshal Sir Hugh Trenchard, and Lords Beatty, Haig, Wilson, Horne and Byng – and to the rear 'a long river' of soldiers, sailors, airmen and merchant mariners, as well as representatives from the Dominion forces and ex-servicemen.[1]

'The column passed into Grosvenor-gardens,' recorded *The Times*, 'between ranks, thousands strong, of silent people – people who crowded pavements, roofs and windows, and flowed in dense, packed masses up side streets and every open space. Then on down Grosvenor-place; behind the gun-carriage the long procession drew out in navy blue and khaki and the blue of the Royal Air Force, and in the sombre clothes of the ex-Service men.'[2]

At 10.45 a.m. the gun-carriage came to a halt in front of a veiled Cenotaph on Whitehall and King George V, the Chief Mourner, stepped forward to place a wreath on the coffin, 'the token of the Nation's Homage'. Then the choir and some of the crowd sang an 'extraordinarily moving' rendition of 'O, God, our help in ages past' – the 'heart-rending' drum roll 'rising through and submerging even the sound of the brass and the voices' – and finally the Archbishop of Canterbury led the mourners in a recitation of the Lord's Prayer. Shortly after the prayer ceased, Big Ben chimed out the hour and the King turned to face the

Cenotaph and, by the touch of a button, released the veils that hid it. 'They fell away,' noted *The Times*, 'and it stood clean and wonderful in its naked beauty.'[3]

For two minutes the 'great multitude bowed its head' in silence. Then bugles played the Last Post and, as the final note died away, the King stepped forward and placed a large wreath at the base of the Cenotaph, its inscription reading: 'In memory of the Glorious Dead. From George R.I. and Mary R. – November 11th, 1920.' Further wreaths were placed beside it by the Prince of Wales, the Prime Minister Lloyd George and representatives of the Colonies, the Dominions and the people of France. Once this was over, and the King, princes and members of government had taken their places in the procession, the gun-carriage and coffin 'passed on towards the Abbey, and the saddest, stateliest, most beautiful ceremony that London has ever seen was over'.[4]

At Westminster Abbey a congregation of 1,000 – including a Guard of Honour of 100 holders of the Victoria Cross – watched reverently

Field Marshal Earl Haig (foreground) and eleven other senior servicemen walk beside the coffin of the Unknown Warrior as it is taken from Victoria Station to Westminster Abbey on 11 November 1920.

as the pall-bearers carried the Union Jack-draped coffin in through the West Door and placed it on cross-struts covering an open grave between the first and second arches of the nave. After a brief funeral service that included Beethoven's 'Equale for Trombones', a reading of the Lord's Prayer, and a lesson taken from the Book of Revelation by Bishop Herbert Ryle, the Dean of Westminster, the pall-bearers stepped forward and, having removed the wreath, helmet, side-arm and Union Jack, lowered the coffin into the grave. Finally, as the Dean spoke the words, 'Earth to earth, ashes to ashes, dust to dust', the King used a silver shell to sprinkle earth from France on to the coffin. 'Of all the great ceremonies which Westminster Abbey has been the scene of recent years,' opined *The Times*, 'this was the most beautiful and the most affecting.'[5]

The burial of the Unknown Warrior – an unidentified soldier killed on the Western Front – in Westminster Abbey on 11 November 1920 was the result of a long campaign by a regimental padre, the Reverend David Railton, MC, to provide a symbolic place of mourning for the families and loved ones of the huge number of British and Commonwealth servicemen who had died with no known grave. The idea first came to Railton in early 1916 as he returned to his billet at Erkingham, near Armentières in northern France, and noticed a grave in the garden with a white cross marked 'An Unknown British Soldier', and in brackets underneath 'of the Black Watch'. He wrote later:

> How that grave caused me to think! I love every inch of Scotland. I had served in the earlier days as a private soldier, in the ranks of the Scottish Territorial battalion. How I wondered! How I longed to see his folk! But, who was he, and who were they? From which of the lonely mystic glens of old Scotia did he come? Was he a citizen of 'Auld Reekie'? Was he one of the grand old 'Contemptibles'? Was he just a laddie – newly joined – aged eighteen, the only son of a shepherd from the far away Highlands? There was no answer to these questions.[6]

To another question, however – 'What can I do to ease the pain of father, mother, brother, sister, sweetheart, wife and friend?' – he soon found the solution: 'Let this body – this symbol of him – be carried reverently over the sea to his native land.' And so the idea of the 'Unknown Comrade' was born in Railton's mind, though he decided not to act upon it while the war was still raging because it would have had 'no personal meaning for those whose relatives fell after that date'.[7]

Instead he waited until August 1920 – by which time the 'rush and noise of "Peace" quarrels seemed to be dying down' – to write and ask the Dean of Westminster 'if he would consider the possibility of burying in the Abbey the body of one of our unknown comrades'. The Dean's initial response was cautiously positive, saying the proposal had made 'a strong appeal to me' but that he was not yet in a position to give a final decision. By 19 October he was. 'The idea which you suggested to me in August,' he wrote, 'I have kept steadily in view ever since . . . It has necessitated communications with War Office, Prime Minister and Buckingham Palace. The announcement which the Prime Minister will, or intends to, make this afternoon, will show you how far the Government is ready to cooperate.'[8]

What the Dean did not mention was the King's initial ambivalence. 'For the moment,' wrote his personal secretary, Lord Stamfordham, on 7 October, 'the King is doubtful about the proposal . . . and is inclined to think that nearly two years after the last shot fired on the battlefield of France and Flanders is so long ago that a funeral now might be regarded as belated, and almost, as it were, re-open the war wound, which time is gradually healing.' Yet he also acknowledged the 'force' of the Dean's argument and was prepared to speak to Lloyd George before making up his mind.[9] The result of that conversation, and of a subsequent Cabinet meeting on 15 October, was to 'accept in principle the proposals contained' in the Dean's 'memorandum'.[10]

The chief task, now, was to select a body to represent the 'Unknown Warrior' (a term the Dean preferred to Railton's suggestion of 'Unknown Comrade'). It was given to Brigadier L. J. Wyatt, commanding British troops in France and Flanders and Director of the War Graves Commission, who 'issued instructions that the body of a British soldier, which it would be impossible to identify, should be brought in from each of the four battle areas – the Aisne, the Somme, Arras and Ypres, on the night of November 7, and placed in the chapel of St Pol'. Shortly after midnight, Wyatt selected one of the bodies – mostly bones sealed in a sack – and, with the help of an aide, Colonel Gell, placed it in the shell of a coffin and screwed down the lid. The remaining bodies were reburied in the nearby military cemetery. 'I had no idea,' wrote Wyatt, 'even of the area from which the body I had selected had come; no one else can know it.'[11]

The following day, at noon, the shell was sent under escort to Boulogne where it was placed 'in a plain oak coffin, with wrought iron bands, through one of which was passed a Crusader's sword from the Tower of London collection'. Covering the coffin was 'the famous "Padre's flag" – the bloodstained Union Jack which had belonged to the Reverend Railton and was used by him as an altar cloth and funeral pall during the war'. Guarded overnight in Boulogne Castle by a company of French infantry, the Unknown Warrior was brought across the Channel to Dover during the night of 9/10 November by the destroyer HMS *Verdun* and thence to Victoria by special train. Accompanying it were 'six barrels of earth from the Ypres Salient . . . so that the body should rest in the soil on which so many of our troops gave up their lives'.[12]

On 11 November 1921, a year after the burial in the Abbey, a permanent gravestone of black Belgian marble (from a quarry near Namur) was unveiled. Part of the inscription reads:

BENEATH THIS STONE RESTS THE BODY
OF A BRITISH WARRIOR
UNKNOWN BY NAME OR RANK
BROUGHT FROM FRANCE TO LIE AMONG
THE MOST ILLUSTRIOUS OF THE LAND
. . . THUS ARE COMMEMORATED THE MANY
MULTITUDES WHO DURING THE GREAT
WAR OF 1914–1918 GAVE THE MOST THAT
MAN CAN GIVE LIFE ITSELF
FOR GOD
FOR KING AND COUNTRY
FOR LOVED ONES HOME AND EMPIRE
FOR THE SACRED CAUSE OF JUSTICE AND
THE FREEDOM OF THE WORLD
THEY BURIED HIM AMONG THE KINGS BECAUSE HE
HAD DONE GOOD TOWARD GOD AND TOWARD
HIS HOUSE[13]

Railton explained the symbolic significance of the Unknown Warrior's Tomb as follows:

473

Those whose loved ones were amongst the 'unknown' know that in this Tomb there may be – there is – resting the body of their beloved. They know also that he is not there himself, though he may often be near . . . No one knows the 'Unknown Warrior's' rank, his wealth, his education, or his history . . . He may have been wealthy, or one whose home was in a slum. He may have been a Public School boy, or a gypsy. Many people have not yet grasped the fact that he may have come from any part of the British Isles, or from the Dominions and the Colonies. And there are still a good few who do not realize he may have been a sailor [or a clergyman] . . . Our Children must be taught most carefully that this one Warrior is just a representative of all Britons who fell in the Great War, known or unknown.[14]

Casualty figures are always contentious, but the most authoritative recent survey by the historians John Ellis and Michael Cox gives the total number of British Empire military fatalities during the First World War at just over 900,000: 702,000 from the British Isles, and the rest from India and the Dominions (among them 62,000 Indians, 59,000 Canadians, 54,000 Australians and 17,000 New Zealanders). A further 2,088,000 were wounded (including 1.66 million Britons).[15] Of those killed, under two-thirds – 588,000 – were buried in named graves. The rest were either buried but not identifiable by name, or not buried at all.[16]

Of all the combatants, Germany suffered the most military deaths: just over 2 million, with a further 5.67 million wounded. Next, in descending order, were Russia (1.8 million killed and 4.95 million wounded), France (1.39 million and 4.32 million), Austria-Hungary (1.02 million and 1.94 million), Italy (462,000 and 955,000), the Ottoman Empire (236,000 and 770,000), Serbia (127,000 and 133,000), Romania (220,000 and 120,000), Bulgaria (77,000 and 152,000), the United States (52,000 and 230,000) and Belgium (38,000 and 45,000). Allied military fatalities were, at around 5 million, about 50 per cent more than the 3.4 million suffered by the Central Powers. In all about 8.4 million servicemen lost their lives (the vast majority in combat), and a further 7 million civilians (just under a million to direct military action and the rest to sickness and starvation). It was the first war in which the total number of deaths in combat was greater than those soldiers lost to disease and illness; and the first to take an exceptionally heavy toll of non-combatants.[17]

It was a war, moreover, with huge geopolitical consequences: it caused the break-up of the German, Russian, Austro-Hungarian and Turkish Empires; it triggered the Russian Revolution that gave birth to the Soviet Union; it forced a reluctant United States on to the world stage; it laid the seeds of conflict in the Middle East by its wholly arbitrary creation of Iraq and, eventually, of Israel; and its harsh Versailles peace settlement was a significant cause of the economic and political turmoil in Germany in the 1920s and 1930s that made possible the rise of Hitler and the Nazis. 'In short,' wrote Hew Strachan, 'it shaped not just Europe but the world in the twentieth century.'[18]

ACKNOWLEDGEMENTS

This book's genesis was a curious affair. At a lunch to celebrate a quite separate literary project, I was asked by my publisher Rupert Lancaster if I'd ever thought of writing about the Great War. Only for about 35 years, I was tempted to answer, since I'd first read Martin Middlebrook's wonderful oral history of the First Day of the Somme. Instead I just said yes, and mumbled something about an idea for TV (which, inevitably, was never made) that would tell the story of the crucial 30 days from the Sarajevo assassinations to the outbreak of war between Austria-Hungary and Serbia (the point at which a general conflict was all but certain). I love it, said Rupert.

What he actually loved, as I soon discovered, was the plan to break history down into individual days. For him, though, the outbreak was only part of the story. He wanted me to cover the whole war from the perspective of all the belligerents: not only those who fought for each side – on the ground, in the air and at sea – but also those who played a vital role on the home front. I agreed and the result is, I hope, a wonderfully eclectic cast of characters that includes emperors, politicians, generals, volunteer soldiers, journalists, suffragettes, munitions workers, nurses, conscientious objectors, mutineers, spies, secret agents, revolutionaries, freedom fighters and patriots – many of whom were prepared to, and did, lay down their lives for their country and their principles.

The fatalities included two of my great uncles, both volunteers keen to do their bit. I'd heard about their sacrifice as a boy, but knew nothing of the details. It was particularly moving, therefore, to read of the death of one of them in a cache of letters written by officers and soldiers who had served with him. The letters had been transcribed by my grandmother and inherited by my father. When I visited my father's house to collect them, he could not remember where they were. But it eventually came to him in the middle of the night and, having recovered them, he left them on my bed. Thus was I able to piece together the last dramatic moments of a young dentist whose soldiers would have, in the words of one, 'followed him anywhere'.

Of the many people who contributed to the book, special thanks are due to the following: Rupert Lancaster and my agent Peter Robinson for cooking up the idea in the first place; Rupert's excellent team at Hodder, including Kate Miles, Juliet Brightmore, Bea Long, Nikki Barrow, Vickie Boff and Peter James; my father Robin David; Bruce Markham-David; my research assistant Holly Harwood; Billy James (for letting me quote from the unpublished memoir of Archibald James); the historian Leanda de Lisle (for the loan of her grandfather Kenelm Dormer's Great War diary); and the staffs of the British Library, London Library, National Archives, National Army Museum, Imperial War Museum, Royal Artillery Museum (Firepower!), Tank Museum and Westminster Abbey Library.

I saw it as a particularly good sign that my wife Louise was not just duty bound but keen to read the manuscript. She later admitted to passing over some of the grimmer descriptions of battle (of which, inevitably, there are many), but enjoyed the less martial entries on the Christmas Truce, the peace movement, conscientious objectors, Mata Hari, the Balfour Declaration, women's suffrage and the grim fate of the Romanov family. So something for everyone, I hope.

Lastly, I should apologize to my dedicatee (and youngest daughter) Natasha. She was promised a novel (like her sisters) but got a book about the most lethal war in our island's history. That's life.

PICTURE ACKNOWLEDGEMENTS

© akg-images: 43/Interfoto, 75, 99/Ullstein Bild, 200/Interfoto, 225/Interfoto, 231/Interfoto, 252/Ullstein Bild, 275, 284 right, 304/Ullstein Bild, 311, 329, 340, 366, 403, 407, 421/Interfoto, 438. Author's Collection: 3, 27. © Corbis: 398/David J & Janice L Frent Collection. © Corbis/Bettmann: 62, 344, 466. © Mary Evans Picture Library: 154/Collection Gregoire, 191/Marx Memorial Library, 213/Tal/Epic, 217/IWM/Robert Hunt Library. © Getty Images: 32, 47, 72, 83, 113, 124/Fairfax Media, 128/Time & Life Pictures, 136, 144/UIG, 257, 318, 336, 350, 353, 470. © Imperial War Museums: 2-3 (prelims), 20-21, 90-91, 184-185, 290-291, 388-389/IWM ART 4485 (detail), 38/ IWM Q70071, 65/IWM Q56325, 81/IWM Q50992, 85/IWM HU35801, 108/IWM Q13682, 162/IWM Q52304, 167/IWM Q32930, 173/IWM HU94153, 177/IWM Q13708, 246/IWM Q744, 268/IWM Q5572, 280/IWM Q001540, 284 left/IWM Q61077, 377/IWM CO2202, 384/IWM Q13213B, 432/IWM Q30016, 443/IWM Q69484, 454/IWM Q9344. © Mirrorpix: 140.

BIBLIOGRAPHY

All sources published in London unless otherwise indicated.

Primary Sources, Unpublished
Official Documents

The National Archives, London (TNA)
Foreign Office (FO):
        Prisoner of War and Aliens Department: General Correspondence, FO 383

Ministry of Munitions (MUN):
        Historical Record Branch, MUN 5

Security Service (KV):
        Personal Files, KV 2

War Office (WO):
        Capital Courts Martial Papers, WO 71
        Distinguished Service Order Register, WO 390
        Regimental War Diaries, WO 95 and 167

Private Papers

Family Papers (FP)
David Papers
Dormer Papers
James Papers
Neely Papers

Royal Artillery Museum, Woolwich
Typescript Account by Sergeant William Groves, RFA

Tank Museum, Bovington
William Dawson, 'Reminiscences of my experiences in the first tank, 1916–18'
Colonel N. M. Dillon, 'Record of Service'

Westminster Abbey Library
Unknown Warrior Papers

Primary Sources, Published

Published Documents, Diaries, Letters and Memoirs

America: Great Crises in our History (12 vols, 1925; this ebook edition 2011)
Asquith, H. H., *Memories and Reflections, 1852–1927* (2 vols, 1928)
Bean, Charles, *Gallipoli Mission* (1948; this edition 1990)
Bloem, Walter, *The Advance from Mons 1914: The Experiences of a German Infantry Officer* (1916; this edition 1930)
Boulton (ed.), James T., *The Selected Letters of D. H. Lawrence* (Cambridge, 2000)
Brittain, Vera, *Testament of Youth: An Autobiographical Study of the Years 1900–1925* (1933; this edition 2009)
Brusilov, A. A., *A Soldier's Note-Book: 1914–1918* (1930)
Cowen, Ruth (ed.), *A Nurse at the Front: The First World War Diaries of Sister Edith Appleton* (2012)
David, Saul (ed.), *Mud and Bodies: The War Diaries and Letters of Captain N. A. C. Weir, 1914–1920* (2013)
Downham, Peter (ed.), *Diary of an Old Contemptible: Private Edward Roe, East Lancashire Regiment: From Mons to Baghdad 1914–1919* (2004)
Dunn, Captain J. C., *The War the Infantry Knew 1914–1919* (1938; this edition 1989)
Durnford, H. G., *The Tunnellers of Holzminden* (Cambridge, 1920)
Emden, Richard van, and Humphries, Steve, *All Quiet on the Home Front: An Oral History of Life in Britain during the First World War* (2003; this edition 2004)
Farmborough, Florence, *Nurse at the Russian Front: A Diary 1914–1918* (1974)
Fokker, Anthony, *Flying Dutchman* (1931)
Haig Diaries and Letters: Gary Sheffield and John Bourne (eds), *Douglas Haig: War Diaries and Letters 1914–1918* (2005)
Hitler, Adolf, *Mein Kampf* (2 vols, Jaico edition, 2012)
Horne, Charles F. (ed.), *Source Records of the Great War* (7 vols, New York, 1923)
Jünger, Ernst, *Storm of Steel* (1920; this edition 2004)

Lawrence, T. E., *Seven Pillars of Wisdom: A Triumph* (1926; this edition 2000)

Ludendorff, General Erich, *My War Memories: 1914–1918* (2 vols, 1919)

Levine, Joshua, *Forgotten Voices of the Somme* (2008; this edition 2009)

MacArthur, Brian (ed.), *For King and Country: Voices from the First World War* (2008)

Melotte, Edward (ed.), *Mons, Anzac and Kut: By An MP – Lieutenant-Colonel the Hon. Aubrey Herbert MP* (Barnsley, 2009)

Norwich, John Julius (ed.), *The Duff Cooper Diaries: 1915–1951* (2005)

Nowlan, K. B. (ed.), *The Making of 1916* (Dublin, 1916)

Pankhurst, Christabel, *Unshackled: The Story of How We Won the Vote* (1959; this edition 1987)

Peel, C. S., *How We Lived Then 1914–1918: A Sketch of Social and Domestic Life in England during the War* (1929)

Philips Price, M., *War and Revolution in Asiatic Russia* (1918)

Reed, John, *Ten Days That Shook the World* (1919; this edition 2011)

Richthofen, Manfred von, *The Red Air Fighter* (1918; this edition 1990)

Sulzbach, Herbert, *With the German Guns: Four Years on the Western Front* (1935; this edition 1973)

Thompson, Julian (ed.), *The Imperial War Museum Book of the War at Sea 1914–1918* (2005)

Weizmann, Chaim, *Trial and Error: The Autobiography of Chaim Weizmann, First President of Israel* (1949)

Willcocks, Lieutenant-General James, *With the Indians in France* (1920)

Contemporary Publications

Bean, Charles, *Official History of Australia in the War of 1914–1918* (2 vols, 1939–40)

Churchill, Winston S., *The World Crisis* (6 vols, 1923–35)

J. E. Edmonds, *History of the Great War: Military Operations, France and Belgium 1914* (2 vols, 1922–5)

Official History of the Ministry of Munitions (10 vols, 1922; this edition 2008)

Newspapers and Journals

The Carthusian
Daily Express
London Gazette
Muslim News
The Times

Secondary Sources
Books and Articles

Adams, Jefferson, *Historical Dictionary of German Intelligence* (Plymouth, 2009)

Akçam, Taner, *A Shameful Act: The Armenian Genocide and the Question of Turkish Responsibility* (New York, 2006)

Andrew, Christopher, *The Defence of the Realm: The Authorized History of MI5* (2009; this edition 2010)

Babington, Anthony, *For the Sake of Example: Capital Courts Martial 1914–1920* (1993)

Badsey, Stephen, *Doctrine and Reform in the British Cavalry, 1880–1918* (2008)

Baker, Anne, *From Biplane to Spitfire: The Life of Air Chief Marshal Sir Geoffrey Salmond KCB KCMG DSO* (Barnsley, 2003)

Barker, Ralph, *The Royal Flying Corps in France* (2 vols, 1994–5)

Barr, James, *Setting the Desert on Fire: T. E. Lawrence and Britain's Secret War in Arabia, 1916–18* (2006)

Baumont, Maurice, *Fall of the Kaiser: The Kaiser with his Generals* (1931)

Berghahn, V. R., *Germany and the Approach of War in 1914* (1973)

Best, Geoffrey, *Churchill and War* (2005)

Best, Nicholas, *The Greatest Day in History: How the Great War Really Ended* (2008)

Bishop, Patrick, *Wings: One Hundred Years of Aerial Warfare* (2012)

Boghardt, Thomas, *The Zimmermann Telegram: Intelligence, Diplomacy and America's Entry into World War I* (Annapolis, 2012)

Brendon, Piers, *The Decline and Fall of the British Empire: 1781–1997* (2007)

Brown, Malcolm, and Seaton, Shirley, *Christmas Truce: The Western Front December 1914* (New York, 1984)

Carlyon, L. A., *Gallipoli* (2002)

Castle, H. G., *Fire over England: The German Air Raids in World War I* (1982)

Clark, Christopher, *The Sleepwalkers: How Europe went to War in 1914* (2012)

Clayton, Anthony, *Paths of Glory: The French Army 1914–18* (2003)

Clifford, Colin, *The Asquiths* (2002; this edition 2003)

Collins, James L., *The Marshall Cavendish Illustrated Encyclopaedia of World War One* (25 vols, 1972)

Cook, Andrew, *M: MI5's First Spymaster* (2004)

Corns, Cathryn, and Hughes-Wilson, John, *Blindfold and Alone: British Military Executions in the Great War* (2001)

Corrigan, Gordon, *Sepoys in the Trenches: The Indian Corps on the Western Front* (2006)

David, Charles Markham, *Seventy Years* (privately published, 2011)

David, Saul, *Military Blunders: The How and Why of Military Failure* (1997)

Duffy, Christopher, *Through German Eyes: The British and the Somme 1916* (2006)

Dupuy, Trevor N., and Onacewicz, Wlodzimierz, *Triumphs and Tragedies in the East 1915–1917* (New York, 1967)

Ellis, John, and Cox, Michael, *The World War I Databook: The Essential Facts and Figures for All the Combatants* (2001)

Ellsworth-Jones, Will, *We Will Not Fight: The Untold Story of the World War One's Conscientious Objectors* (2008)

Englund, Peter, *The Beauty and the Sorrow: An Intimate History of the First World War* (2011)

Farrar, Martin J., *News from the Front: War Correspondents on the Western Front 1914–18* (Stroud, 1998)

Ferguson, Niall, *The Pity of War* (1998)

Figes, Orlando, *A People's Tragedy: The Russian Revolution, 1891–1924* (1996; this edition 1997)

Fraser, David, *Knight's Cross: A Life of Field Marshal Erwin Rommel* (1993; this edition 1994)

Fromkin, David, *A Peace to End All Peace: Creating the Modern Middle East 1914–1922* (1989)

—, *Europe's Last Summer: Why the World Went to War in 1914* (2004)

Gilbert, Martin, *First World War* (1994; this edition 1995)

Gill, Douglas, and Dallas, Gloden, 'Mutiny at Etaples Base in 1917', *Past & Present*, no. 69 (Nov. 1975), pp. 88–112.

Griffiths, Paddy, *British Fighting Methods in the Great War* (1998)

Hammond, Bryn, *Cambrai 1917: The Myth of the First Great Tank Battle* (2008)

Hanson, Neil, *Escape from Germany: The Greatest PoW Break-out of the First World War* (2011)

Harrison, Shirley, *Sylvia Pankhurst: The Rebellious Suffragette: A Crusading Life 1882–1960* (2003; this edition 2012)

Hart, Peter, *The Somme* (2005)

—, *Aces Falling: War above the Trenches, 1918* (2007)

—, *1918: A Very British Victory* (2008)

Haslam, M. J., *The Chilwell Story: 1915–1982, VC Factory and Ordnance Depot* (1982)

Hattersley, Roy, *David Lloyd George: The Great Outsider* (2010)

Hayes, Geoffrey, Iarocci, Andrew and Bechthold, Mike (eds), *Vimy Ridge: A Canadian Reassessment* (Waterloo, Ontario, 2007)

Herwig, Holger H., *The First World War, Germany and Austria-Hungary 1914–1918* (1997)

Hochschild, Adam, *To End All Wars* (New York, 2012)

Holmes, Richard, *The Little Field Marshal: A Life of Sir John French* (1981; this edition 2005)

—, *Tommy: The British Soldier on the Western Front 1914–1918* (2004; this edition 2005)

Hopkirk, Peter, *On Secret Service East of Constantinople* (1994; this edition 2006)

Hore, Captain Peter, *The Habit of Victory: The Story of the Royal Navy, 1545–1945* (2005; this edition 2006)

Horne, Alistair, *The Price of Glory* (1962; this edition 1964)

James Smith, David, *One Morning in Sarajevo: 28 June 1914* (2008)

Joll, James, *The Origins of the First World War* (1984)

Jones, Nigel, *Rupert Brooke: Life, Death and Myth* (1999; this edition 2003)

Keay, John, *Sowing the Wind: The Seeds of Conflict in the Middle East* (2003)

Keegan, John, *The First World War* (1998)

Kershaw, Ian, *Hitler: Hubris 1889–1936* (2001)

Kilduff, Peter, *Red Baron: The Life and Death of an Ace* (2007)

Lewis, Bernard, *Emergence of Modern Turkey* (2001)

Lewis, Geoffrey, *Balfour and Weizmann: The Zionist, the Zealot and the Emergence of Israel* (2009)

Lewis, R., *Over the Top with the 25th* (Halifax, 1918)

Lewis-Stempel, John, *Six Weeks: The Short and Gallant Life of the British Officer in the First World War* (2010; this edition 2011)

Low, G., and Everett, H. M., *The History of the Royal Monmouthshire Royal Engineers* (2 vols, 1969)

Macdonald, Lyn, *They Called It Passchendaele: The Story of the Third Battle of Ypres and the Men Who Fought in It* (1978; this edition 1983)

—, *The Roses of No Man's Land* (1980; this edition 1993)

—, *Somme* (1983)

—, *1914* (1987; this edition 1989)

—, *1915: The Death of Innocence* (1993)

—, *To the Last Man: Spring 1918* (1998)

Mackay, Francis, *Asiago Plateau: Battle in the Woods and Clouds – Italy 1918* (2000)

McMeekin, Sean, *The Russian Origins of the First World War* (Cambridge, Mass., 2011)

Marwick, A., *Women at War, 1914–1918* (1977)

Mead, Gary, *The Doughboys: America and the First World War* (2000; this edition 2001)

—, *The Good Soldier: The Biography of Douglas Haig* (2007)

Middlebrook, Martin, *The First Day of the Somme: July 1916* (1971; this edition 1984)
—, *The Kaiser's Battle: 21 March 1918 – The First Day of the German Spring Offensive* (1978; this edition 1983)

Murphy, Lieut.-Colonel C. C. R., *The History of the Suffolk Regiment 1914–1927* (1928)

Paice, Edward, *Tip and Run: The Untold Tragedy of the Great War in Africa* (2007)

Persico, Joseph E., *11th Month, 11th Day, 11th Hour: Armistice Day 1918: World War I and its Violent Climax* (2004; this edition 2005)

Philpott, William, *Bloody Victory: The Sacrifice of the Somme and the Making of the Twentieth Century* (2009)

Preston, Diana, *Wilful Murder: The Sinking of the Lusitania* (2002; this edition 2003)

Purvis, June, *Emmeline Pankhurst: A Biography* (2003)

Railton, Rev. David, 'The Origin of the Unknown Warrior's Grave', *Our Empire*, November 1931, vol. VII.

Rappaport, Helen, *Ekaterinburg: The Last Days of the Romanovs* (2008)
The Register of the Victoria Cross (1997)

Royle, Trevor, *War Report: The War Correspondent's View of Battle* (Edinburgh, 1987)

Russell, Douglas S., *Winston Churchill: Soldier: The Military Life of a Gentleman at War* (2005)

Sebag Montefiore, Simon, *Jerusalem: The Biography* (2011)

Sheffield, Gary, *Forgotten Victory: The First World War – Myths and Realities* (2002)
—, *The Chief: Douglas Haig and the British Army* (2011)

Shipman, Pat, *Femme Fatale: Love, Lies and the Unknown Life of Mata Hari* (2007)

Silkin, John (ed.), *The Penguin Book of First World War Poetry* (1979)

Smith, Leonard V., *Between Mutiny and Obedience: The Case of the Fifth Infantry Division during World War I* (Princeton, 1994)

Souhami, Diana, *Edith Cavell* (2010; this edition 2011)

Stannard Baker, Ray, *Woodrow Wilson: Life and Letters*, vol. VI: *Facing War 1915–1917* (1938)

Stevenson, David, *1914–1918: The History of the First World War* (2004, this edition 2005)
—, *With our Backs to the Wall: Victory and Defeat in 1918* (2011)

Strachan, Hew (ed.), *The Oxford Illustrated History of the First World War* (1998)
—, *The First World War: To Arms* (Oxford, 2001)
—, *The First World War* (2003; this edition 2006)

Sumner, Ian, *They Shall Not Pass: The French Army on the Western Front 1914–1918* (Barnsley, 2012)

Taylor, A. J. P., *The First World War: An Illustrated History* (1963; this edition 1985)

Terraine, John, *Mons: The Retreat to Victory* (1960)

—, *Douglas Haig: The Educated Soldier* (1963)

—, *The First World War* (1965)

—, *To Win A War: 1918, the Year of Victory* (1978)

Threlfall, T. R., *The Story of the King's* (1916)

Townshend, Charles, *Easter 1916: The Irish Rebellion* (2005)

—, *When God Made Hell: The British Invasion of Mesopotamia and the Creation of Iraq 1914–1921* (2011, ebook edition)

Travers, Tim, *The Killing Ground: The British Army, the Western Front and the Emergence of Modern War, 1900–1918* (1987)

Tuchman, Barbara W., *The Zimmermann Telegram* (1958; this edition 1966)

—, *The Guns of August* (1962)

'The Unknown Warrior', *After the Battle*, No. 6, 1974

VC GC (3 vols, 2013)

Warner, Philip, *The Battle of Loos* (1976)

Weber, Thomas, *Hitler's First War: Adolf Hitler, the Men of the List Regiment, and the First World War* (2010)

Williams, Charles, *Pétain* (2005)

Woodward, David R., *Hell in the Holy Land: World War I in the Middle East* (Lexington, 2006)

Wylly, H. C., *The Loyal North Lancashire Regiment*, vol. II: *1914–1919* (1933)

TV Documentaries

'Wartime Factory Disaster', *Inside Out*, BBC East Midlands, 10 February 2003

Websites

www.1914-1918.net
www.eyewitnesstohistory.com
www.history.com
www.revdc.net
www.shotatdawn.infos
www.uboat.net.wwi
www.victoriacross.org.uk
www.westminster-abbey.org

NOTES

INTRODUCTION

1. Adolf Hitler, *Mein Kampf* (2 vols, Jaico edition, 2012), I, pp. 97–8.
2. Ibid., pp. 99–100.
3. David Stevenson, *1914–1918: The History of the First World War* (2004, this edition 2005), p. 11.
4. Despatch from the German Ambassador in London, 24 July 1914, in *America: Great Crises in our History*, vol. XI: *The Great War 1914–1916* (1925; this ebook edition 2011), p. 261.
5. Stevenson, *1914–1918*, p. 11.
6. Christopher Clark, *The Sleepwalkers: How Europe went to War in 1914* (2012), p. 469.
7. Ibid., pp. 11–12.
8. Ibid., p. 12.
9. Annexe Memoire by Leopold von Berchtold, 2 July 1914, in *America*, XI, p. 201.
10. Letter from the Emperor Franz Joseph to Kaiser Wilhelm II, 2 July 1914, in ibid., p. 145.
11. Stevenson, *1914–1918*, p. 16.
12. Ibid.
13. Ibid., p. 17.
14. Ibid., p. 24.
15. *America*, XI, p. 392.
16. Clark, *The Sleepwalkers*, p. 507.
17. Hew Strachan, *The First World War: To Arms* (Oxford, 2001), p. 83.
18. Ibid., pp. 83–4.
19. Ibid., p. 84.
20. Clark, *The Sleepwalkers*, p. 511.
21. Ibid., pp. 510–11.
22. *America*, XI, p. 401.
23. Clark, *The Sleepwalkers*, p. 512.
24. Quoted in *America*, XI, p. 410.
25. Ibid., p. 431.
26. Clark, *The Sleepwalkers*, pp. 513–14.
27. Ibid., p. 509.
28. Stevenson, *1914–1918*, p. 28.
29. Strachan, *The First World War: To Arms*, p. 91.
30. See V. R. Berghahn, *Germany and the Approach of War in 1914* (1973); James Joll, *The Origins of the First World War* (1984); and David Fromkin, *Europe's Last Summer: Why the World Went to War in 1914* (2004).
31. See, respectively, Samuel R. Williamson Jr, 'The Origins of the War', in Hew Strachan (ed.), *The Oxford Illustrated History of the First World War* (1998); and Sean McMeekin's *The Russian Origins of the First World War* (Cambridge, Mass., 2011).

32. Clark, *The Sleepwalkers*, pp. 561–2.
33. Thomas Weber, *Hitler's First War: Adolf Hitler, the Men of the List Regiment, and the First World War* (2010), p. 16.
34. Hitler, *Mein Kampf*, pp. 98–9.
35. Ibid., p. 100.

PROLOGUE
'Sophie, Sophie, don't die, stay alive for our children!'

1. David James Smith, *One Morning in Sarajevo: 28 June 1914* (2008), p. 168.
2. Ibid., pp. 168–9.
3. Ibid., pp. 169–83.
4. Ibid., p. 71.
5. Stevenson, *1914–1918*, p. 10.
6. Clark, *The Sleepwalkers*, p. 374.
7. James Smith, *One Morning in Sarajevo*, pp. 187–90. Because of their youth, Princip and Čabrinović were given the maximum sentence possible, twenty years, while most of their older co-conspirators were executed. Princip died in prison in April 1918 from tuberculosis.
8. Quoted in Clark, *The Sleepwalkers*, p. 375.
9. Ibid., pp. 375–6.

PART ONE: 1914

4 August 1914: *'Just for a scrap of paper'* – Britain declares war

1. 'The "Scrap of Paper"', Sir Edward Goschen's Official Report, in *America*, XI, p. 841.
2. Ibid.
3. Ibid.
4. Ibid., p. 858.
5. Despatch from the German ambassador in London, 29 July 1914, in *America*, XI, p. 289.
6. Clark, *The Sleepwalkers*, p. 497.
7. Despatch from the German ambassador in London, 1 August 1914, in *America*, XI, p. 326.
8. Clark, *The Sleepwalkers*, p. 531.
9. Ibid., pp. 532–3.
10. Ibid., p. 535.
11. Speech by Sir Edward Grey to the House of Commons, 3 August 1914, in *America*, XI, p. 987.
12. Ibid.
13. Stevenson, *1914–1918*, p. 33.
14. Strachan, *The First World War: To Arms*, p. 95.

6 August 1914: *'Have they all gone to the war?'* – The Cabinet agrees to send the BEF to France

1. Biography of Hugh Bertram Neely, Neely Papers, FP.
2. *Daily Express*, 20 March 1912.
3. Clive Neely to his mother, Kuala Lumpur, 5 November 1914, Neely Papers, FP.
4. 'Married Woman' to Phyllis Neely, 4 September 1914, ibid.
5. Gary Sheffield and John Bourne (eds), *Douglas Haig: War Diaries and Letters 1914–1918* (2005) (hereafter *Haig Diaries and Letters*), p. 52.

6. Stevenson, *1914–1918*, p. 36.
7. *Haig Diaries and Letters*, p. 54.
8. Richard Holmes, *The Little Field Marshal: A Life of Sir John French* (1981; this edition 2005), p. 198.
9. *Haig Diaries and Letters*, p. 54.
10. Ibid.
11. Ibid., pp. 54–5.
12. Ibid., pp. 55–6.
13. Holmes, *The Little Field Marshal*, p. 198.

8 August 1914: *'Your Country Needs You!'* – Kitchener appeals for volunteers

1. Quoted in William Philpott, *Bloody Victory: The Sacrifice of the Somme and the Making of the Twentieth Century* (2009), p. 39.
2. Ibid., p. 46.
3. Peter Hart, *The Somme* (2005), p. 40.
4. Philpott, *Bloody Victory*, p. 46.
5. Quoted in Hart, *The Somme*, p. 41.
6. Quoted in Vera Brittain, *Testament of Youth: An Autobiographical Study of the Years 1900–1925* (1933; this edition 2009), pp. 102–3.
7. Ibid., pp. 103–4.
8. Ibid., p. 104.
9. Saul David (ed.), *Mud and Bodies: The War Diaries and Letters of Captain N. A. C. Weir, 1914–1920* (2013), p. 10.
10. 'Peace' (the second of the war sonnets), in Nigel Jones, *Rupert Brooke: Life, Death and Myth* (1999; this edition 2003), p. 391.

23 August 1914: *'Every shot was meant'* – The Battle of Mons

1. Corporal W. Holbrook, quoted in Lyn Macdonald, *1914* (1987; this edition 1989), p. 99.
2. *The Register of the Victoria Cross* (1997), p. 456.
3. Stevenson, *1914–1918*, p. 53.
4. T. R. Threlfall, *The Story of the King's* (1916), p. 134.
5. Holmes, *The Little Field Marshal*, p. 211.
6. Ibid., p. 217.
7. Stevenson, *1914–1918*, pp. 51–2.
8. Richard Harding Davis's despatch for the *New York Tribune*, in *America*, XI, p. 1597.

29 August 1914: *'The booty is immense'* – The Germans triumph at Tannenberg

1. General Vasily Gurko, in Charles F. Horne (ed.), *Source Records of the Great War* (New York, 1923), II, pp. 188–9.
2. Stevenson, *1914–1918*, p. 64.
3. John Keegan, *The First World War* (1998), p. 155.
4. Ibid., p. 65.
5. Ibid.
6. Strachan, *The First World War: To Arms*, pp. 321–2.
7. Ibid., pp. 325–6.
8. General Paul von Hindenburg, in Horne (ed.), *Source Records of the Great War*, II, p. 182.
9. General Vasily Gurko, op. cit., p. 188.

10. General Paul von Hindenburg, op. cit., p. 185.
11. Ibid.

30 August 1914: *'I have seen the broken bits of many regiments'* – The Amiens Despatch

1. Quoted in Martin J. Farrar, *News from the Front: War Correspondents on the Western Front 1914–18* (Stroud, 1998), p. 19.
2. *Sunday Times*, 30 August 1914.
3. Farrar, *News from the Front*, pp. 4–9.
4. Ibid., pp. 21–2.
5. Ibid., pp. 23–4.
6. Ibid., p. 24.

5 September 1914: *'All that men can do our fellows will do'* – Sir John French commits the BEF to the offensive

1. Strachan, *The First World War: To Arms*, p. 252.
2. Holmes, *The Little Field Marshal*, pp. 238–9.
3. Ibid., p. 239.
4. Ibid., pp. 229–30.
5. Strachan, *The First World War: To Arms*, p. 243.
6. Stevenson, *1914–1918*, p. 58.
7. Ibid., p. 59.
8. *Haig Diaries and Letters*, pp. 70–1.
9. Holmes, *The Little Field Marshal*, p. 240.
10. *America*, XI, p. 2189.

8 September 1914: *'All I have . . . I leave to Miss Mary MacNulty'* – Shot at dawn

1. Private T. Highgate, Capital Courts Martial Papers, The National Archives TNA, WO 71/387.
2. Walter Bloem, *The Advance from Mons 1914: The Experiences of a German Infantry Officer* (1916; this edition 1930), p. 63.
3. Corporal Bernard Denore, 1st Royal Berkshires, quoted in Brian MacArthur (ed.), *For King and Country: Voices from the First World War* (2008), pp. 20–2.
4. Macdonald, *1914*, pp. 197–200.
5. Anthony Babington, *For the Sake of Example: Capital Courts Martial 1914–1920* (1993), pp. 6–7.
6. Cathryn Corns and John Hughes-Wilson, *Blindfold and Alone: British Military Executions in the Great War* (2001), p. 111.
7. Ibid.
8. Private T. Highgate, Capital Courts Martial Papers, TNA, WO 71/387.
9. Ibid.
10. Ibid.
11. Ibid.
12. Ibid.
13. Ibid.
14. Babington, *For the Sake of Example*, p. 6.
15. Corns and Hughes-Wilson, *Blindfold and Alone*, pp. 103–4.
16. Private T. Highgate, Capital Court Martial Papers, TNA, WO 71/387.

22 September 1914: '*We were woken by a terrific crash*' – First blood to the U-boats

1. 'The First Submarine Blow is Struck' by Lieutenant Otto Weddigen, in *America*, XI, p. 2319.
2. www.uboat.net.wwi.
3. 'The First Submarine Blow is Struck' by Lieutenant Otto Weddigen, op. cit.
4. Quoted in Julian Thompson (ed.), *The Imperial War Museum Book of the War at Sea 1914–1918* (2005), p. 74.
5. Ibid., p. 75.
6. Ibid., p. 74.
7. Ibid., p. 75.
8. Ibid., pp. 74–6.
9. 'The First Submarine Blow is Struck' by Lieutenant Otto Weddigen, op. cit.
10. Thompson (ed.), *The War at Sea 1914–1918*, p. 76.

6 October 1914: '*Spy mania everywhere*' – The Fall of Antwerp

1. Lyn Macdonald, *The Roses of No Man's Land* (1980; this edition 1993), p. 40.
2. Winston S. Churchill, *The World Crisis*, vol. I: *1911–1914* (1923), p. 332.
3. Douglas S. Russell, *Winston Churchill: Soldier: The Military Life of a Gentleman at War* (2005), pp. 350–1.
4. Holmes, *The Little Field Marshal*, p. 243.

5. Quoted in Russell, *Winston Churchill*, p. 351.
6. Ibid., p. 352.
7. Ibid., p. 351.
8. Letter from Brooke to Leonard Bacon, in Jones, *Rupert Brooke*, p. 385.
9. Macdonald, *The Roses of No Man's Land*, p. 41.
10. Macdonald, *1914*, pp. 338–9; Russell, *Winston Churchill*, p. 352.
11. Russell, *Winston Churchill*, p. 352.
12. Ibid., p. 353.
13. Churchill, *The World Crisis*, I, p. 364.

25 October 1914: '*He was dragged off the field*' – The Indian Corps to the rescue

1 Quoted in the *Muslim News*, Issue 246, Friday 30 October 2009.
2 Keegan, *The First World War*, p. 143.
3 Gordon Corrigan, *Sepoys in the Trenches: The Indian Corps on the Western Front* (2006), p. 74.
4 Fourth Supplement to the *London Gazette* of 4 December 1914 (7 December 1914, Number 28999, p. 10425).
5 Entry 694, Sepoy Khudadad Khan, *VC GC* (2013), II.
6 Lieutenant-General James Willcocks, *With the Indians in France* (1920), p. 35.
7 Piers Brendon, *The Decline and Fall of the British Empire: 1781–1997* (2007), pp. 256–8.
8 Ibid., p. 253.

31 October 1914: *'The Worcesters saved the Empire'* – First Battle of Ypres

1. Holmes, *The Little Field Marshal*, p. 251.
2. Ibid.
3. Macdonald, *1914*, p. 393.
4. Ibid.
5. Holmes, *The Little Field Marshal*, p. 251.
6. Quoted in Macdonald, *1914*, p. 391.
7. Stevenson, *1914–1918*, pp. 76–7.
8. Weber, *Hitler's First War*, p. 48.
9. Ian Kershaw, *Hitler: Hubris 1889–1936* (2001), pp. 91–2.

4 November 1914: *'The action of a lunatic'* – Lettow-Vorbeck repulses the British at Tanga

1. Edward Paice, *Tip and Run: The Untold Tragedy of the Great War in Africa* (2007), p. 51.
2. Ibid., pp. 52–4.
3. Ibid., p. 55.
4. Ibid., p. 58.
5. Ibid., p. 40.
6. Ibid., p. 388.

6 November 1914: *'May my life be honoured'* – The shooting of a spy

1. Christopher Andrew, *The Defence of the Realm: The Authorized History of MI5* (2009; this edition 2010), p. 65.
2. Ibid., p. 64.
3. Andrew Cook, *M: MI5's First Spymaster* (2004), p. 229.
4. Carl Hans Lody, Capital Courts Martial Papers, TNA, WO 71/1236 (1914).
5. Andrew, *The Defence of the Realm*, pp. 64–5.
6. Ibid., p. 65.
7. Ibid.
8. Lody, Capital Courts Martial Papers, op. cit.
9. Cook, *M*, p. 230.
10. Defence of the Realm Consolidation Act 1914, TNA, MUN 5/19/221/8 (November 1914).
11. Ibid.
12. Adam Hochschild, *To End All Wars* (New York, 2012), p. 155.

9 November 1914: *'The result . . . was never in doubt'* – The sinking of the *Emden*

1. Captain John C. T. Glossop, 'How the German Raider was Destroyed', in *America*, XI, p. 1458.
2. Clive Neely to his mother, Kuala Lumpur, 5 November 1914, Neely Papers, FP.
3. Lieutenant Hellmuth von Mücke, 'The Cruise and Destruction of the "Emden"', in *America*, XI, p. 1425.
4. Glossop, 'How the German Raider was Destroyed', op. cit.
5. Mücke, 'The Cruise and Destruction of the "Emden"', op. cit.
6. Glossop, 'How the German Raider was Destroyed', op. cit.
7. Keegan, *The First World War*, p. 232.

11 November 1914: *'Not a very pleasant bivouac'* – A sapper goes to war

1. 11–12 November 1914, War Diary, No. 2 (Railway) Company, RMRE, TNA, WO 95 4152.
2. 14 November 1914, ibid.
3. 14–17 November 1914, ibid.
4. 18 November 1914, ibid.
5. 7–12 December 1914, ibid.
6. Letter from Second Lieutenant Hugh Neely to his sister Phyllis Neely, December 1914, Neely Papers, FP.
7. Ibid.

8 December 1914: *'Revenge is sweet'* – The Battle of the Falklands

1. Letter from Midshipman McEwan to his mother, in Thompson (ed.), *The War at Sea 1914–1918*, p. 114.
2. Lieutenant Giffard, in Captain Peter Hore, *The Habit of Victory: The Story of the Royal Navy, 1545–1945* (2005; this edition 2006), p. 298.
3. Assistant Paymaster Duckworth, in Thompson (ed.), *The War at Sea 1914–1918*, p. 119.
4. Lieutenant Hammill, in ibid., p. 120.
5. 'The Battle of the Falklands', Vice Admiral Sturdee's Official Report, in *America*, XI, p. 2636.
6. Lieutenant Giffard, in Hore, *The Habit of Victory*, p. 299.
7. Ibid., pp. 299–300.
8. Torpedoman Pratt, in Thompson (ed.), *The War at Sea 1914–1918*, p. 129.

9. Strachan, *The First World War*, I, pp. 478–9.

16 December 1914: *'"Run!" came the order – and we ran'* – German battle cruisers shell Scarborough

1. Quoted in Martin Gilbert, *First World War* (1994; this edition 1995), p. 110.
2. Ibid.
3. Strachan, *The First World War*, I, pp. 428–9.
4. Ibid., p. 430.
5. Ibid.

24 December 1914: *'We marked the goal with our caps'* – The Christmas Truce

1. Quoted in Malcolm Brown and Shirley Seaton, *Christmas Truce: The Western Front December 1914* (New York, 1984), pp. 70–1.
2. Ibid., p. 70.
3. Ibid., p. 130.
4. Ibid., pp. 131–2.
5. Ibid., p. 133.
6. Ibid., p. 134.
7. Quoted in Hochschild, *To End All Wars*, p. 131.
8. Sergeant Barker to his brother, in *The Times*, 24 December 2012.
9. Brown and Seaton, *Christmas Truce*, pp. 39–40.
10. Ibid., p. 112.
11. Ibid., p. 165.
12. Ibid., p. 166.
13. Quoted in Hochschild, *To End All Wars*, p. 132.

14. 25 December 1914, War Diary, No. 2 (Railway) Company, RMRE, TNA, WO 95 4152.
15. David (ed.), *Mud and Bodies*, p. 15.
16. Brittain, *Testament of Youth*, p. 112.
17. Ibid., pp. 114–16.

PART TWO: 1915

1. Quoted in Gilbert, *First World War*, p. 105.
2. Ibid., p. 108.
3. Ibid., p. 121.

24 January 1915: '*A magnificent but dreadful sight*' – The Battle of Dogger Bank

1. Paymaster Miller, in Thompson (ed.), *The War at Sea 1914–1918*, p. 92.
2. Boy Seaman Hayward, in ibid., p. 94.
3. 'By a Survivor from the "Blucher"', in *America*, XI, p. 2871.
4. Captain Chatfield, in Thompson (ed.), *The War at Sea 1914–1918*, p. 95.
5. Ibid., p. 96.
6. Surgeon Lieutenant Carey of HMS *Southampton*, in ibid., p. 97.
7. 'News Account by a Gunner of the "Arethusa"', in *America*, XI, p. 2800.
8. Strachan, *The First World War*, I, p. 436.
9. Ibid., p. 437.

25 February 1915: '*The sound of rifle shots would fill the air*' – The start of the Armenian genocide

1. Taner Akçam, *A Shameful Act: The Armenian Genocide and the Question of Turkish Responsibility* (New York, 2006), p. 144.
2. Quoted in ibid.
3. Ibid., p. 148.
4. Ibid., pp. 2–3.
5. Ibid., p. 142.
6. Ibid., p. 101.
7. Bernard Lewis, *Emergence of Modern Turkey* (2001), p. 356.
8. Akçam, *A Shameful Act*, p. 142.
9. Ibid., p. 143.

4 March 1915: '*Just off to see the Germans*' – Second Lieutenant Hugh Neely leaves for France

1. Telegram from Hugh Neely to Phyllis Neely, 4 March 1915, Neely Papers, FP.
2. Telegram from Hugh Neely to Jack Neely, ibid.
3. Letter from Hugh Neely to his mother, Felixstowe, undated [early February 1915], ibid.
4. Ibid.
5. Hugh Neely to Clive Neely, Felixstowe, undated [early February 1915], ibid.
6. Letter from Hugh Neely to Phyllis Neely, Felixstowe, 16 February 1915, ibid.
7. Letter from Hugh Neely to his parents, 4 March 1915, ibid.

8. Biography of Hugh Bertram Neely, ibid.

9. Lieut.-Colonel C. C. R. Murphy, *The History of the Suffolk Regiment 1914–1927* (1928), pp. 52–3.

10. Ibid., pp. 53–5.

11. G. Low and H. M. Everett, *The History of the Royal Monmouthshire Royal Engineers (Militia)*, vol. II: *1908–1967* (1969), p. 20.

12. 11–12 March 1915, War Diary, No. 2 (Railway) Company, RMRE, TNA, WO 95 4152.

10 March 1915: *'It was hell let loose'* – The Battle of Neuve Chapelle

1. Quoted in Lyn Macdonald, *1915: The Death of Innocence* (1993), pp. 93–4.

2. Trumpeter Jimmy Naylor, quoted in ibid., pp. 95–6.

3. Ibid., p. 96.

4. Holmes, *The Little Field Marshal*, p. 273.

5. Colonel Pritchard, in Macdonald, *1915*, p. 123.

6. Gary Sheffield, *The Chief: Douglas Haig and the British Army* (2011), p. 109.

7. Ibid.

18 March 1915: *'The day had gone against us'* – Churchill's attempt to force the Dardanelles

1. Churchill, *The World Crisis*, II, pp. 222–3.

2. Quoted in Geoffrey Best, *Churchill and War* (2005), pp. 57–8.

3. Quoted in Gilbert, *First World War*, pp. 124–5.

4. Quoted in L. A. Carlyon, *Gallipoli* (2002), p. 68.

5. Quoted in Thompson (ed.), *The War at Sea 1914–1918*, p. 228.

6. Ibid.

7. Commander Acheson, in ibid., p. 229.

8. Midshipman Field, in ibid.

9. Ibid., p. 230.

10. Carlyon, *Gallipoli*, p. 71.

11. Ibid., p. 72.

12. Thompson (ed.), *The War at Sea 1914–1918*, p. 232.

13. Jones, *Rupert Brooke*, p. 415.

1 April 1915: *'Like shooting a sitting rabbit'* – Birth of the fighter plane

1. 'Unpublished Memoir of Sir Archibald James MP, 3rd Hussars, RFC and RAF', James Papers, FP.

2. Ralph Barker, *The Royal Flying Corps in France*, vol. I: *From Mons to the Somme* (1994), pp. 104–5.

3. Quoted in www.history.com/ this-day-in-history/germans-shoot-down-french-pilot-garros.

4. Anthony Fokker, *Flying Dutchman* (1931), pp. 143–4.

5. Ibid., p. 145.

24 April 1915: *'We would have followed him anywhere'* – The Second Battle of Ypres

1. Murphy, *The History of the Suffolk Regiment*, p. 66.

2. Ibid.

3. Hugh Neely's Pay Book, Neely Papers, FP.

4. Letter from Private W. Foreman to Mrs C. Neely, 27 June 1915, ibid.

5. Letter from Captain B. D. Rushbrooke to Mrs C. Neely, 10 May 1915, ibid.

6. Letter from Sergeant W. Pegg to Mrs C. Neely, 23 May 1915, ibid.

7. Ibid.

8. Letter from Lieut.-Col. D. W. McPherson, OC No. 2 Canadian Field Ambulance, to DMS Canadian Expeditionary Force, London, 22 May 1915, ibid.

9. Ruth Cowen (ed.), *A Nurse at the Front: The First World War Diaries of Sister Edith Appleton* (2012), p. 24.

10. Murphy, *The History of the Suffolk Regiment*, p. 69.

11. John Lewis-Stempel, *Six Weeks: The Short and Gallant Life of the British Officer in the First World War* (2010; this edition 2011), pp. 183–4.

12. Telegram from the War Office to Mr W. Neely, 27 April 1915, Neely Papers, FP.

13. Letter from 2nd Lt. R. A. Pargeler to Mrs C. Neely, 25 April 1915, ibid.

14. Telegram from the King and Queen to Mr W. Neely, 3 May 1915, ibid.

15. Letter from Captain B. D. Rushbrooke, op. cit.

16. Letter from Sergeant W. Pegg, op. cit.

17. Letter from Major C. J. Saunders, 1st Suffolks, to Mrs C. Neely, 4 June 1915, Neely Papers, FP.

18. Letter from Private W. Foreman, op. cit.

19. Letter from Guy Neely to Phyllis Neely, 20 May 1915, Neely Papers, FP.

20. Letter from Jack Neely to Phyllis Neely, 11 March [year unknown], ibid.

25 April 1915: '*No one was in charge*' – Anzac Cove

1. Quoted in Carlyon, *Gallipoli*, p. 151.

2. Ibid., p. 138.

3. Ibid., p. 146.

4. Ibid., pp. 177–8.

5. Gilbert, *First World War*, pp. 137–8.

6. Ibid., p. 151.

28 April 1915: '*With mourning hearts we stand united here*' – The International Congress of Women

1. June Purvis, *Emmeline Pankhurst: A Biography* (2003), p. 274.

2. http://www.history.com/this-day-in-history/international-congress-of-women-opens-at-the-hague.

3. Hochschild, *To End All Wars*, p. 140.

4. Purvis, *Emmeline Pankhurst*, p. 268.

5. Hochschild, *To End All Wars*, p. 106.

6. Purvis, *Emmeline Pankhurst*, p. 270.

7. Hochschild, *To End All Wars*, pp. 106–7.

8. Ibid., p. 107.
9. Purvis, *Emmeline Pankhurst*, p. 270.
10. Ibid., p. 275.

1 May 1915: '*We had to wrench our skirts from their clinging hands*' – The Gorlice–Tarnów offensive

1. Florence Farmborough, *Nurse at the Russian Front: A Diary 1914–1918* (1974), pp. 33–6.
2. Stevenson, *1914–1918*, p. 154.
3. Peter Englund, *The Beauty and the Sorrow: An Intimate History of the First World War* (2011), p. 117.
4. Farmborough, *Nurse at the Russian Front*, p. 36.
5. Ibid.
6. Ibid., pp. 36–7.
7. Stevenson, *1914–1918*, p. 153.
8. Ibid.
9. Gilbert, *First World War*, p. 155.
10. Stevenson, *1914–1918*, p. 155.

7 May 1915: '*By heavens, they've done it*' – The sinking of the *Lusitania*

1. Quoted in Diana Preston, *Wilful Murder: The Sinking of the Lusitania* (2002; this edition 2003), pp. 221–2.
2. Ibid., p. 227.
3. Ibid., p. 80.
4. Ibid., p. 88.
5. Quoted in *America*, XI, p. 3013.
6. Gilbert, *First World War*, p. 157.
7. Ibid.
8. Preston, *Wilful Murder*, p. 198.

9. Ibid., pp. 203–4.
10. Ibid., p. 211.
11. Diary of Lieutenant Schweiger in *America*, XI, p. 3062.
12. Preston, *Wilful Murder*, pp. 340, 377.
13. Quoted in Gilbert, *First World War*, pp. 157–8.
14. Ibid., pp. 158–9.

14 May 1915: '*We had not sufficient high explosive*' – The shell crisis

1. *The Times*, 14 May 1915.
2. Holmes, *The Little Field Marshal*, p. 284.
3. Ibid., p. 285.
4. Ibid.
5. Quoted in Trevor Royle, *War Report: The War Correspondent's View of Battle* (Edinburgh, 1987), p. 100.
6. Stevenson, *1914–1918*, p. 232.
7. Ibid.
8. Holmes, *The Little Field Marshal*, p. 286.
9. Quoted in Farrar, *News from the Front*, pp. 68–9.
10. *The Times*, 14 May 1915, p. 104.
11. Holmes, *The Little Field Marshal*, p. 288.
12. Stevenson, *1914–1918*, p. 233.
13. Royle, *War Report*, p. 110.

31 May 1915: '*Only a few houses will be struck*' – London burning

1. Quoted in Shirley Harrison, *Sylvia Pankhurst: The Rebellious Suffragette: A Crusading Life*

1882–1960 (2003; this edition 2012), p. 242.
2. Ibid.
3. Ibid., p. 256.
4. *The Times*, 2 June 1915.
5. *Official History of the Ministry of Munitions* (1922; this edition 2008), vol. X, Part 6, pp. 24–5.
6. Official Report by Flight Sub-Lieutenant Reginald Wharfeford, 8 June 1915, in http://www.victoriacross.org.uk/bbwarnef.htm.
7. Ibid.
8. Hochschild, *To End All Wars*, p. 153.
9. Lawrence to Lady Ottoline Morrell, in James T. Boulton (ed.), *The Selected Letters of D. H. Lawrence* (Cambridge, 2000), p. 106.

7 August 1915: *'It was simply murder'* – The Nek

1. Carlyon, *Gallipoli*, pp. 400–1.
2. Ibid., p. 402.
3. Ibid., p. 404.
4. Ibid., pp. 405, 408.
5. Ibid., p. 399.
6. Ibid., p. 406.
7. Ibid.
8. Ibid., p. 407.
9. Ibid.
10. Ibid., pp. 407–8.
11. Charles Bean, 'The Story of Anzac', *Official History of Australia in the War of 1914–1918* (1940), II, p. 633.
12. The 8th Light Horse lost 234 out of 300 men (including 154 killed); the 10th's casualties were 138, including eighty dead. Figures in Carlyon, *Gallipoli*, p. 408.
13. Ibid., p. 410.

8 August 1915: *'Golden opportunities are being lost'* – Suvla Bay

1. Quoted in Macdonald, *1915*, pp. 450–1.
2. Ibid., p. 450.
3. Carlyon, *Gallipoli*, pp. 348–9.
4. Saul David, *Military Blunders: The How and Why of Military Failure* (1997), p. 59.
5. Ibid.
6. Ibid., p. 60.
7. Ibid., pp. 61–2.
8. Ibid., p. 62.
9. Quoted in Carlyon, *Gallipoli*, p. 376.
10. Charles Bean, *Gallipoli Mission* (1948; this edition 1990), p. 220.
11. Colonel H. C. Wylly, *The Loyal North Lancashire Regiment*: vol. II: *1914–1919* (1933), p. 235.

25 September 1915: *'There seemed to be nothing ahead of us'* – The Battle of Loos

1. *Haig Diaries and Letters*, p. 153.
2. Sheffield, *The Chief*, p. 128.
3. *Haig Diaries and Letters*, p. 153.
4. Quoted in Sheffield, *The Chief*, p. 128.
5. Quoted in Macdonald, *1915*, pp. 504–5.
6. 'The Heroine of Loos', 20 November 1939, 1st Black Watch

War Diary, TNA, WO 167/710.
7. Ibid.
8. David (ed.), *Mud and Bodies*, p. 35.
9. *Haig Diaries and Letters*, p. 155.
10. Ibid.
11. Quoted in Sheffield, *The Chief*, p. 128.
12. Ibid., p. 127.
13. David (ed.), *Mud and Bodies*, p. 34.
14. Ibid., p. 38.
15. *Haig Diaries and Letters*, p. 164.
16. Keegan, *The First World War*, p. 218.
17. Philip Warner, *The Battle of Loos* (1976), pp. 1–2.
18. Quoted in Brittain, *Testament of Youth*, p. 151.
19. Ibid., p. 197.

8 October 1915: *'The whole city was in retreat'* – The fall of Belgrade

1. 'The Last Days of Belgrade', *The Carthusian*, December 1915.
2. Ibid.
3. Ibid.
4. Ibid.
5. Ibid.
6. Ibid.
7. Quoted in Gilbert, *First World War*, p. 208.
8. Ibid., p. 209.

12 October 1915: *'She was killed immediately'* – The execution of Edith Cavell

1. The Testimony of Pasteur Le Seur

in www.revdc.net/cavell/leseur.htm.
2. Ibid.
3. Ibid.
4. Diana Souhami, *Edith Cavell* (2010; this edition 2011), p. 255.
5. Ibid., p. 259.
6. Ibid., p. 283.
7. TNA, FO 383/15.
8. Souhami, *Edith Cavell*, pp. 313–15.
9. TNA, FO 383/15.
10. Souhami, *Edith Cavell*, p. 326.
11. Ibid., p. 328.
12. Ibid., pp. 341–2.
13. TNA, FO 383/15.
14. Souhami, *Edith Cavell*, pp. 364–5.
15. Account by Reverend H. Stirling Gahan, in *America*, XI, p. 3337.
16. The Testimony of Pasteur Le Seur, op. cit.
17. Gilbert, *First World War*, p. 203.
18. TNA, FO 383/15.

22 November 1915: *'Trenches filled with dead and dying'* – The Battle of Ctesiphon

1 Charles Townshend, *When God Made Hell: The British Invasion of Mesopotamia and the Creation of Iraq 1914–1921* (2011, ebook edition), pp. 150–2.
2. Stevenson, *1914–1918*, p. 121.
3. Quoted in Townshend, *When God Made Hell*, pp. 119–20.
4. Ibid., p. 135.
5. Ibid.
6. Ibid., p. 136.
7. Ibid.
8. Ibid., pp. 136–7.

9. Ibid., p. 152.
10. Ibid.
11. Ibid., pp. 148, 155.
12. Typescript Account by Sergeant William Groves, RFA, of Ctesiphon and Kut, Royal Artillery Museum, MD3692.
13. Quoted in Townshend, *When God Made Hell*, p. 159.
14. T/s Account by Sergeant Groves, op. cit.
15. Quoted in Townshend, *When God Made Hell*, p. 160.
16. Ibid.
17. T/s Account by Sergeant Groves, op. cit.
18. Quoted in Townshend, *When God Made Hell*, p. 161.
19. T/s Account by Sergeant Groves, op. cit.
20. Quoted in Townshend, *When God Made Hell*, p. 162.
21. Ibid., p. 173.

1 December 1915: *'I am on the move now'* – Reinforcements reach Gallipoli

1. Macdonald, *1915*, p. 581.
2. Wylly, *The Loyal North Lancashire Regiment*, II, p. 236.
3. Clive Neely to his sister Phyllis, 10 November 1915, Neely Papers, FP.
4. Ibid., 19 November 1915.
5. Wylly, *The Loyal North Lancashire Regiment*, II, p. 236.
6. Macdonald, *1915*, p. 566.
7. Carlyon, *Gallipoli*, p. 509.
8. Ibid., p. 510.
9. Ibid., p. 512.

10. Gilbert, *First World War*, p. 213.
11. Wylly, *The Loyal North Lancashire Regiment*, II, pp. 238–9.
12. Peter Downham (ed.), *Diary of an Old Contemptible: Private Edward Roe, East Lancashire Regiment: From Mons to Baghdad 1914–1919* (2004), pp. 130–1.
13. Ibid., p. 131.
14. Ibid.
15. Ibid., p. 133.
16. Figures quoted in Carlyon, *Gallipoli*, pp. 530–1.
17. Diary entry for 11 July 1916 in John Julius Norwich (ed.), *The Duff Cooper Diaries: 1915–1951* (2005), p. 33.
18. Ibid., p. 532.

Boxing Day 1915: *'The message was not from Roland'* – News from France

1. Brittain, *Testament of Youth*, p. 226.
2. Ibid., p. 231.
3. Ibid.
4. Ibid.
5. Ibid., pp. 232–3.
6. Ibid., pp. 235–6.
7. Ibid., p. 236.
8. Ibid., pp. 240–1.
9. Ibid., p. 241.
10. Ibid.
11. Ibid., p. 242.
12. Ibid., pp. 243–4.
13. Ibid., p. 251.
14. Ibid.
15. Ibid., p. 265.

PART THREE: 1916

1. Stevenson, *1914–1918*, p. 162; Gilbert, *First World War*, p. 221.
2. Quoted in Gilbert, *First World War*, p. 221.
3. Quoted in Sheffield, *The Chief*, pp. 131–2.
4. Stevenson, *1914–1918*, p. 162.
5. Ibid., p. 161.
6. Quoted in Sheffield, *The Chief*, p. 160.

26 January 1916: *'War is a game that is played with a smile'* – A Cabinet minister at the front

1. Quoted in Russell, *Winston Churchill*, p. 370.
2. Ibid., p. 358.
3. Ibid., p. 362.
4. Ibid., p. 363.
5. Ibid., p. 364.
6. Ibid., p. 365.
7. David (ed.), *Mud and Bodies*, p. 50.
8. Quoted in Russell, *Winston Churchill*, p. 369.
9. Ibid., p. 370.
10. Ibid., pp. 371, 374.
11. Quoted in Gilbert, *First World War*, p. 225.
12. Quoted in Russell, *Winston Churchill*, p. 374.
13. Ibid., pp. 377–8.

27 January 1916: *'This vital measure'* – Conscription is introduced in Britain
1. 'The Service Act', *The Times*, 31 January 1916.

2. Stevenson, *1914–1918*, pp. 202–3.
3. Ibid., p. 203.
4. 'Text of the Bill', *The Times*, 8 January 1915.
5. 'The Service Act', *The Times*, 31 January 1916.
6. Ibid.
7. Stevenson, *1914–1918*, p. 204.

16 February 1916: *'No other race of human beings . . . could have performed this feat'* – The fall of Erzerum

1. M. Philips Price, *War and Revolution in Asiatic Russia* (1918), p. 74.
2. Peter Hopkirk, *On Secret Service East of Constantinople* (1994; this edition 2006), p. 197.
3. Ibid., pp. 197–8.
4. Philips Price, *War and Revolution*, p. 79.
5. Ibid., pp. 80–1.
6. Ibid., pp. 81–2.
7. Ibid., p. 82.
8. Ibid., p. 167.
9. Ibid., p. 172.
10. Hopkirk, *On Secret Service East of Constantinople*, pp. 201–2.
11. Philips Price, *War and Revolution*, p. 83.
12. Ibid., p. 84.

21 February 1916: *'A tempest growing ever stronger'* – The Germans attack at Verdun

1. Alistair Horne, *The Price of Glory* (1962; this edition 1964), p. 77;

Stevenson, *1914–1918*, p. 163.

2. Quoted in Horne, *The Price of Glory*, p. 78.
3. Ibid., pp. 78–9.
4. Ibid., p. 85.
5. Ibid., p. 83.
6. Ibid., pp. 84–9.
7. Stevenson, *1914–1918*, p. 163.
8. Horne, *The Price of Glory*, p. 105.
9. Quoted in ibid.
10. Ibid., p. 107.
11. Ibid., pp. 110–25.
12. Stevenson, *1914–1918*, p. 164.
13. Charles Williams, *Pétain* (2005), pp. 125–6.
14. Ibid., pp. 129–30.
15. Ibid., pp. 131–2.
16. Quoted in ibid., p. 138.

9 April 1916: *'Men fell by the dozen'* – The Kut relief force attacks at Sannaiyat

1. Downham (ed.), *Diary of an Old Contemptible*, p. 161.
2. General Maude, quoted in Wylly, *The Loyal North Lancashire Regiment*, pp. 242–3.
3. Downham (ed.), *Diary of an Old Contemptible*, p. 153.
4. Ibid., p. 146.
5. Ibid., p. 147.
6. Ibid., p. 148.
7. Ibid., p. 153.
8. Ibid., p. 157.
9. Ibid.
10. Wylly, *The Loyal North Lancashire Regiment*, p. 242.
11. Townshend, *When God Made Hell*, p. 235.
12. Downham (ed.), *Diary of an Old Contemptible*, p. 160.
13. Ibid.
14. General Maude's diary, quoted in Wylly, *The Loyal North Lancashire Regiment*, p. 243.
15. Downham (ed.), *Diary of an Old Contemptible*, p. 162.
16. Ibid., pp. 162–3.
17. General Maude's diary, quoted in Wylly, *The Loyal North Lancashire Regiment*, p. 243.
18. Ibid.
19. Quoted in Townshend, *When God Made Hell*, p. 235.
20. Downham (ed.), *Diary of an Old Contemptible*, pp. 163–4.
21. Ibid., pp. 164–5.
22. Ibid., p. 165.
23. Quoted in Wylly, *The Loyal North Lancashire Regiment*, p. 243.
24. Supplement to the *London Gazette* of 26 September 1916 (26 September 1916, Number 29765, p. 9417).
25. Wylly, *The Loyal North Lancashire Regiment*, p. 243.
26. T/s Account by Sergeant Groves, op. cit.

24 April 1916: *'Women began to shriek and cry'* – The Easter Rising

1. Charles Townshend, *Easter 1916: The Irish Rebellion* (2005), pp. 157–8.
2. Ibid., p. 158.
3. Ibid., pp. 158–9.
4. Ibid., p. 159.
5. Ibid., p. 160.
6. Ibid., pp. 160–1.

7. Quoted in ibid., p. 165.
8. Ibid., pp. 138–41.
9. Ibid., pp. 141–2.
10. Maureen Wall, 'The Plans and the Countermand', in K. B. Nowlan (ed.), *The Making of 1916* (Dublin, 1916), p. 218.
11. Townshend, *Easter 1916*, p. 143.
12. Ibid., p. 181.
13. Ibid., pp 184–6.
14. Ibid., pp. 195–8.
15. Ibid., p. 208.
16. Ibid., p. 243.
17. Gilbert, *First World War*, p. 242.
18. Townshend, *Easter 1916*, pp. 245–50.
19. Gilbert, *First World War*, p. 242.
20. Townshend, *Easter 1916*, p. 269.
21. Ibid., p. 279.
22. Ibid., p. 281.

29 April 1916: *'A shattering and humiliating experience'* – The fall of Kut

1. Ibid.
2. Townshend, *When God Made Hell*, p. 253.
3. T/s Account by Sergeant Groves, op. cit.
4. Townshend, *When God Made Hell*, p. 243.
5. T/s Account by Sergeant Groves, op. cit.
6. Townshend, *When God Made Hell*, p. 244.
7. Quoted in ibid., p. 248.
8. Ibid., p. 249.
9. Ibid.
10. Ibid., p. 250.
11. Ibid., pp. 251–2.

12. T/s Account by Sergeant Groves, op. cit.
13. Edward Melotte (ed.), *Mons, Anzac and Kut: By an MP – Lieutenant-Colonel the Hon. Aubrey Herbert MP* (Barnsley, 2009), pp. 198–9.
14. T/s Account by Sergeant Groves, op. cit.
15. Quoted in Townshend, *When God Made Hell*, p. 253.
16. Ibid., pp. 306–7.
17. T/s Account by Sergeant Groves, op. cit.
18. Ibid.
19. Figures quoted in Gilbert, *First World War*, p. 248.
20. Downham (ed.), *Diary of an Old Contemptible*, p. 172.
21. 2nd Lieutenant Clive William Neely, The Great War, Lancing College War Memorial.

31 May 1916: *'Were we celebrating a glorious naval victory or lamenting an ignominious defeat?'* – Battle of Jutland

1. Thompson (ed.), *The War at Sea 1914–1918*, p. 295.
2. Ibid., pp. 293–4.
3. Hore, *The Habit of Victory*, p. 306.
4. Thompson (ed.), *The War at Sea 1914–1918*, pp. 298–9.
5. Ibid., p. 299.
6. Hore, *The Habit of Victory*, p. 307.
7. Thompson (ed.), *The War at Sea 1914–1918*, p. 301.
8. Ibid., p. 302.
9. Ibid., pp. 303–6.

10 Ibid., p. 306.

11. Ibid., p. 307.

12. *The Register of the Victoria Cross*, p. 30.

13. Thompson (ed.), *The War at Sea 1914–1918*, p. 308.

14. Hore, *The Habit of Victory*, p. 308.

15. Charles Markham David, *Seventy Years* (privately published, 2011), p. 22.

16. Ibid., p. 307.

17. Ibid., p. 310.

18. Thompson (ed.), *The War at Sea 1914–1918*, pp. 310–14.

19. Ibid., pp. 315–20.

20. David, *Seventy Years*, p. 22.

21. Hore, *The Habit of Victory*, p. 309.

22. Stevenson, *1914–1918*, p. 253.

23. Ibid., p. 254.

24. Ibid.

25. David, *Seventy Years*, p. 21.

26. Neil Weir to his mother, 5 June 1916, in David (ed.), *Mud and Bodies*, p. 60.

27. Brittain, *Testament of Youth*, p. 271.

28. Ibid.

4 June 1916: *'The ceaseless torrent poured westward'* – The Brusilov offensive

1. Gilbert, *The First World War*, p. 253.

2. Anonymous Austrian account of Russian incursions into Hungarian territory during the June 1916 Brusilov offensive, in Horne (ed.), *Source Records of the Great War*, IV, p. 202.

3. Farmborough, *Nurse at the Russian Front*, p. 188.

4. General von Cramon on the Brusilov offensive, in Horne (ed.), *Source Records of the Great War*, IV, p. 197.

5. General A. A. Brusilov, *A Soldier's Note-Book: 1914–1918* (1930), p. 199.

6. Ibid., p. 208.

7. Ibid., pp. 215–17.

8. Ibid., pp. 222 and 238.

9. Stevenson, *1914–1918*, pp. 167–8.

10. Brusilov, *A Soldier's Note-Book*, p. 243.

11. 'An anonymous Polish land-owner's account of Russian incursions in June 1916', in Horne (ed.), *Source Records of the Great War*, IV, p. 202.

12. General von Cramon on the Brusilov offensive, in ibid., pp. 198–9.

13. Brusilov, *A Soldier's Note-Book*, p. 248.

14. Ibid., p. 251.

15. Ibid., p. 257.

16. Stevenson, *1914–1918*, p. 168.

17. Brusilov, *A Soldier's Note-Book*, pp. 248–9.

5 June 1916: *'It began yesterday at Medina'* – The Arab Revolt

1. James Barr, *Setting the Desert on Fire: T. E. Lawrence and Britain's Secret War in Arabia, 1916–18* (2006), p. 26.

2. Ibid.

3. Ibid.

4. Ibid.

5. David Fromkin, *A Peace to End All*

Peace: Creating the Modern Middle East 1914–1922 (1989), p. 218.

6. Hopkirk, *On Secret Service East of Constantinople*, p. 227.

7. Barr, *Setting the Desert on Fire*, pp. 19–21.

8. Ibid., p. 22.

9. Fromkin, *A Peace to End All Peace*, p. 219.

10. Barr, *Setting the Desert on Fire*, p. 24.

11. Ibid., pp. 31–3.

12. Ibid., p. 56.

13. Ibid.

15 June 1916: *'You and I will be burnt at the stake'* – The Boulogne 'Absolutists'

1. Will Ellsworth-Jones, *We Will Not Fight: The Untold Story of World War One's Conscientious Objectors* (2008), pp. 168–9.

2. Ibid., p. 169.

3. Ibid., pp. 169–70.

4. Ibid., p. 170.

5. Ibid.

6. Ibid.

7. 'Text of the Bill', *The Times*, 8 January 1916.

8. Ellsworth-Jones, *We Will Not Fight*, pp. 7–12, 18.

9. Ibid., pp. 71–3.

10. Ibid., pp. 110–11.

11. Ibid., p. 135.

12. Ibid., p. 155.

13. Ibid., pp. 162–5.

14. Ibid., pp. 196–7.

15. Ibid.

16. Ibid., p. 198.

17. Brittain, *Testament of Youth*, p. 272.

1 July 1916: *'Not a man wavered, broke ranks or attempted to come back'* – First day of the Somme: The BEF perspective

1. *Haig Diaries and Letters*, p. 195.

2. Diary of Captain Kenelm Dormer, Irish Guards, Dormer Papers, FP.

3. Martin Middlebrook, *The First Day of the Somme: July 1916* (1971; this edition 1984), p. 115.

4. Ellsworth-Jones, *We Will Not Fight*, p. 185.

5. Middlebrook, *The First Day of the Somme*, p. 151.

6. Ellsworth-Jones, *We Will Not Fight*, p. 185.

7. Ibid., pp. 186–7.

8. Ibid., p. 187.

9. Philpott, *Bloody Victory*, pp. 79–80.

10. Sheffield, *The Chief*, p. 161.

11. Ibid., p. 164.

12. Ibid., p. 165.

13. Ibid., p. 164.

14. Ibid., p. 166.

15. Ibid., p. 167.

16. David, *Military Blunders*, p. 99.

17. Ibid., p. 101.

18. Ibid., p. 104.

19. Ibid., p. 103.

20. Ibid., p. 105.

1 July 1916: *'Only isolated parties got as far as the wire'* – First day of the Somme: The German perspective

1. Middlebrook, *The First Day of the Somme*, p. 111.
2. Christopher Duffy, *Through German Eyes: The British and the Somme 1916* (2006), pp. 135–6.
3. Ibid., p. 136.
4. Middlebrook, *The First Day of the Somme*, p. 171.
5. Duffy, *Through German Eyes*, p. 137.
6. Ibid., p. 140.
7. Ibid., p. 144.
8. Ibid., pp. 144–5.
9. Ibid., pp. 145–7.
10. Ibid., p. 154.
11. Ibid., pp. 162–3.
12. Ibid., pp. 163–4.
13. Ibid., p. 165.
14. Interrogation of fourteen British officers and 160 other ranks at the hospital in Caudry, in ibid., p. 166.
15. Ibid., p. 168.
16. Ibid., p. 169.
17. Philpott, *Bloody Victory*, p. 226.

1 July 1916: *'An atmosphere of tense expectation'* – First day of the Somme: The Home perspective

1. Brittain, *Testament of Youth*, pp. 275–7.
2. Ibid., pp. 274 and 276.
3. Ibid.
4. Ibid., pp. 274–5.
5. Ibid., pp. 276–7.
6. Ibid., p. 278.
7. Ibid.
8. Richard van Emden and Steve Humphries, *All Quiet on the Home Front: An Oral History of Life in Britain during the First World War* (2003; this edition 2004), p. 87.
9. Ibid., pp. 87–8.
10. Ibid., p. 88.
11. http://www.1914–1918.net/brothersdied.htm.
12. Emden and Humphries, *All Quiet on the Home Front*, pp. 89–90.
13. Ibid., pp. 94–5.
14. Brittain, *Testament of Youth*, pp. 281–2.
15. Ibid., p. 44.

14 July 1916: *'The best day we have had this war'* – The assault on Bazentin Ridge

1. David (ed.), *Mud and Bodies*, pp. 65–6.
2. Ibid., p. 66.
3. Ibid.
4. Ibid., p. 67.
5. Ibid.
6. Ibid., pp. 67–8.
7. Duffy, *Through German Eyes*, p. 173.
8. Philpott, *Bloody Victory*, p. 238.
9. Ibid., pp. 239–40.
10. *Haig Diaries and Letters*, p. 206.
11. Ibid., p. 241.
12. Sheffield, *The Chief*, p. 183.
13. Gilbert, *First World War*, p. 266.
14. Ibid.
15. Philpott, *Bloody Victory*, p. 251.
16. Keegan, *The First World War*, p. 319.

15 September 1916: *'It was a phantasmagoric vision'* – The tank attack at Flers

1. Duffy, *Through German Eyes*, p. 215.
2. Ibid., p. 214.
3. Bryn Hammond, *Cambrai 1917: The Myth of the First Great Tank Battle* (2008), pp. 39–41.
4. William Dawson, 'Reminiscences of my experiences in the first tank, 1916–18', Tank Museum, Bovington, RH.86 TC 3 BN 19.
5. Ibid.
6. Ibid.
7. Ibid.
8. Ibid.
9. Philpott, *Bloody Victory*, p. 362.
10. Duffy, *Through German Eyes*, p. 215.
11. Philpott, *Bloody Victory*, p. 359.
12. Ibid., p. 361.
13. Joshua Levine, *Forgotten Voices of the Somme* (2008; this edition 2009), p. 223.
14. Ibid., p. 226.
15. Ibid., pp. 226–7.
16. Duffy, *Through German Eyes*, p. 225.
17. Lieutenant Wilfred Staddon, in Levine, *Forgotten Voices of the Somme*, p. 227.
18. Philpott, *Bloody Victory*, p. 364.
19. Duffy, *Through German Eyes*, pp. 225–6.
20. Philpott, *Bloody Victory*, pp. 364–5; Colin Clifford, *The Asquiths* (2002; this edition 2003), pp. 366–7.
21. Dawson, 'Reminiscences', op. cit.
22. Duffy, *Through German Eyes*, p. 217.
23. Philpott, *Bloody Victory*, p. 367.
24. *Haig Diaries and Letters*, p. 230.
25. Philpott, *Bloody Victory*, p. 368.

24 October 1916: *'I have only one man left!'* – The French recover Fort Douaumont

1. Horne, *The Price of Glory*, p. 301.
2. Ibid., pp. 234–8.
3. Ibid., pp. 301–2.
4. Ibid., p. 306.
5. Ibid., pp. 304–6.
6. Ibid., pp. 306–7.
7. Ibid., p. 307.
8. Ibid.
9. Ibid., pp. 310–11.
10. Stevenson, *1914–1918*, p. 174.
11. Horne, *The Price of Glory*, pp. 228–9.
12. Ibid., p. 313.
13. Ibid., p. 324.
14. Ibid.
15. Ibid., p. 319.

18 November 1916: *'It was snowing hard and freezing'* – The last day on the Somme

1. Hart, *The Somme*, p. 519.
2. Captain Arthur Hardwick, 59th Field Ambulance, quoted in ibid., p. 520.
3. Ibid.
4. Sheffield, *The Chief*, p. 191.
5. *Haig Diaries and Letters*, pp. 231–2.
6. Philpott, *Bloody Victory*, p. 417.
7. *Haig Diaries and Letters*, p. 251.
8. Ibid.
9. Philpott, *Bloody Victory*, p. 410.
10. Hart, *The Somme*, p. 528.
11. Sheffield, *The Chief*, p. 194.
12. Ibid.

13. Philpott, *Bloody Victory*, pp. 628–9.
14. Sheffield, *The Chief*, p. 195.
15. Captain Douglas Jerrold, quoted in Hart, *The Somme*, pp. 502–3.
16. Private Herbert Butt, 4th Canadian Division, in ibid., p. 523.

23 November 1916: *'The Englishman could not help falling'* – A duel in the clouds

1. Barker, *The Royal Flying Corps in France*, I, p. 207.
2. Ibid., pp. 100–1.
3. Ibid., p. 98.
4. Ibid., p. 188.
5. Ibid., p. 170.
6. Ibid., p. 207.
7. Ibid., p. 208.
8. Ibid., pp. 208–9.
9. Manfred von Richthofen, *The Red Air Fighter* (1918; this edition 1990), p. 60.
10. Ibid., p. 95.
11. Ibid., pp. 100–1.
12. Ibid., p. 102.
13. Ibid.
14. Ibid., p. 100.

12 December 1916: *'A basis for the restoration of a lasting peace'* – Germany proposes peace talks

1. Ray Stannard Baker, *Woodrow Wilson: Life and Letters*. vol. VI: *Facing War 1915–1917* (1938), p. 392n; Roy Hattersley, *David Lloyd George: The Great Outsider* (2010), p. 425.

2. Stannard Baker, *Woodrow Wilson*, VI, p. 392.
3. Ibid., pp. 393–4.
4. Hattersley, *David Lloyd George*, p. 425.
5. Stannard Baker, *Woodrow Wilson*, VI, pp. 399–400.
6. Gilbert, *First World War*, p. 303.
7. Brittain, *Testament of Youth*, p. 315.
8. Hattersley, *David Lloyd George*, p. 426.
9. Stannard Baker, *Woodrow Wilson*, VI, p. 407.
10. Brittain, *Testament of Youth*, p. 315.

PART FOUR: 1917

1. Stevenson, *1914–1918*, p. 173.
2. *Haig Diaries and Letters*, p. 256.
3. Ibid.
4. Stevenson, *1914–1918*, p. 174.
5. Ibid.
6. *Haig Diaries and Letters*, p. 256.
7. Hattersley, *David Lloyd George*, p. 428.
8. Stevenson, *1914–1918*, p. 174.
9. Hattersley, *David Lloyd George*, p. 429.
10. Ibid., p. 432.

17 January 1917: *'D'you want to bring America into the war?'* – Intercepting the Zimmermann Telegram

1. Thomas Boghardt, *The Zimmermann Telegram: Intelligence, Diplomacy and America's Entry into World War I* (Annapolis, 2012), pp. 96–7.

2. Ibid., p. 97.
3. Ibid.
4. Hopkirk, *On Secret Service East of Constantinople*, pp. 242–3.
5. Boghardt, *The Zimmermann Telegram*, p. 97.
6. Ibid., p. 101.
7. Ibid., p. 26.
8. Ibid., pp. 60–2.
9. Ibid., p. 65.
10. Ibid., p. 67.
11. Ibid., pp. 77–8.

13 February 1917: *'A haggard look came into her eyes'* – The arrest of a dancer

1. Pat Shipman, *Femme Fatale: Love, Lies and the Unknown Life of Mata Hari* (2007), pp. 276–7.
2. Ibid., pp. 279–80.
3. Ibid., p. 281.
4. Ibid., pp. 3–12 and 50.
5. Ibid., pp. 145–6.
6. Ibid., pp. 186–7.
7. Metropolitan Police Report, 4 August 1917, Mata Hari Papers, TNA, KV 2/1.
8. Ibid.
9. Shipman, *Femme Fatale*, p. 192.
10. Ibid., p. 227.
11. Metropolitan Police Report, 4 August 1917, op. cit.
12. Report from the English Mission at the War Ministry in Paris, 18 November 1917, Mata Hari Papers, TNA, KV 2/1.
13. Shipman, *Femme Fatale*, p. 310.
14. Jefferson Adams, *Historical Dictionary of German Intelligence* (Plymouth, 2009), pp. 289–90.

19 February 1917: *'Texas and Arizona? Why not Illinois and New York?'* – America learns of the Zimmermann Telegram

1. Boghardt, *The Zimmermann Telegram*, pp. 116–17.
2. Ibid., p. 117.
3. Ibid., p. 78.
4. Stannard Baker, *Woodrow Wilson*, VI, p. 458.
5. Hopkirk, *On Secret Service East of Constantinople*, pp. 109, 225 and 242; Barbara W. Tuchman, *The Zimmermann Telegram* (1958; this edition 1966), pp. 18–19.
6. Boghardt, *The Zimmermann Telegram*, p. 105.
7. Ibid., pp. 118–19.
8. Ibid., p. 2.

15 March 1917: *'The people will not understand it'* – Tsar Nicholas II abdicates

1. Orlando Figes, *A People's Tragedy: The Russian Revolution, 1891–1924* (1996; this edition 1997), p. 342.
2. Hew Strachan, *The First World War* (2003; this edition 2006), p. 2.
3. Figes, *A People's Tragedy*, p. 312.
4. Ibid., p. 315.
5. Ibid., p. 340.
6. Ibid., p. 341.
7. Ibid., p. 342.
8. Ibid.
9. Ibid., p. 18.

10. Ibid., p. 343.
11. Strachan, *The First World War*, pp. 235–6.
12. Figes, *A People's Tragedy*, p. 343.
13. Ibid., p. 346.
14. Brittain, *Testament of Youth*, p. 336.

2 April 1917: *'The world must be made safe for democracy'* – Woodrow Wilson's war speech

1. Stannard Baker, *Woodrow Wilson*, VI, p. 509.
2. Ibid., p. 510.
3. President Wilson's Address to Congress, 2 April 1917, in *America*, XII, p. 222.
4. Ibid.
5. Ibid.
6. Ibid.
7. Ibid.
8. *New York Times*, 3 April 1917.
9. Stannard Baker, *Woodrow Wilson*, VI, p. 511.
10. Ibid.
11. Ibid.
12. Ibid., pp. 511–12.
13. Ibid., pp. 512–13.
14. Ibid., p. 513.
15. Ibid.
16. Ibid.
17. Ibid., pp. 513–14.
18. Ibid., p. 515.
19. Ibid., pp. 516–17.
20. Boghardt, *The Zimmermann Telegram*, pp. 182–3.

9 April 1917: *'Everything was smashed in'* – The Canadians at Vimy Ridge

1. David Campbell, 'The 2nd Canadian Division: A "Most Spectacular Victory"', in Geoffrey Hayes, Andrew Iarocci and Mike Bechthold (eds), *Vimy Ridge: A Canadian Reassessment* (Waterloo, Ontario, 2007), p. 174.
2. Paul Dickson, 'The End of the Beginning: The Canadian Corps in 1917', in ibid., p. 41.
3. Campbell, 'The 2nd Canadian Division', pp. 171–2.
4. Ibid., p. 172.
5. Gary Sheffield, 'Vimy Ridge and the Battle of Arras: A British Perspective', in Hayes, Iarocci and Bechthold (eds), *Vimy Ridge*, p. 23.
6. R. Lewis, *Over the Top with the 25th* (Halifax, 1918, this ebook edition 2011), p. 615.
7. Campbell, 'The 2nd Canadian Division', p. 176.
8. Lewis, *Over the Top with the 25th*, p. 616.
9. Campbell, 'The 2nd Canadian Division', p. 177.
10. Entry No. 1144, *The Register of the Victoria Cross*, p. 293.
11. Lewis, *Over the Top with the 25th*, p. 620.
12. Campbell, 'The 2nd Canadian Division', pp. 178–9.
13. Ibid., pp. 179–80.
14. Ibid., pp. 181–2.
15. Sheffield, *The Chief*, p. 214.
16. *Haig Diaries and Letters*, p. 278.
17. Sheffield, 'Vimy Ridge and the Battle of Arras', p. 16.
18. Gilbert, *First World War*, p. 325.

19. Sheffield, 'Vimy Ridge and the Battle of Arras', p. 24.

16 April 1917: *'You won't find any Germans in front of you'* – The first day of the Nivelle offensive

1. Horne, *The Price of Glory*, p. 314.
2. Ibid.
3. Ian Sumner, *They Shall Not Pass: The French Army on the Western Front 1914–1918* (Barnsley, 2012), p. 147.
4. Horne, *The Price of Glory*, p. 314.
5. Anthony Clayton, *Paths of Glory: The French Army 1914–18* (2003), p. 127.
6. Sumner, *They Shall Not Pass*, p. 149.
7. Ibid.
8. Clayton, *Paths of Glory*, p. 128.
9. Sumner, *They Shall Not Pass*, p. 157.
10. Ibid., p. 151.
11. Ibid.
12. Ibid., pp. 151–2.
13. Horne, *The Price of Glory*, p. 315.
14. Sumner, *They Shall Not Pass*, p. 152.
15. Ibid., pp. 152–3.
16. Williams, *Pétain*, p. 149.
17. Ibid., p. 152.
18. *Haig Diaries and Letters*, p. 291.
19. Williams, *Pétain*, p. 152.
20. *Haig Diaries and Letters*, p. 292.
21. Ibid., p. 290.
22. Williams, *Pétain*, p. 156.

29 April 1917: *'They have ruined the heart of the French soldier'* – The start of the French mutinies

1. Williams, *Pétain*, p. 149; Sumner, *They Shall Not Pass*, p. 160.
2. Williams, *Pétain*, p. 156; Sumner, *They Shall Not Pass*, p. 160.
3. Williams, *Pétain*, p. 157.
4. Ibid., pp. 157–8.
5. Ibid., p. 156.
6. Ibid., p. 159.
7. Leonard V. Smith, *Between Mutiny and Obedience: The Case of the Fifth Infantry Division during World War I* (Princeton, 1994), pp. 176–7.
8. Strachan, *The First World War*, p. 243.
9. Smith, *Between Mutiny and Obedience*, pp. 176–7.
10. Sumner, *They Shall Not Pass*, p. 161.
11. Williams, *Pétain*, p. 159.
12. Sumner, *They Shall Not Pass*, p. 161.
13. Smith, *Between Mutiny and Obedience*, pp. 178, 188–91, 195.
14. Williams, *Pétain*, p. 160.
15. Gilbert, *First World War*, p. 334.
16. Horne, *The Price of Glory*, p. 317.

29 April 1917: *'We attacked them by a rush'* – The Red Baron's deadliest day

1. Richthofen, *The Red Air Fighter*, p. 118.
2. Ibid., pp. 118–19.
3. Ibid., p. 118.
4. Peter Hart, *Aces Falling: War above the Trenches, 1918* (2007), p. 45.
5. Ralph Barker, *The Royal Flying Corps in France*, vol. II: *From Bloody April 1917 to Final Victory* (1995), pp. 46–7.

6. Richthofen, *The Red Air Fighter*, pp. 118–19.
7. Ibid., pp. 119–20.
8. Patrick Bishop, *Wings: One Hundred Years of Aerial Warfare* (2012), p. 102.
9. Barker, *The Royal Flying Corps in France*, II, p. 5.
10. Ibid., p. 6.
11. Ibid., p. 20.
12. Ibid., p. 48.
13. Ibid., pp. 48–50.
14. Bishop, *Wings*, p. 102.

25 May 1917: '*I saw dead animals and people lying everywhere*' – Death from above

1. Emden and Humphries, *All Quiet on the Home Front*, pp. 174–5.
2. C. S. Peel, *How We Lived Then 1914–1918: A Sketch of Social and Domestic Life in England during the War* (1929), p. 142.
3. Ibid., pp. 143–4.
4. Emden and Humphries, *All Quiet on the Home Front*, pp. 175–6.
5. Ibid., p. 176.
6. Ibid., p. 177.
7. Ibid., pp. 173–4.
8. Ibid., p. 174.
9. Ibid., p. 178.
10. Ibid., pp. 182, 187–8.
11. Ibid., p. 178.

7 June 1917: '*The earth seemed to tear apart*' – Messines Ridge

1. Lyn Macdonald, *They Called It Passchendaele: The Story of the Third Battle of Ypres and the Men Who Fought in It* (1978; this edition 1983), p. 41.
2. Gilbert, *First World War*, p. 336.
3. Ibid., pp. 41–2.
4. Sheffield, *The Chief*, pp. 223–4.
5. *Haig Diaries and Letters*, p. 299.
6. Sheffield, *The Chief*, pp. 225–6.
7. Macdonald, *They Called It Passchendaele*, p. 44.
8. Gilbert, *First World War*, p. 337.
9. Macdonald, *They Called It Passchendaele*, pp. 45–6.
10. Ibid., pp. 52–3.
11. Ibid., pp. 54–5.
12. *Haig Diaries and Letters*, p. 298.
13. Sheffield, *The Chief*, pp. 226–7.

28 June 1917: '*We lacked not only the training, but the organisation*' – The doughboys arrive in France

1. Gary Mead, *The Doughboys: America and the First World War* (2000; this edition 2001), p. 104.
2. Ibid., p. 105.
3. Ibid., pp. 69–71.
4. Ibid., pp. 72–3.
5. Ibid., pp. 76–8.
6. Ibid., pp. 110–17.
7. Ibid., pp. 117–18.
8. Ibid., p. 96.
9. General John Pershing's Official Report, in *America*, XII, p. 598.
10. *Haig Diaries and Letters*, p. 304.
11. Ibid.

1 July 1917: '*To vanquish is our desire*' – Russia's last throw of the dice

1. Horne (ed.), *Source Records of the Great War*, V, pp. 250–1.
2. General Deniken's Official Report on the Kerensky Offensive, in ibid., p. 264.
3. Holger H. Herwig, *The First World War, Germany and Austria-Hungary 1914–1918* (1997), p. 334.
4. Ibid.
5. Trevor N. Dupuy and Wlodzimierz Onacewicz, *Triumphs and Tragedies in the East 1915–1917* (New York, 1967), p. 72.
6. Figes, *A People's Tragedy*, p. 407.
7. Stevenson, *1914–1918*, p. 325.
8. Figes, *A People's Tragedy*, p. 406.
9. Ibid., p. 416.
10 Ibid., pp. 417–18.
11. Norman Stone, 'Kerensky Offensive', in James L. Collins, *The Marshall Cavendish Illustrated Encyclopaedia of World War One* (1972), VIII, pp. 2449–53.
12. Brusilov's Official Announcements of the Kerensky Offensive, in Horne (ed.), *Source Records of the Great War*, V, p. 253.
13. Ibid.

2 July 1917: *'They shoot a lot and hit a little'* – The Battle for Aqaba

1. David Fromkin, *A Peace to End All Peace: Creating the Modern Middle East 1914–1922* (1989), p. 309.
2. T. E. Lawrence, *Seven Pillars of Wisdom* (1925; this edition 2000), p. 308.
3. Ibid., pp. 308–9.
4. Ibid., p. 309.

5. Ibid., pp. 310–12.
6. Ibid., p. 312.
7. Ibid., p. 313.
8. Barr, *Setting the Desert on Fire*, p. 148.
9. Fromkin, *A Peace to End All Peace*, p. 310.
10. Ibid.

31 July 1917: *'A fine day's work'* – The opening of the Third Battle of Ypres

1. Macdonald, *They Called It Passchendaele*, pp. 99–100.
2. Dawson, 'Reminiscences', pp. 14–15.
3. Colonel N. M. Dillon, 'Record', Tank Museum, Bovington, 069.02 (41) Dillon 9127/1.
4. Ibid.
5. Ibid.
6. Ibid.
7. *Haig Diaries and Letters*, pp. 299–300.
8. Ibid., p. 300.
9. Ibid., p. 301.
10. Stevenson, *1914–1918*, p. 333.
11. *Haig Diaries and Letters*, p. 301.
12. Sheffield, *The Chief*, p. 231.
13. Ibid., p. 228.
14. *Haig Diaries and Letters*, p. 307.
15. Stevenson, *1914–1918*, p. 334.

9 September 1917: *'The Red Cap must have lost his head'* – The Etaples Mutiny

1. www.shotatdawn.info/page31.html.

2. Douglas Gill and Gloden Dallas, 'Mutiny at Etaples Base in 1917', *Past & Present*, No. 69 (Nov. 1975), p. 91.
3. Ibid., pp. 91–2.
4. Ibid., p. 92.
5. www.shotatdawn.info/page31.html.
6. Gill and Dallas, 'Mutiny at Etaples Base in 1917', p. 93.
7. www.shotatdawn.info/page31.html.
8. Ibid.
9. Corporal J. Short, Capital Courts Martial Papers, TNA, WO 71/599.
10. Gill and Dallas, 'Mutiny at Etaples Base in 1917', pp. 97–8.
11. Ibid., pp. 98–102.
12. Brittain, *Testament of Youth*, pp. 385–6.
13. Ibid., p. 386.

15 October 1917: *'She lay prone, motionless'* – Mata Hari's execution

1. Henry Wales, 'The Execution of Mata Hari, 1917', in www.eyewitnesstohistory.com/matahari.htm.
2. Shipman, *Femme Fatale*, p. 367.
3. Ibid.
4. Henry Wales, 'The Execution of Mata Hari, 1917'.
5. Shipman, *Femme Fatale*, p. 367.
6. Ibid., p. 298.
7. Ibid., pp. 320–1.
8. Ibid., p. 355.
9. Ibid., pp. 359–60.

24 October 1917: *'Eviva Germania!'* – The Italian collapse at Caporetto
1. David, *Military Blunders*, pp. 303–4.

2. General von Cramon, 'Caporetto', in Horne (ed.), *Source Records of the Great War*, V, p. 326.
3. Ibid., p. 327.
4. David, *Military Blunders*, p. 303.
5. Ibid., pp. 303–4.
6. Ibid., p. 304.
7. Cramon, 'Caporetto', p. 329.
8. David, *Military Blunders*, p. 306.
9. Ibid., pp. 306–7.
10. Ibid., p. 307.
11. Ibid.
12. David Fraser, *Knight's Cross: A Life of Field Marshal Erwin Rommel* (1993; this edition 1994), pp. 73 and 77.
13. Cadorna's Official Communiqué, 28 October 1917, in Horne (ed.), *Source Records of the Great War*, V, p. 318.
14. David, *Military Blunders*, p. 308.
15. G. M. Trevelyan, 'Caporetto', in Horne (ed.), *Source Records of the Great War*, V, pp. 319–20.
16. David, *Military Blunders*, p. 308.
17. Ibid., pp. 308–9.
18. Ibid., p. 309.
19. Stevenson, *1914–1918*, p. 379.

2 November 1917: *'I knew that this was a great event'* – The Balfour Declaration

1. Chaim Weizmann, *Trial and Error: The Autobiography of Chaim Weizmann, First President of Israel* (1949), p. 262.
2. Ibid.
3. Ibid.
4. Simon Sebag Montefiore,

Jerusalem: The Biography (2011), p. 409.

5. Weizmann, *Trial and Error*, p. 144.

6. Ibid., p. 220.

7. Sebag Montefiore, *Jerusalem*, p. 412.

8. Ibid.

9. Ibid., p. 413.

10. Ibid., p. 414.

11. Ibid.

12. Weizmann, *Trial and Error*, pp. 256 and 262.

13. Ibid., p. 261.

14. Ibid., p. 266.

15. Geoffrey Lewis, *Balfour and Weizmann: The Zionist, the Zealot and the Emergence of Israel* (2009), p. 153.

6 November 1917: *'A very important success'* – The Canadians take Passchendaele

1. Macdonald, *They Called It Passchendaele*, p. 226.

2. Ibid., pp. 226–7.

3. Ibid., pp. 228–9.

4. *Haig Diaries and Letters*, p. 339.

5. Stevenson, *1914–1918*, pp. 334–5.

6. Sheffield, *The Chief*, p. 237.

7. Ibid., p. 238.

8. Ibid., p. 246.

9. Stevenson, *1914–1918*, p. 336.

10. Sheffield, *The Chief*, p. 247.

11. Stevenson, *1914–1918*, p. 336.

12. Sheffield, *The Chief*, p. 247.

13. Low and Everett, *The History of the Royal Monmouthshire Royal Engineers*, II, p. 30.

14. Ibid., p. 23.

15. 'Register of the Distinguished Service Order, 27th October 1917–18th January 1918', TNO, WO 390/6, p. 59.

16. David, *Seventy Years*, p. 39.

7 November 1917: *'Go where you ought to go – into the dustbin of history!'* – The Bolshevik coup

1. Figes, *A People's Tragedy*, pp. 480, 485.

2. Ibid., p. 485.

3. John Reed, *Ten Days That Shook the World* (1919; this edition 2011), p. 58.

4. Ibid.

5. Figes, *A People's Tragedy*, p. 486.

6. Reed, *Ten Days That Shook the World*, p. 55.

7. Figes, *A People's Tragedy*, p. 488.

8. Ibid., p. 491.

9. Reed, *Ten Days That Shook the World*, p. 65.

10. Ibid., p. 66.

11. Ibid., p. 67.

12. Ibid., p. 69.

13. Stevenson, *1914–1918*, p. 383.

9 December 1917: *'The most famous city in the world . . . has fallen to the British Army'* – The capture of Jerusalem

1. Sebag Montefiore, *Jerusalem*, pp. 417–18.

2. Ibid., p. 418.

3. John Keay, *Sowing the Wind: The*

Seeds of Conflict in the Middle East (2003), p. 84.

4. Sebag Montefiore, *Jerusalem*, p. 418.
5. Stevenson, *1914–1918*, p. 339.
6. Sebag Montefiore, *Jerusalem*, p. 416.
7. Ibid.
8. Ibid., p. 417.
9. Ibid., p. 419.
10. Barr, *Setting the Desert on Fire*, p. 208.
11. Ibid.
12. Sebag Montefiore, *Jerusalem*, p. 420.
13. Lawrence, *Seven Pillars of Wisdom*, pp. 462–4.
14. Ibid., p. 464.

PART FIVE: 1918

1. General Erich Ludendorff, *My War Memories: 1914–1918* (1919), II, p. 537.
2. *Haig Diaries and Letters*, p. 358.
3. Stevenson, *1914–1918*, pp. 405–6.
4. Ibid., p. 322.
5. Ibid., p. 324.
6. Ibid., pp. 372–3.
7. Ibid., pp. 373–4.

8 January 1918: *'A world . . . fit and safe to live in'* – Woodrow Wilson's Fourteen Points

1. Mead, *The Doughboys*, Appendix 4, p. 426.
2. Ibid., pp. 426 and 428.
3. Ibid., p. 427; Stevenson, *1914–1918*, pp. 390–1.
4. Mead, *The Doughboys*, pp. 426–7.
5. Ibid.
6. Stevenson, *1914–1918*, p. 392.

7. Ibid., pp. 390–1.
8. Ibid., p. 392.
9. Ibid.
10. Ibid.

6 February 1918: *'An unadvertised triumph'* – Women get the vote

1. Brittain, *Testament of Youth*, p. 404.
2. David Stevenson, *With our Backs to the Wall: Victory and Defeat in 1918* (2011), p. 440.
3. Ibid., p. 447.
4. Christabel Pankhurst, *Unshackled: The Story of How We Won the Vote* (1959; this edition 1987), p. 292.
5. Hattersley, *David Lloyd George*, p. 441.
6. Ibid.
7. Arthur Marwick, *Women at War, 1914–1918* (1977), p. 156.
8. Pankhurst, *Unshackled*, p. 292.
9. Ibid., p. 293.
10. Ibid., p. 294.

3 March 1918: *'Our conditions are hard and severe'* – The German diktat at Brest-Litovsk

1. Figes, *A People's Tragedy*, p. 548.
2. Ibid.; Gilbert, *First World War*, p. 401.
3. Figes, *A People's Tragedy*, pp. 543–4.
4. Ibid., pp. 544–5.
5. Gilbert, *First World War*, p. 398.
6. Ibid., p. 399.
7. Lenin's Address of 23 February 1918, in Horne (ed.), *Source Records of the Great War*, VI, p. 36.

8. Herbert Sulzbach, *With the German Guns: Four Years on the Western Front* (1935; this edition 1973), p. 145.
9. Farmborough, *Nurse at the Russian Front*, p. 387.

21 March 1918: *'Only a few of the enemy had survived the storm'* – The opening of *die Kaiserschlact* ('the Kaiser's battle')

1. Sulzbach, *With the German Guns*, p. 150.
2. David, *Military Blunders*, p. 318.
3. Martin Middlebrook, *The Kaiser's Battle: 21 March 1918 – The First Day of the German Spring Offensive* (1978; this edition 1983), p. 148.
4. Ibid., pp. 149 and 153.
5. Ibid., p. 171.
6. Ibid., p. 172.
7. Stevenson, *1914–1918*, p. 408.
8. Ibid., p. 406.
9. Ibid., p. 407.
10. Sheffield, *The Chief*, p. 261.
11. *Haig Diaries and Letters*, p. 388; Stevenson, *1914–1918*, p. 407.
12. David, *Military Blunders*, p. 317.
13. Middlebrook, *The Kaiser's Battle*, p. 257.
14. Ibid., pp. 257–8.
15. Ibid., pp. 308–9.
16. Ibid., p. 322.
17. *Haig Diaries and Letters*, p. 390.
18. Brittain, *Testament of Youth*, p. 410.
19. Middlebrook, *The Kaiser's Battle*, pp. 332–3.

4 April 1918: *'They won't come any further'* – Operation Michael runs out of steam

1. Peter Hart, *1918: A Very British Victory* (2008), p. 217.
2. Ibid., pp. 217–18.
3. Lyn Macdonald, *To the Last Man: Spring 1918* (1998), p. 344.
4. Stevenson, *1914–1918*, p. 410.
5. Ibid., pp. 410–11.
6. Ibid., p. 412; Hart, *1918*, p. 219.
7. Sheffield, *The Chief*, pp. 279–80.
8. Hart, *1918*, p. 219.
9. Stevenson, *1914–1918*, p. 414.
10. Brittain, *Testament of Youth*, p. 411.
11. Ibid., pp. 411–12.

21 April 1918: *'He was hunched in the cockpit aiming over his guns'* – The Red Baron's last flight

1. Peter Kilduff, *Red Baron: The Life and Death of an Ace* (2007), p. 216.
2. Ibid.
3. Ibid.
4. Hart, *Aces Falling*, p. 168.
5. Ibid.
6. Ibid., p. 169.
7. Ibid., p. 170.
8. Ibid., p. 171.
9. Ibid.
10. Kilduff, *Red Baron*, pp. 230–2.
11. Ibid., p. 233.
12. Ibid., p. 235.
13. Hart, *Aces Falling*, p. 177.

25 April 1918: *'The men remained petrified in their holes'* – The battle for Mont Kemmel

1. Sumner, *They Shall Not Pass*, p. 191.
2. Hart, *1918*, p. 254.
3. Ibid.
4. Ibid., pp. 255–6.
5. Stevenson, *1914–1918*, pp. 412–13.
6. Sheffield, *The Chief*, p. 282.
7. Brittain, *Testament of Youth*, p. 419.
8. Ibid., pp. 419–20.
9. Stevenson, *1914–1918*, p. 414; Stevenson, *With our Backs to the Wall*, pp. 76–7.
10. Ibid., p. 77.

27 May 1918: *'I've never seen anything like it'* – The Germans attack in Champagne

1. Stevenson, *1914–1918*, p. 417; Stevenson, *With our Backs to the Wall*, p. 82.
2. Sumner, *They Shall Not Pass*, pp. 192–3.
3. Stevenson, *With our Backs to the Wall*, p. 83.
4. Ibid.
5. Ibid., pp. 79–80.
6. Ibid., pp. 80–1.
7. Ibid., pp. 81–2.
8. Ibid., p. 84.
9. Ibid., pp. 84–5.
10. *Haig Diaries and Letters*, p. 419.
11. Stevenson, *With our Backs to the Wall*, p. 85; Stevenson, *1914–1918*, p. 418.
12. Stevenson, *1914–1918*, p. 418.
13. Stevenson, *With our Backs to the Wall*, p. 87.

28 May 1918: *'Will the Americans really fight?'* – The doughboys attack at Cantigny

1. Mead, *Doughboys*, p. 233.
2. Ibid., pp. 233–4.
3. Ibid., pp. 234–5.
4. Ibid., p. 235.
5. Ibid., pp. 236–7.
6. Ibid., pp. 214–15.
7. Ibid., p. 15.
8. Stevenson, *1914–1918*, p. 441.
9. Ibid., p. 440.
10. Mead, *Doughboys*, p. 237.

15 June 1918: *'The position was critical'* – The Asiago Plateau

1. Brittain, *Testament of Youth*, p. 439.
2. Ibid.
3. Stevenson, *1914–1918*, p. 415.
4. Ibid., pp. 415–16.
5. Stevenson, *With our Backs to the Wall*, p. 103.
6. Ludendorff, *My War Memories*, II, p. 635.
7. Brittain, *Testament of Youth*, pp. 435–7.
8. Ibid., p. 437.
9. Ibid., pp. 438–9.
10. Ibid., pp. 439–40.
11. Ibid., pp. 442.
12. Ibid., p. 661.

1 July 1918: *'What I saw there I will never forget'* – The Chilwell explosion

1. Emden and Humphries, *All Quiet on the Home Front*, pp. 259–60.
2. Ibid., p. 260.
3. Ibid., p. 259.

4. M. J. Haslam, 'The Chilwell Story: 1915–1982, VC Factory and Ordnance Depot', *RAOC Corps Gazette*, 1982, p. 9; 'Wartime Factory Disaster', *Inside Out*, BBC East Midlands, 10 February 2003.

5. Emden and Humphries, *All Quiet on the Home Front*, p. 256.

6. Ibid., p. 257.

7. Ibid., p. 285; 'Wartime Factory Disaster', op. cit.

8. Haslam, 'The Chilwell Story', p. 45.

9. 'Wartime Factory Disaster', op. cit.

18 July 1918: *'The presidium . . . has sentenced you to be shot'* – The Romanov executions

1. Helen Rappaport, *Ekaterinburg: The Last Days of the Romanovs* (2008), pp. 30 and 184.

2. Ibid., p. 184.

3. Ibid. pp. 184–5.

4. Ibid., p. 186.

5. Ibid., pp. 186–7.

6. Ibid., p. 188.

7. Ibid.

8. Ibid., pp. 188–9.

9. Ibid., p. 189.

10. Ibid., pp. 189–91.

11. Figes, *A People's Tragedy*, p. 635.

12. Ibid., p. 636.

13. Ibid., pp. 637–8.

14. Ibid., p. 638.

15. Ibid., pp. 639–40.

24 July 1918: *'The night air, how good it was'* – Escape from Holzminden

1. Neil Hanson, *Escape from Germany: The Greatest PoW Break-out of the First World War* (2011), pp. 200–1.

2. Ibid., pp. 201–2.

3. Ibid., p. 201.

4. Ibid., pp. 23–4.

5. Ibid., pp. 26–7.

6. H. G. Durnford, *The Tunnellers of Holzminden* (1920), p. 37.

7. Ibid., p. 34.

8. Ibid., p. 156.

9. Hanson, *Escape from Germany*, pp. 128–9.

10. Ibid., pp. 136, 146–7; Durnford, *The Tunnellers of Holzminden*, p. 94.

11. Hanson, *Escape from Germany*, p. 146.

12. Durnford, *The Tunnellers of Holzminden*, p. 91.

13. Ibid., p. 119.

14. Ibid., p. 50.

15. Ibid., p. 124; Hanson, *Escape from Germany*, pp. 204–5.

16. Ibid., p. 207.

17. Ibid., pp. 208–9.

18. Ibid., pp. 220–8.

19. Ibid., pp. 229–30.

8 August 1918: *'The black day of the German Army'* – Battle of Amiens

1. Ludendorff, *My War Memories*, II, pp. 679–80.

2. Hart, *1918*, p. 325.

3. Ibid., p. 326.

4. Ibid., p. 328.

5. Ibid., p. 334.

6. Ibid., p. 333.

7. Ibid., p. 341.

8. Sheffield, *The Chief*, p. 299.
9. Stevenson, *1914–1918*, pp. 419–24.
10. Ibid., pp. 420, 423.
11. Ibid., pp. 424–5.
12. Sheffield, *The Chief*, pp. 295–7.
13. Ibid., p. 426.
14. *Haig Diaries and Letters*, p. 440.
15. Sheffield, *The Chief*, pp. 299–300.
16. Stevenson, *1914–1918*, p. 427.
17. Ibid.; Ludendorff, *My War Memories*, II, p. 683.
18. Ludendorff, *My War Memories*, II, p. 687.

19 September 1918: *'Ninety-four squadrons . . . hurrying forward relentlessly'* – Battle of Megiddo

1. Anne Baker, *From Biplane to Spitfire: The Life of Air Chief Marshal Sir Geoffrey Salmond KCB KCMG DSO* (Barnsley, 2003), pp. 134–5.
2. David R. Woodward, *Hell in the Holy Land: World War I in the Middle East* (Lexington, 2006), p. 195.
3. General Allenby's Report on Fighting at Megiddo, 20 September 1918, in Horne (ed.), *Source Records of the Great War*, VI, p. 341.
4. Baker, *From Biplane to Spitfire*, pp. 136–7.
5. Stevenson, *With our Backs to the Wall*, p. 153.
6. Lawrence, *Seven Pillars of Wisdom*, p. 635.
7. Stevenson, *With our Backs to the Wall*, p. 149.

8. Ibid., p. 150.
9. Ibid., p. 151.
10. Ibid., pp. 151–2.
11. Lawrence, *Seven Pillars of Wisdom*, p. 666.

27 September 1918: *'The old trench warfare was a thing of the past'* – Piercing the Hindenburg Line

1. Hart, *1918*, p. 440.
2. Ibid., pp. 439–40.
3. Ibid., pp. 440–1; Stevenson, *With our Backs to the Wall*, p. 138.
4. Hart, *1918*, p. 442.
5. MacArthur (ed.), *For King and Country*, pp. 393–4.
6. Ibid., pp. 394–5.
7. Stevenson, *With our Backs to the Wall*, p. 138.
8. Stevenson, *1914–1918*, pp. 428–9.
9. *Haig Diaries and Letters*, p. 451.
10. Ibid., p. 453.
11. Stevenson, *1914–1918*, p. 431.
12. *Haig Diaries and Letters*, p. 467.
13. Stevenson, *1914–1918*, p. 431.
14. *Haig Diaries and Letters*, p. 468.
15. Stevenson, *1914–1918*, p. 471.

9 November 1918: *'Long live the German Republic!'* – The Kaiser abdicates

1. Nicholas Best, *The Greatest Day in History: How the Great War Really Ended* (2008), pp. 105–6.
2. Ibid., p. 106.
3. Ibid., pp. 106–7; Stevenson, *1914–1918*, pp. 493–7.
4. Maurice Baumont, *Fall of the*

Kaiser: The Kaiser with his Generals (1931), p. 89.

5. Ibid., p. 90; Best, *The Greatest Day in History*, p. 108.

6. Best, *The Greatest Day in History*, p. 108; Baumont, *Fall of the Kaiser*, pp. 93–6.

7. Baumont, *Fall of the Kaiser*, pp. 96–9; Best, *The Greatest Day in History*, pp. 108–9.

8. Stevenson, *With our Backs to the Wall*, p. 514.

9. Stevenson, *1914–1918*, pp. 472–4.

10. Stevenson, *With our Backs to the Wall*, p. 520.

11. Stevenson, *1914–1918*, pp. 491–4.

12. Best, *The Greatest Day in History*, pp. 116–17.

13. Baumont, *Fall of the Kaiser*, p. 110.

14. Best, *The Greatest Day in History*, pp. 116–17.

15. Ibid., pp. 121–2.

16. Ibid., p. 122.

11 November 1918: 'VICTORY! VICTORY! VICTORY!' – The Armistice

1. Stevenson, *With our Backs to the Wall*, pp. 544–5.

2. Ibid., p. 545.; Best, *The Greatest Day in History*, pp. 84–5.

3. Best, *The Greatest Day in History*, p. 86.

4. Ibid., p. 157.

5. Ibid., p. 162.

6. Ibid., p. 163; Stevenson, *With our Backs to the Wall*, p. 545.

7. Best, *The Greatest Day in History*, p. 164; Joseph E. Persico, *11th Month, 11th Day, 11th Hour: Armistice Day 1918: World War I and its Violent Climax* (2004; this edition 2005), p. 324.

8. Persico, *11th Month, 11th Day, 11th Hour*, pp. 349–51.

9. Sulzbach, *With the German Guns*, p. 248.

10. Weber, *Hitler's First War*, p. 221.

11. Cowen (ed.), *A Nurse at the Front*, pp. 263–4.

12. David, *Seventy Years*, pp. 29–30.

13. Best, *The Greatest Day in History*, p. 205.

14. Persico, *11th Month, 11th Day, 11th Hour*, p. 363.

15. Mead, *Doughboys*, p. 344.

16. Ibid., p. 362.

17. Brittain, *Testament of Youth*, p. 462.

EPILOGUE

1. 'The Burial of the Unknown Warrior', *The Times*, 12 November 1920.

2. Ibid.

3. Ibid.

4. Ibid.

5. Ibid.

6. Rev. David Railton, 'The Origin of the Unknown Warrior's Grave', *Our Empire*, November 1931, vol. VII.

7. Ibid.

8. Ibid.

9. Lord Stamfordham to the Dean of Westminster, 7 October 1920, Muniment Room and Library,

Westminster Abbey, WAM 58667.

10. Interim Report of the Cabinet Memorial Services Committee, 15 October 1920, WAM 58668.

11. 'The Unknown Warrior', *After the Battle*, No. 6, 1974, pp. 48–9.

12. Ibid., pp. 49–51.

13. http://www.westminster-abbey. org/our-history/people/unknown-warrior.

14. Railton, 'The Origin of the Unknown Warrior's Grave'.

15. John Ellis and Michael Cox, *The World War I Databook: The Essential Facts and Figures for All the Combatants* (2001), pp. 269–70.

16. Commonwealth War Graves Commission, *Annual Report, 2009–2010* (2010).

17. Ellis and Cox, *The World War I Databook*, pp. 269–70.

18. Strachan, *The First World War*, p. 331.

INDEX

Page numbers in *italic* refer to illustrations

First published in Great Britain in 2013
by Hodder & Stoughton

An Hachette UK company

1

Copyright © Saul David 2013

Maps © Rodney Paull

A CIP catalogue record for this title
is available from the British Library

ISBN 978 1 444 76335 5

eBook ISBN 978 1 444 76337 9

Typeset by Palimpsest Book Production Limited,
Falkirk, Stirlingshire

Printed and bound by Clays Ltd, St Ives plc

Hodder & Stoughton policy is to use papers that are natural,
renewable and recyclable products and made from wood grown
in sustainable forests. The logging and manufacturing processes
are expected to conform to the environmental
regulations of the country of origin.

Hodder & Stoughton Ltd
338 Euston Road
London NW1 3BH

www.hodder.co.uk

An invitation from the publisher

Join us at www.hodder.co.uk, or follow us
on Twitter @hodderbooks to be a part of
our community of people who love the very
best in books and reading.

Whether you want to discover more about a book
or an author, watch trailers and interviews, have the
chance to win early limited editions, or simply browse
our expert readers' selection of the very best books,
we think you'll find what you're looking for.

And if you don't, that's the place to tell us what's missing.

We love what we do, and we'd love you to be a part of it.

www.hodder.co.uk

 @hodderbooks

 HodderBooks

 HodderBooks